THE UNIVERSITY OF MICHIGAN
CENTER FOR CHINESE STUDIES

MICHIGAN MONOGRAPHS IN
CHINESE STUDIES
NO. 52

INDIVIDUALISM AND HOLISM:

STUDIES IN CONFUCIAN AND TAOIST VALUES

edited by
Donald J. Munro

Ann Arbor
Center for Chinese Studies
The University of Michigan
1985

Published by Center for Chinese Studies
The University of Michigan
Ann Arbor, Michigan 48109-1290

First Edition 1985
Second Printing 1987
Third Printing 1991
Fourth Printing 1996

Printed and made in the United States of America

Cover: Carrie DiLorenzo

♾ The paper used in this publication meets the minimum requirements
of the American National Standard for Information Sciences—
Permanence of Paper for Publications and Documents
in Libraries and Archives ANSI/NISO/Z39.48—1992.

Library of Congress Cataloging-in-Publication Data

Individualism and holism.

Papers presented at a conference held in 1982.
Bibliography: p.
Includes index.
ISBN 0-89264-057-X (alk. paper)
ISBN 0-89264-058-8 (pbk.) (alk. paper)
1. Individualism—Congresses.
2. Holism—Congresses.
3. Philosophy, Confucian—Congresses.
4. Philosophy, Taoist—Congresses.
I. Munro, Donald J.
B824.I53   1985   128′.0951   84-27417
CIP

CONTENTS

Part III: The Whole and the Individual

Acknowledgments

The conference for which the papers in this volume were prepared took place 24-29 June 1981 at the Breckenridge Conference Center belonging to Bowdoin College in York, Maine. The pastoral setting, together with the kindness and professional efficiency of the staff there, nurtured vitality in the formal and informal discussions. We are especially grateful to Mr. Geoffery Stanwood of the Breckenridge Center, who quietly managed the hospitable community so that we could focus on papers written and revisions to be written. The conference was funded by the Committee on Studies of Chinese Civilization of the American Council of Learned Societies with funds provided by the Ford Foundation, and it was also supported by direct grants from the National Endowment for the Humanities and the Center for Chinese Studies, The University of Michigan. Our conference in turn grew out of ideas that had emerged at an earlier planning meeting, graciously hosted by Columbia University.

In ways too numerous to list individually, each writer benefitted from the suggestions and critical insights of discussants who do not have papers in this volume. We acknowledge with gratitude the contributions from Thomas Berry, Riverdale Center of Religious Research; Derk Bodde, Emeritus, Department of Chinese Studies, University of Pennsylvania; Galia S. Bodde; W. T. Chan, Department of Philosophy, Chatham College; Chang Wejen, Academia Sinica, Nankang; Alan Donagan, Department of Philosophy, California Institute of Technology; Robert Eno, Department of Far Eastern Languages and Literatures, The University of Michigan; and Thomas Metzger, Department of History, University of California, San Diego.

A steering committee composed of Irene Bloom, Chad Hansen, and myself made the major decisions about topical structure of the conference, papers to solicit, editorial policy, and publication plans. Able staff support came from Marian Gram and Robert Eno. Certain limitations on conference content were matters of policy, such as the decision not to include papers on Chinese Buddhism, in order to keep the conference topic manageable. Some limitations were beyond our control. These included late changes in the plans of a few expected participants that prevented them from submitting papers. No doubt other limitations or gaps of which we are unaware will be spotted by readers; we look forward to learning from those readers. Overall I take the rap for the deficiencies. No conference organizer or editor ever had the advantage of wiser, more ready, or more generous support from his steering committee. The likelihood is that in the case of a defect, I neglected to follow one of their suggestions.

All of us who participated in the conference owe a debt to Steven Lukes, who clarified so well the Western idea of individualism in his book *Individualism*, New York: Harper and Row, 1973. In addition, in preparing my introduction for this volume I benefitted again from Lukes' work. In trying to understand the idea of holism in Western social sciences and philosophy, I learned from a number of sources, most of all from Alan Ryan, *The Philosophy of the Social Sciences* (New York: Pantheon, 1970), especially from chapter 8, "Wholes, Parts, Purposes, and Functions." I was able to revise and, I hope, enrich the introduction on the basis of criticisms and recommendations from Frithjof Bergmann, Irene Bloom, Chang Ch'un-shu, Kenneth DeWoskin, Robert Eno, and Chad Hansen. I owe a special debt to my friend Frithjof Bergmann, also of the Department of Philosophy, The University of Michigan, for first introducing me to the significance of the German Romantics in any consideration of the idea of individualism in the West. Lukes also enlightened me on this matter when he discussed the Romantics in connection with the value of "self-development." Although Lukes introduced the value of uniqueness in connection with self-development, I go beyond him to claim that uniqueness is really a paramount virtue in Western individualism. Further, self-development in the Chinese case, far from requiring uniqueness, is quite compatible with uniformity. Everyone should cultivate characteristics shared by all.

The careful conference notes prepared by the rapporteurs, Terry Kelleher and Robert Eno, made the editorial work less painful than it would otherwise have been. There was a talented presence throughout the editorial process, namely Barbara Congelosi, formerly editor of the Michigan Monographs on Chinese Studies. The perfectionist's perfectionist, she improved all of the papers in matters of style and substance. In such matters I served as her apprentice. I am also very grateful to Lorraine Sobson and Janis Michael, who, as editors of Michigan Monographs in Chinese Studies, put this book in its final form.

Authors

WOLFGANG BAUER is Professor of Chinese Studies at the Institut für Ostasienkunde-Sinologie of the Universität München.

JUDITH A. BERLING is Associate Professor of the Department of Religious Studies at Indiana University.

IRENE BLOOM is Research Associate in the Department of East Asian Languages and Cultures at Columbia University.

ARTHUR C. DANTO is Johnsonian Professor of Philosophy in the Department of Philosophy at Columbia University.

WM. THEODORE deBARY is John Mitchell Mason Professor of the University at Columbia University.

A. C. GRAHAM is Professor in the Institute of East Asian Philosophies in Singapore.

CHAD HANSEN is Professor of Philosophy in the Department of Philosophy at the University of Vermont.

AMBROSE Y. C. KING is Chair Professor of Sociology and Head, New Asia College, of the Chinese University of Hong Kong.

LEO OU-FAN LEE is Professor of Chinese Literature in the Department of Far Eastern Languages and Civilizations at the University of Chicago.

RICHARD MATHER is Professor Emeritus of East Asian Studies at the University of Minnesota.

DONALD J. MUNRO is Professor of Philosophy in the Department of Philosophy at the University of Michigan.

TU WEI-MING is Professor of Chinese History and Philosophy, Department of East Asian Languages and Civilizations, and Chairman, Committee on the Study of Religion, at Harvard University.

CHRISTINA WHITMAN is Professor of Law at the University of Michigan Law School.

YING-SHIH YÜ is Charles Seymour Professor of History of the Department of History at Yale University.

Introduction

Individualism and Holism: Studies in Confucian and Taoist Values

Donald J. Munro

The notion of "individualism" inevitably creeps into the conversation of Americans who try to compare their country with China. It is something we supposedly have and prize which the Chinese do not now have nor probably ever had. For several generations, noncommunists and communists in China have excoriated individualism as the equivalent of selfishness. For them it is a morally insupportable value, not least because it is thought to fragment societies. Inasmuch as the word "individualism" defines a number of different, though related, value concepts in modern usage, the point of departure for our analysis will be the examination of each of these. This approach will enable us to judge exactly what it is we are supposed to have, whether or not the concept has played a role in Chinese society, past or present, and, if so, what significance has been attached to it.

The word "holism" rarely creeps into anyone's conversation, except, perhaps, that of the sociologist or philosopher. It is a scholarly word. Yet there is considerable overlap between lay remarks about individual interest being subordinate to group interest and the scholar's technical descriptions of what some holisms expect of people. The ideas suggested by the term are not exclusively scholarly. It seems to point to some Chinese ways of thinking about relations among individuals that contrast with our ways. But if anything, it is vaguer than "individualism."

The papers in this volume attempt to get a handle on these terms as they might apply to China by considering how they might fit with discussions of two influential, premodern Chinese philosophical schools. This is not to say that the contributing scholars end up agreeing on how to define individualism in the West—or, for that matter, on how to interpret the Chinese philosophical tradition. The closest they come is to affirm that the ideas of individual and whole ("whole" referring to group, nature, Tao, and the like) are complementary concepts, neither capable of adequate explanation except in terms of the other. Doctrines may differ in their relative emphasis on the one or the other, while agreeing on their interdependency. This fact is reflected in the organization of the present volume.

In spite of our contributors' differing perspectives on how to define individualism and holism, the exercise of applying the terms to China and the debate itself help to clarify the terms. The major beneficiary should be anyone who attempts to compare or contrast the values of our two societies. After considering the findings of these papers, we hope that such a person will close this book feeling better equipped to discuss the topic with some precision and to make appropriate qualifications.

In introducing the papers in this volume, I will begin by considering "individualism" as a technical term, referring to modern Western theories about the good life that are not much older than the eighteenth century. Viewed from this vantage point, individualism encompasses certain specific values, such as uniqueness, privacy, autonomy, and dignity, of which all but the first have been both identified and discussed at length by Steven Lukes.[1] Frequently, when Westerners make judgments about Chinese culture, they are comparing modern European values to those in premodern China. There is nothing wrong in this provided that the person doing the judging is aware of what he is doing. The exercise may be beneficial. For example, it may make the Westerner sensitive to what is different about his values and prevent him from immodestly assuming that what he prizes today has always been prized by rational people everywhere. But there is also the danger that he will assume that Chinese and Europeans have always had radically different world views and values associated with them and, consequently, that they are likely to in the future. In contrast, mindful that our individualistic values are relatively modern, the reader may then find himself free to ask the question: If we compare Europeans before the Enlightenment with premodern Chinese, will we find that their world views and values were also similar in important ways? I believe that the answer will be that they were, tilting in both cases toward holistic world views that were manifested in such values and behavior as social role fulfillment and the tightening of cognitive and affective links with something beyond the self. The most productive way to think about our two cultures, especially when making inferences about the future, is to keep in mind both past similarities and recent divergencies.

After a brief discussion on the applicability to premodern China of individualism as a technical term embracing certain values, I will try to explain what holism is by using examples from the Chinese case. I will introduce the topic of holism by contrasting the differing metaphysical assumptions about persons and groups that are respectively found in modern individualisms and holisms. On a broad level, the contrast concerns the relation between parts and wholes and the many and the one. The values associated with holistic philosophies in China will then be considered. Finally, in part as an aid to readers outside of the China field, I will sketch some historical considerations as background for understanding developments described in the papers.

I. Individualism

Uniqueness

Where Newton affirmed the existence of universal laws of physics, Kant (1724-1804) claimed the existence of universal moral laws. On moral issues, all rational men would identify the same rules as applicable (see Arthur Danto's comment quoted below). This position was shared by most philosophers going back to Plato. It was challenged by Sophists and Epicureans in Greece and Rome and by Renaissance skeptics such as Montaigne (1533-92). Thomas Hobbes (1588-1679) noted that people have different desires and, therefore, can be expected to have different views of the good life. But the mainstream view was rarely challenged in this way until the end of the eighteenth century. The first opponents who succeeded in sowing a lasting legacy on the matter in ethical and political thought were the German Romantics, who flourished at the end of the eighteenth and beginning of the nineteenth centuries. The Romantics stressed the values of uniqueness and *innerlichkeit*, the latter of which suggests introspection and solitude.

Friedrich Schleiermacher (1768-1834) described his revolt against the idea, prominent both in Kant and in his contemporary Johann Fichte (1762-1814), that there is a universal reason which is the same in all men. His opposing insight was that each person combines the attributes of the human in a unique way. For the first time, and for us it was a relatively recent time, influential thinkers treated individual uniqueness of thought and conduct as a primary moral value. This was the contribution of men like Friedrich von Schlegel (1772-1829), Novalis (Friedrich von Hardenberg, 1772-1801), and Friedrich Schelling (1775-1854). One study of Schlegel describes the value in the following way:

> In the fullness of individual differences Schlegel sees a new moral law. Universal sympathy is too narrow a principle for the moral *Gemut*. "The truly spiritual man feels something higher than sympathy." He feels the individuality of the other, which is sacred to him not because it is the other's but because it is individuality. For him every infinite individual is God. For "it is just individuality that is the original and eternal in man; mere personality is not so momentous. To pursue the cultivation and development of this individuality as one's highest calling would be divine egoism."[2]

The moral man should express his uniqueness in his life in a manner akin to the original artist in his creative act.

Uniqueness eventually became one of the principal values of modern individualism, concretely cultivated in American schools through the child-centered curriculum reforms of the Progressive Education Movement. John Stuart Mill and John Dewey were two of the bridges between German ideas and the American audience. For this audience the value was linked to progress: individual variation in people's points of view is precious because it promotes the growth of the progressive society.

Individuality or uniqueness as a value does have a history in China. Confucians wrote so much about what men share, about self-fulfillment as equal to the realization of common moral sentiments and judgments, that it comes as a pleasant surprise to encounter at the end of the Han dynasty (206 B.C.-A.D. 220) the emergence of a cry for diversity. As Yü Ying-shih notes in his paper, "By the end of the Han dynasty singularity [i^a] had become a positive value. A personality would be favorably judged precisely because it was singular, different, or extraordinary. On the other hand, the idea of identity or sameness [t'ung] was held in contempt." Interested in how personalities differ, the elite developed a technique for analyzing and evaluating character. Professor Yü mentions the Jen-wu chih [Treatise on personality], the only surviving characterological work from the early Six Dynasties period (220-589), which emphasizes reaching beyond a person's physical appearance to grasp his spirit. (It was followed in later centuries by works like the Shih-shuo hsin-yü [A new account of tales of the world].)[3] According to this methodology, study of the eyes best reveals the uniqueness that lies in men. Portraiture developed in tandem with the interest in the individual subject's eyes. Professor Yü tells us that the great fourth-century painter Ku K'ai-chih (355-406?) would not dot the pupils of the eyes in an otherwise finished portrait for several years, awaiting the appropriate time to capture his subject's spiritual uniqueness. Professor Mather carries the same theme well into the Six Dynasties period, when concise characterizations of unique traits flourished as a theme of "Pure Conversation" in the elite salons. Unconventional personalities, such as Hsi K'ang (223-262), were expressing their "true selves" in following spontaneous inclinations as they drank wine and, as the stories go, cavorted with pigs in rustic settings.

In contrast, Neo-Confucians would argue that being true to the higher self should imply fairly similar goals on everyone's part. In her paper, Irene Bloom denies that Chu Hsi (1130-1200) ever advocated the abandonment of diversity of personality. Accommodation to the cosmic whole, as she puts it, never invites dissolution of the self or its special traits. It is true that Neo-Confucians recognized that there must be many paths to sagehood because of the wide variety of individual personalities. Chu Hsi quotes one of the eleventh-century Ch'eng brothers on several well-known figures: "Confucius was quite clear and pure of disposition. Yen Tzu was quite happy and at ease. And Mencius was quite a vigorous debater."[4] The descriptions of sage-like characters are fairly rich in remarks about variations in their styles, such as their approaches to teaching, and in the differing effects on others of such styles. Combining these descriptions with those of less noble figures, we have lengthy lists of admirable and not so admirable qualities. The portraits of decent disciples reveal mixtures of the two traits, such as uprightness coupled with backwardness in learning.

But I would argue that in Confucianism the common traits of the sage-like types stand out as the ideal features for people to copy. Most of the differences between people mentioned by the Sung philosophers describe how they vary in terms of distance from a standard of clarity of understanding or from a standard of exact propriety of response to some event. Difference is a fact of life to be coped with and changed if possible. The goals to prize are the common (not the unique) traits of the sages: empathy with things that live, emotional balance, goal commitment, respect for social role responsibilities. Progress in self-cultivation is progress in realizing what men share, such as familial sentiments and the ability to nurture living things. Such progress involves transforming and changing the physical endowment that differentiates people. Although in their philosophical writings Neo-Confucians never exalted uniqueness as an intrinsic value to be prized nor assumed that good people could have different views of the good life, their ranks were peopled by unique individuals. Indeed, there is a tradition going back to the earliest Taoist texts of individuality as eccentricity. Some eccentric Confucians were revered as heroes by their later Confucian peers in part because of their unconventional pursuit of shared Confucian goals. The most famous such hero is Wang Yang-ming (1472-1529), known for the eccentricity, or "madness" (*k'uang*), with which he pursued sagehood. We can place Li Chih (1527-1602) under an odd corner of the umbrella raised by Wang. Li is one of many nonconformists of a second age of diversity, the late Ming (1368-1643). He once wrote, "Each man Heaven gives birth to has his own individual function and he does not need to learn this from Confucius."[5]

Innerlichkeit means to be inner, to have an inner world. It is turning away from the mundane, from convention, from conformity, and especially from material popular culture. It is turning to one's inner resources, out of which self-development grows. This mode of being corresponds precisely to Thoreau's notion of a man not keeping pace with his companions because he hears "a different drummer." For the German Romantics, who emphasized such subjectivity in the creative development of the individual personality, one's own drummer is likely to be different from someone else's.

Some Taoists and Sung and Ming Neo-Confucians also treat subjectivity, i.e., turning away from the material and mundane, as essential to self-development. There are points of convergence on this theme in the papers by Tu Wei-ming and Wolfgang Bauer. They concern the idea of solitariness or being watchful when alone. Bauer traces the shift in the meaning of solitariness from the solitude of the hermit in his retreat to solitude as a Neo-Confucian means of self-discovery. The latter enriched a new form of individualism in the late Ming. Tu provides a concrete example from the Ming in which solitariness was a method of self-cultivation involving the examination of one's motives, said to enhance energy for self-improvement. In both Chinese and Western culture, subjectivity is supposed to enhance sensitivity. However, there are some important differences between the two perspectives on this point. In the Confucian case, the inner resources through which one develops oneself will be the same for all men in many respects (e.g., consciousness of familial sentiments or of the power to create). The Germans made no such presumption. The introspective Confucian would, of course, discover unique things about his own personality, about his motives and emotions. However, though these are important, for the Confucian they are merely the facts determining the challenge of cultivation, not differences to be cherished for their own sake and nurtured as part of self-development. Confucianism, unlike Western romantic thought, never viewed the unique qualities of individuals as a realm of intrinsic philosophical interest.

None of this is to deny that the Confucian, like the Taoist, may find understanding, satisfaction, and development in discipline as a result of solitary practices of self-expression. Calligraphy is the most obvious example. Such activity may provide the individual with a sense of control absent elsewhere in his life and reveal to him particularities about his personality.[6] For the Confucian involved in artistic creativity, the expression of those particularities may be important after he copies and then transcends the models of his masters. Practices like calligraphy are means of reaching the goal of sagehood, and in this sense discovery of one's particular qualities is a significant step in striving towards a universal goal. People differ in the means appropriate to achieve the universal goals. Hence knowing about and expressing particularities of personality in the course of self-development, by these varying means, is a worthy undertaking. This is a qualification to our comments about the relative unimportance of uniqueness as a value in China.

Many European philosophers expected to find uniqueness in the individual's emotional life and the capacity for sameness in his reason. They would have been surprised to realize that Confucians regarded some morally important emotions as the same in all people. The implication is that the European expectations of emotional uniqueness may have been arbitrary, and once the European model is challenged in this way, it in turn raises the complementary question of whether "rational thinking" may differentiate persons as much as the emotions do. In any case, lacking a categorical split between emotion and reason, the Confucians had no difficulty idealizing commonality of the fused cognitive and emotional response by sages to the same situation, while expecting situational variation in such responses by ordinary persons.

Another major difference is that the Neo-Confucian completed the process of self-realization in a communal setting, preferably in public service, where the highly formalized role types were uncongenial to individuality. The Confucian associated the expression of individuality with retirement from public service. The German individualist achieved self-realization in artistic creation or the aesthetic absorption of the world around him. In such creation he drew upon the personal experiences to which his subjectivity sensitized him. Uniqueness of creation was a moral goal central to the German idea of self-realization, but not to the Confucian. In actuality, there was always the possibility that the artistic model of the modern individualist would lead its proponents to a certain uniformity in eccentricity, "Left-Bank chic."

But the most basic point is that the Westerner is likely erroneously to equate subjectivity (in the sense of introspection and solitude) and its role in self-development with individuality or uniqueness. He is likely to do this because of their long association, starting with the Romantics. In China, these two concepts overlapped when it was a question of discovery by the individual of his transitory motives or emotional state. But the Confucian can make a place for subjectivity in self-development without treating uniqueness as something to be preserved or enhanced. Subjectivity is not the same thing as the individuality prized by modern individualism.

Southern Sung (1127-1280) interest in contemplation and solitude was in part the result of the failure of Northern Sung (960-1127) practical political reformist activity. Chu Hsi, a Southern Sung Neo-Confucian, spent nine years in official service. During those nine years, he revived schools, developed curricula, built granaries, promoted tax cuts for the poor, and pushed for local control over supplies in the granaries—clearly an activist when in office. While opposed to devoting "half the day to quiet-sitting," a version of Buddhist meditation, he did recognize the need for some solitary contemplation as part of cultivation. W. T. de Bary has explained that "Neo-Confucian cultivation would, to a remarkable and unprecedented degree, be self-centered—that is, focused on the individual person and carried on in relative isolation."[7] The need for solitude for contemplation sometimes conflicted with the obligation of public service. The tension was especially acute in the case of Wang Yang-ming and some of his followers. However, as Tu Wei-ming illustrates with the example of Liu Tsung-chou (1578-1645), in the long run self-development can only occur in a communal setting. The individual may begin with self-reflection in his solitude but must thereafter return to transform himself with the aid of others, cooperatively helping the cosmic creative process. Subjectivity and the communal life are complementary, not opposed. Silence and the official robe were not incompatible. Even in a special Taoist case discussed by Kuo Hsiang (d. 312), the "court hermit" remains on the job but is able psychologically to withdraw to the mountain forest.

Turning to the modern period, as Leo Ou-fan Lee shows in his paper on "romantic individualism" on the eve of modern China's emergence, things changed briefly when some writers associated with the May Fourth Movement (1919) were particularly preoccupied with their own feelings and experiences to the exclusion of communal activism. They used the terms *ke-jen* and *ke-hsing* (individuality), terms shaped in meaning by contact with Western thought, in discussing the individual's unique personality. The special qualities were not so much character traits as emotions, the writer's own "feelings, moods, visions, and even dreams." They believed that highly personal experience is the building block of literary creation.

Another Chinese advocate of individualism at this time, not extensively discussed by Leo Lee, was Hu Shih (1891-1962). Influenced by his perception of American democracy and John Dewey's philosophy, Hu Shih's individualism centered on the growth of the individual's personality (though his views on the direction of that growth remained unclear) and the intellectual's independent judgment. He juxtaposed such growth and independence to obedience to hierarchical Confucian social roles and to conformity with traditional Confucian values. He believed that the few intellectuals capable of such individualism could gradually transform the

Chinese people as a whole through education. But often leading thinkers such as Liang Sou-ming[8] objected that such individualism is alien to the Chinese, because it requires a conception of rights of the individual in opposition to authority, and such a conception has never existed in China. Returning to Leo Lee's May Fourth period writers, he finds that by the late 1920s, in a manner in tune with the requirements of the spirit, though not the name of the Neo-Confucian legacy, this combination of individuality and subjectivism gave way to renewed interest among intellectuals in units larger than the self: the city, the region, and the country. And even in their earlier days of preoccupation with breaking the constraint of traditional Confucian family roles, they never ignored the social realities of their time.

Privacy

Privacy is one of the foremost values of the modern liberal. It refers to areas of thought and conduct that should not be subject to intrusion by the public or by the government. The liberal can trace the roots of his values to the writings of people like John Locke, John Stuart Mill, and Benjamin Constant. Privacy as it bears on *beliefs* has sources in our religious history. The beliefs in question were originally those concerning religion and ethics. Demand for tolerance is a legacy of the efforts by minority Protestant groups in the seventeenth century, (for example, the Baptists and Socinians) to retain a zone of freedom of religious conscience against civil authorities. In time the range extended to include all beliefs that in the believer's eye do not endanger others. When applied to beliefs, privacy also includes the idea that the individual alone has adequate access to his inner processes. Mental events are private and not directly accessible to other persons. Thus, applied to beliefs, privacy is both a value to be legally protected and a concept in the philosophy of mind. These are different concepts.

Focusing on privacy in the sense of a value to be protected, John Stuart Mill popularized the notion that there is some purely personal or private *conduct* that is none of the public's business. He wrote that "the strongest of all the arguments against the interference of the public with purely personal conduct is that, when it does interfere, the odds are that it interferes wrongly and in the wrong place."[9] Under the influence of Wilhelm von Humboldt (1767-1835), one of the German Romantics, Mill linked the protection of this kind of privacy with the cultivation of the value of uniqueness. His views on this topic are worth quoting at length:

> Few persons, out of Germany, even comprehend the meaning of the doctrine which Wilhelm von Humboldt, so eminent both as a *savant* and as a politician, made the text of a treatise... that, therefore, the object "toward which every human being must ceaselessly direct his efforts, and on which especially those who design to influence their fellow men must ever keep their eyes, is the individuality of power and development"; that for this there are two requisites, "freedom and variety of situations"; and that from the union of these arise "individual vigor and manifold diversity," which combine themselves in "originality."[10]

Originality flourishes where diversity of both opinion and purely personal conduct is permitted to flourish.

For the modern liberal, "purely personal conduct" often concerns personal relationships. Isaiah Berlin referred to negative liberty as involving a "sense of privacy ... of the area of personal relationships as something in its own right."[11] As Christina Whitman shows in her paper, privacy in the modern world has much to do with protecting the individual's ability to form bonds quite unlike those that pertain in public society, particularly in the family setting. The French historian Fernand Braudel wrote that "Privacy was an eighteenth century innovation" and went on to describe changes in the design of family living arrangements which reflected this new value. It was at this time that family dwellings began to include, in addition to a reception and a public room, a private apartment where family members could live as they pleased and, within that, a bedroom as a realm apart. Such arrangements had not existed earlier, in the high cultures of Rome, Tuscany under the Medicis, or France under Louis XIV.[12] Professor Whitman notes that in Confucian idealizations, bonds formed within the family were not viewed as qualitatively distinct from other sorts of social bonds. They were, instead, viewed as models for the varieties of relationships between individual and state. (Yü Ying-shih does remind us, however, of a brief moment during the Six Dynasties period when some individuals idealized the emotional relationship between husband and wife to a previously unencountered degree.)

It is tempting to seize the example of Chinese hermits and other practitioners of withdrawal as evidence of Chinese appreciation for privacy as a value. There is nothing wrong with this provided we remember that privacy as the modern liberal understands it is a recent value with certain connotations that must be sifted out before the comparison will work. First, the hermits did seek a realm free from interference from the aristocratic moralist or government agent. But this does not mean they thought of privacy as a right or as any kind of legitimate privilege that their rulers owed them. There were no arguments for institutionalized protection of privacy. Second, they sought at least occasional protection from intrusion for their complete daily life, rather than specific aspects of it. In the case of the modern liberal, it is his beliefs, his intimate relationships, his mail, for which he seeks privacy. He is usually not seeking any form of general isolation or social distancing. In contrast, privacy of beliefs, relationships, and property are not topics that we associate with Chinese eremitism.

The liberal may seek privacy as an aid to self-development. Angus Graham explains Chuang Tzu's (369?-286? B.C.) rejection of any official role by appealing to the belief that the Taoist who is allowed to be *tu* (alone/ on one's own) "will grow naturally into his own unique shape like water finding its level inside irregular contours."

This is essentially the concern of many poets during the Six Dynasties period. Richard Mather tells us about the desire of poets such as Hsi K'ang and T'ao Ch'ien (365-427?) to escape the "cage" of official life. Withdrawal from worldly concerns was one way to permit the "true self" to develop by itself, a course of development that was expected to be at odds with social norms. Wolfgang Bauer speaks of the hermit who "bars his door," who lives apart as a way of avoiding the obstacles which separate man from nature. In the end, his privacy "aimed not at the preservation of the ego but rather at its expansion and final dissolution in cosmos and nature." Judith Berling alerts us to the fact that, according to Chuang Tzu, after the sage properly fasts his mind, there is no longer a distinct self. We may wonder what kind of self-development Chuang Tzu and the hermits might have had in mind that led, not to the amplification of some personal traits, but rather to the loss of any distinct self. Can it still be called "*self*-cultivation"? Should we speak of Taoists nurturing their characters rather than their selves? Herein lies a paradox in mysticism. To the outside observer the mystic's experience of the world is ineffable, private, the product of self-exploration; yet, for the mystic himself, there may be a *loss* of self.

There are some interesting qualifications to be made with respect to the isolation of Chinese hermits. As Wolfgang Bauer notes, they originally lived in small groups, not in complete isolation. Furthermore, while many early Taoists focused on limiting social and sexual relationships, those limits were never contracted to the point of celibacy. Even Chuang Tzu, whose writings are filled with anecdotes about hermits, allegedly was married. Taoist hermits began to practice celibacy only when Buddhism gained cultural strength, and even then they practiced it erratically. Further qualifying the meaning of social isolation as applied to Chinese eremitism, Professor Mather argues that, while barring their doors, most of the Six Dynasties eccentrics, such as the Seven Sages of the Bamboo Grove (fl. A.D. 262), accepted the traditional portrait of the universe as hierarchical, with a built-in structure based on mutual obligation. In other words, even though social "drop-outs" themselves, they did not reject the cosmological basis for belief in customary social roles, only their current abuses. Yü Ying-shih would argue for a stronger position than Mather's, namely, that the Neo-Taoists *had* shifted from a hierarchical conception of the Tao to a more egalitarian one. Hierarchical order does exist in the world, but it is secondary to some greater reality, "nonbeing" that is void of hierarchy.

Christina Whitman writes that when the ideal state is flourishing, the Confucian may see no need at all for a zone of privacy to promote self-development. The goals of self-control and state control are in this case identical. However, short of that utopia, many Neo-Confucians required periods of isolation for contemplation as part of the process of self-realization.

Some cases of Taoist eremitism had nothing to do with self-development. The motive for withdrawal from public service or retirement from the capital to the small village was often to protect one's life during periods of political intrigue and power struggles. This was particularly true during the Golden Age of eremitism in the third and early fourth centuries. On occasion, the recluse in his wilderness retreat had a positive function quite unconnected with self-development. Bauer relates in his essay a charming anecdote about such an individual who, serving as an "official in the wilderness," purveyor of culture to the mountains, and exemplar of correct relations between man and forest, betrayed this role when he left to become an actual official at the capital.

> [By leaving the Northern Mountain] he had made the red cloud glisten in solitude high in the sky, the bright moon rise lonely, the green pine throw its shadow for no purpose, and the white cloud wander without companion. . . . The hermit's bed surrounded by orchids is empty, and so the crane cries melancholically at night. The hermit disappeared, and in the morning the apes realized this to their dismay.

For Confucians, too, as Professor Bauer shows, the retreat to solitude sometimes had nothing to do with self-development. Heroic officials during the Chou set a precedent for withdrawal to preserve purity of will, that is, to avoid compromising standards by serving a morally corrupt ruler. Moreover, especially during the later dynasties, the Confucian often withdrew out of loyalty to a fallen imperial house, refusing to serve its conqueror.

Autonomy

Autonomy, sometimes associated with the individualistic character of choice making, and sometimes with independence from various influences, is another value that has been associated with modern Western individualism. Its meaning is slippery. One approach holds that a person is autonomous when his actions are the result of his own choices rather than of the restraining causes or threats of some person or thing external to the individual.

There are precursors of this view in the classical period of Greece and Rome. The Epicureans claimed the presence of a free will that liberates man from restraint by fate; his actions are not merely effects of prior states of atoms in his body and environment. They explained it in terms of the will being able to cause a new, swerving motion in the mind's atoms. Early Christianity claimed that men are free to affirm or deny God's laws. It attributed a special responsibility to men in their exercise of free will. Irene Bloom argues that the Augustinian view of free choice is qualitatively different from the earlier Epicurean one. I would add that what is new in Christian thought about free will is God, and the need to make Him blameless for human errors so as to preserve His omnipotence and omnibenevolence. Human evil, including error, are explained in terms of misuse of free will, and God's goodness is retained. Eventually European thinkers developed another approach: man is able to identify reasons for acting and then select choices because he has a faculty of reason that can function independently of the desires and other physical influences. Kant contributed most to the modern Western formulation of this value, describing each person as free to the extent that he is able to legislate moral rules to himself. Autonomy is central to the modern European view of what a person is.

The *Analects* reports that Confucius said, "The commander of the forces of a large State may be carried off, but the will of even a common man cannot be taken from him."[13] Since that time, Confucians have not questioned the possibility of the individual's independence of will. But choice making, or willing, has not often been at the center of ethical concern. The will does not play the key role in identifying what is distinctively human. Humans are distinctive because they have certain feelings (such as love of kin) and because they are able to extend those feelings to other people, outside the family. In this process, they give rise to the variety of virtues, such as loyalty, all of which have roots in kinship love.

One occasion for choice stands out in Confucian works. This is when one chooses commitment to a lifetime goal of self-improvement, called "striving to be a sage" or a true person. For the Neo-Confucian, once this choice is made, the individual's attention shifts to eradicating or removing obstacles: eradicating the polluting selfish thoughts that impede the individual's natural predisposition to follow patterns of proper relations with things. Occasionally, a momentous moral choice confronts the individual; but more likely than not it is the negative choice of whether to resign from office, for any of the reasons described in the section on privacy above. There is little encouragement to test ethical problems by trying unorthodox solutions. The ultimate values always remain the same, so there is no worry about choosing a different life path.

Choice making is discussed in the texts, but it is on the back burner. In the *Chu Tzu yü-lei* [Classified conversations of Master Chu (Hsi)] there is the obvious recognition that everyone "chooses" how to implement general rules in concrete circumstances. In that text, the philosophically important discussion concerns choice when there is a conflict between the objective and constant principles (*ching*) and individual intuitions about the best choice in a specific situation. Some of the *ching*, like social role duties, are both objective or recorded in classics and also innate; others are entirely objective, like ritual rules. There is a commonsensical recognition that where the correct course indicated by a situation is likely to be uncontroversial (and generally agreed), individual choice based on subjective considerations is legitimate. It is fine to ignore the taboo against touching the hand of a female not your wife or from your bloodline in order to save a woman from drowning, and it is fine to drink a summer liquid in winter if the weather turns unseasonably warm. However, even in discussing these examples, Chu Hsi reveals his clear preference for the objectivity of the *ching*. For him these are abnormal situations that should be kept to a minimum: counterexamples that only prove the general supremacy of the *ching*. When the issue involves those *ching* that pertain to social role duties cementing the authority structure, his position is that the ordinary person (who, we might add, wishes to save his skin) had better ignore individual choice entirely and stick to obeying the objective rules. For example, where the *ching* require loyalty to king and the individual's feelings suggest that there is reason to kill him, or the rules require obedience to parents, who select brides, and the individual contemplates choosing to ignore them, Chu Hsi counsels a prudent submission to the authority of the *ching*.[14]

The more morally cultivated you become, the more your actions naturally hit the proper mark without your having to go through the anguish of deciding what rule to apply or how to apply it. Deliberate moral reasoning in the Western sense is a sign of inadequate personal progress rather than the distinctive feature of humankind. In dealing with a number of these issues, Irene Bloom suggests one reason choice making is present but "drained of tension" in China. It is that within Confucianism there is no mind-body problem and thus no attendant conflict between the rules legislated by reason and the choices offered by physical desires.

The central problem in self-cultivation is not the proper exercise of free choice, as is hypothesized in so much of Western ethics. Rather, it is how to remove obstacles that prevent the natural growth of the mind through principle, or that distort incoming impressions. This means that the problem is identifying and then removing selfish thoughts.

At the same time that the issue of autonomy remained a subordinate one for Confucians, some Confucians were interested in questions concerning the will. This interest fits in with the topic of self-cultivation or education, learning how to cleanse the mind of obstacles. In particular, the student was taught to examine his motivational structure so as to become aware of his intentions, the reasons behind them, and what behavior is likely to result. As Tu Wei-ming illustrates with the case of Liu Tsung-chou, this is a way of keeping tabs on one's moral growth.

Kant linked freedom to the exercise of autonomy. Superficially, we can find Taoists interested in a freedom that bears a slight resemblance to Kant's. Richard Mather defines the character *ta* as "total freedom from inhibition" and the Taoists who realize it as "free spirits" (*ta-jen*). They prized the absence of constraints imposed by popular values and customary rules. There is some similarity in this to the attitude of persons during the European Enlightenment who placed their own moral decisions ahead of those of the crowd. But a fundamental difference remains. The Taoist free spirit transcended the limits of ordinary understanding by attaining the cosmic perspective of the man who is intuitively wise. The Enlightenment individualist substituted for it the product of critical, analytical reasoning.

On a deeper level, Kantian autonomy assumes a distinction between reason and desire, and the ability of reason to reject any specific desire. This distinction does not exist in Taoism. Taoist freedom involves forgetting convention and, perhaps, following desire. Thus, there really is no parallel concept of freedom in the Kantian and Taoist cases.

We can learn more about the role of choice making by examining the *Book of Changes*, which many Confucians and Six Dynasties Taoists regarded as a repository of truths. In his paper, Wolfgang Bauer points to the prominence at the very beginning of *Changes* of the individual whose will is "firm as a rock," like a "concealed dragon": "The concealed dragon refrains from action. What does this signify? [He] ... withdraws from the world without regret, cares not that no one seeks him, does what pleases him, and avoids whatever might grieve him. Firm as a rock, he can by no means be uprooted. This is the concealed dragon."[15] Bauer describes some of the Six Dynasties "hermits in town," whose wills were purportedly firm as rocks. They practiced eremitism of attitude while dwelling, not in the forest, but in town. Unlike Confucians, these Taoists did not link this value of autonomy to self-development. The independent wills of these hermits directed them to drunkenness, negligence of duties in office, and the breaking of ritual taboos. As autonomy degenerated into libertinism, their influence lost the broad appeal that might have roused a movement.

Dignity

Like privacy and autonomy, the content that we give the idea of dignity of the individual is a recent Western development. Its roots, however, extend far back in time, to the Platonic claim that reason is the highest part of man, the part that is akin to the divine Ideas. Aristotle claimed that practical and theoretical reason are peculiar to man and, moreover, the "best thing in us." Our later religious tradition enhanced this reason-centered basis for human worth by contributing the doctrine that each person has a divine soul, made in the image of God, and that God loves persons equally. Reason resides in the soul. As Chad Hansen notes in his first essay, the modern notion of dignity also owes much to Kant. For Kant, individuals deserve respect because they have a special ability to know moral principles through reason, and this ability is independent of the rules of any particular culture in which they may live. Thus, dignity and autonomy are linked. Our worth as individuals stems from our ability to act as lawgivers unto ourselves. Not all philosophers have accepted the Kantian position. The utilitarian objection is the best known. But Hansen makes the case that institutionally, especially in our judicial system, the Kantian position has been absorbed. Contemporary legal arguments for retributive punishment presuppose the existence of individuals as rational beings who are able to identify the correct moral course.

There is an assumption of individual worth in the Mencian doctrine that all individuals possess an evaluating mind. Anyone can be a sage like Yao and Shun. (This mind is not like Aristotelian reason. It belongs as much to the realm of the sentiments as it does to cognition, a kind of fusion of knowing that something is right and feeling warmly toward it or knowing something is wrong and hating it.) Carrying the Mencian torch more than a millennium later, Wang Yang-ming's moral psychology implies the worth of the individual. It is anchored in his doctrine of innate knowledge (*liang chih*) equally possessed by all humans. It is also implied by his related claim, in function akin to Descartes' *cogito ergo sum*, that each person can look within and find an indubitable sentiment on which he can build all subsequent moral judgments, thereby finding the path to the impartiality of mind that constitutes sagehood. That sentiment is love of parents. The certainty attaching to insight into the original sentiment infuses acts, the motivation for which can be traced back to that sentiment, assuring us that the acts will be appropriate. And W. T. de Bary believes that Chu Hsi, too, implies a doctrine of individual dignity when he talks about each individual's ability to aid in the cosmic process of creation.

These comparisons have some merit as long as one remembers that the justifications for individual worth are quite different in the two cultures and time periods (reason, divinity of soul, and God's love in the Western rationalist and Christian cases, as opposed to evaluating mind plus moral sentiments or the capacity to become a sage, or heaven as the source of human nature in the Confucian case). The closest explicit Confucian comments about individual worth are like this: Everyone has something he can prize (i.e., his originally good nature); thus, everyone can become a sage.[16] Confucians also spoke about the dignity that attaches to social position and how conduct can sustain or damage that dignity. Yet there remains a divergence in viewpoint on the institutional function of the idea of individual worth between modern Europe and premodern China. In Europe this idea came to underlie the theory and practice of equality before the law. Premodern China not only lacked such a view of law but also positively required differential punishment for the same crime, as a function of the differing hierarchical social roles of culprit and victim. And Chad Hansen points to the Chinese tradition of group responsibility that is consistent with a utilitarian consequentialism. No special concern exists for the individual when it is social order that is paramount.

In the case of the Taoists, assertions about the special worth of each human would elicit derisive hoots. Such claims would be interpreted as but another Confucian attempt to substitute a biased human perspective for the cosmic view. From the standpoint of the Tao, nothing has special worth—or all things have the same worth. How pompous of humans to think that any one of them has worth while a louse does not, or to harp on the former and ignore the latter.

This comparison of modern Western individualistic values with premodern Confucian and Taoist ethical thought has highlighted some core differences between the values of the two cultures. If we are contrasting from the standpoint of time period, the root of our divergence rests in the nineteenth-century German Romantics, who prized individuality as uniqueness and advocated its unfettered cultivation. The Western liberal is probably unaware that prior to the nineteenth century, the acceptance of uniformity in ultimate matters was the norm in Europe. And that is a point of convergence rather than divergence between China and Europe prior to the modern age. In his concluding remarks to this volume, Arthur Danto writes of Immanuel Kant that "the rational being is perceived as a legislator, but then each legislator, or rational being, enacts only those principles each other legislator would enact upon suitable ratiocination, so that in the end everyone must think alike." With suitable modifications, this conclusion would be affirmed by most Confucians as well.

The implications of this point are profound for any modern Western individualist who inherits both elements of the Kantian view on rationality and sameness of thought, and elements of the Romantics. For example, a curious aspect of the association of dignity and autonomy is that the idea of autonomy could serve as an argument to undermine dignity. Kantian autonomy assumes the existence of universal reason, which may imply sameness of moral judgment in all humans. Locked into the *a priori* dictates of such a faculty, the person could be seen as stripped of crucial elements of individuality, thereby losing a portion of his dignity in the process.

If we ignore time frames and contrast cultures, something else stands out. Linked in some way to many of the modern individualistic values is a belief that a faculty of reason is a special trait of humans. This refers to the ability to intuit universal truths and logically to deduce other truths from them. Each individual possesses it, and it gives him personal, unmediated access to truth. Descartes is the modern father of this claim, insisting that "the power of judging well and of distinguishing between the true and the false, which, properly speaking, is what is called good sense, or reason, is by nature equal in all men."[17] The comparable "special" human trait identified by Confucians belongs more to the realm of affect or disposition than to the realm of cognition. The important point about those familial emotions is that they relate the individual to other people. The prominence in China of familial feeling as basic and the prominence in the West of reason have led to differently weighted visions of self-fulfillment. There has been no shortage of Western writers idealizing as most noble the life of reason, of grasping fixed truths and making deductions from them. There has been no shortage of Chinese having the same attitude toward the life of proper relationships, characterized by skill in responding sensitively to others based on knowledge of their situation in a scheme of familylike social nets.

II. Holism

Many advocates of modern individualistic values also adhere to a way of thinking about the individual person that has no influential or well-developed counterpart in China. This works to put even more distance between the premodern Chinese doctrines that we have discussed and the Western advocates of these individualistic values. According to this modern perspective, each individual person possesses key traits independent of any social relations. Those traits may be interests, abilities, or needs. An account of each person can be given without considering society or any unit larger than the individual. Society is an artificial human construct organized to cater to those traits of individuals; it is simply an aggregate of the many individuals so conceived. Thinkers at the beginning of the liberal democratic heritage who are associated with this perspective are Hobbes and Locke. J. S. Mill probably would have rejected it. Contemporary philosophers, political theorists, and sociologists who accept this metaphysical view will insist on explaining a social whole, such as a family, organization, or state, in terms of the psychological orientation and behavior of individuals. Holistic sociology is reduced to psychology.

Holistic theories, in contrast, are those that explain the relation of wholes and parts in a different way. Usually, this means to regard parts as components of integrated structures, which are the wholes. Thus, parts exist only within wholes, to which they have inseparable relations. Let us call this the "part-whole" approach (see the reference to Hansen below). In an organism, one thinks of molecules in relation to cells and organs and tissues rather than of molecules by themselves. As applied to persons, these explanations reject the atomistic way of explaining persons in the Hobbes-Locke model. They insist on understanding persons in terms of their relation to some whole, such as the family, society, Tao, Principle, or Pure Consciousness. Wholes have identity in themselves, meaning that they are not reducible without major qualitative loss of that identity. Some sociologists, including Durkheim, argue for holistic explanations of the relation of individual persons and society. Their position is that "explanations in terms of individual goals, aims, and purposes are necessarily out of place in social science, which should only concern itself with the behavior of social, that is, holistic phenomena."[18]

Another characteristic of holisms is that in many instances they assign purposes or goals to wholes, such as clans, families, or nature. The destiny of individuals is a function of their relation to the whole and its purposes. For the Neo-Confucian in China, a purpose of nature as a whole is the nourishment and perpetuation of creativity and life. However, philosophical Taoists and Ch'an Buddhists are an exception. They do not in any literal sense picture the whole (Tao, or the One Mind) as having a purpose.

Holisms assume that there is a stable structure to the whole in spite of changing parts. For the holistic sociologist, this means that groups exhibit regular behavior because of that structure, in spite of the flux of their individual members.[19] Such a sociologist will be less interested in the goals, behavior, or psychological condition of particular individuals than in the goals, regular behavior, and structure of groups. These group structures will be articulated through a network of relationships, often hierarchical, between different social roles. Finally, and of special interest to us in this volume, certain values are associated with holistic metaphysics and explanations. In the Confucian case, these include role fulfillment, social order, harmony, comprehensive knowledge, and assisting the creative powers of nature. Let us now turn to our overview of holism in China.

In his paper on "Individualism in Chinese Thought," Chad Hansen develops a thesis concerning Chinese holistic theories of explanation. It focuses on their views of language and the metaphysical presuppositions underlying those views. His thesis is that Chinese theories of language presuppose a part-whole way of dividing things, in contrast to certain Western models based on the many-one dichotomy. The former explains things by showing how users of the language divide up wholes. Parts have no inherent principle of individuation. By contrast, the many-one dichotomy involves explanation by referring to the mechanistic behavior of determinate individual, interchangeable units, such as atoms or persons, included in one larger unit. Hansen argues that the metaphysical dominance of holistic, or nonindividuating, models in a culture may be one reason why native scholars construct holistic portraits of society, as did Confucians.

My own essay differentiates three different holisms in the Ch'eng-Chu (twelfth-century) school. Each variant assumes that things exist only as integrated parts of wholes. One holism, which predates the Sung period, explains persons in terms of their occupancy of mutually related social roles that form parts of a hierarchical social order. That order itself is part of a cosmic order, explained by analogy with the family, in which each thing in nature and cosmos has a fixed place, akin to the fixed social places of father, wife, older son, younger son, and so forth in the family. The Chinese term for role is *fen*, literally meaning "portion." It overlaps in meaning to some extent with the Western notion of rights. However, one's *fen* is always conceived of as a share of the whole, such as the Tao, and not as a distinct set of rights belonging to the individual as an individual.

Role fulfillment deemphasizes particular qualities the person may possess as an individual. In the words of one study, "the decisive fact is whether a position can develop whose rights and duties can be excercised not just by one individual in his uniqueness. Only with deindividualization are role norms formed."[20] This Neo-Confucian holism is similar to holisms in traditional societies, identified by Louis Dumont in *Homo Hierarchicus*. Dumont cites an intriguing passage from de Tocqueville that sums up the former's explanation for this kind of holism:

> Among aristocratic nations, as families remain for centuries in the same condition, often on the same spot, all generations become as it were contemporaneous. A man almost always knows his forefathers and respects them: he thinks he already sees his remote descendants and he loves them. He willingly imposes duties on himself towards the former and the latter; and he will frequently sacrifice his personal gratifications to those who went before and to those who will come after him.... As in aristocratic communities all the citizens occupy fixed positions, one above the other, the result is that each of them always sees a man above himself whose patronage is necessary to him, and below himself another man whose cooperation he may claim. Men living in aristocratic ages are therefore almost always closely attached to something placed out of their own sphere, and they are often disposed to forget themselves.[21]

Richard Mather argues in his paper that both Confucians and Six Dynasties Taoists accepted the hierarchical whole as a given.

The Western thinker may mistakenly infer from reference to fixed social roles that he is faced with a totally static holism. However, so strongly did Confucians believe that all things exist in a state of constant growth and change that their image of social roles is one of change as well. The most obvious example is the continual role changes to which each individual is subject, such as from daughter or son to mother or father. The holistic hierarchies about which Louis Dumont wrote are static in that the roles do not change, but they may be dynamic in that any individual's duties towards others change as the individuals change.

Another Neo-Confucian holism rests on the claim that things are linked by being penetrated by a single ordering principle and that the pattern in its entirety is present in each thing. This concept came to Neo-Confucianism by way of Taoism, and the Berling, Mather, and Bauer papers discuss Taoist portraits of the individual in terms of his relation to the Tao. Chinese Buddhism, too, contributed to this holistic metaphysic, as in the T'ien-t'ai notion that all phenomenal things are integrated: the doctrine of "all in one, one in all." The relationship of the One Mind (Buddha) to the disparate phenomena (dharmas) formed an enduring problem for Chinese Buddhist schools.

The part-whole explanation frequently underlies accounts of the mind. For example, some writers, Buddhist and Neo-Confucian, speak of only one cosmic mind, in which individuals share. Lu Hsiang-shan (1139-1193) wrote, "The universe is my mind and my mind is the universe. Sages appeared tens of thousands of generations ago. They shared this mind; they shared this principle. Sages will appear tens of thousands of generations to come. They will share this mind; they will share this principle."[22] This view is astonishingly different from the picture of mind held by most Westerners, that mind is a thing discretely and individually possessed by each person—many minds rather than one mind.

Chu Hsi did not share Lu Hsiang-shan's idea about mind. However, his own account of mind also falls under the part-whole explanatory approach. The whole is all that exists and the parts are linked to each other and to the whole, not as pieces of a pie, but as ropes in a net, relationally. Thus, an important characteristic of the mind is cognitive awareness (*chih-chüeh*). It can be explained only in terms of the principles inherent in it and in other things, which it knows, and in terms of its responses to other things. Ideally, these responses correspond to patterns of relationship eternally fixed. Here lies one of the justifications for official involvement in the educational process. Education, especially in ritual forms, trains people so that the right kinds of emotional and overt responses arise when certain events or things present themselves.

Holistic Values

We began by evaluating the applicability of individualistic values to premodern China. We will now consider values associated with the Chinese holisms described above.

One value is role fulfillment in a hierarchical system, discussed in my paper. This takes priority over most other goods. Duties and legitimate expectations are a function of roles in such a social system, rather than being constructions out of more basic properties (needs, interests, rights) that human beings have apart from any role in a system. In contrast, modern Western individualists characteristically construct duties and expectations out of properties possessed by persons as persons, not as specific role occupants. The individual's particular interests and need to express them give rise to a duty of government to permit that development. His capacity for autonomy leads to his expectation that he will be allowed to exercise it.

A second holistic value includes the previous one but is more comprehensive. As portrayed by Irene Bloom, it is recognition of the ties that people have to other things because they are made of the same physical material and informed by the same ordering principles. They recognize and reaffirm these ties by trying to know as much as possible about other people and things and by developing sympathetic feelings for them. For Mencius and for the Sung Neo-Confucians, the mind is the agency of this communication. This is the primary function of the mind. With this knowledge and sympathy the individual can break down the psychological barriers that prevent him from caring for others and from knowing enough about them to act on these sentiments. However, as Bloom insists, this sympathy does not involve dissolution of the natural boundaries separating the individual self from others.

In this absence of self-dissolution, the Confucian holistic value differs from the Taoist. Judith Berling describes Chuang Tzu's gradual shedding of the social self, self defined in terms of Confucian social roles. As devotion to role fulfillment is replaced by an attitude welcoming all things as of equal value, there is a loss of self, a state coextensive with the Tao. The Chinese Buddhist schools take a similar position. They try to help people stop thinking of the self and dharmas (or phenomenal things) as independent existences. Instead, the person should realize that there is only one reality. Its nature differs from school to school. For example, the "Consciousness Only" school views it as Pure Consciousness.

These Taoist and Buddhist doctrines foreshadow Wang Yang-ming's monism. According to Wang, to distinguish between the mind as subject and the principles of things one seeks to know as objects (a precondition of proper relatedness for Chu Hsi) is to destroy the possibility of attaining the holistic value. He seems motivated by concern about the psychological consequences of distinguishing between subject and object. The subject-object or self-other distinction may cause persons to erect harmful psychological barriers (prejudice, disinterest) between themselves and other things. Thus, the subject-object division is less an epistemological than an ethical issue.

The Confucian texts give the impression that the holistic value of union of self and others is something of which the writer was first negatively aware. That is, the writer reveals himself as having a holistic perspective because he has become disturbed by the physical, psychological, or social separation of one thing (a person, many persons, a mind) from certain other things. As Arthur Danto reminds us, the Confucian value of relatedness manifests itself in the relation between teacher and disciple. They create a microcosm of the community-centered life for society as a whole, to which this value leads.

Closely tied to the preceding value is harmony—specifically, harmony of parts. This can be harmony within the individual psyche, as when all the feelings express themselves in correct measure. It can be harmony within society, as when the occupants of a social group such as a family perform their functions and do not transgress the boundaries of duty or expectations that accompany those functions. A central value that crops up in modern Western individualisms is absent in these Chinese holisms: competition. Some Western accounts of individual rights and of autonomy rationalize or even celebrate competition. One does not find in these Chinese writings any counterpart of the "hidden hand" which, for the Westerner, presumably ensures that social competition will be constructive.

In this volume W. T. de Bary describes a fourth value, the culmination of the learning process that is part of cultivating the nature:

> [It entails] a comprehensive understanding of things in their undifferentiated unity or wholeness [*kuan-t'ung*], which eventually dawns on one (i.e., an understanding which is not necessarily an exhaustive knowledge of things in their particularity but which brings a fusion of cognitive awareness and affective response, overcoming the dichotomy of self and other, inner and outer, etc.)...

Psychologically, nothing seems alien to the person who understands totally how all things link together in unity. To understand these linkages involves in part understanding their rank relationships in a chain of priorities, or understanding which relationships are the building blocks for others. The Confucians refer to the relationships in terms of the plant metaphor; some things are roots and others are branches. As Professor de Bary goes on to explain, the ideal of comprehending and unifying the whole range of knowledge was the aim of several major works of the Sung period, such as Chou Tun-i's *Comprehensive Penetration* (of the *Book of Changes*, or *T'ung shu*) and Ssu-ma Kuang's *Comprehensive Mirror for Aid in Government* (*Tzu-chih t'ung chien*).

One other value, with textual roots in the *Doctrine of the Mean*, was especially important in the Sung and Ming periods. This is cocreativity with heaven and earth. Tu Wei-ming describes Wang Yang-ming's thesis that the person with a sincere will brings life to the objects that he knows and towards which he has some intentional concern. Liu Tsung-chou, building on both insights, treats man's ideal condition as one in which he acts as assistant to heaven and earth in the nurturing process. Personal development for the individual requires his deferring to and enabling the natural patterns of change to be fulfilled. The Confucian served as cocreator by such acts as not cutting grass, sparing tree saplings, saving the lives of pregnant animals, protecting pregnant women, comforting the aged, and nurturing the young. There are few Western philosophers who stress that God requires the assistance of any human in making his natural laws work. An exception is William James, whose God, a lineal descendant of Hegel's God who depends on humans to become conscious, is neither self-sufficient nor absolute.

If we set aside the exceptions noted in the section above on individualism, most of the Confucian and Taoist writings suggest the coimplication of self and other, and coimplication implies organic relation. The clearest evidence for this is in the terms that identify the polarities in Chinese descriptions of the relation between individual and whole. Whole can be family, society, Tao, heaven, and so forth, depending on context. The polarities are self (*chi*) and all things (*wan wu*); self and group (*ch'ün*); many, or parts (*fen shu*), and one (i^b); self and Way (*Tao*); and so forth. These are complementary terms, mutually related by a principle of coimplication. This means that each extreme is defined in terms of or requires the other.

Despite their theoretical stress on holism, Ambrose King reminds us that *in practice*, Confucians lacked a clear definition of the "group." Actual Confucians did not form relationships with a group but with particular individuals. The very idea of the group was vague and elastic. Thus, there is a disjunction between theory and practice which even raises questions about the applicability to concrete society of some of the polarities with which Chinese writers have described the relation of individual and whole.

Nevertheless, in spite of vagueness in their concepts of social groups, at the core of Confucian personal practice there is an interrelation between self-centeredness and dedication to the needs of others. There can be no self-perfection without an effort to perfect others (a position, incidentally, with which Goethe would have agreed and most of the German Romantics disagreed). Empathy for others begins with what seems to be self-absorption. However, introspection may reveal traits in the individual that he shares with others. As the *Analects* tell us, one must use one's own feelings as a guide in treating other people. Rather than finding himself in opposition to the whole, the Confucian fulfills himself through the social process, in cooperation with others.

In the case of the Taoists, the people whose behavior is individualistic often do not adhere to an individualistic metaphysics. Instead, some holistic entity generally plays a crucial role in their account of the good life, whether it be the primitive idealized state portrayed in the last section of the *Tao-te ching* or the Tao itself. Thus, those people who startle us with their eccentric or self-centered behavior or attitudes may nevertheless believe in the existence of a whole that trivializes much of individual human existence.

In contrast, the polarities with which the modern Westerner discusses the topic of the self, such as self and group, individualism and collectivism, or self and nature, often suggest opposition between the poles. There is a suggestion of tension, of the self in danger of constraint by group, or of the self alienated from nature, which it must conquer in order to survive.

The intriguing thing about all of these holistic values, except perhaps for cocreativity, is that they characterize important strands in Western thought from the classical period until about the eighteenth century. The value of role fulfillment was significant in most of what de Tocqueville called the "aristocratic societies." The most influential political utopia during this period was still Plato's *Republic*. Its author has this to say about social roles in his *Republic*: "And is this not the reason why such a city is the only one in which we shall find the cobbler a cobbler, and not a pilot in addition to his cobbling, and the farmer a farmer and not a judge added to his farming, and the soldier a soldier and not a money-maker in addition to his soldiery, and so of all the rest?"[23]

Karl Popper's *The Open Society and Its Enemies* is the most famous modern critique of the holistic political ideal from Plato down to Marx. Popper comments as follows about the holistic metaphysical position associated with Plato's ideal:

> His [Plato's] demand that the individual should subserve the interests of the whole, whether this be the universe, the city, the tribe, the race, or any other collective body, was illustrated in the last chapter by a few passages. To quote one of these again, but more fully: "The part exists for the sake of the whole, but the whole does not exist for the sake of the part.... You are created for the sake of the whole and not the whole for the sake of you." This quotation not only illustrates holism and collectivism, but also conveys its strong emotional appeal of which Plato was conscious.[24]

The value of relatedness is pronounced in the medieval philosophies derived from Plotinus, such as that of Augustine. Later, Plato's dramatic portrait of totalistically integrated knowledge in the *Symposium* was influential among such Italian Renaissance humanists as Marsilio Ficino (1433-99). Many medieval accounts of the state and the cosmos are holistic, based on an organic metaphor. The value of relatedness exists for each person in it. Compare, for example, the following description of a medieval European account with that of a Ch'eng-Chu Neo-Confucian. Though the details do not mesh entirely, the ideas in the passage, of a harmony of things in their assigned places and of the macrocosm-microcosm relation, resonate with those typically held by the Ch'eng-Chu school adherents.

> But as there must of necessity be connections between the various groups and as all of them must be connected with the divinely ordered Universe, we come by the further notion of a divinely instituted Harmony which pervades the Universe Whole and every part thereof. To every Being is assigned its place in that Whole, and to every link between Beings corresponds a divine decree. But since the World is One Organism, animated by one Spirit, fashioned by One Ordinance, the self-same principles that appear in the structure of the World will appear once more in the structure of its every Part. Therefore every particular Being, in so far as it is a Whole, is a diminished copy of the World; it is a *Microcosmus* or *Minor Mundus* in which the Macrocosmus is mirrored. In the fullest measure this is true of every human individual; it holds good also of every human community and of human society in general.[25]

There was an alternative ideal. In the classical period of Greece and Rome, the Epicureans combined a mechanistic and atomistic metaphysics with an ethics based on egoistic hedonism. The latter argued that each person does and should attempt to maximize his own pleasure. The political ideal was the less government the better, so as not to interfere with the individual's choices that lead to his pleasure. But the Epicurean movement had fallen asleep by the fifth century A.D. and was not to reawaken until the eighteenth century. Thomas Jefferson, among others, was an avowed Epicurean. The point is that the holistic vision dominated Europe from the decline of Epicureanism until well into the Renaissance.

From this consideration of holism we may conclude that until the eighteenth century, there was some interesting convergence between the metaphysical assumptions and values of many Western and Chinese philosophies, both most accurately characterized as holistic. In the section on individualism, we noted that prior to the German Romantics, many Europeans shared with the dominant Confucian tradition the expectation that on moral issues all enlightened people would think alike. Individuality in this regard was not an ultimate virtue. Therefore, the great divergencies that we sense, Western individualism versus Chinese collectivism, are to some degree a function of comparing transitional or premodern China with the modern West. Future scholars are left to question the presence of doctrines in pre-Renaissance Europe that helped foster the individualism that eventually emerged there. Future scholarship is also left with the problem of examining a divergency that did exist alongside the agreement: the primacy of reason in Europe as opposed to the Confucian primacy of sentiment and its inseparable ties to cognition. But that road would take us far beyond individualism and holism to an entirely separate issue.

III. The Historical Setting

A comprehensive philosophical study of the rise of Western individualism would refer to its political background. It would mention factions that had endorsed the doctrine of the divine right of kings and their opponents who were concerned about the limits on state power over the individual. Readers of a volume that focuses on Chinese thought may also benefit from a brief description of the historical setting. Many of the thinkers discussed in this volume lived in one of three time periods. Current or recent military dangers and political instability colored each era and fostered a sense of urgency among the intellectuals of the time.

Warring States Period (403-221 B.C.)

The royal Chou house, which had provided political stability during the formative years of Chou dynasty cultural development, had long since lost all power as China entered the fifth century B.C. As the Chou polity dissolved into autonomous feudal states, each striving to establish preeminence, interstate warfare become endemic. Two goals motivated most state rulers. One was to maximize military and economic strength. This implied a policy of expansionism but in time meant for most states strategic defense against the state of Ch'in, which began its inexorable movement east in the middle of the fourth century, during the time of Mencius. The other goal was to imitate in power one of the famous Hegemons: feudal overlords of the seventh century B.C. whose preeminence allowed them to preside over an unruly alliance of feudal heads of state.

Battles were fought with infantry armies. Success depended not only on military prowess but also on the presence of technical skills for irrigation projects, management of government offices, and handling logistical problems for army supply and commerce. State rulers tried to attract the best advisors they could. Though they sought practical measures, philosophically inclined advisors often provided them with other visions. The Hundred Schools of Thought flourished in this climate, its thinkers offering their solutions to state rulers or to the people living in dangerous conditions in their states. For example, the state of Ch'i, at a place called "Below the Ch'i Gate," provided lecture halls and free accommodations to scholars from various schools.

The philosophical importance of the nuclear family, so central to the thought of the time, had been articulated earlier in the thought of Confucius (551-479 B.C.). He recommended that a son cover up the sheep thievery of his father, rather than bring him to state justice. Although clan loyalties were disrupted as many of the large aristocratic lineages were wiped out in the interstate warfare, the family ethic remained strong in the Confucianism of the Warring States period. Confucians insisted on the naturalness of familylike social bonds. Mencius spoke of the innate ability of humans to evaluate social acts in accordance with some objective standard. Goodness was a function of humaneness (rooted in kinship affection) and propriety in certain inescapable social relations. A humane ruler could theoretically extend kinship affection to all people and thereby unify the realm in a humane government.

Other thinkers of the age, such as Chuang Tzu, advised each individual in those dangerous times to prize his own life and not endanger it in precarious social entanglements. Chuang Tzu rejected any ultimacy of social bonds as well as claims about the naturalness or objectivity of hierarchies and standards. He recommended "forgetting" the evaluation of social acts as one step down a road to understanding the individual's union with the Tao.

Late Han and Early Six Dynasties

The flourishing of Neo-Taoism marked a second great age of instability in China, extending from the latter part of the second century A.D. to the early fourth century. It followed nearly a century of prosperity in the late Eastern Han (A.D. 25-220). One problem precipitating the onset of instability was an increase in large landholdings by regional lords, which led to peasant unrest and fragmentation of political power. Another was the usurpation of court power by families of the dowager empresses and eunuchs. The latter initiated two famous purges in A.D. 166 and 169. Yü Ying-shih discusses the role of these purges in transforming many Han intellectuals into escapists or in redirecting their interests to Taoist topics. Religious Taoist bands known as the Yellow Turbans rebelled in 184, contributing to the instability. Regional generals, whose power increased in quashing the revolts, became warlords controlling large parts of China.

The end of the Han empire came in A.D. 220. Great landowning families dominated the countryside from fortified estates which were populated by vast numbers of retainers and private armies. Yet some of the facade of state Confucianism remained intact. Between 240 and 248, three items of the Confucian canon were carved on stone (symbolic of state support). Central governmental positions existed, going in theory to candidates satisfying

Confucian criteria of merit. In actuality, however, the posts were monopolized by members of the great gentry families. This was one source of cynicism among intellectuals. The National University, reopened in the state of Wei (220-265), was in fact a place where incompetent students could go to escape labor conscription.

In addition to this quasi-refeudalization, a north-south division of the country helped to shape the thought trends of the age. In 311 a "barbarian" Hsiung-nu leader sacked Loyang, the capital of the Chin dynasty. Later, refugees set up the Eastern Chin, a site that is today's Nanking. The nature of the split was such that non-Chinese peoples controlled the north and old Han Chinese families the south, where they had administrative responsibility for a large non-Han population.

Confucianism had begun to lose some ground in the second century A.D. as Confucian political institutions became associated with the failure of the state to provide security. A shift in values occurred among intellectuals, moving from overwhelming emphasis on public service to more preoccupation with self and nature. An early Neo-Taoist, Kuo Hsiang, described an ideal which would accommodate both alternatives. It was the court hermit, who performs bureaucratic tasks at court but whose mind is in the mountain forest. By the third and fourth centuries, cynicism rooted in the hypocrisy of official Confucianism and in the dangers of political involvement led some Taoists to a complete rejection of Confucian social responsibilities. The wildly eccentric Seven Sages of the Bamboo Grove provide the most famous example. This period marks the high point of eremitism, of seeking union with the Tao, of wine-enhanced Taoist freedom. Some of these Taoist political utopias were outright anarchic, but, curiously, rulers of states increased the status of hermits by trying to entice them to serve in their governments for the prestige it would bring. Neo-Taoism originally had taken root among disenchanted members of the great northern gentry families. After the fall of the Western Chin, it continued to flourish in the southern capital.

Southern Sung Neo-Confucianism

The philosophical orientation and creativity which emerged during the Sung dynasty (960-1279) must be understood in terms of three developments in the centuries preceding the Sung: the decline of Buddhism, the restoration of state Confucianism, and the invention of wood-block printing.

During the Six Dynasties period, the Indian philosophy of Buddhism grew from a novelty to a dominant intellectual and religious force in China. It reached a peak early in the T'ang dynasty (618-907) when the second T'ang emperor (r. 626-49) initiated a policy of religious and philosophical tolerance. Under his policies Buddhism flourished, and pilgrims continued to journey to India in search of teachers and texts, traveling over Central Asian roads secured by a conquering T'ang-Turkish joint military force.

But Buddhism was unable to sustain its growth. A massive purge of monasteries took place from 841 to 845, and the destruction of temples and laicizing of monks and nuns weakened the institutional (though not the popular) basis of Buddhism as earlier purges had failed to do. Furthermore, Chinese Buddhism was deprived of a critical source of intellectual infusion, namely, the missionary, who carried wisdom from the Indian well-spring. By the end of the T'ang, Buddhism was finished in India, and its northern lands were soon to be subjugated by Moslem invaders. After the mid-eleventh century nearly a thousand years of traffic by Indian missionaries and Chinese pilgrims ground finally to a halt.

The gradual decline in the growth of Buddhism was balanced by a slow reemergence of state Confucianism. Beginning in the T'ang, this reemergence was characterized by symbolic acts of support for Confucianism at the state level, without the simultaneous imposition of rigid ideological orthodoxy on individual thinkers, except in their capacities as examination candidates. Although most T'ang rulers tilted towards Buddhism or Taoism (only the second emperor was to any degree a committed Confucian), the T'ang continued to expand the civil service examination system. That system embodied the Confucian merit criterion. The principle was symbolically important to Confucianism, although the examination system still largely served other interests. Most official positions went to sons of hereditary landowning families or to the sons of incumbent officials. Not only could the leading families, as always, best afford to employ tutors for their sons, but they also had a monopoly on places in the two national universities that produced many of the examination candidates. Other symbolic acts also sustained the momentum of Confucian ideals. In the seventh century, a new edition of the *Five Classics*, sacred to Confucians, was issued to serve as a sourcebook for examination candidates. By the end of the T'ang, Confucianism had gained something of the character of a state cult, with a liturgy, icons honoring Confucian sages of the past (particularly of the Han), and regular ceremonies conducted under official sponsorship. In sum, the centuries preceding the Sung fostered a climate which was not inhospitable or intellectually suffocating to individual Confucians.

Finally, the expansion of wood-block printing made philosophical texts widely available to interested readers. The Buddhist *Diamond Sutra* had been printed in 868. By the tenth century this form of printing had come into its own. In 932 the state ordered the printing of the Confucian canon with commentary, a task completed by the National Academy in 953. Private printers put out examination review guides, dictionaries, and works on medicine and divination. Sung Confucians had access to philosophical books to a degree unknown to their T'ang predecessors.

The Sung period began in 960 under an enlightened emperor who made considerable progress in unifying the country. His younger brother, the next emperor, continued the project. While in the long run non-Chinese tribes in the northern reaches continued to impede the political stability the emperors sought, in the short run the Chinese rulers were able to buy some stability. By the early eleventh century, the price of peace with the proto-Mongol Ch'i-tan (dynastic name, Liao) was tribute in silver and silk. The same was required (starting in 1044) for peace with the Tanguts, who came out of the Tibetan border lands.

A magnificently refined growth did occur during the years of peace. The population rose to one hundred million by 1100. The capital city in eastern Honan, Kaifeng, grew into a genuinely cosmopolitan cultural center, whose skilled artisans exerted an unfortunate attraction on the tribes that were destined to sack it. Other cities grew as well, along with commerce, urban social classes, and a scholar-official class that replaced the old semifeudal aristocracy as the dominant social group. Perhaps a third of the civil servants eventually came into service via the examinations, a great leap from the T'ang dynasty.

There were tensions under the surface. Large budget deficits caused by outlays to maintain a huge army and to pay off potential invaders; malaise in the bureaucracy, caused, among other reasons, by the usual claims of nepotism, corruption, and factionalism; loss of land by peasants to large landholders. These were some of the problems that plagued the early Sung. They preceded the advent of Wang An-shih (1021-86), a reform-minded statesman who attained the highest bureaucratic office in 1073. He issued a flurry of new directives (1069-73) dealing with economic, organizational, military, and educational matters. Among the more famous were: state loans to farmers at planting time, intended to inhibit the landlord-moneylenders' penchant for lending and then foreclosing to increase their own holdings; a state monopoly of commerce; civil service examinations to test practical matters (e.g., knowledge of law and military strategy) and problem-solving ability and thereby to improve the quality of officials. Wang was ousted before his policies could have much effect, but his supporters regained power in 1102. Conservative factions, especially those representing the old northern landowning families, opposed him every step of the way. The famous poet Su Shih (1037-1101) was a part of the conservative backlash. These factional struggles, along with the other tensions, served only to weaken the state. However, the pivotal crisis of the mid-Sung arose from outside the state. The proto-Manchu Jurchen, originally vassals of the Ch'i-tan, conquered their masters and founded a new empire, the Chin. They invaded Sung territories, sacking the capital of Kaifeng in 1127, which marks the beginning of the Southern Sung.

A Confucian philosopher lived during the Southern Sung whose doctrines were destined to be made orthodox (beginning in 1313) for the country as a whole, meaning that they were required knowledge for civil service examination candidates. Chu Hsi condemned the Buddhism that had flourished through the T'ang. He condemned it for its amorality, its renunciation of unavoidable family relations and social obligations, and he traced China's weaknesses in part to this ideological poisoning. He tried to anchor these family and social duties, along with others (including some even inspired by Buddhism), in a new cosmology so that Confucianism could more compellingly fill the morality gap. Furthermore, moved by the failure of Wang An-shih's political reforms and troubled by what he saw as an unresponsive bureaucratic state, Chu subtly shifted the Confucian focus away from exclusive political activism to favor *self*-development, with the emphasis on learning for the sake of self. This included permissiveness toward a certain amount of Buddhist-like solitude and introspective examination of thought. Like so many of his colleagues, his interests and activities were wide-ranging: official for nine years, writer, teacher, school organizer. These catholic interests reflect the urban flowering of the Sung, especially the stimulating intellectual environment fostered by the availability of so many printed books and by contact with fellow scholars in private academies and in the cities.

Many eminent Confucian thinkers followed Chu Hsi. Perhaps the most famous is Wang Yang-ming of the Ming dynasty. Some of the following essays touch on elements of their thought. However, with the rise of Chu Hsi we complete the basic outline of the historical background to much of the tradition examined in this volume. It is time to turn to the essays themselves.

NOTES

1. Steven Lukes, *Individualism* (New York: Harper and Row, 1973).
2. John Herman Randall, Jr., *The Career of Philosophy* (From the German Enlightenment to the Age of Darwin), 2 vols. (New York: Columbia University Press, 1965), 2:235.
3. *Shih-shuo hsin-yü* [A new account of tales of the world], trans. Richard Mather (Minneapolis: University of Minnesota Press, 1976).
4. Chu Hsi and Lü Tsu-ch'ien, *Reflections on Things at Hand*, trans. W. T. Chan (New York: Columbia University Press, 1967), 291.
5. W. T. de Bary, "Individualism and Humanitarianism," in *Self and Society in Ming Thought*, ed. W. T. de Bary (New York: Columbia University Press, 1970), 199.
6. I am indebted to Yi-tsi Feuerwerker for this insight.
7. Chu Hsi criticizes half-day quiet-sitting in the *Chu Tzu yü-lei ta-ch'uan* [Complete edition of the classified conversations of Master Chu], ed. Li Ching-te (1270) (Kyo·:'to Yamagataya Shoshi ed., 1668; reprint ed. in 8 vols., Kyoto: Chubun Shoten, 1973), 62.32b (4:3176) (in the Chung-hua shu-chü ed., see 62.25b 4:2456). The de Bary citation is from his *The Unfolding of Neo-Confucianism* (New York: Columbia University Press, 1975), 14.
8. Jerome B. Grieder, *Hu Shih and the Chinese Renaissance* (Cambridge: Harvard University Press, 1970), 140-41.
9. John Stuart Mill, *On Liberty* (New York: Library of Liberal Arts/ Bobbs-Merrill, 1956), 102.
10. Ibid., 69-70.
11. Isaiah Berlin, *Four Essays on Liberty* (Oxford: Oxford University Press, 1969), 129; quoted in Lukes, *Individualism*, 62.
12. Fernand Braudel, *The Structure of Everyday Life* (New York: Harper and Row, 1981), 308-9.
13. *Analects*, 9:25.
14. In a paper entitled "Chu Hsi on the Standard and the Expedient," prepared for the International Conference on Chu Hsi (Honolulu, Hawaii, 1982), Wei Cheng-t'ung alerts us to the fact that sages alone should rely on individual choice of action in such situations. This paper has helped clarify my thinking about choice in Chu Hsi.
15. Citing John Blofeld, trans., *The Book of Changes* (London: Allen and Unwin, 1965), 86-87.
16. Ch'eng Hao and Ch'eng I, *I-shu* [Written legacy], in *Erh-Ch'eng ch'üan-shu* [Complete works of the two Ch'engs] (SPPY ed.), 25.5a. Kenneth DeWoskin alerted me to the existence of a number of passages discussing how improper behavior can undercut the dignity of social positions. But that is a different matter altogether.

17. C. Adam and P. Tannery, *Oeuvres de Descartes* vi, 1-3; quoted in Norman Kemp Smith, *New Studies in the Philosophy of Descartes* (New York: Russell and Russell, 1963), 73.

18. Alan Ryan, *The Philosophy of the Social Sciences* (New York: Pantheon, 1970), 172.

19. Ibid., 174.

20. Heinrich Popitz, "The Concept of Social Role as an Element of Sociological Theory," in *Role*, ed. J. A. Jackson (Cambridge: Cambridge University Press, 1972), 17.

21. Alexis de Tocqueville, *Democracy in America*, vol. 2, pt. 2, 90-92; cited in Louis Dumont, *Homo Hierarchicus: An Essay on the Caste System*, trans. Mark Sainsbury (Chicago: University of Chicago Press, 1970), 17-18.

22. Cited in Wing-tsit Chan, "The Evolution of the Neo-Confucian Concept of *Li* as Principle," *Tsing-Hua Journal of Chinese Studies*, n.s. (February 1964) 4(2):142.

23. Plato, *Republic* 397e, in *The Collected Dialogues of Plato*, ed. Edith Hamilton and Huntington Cairns (New York: Bollingen, 1961), 642.

24. Karl Popper, *The Open Society and Its Enemies*, 2 vols. (Princeton: Princeton University Press, 1966), 1:100.

25. Otto Gierke, *Political Theories of the Middle Ages*, trans. Frederic William Maitland (Cambridge: Cambridge University Press, 1900), 9.

Glossary

Ch'eng 程

Ch'eng Hao 程顥

Ch'eng I 程頤

chi 己

Ch'i-tan 契丹

chih-chüeh 知覺

Ch'in 秦

ching 經

Chou Tun-i 周敦頤

Chu Hsi 朱熹

Chu Tzu yü-lei 朱子語類

Chu Tzu yü-lei ta-ch'üan 朱子語類大全

Chuang Tzu 莊子

ch'ün 羣

Erh Ch'eng ch'üan-shu 二程全書

fen 分

fen shu 分殊

Hsi K'ang 嵇康

Hu Shih 胡適

i[a] 異

i[b] 一

I-shu 遺書

Jen-wu chih 人物志

ke-hsing 個性

ke-jen 個人

Ku K'ai-chih 顧愷之

kuan-t'ung 貫通

k'uang 狂

Kuo Hsiang 郭象

Li Chih 李贄

Li Ching-te 黎靖德

liang-chih 艮知

Liang Sou-ming 梁漱溟

Liao 遼

Liu Tsung-chou 劉宗周

Lu Hsiang-shan 陸象山

Lü Tsu-ch'ien 呂祖謙

shih-shuo hsin-yü 世說新語

Ssu-ma Kuang 司馬光

Su Shih 蘇軾

ta 達

ta-jen 達人

tao 道

T'ao Ch'ien 陶潛

Tao-te ching   道德經   *Tzu-chih t'ung chien*   資治通鑑

T'ien-t'ai   天台   *wan-wu*   萬物

tu   獨   Wang An-shih   王安石

t'ung   同   Wang Yang-ming   王陽明

T'ung shu   通書

Part I:

Conceptual Problems

Individualism in Chinese Thought

Chad Hansen

Individualism and Individualisms

When we ask if Chinese philosophy is individualistic, we ask an extremely vague question. In the first place, there is the vagueness of degree. Where do we draw the line between individualist and nonindividualist theories? Must a theory be as individualistic as John Stuart Mill's or Robert Nozick's to be classed as individualistic? If we allow relative judgments, then it will be trivially true that Chinese philosophy is individualistic since some will always be more individualistic than others. Secondly, there is ambiguity about subject matter. Our question may be about theories from wholly different fields of philosophy. There can be metaphysically individualistic theories and ethically individualistic theories. We may call a theory "individualist" because it champions the interests of human individuals. We may call another theory "individualist" because it describes the world as made up of irreducible individuals—atoms, bare particulars, or physical objects. Finally, our question may be interpreted as asking whether or not the conceptual structure of Chinese thought is like that of Western individualism in utilizing a contrast between the many (individuals) and the one (universal).

My main concern in this paper is with the last question. Is the conceptual structure (the language) of Chinese philosophy less individualistic than that of the (English-speaking) West? I shall argue that it is and, further, that the structural difference casts doubt on many other claims about individualism in Chinese philosophy. However, before I address the structural question, let me outline how individualistic theories would differ in different branches of philosophy.

Metaphysics. Metaphysical or ontological individualism would include theories about the reality or reality-dependence of particulars vis-à-vis systems, structures, contexts, or frames of reference or of human individuals vis-à-vis social collectives or institutions.

Philosophy of science. Methodological individualism is a theory about how particulars or individuals function in explanations..It addresses the question "Can systems, institutions, and macro-objects be explained solely by reference to the individuals (human individuals or particles) which constitute them?"

Epistemology. Solipsism is an extreme example of individualism in epistemological theory. It holds not only that knowledge is an attribute of individuals but also that one's knowledge is only of one's own mind. Both Western rationalism and empiricism, because they explain knowledge as individual information gathering and/or processing, could be classed as individualistic.

Philosophy of Mind. Psychological egoism is a theory that is an extreme form of individualism in philosophy of mind. However, as with rationalism and empiricism, typical psychological theories that explain behavior solely by reference to properties of individuals can be classed as individualistic.

Ethics. Ethical individualism embraces a host of theories which treat human individuals as central elements in explaining value or obligation. Ethical Egoism, Kantian dignity, and the contract theories' ethical systems are individualistic in contrast with Hegelian Idealism and organic social theories. Utilitarianism is a special case. Typical Anglo-American utilitarianism tends to be individualistic insofar as the total utility is held to be a strict function of the well-being of individuals; but a utilitarian might also calculate on the basis of the well-being of an institution, such as the family, or of communities, economic classes, or the state as a whole.

My concern is not directly with the presence or absence of these theories, but with the language which would be used to articulate any of them. There are several nonequivalent conceptual structures used in formulating and/or rebutting such theories. The statement of philosophical issues depends on structuring dichotomies such as the one-many, permanence-change, reality-appearance, nature-convention contrasts. The contrast which informs most of Western philosophy is the one-many contrast. Although individualism, in the sense of theoretical focus on the "many," is a modern aberration even in the West, the structuring dichotomy is as old as Western philosophy itself. As a positively evaluated trend in Western philosophy, individualism is, as Lukes notes, a relatively recent phenomenon.[1] Plato and classical Western philosophy regarded the universal as knowable, valuable, and real; the individual was unimportant. Individuals were inherently imperfect, limited, and changing, hence less real and knowable than abstract "universals." The move to individualism in Western Europe took place within the framework of the individual versus universal dichotomy.

There are a number of ways to talk about one-many structures. We may talk about sets and members, universals and particulars, collections and individuals. The alternative to one-many structures is part-whole structures. Philosophical Chinese has a part-whole structure rather than one-many structure. The difference is that in one-many structures, the units are treated as interchangeable, fixed in "size," and only externally related. Thus, with individuals comes the notion of a fixed unit—the atom, the quark, the person, the U.N. member, and so forth. To increase the scope of reference we increase the number of units or individuals. Parts, by contrast, are of variable size. Some parts may be parts of other parts. One can refer to more and less inclusive parts of the same whole. A finger is part of a person. So is a hand, an arm, a trunk. Mereological sets—sets which consist of, rather than contain, their members—are part-whole systems.

Scholars typically describe Chinese thought as concrete.[2] I am not quarreling with that characterization. But it is wrong to assume that all and only particulars are concrete. In the Chinese case, both the parts and the wholes are concrete—the general is also the concrete. In speaking, we tend to assimilate "concrete" and "particular" as well as "abstract" and "universal." We tend to trust the one-many contrast as equivalent to the concrete-abstract contrast. The many are the concrete individuals; the one is on a different, more abstract level. The Chinese part-whole contrast is, on the other hand, on just one level (by hypothesis, nonabstract).

So if we want to write about individualism in China, we must make several things specific. We must specify what kind of individualist theory we are writing about and whether or not we are considering as "individualist" a theory which postulates fixed units or one which postulates variable parts. We can then state the problem of degree for each type of theory by using a framework of comparison in the shape of a ladder for each type of theory. The rungs would represent the different structural dichotomies and each point on the horizontal would represent the degree of individualism in the theory. We could then address the question of the degree of individualism of a whole tradition by locating all similar philosophical theories from each tradition somewhere on the grid.

General	*Particular*
*****************************	
one	many
set	member
collective	individual
universal	particular
property	instantiation
*****************************	
whole	part
organism	organ

With the help of the "ladder" structure depicted above, we can now make several claims about individualism in Chinese philosophy.

(1) Chinese philosophy can be placed on different "rungs" from Western philosophy. It uses part-whole contrasts rather than one-many contrasts. The one-many conceptual structure should not be an interpretive model for a language such as Chinese. It is far more natural to interpret theories articulated in Chinese as using a part-whole model.

(2) Although some can be found near both the left and right edges, Chinese philosophers are markedly clustered on the holistic, or general, side.

(3) Both of the above types of contrast form part of a coherent theory of Chinese thought. The differences between Chinese and Western thought can be understood as stemming from a different conceptual structure and different background beliefs.

(4) The assertion of individualistic theories in one field of philosophy (e.g., epistemological) is itself one of the background activities which helps explain the presence or absence of individualistic theories in other fields of philosophy (e.g., ethics). Thus, although ethical individualism is by no means entailed by methodological individualism, we plausibly regard ethical individualism as more likely to emerge where other individualist theories are advanced.

Since there are many schools, movements within schools, and individual philosophers (both well known and obscure) in the Chinese tradition, there will be a significant range of holism-particularism within the Chinese tradition. It is trivially true, therefore, that Chinese philosophy contains "individualism" in the sense that some theories of one or another type, relative to other theories in the tradition, stress particularity. My claim is a more theoretical and semantic one that the object language (Chinese) should be interpreted so that the relevant dichotomy for contrasting theories is not the one-many dichotomy so central to Western thought, but rather the part-whole dichotomy more typical of mereology.

The argument for this proposition does not use inductive generalization. It consists, instead, of an analysis of the structure of the language in which ontological claims and methodological claims are made. I shall argue that both metaphysical theories and methodological (philosophy of science) theories in the Chinese tradition are nonindividualistic. They are more naturally and coherently modeled on a part-whole dichotomy than on a one-many dichotomy. In the conceptual scheme of classical Chinese, the principles of individuation are not fixed and inherent but are variable for each kind of thing. Division of things into individualized, fixed, interchangeable parts is not an essential feature of the nature of the thing. Chinese language, in other words, draws more immediately to a speaker's attention the fact that for each kind of thing, *many* different principles of partitioning are possible. The division of semantic reference is a matter of choice and convenience, not of bare objective nature.

Methodology: Generalizations and Interpretive Hypotheses

Frege, Tarski, and Carnap launched the formal study of interpretation. They characterized an interpretation as a theory of meaning for a formal language, such as logic. Two aspects of this formal, logical view of interpretation stand out: (1) interpretations are theories, and (2) they are theories about whole languages. These insights suggest a radical reevaluation of our view of the meaning of Chinese texts.

(1) That interpretations are theories suggests that, like scientific theories, they are justified by the principle of inference to the best explanation. A particular theory is judged not only by whether or not it explains the data, but also by how elegantly it does so and by how coherent it is with more comprehensive theories. A comprehensive theory of the nature of Chinese thought is, therefore, a constraint on interpretations of particular philosophers. Given a choice between two interpretations of some troublesome doctrine, say, Hsün Tzu's theory of the mind, we should prefer

the interpretation which is most coherent with the best available and most comprehensive theory of the classical period as a whole.

(2) That interpretations are of a language, not of a philosopher or a doctrine, seems counter to the ordinary notion of an interpretation. However, sinologists speak quite comfortably of "the language of the *Lao Tzu*" or "the language of the inner chapters of the *Chuang Tzu*." The formal conception of interpretation which treats interpretation as an explanation of the relation between two languages undermines the distinction between language and theory. It suggests that to have a theory is to use language in a special way. To write a theory is to postulate rules of inference between sentences containing certain theoretical terms and to adopt rules of substitution corresponding to the definitions in the theory.

(3) The formal conception also contradicts the psychological view of interpretation. In the primary, formal sense, we interpret languages, not minds or people. After we have an interpretive theory of the language as an abstract system, we can then go on to give political, sociological, and psychological explanations of why specific individuals used that language in particular ways. The semantic and psychological projects are logically distinct and the semantic project is logically prior to the historical one. Note, however (as we shall see below), that a semantic interpretation must presuppose a psychological similarity (basic rationality) among language users from all cultures.

Eighteenth-century philosophy bequeathed to English a theory of mind and language that is somewhat at odds with this formal approach to interpretation. Dualists from Descartes and Locke down to Chomsky, Fodor, and Katz have supposed that a semantic system must be grounded in some prelinguistic mental form, that we really have an interpretation only when we have translated the language into "mentalese." Similarly, Whorf and Sapir focus on the relation of language and thought. The problem with such theories of interpretation is that we can evaluate mentalese interpretations or theories about private thoughts only by translating them into some shared language like English. Strictly speaking, I offer no theory of Chinese "*thought*," i.e., of psychological processes. I offer instead only a general interpretive theory in my language of the philosophical theories they wrote (and preserved) in theirs.

Just as scientific theories are undetermined by data, interpretations are underdetermined by texts. Sinologists know experientially what Quine argued theoretically—there are many possible ways of interpreting a language.[3] When we translate the language of Mencius in a particular way, we implicitly choose to attribute one set of beliefs to him rather than another. How can we prove which is the correct set of beliefs? We cannot simply say, "This is what Mencius says in the text," because if we had chosen one of the alternative interpretations, we would have had him saying quite different things. Since we have no independent evidence of the beliefs of people from two thousand years ago except for the texts which have been transmitted to us, interpretation seems impossible—unless we adopt a principle for choosing among alternative interpretive theories.

Semantic theorists have proposed two principles for such choices. Donald Davidson has proposed the principle of charity[4] and Richard Grandy has proposed the principle of humanity.[5] The principle of charity says we should choose the interpretation that implicitly assigns to Mencius the set of beliefs which most nearly matches our own. That is, we try to maximize the number of sentences of the *Mencius* which come out true when interpreted into English. The principle of humanity, on the other hand, does not try to make all of Mencius's statements true but rather attempts to make Mencius's pattern of reasoning as similar to ours as possible. So, if we attribute a background assumption which is different from our own, then we should also assume that he disagrees with us in other ways whenever he is reasoning from that assumption. Thus, the principle of humanity may actually require that we interpret texts so some of the sentences seem to us to be false—as long as doing so makes the overall pattern of relationships among Mencius's beliefs like ours. The point is that we should maximize agreement in beliefs only where we share background assumptions. Conversely, when we attribute a theory to Mencius which is different from our own, we should argue that Mencius's background beliefs could lead us to develop a similar theory.

In claiming that the conceptual structure of Chinese is not individualistic, I thus argue that, other things being equal, we should not choose individualistic interpretations of particular doctrines when we have a choice. I will prove the claim by exhibiting a contrasting, nonindividuating interpretative theory of "philosophical Chinese" and illustrating the superiority of its assumptions in explaining other characteristically Chinese philosophical doctrines. Chinese philosophy is nonindividualistic in the sense that it is more coherent to interpret it via a part-whole rather than a one-many contrast. This is not to be understood as an argument that language constrains thought; that is, it is not Whorfian. Rather, it is a theory of how certain kinds of facts about language constrain what may be counted as plausible interpretations. The only causal relation between language and thought assumed by this method is the relation implicit in the principle of humanity. The language is itself a source of background beliefs which could lead to philosophical doctrines—especially doctrines about language. If one mistakes this bland observation about explaining doctrines for linguistic determinism, it can only be because one supposes that all explanations are deterministic.

Nonindividualistic interpretations are always possible for texts written in classical Chinese and interesting philosophical theories (1) of language, (2) of metaphysics, (3) of "scientific" explanation, (4) of epistemology, and (5) of philosophy of mind from that period all reflect elaborate, sophisticated, and coherent nonindividualistic points of view. These theories, originating in the classical period of Chinese thought, all fit most coherently with a part-whole analysis of the structural features of the Chinese language. The burden of proof is thus shifted to any individualistic interpretive theory. It must show why any given doctrine or school should be interpreted as individualistic without appeal to our "prejudice" that only individualism is plausible. The argument for an individualistic interpretation must show that (1) the individualistic interpretation is prima facie possible and equally coherent with other classical philosophical beliefs; and then that (2) some problems or considerations internal to a Chinese part-whole scheme would have made a "one-many" scheme necessary; *and* (3) how Chinese thinkers adapted the part-whole conceptual apparatus to construct such individualistic theories.

Languages and Principles of Individuation

The explanation of the naturalness of a part-whole interpretation of Chinese invokes contrasts between Chinese nouns and Indo-European nouns. Chinese nouns function very much like one set of English nouns, mass nouns, which lack a semantic principle of individuation. Adjectives typically have only a semantic scope. Consider this example: "The water on my desk is cold." Both "water" and "cold" pick out a segment of the world, and the stuff on my desk is part of the intersection of the scope of both terms. Nouns may carry one or two further semantic principles beyond mere scope or extension. Thus, while it makes sense to ask if this is the same water that was here last night, it is not appropriate to ask if it is the same cold. Nouns like "water" have not only a range associated with them but also a criterion of identity. Learning to use "water" involves learning principles for identifying the same water at different times and in different situations.

In addition to semantic scope and a principle of identity, other nouns in English have a principle of individuation. Unlike "water" (which has no inherent principles of division into units), "books," "bottles," "thermometers," and "games" have semantic principles of individuation. We call this second group of nouns "count nouns" since they pick out fixed units which can be counted. The claim that these are the same books that were on my desk last night entails a set of claims about each individual book's being the same *one* that was on my desk last night. We have separate criteria of individuality for Broadway plays and for butterflies, for words and cars, data and diseases, persons and promises.

The contrast between Western languages and Chinese can be explained by focusing on how individuation is related to the notion of a thing-kind. Built into English count nouns is a single principle of individuation. We treat that kind of thing as having natural, fixed, and functionally similar individuals. Individual plays are not to be confused with individual performances of an individual play; individual butterflies are not to be confused with individual growth stages of butterflies. Individualization is normally inherent in English concepts of the types. Claims about the type of thing entail that certain parts of the scope count as individuals of that type.

Chinese nouns do not have built-in principles of individuation. Although the noun syntax of classical Chinese was in transition during the classical period, it ended up most nearly resembling the syntax of mass nouns. That is, like "water," 'rice," "paper," and "grass," typical modern Chinese nouns (1) have no plural, (2) cannot be directly "counted" (preceded by numbers or indirect articles),[6] (3) require no distinction between "many/much" and "few/little," and (4) may be associated with one or more sortals or classifiers which externally provide principles of individuation for various nouns. These features of Chinese nouns are widely known to commentators on Chinese thought, but their significance for philosophical interpretation has seldom been appreciated. Graham, most recently, has claimed that this feature of grammar is significant.

> There are, however, ways in which tense or number may affect the schemas within which we think. The number terminations of nouns encourage us to conceive enumeration primarily as counting of things with the same name, similar to each other and countable only in one way. When we think of parts in a whole, interconnected by relations other than similarity, and divisible and countable in various ways, it is as a special and more complicated case.[7]

For a Chinese writer, then, the world need not be presented as sets of interchangeable objects (substances or particulars) which instantiate properties. It can be structured on part-whole distinctions which are variable. Parts have no given "basic" configuration—no single, inherent principle of individuation. What counts as a part in part-whole explanations is relative to the context. The behavior of a clan can be explained by the behavior of the atomic families which make it up as well as by the behavior of individuals who make it up.

Most commonly, Chinese nouns are simply said to lack plural inflection. Graham is surely right that if that were the only difference, then this fact would have no special significance for explaining the general character of Chinese thought. It would be "merely a translator's problem."[8] However, it is not merely that Chinese nouns lack plural inflections. It is that classical Chinese lacks the operation of grammatical pluralization. Moreover, Chinese nouns are not simply like the English nouns "fish," "sheep," and "deer" in having the same singular and plural form. It is rather that Chinese nouns have the same form for "deer" and "venison," for "sheep" and "mutton," for "tree" and "wood." The nouns not only lack plurals, they are not directly modified by numbers or articles and require neither the many/much nor the few/little distinction.[9] The grammar of all Chinese nouns is most like that of English mass nouns.

Thus, an interpretive theory which allows that Chinese nouns do not have inherent principles of individuation is prima facie more plausible than individualist alternatives. An argument is required before we can accept the interpretive hypothesis that, for example, a Confucian ethical commitment to humanity (jen^a) is an ethical commitment to human individuals. Lacking such an argument, the nonindividualistic reading is always to be preferred on grounds of coherence with Chinese grammar.

Chinese Theories of Language

The Chinese theories of language developed in the classical period in China, i.e. the theories of the Neo-Mohists, are nonindividualistic in the sense that they focus on the scope or range of terms and not on individual objects or the properties, qualities, and attributes of individual objects. All descriptive predicates—common nouns, mass nouns, adjectives, and intransitive verbs—comprehend a range, scope, or extent. Understanding the descriptive predicate involves being able to distinguish between what is included in the scope and what is not. Knowing a term requires the ability to make a conceptual figure-ground distinction—how to distinguish what the term picks out from what it simultaneously excludes. Unless we can tell both what is and what is not "the thing in question," we cannot be said to "know" (the use of) the term.

The Neo-Mohists' conception of language is based on this contrast theory of descriptive terms. They take it to be inherent in names that each name has a converse from which it is distinguished. Graham has remarked on this feature of Mohist semantic theory.

> All issues are between *shih* "is-this" and *fei* "is-not" (typically, "ox" and "non-ox"), alternatives of which to affirm one of certain things is to affirm the converse (*fan*) of all the rest (A 72). Disputation is defined as "contending over converse claims" (A 74), not, as a Westerner would have been inclined to expect, contending over contradictory statements about the same things.[10]
>
> The converse of applying the name "ox" to one kind of thing is that all other things must be called "non-oxen"... As the *Explanation* of A 73 notes, it is essential that the combination of "X" and "non-X" is all-inclusive, so that everything which lacks the characteristics of X is classed as non-X.[11]

A similar assumption is evident in the synoptic *Mo Tzu* as well. Mo Tzu says that it is necessary to have standards of language if we are to understand *pien* (distinction).[12] He treats knowing as knowing pairs of opposite terms and being able to distinguish between the "stuffs" which bear each name. The most prominent example is Mo Tzu's discussion of the blind man's knowledge of "black/white." The blind man has control of the terms "black" and "white" and he uses them very much as other speakers do, but to know black and white is to be able to "divide" them and to choose them.[13] In stressing only scope in talking about language, the Mohists do not clearly distinguish between adjectives and nouns. In fact, classical Chinese philosophers in general thought of all words as names—including such quantifiers as *chin* (all) and *huo* (some).[14] The model of the proper name ultimately dominates theorizing about language in ancient China. A name "X" designates or picks out a segment of reality and separates or distinguishes it from "non-X." Thus, to learn a name is to learn to divide, discriminate, or categorize stuff. That explains why the Mohists refer to the study of names as *pien* (linguistic discrimination). The approach of the Mohists points to an implicit ontology of a whole divided into parts or segments to which we refer by using terms of conventional language. The ontology, in other words, is a part-whole, rather than a one-many, ontology.

Taoism, of course, also presupposes this view of the nature of naming. Names come in contrasting pairs which "divide" the world into parts, thereby engendering attitudes (desires or dislikes) toward things. The attitudes cause *wei* (action)—deliberate or conventionally motivated behavior.[15] Students of

Taoism will recognize this doctrine as the underlying theory of language in the *Tao-te ching*.

The theory of language and the use of a part-whole contrast fit neatly together. The whole is divided into parts—X and non-X—by words. Words define scopes or ranges rather than point to a collection of individual objects. The Mohists recognize that there are various ways of employing language to slice the world up into kinds (*lei*).

The parts (kinds of things) can themselves be further divided with no presupposition that one must eventually arrive at indivisible atoms. The technical terms used to structure this part-whole analysis are among the very first technical terms introduced in the Mohist canon.

> C. A *t'i* (unit/individual/part) is a portion in a *chien* (total/collection/ whole).

> E. (For example, one of two, or the starting-point of a measured length.)[16]

Graham comments that *t'i* is "used of all countable units, whether part or whole, individual and class, sub-class and class (for none of which are there any special terms)." Further, "any *chien* may in turn be treated as a *t'i* and counted as one in a new total (B 12, 59)."[17] Of course, that a term functions indiscriminately as "part," "individual," and "subclass" means that it is different from our ordinary concept of "individual." *T'i* are parts of *chien*, not tokens of types. In fact, not individual concepts but "species terms," such as "ox" and "horse," are standard examples of *t'i*. When used, for example, of animals, *t'i* most frequently corresponds not to individual beasts but to the species, the natural kinds of animals. "Horse" and "ox" are names of *t'i* which form a *chien* (compound) called by the compound name "ox-horse." In the following passage, for example, each species or kind is treated as a "one" relative to the "two" (compound) which combines both species. "Moreover, if neither oxen nor horses are two, but oxen and horses are two, then, without the oxen being the non-oxen or the horses being the non-horses, there is no difficulty about 'Oxen and horses are non-oxen and non-horses'."[18]

When not directed at a species, *t'i* might be used to describe parts of species, for example, in ethics. The Mohists define the Confucian kinship virtue, *jen*, as *t'i*-love (love of the part) to contrast with the Mohist ideal of *chien*-love (love of all humanity). Mo Tzu's utilitarianism is not based on valuing the well-being of individuals as opposed to that of humanity. It requires argument to justify the interpretive hypothesis that Mo Tzu's reference to "love of man" translates into love of individuals. There are a number of other puzzling passages dealing with reference to species (typically using "horse" as the example) in the Mohist chapter on "Names and Objects" which further illustrate this tendency to treat whole species as one—as a *t'i*.[19] The argument for individuating by types or kinds is articulated in Canon B12.

> C. Things marked off as a group are one unit [*t'i*]. Explained by: both being as one, being this thing specifically.

E. 'Both being as one': for example, 'oxen and horses have four feet'. 'Being this thing specifically': they fit 'ox' or 'horse'. If you count oxen as an item and horses as an item, oxen and horses are two. If you count oxen and horses as an item, oxen and horses are one. (For example, counting the fingers. The fingers are five but the five are one.)[20]

Thus, the Neo-Mohists do not regard individuation in our sense as an inherent feature of the account of how language works. It can be varied according to contextual purpose. Explanation in terms of individuals would, in fact, seem quite arbitrary given this view of language.

This hypothesis about noun intensions does not mean that Chinese cannot express the notion of numerical identity and difference based on spatio-temporal contiguity. That is, there is clearly a concept of a physical object-unit (i.e., an individual) which persists through change in position and through qualitative change. So, in fact, a concept of numerical identity is explicitly distinguished from identity of kinds (*t'i*). The Mohists list both among the types of sameness and difference.

C. *T'ung* (same).Identical, as [parts; *t'i*], as together, of a kind.

E. There being two names but one object is sameness of 'identity'. Not being outside the total is sameness 'as [parts]'. Both occupying the room is the sameness of being 'together'. Being the same in some respect is sameness in being 'of a kind'.

C. *Yi* (different). Two, not [parts], not together, not of a kind.

E. The objects, if the names are two, necessarily being different is being 'two'. Not connected or attached is 'not parts'. Not in the same place is 'not together'. Not the same in a certain respect is 'not of a kind'.[21]

Further, for each numerically distinct object, or for each kind of thing, there are various ways of dividing into *t'i*. What can be divided into parts on one level can be regarded as a single whole on another level.

C. One is less than two but more than five.Explained by: establishing the level.

E. Five has one in it; one has five in it, twelve in it.[22]

Proper names, of course, typically pick out the spatially contiguous, "ordinary" physical objects for Chinese speakers as for us. The Neo-Mohists recognize this in their distinctions among kinds of names (Canon A178). Hsün Tzu, following the Mohists, presents a picture of the relation of language and reality which is characterized primarily in terms of breadth or narrowness of range. At the same time, however, he recognizes the numerical identity of objects as a sort of lowest-level particularizing.

Wu (stuff) includes that which has the same structure and different location and that which has different structure in the same location. These can be distinguished. That with structure alike in different locations, although it can be combined, we call it two things. When the structure

changes yet the thing is not distinguished as constituting something
different, we call it transformation. When there is a transformation
without distinction, we call it one thing.[23]

So, according to Hsün Tzu, spatially distinct stuffs either can be regarded
as "two" or can be combined. Further, the same thing can change and still be
regarded as "one." Referring to individual objects that persist through time is
therefore possible in Chinese. But, unlike English, that is neither the only nor
the dominant conceptual scheme in the language. In fact, that Hsün Tzu
should have felt it necessary to make this kind of point explicit and that he
should have formulated it in the way he did indicates that he regards
individuation as an optional and peripheral aspect of a language. That is why
he so pointedly allows that we can either combine spatially separate things or
we can regard them as "two." Individuation is possible in Chinese language,
but it would not have seemed as "intuitive" or "rock-bottom" obvious to a
writer using Chinese language. It would be primarily associated with the
possibility of having different "names" and would, secondarily, be regarded as
an optional way of cutting up the world.

The contrast with Western languages is that a particular semantic
principle of individuation is built into each common noun. Western
philosophers discovered that individuation criteria are variable and relative to
a language only after sophisticated and technical logical constructions
exhibited the possibility of mereological languages. It was more natural for
Western philosophers to write in ways which treat individuals as fundamental,
prelinguistic aspects of the structure of reality.

This naturally makes us more inclined to insist that a "real" explanation
must explain in terms of the individual units in some whole—whether they be
atoms in physical objects or individuals in society. Chinese theorists regard it
as natural to explain by showing how we distinguish and divide wholes. We
explain by fitting the parts into the larger structures. The tendency of Chinese
writers to focus on opposites and on theories of balance among elements is a
reflection of this aspect of their approach to philosophical and scientific
explanation.

Metaphysics and Explanation

The typical pattern of Chinese metaphysical explanation emerges in the
familiar top-down form in the *Tao-te ching*: "*Tao* gives rise to 'one'. 'One'
gives rise to 'two'. 'Two' gives rise to 'three'. 'Three' gives rise to the 'ten
thousand things'."[24]

This typical account of things goes from the whole to the parts. A
metaphysical doctrine of the sort described in the *Tao-te ching* passage can be
found in the *I ching* [Book of changes].

Therefore in the system of Change there is the Great Ultimate. It generates
the Two Modes (yin and yang). The Two Modes generate the Four Forms
(major and minor yin and yang). The Four Forms generate the Eight
Trigrams. The Eight Trigrams determine good and evil fortunes. And
good and evil fortunes produce the great business (of life).[25]

Explanation in this typical Chinese model consists in giving the roles or balance of contrasting concepts in some greater inclusive whole, which is itself a part of a greater whole, and so on, until one reaches the "everything" concept—be it the Great Ultimate, the Tao, Nonbeing, or the Buddha Nature.

Benjamin Schwartz contends that one of the key differences between Chinese and Western thought involves reductionism.[26] Western thought is reductionist in that its method of explaining a macrophenomenon consists in redescribing it in terms of the behavior or properties of smaller entities which constitute it. Chinese thought, Professor Schwartz points out, is not reductionist in this sense. That is to say, there is no tendency toward methodological "atomism" in Chinese cosmologies or in Chinese social or political theories.

Professor Schwartz, in my view, is not saying that Chinese metaphysical theories are never reductionist in the logical sense, but rather that they are not *micro*reductionist. Reductionism is a formal logical concept that does not require that explanation be in terms of the behavior of small particles. Any theory (T) is reduced to another (T') if and only if every theorem of T can be proved from the axioms of T' (possibly with the aid of "bridge laws," which specify the reference of the terms of T in the vocabulary of T'). The axioms of T' might deal with large forces (say, yin and yang) or with small objects (say, quarks and leptons). T' may explain the phenomena described in T either by treating them as part of a more comprehensive system or as comprised of smaller independent systems. Logically, therefore, we should distinguish between macroreduction and microreduction. "Organicism" and "holism" are versions of macroreduction. Atomism in science and individualism in sociology, psychology, and political theory are versions of microreduction. Holism would say that a phenomenon, P, can be explained by the laws describing the larger phenomenon of which P is a part. Atomism or individualism would say the phenomenon is explained by the laws governing the behavior of standard, interchangeable units which are included in the whole.

Chinese metaphysical theories are logically reductionist in the sense that they purport to translate ordinary descriptions of events (e.g., it appeared to someone that there was a ghost in the vicinity) in terms of a restricted set of metaphysical terms (e.g., there was a concentration of yang in the vicinity). However, the reductive explanations offered are neither atomist nor individualist. The explanatory concepts are encompassing concepts rather than particular ones. Particular events are explained as reflecting some cosmic balance of yin-yang forces.

By contrast, atomistic or individualistic reduction—microreduction—has been characteristic of traditional Western scientific explanation. (Some post-Einsteinian theories are more "holistic," e.g., unified field theory.) Such microreduction seems to be largely absent, as Schwartz suggests, from Chinese metaphysics and cosmology. It should be observed, however, that a yin-yang or *ch'i* metaphysical system could be construed as an appeal to "underlying structure." Although yin and yang are general concepts, they do not necessarily explain by invoking some notion of an organic, "macro" homeostasis of yin and yang. It was typical for metaphysical explanations of change to refer to the overall balance of forces, but some Chinese cosmologists, e.g., Wang Ch'ung, often formulated reductions which clearly assume that the configurations of yin and yang are outcomes of chance. Hence, the reduction worked by yin-yang theories might still be "down" in direction.

We can nonetheless preserve a contrast between the characteristic style of reduction in Western science and Chinese traditional "proto-science" because downward, or nonholistic, reduction need not be individualist reduction. That is, typical microreduction (atomism) in Western theories of nature depends on analyzing the constitution of the macroobject into individuals—fixed, interchangeable units. Yin and yang, like other Chinese nouns, do not have individuating principles. They are not viewed as corpuscles. So downward yin-yang explanations would at best invoke a part-whole, rather than an individual-collective, contrast.

The above observations about language and philosophy of language help us understand this difference in explanatory attitude. It counts as an explicable disagreement between traditions of the sort required by the principle of humanity. Some of the considerations which would stimulate Chinese thinkers to adopt a holistic view of explanation would not be considerations for someone writing another language like English. That the Chinese language is of a certain sort provides a consideration that motivates a part-whole, rather than a one-many, theory of the nature of language. That the theories of language advanced presupposed a part-whole ontological structure is, in turn, a consideration which affects methodological and metaphysical doctrine formation. That methodological and metaphysical doctrines are holistic or nonindividuating makes it, finally, more likely that Chinese political actors will tend to construct holistic or nonindividuating models of society and social process.

Western individualistic political theory starts from Hobbes's analysis of society as consisting of mutually disinterested individuals. That analysis was motivated by his presupposition that the model for explaining society was similar to the model of Newtonian science. Hobbes used a parallel to the atomistic explanations characteristic of the new science of his day. It seemed that all "real" explanation would break larger objects into individual parts and explain the larger object in terms of the laws governing the parts. The individual components, then, following their own microlaws, would interact in ways which would result in the macrophenomena. Similarly, the social development of sovereign political authorities and the rule of law, courts, and legislatures was also a natural event explainable solely in terms of the self-contained, self-interested behaviors of the individuals who make up the society. The laws of society are consequences or sums of the behaviors of individuals following the natural laws which govern them in the same way that the laws of macroobjects are consequences of the natural laws governing the atoms.

We would not expect a Hobbesian explanation to develop in the Chinese context. Confucians view the state as a natural unit analogous to the family;

the state is characterized by hierarchically, functionally defined, and interrelated parts rather than by its members (individuals) and the sum of their isolated behavior. In another chapter in this volume I argue that although there is a kind of state of nature justification of authority in Chinese political theory, it is nonindividualistic. I shall say no more about individualism in political theories now except to conclude that we should not be surprised to find that explanatory political theory in China is nonindividualistic. Indeed, the burden of proof is on anyone who assumes (by looking at some superficial resemblance to Hobbes) that any particular Chinese ethical or political theory is individualistic.

Some Nonholistic Systems

It would be misleading to insist that all Chinese philosophies have constructed only holist metaphysical systems. There have, in my view, been a string of connected systems of microreduction. The string starts with Chuang Tzu. Chuang Tzu's relativism grows out of the awareness that there are an unlimited number of unique perspectives from which to use language. No perspective is privileged. The ten thousand differences blow their own way; the myriad feelings simply are presented before us, the heart shoots out its judgments like bolts from a crossbow: there is no ultimate source. *Tao*, the way things are, is just the accidental sum of all the *tao*s of the parts. We make the way by walking it.

A nonholistic view of Chuang Tzu is admittedly controversial. However, the next link in the chain is widely accepted. The most influential early commentary on the *Chuang Tzu*, by Kuo Hsiang, reflects this kind of particularism in contrast to the holistic system erected by Wang Pi. Whereas Wang Pi traces all explanation to "basic substance" (*pen-t'i*), Kuo Hsiang appears to be much less organic. Chan's characterization perhaps overstresses the seemingly individualistic aspects of Kuo Hsiang.

> Things exist and transform themselves spontaneously and there is no other reality or agent to cause them. Heaven is not something behind this process of Nature but is merely its general name. Things exist and transform according to principle, but each and every thing has its own principle. Everything is therefore self-sufficient and there is no need of an overall original reality to combine or govern them, as in the case of Wang Pi. In other words, while Wang Pi emphasizes the one, Kuo emphasizes the many. To Wang Pi, principle transcends things, but to Kuo, it is immanent in them.[27]

The ring of individualism in this account is a little misleading because it is more plausible to treat Kuo Hsiang (and Chuang Tzu) as writing about *thing-kinds* producing themselves than of individual things producing themselves; theirs is a relatively commonsense view about creation and procreation of species. Sheep produce sheep; flies produce flies. "The many," for purposes of interpreting Chuang and Kuo, are not the individual physical objects, but the many stuffs denoted by the terms of the language. The one is not a universal or type, but the whole out of which the stuffs are carved. Chan might better have said, "While Wang Pi emphasizes the one, Kuo emphasizes the parts." A perfectly coherent part-whole reading of Chuang Tzu and Kuo Hsiang is clearly preferable to a Western (Platonic) one-many reading.

The Kuo Hsiang nonholistic paradigm seems to be repeated in the Hua-yen doctrine of mutual implication of all dharmas because it makes the realm of dharmas (*dharmadhatu*) an outcome of the parts. Chu Hsi's Neo-Confucian adaptation of this view (individualistic in the same sense as its counterpart, Leibnitzian monadology) holds that the *li* (principle) of each thing (thing-kind) entails the totality of all principles. Each of these doctrines may be viewed as relatively "particularist" in comparison with other Chinese philosophers. The explanations are downward, to be sure, but they are not individualistic. The explanations start, not with particulars, but with parts.

What I am claiming, then, is not the total absence of a mode of explanation in which wholes are understood as merely sums of the parts, but the relative dominance of the culture by the macro mode of explanation. Hsün Tzu can formulate individualistic principles for dividing up stuffs, but he qualifies his description by stressing the optional nature of individuating in any particular way. It would not seem as obvious that explanation by decomposition into components was "real" explanation when semantic schemes of dividing were viewed as optional, arbitrary, and changeable. Individualism in explanations gets much of its plausibility from the fact that we can state laws about stable, interchangeable, component parts—individuals. It is thus no mere coincidence that nonholistic metaphysical systems in China tend to appeal either to chance or to totalistic monadology.

Philosophy of Mind and Knowledge: The Individual Person

The main focus of our concern about "individualism" in China is individualism in normative theories—theories about the worth and dignity of individuals and the status of individual claims in a normative structure. Of course, one could advocate individualism in this sense without necessarily believing in reductive or methodological individualism. This is plausibly the position of John Dewey and the new liberalism of T. H. Green. That is, they favor individualism in political systems and think political systems should be structured to foster individualism. Yet they are critical of the claims of descriptive individualism and, in fact, tend to criticize classical individualist analyses of personality and society as actually undermining the values a prescriptive individualism would require. Still, Dewey and Green get their value system from a tradition which generated both descriptive and prescriptive theories. While it is logically possible that the prescriptive theory might be held and the descriptive one rejected, we justifiably regard the cultural emergence of the prescriptive without the concurrent development of the descriptive as unlikely. It is possible to say that all value resides in individuals without implying that individuals are the basic elements in explanations of a social structure, but it would be surprising to find a culture with almost no descriptive individualism which had an important tradition of prescriptive individualism.

In any case, the only uncontroversial historical example we have of the emergence of individualism as a prescriptive doctrine is Western Europe, where various other individualistic forms of analysis were common. An interpretive theory which treated Chinese metaphysics and philosophy of language as nonindividualistic and then held that the ethical and political theories *were* individualistic would be prima facie less plausible than a more comprehensive and coherent theory. It would require specific argument to explain why ethical and political theories would be structured by a conceptual dichotomy different from that of the explanatory theories.

One of the main independent considerations which might motivate individualism in ethics and politics is the kind of individualism found in Western philosophy of mind and epistemology—that is, the view that individual humans are relatively self-sufficient information gatherers and processors and that human agency is fundamentally autonomous. Thus, it is not only that Hobbes believes that the atomic model is the most promising explanatory model for understanding the behavior of large social objects. His belief is buttressed by a number of parallel cultural views about the concept of a person—views which contributed to the belief that each human individual, especially in his or her conscious processes, is an independent explanatory factor. Descartes had formulated a conception of mind and mental processes in which each person's ideas, desires, and will were private—in principle inaccessible to other persons or to society. Hobbes developed this picture of individuals into an account of independence of action and desire which stripped the individual of all but egoistic motives. All motives, desires, and ideas are rooted in the individual ego and directed at internal mental states which are wholly private—within the individual.

Hobbes's prescriptive theory was not, of course, liberal individualism. Locke's was. Still, Locke's theory of human nature (philosophy of mind) continued the trend away from recognizing any social component in human mental processes. In his view, our conscious life consists in being presented with ideas—sensations and concepts. We get our ideas from experience of the world. That experience is essentially private and unmediated by cultural or social forces. We experience the world and our reason (reason, too, is presocial and purely internal to each human) collects, associates, and abstracts from experience to stock our mind with concepts. Language is merely a conventional way to tell our neighbor what concepts, impressions, feelings, desires, intentions, and so forth, we have. It has no effect on the conscious process at all. Meaningful language requires the prior existence of a stock of ideas and desires which we privately collect and store in our minds.

Let us now consider a philosopher from China who is often interpreted as individualistic and who deals with the relation of language and thought— Chuang Tzu. The interpretation of Chuang Tzu given above reflects the antisocial, antiholistic tendency that distinguishes Chuang Tzu from most other philosophers of the period. Its antisocial character, however, is not so much individualist as particularist. Points of view are not attached to historical, persisting individuals. For each individual there are multiple points of view which change with time, location, audience, etc. Thus, it is not *my* point of view which lies at the base of his system, but *this* one. The "this" is to be identified, not with an atomic human, but with a particular context of expression. Thus, at some other time, you may occupy this perspective, and I will occupy some other. The point is that we ought not to presuppose that the individual-society dichotomy is the relevant one for talking about Chuang Tzu's relativism. Chuang Tzu's system rests instead on a distinction between the social-conventional and the "natural." It is our own cultural heritage that presupposes that the natural, or unconventional, must be the individual.

Chuang Tzu may legitimately be likened to the ancient Greek Sophists. In some sense he may be construed as saying that "man is the measure of all things." What is significant is that it is not *individual* persons who are the measure. Chuang Tzu's view is that evaluation in language (*shih* and *fei*) is from some human perspective. It is *we*, rather than Chuang Tzu, who assume that a particular perspective must be that of a human individual. For Chuang Tzu, perspectives are associated with systems of assigning *shih* and *fei*, that is, with schools of thought which, like the Mohist and Confucian schools, divide things into descriptive or evaluative classes. Perspectives might also be identified with species. The perspective of a human is contrasted to that of deer and fish.

Chuang Tzu's perspectives are not individualistic in the sense of focusing on human individual subjectivity. Nor is his antisocial relativism based on epistemological individualism. He does not have a view of knowledge as a subjective, private representation of the perspective of a single human individual mind. He views knowledge as relative to all kinds of features of the social and natural context. At the base of his system lie the sounds of nature, among which are human voices. The sounds are produced by natural processes involving natural human animals in localized contexts.

Chuang Tzu's view of the mind is, in fact, the direct opposite of Locke's. For Chuang Tzu, a mind consists of propensities to approve (*shih*) and disapprove (*fei*). There is no fixed, privately accessible reason that organizes subjective "raw experience" into these structures of approval. The structures the mind uses are learned transmissions from the past and are enshrined in our culture; these structures are learned or acquired in the process of "completing" the evaluating mind. The mind is not innate, but acquired.

Chuang Tzu is not unique among classical Chinese philosophers in seeing humans as shaped by their absorption of values from a social nexus. Confucius had earlier taught that human nature is "established by" conventional rules of behavior. Chuang Tzu merely added to this Confucian view the relativistic awareness that we could be shaped by many different structural systems. So we can *shih* and *fei* in one way and be Mohists, and *shih* and *fei* in another way and be Confucians.

Like Lao Tzu, Chuang Tzu comprehends desires as feelings generated by systems of naming, distinguishing, and evaluating, not as unexplained emanations from particular human individuals. In other words, desires are socially shaped, not purely natural. Our knowledge is not a direct, unmediated relation between our subjectivity and the world; it consists rather in mastering and perfecting a social ritual—a way of uttering names, distinguishing objects, and behaving.

Chuang Tzu's view is close to that of the Greek Sophists in that both emphasize conventional skills rather than representational knowledge. Chuang Tzu's antisocial views are reflected in his insistence that there is a wide range of possible systems of reaction. The system that appears dominant in the society—the conventional Confucian way—has no special warrant. There is an infinite number of ways to *shih* and *fei*. Chuang Tzu's relativistic system, however, even with its antisocial undertone, is not the same as the claim that individual experiences, conjoined with the operations of a faculty of reason which is complete and innate in each individual, are the source of all knowledge.

Knowledge in the Chinese tradition is essentially skill-knowledge, "knowing (how) to." It is not primarily propositional or factual knowledge. Chuang Tzu's particularism arises from an egalitarian view of skills—not an egalitarian view of human individuals. No skill provides an absolute reference point from which one may rank other skills. A butcher may know the secret of life as well as a political statesman or a philosopher.

Individualism and Egoism

The only uncontroversial instance of the emergence of ethical individualism as a major intellectual movement is found in the Western tradition, in which there was also reductive individualism in metaphysics and philosophy of science, in which there was wide acceptance of psychological egoism, and in which epistemological and psychological solipsism were considered the commonsense models for explaining people's behavior. The examples of Dewey and Green remind us that one can be committed to freedom and dignity of individuals without accepting these other forms of individualism. However, those examples emerged from a cultural setting in which normative individualism was already well entrenched. It is doubtful that individualism as a normative theory would be likely to emerge and achieve dominance in a cultural milieu which has none of these other, concomitant individualist doctrines.

I have argued that part-whole interpretations of normative doctrines are to be preferred over individualist (one-many) interpretations. Philosophical doctrines written in classical Chinese can always be given elegant part-whole interpretations, and such interpretations are more compatible with the structure of the language. Furthermore, relatively sophisticated and coherent part-whole theories of language which closely reflect that language structure were constructed in the classical period and were well known to the classical Chinese philosophers. And the dominant type of metaphysical or explanatory theory also develops the part-whole approach. Finally, theories of human nature, motivation, and knowledge do not rest on a conception of the atomic individual so characteristic of Western political theory. I conclude, following the principle that we choose interpretations according to a principle which preserves coherence among assumptions and beliefs (the principle of humanity), that any interpretive claim that some philosopher or doctrine is equivalent to Western normative individualism should be met with initial skepticism. Given the possibility of a nonindividualist reading and the existence of perfectly plausible nonindividualist theories in metaphysics, methodology, and philosophy of mind, it must be shown why any particular philosopher would have been motivated to postulate Western-style individualism. Those who advocate such an interpretation may ultimately be able to demonstrate that no coherent nonindividualist interpretation of some text or other is possible, but until this has been shown, we may justifiably generalize that there is no individualism in Chinese philosophy.

NOTES

1. Steven Lukes, *Individualism* (New York: Harper and Row, 1973), 1.
2. Haijima Nakamura, *Ways of Thinking of Eastern People: India China Tibet Japan* (Honolulu: East-West Center Press, 1964), 177.
3. W. V. O. Quine, *Word and Object* (Cambridge: M. I. T. Press, 1960).
4. Donald Davidson, "Truth and Meaning," *Synthese* (1967), 17(3):304-23.
5. Richard Grandy, "Reference, Meaning and Belief," *The Journal of Philosophy* (1973), 70(14):439-52.
6. Prior to the Han dynasty (206 B.C.), Chinese nouns could be directly modified by number or might be counted with the use of sortals. Nouns were also directly preceded by demonstratives, unlike modern Chinese. See Chad Hansen, *Language and Logic in Ancient China* (Ann Arbor: University of Michigan Press, 1983).
7. A. C. Graham, *Later Mohist Logic, Ethics and Science* (Hong Kong and London: The Chinese University Press and The School of Oriental and African Studies, University of London, 1978), 29.
8. Ibid.
9. See n. 6 above.
10. Graham, *Mohist Logic*, 39. Note that the term Graham translates here as "disputation" is what I refer to as distinction or linguistic discrimination (*pien*).
11. Ibid., 318.
12. Mo Tzu, *A Concordance to Mo Tzu*, Harvard-Yenching Institute Sinological Index Series, supp. no. 21 (Taipei: Chinese Materials and Research Aids Service Center, Inc., 1974), 56/35/6-7.
13. *Mo Tzu*, 83/47/23-24.
14. Graham, *Mohist Logic*, 35.
15. The first two chapters of the *Tao-te ching* present the classic Taoist statement of this view.
16. Graham, *Mohist Logic*, 265.
17. Ibid.
18. Ibid., 439.
19. Ibid., 491-93.
20. Ibid., 363.
21. Ibid., 334. I have changed Graham's translation of *t'i* from "units" to "parts" in line with my views expressed above. These definitions make clear that *t'i* sameness and difference are distinct from numerical or unit identity. Graham appears to reason that the definition of *t'i* (A2) as divisions with a *chien* (compound) followed by an explanation "like one in two"

justifies his frequent reference to a *t'i* as "countable units," but as I have argued, the fact that *t'i* functions without discriminating, for example, members from subsets shows that it is not our ordinary concept of individual or "countable unit."

22. Graham, *Mohist Logic*, 431.

23. Hsün Tzu, *A Concordance to Hsün Tzu*, Harvard-Yenching Institute Sinological Index Series, vol. 22 (Taipei: Chinese Materials and Research Aids Service Center, Inc., 1966), 22/84/27-29.

24. *Tao-te ching*, chap. 42.

25. Wing-tsit Chan, *A Source Book in Chinese Philosophy* (Princeton: Princeton University Press, 1963), 267 (*I-ching*, chap. 11).

26. Benjamin Schwartz, "Reductionism in Chinese Philosophy," *The Journal of Chinese Philosophy* (March 1973), 1(1):27-44.

27. Chan, *Source Book*, 317.

Glossary

ch'i 氣

chien 兼

chin 盡

Chu Hsi 朱熹

Chuang Tzu 莊子

fan 仮

fei 非

Hsün Tzu 荀子

Hua-yen 華嚴

huo 或

I ching 易經

jen[a] 人

jen[b] 仁

Kuo Hsiang 郭象

Lao Tzu 老子

lei 類

li 理

Mo Tzu 墨子

pen-t'i 本體

pien 辯

shih 是

tao 道

Tao-te ching 道德經

t'i 體

t'ung 同

Wang Ch'ung 王充

Wang Pi 王弼

wei 爲

wu 物

yi 異

The Individual and Group in Confucianism:
A Relational Perspective

Ambrose Y. C. King

Confucius developed a humanistic ethics in a man-centered world.[1] For a Confucian, the basic concern is the social life here and now. How to establish a secular harmonious world is the basic theoretical and practical question the Confucians have to address. Confucians focus on the organic relationship between the individual and society and consider the two inseparable and interdependent. As we shall see, the problem is that "society" is only vaguely defined, as is the idea of "group" if one is referring to a unit larger than the family.

Jen, "perfect virtue" (James Legge), or "benevolence" (D. C. Lau), is the highest attainment of moral cultivation.[2] In Confucian ethics, jen can only be achieved by the efforts of the individual self (chi). This means that Confucius regards the individual as an active self which is capable of reaching a state of moral autonomy and achieving sagehood. The cornerstone of Confucian ethics, shu, or "reciprocity," in the last analysis can only be accomplished or performed by the individual self.[3] According to Confucius, shu means that "what you do not want done to yourself, do not do to others." In fact, shu, or the emphatic capacity to take the role of others, is the architectonic concept in Confucian ethics.[4] In this sense, Confucian ethics is heavily characterized by what may be called "self-centered voluntarism," which we will discuss later. Not surprisingly, Confucianism is distinctly concerned with the concept of self-cultivation.[5] Indeed, the moral autonomy of the self is unequivocally affirmed by Confucians. To be a gentleman (chün-tzu) one must be able to assert oneself against all kinds of pressure, from both within and without.

Let us turn our attention to the relationship between the individual and the group. To start with, Confucians never see the individual man as an isolated entity; man is defined as a social being.[6] Indeed, as Hu Shih quite correctly states, "In the Confucians' human-centered philosophy, man cannot exist alone; all actions must be in a form of interaction between man and man."[7] Without doubt, "to be a man among men" is Confucius's fundamental aim. There can be no fulfillment for the individual in isolation from his fellow men. Jen would be nothing if it could not be placed in the context of the social world. The fact is that "jen can only be cultivated and developed in interhuman relationships, i.e., in a social context."[8] From the Confucian viewpoint, the most fundamental relationships are the *wu-lun* (five social dyads, or five cardinal relations). These five relationships and their appropriate tenor are *ch'in* (affection) between parent and child; *i* (righteousness) between ruler and subject; *pieh* (distinction) between husband and wife; *hsü* (order) between old and young; and *hsin* (sincerity) between friends.[9] The five cardinal relations have been considered the basic norms of Chinese social order. C. K. Yang writes:

> These five cardinal relations, centering upon kinship ties, formed the core of social and moral training for the individual almost from the beginning of his consciousness of social existence until he became so conditioned to it that his standard of satisfaction and deprivation was based upon it.[10]

The five cardinal relations thus comprise the "central value system," to use Bellah's concept, of Confucian society.[11]

Among the five cardinal relations, three belong to the kinship realm. The remaining two, though not family relationships, are conceived of in terms of the family. The relationship between the ruler and the ruled is conceived of in terms of father (*chün-fu*) and son (*tzu-min*), and the relationship between friend and friend is stated in terms of elder brother (*wu-hsiung*) and younger brother (*wu-ti*). True enough, the true cardinal kinship relations are only the major family relationships, and there are many more. In the *Erh ya*, the oldest dictionary of the Chinese language, there were more than one hundred specific terms for various family relationships.[12] Many nonfamily social relationships were patterned after the family system in terms of structure and values. For example, the relationship between teacher and student operated on a simulated father-and-son basis and thus formed a quasi-kinship bond. The Chinese family system as such was thus viewed as "the social system of China."[13] Talcott Parsons has termed China a "familistic" society, one in which the family, and the kinship system deriving from it, has an unusually strategic place in the society as a whole.[14]

In the Confucian family system, the father-son relationship is most important. The principle of *hsiao* (filial piety) is at the very center of personal, family, and social existence.[15] While there are other cultural ideals in the Confucian teaching, "filialism was the source of the predominant identity of traditional China, a basic ideal against which any other form of self image had to be judged."[16] It should be mentioned that in the Confucian value system, each individual role is not placed in an absolute hierarchical context. The five pairs in the five cardinal relations were originally symmetrical (i.e., equal) relationships. But in the influential *Hsiao ching*, the *hsiao* concept was pushed into the center of the Chinese ethical system. There was no recognition of the independent existence of the individual; the individual was submerged into the familistic ethics.[17] The symmetrical father-son relation thus became asymmetrical in nature.[18] Furthermore, this asymmetrical authority relationship, which became a socially accepted version of the Confucian family ethics, was given institutional support by the Chinese legal system.

Throughout the dynasties, as is well documented and argued by Ch'ü T'ung-tsu, Chinese laws underwent a process of "Confucianization" whereby the hierarchical harmony of the family was upheld as an unquestionable value.[19] John C. H. Wu writes:

> Traditionally, a Chinese seldom thought of himself as an isolated entity. He was his father's son, his son's father, his elder brother's junior ... in other words, an integral member of his family. He was a concrete individual person who moved, lived, and had his being in the natural milieu of the family.... Each family had a head, to whom his wife, his children, his daughter-in-law, his grand-children, and the domestics owed unquestioning obedience. I know of no other system of law which is so meticulous in enforcing the duties of filial piety.[20]

To be sure, the individual is not wholly absent in the Chinese family. This is true particularly in comparison with the role of individual in the Japanese family, where the individual was completely submerged by the family as a unit.[21] However, the emphasis on hierarchical harmony in the Chinese family inevitably tends to place structural constraints on the individual. Kenneth Abbott writes: "Individualism exists, but it is interiorized and cannot be socially expressed.... Self-cultivation differs from self-actualization in that the first is orderly and the second is spontaneous."[22]

In the family, the individual is hesitant to take a self-assertive stand for fear of being viewed as disruptive of harmony. Richard Wilson argues that the Chinese social system is distinctive in its singular focus on group loyalty and the intensity with which ideals of loyal behavior (such as sacrifice for the collective good) are held.[23] Regarding the status of the individual in the family, C. K. Yang's analysis finds that

> the Western concept of individualism ... runs directly counter to the spirit of the traditional Chinese family and is incompatible with the traditional loyalty to it.... Self cultivation, the basic theme of Confucian ethics traditionally inculcated in the child's mind from an early age, did not seek a solution to social conflict in defining, limiting, and guaranteeing the rights and interests of the individual or in the balance of power and interests between individuals. It sought the solution from the self-sacrifice of the individual for the preservation of the group.[24]

Yang's analysis shows that individual autonomy was indeed emphasized in the Confucian conception of man. But the basic fact is that the individual had to be socially and structurally located in the family, which was the primary social reality for Chinese in traditional times. The family, not the individual, was continually stressed as a hierarchical whole. Liang Sou-ming's claim that "the greatest shortcoming of Chinese culture is that the individual can never be discovered" is therefore understandable.[25] Chang Tung-sun also views the individual in Chinese culture as a "dependent being."[26]

Indeed, it is no accident that K'ang Yu-wei saw the "abolition" of the traditional family as a condition for proper performance of modern public duties,[27] and that T'an Ssu-t'ung vehemently attacked the *kang-ch'ang* (moral laws) and made an uncompromising call to "burst out the net" of Confucian social bonds.[28] During the May Fourth Movement, a cultural attack was launched on filialism, resulting in a questioning of the Confucian family norms of obedience and authority, at least in the intellectual circles.

Elasticity of the Group

The strong group orientation of the Chinese is treated as an almost unequivocal fact by most, if not all, social scientists, particularly sociologists. The group, so the sociologists of Durkheimian persuasion would argue, has an autonomous life of its own, external to the individual. The Chinese family as the predominant social unit has a structural force which bends the individual to a role of dependency. This sociological fact can hardly be denied. There is a limit, however, to the function of social structure in shaping the individual's behavior. The structural conception of human society, though not wrong, is simply not sufficient. H. Blumer writes from a symbolic interaction viewpoint: "Social organization is a framework inside of which acting units develop their actions. Structural features, such as 'culture,' 'social system,' 'social stratification,' or 'social roles,' set conditions for their action but do not determine their action."[29]

A structural analysis of Chinese behavior (especially Chinese family behavior) will tend to produce an over-Confucianized view of Chinese society. By "over-Confucianized" we mean that the individual's action is consciously or unconsciously interpreted as the result of a complete internalization of Confucian norms and values. The fundamental weakness of the structural conception of Chinese society lies in its failure to recognize that the individuals who comprise the society have selves, which are particularly stressed, as shown above, in Confucian ethics.

The Confucian concept of *cheng-ming* (rectification of names), which means the correspondence of names and reality, aims at achieving social harmony through a well-defined role system. In the Confucian's ritualistic social relations, each person is assigned a proper place. A considerable amount of conduct can thus be explained by roles. But, as Dennis Wrong rightly argues, a human being is never merely a role-player,[30] and Chinese behavior cannot be understood through the sheer analysis of the Confucian values and norms. This is true not only because a complete Confucianization is impossible but also because there are inconsistent values and norms within the Confucian ethics. Indeed, there are tensions and conflicts between Confucian cultural aspirations and structural norms. The conflict between loyalty and filial piety,[31] the conflict between universalistic virtue (*kung*) and familistic morality,[32] and the very basic tension between *jen* and *li* (propriety)[33] are cases in point. Most conspicuous is the conflict between the value of individual autonomy and the norm of familistic obedience. All of these tensions and conflicts occur "when cultural values are internalized by those whose position in the social structure does not give them access to act in accord with the values they have been taught to prize."[34] These are examples of "sociological ambivalence" par excellence, to use Merton and Barber's terminology.[35] The concept of sociological ambivalence makes a significant contribution to the understanding of the dynamics of the structure of social roles.[36] It helps make more intelligible behavior which cannot simply be attributed to fixed Confucian roles and prescriptions. Ralph Turner's conception of role-making is another important corrective to the static and overly deterministic conception of roles.[37] Turner views the role relations as "fully interactive" rather than merely the extension of normative or cultural deterministic theory; actual role transactions are more or less the result of a stable working compromise between ideal prescription and a flexible role-making process—between the structural demands of others and the requirements of one's own purpose and sentiments.[38] In the analysis of Confucian role behavior, Turner's dynamic view of roles is essential, particularly because of the fact that Confucianism attaches a good deal of autonomy to the individual self. The Confucian *chi*, a dynamic entity, is capable of modifying and creating its role relations with others. This recognition of the voluntaristic nature of the self and the dynamic of role structure is particularly important when we begin to examine the relation between *chi* (self) and *ch'ün* (group).

Confucians classify the human community into three categories: *chi*, the individual; *chia*, the family; and *ch'ün*, the group.[39] For a Confucian, the emphasis is on the family, and for this reason Confucian ethics have developed an elaborate role system on the family level. Relatively speaking, the Confucian conception of *ch'ün* is the least articulate. It should be pointed out that, conceptually, the family is also a group. For the purpose of analytical distinction, "family" might be termed "familistic group," while the *ch'ün* is a "nonfamilistic group," or simply "group." Insofar as Confucian theory is concerned, there is no formal treatment of the concept of *ch'ün*. *Ch'ün* remains an elusive and shifting concept. Fei Hsiao-t'ung correctly argues that the boundary between *chi* and *ch'ün* is relative and ambiguous; in the Chinese tradition, there is no group boundary as such—the outer limit of the group is the vague concept of *t'ien-hsia*.[40] Barbara Ward has also pointed out that one feature of Chinese social structuring is the relative lack of clear boundaries for defining an "in-group."[41] Even the term *chia*, which describes the basic social unit, is conceptually unclear. Sometimes it includes only members of a nuclear family, but it may also include all members of a lineage or a clan. Moreover, the common expression *tzu chia jen* ("our family people") can refer to any person one wants to include; the concept of *tzu chia jen* can be contracted or expanded depending upon the circumstances. It can theoretically be extended to an unlimited number of people and thereby becomes what is called *t'ien-hsia i-chia* ("all the world belongs to one family").[42] The fact that "group" has no definable boundary has, I would argue, significant theoretical implications for the consideration of the issue of holism versus individualism. The very ambiguity or elasticity of the family group would give the individual ample room for maneuver in constructing his network of kinship relations. The boundaries of both the family and other groups are thus very much dependent upon the decision of the *chi* (self).

According to Benjamin Schwartz, there is a set of polarities in the Confucian social ethics. A central one is the polarity of self-cultivation (*hsiu-shen*, or *hsiu-chi*) and the ordering and harmonizing of the world (*chih-kuo p'ing t'ien-hsia*).[43] The *Problematik* of Confucianism explored by Schwartz opens up new dimensions of Confucian social thought which await further articulation. It seems to me that Confucian social ethics has failed to provide a "viable linkage" between the individual and *ch'ün*, the nonfamilistic group. The root of the Confucian *Problematik* lies in the fact that the boundary between the self and the group has not been conceptually articulated.

As has been noted above, Confucians place a high value on the adjusted equilibrium and social harmony. But a closer look makes it clear that the Confucian social order is constructed upon the concept of *lun*, which can be interpreted as a set of rules governing social relations and is primarily concerned with the problem of *pieh*, or differentiation among role relations. A noted sociologist sees *lun* as *ch'a-hsü*, denoting a differentiated status order. The phrase *pu shih ch'i lun* means that every role relation is properly in order; more specifically, it means that the role relations are differentiated according to the degree of intimacy attaching to the individual concerned. *Lun* covers a wide range of social relations, in which the *chi*, or self, is at the center.[44] In other words, *jen-lun* is the sum total of a person's network of role relations, while *wu-lun* constitutes the basic principle of a person's network of primary role relations. What must be emphasized here is that while Confucian ethics teach how the individual should be related to other particular roles through the proper *lun*, the issue of how the individual should be related to the "group" is not closely examined. In other words, the individual's behavior is supposed to be *lun*-oriented; the *lun*-oriented role relations, however, are seen as personal, concrete, and particularistic in nature. It is here that the nature of the relationship between the individual and the group becomes difficult to characterize simply. As mentioned earlier, since the boundary of the group very much depends upon the individual, who is the architect in role-relation construction, all apparently group values and interests also center around the self. Fei Hsiao-t'ung calls this *tzu-wo chu-i* (roughly translated as "egoism"). In his view, *tzu-wo chu-i* was no monopoly of the school of Yang Chu, who would not give up a hair from his shank even to gain the entire world. Confucianism also subscribed to this concept. However, Fei is fully aware of the difference between the Yang Chu school and Confucianism; the former, according to him, neglected completely the relativity and elasticity of *tzu-wo chu-i*, thus focusing solely on the self, while the latter was fully cognizant of the relativity of the *tzu-wo chu-i* and could extend the self to family and country according to the needs of situation.[45] It is no accident that Confucianism, irrespective of its different strains, emphasizes the concept of *k'o chi* (overcoming one's self). And *k'o chi fu li* (to return to the observance of rites through overcoming the self) is considered to be the way to achieve *jen*.[46] This ethical principle obviously aims at making the individual self sensitive to his moral relatedness to others. The significant point is that in Confucianism, though the concept of group is recognized, the individual tends only to identify his moral relation with particular individuals of the group, not with the group per se. *Lun* exists only in relation to individuals, not in relation to the group. This singular fact defies the simplistic application of the Western terms "individualism" and "holism" (or "collectivism") to the Chinese phenomenon.

Relational Orientation of the Individual

Among scholars who have interpreted the inner logic of the Chinese social system, Liang Sou-ming is one of the most perceptive. After painstaking efforts to compare the Chinese social system with others, Liang Sou-ming came to the conclusion that Chinese society is neither *ko-jen pen-wei* (individual-based) nor *she-hui pen-wei* (society-based), but *kuan-hsi pen-wei* (relation-based). In a relation-based social system, the emphasis is placed on the relation between particular individuals: "The focus is not fixed on any particular individual, but on the particular nature of the relations between individuals who interact with each other. The focus is placed upon the relationship."[47] In other words, in the Confucian system, man is socially situated in a relational context—man is a "relational being." Pan Kuang-tan, a sociologist, has convincingly argued that the Chinese humanistic value system pays enormous attention to the "other man." Confucian thinking, he writes, is deeply concerned with one basic principle, which consists of two primary problems: the kind of differentiation to be made between individuals and the kind of relations to be established between individuals. He said the totality of these two issues is the principle of *lun*.[48] The essence of *lun* lies in the differentiated relationship between particular individuals. We might thus say that the Chinese individual is a relational being who conceives of the "other man" in concrete and differentiated relational terms. With a relational orientation, the individual is certainly not an isolated entity; he must be a "social" being. However, his "social characteristics" can only be meaningfully expressed through differentiated relational terms. According to Confucians, there are many kinds of relations between individuals: "Some of them are preordained givens, while others are voluntarily constructed; the father-son and brother-brother relations belong to the former type, husband-wife and friend-friend relations belong to the latter type. Every kind of relation is *lun*."[49] Under various kinds of *lun*, each individual has differentiated, particularistic relations with other concrete individuals. Regardless of whether the *lun* is a preordained given or voluntarily constructed, each individual is expected to perform his particular role in the relational context. What should be stressed here is that in the relational context, the individual's relations with others are neither independent nor dependent but *interdependent*. Thus, the individual self is not totally submerged in the relationships. On the contrary, the individual has considerable social and psychological space for action. Indeed, apart from the preordained *lun*, for example, the father-son *lun*, in which individual behavior is more or less prescribed by the fixed status as well as fixed responsibilities, an individual has considerable freedom in deciding whether or not to enter into voluntarily constructed relationships with others at all; and the individual self is also capable of shaping, if not fixing, what kinds of relationships to have with others. In a word, the self is an active entity capable of defining the roles for himself and others and, moreover, of defining the boundaries of groups of which the self is at the center. It is clearly no accident that social phenomena such as *la kuan-hsi* (to establish relationships with others) and *p'an chiao-ch'ing* (to relate oneself to others) are so prevalent in Chinese society.[50] These social phenomena attest to the individual's freedom of action in constructing a personal relational network.[51] At this juncture, it must be stressed again that in constructing a personal network, the emphasis is placed on the *particular* relations between oneself and other *concrete* individuals. The individual interacts with others always on a particularistic relational basis. In this kind of social communication, the Confucian norms of *shu*, or reciprocity, and the so-called *hsieh chu chih tao*, or the "principle of the measuring square" (a more elaborate version of *shu*)[52] have served as a principal ethical guide. The key word to both *shu* and *chi chü chih tao* is *t'ui* (to infer).[53] Indeed, the kernel of Confucian ethics is an ethics of *t'ui chi chi jen*, which means to infer another's wants and desires from one's own wants and desires. According to the Confucian mode of thinking, one can infer from the self to the family, from the family to the country, and from the country to *t'ien-hsia*. However, most of the Confucian values and norms are not universal and comprehensive in nature; even the most all-encompassing virtue, *jen*, can hardly be interpreted as an overall ethical commandment. Fei Hsiao-t'ung went so far as to argue that, because of the lack of a well-defined concept of group, Confucianism could not develop a comprehensive, universal system of morality.[54] Fei's argument is probably untenable, but we have to point out that the basic virtues—*hsiao*, or filial piety; *t'i*, or fraternal subordination of the younger brother; *chung*, or loyalty; and *hsin*, or sincerity—are all moral elements of private personal relationships. Reischauer's observations are pertinent here:

> The Chinese clearly recognized universal principles, but tempered them with strong particularistic considerations. The five basic Chinese relations were all specific ones and not applicable universally.... Among the virtues most emphasized were filial piety, loyalty, and love, or human-heartedness, but to the Chinese this love was not applied uniformly to strangers as well as relatives but was carefully graded according to the nature of the specific relationships. There was no thought of loving one's neighbor as oneself.[55]

The Confucian individual knows how he should deal with the other only after he knows what particular relations the other has with him. The uneasiness and discomfort of the Chinese with strangers are widely recognized.[56] This phenomenon can be attributed in part to the fact that "stranger" as a role category is too ambiguous to be located in any *lun* relations of Confucian ethics. It explains why the intermediary is so widely used by Chinese as a cultural mechanism in the social engineering of relation-building. Through the intermediary, the individual is able to associate strangers on relational terms. Indeed, it could be argued that Confucianism does not provide the individual with ethical guidance in dealing with "strangers" with whom one has no particular relations. As a result, the Chinese who appear to conform to the "cult of restraint," to borrow Lifton's concept,[57] might be just as aggressive as any non-Chinese in the world beyond the "concrete" family. Eberhard writes:

> As the Chinese must suppress all aggression within the family, the outer world is the field in which aggression finds its outlet.... Only with complete strangers, such as in encounters in a modern big city, or in a foreign country where one is sure that the contact is casual and not lasting, is the individual free and can discharge his aggression directly as the individual in Western society may feel free to do. What counts in such contacts is aggressive intelligence, making the most of every chance as often as one can without risking too much. The biographies of Chinese immigrants, especially Chinese businessmen in other societies testify to this.[58]

Indeed, in the outer world, when the individual faces an amorphous entity called group or society, he finds himself no longer structurally situated in a relation-based social web. In this setting the Confucian value and norms would seem to him not morally abiding and relevant. The common saying *jen pu wei chi, t'ien chü ti mieh* ("If one does not think of his own interest, neither heaven nor earth will save him"), by no means a socially embarrassing statement, only becomes thinkable and understandable in a relation-free social context. It is a recognizable social phenomenon that the Chinese individual often ceases to be a "social being" in the true Confucian sense in relation to either the stranger or the *ch'ün* (group); that is to say, he often fails to take the stranger or the group as a serious relational object and is thus incapable of relating himself to the stranger or the group in interdependent terms. As a result, the individual might not feel that it is socially restrained or ethically illegitimate to see things from his own moral or strategic perspective. In this sense, Fei Hsiao-t'ung's characterization of *tzu wo chu-i*, or "egoism," may be justifiable. And it is no wonder that *tzu wo chu-i* becomes rampant when the individual's life moves more and more away from the family as industrialization and urbanization progress in modern China. Furthermore, the term individualism, not surprisingly, has been unfortunately defined in Chinese society as "individual firstism" or "undisciplined liberalism," meaning "placing personal honors, status and interests above other things."[59] The phenomenon of "individualism" has become so serious in Taiwan, a rapidly modernizing industrial society, that there was in 1981 an intellectual outcry to establish *ti liu lun* (the sixth cardinal relation), namely *ch'ün-chi lun* (the relationship between the individual and the group or the society), in addition to the traditional five cardinal relations.[60] The very idea of seeking to establish a new *lun* for the relationship between the individual and the group or the society testifies again to the fact that, due to the lack of a clearly defined concept of *ch'ün*, the Confucian paradigm has not provided a "viable linkage" between the individual and the group. Thus, neither holism nor individualism could find a central place in the Confucian mode of thinking. However, for good or bad, the Confucian relational perspective did provide the Chinese with a way of creating a long-standing social system in which the individual, who is a relational being endowed with a self-centered autonomy, finds himself placed in a complicated and humanly rich relational web he could hardly afford to escape.

NOTES

1. Frederick W. Mote, *Intellectual Foundations of China* (New York: Knopf, 1971), 45.
2. Lin Yü-sheng, "The Evolution of the Pre-Confucian Meaning of *Jen* and the Confucian Concept of Moral Autonomy," *Monumenta Serica* (1974-75), 31:184.
3. Reciprocity as a moral principle has been applied to social relations of all kinds, and it provides a common ground for both gentlemen and small men. See Lien-sheng Yang, "The Concept of *Pao* as a Basis for Social Relations in China," *Chinese Thought and Institutions*, ed. John K. Fairbank (Chicago: University of Chicago Press, 1957), 291-309.
4. In the *Analects* (4:15), it is stated: "*Shan*. My doctrine is that of an all pervading unity. The disciple Tsang replied 'yes.' The Master went out, and the other disciples asked, saying, 'What do his words mean?' Tsang said, 'The doctrine of our Master is loyalty and reciprocity—this and nothing more'" (translation slightly adapted from James Legge, trans., *The Chinese Classics*, 5 vols. [Hong Kong University Press, 1960], 1:168-69). Also in the *Analects*: "Tsze-kung asked, saying, 'Is there one word which may serve as a rule of practice for all one's life?' The Master said, 'Is not reciprocity such a word? What do you not want done to yourself, do not do to others'" (15:23; translated in Legge, *Chinese Classics*, 1:301).
5. Robert J. Lifton, *Thought Reform and the Psychology of Totalism* (Middlesex, England: Penguin Books, 1967), 445.
6. Charles A. Moore, "Introduction: The Humanistic Chinese Mind," in *The Chinese Mind*, ed. Charles A. Moore (Honolulu: University of Hawaii Press, 1967), 5.
7. Hu Shih, *Chung-kuo che-hsüeh shih ta-kang* [An outline of the history of Chinese philosophy] (Shanghai: Commercial Press, 1919), 116.
8. Lin Yü-sheng, "The Pre-Confucian Meaning of *Jen*," 193.
9. Ruey Yeh-fu, "The Five Social Dyads as a Means of Social Control," *Journal of Sociology*, Taipei (April 1967), 3:53.
10. C. K. Yang, *Chinese Communist Society: The Family and the Village* (Cambridge: M.I.T. Press, 1959), 7.
11. Robert N. Bellah, *Tokugawa Religion* (Boston: Beacon Press, 1970), 178.
12. Fung Yu-lan, *A Short History of Chinese Philosophy*, ed. Derk Bodde (New York: The MacMillan Company, 1964), 21.
13. Ibid.
14. Yang, *Chinese Communist Society*, v.
15. Fung Yu-lan has called it "the ideological basis of traditional society." See Fung Yu-lan, "The Philosophy as the Basis of Traditional Chinese Society," in *Ideological Differences and World Order*, ed. F. S. C. Northrop (New Haven: Yale University Press, 1949), 18.
16. Lifton, *Thought Reform*, 419.
17. Hu Shih, *Chung-kuo che-hsüeh*, 129.
18. The difference between symmetrical and asymmetrical rule, according to Goffman, is as follows: "A symmetrical rule is one which leads an individual to have obligations or expectations regarding others that these others have in regard to him.... An asymmetrical rule is one that leads others to treat and be treated by an individual differently from the way he treats and is treated by them." Erving Goffman, *Interaction Ritual* (London: Allen Lane, The Penguin Press, 1972), 52-53.
19. Ch'ü T'ung-tsu, *Chung-kuo fa-lü yü Chung-kuo she-hui* [Chinese law and society] (Hong Kong: Lung Mun Shu-chü, 1967).
20. John C. H. Wu, "The Status of the Individual in the Political and Legal Traditions of Old and New China," in *The Chinese Mind*, ed. Moore, 346.

21. Chie Nakane writes: "The Japanese family system differs from that of the Chinese system, where family ethics are always based on relationships between particular individuals, such as father and son, brothers and sisters, parents and children, husband and wife, while in Japan they are always based on the collective group, i.e., members of a household, not on the relationships between individuals." Chie Nakane, *Japanese Society* (Middlesex, England: Penguin Books, 1973), 14.

22. K. Abbott, *Harmony and Individualism* (Taipei: The Orient Cultural Service, 1970), 57.

23. Richard W. Wilson, *Learning to Be Chinese* (Cambridge: M.I.T. Press, 1970), 20.

24. Yang, *Chinese Communist Society*, 172.

25. Liang Sou-ming, *Chung-kuo wen-hua yao-i*, [The essential features of Chinese culture] (Hong Kong: Chi-cheng T'u-shu Kung-ssu, 1974), 260.

26. Ibid., 90.

27. K'ang Yu-wei, *Ta t'ung shu* [The book of the grand unity] (Peking: Ku-chi Ch'u-pan-she, 1956).

28. T'an Ssu-t'ung, *Jen-hsüeh* [A study of *jen*] (Peking: Chung-hua Shu-chü, 1958).

29. H. Blumer, "Society as Symbolic Interaction," in *Human Behavior and Social Processes*, ed. Arnold M. Rose (Boston: Houghton-Mifflin Company, 1962), 189-90.

30. Dennis H. Wrong, "The Oversocialized Conception of Man in Modern Sociology," *American Sociological Review* (1961), 26:183-93.

31. Fung Yu-lan, *Hsin shih-lun* [A new discussion of the issues of the practical world] (Taipei: Commercial Press, 1967), 78-79.

32. C. K. Yang, "Some Characteristics of Chinese Bureaucratic Behavior," in *Confucianism in Action*, ed. D. S. Nivison and A. F. Wright (Stanford: Stanford University Press, 1959), 134-64.

33. Lin Yü-sheng, "The Pre-Confucian Meaning of *Jen*," 194.

34. Robert K. Merton and E. Barber, "Sociological Ambivalence," in *Sociological Theory, Values and Sociocultural Change*, ed. E. A. Tiryakian (New York: Harper Torchbooks, 1967), 98.

35. "In the most extended sense, sociological ambivalence refers to incompatible normative expectations of attitudes, beliefs and behavior assigned to a status or to a set of statuses in a society. In its most restricted sense, sociological ambivalence refers to incompatible normative expectations incorporated in a single role of a single social status" (ibid., 94-95).

36. "From the perspective of sociological ambivalence, we see a social role as a dynamic organization of norms and counter-norms, not as a combination of dominant attributes (such as affective neutrality or functional specificity). We propose that the major norms and minor counter-norms alternatively govern role-behavior to produce ambivalence" (ibid., 103).

37. R. Turner, "Role-Making: Process Versus Conformity," in *Human Behavior and Social Processes*, ed. Rose, 149.

38. Walter Buckley, *Sociology and Modern Systems Theory* (Englewood Cliffs: Prentice-Hall, 1967), 148-49.

39. Cheng Te-k'un, *The World of the Chinese—Struggle for Human Unity* (Hong Kong: The Chinese University Press, 1980), 116.

40. Fei Hsiao-t'ung, *Hsiang-tu Chung-kuo* [Peasant China] (Taipei: Lu-chou Ch'u-pan-she, 1967), 29.

41. B. E. Ward, "Sociological Self-Awareness: Some Uses of the Conscious Model," *Man*, 1968, 1:201-15.

42. Fei Hsiao-tung, *Hsiang-tu Chung-kuo*, 24.

43. Benjamin Schwartz, "Some Polarities in Confucian Thought," in *Confucianism in Action*, ed. Nivison and Wright, 50-62.

44. Fei Hsiao-tung, *Hsiang-tu Chung-kuo*, 27-28.

45. Ibid. Fei's views on the Chinese are somewhat different from that of Francis Hsu. Contrasting the Chinese and American views of the individual, Hsu writes, "In the American way of life the emphasis is placed upon the predilections of the individual, a characteristic we shall call individual-centered. This is in contrast to the emphasis the

Chinese put upon an individual's appropriate place and behavior among his fellow men, a characteristic we shall term situation-centered. Being individual-centered, the American moves toward social and psychological isolation. Being more situation-centered, the Chinese is inclined to be socially and psychologically dependent on others." Francis L. K. Hsu, *American and Chinese, Two Ways of Life* (New York: Abelard-Schurman, 1953), 10.

46. *The Analects*, trans. D. C. Lau (Middlesex, England: Penguin Books, 1979), 12:1 (112).
47. Liang Sou-ming, *Chung-kuo wen-hua yao-i*, 94.
48. Pan Kuang-tan, *Cheng-hsüeh chu yen* [Comments on political issues] (Shanghai: Kuan-ch'a She, 1948), 133.
49. Hu Shih, *Chung-kuo che-hsüeh*, 116.
50. Surprising or not, in the People's Republic today, the personal relationship is still as crucial a factor in social communication as ever. There is even a newly coined term, *kuan-hsi hsüeh*, denoting such a social phenomenon. See *Renmin ribao*, 29 September 1981. For a systematic treatment of Chinese interpersonal relationships, see Ambrose Y. C. King, "Jen chi kuan-hsi chung jen-ch'ing chi fen-hsi" [An analysis of *jen-ch'ing* in interpersonal relationships], in *Collection of Papers of the International Conference of Sinology* (Taipei: Academia Sinica, 1981), 413-28.
51. The common belief in China that individuals are capable of constructing their own relational networks is often neglected by social scientists studying personality in that society. For a systematic elaboration of this topic, see Ambrose Y. C. King and Michael H. Bond, "A Confucian Paradigm of Men: A Sociological View" (Paper delivered at the Conference on Chinese Culture and Mental Health held at the East-West Center, Honolulu, Hawaii, March 1982).
52. "What a man dislikes in his superiors, let him not display in the treatment of his inferiors; what he dislikes in his inferiors, let him not display in the service of his superiors; what he hates in those who are before him, let him not therewith precede those who are behind him; what he hates in those who are behind him, let him not therewith follow those who are before him; what he hates to receive on the right, let him not bestow on the left; what he hates to receive on the left, let him not bestow on the right—this is what is called 'The principle with which, as a measuring square, to regular one's conduct'" (*Ta-hsüeh* [The great learning], chap. 10; translated in Legge, *Chinese Classics*, 1:373-74).
53. Hu Shih, *Chung-kuo che-hsüeh*, 112.
54. Fei Hsiao-t'ung, *Hsiang-tu Chung-kuo*, 37.
55. Edwin O. Reischauer, *The Japanese* (Tokyo: Charles E. Tuttle Company, 1978), 138-39.
56. King and Bond, "A Confucian Paradigm of Men," 15.
57. Lifton, *Thought Reform*, 453.
58. Wilfram Eberhard, *Moral and Social Values of the Chinese: Collected Essays* (Taipei: Cheng-wen Publishing Company, 1971), 8, 11.
59. Lifton, *Thought Reform*, 435.
60. The idea of establishing a new *lun* on the relationship between the individual and society was first proposed in Li Kuo-ting's lecture entitled "Pa-shih nien-tai she-hui hsüeh-che mien-tui ti t'iao-chan" [The challenge facing the sociologists of the eighties] (Paper delivered at the Annual Meeting of the Chinese Sociological Society, Taipei, March 1981). This was reported and discussed widely in Taiwan. See *United Daily News*, 16 March 1981.

Glossary

ch'a-hsü 差序

Chang Tung-sun 張東蓀

Cheng-hsüeh chu-yen 政學罪言

cheng-ming 正名

chi 己

chia 家

chih kuo p'ing t'ien-hsia 治國平天下

ch'in 親

Ch'ü T'ung-tsu 瞿同祖

ch'ün 羣

ch'ün-chi lun 羣己倫

chün-fu 君父

chün-tzu 君子

chung 忠

Chung-kuo che-hsüeh shih ta-kang 中國哲學史大綱

Chung-kuo fa-lü yü Chung-kuo she-hui 中國法律與中國社會

Chung-kuo wen-hua yao-i 中國文化要義

Erh ya 爾雅

Fei Hsiao-t'ung 費孝通

Fung Yu-lan 馮友蘭

Hsiang-tu Chung-kuo 鄉土中國

hsiao 孝

Hsiao Ching 孝經

hsieh chü chih tao 絜矩之道

hsin 信

Hsin shih-lun 新事論

hsiu-chi 修己

hsiu-shen 修身

hsü 序

Hu Shih 胡適

i 義

jen 仁

Jen chi kuan-hsi chung jen-ch'ing chih fen-hsi 人際關係中人情之分析

Jen-hsüeh 仁學

jen-lun 人倫

jen pu wei chi, t'ien chü ti mieh 人不爲己天誅地滅

kang-ch'ang 綱常

K'ang Yu-wei 康有爲

k'o chi 克己

k'o chi fu li 克己復禮

ko-jen pen-wei 個人本位

kuan-hsi hsüeh 關係學

kuan-hsi pen-wei 關係本位

kung 公

la kuan-hsi 拉關係

li 禮

Li Kuo-ting 李國鼎

Liang Shu-ming 梁漱溟

lun 倫

Pa-shih nien-tai she-hui hsüeh-che mien-tui ti t'iao-chan 八十年代社會學者面對的挑戰

p'an chiao-ch'ing 攀交情

Pan Kuang-ta 潘光旦

pieh 別

pu shih ch'i lun 不失其倫

she-hui pen-wei 社會本位

shu 恕

Ta-hsüeh 大學

Ta t'ung shu 大同書

T'an Ssu-t'ung 譚嗣同

t'i 悌

ti liu lun 第六倫

t'ien-hsia 天下

t'ien-hsia i-chia 天下一家

t'ui 推

t'ui chi chi jen 推己及人

tzu-chia jen 自家人

tzu-min 子民

tzu-wo chu-i 自我主義

wu-hsiung 吾兄

wu-lun 五倫

wu-ti 吾弟

Yang Chu 楊朱

Part II:

The Individual and the Whole

The Right to Selfishness:
Yangism, Later Mohism, Chuang Tzu

A. C. Graham

In the richness and variety of pre-Han thought there are a number of tendencies which never firmly established themselves in the later tradition. Among them, can we recognize any of the trends which in our own tradition have been called "individualism"? It is natural to think first of Yang Chu, familiar as the archetypal Chinese egoist, but about whose life we seem to have scarcely any solid evidence. For most of the last two thousand years, this thinker, who can be dated only vaguely to about 350 B.C., has been judged by a single reference in *Mencius*: "Yang Tzu was in favor of 'every man for himself' [*wei wo*]; if he could have benefited the world by plucking one hair of his body he would not have done it. Mo Tzu loved everybody; if he could have benefited the world by wearing himself smooth from the crown to the heels he would have done it."[1]

The "Yang Chu" chapter of *Lieh Tzu* (ca. A.D. 300), which expounds a hedonist philosophy, is generally acknowledged to have nothing to do with the pre-Han thinker, but it does preserve an important fragment of probable Mohist origin,[2] a dialogue between Yang Chu and Ch'in Ku-li, chief disciple of Mo Tzu. A list of the doctrines of ten philosophers in the *Lü-shih ch'un-ch'iu* [Mr. Lü's Spring and Autumn Annals] (ca. 240 B.C.) has the item: "Yang Chu valued self" (*kuei chi*).[3]

A historical sketch in the *Huai-nan Tzu* (ca. 130 B.C.) puts Yang Chu between Mo Tzu and Mencius and is the most informative of the summaries of his doctrine: "Keeping one's nature intact [*ch'üan hsing*], protecting one's genuineness [*pao chen*], not letting one's body be tied by other things, these were the doctrines of Yang Tzu, but Mencius denied them."[4]

A curious feature of all these quotations is that they describe Yang Chu's philosophy only in contrast with that of some other thinker or thinkers. There are plenty of other references to Yang Chu scattered over the literature, but they turn up in the sorts of stories which might be told about anyone. A suspicion arises that here it is not so much that Mencius and the rest of them wanted to tell us what Yang Chu taught as that they needed a name to label the teaching, it being the convention to call each school after a supposed founder. No writings of Yang Chu are listed in the Han bibliography; perhaps one should not think of an organized school with a book and a founder but rather of a movement with various teachers, among whom Yang Chu attracted the most attention outside but not necessarily within the group. This suspicion has become stronger since, with increasing sensitivity to the varied strands of thought in composite works, scholars have begun to identify a "Yangist" literature of the late third century B.C. This literature gives firm substance to a philosophy long known only by its slogans, and makes it possible for the first time to discuss seriously the degree to which the doctrine fits Western conceptions of egoism or individualism.

Fung Yu-lan, in his great *History of Chinese Philosophy*, showed that the doctrines ascribed to Yang Chu, those of valuing self, keeping one's nature intact in order to live out one's term, preferring the health and survival of the body to external possessions, are expounded at length in certain chapters of the syncretistic *Lü-shih ch'un-ch'iu*, e.g., "Pen sheng" [Treating life as basic], "Chung chi" [Giving weight to self], "Kuei sheng" [Valuing life], "Ch'ing yü" [The essential desires], and "Shen wei" [Being aware of what one is for].[5] But although the name of Yang Chu is used elsewhere in the same book to label the doctrine of "valuing self," the actual Yangist chapters do not mention him, appealing instead to other names from the fourth century B.C., Tzu Hua Tzu and Chan Tzu.[6] We find the same apparent anomaly with a block of chapters in the *Chuang Tzu*, more recently identified as Yangist by Kuan Feng.[7] These are chapters 28 through 31, "Jang wang" [Yielding the throne], "Tao Chih" [Robber Chih], "Shuo chien" [Discourse on swords], and "Yü fu" [Old fisherman]. Kuan Feng excludes the "Discourse on Swords" from the Yangist identification, but since it can be read as a variation on the theme of preserving life this seems unnecessary. These chapters are distinguished from all others in the *Chuang Tzu* by the form of their titles (two words summing up the theme) and are the very first to have been recognized as spurious, by Su Shih back in the Sung dynasty.[8] They have never looked Taoist and probably got into the book only because the story in "Discourse on Swords" had Chuang Tzu as hero. Because these chapters never mention Yang Chu, it had not previously occurred to students of *Chuang Tzu* to classify them as Yangist. But now that Kuan Feng has done so, it is immediately obvious that they treat the same Yangist themes as the *Lü-shih ch'un-ch'iu* chapters do, including "protecting genuineness," which is expounded in "Old Fisherman." Moreover, whereas the eclectic *Lü-shih ch'un-ch'iu* blurs the outlines of the doctrines which it syncretizes, this series is a direct and uncompromising expression of the Yangism of the late third century B.C.

At the Harvard Conference on Chinese Thought in 1976 I called the philosophy of these chapters "individualism" and met with criticism for using a term with so many misleading Western associations. At the conference for which this paper was written, individualism was the actual theme, and use of the term would, of course, beg the whole question. In any case, I have since got into the habit of calling these chapters the "Yangist Miscellany." They seem closely linked to the very distinctive "primitivist" essays (*Chuang Tzu*, chaps. 8–10 and the essay which introduces chap. 11) dated with unusual precision to the time of civil war after the fall of the Ch'in (209–202 B.C.), and there is other evidence that they come from the same period.[9] The "Primitivist" refers to a contemporary revival of "Yang and Mo" and also to the "disputation" (*pien*) of Yang and Mo.[10] The *pien* of the later Mohists is known from the dialectical chapters of Mo Tzu to have been a highly rational kind of argumentation, but schools other than the Sophists and Mohists conceived the art of persuasion called *pien* as rhetoric rather than logic and also used the word adjectivally in the sense of "subtle and eloquent." The dialogues of "Robber Chih," "Discourse on Swords," and "Old Fisherman" are all disputation in this sense, and the primary participants, Robber Chih and Confucius, both have their command of words described by the adjectival *pien*.[11] The characteristic device of this rhetoric is the apt historical example. The first of the three dialogues in "Robber Chih" incorporates a series of fourteen anecdotes classified in three sets, at the end of which Robber says to Confucius, "If you tell me stories about men, you will find none better than these."[12] The next has a string of eight, all concluding with "these are what earlier generations handed down and recent generations tell";[13] and "Yielding the Throne" consists solely of two series of anecdotes, each in chronological order, apparently intended as illustrations in debate and some in fact utilized elsewhere in the "Yangist Miscellany."[14] Thus, we have an exact parallel to what happens in the *Lü-shih ch'un-ch'iu*: four chapters which never mention Yang Chu preserve the argumentation described elsewhere in the same book as the disputation of the Yangists.

With the aid of these documents, the slogans ascribed to Yang Chu in the *Lü-shih ch'un-ch'iu* and *Huai-nan Tzu* assume a clear meaning. To "keep one's nature intact" is to look after health and life; man's "nature" (*hsing^a*) is understood as the principle by which he is born, grows to fulfill his proper physical shape, and lives out his term. ("It is the nature of man to live long; others things disorder him so he fails to live long.")[15] The value of life is taken as central, and this has various ramifications. Life is preserved by never going beyond a moderate satisfaction of the essential desires, which are those of the eyes, ears, and mouth for the five colors, five sounds, and five tastes;[16] it is absurd to sacrifice it on some trivial point of pride or honor, as in the anecdotes of crazy suicides which comprise the second series in "Yielding the Throne" and are cited with derision by Robber Chih.[17] It is absurd, too, as we learn from "Discourse on Swords," for a lord to waste the lives of retainers in swordfighting for sport. "Protecting genuineness," as expounded in "Old Fisherman," is preserving the integrity of the emotions, sorrow, anger, and fellow feeling, from being undermined by Confucian ritualism.[18] As for "not letting one's body be tied by other things," since the body is not replaceable but external possessions are the latter must be sacrificed for the former. This is the theme of "Giving Weight to Self": "Now as a possession of mine, my life benefits me supremely. Grade them as more or less valuable, and not even the throne of the empire deserves to be compared with it; grade them as more or less important, and not even the wealth of being possessor of the empire can be taken in exchange for it."[19]

From this and other passages identified as Yangist it can be seen that Ku Chieh-kang was right in arguing that Mencius misrepresented Yang Chu.[20] It was not that the Yangist would not lift a finger to help the world; the point was that he would not accept the least injury to the body, even the loss of a hair, for the sake of any external possession, even the throne of the empire. At the time when Ku Chieh-kang was writing, he was aware of only one clear piece of evidence, a reference by Han Fei (also from the late third century B.C.) to hermits who "will not give a hair of the leg in exchange for that greatest of benefits, the empire" because they "give more weight to life than to things [i.e., possessions]."[21] But "Valuing Life" and "Yielding the Throne" include the story of Tzu-chou Chih-fu, who refused the offer of the throne by Yao rather than risk neglecting an ailment, and both note approvingly: "The empire is the weightiest thing of all, but he would not do harm to his life for the sake of it, and how much less for anything else!"[22]

Robber Chih, who wants only to satisfy his sensual desires and live out his full term, refuses to be legitimized as ruler of a state on the grounds that thrones are soon lost: "Is it not because the benefit to one is too great?"[23] Elsewhere in "Robber Chih" we are told that when Yao and Shun tried to give away their thrones "it was not out of kindness to the world, but because they would not for the sake of glory do harm to life"; and that when the intended beneficiaries refused, "it was not a vain renunciation, it was that they would not by undertaking the task do harm to themselves."[24]

Why did Mencius say that Yang Chu refused to give a hair to benefit the world? Ku Chieh-kang may have been right in suggesting that Yang Chu did use the phrase *li t'ien-hsia*, but not in the sense of "benefiting the world"; Yang's meaning was probably closer to "treating the world as a benefit [to oneself]."[25] However, there is a simpler explanation which bears directly on the question of what kind of "egoism" or "individualism" Yang Chu represents. To refuse a throne may be seen, from one point of view, as a high-minded renunciation of a benefit to oneself; from another, as a selfish refusal to undertake responsibility for benefiting the people. Rather than misrepresenting Yang Chu's philosophy, Mencius may be exposing what he sees as the doctrine's selfish implications, which Yang Chu is trying to hide. This explanation is supported by the dialogue of Yang Chu and the Mohist Ch'in Ku-li, in which the latter attacks from the same direction as Mencius.[26]

> "If you could help the whole world by sacrificing one hair of your body, would you do it?"
> "It would take more than one hair to help the world."
> "But supposing it did help, would you do it?" Yang Chu did not answer him.

Yang Chu is embarrassed, but a disciple of his recovers the offensive.

> "If you could win a thousand pieces of gold by injuring your skin and flesh, would you do it?"
> "I would."
> "If you could gain a kingdom by cutting off one limb at the joint, would you do it?"
> Ch'in Ku-li was silent for a while.

What the Yangist calls "gaining a kingdom" is what the Mohist called "helping the world," and neither quibbles over the other's formulation. It is clear that the Yangist is not thinking in terms of preferring himself to other selves, but of each man preferring the welfare of his own body to the things which are mere means of its support. The contrast is always between "self"(*wo* or *chi*) and "things" (*wu*^a). The Yangist does not welcome being supposed indifferent to the good of the world, but when pressed he cannot deny that he sees a throne (in more practical terms, an office) simply as a "thing," a possession, to be accepted or rejected on the basis of its consequences to his own health and longevity. We may say, then, that the Yangist lives his own life and decides for himself whether or not to take office and run the risks of competing for power and wealth. He affirms what for Confucians and Mohists is a right to selfishness.

Turning now to the Mohists, an earlier school which originated in the late fifth century B.C., it goes without saying that they are no defenders of the right to selfishness, but they do approach individualism from another direction. In Confucianism, behavior is prescribed according to social categories, and *i*^a, "duty" or "righteousness," is seen as related to its homophone *i*^b, "appropriate," in the sense of an act appropriate to one's station as ruler or minister, father or son, husband or wife. But the Mohists reduce all moral rules to the single principle of *chien ai*, "universal love," or more literally, "love of everyone,"[27] implying that the love of any one person is duplicated for every other. This principle is perceived in all social relationships:

> Supposing everyone in the world loved one another, and loved others as they loved themselves, would there still be unfilial people? If they regarded father and elder brother or ruler as they regarded themselves, to whom would they behave unfilially? Or would there still be uncompassionate people? If they regarded younger brother and son or minister as they regarded themselves, to whom would they behave uncompassionately?[28]

An ethic based on extending to other individuals the kind of love everyone has for himself would seem to qualify as some kind of "individualism." This impression is strengthened by consideration of the later Mohist systematization of the ethic in the dialectical chapters of *Mo Tzu*. We may note in the first place that a new definition of *i*^a, "righteous," severed all former connections with *i*^b, "appropriate [to social station]": "The 'righteous' is the beneficial."[29] The love of man is typified on the one hand by self-love, on the other by the love of Tsang and Huo (abusive names for bondsman and bondswoman), persons too humble to be loved for anything but their humanity. This love of man, though the same for all, is born from thinking about the benefit of different individuals in different circumstances:

> The loving which involves benefiting is born of thinking. Yesterday's thinking is not today's thinking, yesterday's love of man is not today's love of man. The love of man involved in loving Huo is born from thinking about Huo's benefit, not from thinking about Tsang's benefit; but the love of man involved in loving Tsang is the love of man involved in loving Huo. Even if to get rid of the love of them would benefit the world one cannot get rid of it.[30]

It is frequently stressed that the love of a person is for his own sake, not for praise, reward, or other benefits to oneself. To make this point, self-love is taken as a paradigm:

> Love of oneself is not for the sake of making oneself useful. It is not like loving a horse.... Love of man does not exclude oneself. I am myself among those I love.... Tsang's love of himself is not for the sake of the others who love him.[31]

Each person is to be loved according to his worth, which is equivalent to the degree to which he is righteous; righteousness is judged according to a person's intent and ability to benefit others, irrespective of whether he gets office and actually does benefit them.[32] "No external condition can make me more beneficial."[33] Differences of kin and stranger, self and other, men of the present and of other ages, are all irrelevant to the degree of love. The later Mohists do not deny that it is to the benefit of all that each person has his own social role (fen, lit., "portion") imposing special duties towards certain categories, his own kin, elders, ruler, creditors. But these are a matter of "doing extra" (hou), not of "extra love" (hou ai). It is laid down explicitly that we owe no more love to our own parents than to the parents of others.[34] The fitting of conduct to social status, which in Confucianism is central to morality, is thus treated as secondary to the moral relations between individuals.

There are other respects in which the Mohists are utterly remote from anything that we could call individualism. In the first place, they care nothing for individuality as such. Mo Tzu is indeed unique among pre-Han philosophical books in its meagreness of personal anecdote, indifference to the inner life, impersonality of style, and its failure to convey the faintest intimation of what it felt like to live the philosophy. It is hardly an exaggeration to say that for the Mohists, individuals are interchangeable units differing only in their circumstances and their moral worth. Consequently, no moral problem arises for them in the sacrifice of one man for the benefit of others; it is even said that "if a man's life or death are equally beneficial [that is, if his death would benefit the world just as much as his survival would], there is nothing to choose between them."[35] Nor do they have any conception of freedom as a prerequisite for individual self-realization. The worth of the individual in Mohism is, in the first place, the humanity for which he is loved, a quality shared, of course, with all other men; secondly, it is his social value in terms of his benefit to others, which is realized through the disciplines of an authoritarian political system. But these considerations do not affect the rather surprising fact that the later Mohist ethic, the mostly highly rationalized in the history of Chinese thought, is developed throughout in terms of benefit to individuals and, indeed, hardly finds room for any group except the "world" (t'ien-hsia), which is the totality of individuals. It is tempting to connect this anomaly with the evidence that Mohism was the first great irruption into literary culture of a low social class, the craftsmen.[36] We know too little about the social history of the time to make confident comparisons with the social background of Western individualism, but it is hard to suppress the notion that there is something of the "Protestant ethic and spirit of capitalism" about the Mohists, manifested in their thrift, utilitarianism, puritanism, rationalism, fear of the undermining of endeavor by fatalism, and faith in heaven as a god who punishes the wicked.

The Yangists, based on what little we know of their social origins, would have come from a higher class than the Mohists, since they assume that the crucial choice in life is whether or not to benefit the empire by taking part in its government. The same applies to the Taoists, whose philosophical justification for withdrawing to private life soon superseded the Yangist. Their position is first documented in the late fourth century in the "Inner Chapters" of *Chuang Tzu*, the only ones in the book which can be confidently attributed to Chuang Tzu himself. (*Lao Tzu*, whatever its date, does not concern us here because it represents the political branch of Taoism.) There is some reason to suspect that Chuang Tzu himself was at one time a Yangist; that would help explain why he appears in the Yangist "Discourse on Swords." Moreover, one episode in the "Outer Chapters" may actually be read as an account of his crisis of conversion from Yangism.[37] This is the anecdote of Chuang Tzu stalking a huge magpie which turns out to be after a mantis which is itself pouncing on a cicada, at which point he is himself chased out of the park by a gamekeeper.[38] In this troubling story, the only one about him in which he doubts himself, Chuang Tzu discerns that it is against the order of things to succeed indefinitely in protecting one's life and escaping ties with other things ("It is inherent in things that they are tied to each other.") Here Chuang Tzu seems to be taking the first step away from the Yangist obsession with life and health of the body toward the reconciliation with death and with bodily mutilation that is so characteristic of his mature thought. The Yangist themes of longevity, genuineness, and avoiding ties do, of course, persist in philosophical Taoism, but the first is perceived only as a consequence which may follow if you do *not* aim at it (and if it does not follow, accept that too), when you surrender to the spontaneous course of life as it carries you towards death. "Even things out on the whetstone of heaven, adapt to them and let the stream find its own channels, this is the way to last out your years. Forget the years, forget duty, be quivered into motion by the Limitless, and so find things their places in the Limitless."[39]

It is essential to Chuang Tzu's attitude that instead of spending one's time like a Yangist, making pettifogging calculations of benefits and harms to one's own body, one joyfully immerses in the spontaneous flow and refuses to analyze and distinguish alternatives such as benefit and harm, self and other. The Taoist is without self (*wu chi*).[40] That is the polar opposite of the Yangist "valuing self" and, one might suppose, of any kind of individualism. But it is not the least of the paradoxes of Taoism that, unlike Mohism, which philosophizes in terms of individuals, Taoist doctrine encourages individuality in practice more than any other Chinese view of life. Chuang Tzu himself stands out in the literature as the most strikingly individual character in pre-Han China, and he became a dominant influence in the age when personal idiosyncrasy was most prized, the third and fourth centuries A.D.

That this is no accident may be seen in the familiar Taoist metaphor of water, implicit in the *Chuang Tzu* passage just quoted. The Taoist, without thinking of self, will grow naturally into his own unique shape like water finding its level inside irregular contours, while the rest of us become alike by trying to live according to the same fixed standards as everyone else. A term in the vocabulary of *Chuang Tzu* which relates to individuality is *tu*, "alone," often used verbally ("be alone/on its own") and even nominalized ("the Alone/Unique"). It may be used to refer to the Tao itself (the sage "sees the Alone" or "stands up in the Alone"),[41] yet also to express the perfect independence of the man who lives according to the Tao.

> When Kung-wen Hsüan saw the Commander of the Right he said in amazement, "What man is this? Why is he so singular?[42] Is it of heaven or of man?" "It is of heaven, not of man. Heaven's engendering is a causing to be *alone* [/unique]; the guise which is of man assimilates us to each other. By this I know it is of heaven, not of man."[43]

> In *aloneness* he perfects what is from heaven in him.[44]

> From the engraved and polished he returned to the unhewn, and solidly *alone* [/unique] stood up in his own shape.[45]

> He departs *alone*, he comes *alone*; this one calls "existing *alone*." It is the man who exists alone that one calls "noblest of all."[46]

> When a great sage governs the empire, he sets free the people's hearts and enables them to become perfect in what they were taught and replace their customs. They all extinguish the predatory in their hearts, they all push forward their *lone* [/unique] intents, as though it were their nature to be doing it of themselves, and they do not know how it comes to be so.[47]

We find *tu* with *hsing*[b], "conduct," used pejoratively of the willful behavior of a spoiled prince: "He is young in years, *alone* [/wayward] in conduct."[48] But we also find it used in praise of the Taoist sage: "Only one who is clear about man, clear about spirits, is able to conduct himself *alone*."[49]

When a disciple of Confucius finds two Taoists pleating silkworm frames and making music beside the corpse of a friend, he asks the Master about "extraordinary men" (*chi jen*) and is told: "Extraordinary men are extraordinary in the eyes of men but ordinary in the eyes of heaven."[50]

It appears, then, that we may distinguish two kinds of exception in pre-Han thinking to the prevailing assumption that a man is the sum of his social functions and derives all his value from the appropriateness of his acts to his role as father or son, ruler or minister. The Yangists, and then Chuang Tzu, affirm that it is not irresponsible but, on the contrary, high-minded to drop out, temporarily or permanently to scorn wealth and power, and live your own life. They initiate the one form of individual assertion which won a permanent and acknowledged place in Chinese culture. Mohism, on the other hand, cares nothing for private life and is as moralistic and as socialized as Confucianism and considerably more authoritarian politically; yet it treats all the traditional duties of social categories as second to moral relations between individuals. In this as in other respects, Mohism is the great anomaly, a philosophy from the creative ferment before Chinese civilization decided where to draw its boundaries, ejected from the tradition from the Han onwards, and tantalizing the Westerner with the feeling that it seems to be straying in the direction of his own.

NOTES

1. *Mencius*, 7A:26.
2. I argue its Mohist origin in "The Dialogue between Yang Ju and Chyntzyy," *Bulletin of the School of Oriental and African Studies*, 1959, 22(2):291-99.
3. Hsü Wei-yü, *Lü-shih ch'un-ch'iu chi-shih* [Collected explanations of *Mr. Lü's Spring and Autumn Annals*] (Peking: Wen-hsüeh Ku-chi K'an Hsing She, 1955), 17.30b.
4. *Huai-nan Tzu* (SPTK ed.), 13.7a-b.
5. Hsü Wei-yü, *Lü-shih* 1.6a-14b, 2.4b-11b, 21.8a-10b.
6. Ibid., 2.7a, 21.9b-10b.
7. Kuan Feng, "*Chuang Tzu* 'wai tsa p'ien' ch'u t'an" [Preliminary inquiry into the "outer" and "mixed" chapters of *Chuang Tzu*], in *Chuang Tzu che-hsüeh t'ao-lun chi* [Collection of discussions of Chuang Tzu's philosophy] (Peking: Chung-hua Shu-chü, 1962), 89-96.
8. See Chang Hsin-ch'eng, *Wei shu t'ung k'ao* [General inquiry into forged books], rev. ed. (Shanghai: Shang-wu Yin Shu Kuan, 1957), 834.
9. I have discussed the date of the primitivist and Yangist chapters in "How Much of Chuang-tzu did Chuang-tzu Write?," in *Studies in Classical Chinese Thought*, ed. Henry Rosemont, Jr., and Benjamin I. Schwartz, *Journal of the American Academy of Religion* Thematic Issue (September 1979), 47(3):459-501.
10. *A Concordance to Chuang Tzu*, Harvard-Yenching Institute Sinological Index Series, supp. no. 20 (Cambridge: Harvard University Press, 1956), 21/8/7; 24/10/26-28; 33/12/98.
11. Ibid., 8/29/7-8; 81/29/18, 33.
12. Ibid., 82/29/47.
13. Ibid., 83/29/75.
14. See also Graham, "How Much of Chuang-tzu?," 483-84.
15. Hsü Wei-yü, *Lü-shih* 1.6b, 7a.
16. Ibid., 2.8-11b.
17. *Chuang Tzu*, 79/28/68-80/28/87; 82/29/41-45.
18. Ibid., 87/31/32-39.
19. Hsü Wei-yü, *Lü-shih* 1.11a.
20. Ku Chieh-kang, "Ts'ung *Lü-shih ch'un-ch'iu* t'ui-ts'e *Lao Tzu* chih ch'eng shu nien-tai" [Inferring from *Mr. Lü's Spring and Autumn Annals* the date of composition of *Lao Tzu*], in *Ku shih pien* [Arguments over ancient history], ed. Lo Ken-tse, 7 vols. (Hong Kong: Tai Ping Book Company, 1963), 4:462-520.
21. *Han-fei Tzu* (SPTK ed.), 19.8b.
22. Hsü Wei-yü, *Lü-shih* 2.4b, 5a. *Chuang Tzu*, 76/28/1-3.
23. *Chuang Tzu*, 81/29/27.
24. Ibid., 84/29/90-92.
25. *Li* is translatable as "to benefit" before animate objects, but "to use for one's own benefit" before inanimate objects. Throughout the concordanced pre-Han texts, *li t'ien-hsia* is "benefit the world," with *t'ien-hsia* treated consistently as animate; and the accounts of Yang Chu's doctrines in *Mencius* (7A:26) and *Lieh Tzu* (SPTK ed., 7.4b) both enforce this interpretation by parallelism. Previously, therefore, I doubted the grammatical acceptability of Ku Chieh-kang's proposal (Graham, "Dialogue between Yang Ju and Chyntzyy," 295). But I have since noticed in the *Lü-shih ch'un-ch'iu* a case of *li t'ien-hsia* where Ku Chieh-kang's interpretation is demanded by the parallelism (Hsü Wei-yü, *Lü-shih* 20.3a). With this kind of ambiguity one would guess that the two usages were phonetically

distinguished in speech, but that only one was allowed in literary language (except where parallelism removed all danger of misunderstanding). If Yangism began like Confucianism and Mohism as oral teaching, it is conceivable that slogans about refusing to use the world for one's profit might be unambiguous in speech and yet seem to reverse their meaning as soon as they are written down.

26. *Lieh Tzu* (SPTK ed.), 7.4b, 5a.

27. *Chien*/*KLIAM appears to be related to *ko*/*KLÂK ("each") in the same way as *yu*/*GIÛG ("there is") to *huo*/**G'WƏK ("some"), *wu*^{b}/*MIWO ("there is not") to *mo*/*MÂK ("none"), and *shu*/*DIÔK ("which?") to *shei*/*DIWƏR ("who?"). We might even risk a paradigm with *ai* ("love"): *yu ai*, "love some"; *wu ai*, "love none"; *shei ai*, "love whom?"; *chien ai*, "love everyone"; *huo ai*, "some love"; *mo ai*, "none love"; *shu ai*, "which loves?"; *ko ai*, "each loves." The second series would be derived from the first by addition of a final -K.

28. *A Concordance to Mo Tzu*, Harvard-Yenching Institute Sinological Index Series, supp. no. 21 (Cambridge: Harvard University Press, 1948), 22/14/12-13.

29. Ibid., 65/40/3, translated in my *Later Mohist Logic, Ethics and Science* (Hong Kong and London: Chinese University of Hong Kong and University of London, 1978), 270.

30. *Mo Tzu*, 76/44/41-43 (*Logic*, 247).

31. *Mo Tzu*, 68/42/4; 75/44/17, 21 (*Logic*, 270, 256).

32. See *Logic*, 50.

33. *Mo Tzu*, 76/44/45 (*Logic*, 249).

34. See *Logic*, 48, 49.

35. *Mo Tzu*, 75/44/7 (*Logic*, 251).

36. See *Logic*, 6-8. For a very different view of Mohism, cf. Robin R. E. Yates, "The Mohists on Warfare," in *Studies in Classical Chinese Thought*, ed. Rosemont and Schwartz, 549-603, who claims that "it was the group that was considered the moral entity, rather than the individual with his own status differentiation and internal life" (562). Yates is skeptical of the now widely held view that the movement was rooted in the artisan class (587).

37. I picked up this suggestion in some form in conversation with Lee Yearley.

38. *Chuang Tzu*, 54/20/61-68.

39. Ibid., 7/2/91-92.

40. Ibid., 2/1/22; 28/11/66; 43/17/66. But being without self or "forgetting self" (30/12/45) or "emptying self" (52/20/24) does not prevent a Taoist from refusing, like a Yangist, to "harm himself for the sake of things" (44/17/48) or "give himself in exchange for things" (68/24/73). See also 15/6/12: "One who in pursuit of fame loses himself is not a Knight. . . . These are men who served what served others, suited what suited others, not men who suited themselves with what was suited to themselves."

41. Ibid., 17/6/41; 55/21/25.

42. *Chieh* ("single"), used in ibid., 61/23/10, of an animal which has strayed from its kind, surely refers to some singularity of body or mind. The idea that it means "one-footed" (suggested by the many stories of cripples in *Chuang Tzu*) seems to be no more than an inheritance from the earliest commentators which more recent editors have failed to shake off.

43. Ibid., 8/3/12-14.

44. Ibid., 14/5/55.

45. Ibid., 21/7/31.

46. Ibid.. 28/11/63.

47. Ibid., 31/12/50-51.

48. Ibid., 8/4/1.

49. Ibid., 63/23/49.

50. Ibid., 18/6/73-74.

Glossary

Chan Tzu　詹子

Chang Hsin-ch'eng　張心澂

chi　己

chi jen　畸人

chieh　介

chien ai　兼愛

Ch'in Ku-li　禽滑釐

Ch'ing yü　情欲

ch'üan hsing　全性

Chuang Tzu　莊子

Chuang Tzu che-hsüeh t'ao-lun chi
莊子哲學討論集

Chuang Tzu 'wai tsa p'ien' ch'u tan
莊子└外雜篇┐初探

Chung chi　重己

fen　分

Han Fei　韓非

Han Fei Tzu　韓非子

hou　厚

hou ai　厚愛

hsing　性

hsing　行

Hsü Wei-yü　許維遹

Huai-nan Tzu　淮南子

huo　或

i　義

i　宜

Jang wang　襄王

ko　各

Ku Chieh-kang　顧頡剛

Ku shih pien　古史辨

Kuan Feng　關鋒

kuei chi　貴己

Kuei sheng　貴生

Lao Tzu　老子

li t'ien-hsia　利天下

Lieh Tzu　列子

Lo Ken-tse　羅根澤

Lü-shih ch'un-ch'iu　呂氏春秋

Lü-shih ch'un-ch'iu chi-shih　呂氏春
秋集釋

mo　莫

Mo Tzu　墨子

pao chen　保眞

Pen sheng　本生

pien　辯

shei   誰   Tzu-chou Chih-fu   子州支父

Shen wei   審爲   Tzu Hua Tzu   子華子

shu   孰   *Wei shu t'ung k'ao*   僞書通考

Shuo chien   說劍   *wei-wo*   爲我

Su Shih   蘇軾   *wo*   我

Tao Chih   盜跖   *wu*   物

t'ien hsia   天下   *wu*   無

Tsang and Huo   臧獲   *wu chi*   無己

Ts'ung *Lü-shih ch'un-ch'iu* t'ui-ts'e   Yang Chu   楊朱
Lao Tzu chih ch'eng shu nien-tai
從呂氏春秋推測老子之成書年代   *yu*   有

                                     Yü fu   漁父
tu   獨

Privacy in Early Confucian and Taoist Thought

Christina B. Whitman

"Privacy" is a term that eludes definition,[1] perhaps because it has been used to encompass so much of what Western liberal thought finds essential to human dignity.[2] Most vaguely stated, it refers to certain aspects of "the right to be left alone,"[3] although it is not coextensive with that phrase.[4] In order to clarify the inquiry of this paper into the value of privacy in Confucian and Taoist thought, I shall begin by distinguishing among several possible approaches.

(1) At one level, "privacy" is merely descriptive. It distinguishes between what is open or overt and what is concealed. The existence of the concept of privacy in this sense is a subject for sociologists and anthropologists—those who study manners, living conditions, and taboos concerning body parts and sexual activities. In another neutral usage, "privacy" distinguishes family life from "public" life.[5] The latter is the sphere of culture and politics; the former, the sphere which tends to the necessities of survival. "Privacy" in these neutral, descriptive senses can be found to some degree in all cultures.[6]

(2) "Privacy" may represent a claim of right—for example, a right to be free from certain government actions or a right to government protection from private actors. Whether premodern Chinese thought accommodates or supports such claims of right will not be of primary concern here.

(3) Related to but distinct from the question of claims of right is the question whether a concept of "privacy" as valuable or desirable exists in traditional China. The subject of my inquiry is privacy as a value, rather than privacy as a claim of right. Do early Confucians and Taoists view privacy as worthy of emulation? I put to one side for the moment the question whether this value, if it does exist, is seen as supporting a claim against the government for protection or for forbearance from action.

Only three aspects of the broad concept "privacy" will be explored in this essay: privacy as providing a sphere for intimate personal relationships with family and friends, privacy as freedom from surveillance for purposes of gathering personal information, and privacy as freedom from interference by government or social controls. These concepts describe quite different concerns. They are often grouped together under the single term "privacy," but not without some strain.[7]

Because "privacy" takes a variety of forms in Western thought, it is not surprising that there is no perfectly parallel concept in classical Chinese writings. It is more interesting to ask whether there are Chinese counterparts to the more specific formulations of the terms, and whether early Chinese schools of thought cherish values that are inconsistent with the development of an appreciation of privacy comparable to that now found in the West.

Our own concern with privacy, or at least our urgency in defense of the concept, is in large part a twentieth-century phenomenon. In the United States, privacy has achieved independent status as a legal right only in the last eighty years,[8] and its position is far from secure.[9] The recent increase in attention to privacy in America can be attributed to the development of new means of intruding into people's lives: modern technology permits surveillance without detection on a scale that was previously inconceivable, the mass media compete for audiences by trafficking in information about the personal foibles and intimate relationships of prominent individuals, and the behavioral sciences give academic respectability to inquiries into the most mundane habits of ordinary people. It can also be argued that privacy is taken more seriously now because it is more attainable in a modern, industrial society than at any other stage in human history. People no longer need live out their lives in a small community with a long memory. Mobility and urbanization permit anonymity, which, in turn, guarantees a certain amount of privacy.

A comparison between a modern Western value and its counterpart, if any, in very early Confucian and Taoist belief is inevitably somewhat strained. But it serves a purpose. If nothing else, it helps us to define what is unique about our own views, thereby keeping us from assuming that our talk about privacy refers to some universally shared, thus necessarily correct, human value.

A comparison across cultures and across centuries reveals that even twentieth-century articulations of the value of privacy draw on assumptions about human nature and the relationship of the individual to society that go beyond modern innovations. In many respects, our concern with privacy reflects values that exist in earlier Western thought and that have counterparts in premodern China. Many, maybe most, of the activities that lead us to esteem privacy and the "private" life were also of greatest importance in early China—family, friends, self-development, introspection. Indeed, there may be more that joins us than distinguishes us.

But there is one characteristic of our current approach that is inconsistent with early Confucian and Taoist perspectives, though not with all Chinese thought. That characteristic is the tie between the value of privacy and certain notions of human autonomy. In particular, our twentieth-century devotion to privacy reflects our modern belief that a human being is fully autonomous only if he is free to discover what is distinctive about himself as an individual. This goes beyond choice of a unique life-style. Rather, it reflects one strain in

Western thought of the last two centuries that holds that man understands himself best when he sees himself as separate from other men. This is not a universally accepted view, even in twentieth-century America; indeed, we are deeply ambivalent about both the theory and its manifestation in arguments for privacy.

In summary, we value privacy because it permits each person to discover and develop what is unique about himself. Our notion of privacy allows the individual to stand apart from all others. Confucians and Taoists do not give the goal equal emphasis. They, too, value intimate relationships and self-discovery, but the reasons behind these values are inconsistent with our emphasis on individual uniqueness.

Linguistic Analogues

Although there is not, as I have suggested above, any neat analogue to the broad term "privacy" in the classical texts of Confucianism and Taoism, there are usages reminiscent of that concept.

Some of these are neutral, descriptive usages. The context, rather than the concept, provides negative or positive value. *Yin* (to hide, put aside, or cover) is used in that sense in the *Analects*: "The Master said, 'My followers, I know you believe that I am hiding something from you. I am hiding nothing from you'" (*yi wo wei yin hu, wu wu yin hu erh*).[10] And in the *Chung-yung*: "[Shun] loved to question others and to ponder their words.... He put aside [*yin*] what was error in them and made much of what was good."[11] But *yin* is also used in the *Analects* to refer to an inappropriate secretiveness: "There are three errors which may be made in service to a gentleman. One may speak before his turn; this is called *tsao*. One may not speak when one's turn comes; this is called *yin*...."[12]

Szu comes closest to signifying "privacy" in the Western sense. Although it most often has unfavorable connotations (among its meanings are "adultery," "male/female sex organs," and "urine"), it can also be used in a neutral way. For example, *szu* signifies family, as opposed to communal, ownership in Mencius's description of the well-field system: "The public fields are in the center, and eight families each have one hundred *mu* for their own use" (*pa-chia chieh szu pai-mu*).[13] Mencius also uses *szu* to refer to unauthorized, and thus improper, actions:

> Suppose there were an officer here, with whom you were pleased, and suppose that without telling the king, all on your own [*szu*], you gave him your salary and your rank, and suppose that the officer, also without the king's command and all on his own [*szu*], passed them on to his son—would this be permissible?[14]

Szu is often used to refer to the pursuit of private interests and, in this sense, implies selfishness. Both Mencius and Hsün Tzu, although they disagree fundamentally about the basic goodness of human nature, disparage conduct of this sort and argue that the external environment should not be structured in such a way as to drive men to pursue private interests at the expense of society as a whole. Lao Tzu also condemns the pursuit of *szu*, although he is, as is his wont, more ironic: "Is it not precisely because he does not pursue personal ends that the sage can achieve his personal ends?" (*fei i ch'i wu szu yeh, ku neng ch'eng ch'i szu*).[15] And, "[Let the people] regard simplicity and hold fast to the uncarved block, let them have few personal ends [*shao szu*] and little desire."[16]

Szu is primarily a negative concept in both Confucian and Taoist texts, but there are other concepts that are akin to "privacy" and yet are regarded more positively. Confucius looks favorably on concealment when it reflects family loyalties, even at the expense of the state:

> The Duke of She said to Confucius, "Among our people there are men who are upright. If their father has stolen a sheep, they will report him." Confucius said, "Among my people those who are upright are not like that. A father will conceal [*yin*] his son's wrongdoing, and a son will conceal [*yin*] his father's wrongdoing. Their uprightness lies in this."[17]

And Confucius urges withdrawal from public life in calamitous times: "When the Way does not prevail, then hide [*yin*]."[18]

Of greater significance is the Confucian emphasis on introspection (*nei-hsing*) as one means of self-cultivation: "When you see a worthy man, emulate him. When you see one who is not worthy, then look within" (*nei tzu-hsing*).[19] "If when he looks within [*nei-hsing*] he finds no blemish, why should he be anxious, why should he fear?"[20] "If your goals are not achieved, you should always turn within to seek the cause within yourself."[21] "Therefore the superior man examines his own heart [*nei-hsing*] to see that there is no blemish there."[22]

The Taoists also stress the virtues of inwardness and of things concealed. The first line of the *Tao-te ching* is "The Tao that can be described is not the constant Tao." There is also: "The Tao is hidden [*yin*] and has no name";[23] and "Therefore the sage knows himself and does not reveal himself" (*pu tzu-hsien*).[24]

Reserve and withdrawal, and even the keeping of confidences, are valued in these texts, but, as we shall see, these references do not form a coherent concept precisely analogous to our "privacy." The discrepancy arises from different views about the ends to be served by introspection and withdrawal from public life. In Confucian and Taoist thought, the ultimate purpose is union of the individual with something greater—the natural ordering of men and nature, in Confucianism; or the all-encompassing Tao, in Taoism. In contemporary Western thought, withdrawal is prized primarily because it allows the individual to define himself as unique, distinctive, and autonomous.

Privacy for Intimate Relationships

The first form of privacy that I will discuss is privacy for family and friendship. Privacy of this sort is defended as providing a necessary context for intimate relationships, for the building of personal bonds.[25] Privacy is said to be valued because it allows people the freedom to define these relationships in ways that suit their own needs, relatively immune from social constraints.[26] Privacy permits relaxation and thus a certain degree of freedom from the burden of others' expectations. It also allows individuals to choose to expose themselves to different degrees with different people, creating a range of more or less intimate relationships.

Family and friends are of immense importance in China, as everywhere. The central role of the family in Confucianism gives it far greater doctrinal importance than it has in most Western systems of thought, and friendship is given even greater importance in Confucian poetic texts. Even Taoist poets mourn the loneliness of a reclusive life: "Those who have left I cannot reach. For those who will come I cannot stay."[27] "Where is my friend, now kept from me by mountains and hills?"[28]

Yet, Confucian and Taoist thinkers articulate reasons for valuing these personal relationships that are quite unlike the pursuit of intimacy, self-definition, and freedom of development that is at the core of the Western theory of privacy. The Confucian articulation and, in a different way, the Taoist articulation are inconsistent with our belief that even an ideal state must leave a space for an intimate side of life, shared with family and friends. This belief is based on the conclusion that only such an entirely separate sphere can serve the nonpublic needs that are a part of every human being.

In early Confucian thought, family life is not seen as providing an opportunity for special ties unlike any experienced elsewhere. Instead, it is said to replicate natural hierarchies that ideally dictate all human organization, including the bond of a citizen to his ruler. The family is a model for relationships between individuals and the state. The *Ta-hsüeh* [The great learning] provides one of the most explicit expressions of the family's place as a basic unit of the political structure:

> [The ancient sages] who wished to govern well their states would first bring order to their families.[29]

> What is meant by "To govern well one's state one must first bring order to one's family" is: there has never been a man who could not instruct his family but could instruct the people. Therefore, the superior man achieves instruction for his own state without going beyond his own family.[30]

The theme in these selections is that modes of conduct appropriate for the family life are also those appropriate to politics and rule. The ruler should treat his subjects as a father would his sons, and a child's feelings toward his parents mirror those of the subject to his ruler. The state is thought of as a large family, and relations among family members are not different in kind from political relationships. This suggests that compassion and care should play a significant role in political life, but it also suggests that intimacy is not the predominant aspect of family life.

Therefore, family life does not exist in a completely separate sphere. There is a distinction between family life (*nei*) and the public life of the world (*wai*), but the rules governing these areas overlap. Through his ties to his family, the individual, at least in theory, cannot draw totally apart, leaving the rest of the world behind. Instead, he learns and affirms his social nature and his social role. In instructing King Hsüan of Ch'i, Mencius described the extension of family feeling to all mankind:

> The *Book of Poetry* says:
>   He was a model to his wife,
>   And to his elder and younger brothers.
> With this he governed his home and his nation.
> This means that you should extend your affections to all these others.
> Therefore, if you put forth your natural warmth, that will be sufficient to
> protect all within the four seas.[31]

The mutual support of loyalties between family and state, with the ruler as the ultimate father, did not always work in practice as it was described in theory. Family feeling could become so strong that it would interfere with political obligations. Confucius's example, quoted above, of the "upright" sons who protect their thieving fathers suggests that it might have been regarded as most honorable to put family affections before loyalty to the state. Legal codes from the Han dynasty on tolerated family loyalties at the expense of the state. In practice, we have reason to believe, men found it easier to identify with family and village than with the more remote government of the ruler. The family, then, could serve as a refuge into which the individual could withdraw from a hostile world. But this was seen as the "negative" aspect of family life. It remains significant that this strong sense of family bonding was justified in most early Confucian texts, not because it is natural and necessary for groups of people to set themselves off from society, but because these bonds could, and should, serve as a means of drawing people of all families toward each other in a natural social hierarchy, universally accepted because it reflects universal family experiences.

There is an additional respect in which the Confucian view of personal relationships appears to be inconsistent with our expectations of the ends to be served by privacy for intimate relationships. As I have indicated above, an argument made in support of this form of privacy is that it allows an individual to structure each relationship in a different fashion. That is, privacy provides the conditions for developing relationships of varying degrees of intimacy. It allows a person to use the disclosure of personal information as a way to increase intimacy. As intimacy deepens, the people involved come closer together by revealing more of themselves. Privacy permits one person to have a range of relationships—from relatively impersonal business relationships, in which little personal information is shared, to the extreme intimacy of marriage and enduring friendship. Theoretically, the latter are most free of the constraints created by abstract concepts of role because the unique qualities of the individuals involved are most revealed.

In short, privacy permits variety and deviation from social expectations. Noninterference, at least theoretically, allows friendships and family roles to develop in an open-ended fashion. Western realities may depart from theory as much as Chinese realities. In practice, many intimate relationships in our own society follow set patterns decreed by societal expectations which have been assimilated by the individuals involved. But when we focus on ideals, the contrast with Confucianism is marked. The early Confucian texts do not interpret family life as open-ended. Instead, society—including the family—is seen as functioning in quite specific patterns that are understood to be universal because they are innate in human nature. It is precisely because these patterns are thought to exist in every family group that the family can be used as a model for the organization of the state. There is little, if any, expectation of individual variation.

Early Taoism places no comparable emphasis on family and social bonds. Indeed, such ties are regarded as reflecting distinctions and discriminations that are inconsistent with a real understanding of the unitary Tao. Lao Tzu and Chuang Tzu valued solitude above all else. The closest analogue in Taoist thought to familial or friendship privacy is found, not in these texts, but in the more poetic and less philosophical manifestations of Taoism. In the latter group of texts there is an acknowledgement of the importance of friendship, and in this acknowledgement, as in some Confucian poems, friendship is portrayed as a preferable alternative to conventional, public society. Friendship allows withdrawal. The Seven Sages of the Bamboo Grove, a group of eccentrics who lived in the tumultuous third century A.D., are one obvious manifestation of this perspective.

But this vision of friendship, like the Confucian understanding of the family, remains basically inconsistent with our theory of privacy for the sake of intimacy. First, in Taoism, as in Confucianism, withdrawing with a group of intimates is not regarded as an inevitable human response of the sort that would be appropriate, even necessary, in a properly functioning society. Instead, withdrawal is regarded as a means of survival, an unfortunate necessity in troubled times. Again, the Seven Sages provide a useful example. They lived in a time when men who took positions of prominence lived precariously. Avoidance of social ties and obligations was a means of self-preservation, and those who took this avenue were understood to risk great loneliness.[32] Thus, survival, rather than intimacy, is the primary justification for this version of Taoist withdrawal.

Second, the form that "withdrawal" from society took among Neo-Taoists in the time of the Seven Sages does not really have much to do with privacy at all. Instead, these men survived (to the extent that they were successful) by becoming eccentrics and exhibitionists. One of them, Liu Ling, was known for wandering nude about his house. He always traveled with a servant who carried a flask, for drinking, and a shovel, which could be used, if necessary, to dig Liu's grave. This was not a man who craved privacy.

Third, and most significant, to the extent that Taoist withdrawal is not an aberrant manifestation but is rooted in classical Taoist doctrine, it represents a turning away from society for union with something (the Tao) that goes beyond the transitory ties of friendship. Submerging one's self in the Tao is tied to the quest for survival, for, it is argued, the only way to defeat the fear of death is to forego one's attachment to life. Friendship, then, is not valued as an end in itself; far less is it seen primarily as a route by which an individual can discover and define his uniqueness. The ultimate goal is to rise above attachment—attachment to one's own uniqueness and attachment to one's friends—and to understand that all are part of the single Tao: "A man with special attachments is not a man of love."[33] As a man comes to understand the Tao, he becomes more truly himself and, Chuang Tzu at least would emphasize, he comes to appreciate his individuality within this wholeness. Communion with the Tao is not conformity. Yet, it is significant that one's true self, one's individuality, can be best understood only through attention to that which is in all things.

In conclusion, both early Confucianism and early Taoism value intimate relationships, but the ultimate goal in both philosophies is to rise above particular human ties to achieve a greater union—be it with all men in a society ordered according to the patterns innate to human nature or with the Tao. Neither school conceives of friendship and family life as a self-contained part of life, distinct from all other activities but essential as an avenue for personal growth. In Confucian thought, this area of life is not separate. In Taoism, a separate realm would not be necessary in an ideal state, for an individual need not withdraw to be part of the Tao. Indeed, one who has achieved perfect understanding of the Tao would not make the sorts of discriminations that form the basis of personal achievements.

Yet, it is with respect to this form of privacy that we come closest to early China, for this privacy for intimate relationships is privacy at its most "social." By definition it involves relationships among people. Freedom from surveillance and freedom from social control, which I will discuss next, emphasize instead the self-sufficient autonomy of each individual. This is not to say that autonomy, in the sense of self-fulfillment and freedom from constraint, is irrelevant to familial and friendship privacy. Individual autonomy can be exercised through one's choice of friends and in one's free adoption of a particular family role. Early Confucianism and Taoism also recognize that people play many roles. The difference lies in the ultimate goal understood to be furthered through these roles. In the Chinese philosophies, the goal is union, not uniqueness.

Freedom from Surveillance

Another common understanding of privacy is freedom from observation or surveillance. Typically this refers to protection from efforts to gather information about hidden aspects of an individual's life. Privacy in this sense is valued, again, because it promotes autonomy. Privacy allows for self-definition, choice of behavior, and expression free of social pressures. Privacy leaves room for nonenforcement of social norms—as, for example, those concerning aberrant sexual conduct. To some extent, the call for privacy in this sense reflects the post-Freudian belief that certain human characteristics are beyond the control of society and thus not properly of concern to institutions that could impose sanctions. There is, of course, an overlap with privacy for intimate relationships; one aspect of such privacy is the right to be free from observation while with friends and family.

Although much of the current concern with surveillance is uniquely modern, caused by new techniques for monitoring and collecting data on people's activities, this concern does rest on more broadly applicable views about the proper ends of government and society's capacity to affect behavior. These views are inconsistent with certain core assumptions of Confucianism and Taoism.

Confucianism and, to a lesser extent, Taoism are primarily concerned with the role of government as a moral influence on individual behavior. That emphasis entails two assumptions—that a certain degree of moral consensus is possible and that society can play a significant role in guiding an individual's moral life. The form which this guidance takes differs profoundly between the two schools of thought. In Taoism, as we shall see, it looks more like nonguidance.

Confucian ideology stresses an ordered society, built on a system of parallel hierarchies, which guides man through moral example toward correct attitudes and correct behavior. Given this framework, the idea of a separation between things properly of government concern and those of no concern to anyone but the individual is unintelligible. The implications of this perspective can best be seen in the debate between the early Confucians and the Legalists. The Legalists urged the establishment of clear "legal" rules of behavior and were, by implication, willing to tolerate some "private" areas which would not be addressed by these rules or at least not observed by the enforcers. The Confucians rejected the Legalist position precisely because it left some areas free. Persuasion was preferred to compulsion as a means of regulating behavior—not because it would leave more room for deviance from social norms, but because it would result in more consistent conformity. Persuaded men conform even when the enforcer is not around, while law controls only through fear of sanction.

> Therefore the superior man will watch himself when he is alone. But the small man—when he is alone and idle he will do evil without limit. Only when he sees a superior man does he try to hide his misdeeds.[34]

Thus, Confucian views are inconsistent with the belief that freedom from government surveillance is desirable. This is not to say that surveillance itself is considered to be a good thing. On the contrary, it is viewed as ineffective, and a decreased reliance on legal sanctions may lead to less surveillance in fact. But Confucianism is willing to tolerate, indeed advocates, the pervasive, all-encompassing degree of social control that is abhorrent to the opponents of surveillance. Moral education replaces law for the Confucians because they are willing to accept a state ideology that dictates all significant aspects of human conduct; this ideology is acceptable because it is believed to reflect moral dictates also found in each individual, i.e., it is natural. Confucians are willing to say that, if the state is running properly, there need be no room for individual moral choices that differ from those made by society. An interesting example of the difference between Confucian and Western perspectives on this point can be found in their respective attitudes toward criminal confessions. The Fifth Amendment of the United States Constitution provides that no person "shall be compelled in any criminal case to be a witness against himself." In part, this is justified as a privacy right—the right to refuse to aid the government in obtaining information against one's self. Such freedom from self-incrimination is not acknowledged in China, where confessions have been encouraged, at least since the T'ang dynasty, by reductions of punishment. The Ch'ing-dynasty code even permits the use of torture to extract confessions of guilt.

Taoism, unlike Confucianism, does not contemplate the achievement of a moral consensus. Chuang Tzu sees no role for government at all, and Lao Tzu, who does, explicitly values noninterference. In Lao Tzu's view, failure to govern is the ideal form of government and the form most likely to be successful: "Through nonaction lay hold of all under heaven."[35] As in Confucianism, the ruler guides his people, but he guides them toward nonaction by being himself a model of nonaction.

At first glance, this may look like an argument for freedom from government surveillance, and it is. But it is not an argument for privacy of the sort that we are familiar with. Lao Tzu does not contemplate that freedom from observation will allow room for the development, on the part of each human, of a unique sense of self. The advantage of noninterference for him is that it furthers the elimination of distinctions among individuals. My explication of the third form of the value of privacy will help to clarify this point.

Freedom from Control

Privacy, defined most broadly, is freedom from social control—that is, freedom from interference by the state, other institutions, or other people. The two forms of privacy discussed above are more specific subsets of this generalized value.

Privacy as freedom from social control is valued because we see it as essential to the individual uniqueness which we understand to be essential to moral autonomy. Privacy permits individuals to think and do as they please— to develop their own "true," and "unique," personalities. Our insistence that uniqueness is essential to autonomy assumes that individuals can and should exercise moral choice in a variety of different ways (or that no society can be sure of the proper moral choice) and that personal development should be guided by these choices rather than by what we consider to be externally imposed roles and expectations.

Autonomy of this sort need not be equivalent to selfishness, or the pursuit of private gain, for an individual may choose to pursue ends that go beyond his own interests, or even beyond those of a narrowly defined group, such as his family. But this view does focus on the individual at the expense of the overall functioning of society: "autonomy" emphasizes the development of personal character, especially the unique qualities and aptitudes of each individual. A view premised on moral autonomy is willing to tolerate, in pursuing that goal, departure from social norms.

There is much in early Confucianism and Taoism that is resonant of this view. A key Confucian concept is the cultivation of the self, and this cultivation takes place, in part, through introspection. The goal of self-cultivation is often described as a state of tranquility. Tranquility implies a lack of external interference. Mencius, for instance, gives instructions on "remaining unmoved in one's mind" (*pu-tung hsin*), free from biases and fears generated by the world in which man lives. The *Ta-hsüeh* also preaches tranquility, a state made possible by the moral knowledge that is arrived at through introspection: "Only when you know where to rest can you be calm. Only when you are calm can you be quiet. Only when you are quiet can you be at peace. Only when you are at peace can you be thoughtful. Only when you are thoughtful can you achieve the end."[36] The Taoists, too, seek tranquility. Chuang Tzu talks of freeing the mind and achieving a tranquil state:

> Yen Hui replied, "I cast away my arms and legs. I dismiss my wisdom. I separate myself from my body and get rid of my mind, to become one with the great Tao. This is called sitting and forgetting."[37]

> The perfect man uses his mind like a mirror. He neither grabs nor welcomes.[38]

Although a common symbol of Neo-Taoism is the hermit (*yin-che*) who has cut himself off from the world, neither Chuang Tzu nor the Confucians are talking about physical withdrawal. For Chuang Tzu, "tranquility" is, rather, adaptation to all that comes. For the Confucians, it comes from, among other things, understanding one's natural role in the world.

In Taoism, as I noted above, the emphasis on adaptation leads to the argument that a wise ruler (who will, by definition, also be a sage) is tolerant and does not interfere:

> Therefore it is said that the ancients who tended the empire had no desires and the empire was complete. They did not act and all things were transformed. They were deep and quiet and all the people were calm.[39]

In the *Tao-te-ching*, this sort of rule is advocated because it leads to a peaceful, if somewhat boring, society: "The neighboring state is so very close that they could hear the sounds of each others' cocks and dogs, but the people would grow old and die without having gone there."[40] Noninterference, in Lao Tzu's view, is a device for social control. In *Chuang Tzu,* on the other hand, there is a suggestion, more familiar to Western proponents of privacy, that noninterference will lead to vigor and variety: "To treat things that are different as if they were the same is to be great. To act without limiting one's uniqueness is to be broad. To be many without being the same is to be rich."[41]

Thus, we find in early Confucianism and Taoism: (1) a strong emphasis on self-development; (2) arguments for nonaction, noninterference, or tolerance; and (3) a suggestion, in Chuang Tzu, that this is appropriate because it allows variety to flourish. The first point is particularly important because it suggests that some value is placed on the moral autonomy of the individual. Indeed, both Confucianism and Taoism contemplate that there will be times when the good man will not support the state. However, it is significant that neither philosophy contemplates that such opposition will be necessary or appropriate in an ideal state. In a properly ordered state, the knowledge and personal growth that come through introspection will still be necessary, but they will bring the individual into harmony with his social environment.

Confucianism and Taoism appreciate that men have a rich internal life, but this does not, in these philosophies, lead to the conclusion that society must permit a private sphere for individual development free from social control. The attention in China to self-cultivation does not reflect a judgment that the cultivation process is ultimately valuable because it permits deviations from social norms and allows each individual to develop distinctive values and beliefs. Self-determination in this sense, with emphasis on what is unique rather than on what is shared, is not the end to be achieved. This is of critical importance, for freedom from interference without the expectation that people, when left to themselves, will go different ways, is not what we mean when we talk about "privacy."

I will elaborate on this point, first in terms of Confucianism. Through introspection, the Confucians hold, the individual comes to understand ethical ideas, but these ideas are defined in terms of social relationships. Autonomy is valued, but men acting autonomously are expected to discover what is shared rather than what is unique. The end of self-cultivation is to understand natural hierarchies and to appreciate one's proper place in these hierarchies. Understanding, although achieved by looking within, makes the individual aware of what he has in common with other men. Every man, it is believed, finds the same feelings, the same moral imperatives, and the same impetus toward proper conduct. There is no sharp division between what an individual thinks and does in public and what he thinks and does in private. Cultivation of the self illuminates both public and private roles. The proper result is not deviance, but conformity—conformity to the natural distinctions that pervade all of life.

Moreover, the ultimate goal of self-cultivation, to a Confucian, is not private, but public: to take one's proper place in society, and to stand as a model for others. This is the route to a properly ordered world:

> Tzu-lu asked about the superior man. Confucius replied, "He trains himself to be reverent." Tzu-lu said, "Is that all?" Confucius said, "He trains himself to bring peace to other men." Tzu-lu said, "Is that all?" Confucius replied, "He trains himself to bring peace to all people. Even Yao and Shun could find no fault in that."[42]

In a sense, then, the early Confucians contemplate actual autonomy of life-style as well as moral autonomy. Where society does not accurately reflect the natural hierarchies, man will go his own way when he looks within. But in an ideal society, there is no distinction between what is accomplished by social control and what is accomplished by self-control.

The Taoists, on the other hand, in urging that men look for the "Tao within," do not expect that the contemplative will discover a natural hierarchy, or indeed, any natural distinctions. Nor do they expect that one who achieves realization will or can direct the insights of others. But there is still, as in Confucianism, an expectation that man, when left alone, will discover what is shared. The Taoist takes this even further than the Confucian, for the Taoist sage comes to understand that he is one with all things. The Confucian turns from private ends (*szu*) to understanding public distinctions. The Taoist turns from private ends to understanding that there are no distinctions.

The Six Dynasties Taoist texts contemplate that the wise man will preserve himself by withdrawing. This emphasis on self-preservation, most explicit in poetic Taoism, does indicate a certain attention to private ends. But, as described in the philosophical texts, it is not a distinct human personality that is being preserved. Rather, escape from the vicissitudes of the world becomes possible when the sage realizes that his unique qualities, even his body, are unimportant: "The only reason why I suffer pain is that I have a body; if I had no body, what pain would I have?"[43] What is important is the permanent and universal Tao, not its temporary manifestation in human beings. In an ideal society, the ruler-sage will leave his subjects alone. He will do this not because leaving them alone is a desirable thing in itself (the end of Taoism is the elimination of desire), but because it is the best way to help them find the Tao.

In both early Confucianism and Taoism, freedom from interference is seen as necessary to personal development, but the goals of personal development are not open-ended and do not, ultimately, vary from person to person. The individual is led, instead, to something beyond himself which is shared by all men. This does not mean annihilation or loss of individuality. Rather, one becomes more truly one's self through understanding what is shared. In an ideal society, freedom from social control is not particularly important, for the ends of society and the ends of self-cultivation are identical.

Conclusion

There are certain concepts, valued by early Confucians and by Taoists, that might, at first glance, suggest that privacy as we understand it is perceived as desirable. These concepts include friendship, family bonds, noninterference, self-cultivation, introspection, and withdrawal from society. But a closer look reveals that the end we in twentieth-century western society seek to advance by respecting privacy has no counterpart in early Confucian or Taoist thought. The key to this lack of fit lies in our view that privacy allows an individual to exercise free choice as part of a process of self-determination that has little to do with the larger world. Privacy of family and of friendship allows personal definition of intimate relationships. Freedom from observation provides room to experiment and to deviate from accepted behavior. Privacy that hinges on freedom from social control allows each individual to develop in a distinctive direction that best fits his unique characteristics. These justifications reflect our view of the individual (we prize the unique) and our view of society as furthering the considered choices and the self-knowledge of distinctive individuals. It also explains the ambivalence and even confusion about privacy found in the West, for privacy, for us, is ultimately justified by a sort of radical selfishness.

Early Confucian texts do not balk at pressures to conform because they accept the existence and desirability of pervasive social norms. Privacy merely hinders the achievement of the ideal society when it gives room for nonenforcement of norms or the development of peculiar, and thus irrelevant, characteristics. Little value is placed on a unique sense of self. What a man learns when he looks within brings him back to society.

Taoism initially appears to be more receptive to the theory of privacy, for it talks of tolerance and opposes conformity. However, the goal in Taoism, too, is to find what is common to all men. The Taoists differ from the Confucians in rejecting the necessity of social norms and hierarchy. However, something other than the individual's own freely made choices—namely, the Tao that is in both the individual and all things—determines the direction of individual development.

NOTES

1. The literature is vast. See Judith J. Thomson, "The Right to Privacy," *Philosophy and Public Affairs* (Summer 1975), 4(4):295-314; Thomas Scanlon, "Thomson on Privacy," *Philosophy and Public Affairs* (Summer 1975), 4(4):315-22; Edward J. Bloustein, "Privacy as an Aspect of Human Dignity: An Answer to Dean Prosser," *New York University Law Review* (December 1964), 39(6):962-1007; William L. Prosser, "Privacy," *California Law Review* (August 1969), 48(3):383-423.
2. See Bloustein, "Privacy as an Aspect of Human Dignity."
3. "Privacy" was so described in the law review article credited with giving the concept legal respectability in the United States. See Samuel D. Warren and Louis D. Brandeis, "The Right to Privacy," *Harvard Law Review* (December 1890), 4(5):193-220.
4. Anglo-American law has for centuries protected individuals from other violations of "the right to be left alone" without acknowledging any right to privacy. For example, the common law provides causes of actions for intentional touching, called battery, *Vosburg* v. *Putney*, 80 Wis. 523, 50 N.W. 403 (1891); negligently caused harm to one's person, *Brown* v. *Kendall*, 60 Mass. (6 Cush.) 292 (1850); and false and defamatory communications, *Thorley* v. *Lord Kerry*, 4 Taunt. 355, 128 Eng. Rep. 367 (1812). Indeed, all of the common law of torts can be described as vindicating "the right to be left alone."
5. See Hannah Arendt, *The Human Condition* (Chicago: The University of Chicago Press, 1958), 22-37.
6. John M. Roberts and Thomas Gregor, "Privacy: A Cultural View," in *Nomos XIII: Privacy*, ed. J. Roland Pennock and John W. Chapman (New York: Atherton Press, 1971), 199-225.
7. See Prosser, "Privacy." The American constitutional law of privacy (e.g., *Roe* v. *Wade*, 410 U.S. 113 [1973], holding state criminal abortion legislation to be a violation of a constitutional right to privacy) and the common-law recognition of a right to recover for violations of a right to privacy (e.g., *Melvin* v. *Reid*, 112 Cal. App. 285, 297 P. 91 [1931], cause of action for public disclosure of embarrassing private facts; and *Galella* v. *Onassis*, 487 F. 2d 986 [2d Cir. 1973], cause of action against "paparazzo" photographer for following plaintiff and other harassment) have developed totally independently of each other. The former deals with government intrusions upon citizens' choices in private matters, such as family planning. The latter addresses disputes among individuals arising out of conduct

that, for example, exposes the plaintiff to unwanted public attention.

8. The most famous early decision recognizing the right of privacy is *Pavesich* v. *New England Life Insurance Co.*, 122 Ga. 190, 50 S.E. 68 (1905).

9. See Harry Kalven, Jr., "Privacy in Tort Law—Were Warren and Brandeis Wrong?" *Law and Contemporary Problems* (Spring 1966), 31(2):326-41. Kalven does not question the value of privacy. He describes it as "one of the truly profound values for a civilized society" (326). But he questions whether this value should be protected by giving those who are deprived of privacy a cause of action for damages in tort.

10. *Analects*, 7:23.

11. *Doctrine of the Mean*, sec. 6.

12. *Analects*, 16:6.

13. *Mencius*, 3A:3:19.

14. Ibid., 2B:8:1.

15. *Lao Tzu, chang* 7, in *Ssu-pu ts'ung-k'an* (SPTK) [Comprehensive collection of the four topics] (Shanghai: Shang-wu Yin-shu-kuan, 1937-38), pt. 49(3), *shang* 4a.

16. Ibid., *chang* 19, in SPTK, pt. 49(3), *shang* 9b.

17. *Analects*, 13:18.

18. Ibid., 8:13.

19. Ibid., 4:17.

20. Ibid., 12:4.

21. *Mencius*, 4A:4:1.

22. *Doctrine of the Mean*, sec. 33, in Wan Hsin-ch'üan et al. (ed.), *Ta-hsüeh chung-yung ching-chu* (THCYCC) [Annotated edition of *The Great Learning* and *The Doctrine of the Mean*] (Taipei: Cheng-chung Shu-chü, 1969), 111.

23. *Lao Tzu, chang* 41, in SPTK, pt. 49(3), *hsia* 3b.

24. Ibid., *chang* 72, in SPTK, pt. 49(3), *hsia* 17b.

25. Charles Fried, *An Anatomy of Values: Problems of Personal and Social Choice* (Cambridge: Harvard University Press, 1970), 140-44.

26. See ibid., 142.

27. Juan Chi, "Yung huai shih" [Poems of deepest feeling], no. 32, in Huang Chieh (ed.), *Juan pu-ping yung-huai-shih chu* [Annotated edition of *Poems of Deepest Feeling by Juan Chi*] (Hong Kong: Shang-wu Yin-shu-kuan, 1961), 42.

28. Hsi K'ang, "Tseng Hsiu-ts'ai ju-chün shih-chiu-shih" [Nineteen poems presented to a first degree graduate on his entering the army], no. 8, in Ting Fu-pao (ed.), *Ch'üan Han San-kuo Chin Nan Pei Ch'ao Shih* [Collected poems of the Han dynasty, the period of the Three Kingdoms, the Chin dynasty, and the period of the Northern and Southern dynasties] (Taipei: I-wen Yin-shu-kuan, 1960?), 286.

29. *Ta-hsüeh*, in THCYCC, 5.

30. Ibid., 24.

31. *Mencius*, 1A:7:12.

32. Juan Chi, "Yung huai shih," no. 1, in *Juan pu-ping yung-huai shih chu, supra,* 1-2.

33. *Chuang Tzu*, chapter 6, in SPTK, pt. 49(6), *chüan* 3, 4b-5a.

34. *Ta-hsüeh*, in THCYCC, 21.

35. *Lao Tzu, chang* 57, in SPTK, pt. 49(3), *hsia* 10a.

36. *Ta-hsüeh*, in THCYCC, 4.

37. *Chuang Tzu*, chapter 6, in SPTK, pt. 49(6), *chüan* 3, 26b.

38. Ibid., chapter 7, in SPTK, pt. 49(6), *chüan* 3, 35b-36a.

39. Ibid., chapter 12, in SPTK, pt. 49(7), *chüan* 5, 2a.

40. *Lao Tzu, chang* 80, in SPTK, pt. 49(3), *hsia* 20b.

41. *Chuang Tzu*, chapter 12, in SPTK, pt. 49(7), *chüan* 5, 2b.

42. *Analects*, 14:45.

43. *Lao Tzu, chang* 13, in SPTK, pt. 49(3), *shang* 6b.

Glossary

Cheng-chung shu-chü 正中書局

Ch'üan Han San-kuo Chin Nan-pei-ch'ao Shih 全漢三國晉南北朝詩

Chuang Tzu 莊子

Chung-yung 中庸

fei i ch'i wu ssu yeh, ku neng ch'eng ch'i ssu 非以其無私邪故能成其私

Hsi K'ang 嵇康

Hsüan (King of Ch'i) 齊宣王

Hsün Tzu 荀子

Huang Chieh 黃節

I-wen yin-shu-kuan 藝文印書舘

Juan Chi 阮籍

Juan pu-ping yung-huai-shih chu 阮步兵詠懷詩註

Lao Tzu 老子

Lui Ling 劉伶

nei 內

nei-hsing 內省

nei tzu-hsing 內自省

pa-chia chieh ssu pai-mu 八家皆私百畝

pu-tung hsin 不動心

pu tzu-hsien 不自見

Shang-wu yin-shu-kuan 商務印書舘

shao ssu 少私

Shun 舜

ssu 私

Ssu-pu ts'ung-k'an 四部叢刊

Ta-hsüeh 大學

Ta-hsüeh chung-yung chu 大學中庸注

Tao-te ching 道德經

Ting Fu-pao 丁福保

tsao 躁

"Tseng hsiu-ts'ai ju-chün shih-chiu shou" 贈秀才入軍十九首

Tzu-lu 子路

wai 外

Wan Hsin-ch'üan 萬心權

Yao 堯

Yen Hui 顏回

yi wo wei yin hu, wu wu yin hu erh 以我為隱乎吾無隱乎爾

yin 隱

yin-che 隱者

"Yung Huai Shih" 詠懷詩

Self and Whole in Chuang Tzu*

Judith Berling

The philosophers of late Chou China debated a series of issues which centered around the nature of the individual's commitments or obligations to the social order. These discussions engendered a range of positions on human nature, the basis of polity, education, ritual propriety, and legal institutions. It was the Taoists, and Chuang Tzu in particular, who questioned whether the individual's primary moral obligations were to social institutions, such as family and state. In the context of classical Chinese philosophy, Chuang Tzu seems to be the champion of the individual. Like Western individualists, he advocates freedom from the restrictions of public obligations and raises a standard against "wan conformity."[1] Although the Western concept of individualism entails certain institutionalized legal rights to protect the self-expression of a responsible individual in artistic or religious forms or in a distinctive life-style, Chuang Tzu's argument for freedom does not entail either legal rights or a psychological notion of self-expression or personal choice. Chuang Tzu's position is a call not for the rights of the individual, but for a shift of attention from social and political issues to another dimension of life.

A close examination of Chuang Tzu's thought as presented in the "inner chapters"[2] will demonstrate that although a central concern is freedom, freedom or the lack thereof is integrally related to the person's understanding of the larger whole in which he or she participates.[3] Like other Chinese philosophers, Chuang Tzu sees the person as fundamentally related to a larger whole, but he differs with them as to the nature of that whole and of the person's relationship to it. His criticism of the Confucians and the Legalists demonstrates that he rejects the philosophy of holism as defined by Louis

---

*References to the *Chuang Tzu* are given parenthetically after the citation. Because sections are long and repetitious, I have cited an indexed text with numbered lines. References are to *Chuang Tzu yin-te* [Index to *Chuang Tzu*], edited and published by Huang-tao wen-hua yu-hsien kung-ssu (Taipei, 1971). For example, "1.41-42" means chapter 1, lines 41 and 42. The second half ("W35") refers to the appropriate page in Burton Watson, trans., *The Complete Works of Chuang Tzu* (New York: Columbia University Press, 1968). All of the passages quoted in the text are my own translations, for which I bear full responsibility. Watson is cited as an alternative translation in order to provide the reader with ready access to context.

Dumont in his famous study of Indian society.[4] For Dumont, holism is a view of a hierarchical society with clearly defined social roles enforced by institutional arrangements and laws which are, in turn, sanctioned by religious canons and prescribed ritual behaviors. Virtually every element of Dumont's notion of holism is rejected by Chuang Tzu. The latter's conception of the whole is based on a different set of premises and defines a theoretical limit of perfection[5] and a soteriological goal of freedom, both of which lie beyond the boundaries of the conventional institutions and values of the society.

This paper will explore three different levels of insight into the relations between self and whole as revealed in the writings of Chuang Tzu. The first has to do with the false layers of the extrinsic or socialized self, which is tied to an unquestioned acceptance of the conventional world and its institutions. This view is the medium through which Chuang Tzu refutes the positions and assumptions of other schools of classical Chinese thought. The second portrays the perfected self, a radically free being whose qualities and whose world are presented in paradoxical and fantastic imagery. It is on this level that the theoretical limit and soteriological goal of Chuang Tzu's thought are articulated. The third level provides concrete examples of the Taoist's approach to living in the world. These passages describe a gradual process by which one moves in the direction of the theoretical limit.

Issues in the Interpretation of Chuang Tzu

Chuang Tzu's place of honor in the Chinese heritage does not rest solely on his renown as a philosopher; he is also celebrated as one of the greatest writers of prose in Chinese history. This is not, however, to suggest that his writings can be separated or classified by genre; his philosophy is embedded in his prose style, and his "literature" expresses his philosophy. Chuang Tzu engages in sophisticated, informed, and tightly reasoned philosophical debate with the positions current in his day, but his writings do not limit themselves to this form of philosophical discourse. As A. C. Graham has noted, "he is as much a poet as he is a philosopher."[6] Graham also comments, "By mocking reason and delighting in the impossibility of putting his message into words, the Taoist seems to withdraw beyond the reach of discussion and criticism."[7] I concur both with Graham's statement of the problem and with his conviction that modern scholars cannot let the matter rest there.

Chuang Tzu's refusal to define straightforward principles or rules for life is part and parcel of his philosophy. His approach to life is presented as a skill or art, not as a set of rules.[8] In order to avoid presenting his philosophy as a set of principles, Chuang Tzu resorts to satiric stories and fantastic imagery. These elements of his writings are not philosophical discourse, and for this reason they are more effectively approached through literary analysis. This is by no means to imply that Chuang Tzu is not a consistent and rational thinker. On the contrary, his compelling literary technique is brilliantly employed in the service of logical argument or as the vehicle by which to present a philosophical position (e.g., live spontaneously) without stating it as a principle. To explain prosaically a philosophical position might risk oversimplifying it, thereby presenting it to the reader as something less challenging than what Chuang Tzu has in mind.

A large portion of Chuang Tzu's philosophical arguments are presented in the form of dialogues between Chuang Tzu, or an eccentric Taoist teacher, and an interlocutor. As in the case of Socratic or Confucian dialogues, Chuang Tzu's dialogues contain not only logical arguments, but lively wit; the interlocutor's statements are gently satirized to expose their inadequacies. In addition, the dialogues make use of flagrantly "fictional" elements. Their author often ascribes outrageous positions or statements to famous personages, such as Confucius or one of his major disciples, or turns his opponents into spokesmen for his own position. He also sets up as his "teachers" such unlikelies as maimed criminals or a hunchbacked hag, figures who, according to conventional Chinese expectations, would never be teachers. These satirical elements are, strictly speaking, external to the argument, but the overturned expectations or profound ironies add to the power of the presentation. Chuang Tzu uses these devices to detach readers from unexamined conventional attitudes in order to open their minds to his philosophical positions.

If ignoring the literary dimension of the dialogues results in missing the power of Chuang Tzu's message, ignoring the literary dimension of the fantastic passages leads to dismissing or circumventing the statement of the theoretical limit and soteriological goal of Chuang Tzu's thought. These passages have troubled commentators and scholars because they are stubbornly resistant to philosophical analysis; they appear to be wild flights of fancy. Some have tried to dismiss them as mere allegory, arguing that an intelligent man like Chuang Tzu could not possibly believe such fantastic things.[9] Others, while well aware that such passages establish the theoretical limits of Chuang Tzu's thought, have confined themselves to the more tractable passages.[10] While I can well understand the practicality of the latter position, I believe that these passages are too important to be circumvented.

The fantastic passages are not conveniently segregated from the rest of Chuang Tzu's work. They are, on the contrary, integrated with the philosophical statements and the dialogues, and they pervade the "inner chapters"—considered to be the authentic core of the work—as well as the more dubious "outer chapters." We must therefore assume that they were intended to contribute in some way to the philosophical presentations they accompany. The fantastic passages serve, moreover, an important philosophical purpose by putting the more straightforward and "reasonable" passages into their proper context. Chuang Tzu argues that a valid approach to life cannot be reduced to a simple set of rules; this is why, as Graham has demonstrated, whenever one of Chuang Tzu's stories seems to present a straightforward moral, it is contradicted in the next section, as if to demonstrate that the meaning is more elusive.[11] The fantastic passages serve a similar purpose. Although some stories or dialogues suggest how a Taoist would approach life, these are juxtaposed with fantastic stories which clearly indicate that the "practical suggestions" are only faint reflections of something far more rare and challenging—an art of living which is not simple. The fantastic stories serve as a reminder that Taoist perfection is transcendent, never to be fully realized in the normal course of life.

The Socialized Self and the Conventional World

Chuang Tzu's opponents, in particular the Confucians and the Legalists, believed that the individual was to be defined and understood in terms of formalized relationships with others through established social forms. In Chuang Tzu's opinion, this view defined a person in terms of externals, which were by definition extrinsic to the inner essence of the person. Although Confucians and Legalists differed on how to define the nature of the social world to which the individual was related, they were in accord with respect to stressing the public relatedness and obligations of the individual.

The Legalists saw the individual primarily as a citizen of the state, and they believed that the individual's will must be subordinated to that state. After all, if the state were to be destroyed, the individual's life and livelihood would also be endangered. The state, from a Legalist standpoint, consisted primarily of laws and institutions, the norms and structures of polity which make up the government. The individual was to be inculcated with the laws of the society and amply rewarded for conformity and strictly punished for any deviation. The good individual was obedient and fiercely loyal to the society. Wrongdoers were to be shown no mercy, since their deviance from the laws threatened the stability of the society.

The Confucians also believed that humans were fundamentally social creatures with social obligations, but they saw these formalized obligations as moral norms that formed the basis of a civilized culture. The individual was to be educated in the ritual proprieties of the culture, as described in the classics, in order to learn how to fulfill the obligations of the five cardinal relationships: ruler-subject, parent-child, husband-wife, elder-younger, and friend-friend. These relationships were believed to be the normative patterns for all human relationships. By following the ritual norms, which embody the wisdom and ethics of the civilization, a person refined his or her character. The metaphor for moral refinement, through education and self-cultivation, was the polishing of a jade stone until the rough edges were smoothed away and the luminescence of the stone shown through.[12] The Confucians argued that such cultivation—socialization to the established norms of the society—created persons of moral character and integrity and fulfilled one's innately good human nature. From Chuang Tzu's point of view, this socialization through the external process of ritual and the learning of the classics constituted the imposition of something extrinsic on top of the inner self.

The problem for Chuang Tzu with this view lay in looking outward into a hierarchical society with defined norms and roles which distort and unnaturally limit human potential. He found such a view of the human world too constricting in that it unquestioningly accepts preestablished hierarchies and norms and further assumes that the order of which humans are a part can be institutionalized and defined in laws, rituals, or the classics. Chuang Tzu's arguments imply that in order to find the free and autonomous self, one has to break free from the institutions and conventions of the social world. In order to establish his position, he systematically exposes the arbitrariness and superficiality of these extrinsic layers.

The first of these layers is comprised of the labels attached to individuals by society. These labels represent judgments which in no way touch or reflect the real self. This is true even when they serve as considered societal judgments of the person's behavior, as in the label "criminal." This particular label is based on the laws of society as arbitrated by its accepted authorities and institutions; the Legalists, for instance, would insist that such labels are valid because they are the only way to maintain social order. They are applied with "justice." In Chuang Tzu's day, Chinese criminals were often mutilated or marked with a tattoo or brand. This is a dramatic example of the reality and potential impact of social labeling; the branded criminal could never entirely clear the slate because the mark was always visible, proclaiming his or her transgression to society at large, which was all too ready to shun him or her on this account. The external marks, which in his day carried the conventional label of criminal or deformed, in his writings become attributes of the wise and spiritual.

In like manner, Chuang Tzu suggests that all labels—beautiful and ugly, good and bad, big and small—are superficial and arbitrary; they are based on appearances, conventions, and a limited point of view; there is no valid standard for such labels. The philosophical argument for this is made in his second chapter, "Ch'i-wu lun" [On seeing things as equal].[13] In his satirical attacks on social labels, however, Chuang Tzu stresses not just their arbitrariness, but their superficiality. For instance, Chinese convention assumed that nobility of character would show in a refined, dignified, and attractive demeanor, a certain delicacy of manner. In other words, the labels "dignified" and "wise" were linked in the popular mind. Chuang Tzu's "sages" and "teachers,"[14] however, are depicted as ugly, repulsive, and irreverent—anything but noble and dignified.

A second layer of the socialized self consists of the various roles and functions designated by society. From society's point of view, the citizen's contribution lies in the fulfillment of his or her social and economic roles; this is how one becomes a useful and responsible member of the society. These contributions are made within existing institutional frameworks of society and are measured and shaped by social and economic practices. Everything has its uses, and everyone his or her function.

Chuang Tzu attacks this attitude as dangerous and enervating. To view things only in a functional manner, he argues, is to miss the things themselves, to fail to see their essence, their beauty, and their potentialities. It is a failure of imagination. Chuang Tzu exposes the inadequacy of this position in a dialogue with Hui Tzu, the famous logician. Hui Tzu had a gourd so large that it was useless in its traditional roles as water jug or dipper, so he destroyed it. Chuang Tzu chided him: "Now you had a gourd big enough to hold five piculs. Why didn't you consider making it into a great tub to float on the rivers and lakes instead of worrying that it was too unwieldy to use for a dipper? Your mind must still be tangled!" (1.41-42; W35). Hui Tzu's excessively utilitarian mindset lacks imagination and a sense of fun: why not enjoy the gourd and celebrate its extraordinary properties, instead of lamenting its failure to fit the preconceived mold?

The obsession with utility and function is not only a matter of missed opportunity; it saps life and energy. Chuang Tzu suggests that the effort to make a contribution simply uses one up, consumes the life force, and leads to an early death. This position is established in the dialogue of a carpenter with a huge, gnarled tree, which the carpenter dismisses as useless. That night the tree appears to the carpenter in a dream and berates him roundly for thinking it less valuable than straight lumber trees; according to the tree, being useful simply subjects one to abuse and "the tearing and striking of the common mob" (4.71; W64). The tree maintains that it has cultivated uselessness; it enjoys it, and it relishes its old age and quiet life. The carpenter's apprentice is confused: "If its intent is to be useless, why is it helping to mark the village shrine?" The carpenter retorts, "It is a secret. Better not to speak. It's only resting there.... It protects itself in a different way from ordinary people. If you try to judge it by the standards of duty, you'll be far off!" (4.73-75; W64-65). The tree refuses to be defined by its function and is simply living.

Just as the tree would be harmed if it allowed itself to be used, so people harm themselves by believing that they must contribute to society. Such people sap their energy and kill themselves by not knowing the limitations of what they can realistically accomplish. They let their lives be run by noble aspirations and aims, which—even if not fueled by a desire for fame and recognition—are often beyond their capabilities. Chuang Tzu depicts Yen Hui, the favorite disciple of Confucius, confiding to his master his plan to reform the ruler of Wei. Instead of encouraging Hui in his noble goals, Confucius gives him a lecture on the trouble he will get into (4.1-34; W54-58). In a similar vein, Yen Ho, who has been appointed tutor to the son of the duke of Wei, is warned by his mentor:

> Don't you know about the praying mantis? It waved its arms angrily in the tracks of the approaching carriage, unaware that it had no chance of stopping it. Such was the high opinion it had of its talents. Be careful! Be cautious! If you offend the ruler by parading your talents, you will be in danger (4.59-60; W62-63).

The satirical image of the high-minded Confucian reformer as a praying mantis angrily flagging down a carriage is Chuang Tzu's way of bursting the bubble of Confucian moral aspiration and of undermining the reformist zeal of the Mohists. The desire to be useful, although well intentioned and noble, is dangerous and possibly even fatal. It allows externals (the needs of society) to define the self and is thus as extrinsic to the real self as social judgments.

It is virtually impossible to function in a society entirely free of roles, and this is especially true of the workplace. However, Chuang Tzu's examples do not idealize the wealthy idle who can afford to be "above it all." Many of his "teachers" are lower-class artisans, virtual servants in the society of their day. Chuang Tzu's examples include a wheelwright, a cook, a woodcarver, a ferryman, a cicada catcher, a gamecock trainer, and a tiger trainer. These men were economically dependent on their wealthy patrons; they had to please them in order to continue earning a living. However, in order to discover the secret of their craft, these artisans must transcend external social and economic pressures. Woodworker Ch'ing, who carves bell stands so skillfully that people think they were made by gods or spirits, confides that he "fasts" in order to forget: (a) rewards, titles, and stipends (the economic and social rewards of his work); (b) praise, blame, skill, clumsiness (approval from self and others for his achievements); and (c) limbs and body (his physical self, the hand which does the carving). When these are forgotten, the ruler and court (his patrons) no longer exist for him; they lose their power over him; he is no longer *their* woodcarver (19.56-58; W205). The external aspects of his role get in the way of true creativity; they are extrinsic to Ch'ing as a woodcarver.

In Chuang Tzu's view, the labels imposed by society and the roles and functions assigned to or assumed by an individual are learned; they result from a socialization process that shapes the person by adding layers of attitudes and behaviors which obscure the inner self. The role definitions are products of the collective human experience in a culture or society. Rather than celebrating these as the wisdom of tradition, tested by time and therefore to be emulated, as did the Confucians, Chuang Tzu questions the validity of the civilized perspective of culture as refining the person into a *chün-tzu*, a gentleman or perfected person in the Confucian mode.[15]

Chuang Tzu's teachers and sages are irreverent, sarcastic, and blatantly impolite; they avoid the indirections and niceties of courtesy and often offend the proper. Chuang Tzu portrayed himself shocking his acquaintances by dropping the ritual mourning for his wife and instead sitting on the floor with legs akimbo, pounding on a tub and singing (18.15; W192).[16] Proper mourning was, in Confucian eyes, the most sacred of ritual obligations. Chuang Tzu taunts the Confucians by casting Confucius himself in the role of defending those who flout the mourning rituals. In Chuang Tzu's example, Confucius's disciple is scandalized by the behavior of the friends of Sang-hu at his funeral. They were working (weaving frames for silkworms), playing instruments, and singing, and thereby violating three taboos. When the disciple complains to Confucius, he answers,

> They are men who wander beyond the realm; I am one who wanders within it. Beyond and within can never meet. When I sent you to pay condolences, I was stupid. Just now they have joined with the creator in their human forms to wander in the single ether of heaven and earth (6.66-68; W86-87).

Chuang Tzu's Confucius praises these rebels for being beyond the "stupidity" of paying condolences. Although not cast in the form of a philosophical argument, Confucius's statement asserts that conformity to ritual proprieties lies within the realm of distinctions, of not treating all things and perspectives as equal; hence, it is superficial and false.

Thus, even "decent behavior," propriety, and culture are conceived as layers extrinsic to the self. They have nothing to do with the art of living. In a similar vein, Wheelwright P'ien scorns book learning and the classics, which he considers to be the "dregs of the ancients" (13.68-74); W152-53).[17] If the ancients had any true learning, if they understood the skill of living, they could not have put it into words. To look to the classics for models of civilized behavior is to look to a dead and fossilized past. The Confucians, from Chuang Tzu's point of view, have a distorted view of learning; they are still trying to add something from the outside instead of letting the inner self shine through.

Having questioned the validity of accepting social labels, of devoting oneself to external causes, and of conforming to ritual proprieties and trusting the "wisdom" contained in books, Chuang Tzu goes on to question an aspect of the self which most humans would consider a given—that is, our humanness itself. The human perspective lies beneath any specific culture. It is embodied in our penchant for making distinctions. Often it is also tied to the accident of our physical form, in which case to accept the human point of view as normative because we have experienced no other is then to equate ourselves with our physical form. However a human being has not only a body, but a mind; a human has a unique capability to transcend the limits of physical existence and imagine himself or herself in another place, time, or form. Chuang Tzu challenges us to take advantage of our full imaginative potential by not limiting our capacity for empathy and openness.

He questions the normativeness of the human point of view: "Monkeys pair with monkeys, deer consort with deer, and fish wander with fish. Men think that Mao-ch'iang and Lady Li were beautiful, but if fish saw them they would swim away, and if deer saw them they would run off. Of these four, which knows the true beauty of the world?" (2.68-70; W46). The passage humorously demonstrates that humans have the capability to see Mao-ch'iang from the viewpoint of a fish; we are not limited to the human perspective.

Chuang Tzu also records experiences which transcend the limits of the body. Almost all people have dreamt they were an animal, but Chuang Tzu goes on to question whether he is a man dreaming he is a butterfly, or a butterfly dreaming he is a man (2.94-96; W49). He has the courage and imagination to suppose he might *be* the butterfly; in that imaginative act he transcends both his humanness and his identity as someone called Chuang Tzu. This is not threatening or distressing to him; whether as Chuang Tzu or as the butterfly, he is very much alive and endowed with wit and grace.

Unwillingness to imagine assuming a nonhuman form or perspective traps one in the realm of arbitrary distinctions. Humans cling to what they see as a privileged position, but this only shows their narrowness and audacity.

Now when a great smith is casting metal, if the metal should leap up and say, "I must be made into a Mo-yeh"![18] the smithy would surely regard it as very inauspicious metal. Now, having had the audacity to take on human form once, if you should say, "Only a man! Nothing but a man!" the creator would surely regard you as a most inauspicious person (6.58-59; W85).

The accident of having taken on human form provides a person with the capability to understand that such a form is only one perspective; the autonomous, perfected self is free even of the limitations of humanness and physical existence because it has the courage of imagination.

The Perfected Self and the Tao

Chuang Tzu's ideal of the perfected self, the theoretical limit and soteriological goal of his philosophy, is presented in a series of images and anecdotes which portray the transcendence of the perfected self. These passages do not provide a succinct definition of this self, since the perfected self does not exist in the order of reality characterized by labels and concepts which may be grasped by the mind through discursive language. Concepts and language belong to the socialized self, to the realm of distinctions and unequal perspectives. Instead of appealing to reason in these passages, Chuang Tzu appeals to imagination, the ability to transcend the boundaries of past experience and even of common sense.

In order to convey the transcendence—the radical otherness—of the perfected self, Chuang Tzu uses fantastic imagery and shocking or exhilarating views of a reality beyond the boundaries of sensible reality. Many readers are troubled by these passages and wish to dismiss them as mere allegory or poetry. But Chuang Tzu has anticipated this response and defends against it. He makes his argument in the dialogue between Chien Wu and Lien Shu. Chien Wu is a reasonable man who complains about the crazy statements of Chieh Yü.

> Chien Wu said to Lien Shu, "I heard a statement from Chieh Yü so vast there was no placing it. It went off and never came back [to reality]. I was startled by his words—endless like the Milky Way and greatly unlike anything; they never approach the human condition!"
>
> Lien Shu asked, "What did he say?"
>
> "He said, 'There is a holy man [*shen-jen*] living on distant Ku-she Mountain. His flesh is like ice or snow, and he is meek and shy like a young maiden. He doesn't eat the five grains, but sucks the wind, drinks the dew, mounts the clouds and mist, rides a flying dragon, and wanders beyond the four seas. His spirit concentrated, he can keep creatures from sickness and plague and make the harvest plentiful.' I thought all this was wild and refused to believe it."
>
> "So!" said Lien Shu. "One can't expect a blind man to view beautiful patterns or a deaf man to listen to bells and drums. Are blindness and deafness confined to the body? The understanding has them too, as your words just now have shown" (1.27-32; W33).

The holy man of Ku-she is said to be a fantastic creature with supernatural powers. Chien Wu has every reason to be skeptical about this description, since it defies reason and common sense. However, rather than affirm his skepticism, Lien Shu accuses him of being "deaf" and "dumb" in his understanding. Chien Wu will not open his mind to a greater reality; he closes his imagination and uses the ordinary experience of the past as his measure. The holy man, however, surpasses even the greatest sages of history. Lien Shu says, "You could mold a Yao or Shun from just his dust and chaff. How would he be willing to concern himself with ordinary things?" (1.33-34; W34)

In this dialogue, Chuang Tzu's spokesman, Lien Shu, does not attempt to bring the holy man into the purview of reality; he does not offer more information or evidence which would make the description reasonable. Nor does he advocate belief in the story on the grounds that some things can be accepted only through a leap of faith. According to Lien Shu, the problem is not a lack of faith, but blindness and deafness in understanding, a closed mind and imagination.

The fantastic images of the perfected self portray a level of freedom which transcends even popular images of freedom, such as the story that Lieh Tzu could fly.

> Lieh Tzu could wander riding the wind with airy skill, but after fifteen days he returned. He was never one to fret about seeking good fortune. Although he was able to avoid walking, he still had to depend on something. If he had only mounted the truth of heaven and earth, ridden the changes of the six ethers, and wandered through the boundless, then how would he have depended on anything? (1.19-21; W32)

Chuang Tzu questions whether flying is an adequate image of freedom. It is after all a relatively tame image; children, poets, and dreamers have all imagined being able to fly on the wind like birds and kites. Chuang Tzu sees Lieh Tzu's flying as simply an extension of walking. "Although he was able to avoid walking, he still had to depend on something." But what would it mean to fly without depending on anything? Is that not an image of true freedom? Such freedom would transcend not only the limitations of human mobility (the things which hold us down), but also those things we depend upon in order to conceive of freedom. The purpose is not to give us a more realistic or comprehensible view of freedom but rather to make clear the limits of the freedom which we have already imagined.

The perfected self also transcends the dangers and "mean and trembly fears" (2.10-11; W37)[19] of ordinary mortals.

> The perfected self is spirit-like [shen]. Though the great swamps blaze, they cannot make it hot; though the great rivers freeze, they cannot make it cold; though swift lightning splits the mountains and howling gales shake the sea, they cannot startle it. It rides the clouds and mist, straddles the sun and moon, and wanders beyond the four seas. Even life and death have no effect on the self, much less the rules of profit and loss (2.71-73; W46).

Because it considers all things to be equal, cold and hot, stormy and calm, makes no difference; the perfected self remains calm and unflustered amidst the things which trouble ordinary persons. Having that equanimity, it wanders freely throughout the universe, unhindered and unthreatened.

The freedom of the perfected self (the sage) comes from the fact that he or she makes no distinctions: "Therefore the sage does not follow [such distinctions], but illuminates *all* in heaven. He too recognizes a 'this,' but a 'this' which is also a 'that,' a 'that' which is also a 'this'" (2.29; W40). Freedom occurs not by accepting the fixed limitations of one's place in the hierarchical structure of the whole (as in Dumont's holism), but rather by flowing with changes, assuming new perspectives, identifying "this" with "that," and freeing one's imagination and mind from the hold of the past.

The radical freedom of the perfected self implies a radically different whole, "all in heaven," the Tao. Since Chuang Tzu's concept of Tao has been extensively discussed in previous scholarship,[20] I will limit my remarks on this topic to a few points which demonstrate how the notion of the Tao is complementary to the notion of the radical freedom of the perfected self.

Chuang Tzu does not overtly discuss the Tao, for, like the perfected self, it is beyond distinctions, concepts, and labels. There is really nothing to be said about the whole. However, some of the qualities of the Tao may be deduced from his writings. The Tao is a vast and unified whole which includes all perspectives and all reality, giving all realities equal value. The Tao's vastness exposes the relativity and triviality of all normal distinctions. No single consciousness is large enough to encompass all possible positions simultaneously; yet that is precisely what the Tao does. It is neither a thing (which must have a locus in time and space) nor a mind (which must locate things in time and space to differentiate one from the other). The Tao merely is, and it lets all things be; it is the space or void in which all things and perspectives find room. Just as from an ordinary human standpoint it is useless to distinguish between big and small grains of sand, so from the viewpoint of the Tao are there no distinctions; they are too insignificant. These "trivial" distinctions include social hierarchies, ranks, labels, and relationships.

The Tao is also changing, a dynamic, pulsating flux of nature and of life. From any one perspective, the change may seem to be random and arbitrary. However, this is only because the perspective is too limited; our normal ways of thinking and seeing cannot embrace the order of the Tao. To be able to appreciate the movements of the Tao, humans have to be willing to let go of their perspectives, to change and adapt, to consider possibilities that are utterly new and beyond common sense and past precedent.

Living Skillfully

The poetic and fantastic descriptions of the perfected self strain the imagination. They do not offer a definition of this reality which is philosophically satisfying. However, if the fantastic passages portray the radical transcendence and theoretical limit of his ideal, in other passages Chuang Tzu depicts the process of moving toward the perfected self by cultivating the art or skill of living.

The art of living is portrayed in examples of skillful artisans; of these, only the story of Cook Ting is found in the undisputed inner core of the work, but stories outside of the core may be used to expand upon the ideas presented in the example of Cook Ting. Ting was so skillful that he never wore out his cleaver. He described how he approached the act of butchering an ox: "I approach it with my spirit, and don't look with my eyes. Perception and understanding cease, and spirit moves where it will" (3.6; W50-51). Behind the physical body, the senses, and the discriminating mind is spirit. Spirit "looks" (i.e., is conscious) and it is an active agent in creation (it moves where it will).

The term "spirit" (*shen*) has more than one meaning in the writings of Chuang Tzu. On the one hand it means spiritlike, numinous, as in "ghosts and spirits" (*kuei-shen*). Ghosts and spirits are portrayed as forces which dwell in the land and sometimes cause trouble (see, for example, 4.33; W58; and 16.6; W172). On the other hand, spirituality is a quality of mind which "sees" (envisions), illumines, soars, and transcends; spirit is that core of consciousness not tied down by the physical self. It is an inner quality; Chuang Tzu chides Hui Tzu, the logician, for treating his spirit "like an external thing" by rationalizing and objectifying his thoughts and feelings (5.59; W76). Spirit is a quality of the inner self that lies beneath the layers of mind and things; it is the spirit which one tries to release or recover by moving toward the ideal of the perfected self.

Moving beyond the inner chapters of the work, there are other passages which clarify the notion of spirit and its relationship to the perfected self.[21] Spirit is cultivated by nourishing the mind through inaction, reaching behind the body and intelligence (the discriminating mind). In such a state, mind and spirit are liberated (11.54; W122). If one is able to put heaven and earth outside the self and forget things, spirit will have no cares (13.63; W151). Spirit is nurtured in a state of stillness and quiescence (11.36-37; W119), which create an inner calm, a mind like a mirror.

> The sage is still not because he takes stillness to be good. The myriad things are insufficient to distract his mind; that is why he is still. Still water clearly reflects the beard and eyebrows. An even water level is what the great carpenter takes his measure from. If the stillness of water can possess such clarity, how much more must spirit [*ching-shen*]? The sage's mind is still. It is the mirror of heaven and earth, the looking glass of the ten thousand things (13.2-4; W142).

Spirit is also expansive. It soars and enjoys; as opposed to the man of virtue, "the man of spirit lets his spirit ascend and mount the light. His bodily form dissolves and is gone.... He lives out his fate, exhausting his circumstances. He rests in the joy of heaven and earth, while the myriad affairs of the world melt away" (12.76-77; W137). The "man of spirit" is another term for the perfected self, which wanders free and easy through heaven and earth.

In one passage, spirit is explicitly identified with inborn nature, which determines the "rules and standards" of each thing (12.39; W132). Scholars of Chuang Tzu, most notably Fung Yu-lan, have argued that for Chuang Tzu, the Tao is the inborn nature of each thing; each thing has the Tao of its particular nature, which comes from, and is an aspect of, the one Tao which unites all.[22] Inborn nature is an inner spiritual core which can experience fundamental unity with the Tao.

In order to reach and liberate that inner spiritual core, Chuang Tzu offers examples of "fasting of the mind" (*hsin-chai*). The fasting episodes manifest a common structure: laying down, forgetting, or putting outside of oneself the extraneous layers, feelings, and concerns which characterize the socialized self, and moving toward or uncovering the inner core of spirit or inborn nature (Tao).

In the section above on the socialized self, I noted that Woodworker Ch'ing, in his task of carving bell stands, fasted in order to forget any thought of rewards, praise, patronage, or manual skill—in short, those things which comprise his socialized and physical self. He cannot simply say "I will no longer think of these things." Changing ingrained habits of mind requires discipline, fasting.

In the inner core of Chuang Tzu's writings, there are three important examples which define fasting of the mind. The Woman Crookback taught someone to "put outside of himself" in successive stages the realm, things, and life (6.36-40; W82-83). This refers to a process of distinguishing the real (inner) self from the extraneous layers provided by the realm (the world and its institutions and expectations), things (material objects and ideas, which fan desires and aspirations), and life (the physical self and the sensory experiences which make up daily existence). In order to get him to do this, Woman Crookback says she "sustained a lengthy instruction," seeking to inculcate in him a new mental attitude.

Two dialogues between Confucius and his beloved disciple Yen Hui clarify what is entailed in the mental discipline of fasting, what is "set aside." Confucius describes fasting:

> Let your will be as one! Don't listen with your ears; listen with your mind. No, don't listen with your mind, but listen with your vital energy [*ch'i*]. Listening stops with the ears, the mind stops with classifying, but vital energy is empty and waits on all things. Only the Way gathers in emptiness. Emptiness is called fasting of the mind (4.26-28; W57-58).

Making the will one is an act of concentration. Concentrated, one moves behind the senses (ears) and the discriminating mind to listen with *ch'i*; one directs the listening inward, as in meditation. *Ch'i* in early Chinese philosophy carried several meanings: breath or air; the source of vitality, the life force of things; the cosmological "stuff" of the universe, which expands into air (the void) and contracts to form things. *Ch'i* as breath or void is empty, the "space" within which things appear; within the body, it is the breath and energy which is present even when the body is perfectly still. In this passage, emptiness is the innermost core of the vitality or energy of the person, lying behind all of the activities of the conscious mind.

In the second dialogue, Yen Hui discusses what happens when he "sits down and forgets everything." "I smash limbs and body, expel intelligence, cast off form, drive away understanding, and unite with the great thoroughfare" (6.92-93; W90). He moves behind the physical self, behind intelligence and understanding (functions of the conscious mind) and notions of form (of both self and things), and unites with the Way (symbolized here as the "great thoroughfare"). In this passage, fasting transcends not only body and mind, but the separation of self and other; there is no longer a distinct self. As Yen Hui put it, "Before I was able to hear this, I was certainly Hui. Now that I have been able to, there is not yet a Hui. Could you call that emptiness?" Confucius replied, "That exhausts it!" (4.28-29; W58).

At the end of the process of fasting the mind, then, is emptiness and the Way; in that place there is no self and other, no body and limbs. Woodworker Ch'ing describes this as a state of total concentration and receptivity: "Skill is concentrated and all outside distractions dissipate" (19.58; W206). Woman Crookback is more poetic; her student, she claims, was able in the end to penetrate the dawn, see his solitude, do away with past and present, and enter where there is no life or death (6.40-41; W83). Emptiness, she suggests, is not simply stillness; it is a window on a realm of light and detachment beyond time and physical existence.

Self and Whole in the Taoist Art of Living

Although the passages on fasting of the mind clarify the process of cultivating the perfected self, they do not explicitly address the issue of the relationship of the self to the whole. In this section, I will analyze examples which suggest how a Taoist practicing this "art of living" might approach some of these issues.

It is clear that the Taoist seeks freedom from the restrictions and conventions of the socialized self, societal labels, and external expectations, yet this does not mean that the Taoist renounces or leaves the world. Take the case of Woodworker Ch'ing. Although he has forgotten the financial rewards, the demands of patrons, and his own fears of success or failure, he has not rejected his job; he is still a producer of bell stands which serve a useful function in society. In like manner, all of Chuang Tzu's artisans are productive members of society; they do their jobs responsibly. What is different is their attitude toward society and the demands of their jobs. By turning their focus away from the social and economic demands of their jobs and the specific rules and techniques they entail, the artisans become mentally free to concentrate on the skill of their craft; they have elevated their work to an art. In a brilliant essay on Chuang Tzu, Hsü Fu-kuan has argued that Chuang Tzu's examples of artisans are metaphors for the art of living. If the artisans could transform their lives, like their crafts, into art, they would be Taoist sages. The Way teaches the art of living.[23]

The example of Chuang Tzu's response to his wife's death serves as an illustration of how the attitude of the artisans might be extended to a noncreative, nonartistic situation. As Chuang Tzu portrays it, his own unorthodox behavior was not a simple matter of rebellion against ritual forms; it was a considered response to the reality of his wife's death. "When she first died," he writes, "do you think I wasn't sad like anyone else?" But then he looks into the fact that before she was his wife, or indeed a human being, she had come from the undifferentiated chaos of nature and Tao; her birth, life, and death were simply small events in a much larger process of natural evolution. He concludes:

> It's just like the progression of the four seasons, spring, summer, fall, winter. This person is now going to sleep peacefully in a vast room. If I were to follow after, bawling and sobbing about it, I would consider myself unclear about life. So I stopped (18.18-19; W192).

Chuang Tzu loved his wife, and he admits that he missed her and grieved for her on her death. But he is able to take a larger view, to see her not just as the woman he loved and lived with for so many years but as part of the Tao. He does not focus on what has been taken away from him, nor does he insist on holding to the perspective of the husband-wife relationship. He perceives her passing as part of change, which is larger than his life or hers. From this larger perspective, her life is only a tiny part of a much larger process which affirms life as a whole rather than the existence of any particular thing or person. Chuang Tzu did not rationalize away his grief by giving her death philosophical meaning; he was willing to let go of his own particular perspective (of himself, of her, of their relationship) and see the larger picture; he was open and flexible, accepting and affirming change as a part of life.

Chuang Tzu's response to his wife, both loving her and accepting her death, demonstrates that his position is different from either holism or renunciation as defined by Dumont in his discussion of Indian society. Dumont argues that Indian society is basically holistic, defining an individual's status and obligations through ritual and legal norms which define the hierarchical structures of the society. Those who rejected such strictures in Indian society became renouncers, leaving behind family, property, caste—all social, ritual, and economic obligations—in favor of seeking personal purity and salvation. Dumont would argue that world renunciation was a product of the hierarchical values and holistic social system of India.[24] While on the surface many of Chuang Tzu's stories might suggest that his teachers and sages had, in fact, rejected society, a closer examination shows that this is not so. Not only are the artisans productive members of the society, but Chuang Tzu's attitude toward his wife in no way rejects or undermines the institution or the commitment of marriage. The Taoist can live in the world and have serious and meaningful relationships with others, but he or she functions in these relationships with a freedom which comes from cultivation of the art of living.

Chuang Tzu's approach to relationships is aptly illustrated in an example which deals with four friends. As we might expect of persons freed from the strictures of labels and conventions, these friends are not attracted to each other on the basis of appearances. They cut through the surface layer to recognize and celebrate the fundamentally free orientation of their companions.

> "Who can look on nonbeing as his head, on life as his spine, and on death as his rump? Who knows that life and death, preservation and annihilation, are a single body? I will be his friend!" The four looked at each other and smiled. None felt any disagreement in his heart, and so the four became friends (6.45-47; W84).

After a while, one of them was afflicted with a crippling disease; when his friend asked if he resented it, he replied:

> No, what would I hate? As the changes progress, perhaps in time it will transform my left arm into a rooster; then I'll keep watch on the night. Another change may transform my right arm into a crossbow pellet, and I'll shoot down an owl to roast. Another change may transform my buttocks into cartwheels; then with my spirit for a horse, I'll be able to ride on them. What need will I have for a carriage again? (6.50-52; W84).

The example of the four friends presents a vivid image of Chuang Tzu's view of the relationship of self to whole. The four friends are mutually bound by their unconventional views; they do not see themselves in terms of their individual identities or their social roles. They are not clear, individuated adults, as understood in terms of modern psychology.[25] Instead, they experience themselves as part of the universal process of life and death. The sick friend demonstrates the implications of this view; he is open to the threatening and uncomfortable change being visited upon his body. However, like Chuang Tzu facing his wife's death, he experiences the change not as the mutilation of a body which forms his identity, but as part of a larger process of change. His rather fantastic images to describe the directions the changes might take only serve to underscore how little attached he is to his body or his present form of existence. He can accept and celebrate whatever comes, however arbitrary or meaningless it might appear from the perspective of a single individual. His identity is not that of an individual, as understood in Western individualism, but that of a participant in the flow of life; he and his friends are fully attuned to that flow.

The openness of the Taoist is not openness to the pressures of society, but to what comes naturally from living. Thus, when a ruler sends emissaries to the river where Chuang Tzu is fishing to ask him to administer his state, Chuang Tzu refuses.

> Chuang Tzu held on to the fishing pole and, without turning his head, said, "I have heard that there is a sacred tortoise in Ch'u that has been dead now for three thousand years. The king keeps it wrapped in cloth and boxed, and stores it in the ancestral temple. Now would this tortoise rather be dead and have its bones honored? Or would it rather be alive and drag its tail in the mud? . . . Go away! I will drag my tail in the mud" (17.81-84; W188).

To accept such an honored post would pull Chuang Tzu into the realm of the socialized self; he would be devoting his energies and his vitality to improving social institutions, which are in the end only arbitrary arrangements. This effort would exhaust him, cut him off from the true world of which he is a part, i.e., the dynamic flux of life in the Tao.

Is there no way, then, for the true Taoist to make a difference in the political realm? There is an example in chapter 21[26] in which King Wen invites an old man he saw fishing to take over the realm. Although the man changed none of the laws or policies, within three years political cliques had disappeared, bureaucrats no longer competed for recognition, and people no longer cheated on weights and measures. When the king asked the old man how to extend these methods to the world, the man looked blank and disappeared, never to be heard from again (21.47-55; W228-30). The example suggests that a Taoist, if not interfered with, might be able to effect positive changes, but these would be destroyed by any attempt to institutionalize them. The freedom of the Taoist, likewise, cannot be legislated or institutionalized; it is quite unlike the rights and liberties of Western individualism. The freedom and methods of the Taoist are effective and skillful precisely because they transcend institutionalization and conceptualization.

Although Chuang Tzu seems vulnerable to charges of political irresponsibility, I believe that his position is consistent with his philosophy. Chinese thought in his day was overwhelmingly concerned with political issues and values. Both the style and substance of Chuang Tzu's writings deflected attention from those issues to the psychological, aesthetic, and spiritual realm, which were neglected dimensions of life. Chuang Tzu's art of living cultivates emotional inner peace, appreciation of the beauty and experience of life in itself, and an orientation toward the source and unity of life and being which transcends the petty problems of the mundane world and the institutions of society. He sought to clarify the inner dimensions of the self and the spiritual dimensions of the whole. As Hsü Fu-kuan has argued, Chuang Tzu's philosophy deals with the aesthetic spirit of Chinese thought.[27] The experience of the Tao is analogous to the creativity of the artist and aesthetic appreciation of the observer. What one expresses in the Taoist art of living is the Tao which forms the self-nature of all things and the unity of all being. The art of living cultivates the unity of life in its dynamic flux.

Conclusion

Because the Taoist art of living entails a notion of self and whole far different from the conventional view, it is difficult for one who so aspires to maintain a balance between uncovering the inner core of the self and being open to the whole of life. Graham has proposed the principle "respond with awareness" as a summary of the Taoist's approach to life.[28] Even that principle, as aptly as it captures the spirit of Chuang Tzu's position, offers little guidance as to maintaining balance and perspective while aspiring to cultivate the holistic awareness of the Taoist sage. These difficulties caused problems among followers of Chuang Tzu during the Six Dynasties period.[29] Those who saw the changes of Tao as including the flux of history saw in the *Chuang Tzu* a call to rationalize and accept all social and political developments, whether or not they accorded with the time-honored values of Chinese society. That is, they understood Chuang Tzu as advocating accommodation with history and the social order; Tao embraces all change, so nothing can lie outside of its moral purview. On the other hand, during the same period, some thinkers saw in Chuang Tzu's thought a call to eccentricity, to following spontaneously the inner impulses, the changes of the Tao in the inner self. These thinkers refused to be involved in social institutions, since these did not emanate from inner impulses. They flouted social convention and made a cult of the eccentric and bizarre. Neither of these positions does justice to the balance of Chuang Tzu's position. One is slanted toward holism (accommodation with society), the other toward radical individualism. Chuang Tzu's Taoist, however, leans toward neither side of the dichotomy. The Taoist is independent of arbitrary conventions and values but is supremely aware of and responsive to other positions and perspectives in the whole of life.

NOTES

1. My discussion of individualism is deeply indebted to Steven Lukes, *Individualism* (New York: Harper and Row, 1973). This remark is from 57.
2. The text of the *Chuang Tzu* poses problems of authenticity; textual scholarship has shown many sections to be spurious or extremely dubious, and some seem to have emanated from rival schools. For a recent analysis of these problems, see A. C. Graham, "How Much of *Chuang Tzu* Did Chuang Tzu Write?," in *Studies in Classical Chinese Thought*, ed. Henry Rosemont, Jr., and Benjamin I. Schwartz, *Journal of the American Academy of Religion* (thematic issue) (September 1979), 47(3S):433-48. The first seven chapters, or *nei-p'ien*, have long been regarded as the authentic core of the work; most of my citations will be from these chapters. When I have gone beyond them, I have tried to choose selections which are consistent with the ideas expressed in the core. Whenever passages are cited from outside the core of Graham's "mixed chapters," which he regards as largely products of Chuang Tzu's school, I will specify Graham's judgment of the status of that portion of the text.
3. I am indebted to Professor Donald Munro for suggesting that I pursue the notion of the complementarity of self and whole in Chuang Tzu's thought.
4. Louis Dumont, *Homo Hierarchicus: The Caste System and Its Implications*, trans. Mark Saisbury et al. (Chicago: University of Chicago Press, 1980).
5. For the term "theoretical limit" I am indebted to an essay by A. C. Graham, "Taoist Spontaneity and the Dichotomy of 'Is' and 'Ought,'" in a conference volume, *Experimental Essays on Chuang Tzu*, ed. Victor H. Mair (Honolulu: University Press of Hawaii, 1983), 75, 18.
6. Ibid., 3.
7. Ibid.
8. Ibid., 7.
9. Holmes Welch, *Taoism: The Parting of the Way* (Boston: Beacon Press, 1966), 89-95.
10. Graham, "Taoist Spontaneity," 3-4.
11. A. C. Graham, "Chuang Tzu's Essay on Seeing Things as Equal," *History of Religions* (November 1969-February 1970), 9(2-3):138.
12. *Analects*, 1:15. The image is taken from a verse in the *Classic of Poetry*.
13. Graham, "Chuang Tzu's Essay on Seeing Things as Equal," 137-59.
14. Chuang Tzu satirizes the sages and teachers of the Confucian mold, but he does not develop or portray a serious alternative; there is no sustained, realistic portrait of an ideal Taoist in his writings. Thus, his "sages" and "teachers" serve either to satirize Confucian ideals or to embody one aspect of the Taoist ideal. Because of the strong satiric dimension, I have put these terms in quotation marks.

15. Tu Wei-ming, *Centrality and Commonality: An Essay on Chung Yung*, Society for Asian and Comparative Philosophy Monograph Series, no. 3 (Honolulu: University Press of Hawaii, 1976), chap. 2.

16. This passage is from chapter 18, which Graham does not classify as belonging to any identifiable school.

17. Graham classifies chapter 13 as belonging to the syncretist school. See "How Much of *Chuang Tzu* Did Chuang Tzu Write?," 487-95.

18. Mo-yeh is a sword of legendary strength, the Excalibur of Chinese tradition.

19. In this case I have followed Burton Watson's translation, which captures perfectly the sense of the phrase.

20. Fung Yu-lan, *History of Chinese Philosophy*, trans. Derk Bodde, 2 vols. (Princeton: Princeton University Press, 1952), 1:221-45; Max Kaltenmark, *Lao Tzu and Taoism*, trans. Roger Greaves (Stanford: Stanford University Press, 1969), chap. 4; Graham, "Chuang Tzu's Essay on Seeing Things as Equal"; Hsü Fu-kuan, *Chung-kuo i-shu ching-shen* [The spirit of Chinese art] (T'ai-chung: Ssu-li Tung-hai Ta-hsüeh, 1967).

21. In trying to clarify Chuang Tzu's concept of spirit, I am forced to venture into chapters which Graham classifies as belonging to rival schools. He classifies chapters 11 and 12 as "primitivist documents," and chapters 13 and 15 as "syncretist documents." See "How Much of *Chuang Tzu* Did Chuang Tzu Write?," 475-81, 487-95. The reader is cautioned that this part of my discussion is thus on rather tenuous ground.

22. Fung Yu-lan, 1:223-25.

23. Hsü Fu-kuan, 52-53, 123, 129-31.

24. Louis Dumont, esp. the introduction, 4-8.

25. Some psychologists, e.g., Carl Jung and Abraham Maslow, have concepts of self which transcend the individuated self, but the mainstream of psychology and psychiatry is interested in a healthy, individuated adult.

26. Graham does not classify chapter 21 as belonging to any identifiable rival school.

27. Hsü Fu-kuan, *Chung-kuo i-shu ching-shen*, chapter on Chuang Tzu.

28. Graham, "Taoist Spontaneity," 11-15.

29. See Fung Yu-lan, *History of Chinese Philosophy*, vol. 2, chaps. 5 and 6, and Richard B. Mather, "The Controversy over Conformity and Naturalness During the Six Dynasties," *History of Religions* (November 1969-February 1970), 9(2-3):160-80.

Glossary

ch'i 氣

Ch'i-wu lun 齊物論

Chieh Yü 接輿

Chien Wu 肩吾

Ch'ing 慶

ching-shen 精神

Chuang Tzu 莊子

Chuang Tzu yin-te 莊子引得

chün-tzu 君子

Chung-kuo i-shu ching-shen 中國藝術精神

hsin-chai 心齋

Hsü Fu-kuan 徐復觀

Hui Tzu 惠子

kuei-shen 鬼神

Li 麗

Lieh Tzu 列子

Lien shu 連叔

Mao-ch'iang 毛嬙

Mo-Yeh 鏌鋣

nei-p'ien 內篇

P'ien 扁

Sang-hu 桑戶

shen 神

shen-jen 神人

Shun 舜

Tao 道

Ting 丁

Wen 文

Yao 堯

Yen Ho 顏闔

Yen Hui 顏回

Individualism and the Neo-Taoist Movement in Wei-Chin China

Ying-shih Yü

Both "individualism" and "holism" are Western concepts whose introduction into Chinese intellectual discourse is a matter of only recent historical development.[1] But this does not mean that as categories of analysis these two concepts are totally inapplicable to the study of early Chinese thought. As a matter of fact, we find in the long history of Chinese political and social thought a wide range of views which can be legitimately characterized as either holistic or individualistic. In this study, the Neo-Taoist movement since the end of the Han dynasty will be explored as an example of one type of Chinese individualism.

Crisis in Social Relationships at the End of the Han

Throughout the Han period, the central issue in Chinese political and social thinking was the problem of collective life at various levels. The problem of the individual, which had figured prominently in classical thought in pre-Ch'in times, ceased to be a matter of major concern to the Han-dynasty Chinese theorists. As a result, the best-known Chinese theory of social relationships—the so-called "three bonds and six rules" (san-kang liu-chi)—reached its definitive formulation during this period. The "three bonds" refers to the relationships between ruler and subject, father and son, and husband and wife, whereas the "six rules" pertain to those between paternal uncles, elder and younger brothers, other relatives of the same surname, maternal uncles, teachers, and friends. What is meant by these "bonds" and "rules"? The *Pai-hu t'ung-te lun* [Comprehensive discussions in the White Tiger Hall] provides the following answer: "A bond gives orderliness; a rule regulates. What is greater is the bond; what is smaller is the rule. They serve to order and regulate [the relations between] superiors and inferiors, and to arrange and adjust the way of mankind."[2] As the quotation makes apparent, the theory is exclusively concerned with the establishment of order in all social groups, from family to state. Though unmistakably Legalist in origin, the idea of the "three bonds" was nevertheless fully incorporated into Han Confucian ideology.[3] Under the Legalist influence, Han Confucianism also systematically developed the *li*[b] (rites; rituals) in a way similar to the development of the Legalist *fa* (laws). Whatever the differences may have been between the *li*[b] and the law, there can be little doubt that during the Han period they both functioned, each in its own way, as external constraints on the individual. *Li*[b] and law later became so closely associated that by A.D. 94 the Han Commandant of Justice could even characterize the two as "the outside and the inside of the same thing."[4]

If we take the Han period to be essentially an age of collectivism, then the end of the Han dynasty witnessed the rise of individualism. As a matter of fact, the period from the end of the second century to the early decades of the fourth century was the only epoch in Chinese history in which individualism flourished, not only in the realm of thought but also in the world of action. In order to understand this important historical development, we must begin our account with the profound social and intellectual crisis which began at the end of the Han dynasty.

The crisis took place primarily in the realm of social relationships in some radical circles of the elite class and may best be described as dissolution of the "three bonds." Let us first examine the ruler-subject relationship. By the second half of the second century A.D., there were indications that the idea of universal kingship was under fire. In 164 when Emperor Huan of Han made an imperial visit to Yün-meng (in modern Hupeh), he attracted a large crowd from the neighborhood. There was, however, one old man from Han-yin who continued to work in the field as if nothing was happening. Surprised, a member of the imperial entourage asked the old man why he alone showed no interest in looking at the emperor. The old man said:

> May I ask: What is our purpose in establishing the Son of Heaven? To bring order to the world? Or to bring chaos to it? Do we establish the Son of Heaven with the hope that he would treat us with paternal love? Or must we enslave the whole world in order to provide the needs of the Son of Heaven? Formerly, the sage-kings in governing the world, had only thatched huts for shelter. Nevertheless, the people lived in peace. Now, look at your ruler. He forces the people to work hard so that he can live in self-indulgence and enjoy leisurely trips without limit. I am ashamed for you. Yet you have the nerve to ask me to look up to him with reverence.[5]

This passage immediately raises the question of the legitimacy of universal kingship. Here the authority to rule is based, not on the idea of the "Mandate of Heaven," but on the Taoist theory of the state of nature. Thus, when a ruler fails to fulfill the obligations of his part, he has violated the contract and disqualified himself from the throne. The view of the old man from Han-yin, therefore, not only alludes to the disintegration of political order but also anticipates the type of anarchism that was to dominate Chinese political thinking in the next two centuries, as exemplified particularly by the ideas of Juan Chi (210-263) and Pao Ching-yen (fourth century A.D.).

In his famous "Ta-jen hsien-sheng chuan" [Biography of the great man] Juan Chi says:

> For there were no rulers and everything was in order; there were no officials, and every matter went well.... Once rulers were instituted,

oppressions arose; once officials were appointed, robbery began. Detached and apart, they instituted the rites and the laws by which to impose the bonds on the common people. . . . The utmost of heaven, earth, and the myriad things are exhausted in order to supply their insatiable sensual desires.[6]

There can be little doubt that this anarchist declaration was a culmination of the line of thinking implicit in the words of the old man from Han-yin.[7] Later, Pao Ching-yen further developed the anarchist theme by undermining the traditional theoretical foundations of political order. He was the first thinker openly to challenge the myth of the Mandate of Heaven. Political order was not imposed on man by heaven. Rather, it arose from the simple fact that "the strong suppressed the weak until the weak submitted to them; the clever outsmarted the stupid until the stupid served them." Following the ideas of early Taoists, especially Chuang Tzu, he described the joys of the state of nature as follows:

In remote antiquity, rulers and sujects did not exist. Wells were dug for drinking, and fields tilled for food. At sunrise, the people went out to work; at sunset they came home to rest. Movement was free and without restriction, and desires did not go unfulfilled. Competition and planning were unknown, as were honor and disgrace.[8]

Here Pao Ching-yen clearly placed freedom of the individual above social order.

From the second century to the fourth, it may be noted, this type of anarchistic thought gained currency in China. In the *Lieh Tzu* there is a utopian country called "Utmost North," where "old and young live as equals, and no one is ruler or subject."[9] The most celebrated utopia in Chinese literature, T'ao Ch'ien's (372-427) Peach-Blossom Fountain, is also a community characterized by the absence of the ruler-subject relationship, as was rightly observed by Wang An-shih (1021-1086) long ago.[10] It was on account of this authority crisis that conservatives like Kuo Hsiang (d. 312), Ko Hung (253?-333?) and Yüan Hung (328-376) found it necessary to come to the defense of political order. In their view, a community without a ruler would inevitably end in either chaos or disintegration.[11] The fact of the defence itself testifies to the great popularity, hence the great danger, of anarchist ideas in this period.[12]

On the other hand, universal kingship was experiencing a crisis not only as an idea but also as an institution. The reference to the Han emperor as "your ruler" by the old man from Han-yin suggests that in his view no ruler-subject relationship ever existed between the emperor and himself. That such a view gained considerable currency in China at the end of the Han should occasion no surprise. For by the second century A.D., the ruler-subject bond had acquired, in actual practice, a particularized, personal character. To illustrate this point, let me proffer one interesting example. In A.D. 199 Liu Piao, the overlord of Ching-chou, decided to send a local assistant named Han Sung to the imperial court as his personal envoy. But Han said to Liu:

When one commits oneself to a ruler-subject relationship, one is bound by it till death. Since I have pledged my allegiance to you, I place myself completely in your service even at the risk of my life.... Now Your Excellency sends me to the capital. Should it so happen that the Emperor offers me a position which I cannot decline, then I would become His Majesty's subject and Your Excellency's former subordinate. As a man owes his primary loyalty to the ruler he is currently serving, I am afraid that my duty would then require me to obey His Majesty's orders. Therefore I would no longer be able to devote my life to Your Excellency.[13]

Han Sung's words show clearly that by the end of the Han a man did not take the emperor as his ruler until he actually accepted the latter's official appointment. Thus, the ruler-subject relationship in second-century China, like the feudal lord-serf bond in medieval Germanic culture, became essentially personal in nature.[14] At any given time, a man had only one particular ruler to serve; and it made no difference whether the ruler was an emperor or a local lord. This new development is further illustrated by the following, widely circulated saying of the time: "When a family has served a lord for two generations, they regard him as their master (*chu*), and for three generations they regard him as their ruler (*chün*)."[15] All of these examples point to the conclusion that the emperor had ceased to be perceived as a universal king.

An equally profound crisis was also taking place in familial relationships. First of all, the idea of *hsiao*, or filial piety, being interpreted in purely biological terms was seriously questioned by late Han scholars. Taking up an argument first formulated by the critical thinker Wang Ch'ung (A.D. 27-ca. 100), K'ung Jung (A.D. 153-208), a descendant of Confucius, reportedly made the following startling remarks about the parent-child relationship:

> Why should there exist a special kind of affinity between father and son? Originally the father merely intended to satisfy his desire. What exactly is the relationship between mother and son? A son in his mother's womb is no different from a thing in a bottle. Once the thing comes out of the bottle, the two become separate and no longer related.[16]

Later, when Juan Chi was told that a man had murdered his mother, he immediately remarked, "It is conceivable if someone kills his father, but this man has indeed gone too far as to kill his mother!"[17] Such radical ideas may well have reflected, to a considerable extent, a real crisis in the father-son relationship. At any rate, it had become proverbial by the end of the Han that "those who have been recommended to office on the merit of filial piety often turn out to live separately from their fathers."[18]

There were signs that the husband-wife relationship was also undergoing a fundamental change during the Wei-Chin period. To begin with, it is important to point out that, like the idea of filial piety, the traditional view that *te*, or virtue, was the most essential quality of women also became subject to dispute. Hsün Tsan, who lived in the first quarter of the third century, startled his contemporaries with the unorthodox view that "a woman's virtue is not worth praising; her beauty should be considered the most important thing."[19] As a matter of fact, elite women during this period generally disregarded the Confucian rules of propriety. Instead of devoting themselves exclusively to household work, they now became actively involved in society. For instance, in about 194, when Hsia-hou Tun, governor of Ch'en-liu, gave an official banquet in honor of his newly appointed subordinate, Wei Chen, the invitation also included Wei's wife. Wei, however, being a conservative, criticized the practice as "a custom of the age of decadence which does not agree with the established ritual (*li^b*)."[20] But this "custom" persisted and spread over the next two centuries. Writing in the early years of the fourth century, Ko Hung complained that women of his day no longer attended to their household duties. Instead, they were busy taking part in all kinds of social gatherings, especially informal, mixed parties at which they enjoyed conversation, drinking, and music in the company of men. Moreover, it even became fashionable among friends to greet the host's wife in the inner chamber (*ju-shih shih ch'i*).[21] The new life-style of elite women of the period is best described in the official history of the Chin dynasty:

> With their make-up and hair-dress and clothing finery, they depend entirely on maids and servants to do for them; they know nothing of women's work in the tasks of silk and linen making, nor of the household work of preparing foods and wines. They marry prematurely; they act just as they feel. Consequently they admit no shame for licentious transgressions, and have no compunctions about displaying faults of jealousy. Their fathers and old brothers do not reproach them, nor does the world condemn them.[22]

The Discovery of the Individual

The foregoing discussion of the political and social crisis provides us with the historical background against which the rise of individualism during the Wei-Chin period may be evaluated. In his well-known study of the development of the individual in Renaissance Italy, Jacob Burckhardt points out that in the Middle Ages, "man was conscious of himself only as a member of race, people, party, family, or corporation—only through some general category." It was in Renaissance Italy that man first "became a spiritual *individual*, and recognized himself as such."[23] Almost the same can be said of the spiritual transition from Han collectivism to Wei-Chin individualism, for the breakdown of Confucian ritualism at the end of the Han was also closely linked to the self-discovery of the individual.

In the first place, it is significant to note that the classical Taoist idea about the importance of individual life was rediscovered in the second century. The great Confucian scholar Ma Jung (79-166), in a critical and decisive moment of his life, said to a friend with a sigh: "The individual life of man is indeed more cherishable than the entire world. It is not in accord with the teaching of Lao Tzu and Chuang Tzu to risk my priceless life on account of a negligible moral point."[24] It was no accident that he became one of the earliest commentators of the *Lao Tzu* and the *Huai-nan Tzu*, thus anticipating Wang Pi (226-249) by a century.

The search for the authentic self gradually led to the emergence of a type of personality which, to borrow Burckhardt's phrase, neither knew "of false modesty or of hypocrisy," nor was afraid of singularity, of being unlike others. For instance, Tai Liang (late second century) was once asked by a friend: "Who in the contemporary world, in your own view, would be your peer?" Tai replied: "I compare myself to Confucius from Eastern Lu and the Great Yü from Western Ch'iang. I stand alone in the world, and none is qualified to be my peer."[25] Mi Heng praised K'ung Jung as "Confucius not dead" and K'ung Jung returned the compliment by calling Mi Heng "Yen Hui back to life." Neither felt the need to feign modesty.[26] By the end of the Han dynasty, singularity (i^a) had become a positive value. A personality would be favorably judged precisely because it was singular, different, or extraordinary.[27] On the other hand, the idea of identity, or sameness (t'ung), was held in contempt. In a famous essay on "Harmony and Identity," (Pien ho t'ung lun) Liu Liang (d. ca. 180) even formulated a radical thesis saying that "all faults arise from identity."[28]

The development during this period of the art of characterology also attests to the growth of individualism. "Characterology" refers to the technique of analyzing, evaluating, and judging the character and ability of an individual—a practice that had originated in the Han local recommendation system. The judgment thus passed on a person by his own community served as a basis for deciding whether he would qualify for recommendation to office. One basic assumption of this type of characterology was that personal character and ability differ from individual to individual. By the late second century, the art of characterology had acquired, so to speak, a separate life of its own, though it continued to serve the purpose of the recommendation system during the Wei-Chin period. At the end of the Han there appeared a number of characterologists whose profound insight and sound judgment made them legends in their own time. Among them were Kuo T'ai (better known as Ling-tsung, 128-169) and Hsü Shao (ca. 153-198), who distinguished themselves by characterizations which were always terse and to the point. It is particularly important to point out that in making characterizations their approach was not only physiognomical but psychological as well, with the purpose of capturing the spirit (shen) of the individual. This point is fully borne out in Liu Shao's (early third century) Jen-wu chih [Treatise on personalities], the only characterological work that has survived from this period. Liu's treatise begins with an analysis of man's feelings (ch'ing^a) and his nature (hsing), which are, in his view, the basis of personality. With regard to physiognomical observations, the emphasis is placed on going beyond the physical appearance of a person to reach his spirit. In order to do this the entire observational process must end in the study of the eyes, which alone convey the spirit of a person. In Liu Shao's own words, "Every person has a body; every body possesses a spirit. Our study of a person will be exhaustive only when we are able to understand his spirit."[29] Needless to say, characterology must have contributed immensely to the growth of self-awareness of the individual during and after the last decades of Han China.

Closely related to the art of characterology was the development of portraiture, another unmistakable sign of the rise of individualism. The discovery of the individual in the West since the later Middle Ages is evidenced by the emergence of a new type of portraiture which depicted "a concrete image and a human personality in all its individuality."[30] A similar change also took place in Wei-Chin China. Figure painting, to be sure, was no invention of this period; it existed long before the Han dynasty. However, judging from the Han products brought to light by modern archaeology, these are, by and large, portraits of worthies which were intended to be morally inspiring. As the poet Ts'ao Chih (192-232) put it, "When one sees pictures of the Three Kings and Five Emperors, one cannot help assuming an attitude of respect and veneration.... By this we realize that painting serves as a moral guide."[31] This didactic tradition in portraiture, it must be emphasized, did not totally disappear with the end of the Han. Nevertheless, a new, individualistic type of figure painting clearly made its debut during the Wei-Chin transition. Under the influence of characterology, the artist set out to capture the spiritual individuality of the human person. How to "convey the spirit" (*ch'uan-shen*) became the central problem of portraiture, and the artistic representation of the eyes was once again at the heart of this endeavor. The famous story about Ku K'ai-chih, the great fourth-century master of portraiture, will serve to illustrate this point.

> Ku K'ai-chih would paint a portrait and sometimes not dot the pupils of the eyes for several years. When someone asked his reason, Ku replied, "The beauty or ugliness of the four limbs basically bears no relation to the most subtle part of a painting. What conveys the spirit and portrays the likeness lies precisely in these dots."[32]

Thus, in representing a human personality in all its individuality, it was on the spiritual uniqueness, rather than on the physical likeness, of his subject that the Wei-Chin artist chose to focus.[33] In the West, individual self-discovery was often accompanied by a proliferation of personal verse, especially lyric poetry, through which the emotions of the individual sought expression. Historical examples of this correlation may be found in early Greece and the later Middle Ages as well as in Renaissance Italy.[34] Interestingly enough, the time of the Han-Wei transition also witnessed the emergence of poetic individuality in China. This was the age in which Chinese poets were mainly concerned with expressing their personal feelings in the face of life's joys and sorrows. For example, the "Nineteen Old Poems" (Ku-shih shih-chiu shou) generally considered products of the Latter Han period, show in a highly personal way their authors' inner experiences with the fleetingness of life, the sadness of parting, the emptiness of fame, etc.[35] Starting in the Chien-an period (196-219) with the appearance of Ts'ao Ts'ao and his two sons (Ts'ao P'i and Ts'ao Chih) on the historical scene, a new chapter in Chinese literature was clearly inaugurated. Han rhyme-prose (*fu*), which was predominantly political in character, lost much of its original vitality and importance. Pentameter verse of a personal and lyrical variety, in the tradition of the "Nineteen Old Poems," now became the main vehicle of literary art,[36] owing to a large extent to the influence of the new poetry of the three Ts'aos. Even Ts'ao Ts'ao in his poetic moments was not totally free from a smack of pessimism and individualism.[37]

But, perhaps, it is in Juan Chi's eighty-two "Poems of My Heart" (Yung-huai shih) that we meet Chinese lyric in its full maturity. Striving to express thoughts and sentiments from the innermost reaches of his heart, he was not only personal but also, at times, autobiographical.[38] This was also true of many other poets of his time. Hsi K'ang's "Dark Indignations" (Yu-fen), and "Stating My Aspirations" (Shu-chih), as well as several of his poems to friends, are all classic examples. Both self-discovery and self-revelation figured centrally in Wei-Chin individualism.

Before moving on to the realm of philosophical thought, I wish to examine briefly some of the new expressions in interpersonal relations. A digression in this direction is valuable because, as modern studies have amply shown, the Wei-Chin period is characterized in particular by the interesting fact that ideas and social realities were closely interlocked.[39]

Side by side with the breakdown of the Confucian social order during the last years of the Han a new type of personal relationship began to take shape. According to Ko Hung's observation, personal relationships toward the end of the Han were characterized by "closeness" (ch'in-mi) or "intimacy" (ch'in chih). In a gathering of friends, Ko Hung tells us,

> people no longer bother to exchange greetings when they see each other. A guest may come to the house and hail the servants; a host may look at the guest while calling the dog. If someone does not act in the same way, he would be considered as having failed to establish intimacy with others. As a result he would be rejected by his own circle.[40]

Close personal relationships also developed in the literary circles. Warm feelings among friends were generally expressed through two vehicles: the verse and the letter. The letter as a means of sharing one's innermost thoughts and emotions was practically unknown in ancient times. As far as can evidentially be determined the purely personal type of letter first appeared in the Chien-an period. Particularly representative, according to Professor Ch'ien Mu, are some of the letters of Ts'ao P'i and Ts'ao Chih.[41] Since the letter provided the individual with an important emotional outlet, both receiving a letter from and writing one to a personal friend were a major source of joy. Thus, in his "Letter in Reply to Fan Ch'in," (Ta Fan Ch'in shu) Ts'ao P'i says, "It gives me so much delight and laughter reading your letter that I can hardly control myself."[42] Ts'ao Chih's letter to his best friend Ting I (whose courtesy name is Ching-li) articulates a similar sentiment: "As I am writing this letter to you in a great mood, I hold my brush with delight. Expressing words from my heart amidst laughter is indeed the extreme of joy."[43]

Personal correspondence brought two friends close by making them completely open with each other. It contrasts sharply with the type of correspondence we find in the earlier periods, which is almost invariably formal, impersonal, and business-oriented. Exactly the same thing can be said of the exchange of poems between friends. Moreover, it is significant to note that, according to the Wen-hsüan (chuan 24-26), poetic exchange (tseng-ta) was a completely new device in Chinese culture, first introduced in the Chien-an era. It was therefore another form in which individual self-awareness manifested itself.

The same sort of intimacy also characterized familial relationships. The following story from the *Shih-shuo hsin-yü* is a vivid expression of the emergence of a new type of husband-wife relationship:

> Wang Jung's (234-305) wife always addressed Jung with the familiar pronoun "you" [*ch'ing*[b]]. Jung said to her, "For a wife to address her husband as 'you' is disrespectful according to the rules of etiquette. Hereafter don't call me that again." His wife replied, "But I'm intimate with you and I love you, so I address you as 'you.' If I didn't address you as 'you,' who else would address you as 'you'?" After that he always tolerated it.[44]

For the English reader, it is perhaps necessary to point out that every "you" in this translated passage is *ch'ing*[b] in the original Chinese text. It may further be noted that usage of the word *ch'ing*[b] as an intimate pronoun was common only during the Wei-Chin period of Chinese history.[45]

Another family bond, the father-son relationship, also took a decidedly new turn at this time. Hu-mu Fu-chih (ca. 264-ca. 312), a second-generation leader of Neo-Taoist conversationalists, was particularly noted for his excessive love of "freedom" (*ta*). But in this respect he was surpassed by his son, Ch'ien-chih, who even went so far as to call him by his first name. While this practice shocked many contemporaries, the father himself took the matter in stride.[46]

The two examples cited above must not be taken as isolated and exceptional cases. On the contrary, they clearly indicate that a profound change in interpersonal relations had taken place in some quarters of the elite society during this period. Toward the end of the third century, Shu Hsi, in a remarkable piece of literary imagination, revealed vividly his unique vision of paradise on earth. Surprisingly, he described his utopia as a place where "all the wives address their husbands as 'you' [*ch'ing*[b]]; all the sons call their fathers by first names."[47] This is proof that intimacy as a guiding principle in family life was becoming widespread. While intimacy may not have been a condition of the development of individualism in the West, in the case of Wei-Chin China it clearly helped to set the individual free from the various collectivist bonds that had evolved through the centuries of the Han dynasty.

The Transition from Confucianism to Neo-Taoism

Having traced the emergence of individualistic expression in interpersonal relations of the period, we must now proceed to examine the problem of individualism in the realm of thought. In this section I shall try to show that, apart from the generally accepted political interpretation, the transition from Confucianism to Neo-Taoism in the Wei-Chin period may be more sensibly viewed as an outgrowth of the discovery of the individual. Moreover, the evidence indicates that the type of philosophic discourse which was to dominate the Neo-Taoist movement from the middle of the third century on had already begun well before the end of the Han.

As is generally acknowledged, Chinese philosophical thought in the third century underwent a radical transformation. Traditionally, this transformation has been characterized as a transition from Confucian classical scholarship (*ching-hsüeh*) to Neo-Taoist metaphysics (*hsüan-hsüeh*). This is undoubtedly an accurate description. However, the question we must ask is whether this philosophical shift was linked to the rise of individualism and, if so, in what sense and to what extent? The commonly accepted view with regard to the transition has focused predominantly on political events. According to this view, repeated persecutions of critical and dissident intellectuals by the eunuchs of the imperial court following the two great *tang-ku* purges in 166 and 169 gradually transformed the former from political activists to intellectual escapists. After the end of the Han, such persecution intensified under the repressive Legalist politics of the (Ts'ao) Wei dynasty. For many members of the elite, survival demanded a turn away from their Confucian commitments to social and political order; refuge was found in the metaphysical speculation of Lao Tzu and Chuang Tzu which had no immediate bearing on the worldly affairs of their time. As a result, the political discourse of "Pure Criticism" (*ch'ing-i*) in the second century gave way to the philosophical discourse of "Pure Conversation" (*ch'ing-tan*) in the third. The intellectual transition from Confucian classical scholarship to Neo-Taoist metaphysics was thereby realized.[48]

While much of this well-established view is indeed accurate, it nevertheless fails to take sufficient account of the positive contributions of the Han-Wei intellectuals toward the rise and growth of the movement. It is not entirely true that the intellectuals of the period were coerced into Neo-Taoism by political circumstances; many actually chose to develop this new mode of discourse as a natural outgrowth of their recent self-discovery as individuals. This contention is supported not only by the fact that "conversation" evolved as a way of life for the Han-Wei intellectuals, but also by the central philosophic issues which were to be crystallized later in Neo-Taoism (see below).

To begin with, it may be pointed out that the historical relationship between Pure Criticism and Pure Conversation in the traditional view appears to have been somewhat misrepresented. Like the verse and the letter, conversation acquired new importance in the middle of the second century as a medium through which ideas were exchanged between intellectuals. It was not the case, as has often been assumed, that conversation at this time focused only on political and characterological criticisms and then, as a result of the persecution of its practitioners, shifted to philosophical discussion in the third century. On the contrary, the evidence clearly indicates that both elements were already present in late Han conversations. As Wang Fu (90?-165?) complained, "Scholars nowadays like to talk about matters concerning vacuity and nonbeing [*hsü-wu*]."[49] So, by the middle of the second century at the latest, it had already become an established practice for intellectuals to discuss Taoist philosophical topics in their daily conversations. In A.D. 159, Chou Hsieh, who had from youth admired Lao Tzu's teachings of "mystery and vacuity" (*hsüan-hsü*), earned a great reputation for his generous hospitality. He always invited friends to his home and enjoyed conversations and other entertainments with them.[50] This early case clearly shows how reorientation in thought (i.e., the shift from Confucian learning to Taoist philosophy) and conversation as an art had combined to form an important part of the elite's new life-style.

The phenomenal growth of the student body in the Imperial Academy (T'ai-hsüeh) in the middle of the second century also contributed to the rise of this new mode of intellectual discourse. After A.D. 146, as the *Hou-Han shu* succinctly summarizes it, "students in the Academy steadily increased to over 30,000. However, they gradually turned away from textual analysis [*chang-chü*, lit., "sentences"] of the Classics and came to venerate what was frivolous and ornate (*fou-hua*); the Confucian mode of learning was thus on the wane."[51] It is probably inappropriate to identify the "frivolous and ornate" type of intellectual pursuit with "pure conversation," which was to be referred to pejoratively as "frivolous and vacuous" (*fou-hsü*) in the third century. Nevertheless, there are sure indications that it may well have been a prototype of the latter. For instance, when Fu Jung came to study at the Imperial Academy in 168, his intellectual brilliance immediately drew the attention of Li Ying, a leader among the officials. Each time Fu Jung came to call, Li Ying listened to his talk with such intense interest that he sent other guests away in order to avoid distractions. The conversation between Li and Fu always ended with the former holding the latter's hands and sighing with admiration. It is particularly significant that Fu Jung's style of conversation is vividly depicted as follows: "Wearing a kerchief and swinging his sleeves, his words gushed forth like clouds."[52] As is immediately apparent, this is a typical description of Pure Conversation as we encounter it in later literature, except that from the late third century on the "fly-whisk" (*chu-wei*) was to replace the "sleeves" as an inseparable accoutrement of the conversationalist.[53] Fu Jung's conversation was extremely influential in the Imperial Academy. His dormitory room was always swarming with visitors. Very much annoyed, a neighbor once chided him thus: "Is it the intention of the Son of Heaven to found this Imperial Academy just for people to engage in conversations?"[54] It is difficult to imagine that all these spirited conversations were devoted exclusively to discussions on politics and personalities (*ch'ing-i*) and had nothing to do with the fermentation of new thought (*ch'ing-t'an*) which was underway at the time.

In fact, philosophic reasoning was part and parcel of late Han conversation. The case of a young poet named Li Yen (150-177) may be taken as an illustration. He is described as a person who was, among other things, sharp in language and skilled in enunciating principles (*li*[a]).[55] Here the association of speech with enunciation of principles is particularly noteworthy. As far as we know, this small but solid piece of evidence provides the earliest historical link between the art of conversation and the emergence of a new mode of thinking in late Han times. It antedates by a century the kind of analysis of "names and principles" (*ming-li*) that was central to the Wei-Chin pure conversation.[56]

Historically, the relationship between the art of speech and philosophic reasoning was a symbiotic one; both owed their development to the practice of late Han characterology. According to Liu Shao, two important ways of evaluating the native intelligence of an individual are to "observe his speech" and "examine his argument." "Speech" reveals the quality of a man's training in language and "argument" that of his reasoning power.[57] Moreover, Liu Shao also relates both speech and reasoning to analysis of "principles" (*li*ᵃ). He distinguishes four categories of "principles": cosmological principles (*tao-li*), principles of social institutions (*shih-li*), moral principles (*i-li*), and principles of human feelings (*ch'ing-li*). In his view, the main obstacle to a reasonable settlement in intellectual discussions often arises from the confusion of categories of principles on the part of the discussants. Once this obstacle is removed, however, it is possible to determine which side is truly convincing on the linguistic level (*tz'u-sheng*) as well as on the philosophical level (*li-sheng*).[58] Since Liu Shao's work is generally thought of as a synthesis of the characterological principles that evolved from the middle of the second century, the influence of Liu's discussions in the *Jen-wu chih* on the origins of the Pure Conversation movement must be taken seriously. They show clearly how late Han conversation had in practice been pushed, step by step, into the realm of thought by its own inner logic. It is important to point out that Wei-Chin Pure Conversationalists basically discussed philosophical topics in terms of Liu Shao's categories of "principles." Moreover, the two terms *tz'u-sheng* (lit., "superior in linguistic skill") and *li-sheng* (lit., "superior in philosophical reasoning") are also highly illuminating. They indicate unmistakably that a major technical feature of later Pure Conversation had already been developed in late Han intellectual discussions, namely, a "reasonable settlement" had to be reached in a conversation so as to decide which of the participants was "superior" in language and reasoning. Actually, from the fourth century on, Pure Conversation became a standard intellectual game (like *wei-ch'i*, Chinese chess) played by two or more participants. More often than not, someone would in the end emerge triumphant—either linguistically or logically or both. The transition from Confucian classical learning to Taoist metaphysics may well have been precipitated by political events. But a purely political interpretation of an intellectual movement of this magnitude can hardly stand up to close scrutiny.

By the last two decades of the second century, it was becoming quite clear that Han conversationalists were already intensely absorbed in philosophical discussions. The sudden surge of interest in Wang Ch'ung's *Critical Essays* (Lun-heng) attests to this profound change of intellectual atmosphere. The *Critical Essays* owed its great popularity during this period primarily to the efforts of two leading scholars. The first one is Ts'ai Yung (132-192), who discovered the work sometime between 179 and 189 while residing in Kuei-chi (in modern Chekiang), the home town of Wang Ch'ung. Ts'ai so cherished the work that he always kept it to himself as an "aid to conversation" (*t'an-chu*). The second one is Wang Lang (d. 228), who obtained a copy of the *Essays* when he was serving as prefect of Kuei-chi from 193 to 196. After his return to the north, as the story goes, his marked improvement in intellectual powers took all his old friends by surprise. When they pressed him for an explanation, he confessed that he had been greatly benefited by the *Critical Essays*.[59] The accuracy of these perhaps somewhat dramatized accounts is corroborated by other evidence. Earlier in this study, we quoted a startling statement of K'ung Jung's questioning the Confucian idea of filial piety—a statement based entirely on Wang Ch'ung's argument. In view of the intimate friendship between K'ung Jung and Ts'ai Yung, it is almost certain that the former must have owed his discovery of the *Critical Essays* to the latter.[60] Wang Lang's discovery of the same work also contributed indirectly to the rise of Pure Conversation of Wang Pi and Ho Yen. Wang Lang's son Wang Su (d. 256), a leading classical scholar of the period, played a crucial role in turning the study of the *I-ching* [Book of changes] in a new direction. He brought a newly developed cosmological framework to bear on the interpretation of that unique Confucian classic (which was destined to form, along with the *Lao Tzu* and the *Chuang Tzu*, the "three metaphysical works" (*san-hsüan*) of the Wei-Chin era). Wang Su's interpretation was largely followed by Wang Pi in the latter's commentary to the *Book of Changes*.[61] Thus, it is clear that Wang Ch'ung's merciless dissection of Confucian values, his pointed rejection of the teleological view of the cosmos, and, above all, his emphasis on the Taoist idea of "naturalness" (*tzu-jan*) were already dominant themes of late Han intellectual discourse. Through conversationalists like Ts'ai Yung, K'ung Jung and Wang Lang, the *Critical Essays* exerted a shaping influence on the philosophical development of Pure Conversation. The simple fact that Ts'ai Yung used the *Critical Essays* as an "aid to conversation" proves that conversations among intellectuals had assumed a philosophic tone even before the end of the second century.[62]

This active and enduring interest in the exploration of the world of ideas suggests that there was indeed something profound in the consciousness of the conversationalists that sustained it. From the point of view of this study, I am inclined to think that this striking historical phenomenon can be most sensibly explained in terms of the rising individualism of the period. Through the process of self-discovery, the spiritually liberated individual embarked on a search for a new world order in which he might feel completely at home. As clearly shown in Liu Shao's four categories of "principles" listed above, the individual was seeking to redefine the relationship of the ego to the cosmos, to the state, to the moral order, and to other individuals. Enunciation of "principles" (*li*) of these categories, as we shall see, figured centrally in the philosophic discourse throughout the period. This was the case because the liberated individual refused to settle for anything less than a total understanding of these relationships. Obviously, such principles could nowhere be found in Confucian classical scholarship as it was received in the second and third centuries; it had by then degenerated into meaningless fragments of textual analysis. On the other hand, Taoism, with its ontological concept of "nonbeing" (*wu*), its cosmological views of "nonaction" (*wu-wei*) and "naturalness" (or "spontaneity," *tzu-jan*), its political and social ideal of "nongoverning"(*wu-chih*), and, most importantly, its general emphasis on the freedom of the individual, provided the Wei-Chin individualist with precisely the right kind of spiritual resources. This point will become clear as we identify the central issues in Neo-Taoist philosophy.

Individualism in Pure Conversation

Needless to say, this is not the place to discuss Neo-Taoism in all its diversity and complexity. What follows will simply try to show, through a brief analysis of three pairs of key concepts in Pure Conversation, that there was a close connection between the discovery of the individual on the one hand and the Neo-Taoist mode of thinking on the other. These three pairs are, respectively, "non-being" (*wu*) and "being" (*yu*), "naturalness" or "spontaneity" (*tzu-jan*) and the "teaching of names" (*ming-chiao*), and "feelings" (*ch'ing*[a]) and "rituals" (*li*[b]). I understand all three pairs as having primarily to do with the problem of the individual vis-à-vis order, but at different levels. Structurally, all three pairs share a similar internal relationship. Just as the origin of being is based on nonbeing, that of the "teaching of names" is based on "naturalness" and that of "rituals" on "feelings." In other words, in the Neo-Taoist view, nonbeing, naturalness, and feelings are taken to be ultimate and primary whereas being, the "teaching of names," and rituals are derivative and secondary. In terms of schools of thought, the first triad has traditionally been identified with Neo-Taoism and the second with Confucianism. In the present context, however, it may be more fruitful to associate nonbeing, naturalness, and feelings with the problem of the individual, and being, the "teaching names," and rituals with that of order. I am fully aware that in historical inquiry such neat dichotomies can be made only at the risk of oversimplification. Nevertheless, in this case, the risk is a calculated one.

Let us first look at the Neo-Taoist cosmology. According to the *Chin-shu*,

> During the Cheng-shih reign [240-248] of the Wei dynasty, Ho Yen, Wang Pi, and others followed the teachings of Lao Tzu and Chuang Tzu. They established the theory that heaven, earth, and all the myriad things have the basis of their existence in nonbeing. That which is called nonbeing is the beginning of things and the completion of affairs: it exists everywhere. It is by virtue of nonbeing that the yin and the yang transform into life, all the myriad things take their forms, the worthy establishes his moral worth, and the unworthy [i.e., the common man] keeps his person from being injured.[63]

This central thesis is well explained by Kung-chuan Hsiao,

> Ho Yen's statement "Heaven, earth, and all the myriad things have the basis of their existence in nonbeing," is adequate to sum up the cosmology of the Wei-Chin Taoist school. That is, *wu* or "nonbeing" is the ontological reality of the cosmos. In the "beginning of things and the completion of affairs" it is *yu* or "being" that is produced by it. Nonbeing produces [generates], and is being; that concept is not necessarily in conflict with that of *Tao*. ... "Hsiahou Hsüan [209-245] said: heaven and earth spontaneously move in their cycles; the Sage spontaneously functions. By spontaneity is meant the *Tao*."

To speak in terms of heaven's and earth's and the myriad things' spontaneous cycles of movement and of production, heaven and earth do not purposely produce the myriad things, nor do the myriad things know for what they are produced. Heaven and earth [according to Wang Pi], "take no purposive action with respect to the myriad things, and each of the myriad things adapts to its own functioning."[64]

We can easily see, from the views of Ho Yen, Wang Pi, and Hsia-hou Hsüan quoted above, that the Wei-Chin Taoists defined the relationship of the individual to the cosmic order in a totally new way. As we know, cosmology during the Han period had been both teleologically and hierarchically oriented. Under the Han cosmological system, heaven not only produces all things, including man, with predetermined purposes, but also imposes a hierarchical order on them. Thus, on the one hand, Tung Chung-shu states, "Heaven and earth produce the myriad things for the purpose of nourishing man."[65] On the other hand, he says that heaven is the "great-grandfather" of the common man; that the common man has access to heaven only through the intermediary of the emperor, that is, the Son of Heaven.[66] Now, in Neo-Taoist cosmology, teleology is wholly rejected owing, at least partly, to the influence of Wang Ch'ung.[67] Heaven and earth no longer produce things. On the contrary, like all the myriad things, they are also produced by nonbeing, the ontological reality of the cosmos. Consequently, the concept of Tao also underwent a fundamental change. It was identified, not with what Tung Chung-shu called "the Way of Heaven," but with the ontological creativity of nonbeing which functions spontaneously. In other words, *wu, tzu-jan,* and Tao all became synonymous. From the point of view of the individual, this new conception of the cosmos assures the ego of its inner freedom. For, in the realm of being, every individual thing comes into being by itself, moves in its natural course, and "adapts to its own functioning." Things are not produced by a higher creator with a predetermined purpose. As Kuo Hsiang says, "Throughout the realm of things, there is nothing... which is not 'self-transformed.' Hence the creating of things has no Lord; everything produces itself and does not depend on anything else. This is the normal way of the universe."[68] Indeed, this is a remarkable statement concerning the self-development and self-sufficiency of the individual made on a cosmic scale.

Neo-Taoist cosmology also throws light on the problem of order. The hierarchical conception of Tao in the Han period was considerably modified. Since, as we have seen, Tao is redefined as nonbeing and spontaneity in Neo-Taoist thought, neither the Son of Heaven nor the sage is in a position to claim a monopoly on it. Every individual thing in the world, high or low, great or small, worthy or unworthy, is immediate to Tao because nonbeing is the basis of existence for all things. This does not mean, however, that Neo-Taoists did away with the idea of order completely in their cosmos. Order does exist, but it exists only in the realm of being and is therefore secondary. Moreover, it is present in a way that fully accords with the principle of naturalness. On this point, again, Kuo Hsiang is our reliable guide: "For the one whom the age takes to be worthy becomes the ruler, while those whose talents do not correspond to the demands of the age become servitors. It is analogous to the heavens' being naturally high and earth naturally low, the head being naturally on top and the feet occupying naturally the inferior position."[69] It must be noted that Kuo Hsiang's emphasis here is placed unequivocally on the naturalness of order. However, as a Neo-Taoist thinker his ultimate concern was not with order but with the individual. Thus, in the very beginning of his commentary to the *Chuang Tzu*, he writes,

> Although the great is different from the small, yet if they all indulge themselves in the realm of self-fulfillment, then all things are following their own nature and doing according to their own capacity; all are what they ought to be and equally happy. There is no room for the distinction of superior and inferior.[70]

Clearly, it was this Neo-Taoist vision of the freedom of the individual that necessitated the emergence of a new cosmological system in which all beings must be self-determining as well as self-fulfilling.

Of the three paired concepts of opposites, *tzu-jan* (naturalness) and *ming-chiao* (the teaching of names) have been the most extensively discussed in modern historical scholarship. There is therefore no need to go into all the ramifications of this pair in the present essay. This pair shall be examined only insofar as it sheds light on the problem of the individual vis-à-vis order. In a broad sense, the scope of this pair overlaps with that of nonbeing and being on the one hand and that of feelings and ritual on the other. In a narrower sense, however, it deals primarily with the relationship of the individual to political order, i.e., the state. By and large, modern historians have tended to emphasize the political implications of the controversy over naturalness and the teaching of names. For the sake of clarity, I shall use this paired concept in its narrow sense.

In his commentary on the sentence "When there first were institutions and regulations, there were names," Wang Pi says "When the uncarved block was dispersed . . . there were officials and rulers. When institutions and regulations, officials and rulers are initiated, it is impossible not to establish names and statutes by which to determine superior and inferior; therefore when first there are institutions and regulations, there will be names."[71] This is Wang Pi's understanding of the origins of political order. Here, the "uncarved block" (*p'u*), a term used in the Lao Tzu, is a symbol of the primordial naturalness. Like nonbeing, from which being arises, naturalness provides political order with its existential basis. As Ch'en Yin-k'o rightly points out, the term "names" in this passage is identifiable with that in the teaching of names.[72] If the teaching of names, i.e., political order, originates in naturalness, it then follows that, ideally, it must model itself on the way naturalness operates, which is through "nonaction" (*wu-wei*). Nonaction, however, does not imply a total absence of political order.[73] As a matter of fact, the notion of the necessity of political order was, on the whole, not seriously disputed by leading Neo-Taoist thinkers of the period, with the possible exception of Juan Chi. Even the radical Hsi K'ang had a very clear idea of what an ideal political order should be. As he described it:

The Sage comes as though inevitably to rule over the empire without intending to do so, hence takes the [mind of] all the myriad things as his own mind. He leaves all the forms of life to themselves, and guides his own person by means of the *Tao*, being therein the same as all the world in gaining his own fulfillment. Effortlessly, he takes the absence of involvement in his work; calmly, he looks upon the empire as a commonality.[74]

Thus, the political order that grows out of primordial naturalness and works through nonaction is a minimal order. In terms of general features, if not of concrete conditions, it is quite reminiscent of the minimal state arising from the state of nature in the Lockean tradition. Hsi K'ang's view may be fruitfully compared to Kuo Hsiang's formulation of the same thesis.

If the realm were to lack an enlightened ruler, then nothing would be able to reach its fulfillment. Such fulfillment as there now is must be accounted the achievement of enlightened rulers. Yet that achievement lies in his nonaction and in turning responsibility back to the world. All the [constituent parts] of the world having obtained autonomy, the consequence is that their [individual fulfillment] does not appear to be the achievement of the enlightened ruler.[75]

Both Hsi K'ang and Kuo Hsiang are talking about the minimal political order of nonaction. However, there appears to be a subtle difference: the former, apparently more concerned with the self-fulfillment of the individual, sees an invisible hand in the order of nonaction; the latter, emphasizing the function of the "enlightened ruler," attributes the order to the work of a hidden hand.[76] But, whether by an invisible hand or a hidden hand, maintaining order is hardly ever the central issue in the Neo-Taoist political philosophy. For Neo-Taoists like Wang Pi, Ho Yen, Hsi K'ang, and Kuo Hsiang, political order was at best a "necessary evil."[77] There can be no doubt that as far as the problem of the individual vis-à-vis order was concerned, their emphasis was always on the former, not the latter. As Kuo Hsiang remarked, "The value of a sage-king does not lie in his ability to govern. It lies in the fact that through nonaction he allows each individual thing to undertake its own action."[78]

According to this view, then, political order can be justified on the sole ground that it makes possible self-fulfillment for each and every individual. In other words, the state exists for the sake of the individual, but not vice versa. The language of Neo-Taoist philosophy also attests overwhelmingly to its individualistic mode of thinking. Terms like self-fulfillment (*tzu-te*), self-containment (*tzu-tsu*), self-transformation (*tzu-hua*), self-control (*tzu-chih*), self-action (*tzu-wei*), self-completion (*tzu-ch'eng*), self-adjustment (*tzu-shih*), self-complacency (*tzu-tsai*), etc., abound in Neo-Taoist texts. If language is a reliable index to thought, then the emergence of these new linguistic expressions clearly indicates the direction in which Chinese intellectual history was moving after the end of the second century.

Finally, we come to the last pair of our concepts of opposites, feelings versus rituals. The bearing of this pair on the problem of the individual vis-à-vis order is self-evident and requires no elaboration. The controversy over feelings and rituals was most immediately relevant to the social reality of the time. As our earlier discussion of the changing interpersonal relationships clearly shows, the free and spontaneous flow of personal feelings between husband and wife or father and son inevitably led to transgressions of the "rules of etiquette" (li^b). This was the most protracted of all controversies during this period; it began in the second century and continued well into the fourth. As a matter of fact, the controversy was even more intense in the fourth century than in the third. Debates about mourning rites, for instance, dominated the intellectual discourse of the Eastern Chin period (317-419).[79] The truth is that while the problem of freedom of the individual versus order had been basically resolved in the political domain with the founding of the Western Chin dynasty, a regime of "nonaction" very much catered to the interests of the elite. No *modus vivendi*, however, was worked out in the social sphere until more than a century later. Ch'en Yin-k'o's famous thesis that by the early fourth century Pure Conversation had evolved into an intellectual game played by the elite with no reference to actualities of life is valid only on the political level.[80] On the social level, especially in family and clan relationships, the problem of feelings versus rituals was still very real.

The relationship of "feelings" and "rituals" was probably first called into question in the late second century in connection with Tai Liang's mourning for his mother. Like Juan Chi a century later, Tai Liang, while observing the mourning period, helped himself to meat and wine and wept only when truly overcome by grief. Someone asked him if he was performing the right kind of rites, to which he replied, "Yes. Rites are to keep feelings from going to excess. If feelings are not excessive, what is the need to talk about rites?"[81] As this case clearly shows, in the initial stages of the controversy, a high tension between "feelings" and "rituals" already existed. The two were not yet, however, diametrically opposed to one another. Unlike Juan Chi's radical anti-ritualism, Tai Liang's rejection of li^b was only partial and conditional.

We have reason to believe that, psychologically, the tension between human emotions and ritual originated in the sudden release of personal feelings or emotions that accompanied the self-discovery of the individual after the late second century. The traditional ritual system apparently lacked sufficient flexibility to respond to the deluge of new feelings being allowed expression.

In the realm of ideas, this tension manifested itself essentially in two ways: a fresh interest in the function of feelings in man and a new emphasis on the importance of the spirit, as opposed to the letter, of rituals. As we know, with regard to the idea of "feelings" in Han thought, Tung Chung-shu's view that human nature is good but human feelings are bad had been accepted as more or less orthodox.[82] It is therefore highly significant that at the end of the Han, Hsün Yüeh (148-209) in his *Shen-chien* quoted with emphatic approval the heterodox view of Liu Hsiang (77-6 B.C.) that "since human nature corresponds to human emotions, the one cannot be all good and the other all bad." As he further remarked, if one asserted that human feelings are all bad, then he would have to say that sages like Yao and Shun had no feelings.[83]

This leads us directly to Wang Pi's influential theory concerning the emotions of the sage.

> Where the sage is vitally superior to other men is in his spirit-like intelligence, but where he is like other men is in having the five emotions. Being superior in his spirit-like intelligence, he is able to identify himself with the harmonious whole, so that he is imbued with nonbeing; but being like others in his five emotions, he cannot but react to things with emotion. The emotions of the sage are such that though he reacts to things, he is not ensnared by them. It is a great error, consequently, to say that because he is not ensnared by things, he therefore has no [emotional] reactions to them.[84]

Two observations may be made about Wang Pi's theory. First, it clearly indicates, in conjunction with Hsün Yüeh's view, that during the first half of the third century new philosophical attention was being paid to the problem of "feelings," though we do not know for sure that Wang Pi had access to Hsün Yüeh's work. Second, the theory admirably serves as a justification of the ever-growing importance of personal feelings in the social life of the day. Evidence shows that by the middle of the fourth century it became one of the most central philosophical topics in Pure Conversation, a testimony to its great popularity.[85]

On the other hand, "rituals" as an idea also received critical reexamination in the hands of philosophers. In his commentary on the phrase "the meaning of rites [li^b]" in the *Chuang Tzu*, for example, Kuo Hsiang (d. 312) had this to say:

> For the person who knows the meaning of the rites must roam beyond the realm so as to keep order in the mundane sphere, must cling to the mother in order to preserve the son, must acknowledge his feelings and straightaway act accordingly. Should he display anxiety about his reputation or be restricted by the formalities, then his filial piety will not be sincere and his compassion will not be genuine. Father and son, elder brother and younger [as formalized relationships, make one] hold feelings that lead to mutual deceptions. How can that be the larger meaning of the rites?[86]

Here Kuo Hsiang charged that the Confucian ritual system of his time was devoid of meaning because it could no longer freely express the true feelings of man. Quite to the contrary, it had been formalized to the point of sheer artificiality.[87] Kuo Hsiang's interpretation of "rituals" and "feelings" as antithetical to each other proves beyond dispute that in the early fourth century the Neo-Taoists were still grappling with the problem of freedom of the individual in the face of a strong and deep-rooted Confucian ritual order.

The Neo-Taoist revolt against the ritual order was more radical, widespread, and profound than its attack on the political order. The reason for this is not difficult to see. The conflict between feelings and rituals arose, after all, from the everyday experiences of the spiritually liberated individual who was caught between the growing need to express freely and openly his personal feelings on the one hand and the inadequacy of the existing ritualistic forms on the other. Naturally, the Neo-Taoist individualist would not hesitate to do away with "rituals" whenever and wherever they proved to be in the way of free emotional expression. Thus, when someone chided Juan Chi for having violated rituals by saying goodbye to his sister-in-law, he replied "Were the rites established for people like me?"[88] In response to a criticism of his excessive grief over the loss of a son, Wang Jung said, "A sage forgets his feelings; the lowest beings aren't even capable of having feelings. But the place where feelings are most concentrated is precisely among people like ourselves."[89] Needless to say, for individualists like Juan Chi and Wang Jung, it was far more meaningful to be true to one's authentic self than to conform to a stereotyped social norm. It was precisely this search for inner authenticity that turned individualists of the period away from Confucian ritualism.

An inside view that links the rise of Neo-Taoism to the self-discovery and self-awareness of the individual has been provided by Hsi K'ang. In a debate on the nature of Confucian learning, he explained why the Six Classics were unacceptable to him:

> The emphasis of the Six Classics is placed mainly on repression whereas human nature experiences joy in the following of desires. Repression goes against a man's inclinations; he attains to naturalness by following his desires. Therefore it follows that attainment of naturalness does not come from the repressive Six Classics and preservation of man's nature does not need a base in rituals and laws which run counter to feelings.[90]

Thus, in the final analysis, it was Hsi Kang's profound resentment of ritualistic repression that led him to reject Confucianism. In a letter to a friend, he further explained how he was drawn to the Taoist view.

> Further, I was long left to my own devices, and my disposition became arrogant and careless, my bluntness diametrically opposed to etiquette; laziness and rudeness reinforcing each other.... Besides, my taste for independence was aggravated by my reading of Chuang Tzu and Lao Tzu; as a result my desire for fame and success grew daily weaker, and my commitment to freedom increasingly firmer.[91]

Here, we are told, it was love of independence and freedom that pushed him to Taoism. These two self-revelatory accounts are complementary, and together they reveal most vividly the inner dimensions of the rise of the Neo-Taoist movement.

In view of the evidence we have examined thus far, the transition from Confucian classical scholarship to Neo-Taoist metaphysics may be more intelligently interpreted as what Michel Foucault calls a "rupture" in Chinese consciousness. It was clearly the case that Neo-Taoist metaphysics was established not in the places formerly occupied by Confucian classical scholarship, but in an area where the latter simply did not exist.[92] Han Confucianism was ultimately concerned with the collective life in an imperial order, and Wei-Chin Neo-Taoism with the problem of freedom of the individual. The transition from one to the other was by no means a smooth one. Viewed from this perspective, it may justifiably be contended that the central historical significance of the development of Pure Conversation lies in the emergence of a totally new mode of discourse—an individualistic mode of discourse which superseded the old, collectivistic one of the Han period.

Reconciliation between Taoist Individualism and Confucian Ritualism

So as not to overstate the case of Wei-Chin individualism, we must, in concluding, say something about the ritualistic side of the coin. Throughout the period under consideration, Confucian ritualism with its marked emphasis on moral order and conformity never ceased to be a social and intellectual force with vigor and vitality. Side by side with the new individualistic type of familial relationships described above, there also existed a sharply contrasting type of family order. The case of Ho Tseng (199-278) may be proffered as an illustrative example. His was probably a family life of the most ritualistic kind. He was not only a well-known filial son of the day but also maintained a highly formalized relationship with his wife throughout his life. In his old age, we are told, he saw his wife only two or three times a year; each time he was formally dressed and treated her in strict accordance with the Confucian etiquette between host and guest.[93] He was clearly following a ritualistic tradition of the Han period which managed the private household in the manner of the "government office."[94] Little wonder that he found Juan Chi's transgression of mourning rites absolutely intolerable and proposed to have him banished "beyond the sea."[95]

Interestingly, there are also indications of a struggle between Confucian ritualism and Neo-Taoist naturalism as two competing ways of life. The following story will help to illuminate this contest.

> Wang Jung and Ho Ch'iao [d. 292] experienced the loss of a parent at the same time, and both were praised for their filial devotion. Wang, reduced to a skeleton, kept to his bed; while, Ho wailing and weeping, performed all the rites. Emperor Wu [r. 265-290], remarked to Liu I, "Have you ever observed Wang Jung and Ho Ch'iao? I hear that Ho's grief and suffering go beyond what is required by propriety, and it makes me worry about him."
>
> Liu I replied, "Ho Ch'iao, even though performing all the rites, has suffered no loss in his spirit or health. Wang Jung, even though not performing the rites, is nonetheless so emaciated with grief that his bones stand out. Your servant is of the opinion that Ho Ch'iao's is the filial devotion of life, while Wang Jung's is the filial devotion of death. Your Majesty should not worry about Ch'iao, but rather about Jung."[96]

In the final analysis, the struggle is clearly reducible to a contest between "rituals" (li^b) and "feelings" ($ch'ing^a$). But the story is unmistakably pro-Taoist in tone. The judgment that Wang Jung surpassed Ho Ch'iao in filial devotion suggests that Neo-Taoist naturalism could beat Confucian ritualism on the latter's own ground. On the other hand, the story also reveals that at the end of the Western Chin, Confucian ritualism, though crippled by a social and spiritual crisis that had lasted for a century, was still very much alive.

The controversy over "feelings" and "rituals" was carried to the south by Western Chin emigrés in the early decades of the fourth century. It took at least another century to bring the debate to a conclusion. The end of the controversy was not as visible and colorful as the beginning had been, but from the historical point of view it was as important.

By the middle of the fourth century, Neo-Taoist naturalism and Confucian ritualism began to show signs of reconciliation. We find, for example, that the idea of "rituals" was no longer being treated with contempt and resentment by the elite. On the contrary, they came to the realization that interpersonal feelings cannot be meaningfully and fully expressed without a sensitive ritual system in the first place. Thus, speaking of both the ruler-subject and the father-son relationships, Yüan Hung (328-376) could now say that their handling required the presence of both "feelings" and "rituals" at the same time.[97] How is such a drastic change in attitude to be accounted for? To answer this question, attention must be drawn to a quiet but enduring movement in ritual reforms traceable to as early as the middle of the third century. It is particularly significant that the emphasis of the reform movement was focused quite specifically on the mourning rites, the very battleground on which, as we have seen, wars had been fought between Confucian ritualists and Neo-Taoist naturalists. The movement was by no means a Confucian monopoly. As a matter of fact, Neo-Taoist participants were just as active in it. Especially with the founding of the refugee regime in the south, the study of the mourning rites gained an unprecedented popularity. Leading specialists in the field included not only Confucianists and Neo-Taoists but Buddhists as well.

Ritual studies during the period are too complicated to be discussed here. For our purposes, however, it will suffice to note that the spirit of the reform movement consisted in the particularization of the rites with a view to satisfying, as much as possible, the individuated feelings of the members of each mourning community.[98] In this way, the reformists claimed that they had completely renovated the ritual system, thereby making it, once again, an effective vehicle for the free expression of personal feelings. Thus, we see that along with the self-discovery and self-awareness of the individual, there was also a genuine search for ritualization throughout the Wei-Chin period. Ironically enough, even Pure Conversation, the very symbol of Wei-Chin individualism, became highly ritualized in the course of its development. To qualify as a Pure Conversationalist, for instance, one had to be trained in the art of speech, including voice and logic,[99] to know how to gesticulate the fly-whisk properly,[100] to be well versed in the three metaphysical works (the *Book of Changes*, the *Lao Tzu*, and the *Chuang Tzu*), and, above all, to belong to the elite circle.[101] Wang Seng-ch'ien's (426-485) letter to his son contains the following interesting admonition:

> You have read only about five feet each of the scrolls of the *Lao Tzu* and the *Book of Changes*. You have neither known what Wang Pi and Ho Yen had to say, nor the differences between the commentaries of Ma [Jung] and Cheng [Hsüan], nor [Wang Pi's] [*Lao Tzu*] *chih* [-*lüeh*] and [*Chou-i*] *li* [-*lüeh*]. And yet you have already picked up the fly-whisk and self-styled as a Conversationalist. Nothing is more dangerous than this. Suppose Prefect Yüan [Tsan, 420-477] asks you to talk about the *Book of Changes*, Palace Secretary Hsieh [Chuang, 421-466] challenges you to a discussion on the *Chuang Tzu*, or Mr. Chang [Hsü, 433?-490?] questions you about the *Lao Tzu*, can you answer by admitting that you have not read them? Pure Conversation is like the game of archery: the player must always be aware of the marks already hit by others. A player who knows nothing about them simply loses the game.[102]

This is a most vivid account of the basic intellectual qualifications of a Pure Conversationalist. Clearly, by the middle of the fifth century, Pure Conversation had developed a ritual framework of its own. It fits remarkably well with Foucault's description of the societies of discourse "whose function is to preserve discourse by producing it in a restricted group."[103] Thus, with the teaching of names firmly established on the basis of naturalness, and "rituals" on that of "feelings," as it were, a balance between order and individuality was restored at long last.

NOTES

1. See Lu Hsün, "Wen-hua p'ien-chih lun" [On extremities in cultural development], in *Lu Hsün ch'üan-chi* [Complete works of Lu Hsün], 20 vols. (Peking: Jen-min Wen-hsüeh Ch'u-pan She, 1973), 1:45-46.

2. *Pai-hu t'ung-te lun* [Comprehensive discussions in the White Tiger Hall] (Ssu-pu ts'ung-k'an ch'u-pien so-pen ed.), 7.58; Fung Yu-lan, *A History of Chinese Philosophy*, trans. Derk Bodde, 2 vols. (Princeton: Princeton University Press, 1953), 2:44.

3. Yü Ying-shih, *Li-shih yü ssu-hsiang* [History and thought] (Taipei: Lien-ching Ch'u-pan Shih-yen Kung-ssu), 39-41.

4. *Hou-Han shu* [History of the Latter Han], punctuated ed., 12 vols. (Peking: Chung-hua Shu-chü, 1959), 5:1554; T'ung-tsu Ch'ü, *Law and Society in Traditional China* (Paris: Mouton, 1961), 279.

5. *Hou-Han shu*, 10:2775.

6. *Juan Chi chi* [Collected works of Juan Chi] (Shanghai: Ku-chi Ch'u-pan She, 1978), 66. For English translation, see Kung-chuan Hsiao, *A History of Chinese Political Thought*, trans. Frederick W. Mote, 2 vols. (Princeton: Princeton University Press, 1979), 1:622-23; and Donald Holzman, *Poetry and Politics, The Life and Works of Juan Chi, A.D. 210-263* (Cambridge: Cambridge University Press, 1976), 195-96.

7. For more details, see Yü Ying-shih, "Ming-chao wei-chi yü Wei-Chin shih-feng ti chuan-pien" [Social crisis and the changing life-style of the intellectuals of the Wei-Chin period], originally published in *Shih-huo* (November 1979), 9 (7-8):2-4; now collected in *Chung-kuo chih-shih chieh-ts'eng shih-lun* [Historical studies of the Chinese intellectual class] (Taipei: Lien-ching Ch'u-pan Shih-yeh Kung-ssu, 1980), 333-37.

8. *Pao-p'u tzu* [Writings of Ko Hung], 4 vols. (Wan-yu wen-k'u ed.), 4:773-74; English translation in Wolfgang Bauer, *China and the Search for Happiness*, trans. Michael Shaw (New York: Seabury Press, 1976), 138-39.

9. Yang Po-chün, *Lieh Tzu chi-shih* [Comprehensive annotations of the *Lieh Tzu*] (Shanghai: Lung-men Lien-ho Shu-chü, 1958), 102; A. C. Graham, trans., *The Book of Lieh Tzu* (London: John Murray, 1960), 102. As Graham rightly points out in his introduction, the consensus among scholars in China is that the *Lieh Tzu* is a product of the third century A.D. (1). Most of these scholarly opinions are now conveniently collected in Yang Po-Chün's *Lieh Tzu chi-shih*, 185-245.

10. *Wang Wen-kung wen-chi* [Collected works of Wang An-shih], 2 vols. (Shanghai: Jen-min Ch'u-pan She, 1974), 2:439. See Ch'en Yin-k'o, *T'ao Yüan-ming chih ssu-hsiang yü ch'ing t'an chih kuan-hsi* [The thought of T'ao Ch'ien and its relationship with pure conversation] (Chengtu: Harvard-Yenching Institute, 1945), 52-53.

11. See passages quoted in Yü Ying-shih, "Ming-chiao wei-chi," 336 and n. 6.

12. For a general study of Wei-Chin anarchism, see T'an Chia-chien, "Lüeh lun Wei-Chin shih-ch'i ti wu-chün-lun ssu-ch'ao" [A brief discussion of anarchical ideas in the Wei-Chin period], *Chung-kuo che-hsüeh* (March 1980), (2):120-36.

13. *Fu-tzu* [Writings of Fu Hsüan], quoted in *San-kuo chih* [History of the Three Kingdoms], punctuated ed., 5 vols. (Peking: Chung-hua Shu-chü, 1959), 2:213; *Tzu-chih t'ung-chien* [Comprehensive mirror for aid in government], punctuated ed., 20 vols. (Peking: Chung-hua Shu-chü, 1956), 5:2018-19.

14. Colin Morris, *The Discovery of the Individual, 1050-1200* (London: S.P.C.K. for the Church History Society), 160.

15. *Wei shu* [History of Wei], quoted in *San-kuo chih*, 1:260.

16. *Hou-Han shu*, 8:2278.

17. *Chih shu* [History of Chin], punctuated ed., 10 vols. (Peking: Chung-hua Shu-chü, 1974), 5:1360.

18. *Pao-p'u tzu*, 3:509.

19. Richard B. Mather, trans., *Shih-shuo hsin-yü, A New Account of Tales of the World* (Minneapolis: University of Minnesota Press, 1976), 485.

20. *San-kuo chih*, 3:647. See Mori Mikisaburō, "Gi-Shih jidai ni okeru ningen no hakken" [The discovery of man in the Wei-Chin period], *Tōyō bunka no mondai* (June 1949), (1):146-47.

21. *Pao-p'u tzu*, 3:598-603.

22. *Chin shu*, 1:136; English translation in Kung-chuan Hsiao, *Chinese Political Thought*, 635-36.

23. Jacob Burckhardt, *The Civilization of the Renaissance in Italy*, trans. S. G. C. Middlemore (London: Phaidon Press, 1951), 81. Although Burckhardt's thesis has been variously modified, his basic view of Renaissance individualism still holds well. See Ernst Cassirer, *The Individual and the Cosmos in Renaissance Philosophy*, trans. Mario Domandi (Philadelphia: University of Pennsylvania Press, 1972), 35-36; Paul Oskar Kristeller, "Changing Views of the Intellectual History of the Renaissance since Jacob Burchkhardt," in *The Renaissance, a Reconsideration of the Theories and Interpretations of the Age*, ed. Tinsley Helton (Madison: University of Wisconsin Press, 1961), 30.

24. *Hou-Han shu*, 7:1953.

25. Ibid., 10:2773.

26. Ibid., 8:2278.

27. See T'ang Yung-t'ung, *Wei-Chin hsüan-hsüeh lun kao* [Preliminary discussions of the mysterious learning of the Wei-Chin period] (Peking: Jen-min Ch'u-pan She, 1957), 8.

28. *Hou-Han shu*, 9:2635-39.

29. *Jen-wu chih* [Treatise on personalities] (Ssu-pu ts'ung-k'an ch'u-pien so-pen ed.), *shang* 4-6. Cf. J. K. Shryock, *The Study of Human Abilities, The Jen Wu Chih of Liu Shao* (New Haven: American Oriental Society, 1937), esp. 99-100.

30. See Walter Ullman, *The Individual and Society in the Middle Ages* (Baltimore: The Johns Hopkins Press, 1966), 105; Morris, *Discovery of the Individual*, 86-95.

31. Quoted in William Willets, *Chinese Art*, 2 vols. (Harmondsworth, Middlesex: Penguin Books, Ltd., 1958), 2:582. For Ts'ao Chih's original text, see Yü Chien-hua, ed., *Chung-kuo hua-lun lei-pien* [Chinese art criticism: a classified compilation], 2 vols. (Hong Kong: Chung-hua Shu-chü, 1973), 1:12.

32. Mather, *New Account of Tales of the World*, 368.

33. See the interesting story about Ku K'ai-chih adding three hairs to the cheek of the person in a portrait in order to catch his "spirit" (ibid., 367).

34. See Bruno Snell, *The Discovery of the Mind, The Greek Origins of European Thought*, trans. T. B. Rosenmeyer (New York: Harper and Brothers, 1960), chap. 3; Morris, *Discovery of the Individual*, 68-70; Burckhardt, *Civilization of the Renaissance*, esp. 184-88.

35. Sui Sen-shu, *Ku-shih shih-chiu shou chi-shih* [Comprehensive annotations of the nineteen old poems] (Hong Kong: Chung-hua Shu-chü, 1958).

36. Yü Kuan-ying, "Lun Chien-an Ts'ao-shih fu-tzu ti shih" [The poetry of Ts'ao and his two sons in the Chien-an period], *Wen-hsüeh i-ch'an tseng-k'an* (Peking, 1955), (1):137-58.

37. Étienne Balazs, *Chinese Civilization and Bureaucracy*, ed. Arthur F. Wright (New Haven: Yale University Press, 1964), 177.

38. According to the classification of Chang Chih-yüeh, thirteen out of the eighty-two are autobiographical poems. See his "Lüeh lun Juan Chi chi ch'i *Yung-huai shih*" [A brief discussion of Juan Chi and his *Poems of the Heart*], in *Wei-Chin Liu-ch'ao shih yen-chiu lun-wen chi* [A collection of studies on poetry of the Wei-Chin and Six Dynasties period] (Hong Kong: Chung-kuo Yü-wen Hsüeh-she, 1969), 66.

39. I refer mainly to the works of Ch'en Yin-k'o, T'ang Yung-t'ung, and T'ang Chang-ju.

40. *Pao-p'u tzu*, 3:604.

41. Ch'ien Mu, "Tu *Wen-hsüan*" [On reading the *Wen-hsüan*], in his *Chung-kuo hsüeh-shu ssu-hsiang shih lun-ts'ung* [Studies in Chinese intellectual history], 8 vols. (Taipei: Tung-ta T'u-shu Kung-ssu, 1977), 3:107.

42. Yen K'o-chün, *Ch'üan shang-ku san-tai Ch'in Han San-kuo Liu-ch'ao wen* [Complete prose from antiquity to the end of the Six Dynasties], 5 vols. (Peking: Chung-hua Shu-chü, 1958), 2:1088.

43. Ibid., 1141.

44. Mather, *New Account of Tales of the World*, 488.

45. See Chang Hao, *Yün-ku tsa-chi* [Miscellaneous notes by Chang Hao] (Shanghai: Chung-hua Shu-chü, 1958), 97; Chou Fa-kao, *Chung-kuo ku tai yü-fa: ch'eng-tai p'ien* [A historical grammar of ancient Chinese: substitution] (Taipei: Academia Sinica, 1959), 83-84. See also Mather, *New Account of Tales of the World*, 161, where the intimate "you" is used to a friend.

46. *Chin shu*, 5:1379-80; Mather, *New Account of Tales of the World*, 12.

47. Yen K'o-chün, *Ch'üan Shang-ku wen*, 2:1962.

48. For this standard view, see Ch'en Yin-k'o, "'Hsiao-yao yu' Hsiang-Kuo i chi Chih-tun i t'an-yüan" [An inquiry into the origins of Hsiang-Kuo's and Chih-tun's interpretations of the "Hsiao-yao yu" chapter in the *Chuang Tzu*], *Ch'ing-hua hsüeh-pao* (April 1937), 12(2):309, and *T'ao Yüan-ming chih ssu-hsiang*, 3; T'ang Yung-t'ung, "Tu *Jen-wu chih*" [On reading the *Treatise on Personalities*], in *Wei-Chih hsüan-hsüeh lun kao*, 16; Aoki Masaru, "Seidan" [Pure conversation], in *Aoki Masaru zenshū* [Complete works of Aoki Masaru], 10 vols. (Tokyo: Shunjū Sha, 1969), 1:208-40.

49. Wang Fu, *Ch'ien-fu lun* [Wang Fu's essays], annotated by Wang Chi-p'ei (KHCPTS ed.), 11 and Wang Chi-p'ei's note.

50. *Hou-Han shu*, 7:2031.

51. Ibid., 9:2547.

52. Ibid., 8:2232.

53. Mather, *New Account of Tales of the World*, 56.

54. *Hou-Han shu*, 9:2481.

55. Ibid., 9:2647. For more examples of this kind, see the case of Hsieh Chen and Pien Jang (ibid., 8:2230) and that of K'ung Kung-hsü (ibid., 8:2258).

56. Fung Yu-lan, *A History of Chinese Philosophy*, 2:175-79.

57. Liu Shao, *Jen-wu chih, shang*, 22-23.

58. Ibid., *shang*, 11-12.

59. *Hou-Han shu*, 6:1629.

60. Ibid., 8:2277.

61. For Wang Su's influence on Wang Pi, see Meng Wen-t'ung, *Ching-hsüeh chüeh-yüan* [Origins of Confucian classical scholarship] (reprint, Taipei: Commercial Press, 1966), 38. Ts'ai Yung probably contributed more than anyone else to the widespread circulation of Wang Ch'ung's *Lun-heng*. For instance, after his death, Ts'ai's entire library was obtained by Wang Yeh, Wang Pi's father. It is therefore more than probable that Wang Pi had direct access to Ts'ai's copy of the *Lun-heng* (see *Po-wu chi*, quoted in *San-kuo chih*, 3:796). On the other hand, Juan Yü, Juan Chi's father, had been a disciple of Ts'ai (*San-kuo chih*, 3:600). This important fact explains why both Juan Chi and his nephew Juan Hsiu were so familiar with the ideas of Wang Ch'ung. For details, see Yü Ying-shih, *Chung-kuo chih-shih*, 339, n. 7.

62. Miyazaki Ichisada thinks that the transition from Pure Criticism took place in the early decades of the third century; see his "Seidan" [Pure conversation], *Shirin* (January 1946), 31(1):5. Shiba Rokurō classifies late Han "conversation" in terms of two different types he calls "critical conversation" and "inquisitive conversation." The former focused on personalities, the latter on ideas. He further states that the former flourished during the reigns of Emperors Huan (147-167) and Ling (168-188) and the latter during the reigns of Emperors Lin and Hsien (189-220); see his "Kō-Kan makki no danron ni tsuite" [On conversations at the end of the Han], *Hirojima daigaku bungakubu kiyō* (October 1955),

(8):213-42. I have examined this question in considerable detail in "Han-Chin chih chi shih chih hsin tzu-chüeh yü hsin ssu-ch'ao" [Self-awareness of the literati and the new tide of thought in the Han-Chin period], originally published in *Hsin-ya hsüeh-pao* (August 1959), 4(1):50-60, now included in my *Chung-kuo chih-shih*, 236-49. For a more thorough study, see Okamura Shigeru, "Kō-Kan makki no heiron-teki kifū ni tsuite" [On the critical spirit at the end of the Han], in *Nagoya daigaku bungakubu kenkyū ronshū* [A collection of studies by the Faculty of Arts, Nagoya University] (Nagoya University Press, 1960), 67-112.

63. *Chin-shu*, 4:1236. For a good general discussion of the idea of nonbeing and its relationship to the self-awareness of the individual in this period, see Matsumoto Gamei, "Gi-Shin ni okeru mu no shisō no seikaku" [The nature of the idea of nonbeing in the Wei-Chin period], *Shigaku Zasshi* (February 1940), 51(2):13-42; (March 1940), 51(3):74-105; (April 1940), 51(4):63-90. However, Professor Ch'ien Mu is one of the earliest modern scholars to characterize Wei-Chin Neo-Taoism in terms of the self-awareness of the individual. See *Kuo-hsüeh kai-lun* [A general introduction to Chinese scholarship and thought], 2 vols. (Shanghai: Commercial Press, 1931), 1:150.

64. Kung-chuan Hsiao, *Chinese Political Thought*, 1:610-11. For a general study of the thought of Ho Yen and Wang Pi, see Itano Chōhachi, "Ka An O Hitsu no shisō" [The thought of Ho Yen and Wang Pi], *Tōhō gakuhō* (March 1943), 14(1):43-111.

65. *Ch'un-ch'iu Fan-lu* [Deep significance of the *Spring and Autumn Annals*] (Wan-yu wen-k'u ed., 2 vols.), 1:85. See also *Han shu* [History of the Former Han], punctuated ed., 8 vols. (Peking: Chung-hua Shu-chü, 1962), 6:2516. Tung Chung-shu never explicitly stated for what purpose heaven finds it necessary to produce man. However, he believed that heaven endows man with a nature so that he can practice *jen* (humanity) and *i*[b] (righteousness) (*Ch'un-ch'iu fan-lu*, 1:28). He further held that "humanity" is the embodiment of heaven's will and "righteousness" that of heaven's principle (ibid., 2:175). Therefore, if hard pressed, he probably would say that heaven creates man for the purpose of bringing itself to moral perfection.

66. *Ch'un-ch'iu fan-lu*, 2:175.

67. See Wang Ch'ung's essay on "Tzu-jan" [Spontaneity], in *A Source Book in Chinese Philosophy*, trans. Wing-tsit Chan (Princeton: Princeton University Press, 1963), 296-99.

68. Kuo Ch'ing-fan, *Chuang Tzu chi-shih* [Comprehensive annotations of the Chuang Tzu], 4 vols. (Peking: Chung-hua Shu-chü, 1961), 1:111-12; English translation in Fung Yu-lan, *A History of Chinese Philosophy*, 2:210.

69. Kuo Ch'ing-fan, *Chuang Tzu chi-shih*, 1:58; English translation in Kung-chuan Hsiao, *Chinese Political Thought*, 1:612.

70. Kuo Ch'ing-fan, *Chuang Tzu chih-shih*, 1:1; English translation slightly modified from Fung Yu-lan, *Chuang Tzu, A New Selected Translation with an Exposition of the Philosophy of Kuo Hsiang*, 2d ed. (New York: Paragon Book Reprint Corp., 1964), 27.

71. Kung-chuan Hsiao, *Chinese Political Thought*, 1:612.

72. Ch'en Yin-k'o, *T'ao Yüan-ming chih ssu-hsiang*, 5-6.

73. Kuo Hsiang says: "Nonaction does not mean that [the ruler] just sits there silently with arms folded. Rather he allows each individual thing to undertake its own action so that, ultimately, it may rest in the true form of its nature and life" (Kuo Ch'ing-fan, *Chuang Tzu chi-shih*, 2:369). For a general study of the thought of Kuo Hsiang, see Murakami Yoshimi, "Kaku Chō no shisō ni tsuite" [On the thought of Kuo Hsiang], *Tōyōshi kenkyū* (May 1941), 6(3):1-28.

74. Tai Ming-yang, *Hsi K'ang chi chiao-chu* [Collected works of Hsi K'ang, with collations and annotations] (Peking: Jen-min Wen-hsüeh Ch'u-pan She, 1962), 171; translated in Kung-chuan Hsiao, *Chinese Political Thought*, 1:618.

75. Kuo Ch'ing-fan, *Chuang Tzu chi-shih*, 1:296; translated in Kung-chuan Hsiao, *Chinese Political Thought*, 1:616-17.

76. For the distinction between "invisible hand" and "hidden hand," I have followed Robert Nozick, *Anarchy, State, and Utopia* (New York: Basic Books, Inc., 1974), 18-20.

77. Kuo Ch'ing-fan, *Chuang Tzu chi-shih*, 2:348. Commenting on the statement that "the sage brings little benefit to the world, but much harm," Kuo Hsiang says: "How true is this statement: Although this statement is true, we nevertheless cannot do without the sage. For before all types of knowledge have disappeared from the world, we still need the Way of the sage to control them. If all other kinds of knowledge are around while the sagely knowledge alone is gone, then the world would suffer more harm than it does because of the sage. It therefore follows that in spite of the fact that the sage brings much harm to the world, it is still far better than a world without the sage in which disorder reigns supreme."

78. Ibid., 2:364.

79. See Mou Jun-sun, *Lun Wei-Chin i-lai chih ch'ung-shang t'an-pien chi ch'i ying-hsiang* [Conversation and debate since the Wei-Chin period and their influence] (Hong Kong: The Chinese University of Hong Kong Press, 1966).

80. See Ch'en Yin-k'o, *T'ao Yüan-ming chih ssu-hsiang*, 2; T'ang Chang-ju, *Wei-Chin Nan-pei ch'ao shih lun-ts'ung* [Studies in the history of the Wei, Chin, and Northern-Southern dynasties] (Peking: San-lien Shu-tien, 1955), 336-39. This view is followed by Richard Mather in "The Controversy over Conformity and Naturalness during the Six Dynasties," *History of Religions* (November 1969/February 1970), 9(2-3):161.

81. *Hou-Han shu*, 10:2773.

82. Fung Yu-lan, *A History of Chinese Philosophy*, 2:32-33.

83. *Shen-chien* [Extended reflections] (Ssu-pu ts'ung ch'u-pien so-pen ed.), 5:32-33; translated in Ch'i-yün Ch'en, *Hsün Yüeh and the Mind of Late Han China* (Princeton: Princeton University Press, 1980), 187-88.

84. Ho Shao's biography of Wang Pi, quoted in the commentary of *San-kuo chih*, 3:795; translated in Fung Yu-lan, *A History of Chinese Philosophy*, 2:188. For an excellent discussion of the philosophical significance of this thesis, see T'ang Yung-t'ung, *Wei-Chin hsüan-hsüeh lun kao*, 72-83.

85. For example, see Mather, *New Account of Tales of the World*, 122.

86. Kuo Ch'ing-fan, *Chuang-tzu chi-shih*, 2:260; English translation slightly modified from Kung-chuan Hsiao, *Chinese Political Thought*, 1:636-37. It is significant to point out that in his commentary to the Confucian *Analects*, Wang Pi also stressed the importance of the "meaning" as opposed to the mere forms of the "rites." He specifically remarked that "all the five grades of mourning rites must each fit the feelings of the individual mourner" (quoted in Huang K'an, *Lun-yü chi-chieh i-su* [The *Analects*, annotations and interpretations], reprint [Taipei: Kuang-wen Shu-chü, 1968], 2.4a-b). This point, as will become clear below, bears importantly on the reform movement in mourning rites of the period.

87. See Graham, *Lieh-tzu*, 145.

88. Mather, *New Account of Tales of the World*, 374.

89. Ibid., 324.

90. Tai Ming-yang, *Hsi K'ang chi chiao-chu*, 261.

91. Ibid., 117-18; English translation by J. R. Hightower in *Anthology of Chinese Literature from Early Times to the Fourteenth Century*, ed. Cyril Birch (New York: Grove Press, 1965), 163.

92. Michel Foucault, *The Order of Things, An Archaeology of the Human Sciences* (New York: Vintage Books, 1973), 207. See also Hayden V. White, "Foucault Decoded: Notes from Underground," *History and Theory* (1973) 12(1):23-54.

93. *Chin shu*, 4:997.

94. *Hou-Han shu*, 3:573, 4:1119. See also the illuminating discussion by Ku Yen-wu in his *Jih-chih lu* [Notes of daily accumulation of knowledge] (Wan-yu wen-i'u ed., 12 vols.), 5:40.

95. Mather, *New Account of Tales of the World*, 372.

96. Ibid., 10-11.

97. *Chin shu*, 8:2396. See also T'ang Chang-ju, "Wei-Chin hsüan-hsüeh chih hsing-ch'eng chi ch'i fa-chan" [The rise of Wei-Chin mysterious learning and its development], in *Wei-Chin Nan-pei ch'ao*, esp. 336-37.

98. A comprehensive study of mourning rites in this period is provided by Fujikawa Masakazu in *Gi-Shin jidai ni okeru sōfukurei no kenkyū* (Tokyo: Keibun Sha, 1960). For more details about this movement in ritual reforms, see Yü Ying-shih, *Chung-kuo chih-shih*, 358-72.

99. For speech and voice, see examples listed and discussed in Yü Ying-shih, *Chung-kuo chih-shih*, 243-49; for the importance of logic in conversation, see Ho Ch'ang-ch'ün, *Wei-Chin ch'ing-t'an ssu-hsiang ch'u-lun* [A preliminary discussion of the ideas in Wei-Chin pure conversation] (Shanghai: Commercial Press, 1947), 7-8.

100. See Chao I, "Ch'ing-t'an yung chu-wei" [The use of fly-whisk in pure conversation], *Nien-erh shih cha-chi* [Notes on twenty-two dynastic histories], collated ed. (Taipei: Hua-shih Ch'u-pan She, 1977), 167-68.

101. For example, Ch'en Hsien-ta, a military man of humble social origin, told his son: "The fly-whisk is something belonging exclusively to such distinguished families as the Wangs and the Hsiehs. It is not the sort of thing that you should carry around." See *Nan-Ch'i shu* [History of the Southern Ch'i], punctuated ed., 3 vols. (Peking: Chung-hua Shu-chü, 1972), 2:490.

102. Ibid., 2:598. The text does not give personal names for these three conversationalists. The identifications of Yüan Tsan, Hsieh Chuang, and Chang Hsü have been established as a result of an extensive search in various biographies of the dynastic histories. My reasons for these identifications may be briefly stated as follows.

In Wang Seng-ch'ien's biography, Yüan Shu (408-453) and Hsieh Chuang are mentioned as Wang's intimate friends (2:591). However, Yüan Shu died too early to fit into the picture. On the other hand, the identification of Hsieh Chuang is unmistakable because he is referred to in the letter by his official title *Chung-shu* (*ling*) (Prefect of the Palace Secretariat), a position he did in fact hold (*Sung shu* [History of Sung], punctuated ed., 8 vols. [Peking: Chung-hua Shu-chü, 1974], 8:2167-77). Therefore, the letter must have been written sometime before Hsieh's death in 466 when Wang was about forty, an age old enough to have a son in his late teens or early twenties. Yüan Tsan was Yüan Shu's nephew. He changed his personal name to Tsan after the famous Pure Conversationalist Hsün Tsan of the third century. Moreover, he served as prefect of various provinces and was well known for his study of the *Book of Changes* (*Sung shu*, 8:2229-34). This fits perfectly well with the reference in the letter. As for Chang Hsü, he was a man from Wu-hsing with a great reputation as a Pure Conversationalist. Although he was particularly known for his knowledge of the *Book of Changes*, there can be little doubt that he must also have been versed in the *Lao Tzu* (*Nan-Ch'i shu*, 2:600-602). His first cousin Chang Jung (444-497), for instance, was a famous Neo-Taoist conversationalist with a special interest in the *Lao Tzu* (ibid., 3:721-30). The simple fact that both Wang Seng-ch'ien's and Chang Hsü's biographies are included in the same chapter also indicates a close relationship between the two men.

Without giving his reasons, however, Professor Ch'ien Mu has identified the three conversationalists as Yüan Tsan, Hsieh Fei, and Chang Hsü (*Kuo-hsüeh kai-lun*, 1:163). The first and third identifications agree with my findings. However, his identification of Hsieh *chung-shu* as Hsieh Fei (441-506), son of Hsieh Chuang, may be in error. To raise an obvious objection, Hsieh Fei started his bureaucratic career in 483 and was appointed to the position of *chung-shu ling* as late as 489 or 490, by which time Wang Seng-ch'ien had already been dead for four or five years. Wang could not have possibly referred to Hsieh Fei by this official title (see *Liang shu* [History of Liang], punctuated ed., 8 vols. [Peking: Chung-hua Shu-chü, 1974], 1:261-64).

103. Alan Sheridan, *Michel Foucault, The Will to Truth* (London and New York: Tavistock Publications, 1980), 127.

Glossary

Aoki Masaru　青木正男

Aoki Masaru zenshū　青木正男全集

Chang Chih-yüeh　張志岳

chang-chü　章句

Chang Hao　張昊

Chang Hsü　張緒

Chang Jung　張融

Chao I　趙翼

Ch'en Hsien-ta　陳顯達

Ch'en Yin-k'o　陳寅恪

Cheng Hsüan　鄭玄

Ch'ien-chih [Hu-mu]　謙之〔胡母〕

Ch'ien-fu lun　潛夫論

Ch'ien Mu　錢穆

ch'in-chih　親至

ch'in-mi　親密

Chin shu　晉書

ch'ing[a]　情

ch'ing[b]　卿

ching-hsüeh　經學

Ching-hsüeh chüeh-yüan　經學抉原

Ch'ing-hua hsüeh-pao　清華學報

ch'ing-i　清議

Ching-li　敬禮

ch'ing-li　情理

ch'ing-t'an　清談

"Ch'ing-t'an yung chu-wei"　清談用塵尾

Chou Fa-kao　周法高

Chou Hsieh　周顒

Chou-i li-lüeh　周易例略

chu　主

chu-wei　塵尾

Ch'üan Shang-ku San-tai Ch'in Han San-kuo Liu-ch'ao wen　全上古三代秦漢三國六朝文

ch'uan-shen　傳神

Chuang Tzu　莊子

Chuang Tzu chi-shih　莊子集釋

chün　君

Ch'un-ch'iu fan-lu　春秋繁露

Chung-kuo che-hsüeh　中國哲學

Chung-kuo chih-shih chieh-ts'eng shih-lun　中國知識階層史論

Chung-kuo hsüeh-shu ssu-hsiang shih lun-ts'ung　中國學術思想史論叢

Chung-kuo hua-lun lei-pien 中國畫論類編

Chung-kuo ku-tai yü-fa: ch'eng-tai p'ien 中國古代語法稱代篇

chung-shu ling 中書令

fa 法

fou-hsü 浮虛

fou-hua 浮華

fu 賦

Fu Jung 符融

Fu-tzu 傅子

Fujikawa Masakazu 藤川正數

"Gi-Shin ni okeru mu no shisō no seikaku" 魏晉における無の思想の性格

Gi-Shin jidai ni okeru sōfukurei no kenkyū 魏晉時代における喪服礼の研究

"Gi-Shin jidai ni okeru ningen no hakken" 魏晉時代における人間の発見

"Han-Chin chih chi shih chih hsin tzu-chüeh yü hsin ssu-ch'ao" 漢晉之際士之新自覺與新思潮

Han Sung 韓嵩

Han shu 漢書

Hirojima daigaku bungakubu kiyō 廣島大學文學部紀要

Ho Ch'ang-ch'ün 賀昌羣

Ho Ch'iao 和嶠、

Ho Shao 何劭

Ho Tseng 何曾

Ho Yen 何晏

Hou-Han shu 後漢書

Hsi K'ang 嵇康

Hsi K'ang chi chiao-chu 嵇康集校注

Hsia-hou Hsüan 夏侯玄

Hsia-hou Tun 夏侯惇

hsiao 孝

"'Hsiao-yao yu' Hsiang-Kuo i chi Chih-tun i t'an-yüan" 逍遙遊向郭義及支遁義探源

Hsieh Chen 謝甄

Hsieh Chuang 謝莊

Hsieh Fei 謝朏、

Hsin-ya hsüeh-pao 新亞學報

hsing 性

Hsü Shao 許劭

hsü-wu 虛無

hsüan-hsü 玄虛

hsüan-hsüeh 玄學

Hsün Ts'an 荀粲

Hsün Yüeh　荀悦

Hu-mu Fu-chih　胡母輔之

Huai-nan Tzu　淮南子

Huan [ti]　桓帝

Huang K'an　皇侃

i[a]　異

i[b]　義

I ching　易經

i-li　義理

Ituno Chōhachi　板野長八

jen　仁

Jen-wu chih　人物志

Jih-chih lu　日知錄

ju-shih shih ch'i　入室視妻

Juan Chi　阮籍

Juan Chi chi　阮籍集

Juan Hsiu　阮脩

Juan Yü　阮瑀

"Ka An O Hitsu no shisō"　何晏王弼の思想

"Kaku Chō no shisō ni tsuite"　郭象の思想について

Ko Hung　葛洪

"Kō-Kan makki no danron ni tsuite"　後漢末期の談論について

"Kō-Kan makki no heiron-teki kifū ni tsuite"　後漢末期の評論的気風について

Ku K'ai-chih　顧愷之

"Ku-shih shih-chiu shou"　古詩十九首

Ku-shih shih-chiu shou chi-shih　古詩十九首集釋

Ku Yen-wu　顧炎武

K'ung Jung　孔融

K'ung Kung-hsü　孔公緒

Kuo Ch'ing-fan　郭慶藩

Kuo Hsiang　郭象

Kuo-hsüeh kai-lun　國學概論

Kuo T'ai　郭泰

Lao Tzu　老子

Lao-tzu chih-lüeh　老子指略

li[a]　理

li[b]　禮

li-sheng　理勝

Li-shih yü ssu-hsiang　歷史與思想

Li Yen　酈炎

Li Ying　李膺

Liang shu　梁書

Lieh-tzu　列子

Lieh-tzu chi-shih 列子集釋

Lin-tsung 林宗

Liu Hsiang 劉向

Liu I 劉毅

Liu Liang 劉梁

Liu Piao 劉表

Liu Shao 劉劭

Lu Hsün 魯迅

Lu Hsün ch'üan-chi 魯迅全集

"Lüeh lun Juan Chi chi ch'i *Yung-huai shih*" 略論阮籍及其詠懷詩

"Lüeh lun Wei-Chin shih-ch'i ti wu-chün-lun ssu-ch'ao" 略論魏晉時期的無君論思潮

"Lun Chien-an Ts'ao-shih fu-tzu ti shih" 論建安曹氏父子的詩

Lun-heng 論衡

Lun Wei-Chin i-lai chih ch'ung-shang t'an-pien chi ch'i ying-hsiang 論魏晉以來之崇尚談辯及其影響

Lun-yü chi-chieh i-su 論語集解義疏

Ma Jung 馬融

Matsumoto Gamei 松本雅明

Meng Wen-t'ung 蒙文通

Mi Heng 禰衡

ming-chiao 名教

"Ming-chiao wei-chi yu Wei-Chin shih-feng ti chuan-pien" 名教危機與魏晉士風的轉變

ming-li 名理

Miyazaki Ichisada 宮崎市定

Mori Mikisaburō 森三樹三朗

Mou Jun-sun 牟潤孫

Murakami Yoshimi 村上嘉實

Nagoya daigaku bungakubu kenkyū ronshū 名古屋大學文學部研究論集

Nan-Ch'i shu 南齊書

Nien-erh shih cha-chi 廿二史箚記

Okamura Shigeru 岡村繁

Pai-hu t'ung-te lun 白虎通德論

Pao Ching-yen 鮑敬言

Pao-p'u tzu 抱朴子

"Pien ho t'ung lun" 辯和同論

Pien Jang 邊讓

Po-wu chi 博物記

p'u 樸

san-hsüan 三玄

san-kang liu-chi 三綱六紀

San-kuo chih 三國志

"Seidan" 清談

shen 神

Shen-chien 申鑒

Shiba Rokurō 斯波六郎

Shigaku zasshi 史學雜誌

Shih-huo 食貨

shih-li 事理

shih-shuo hsin-yü 世說新語

Shirin 史林

"Shu-chih" 述志

Shu Hsi 束晳

Shun 舜

Sui Sen-shu 隋森樹

Sung shu 宋書

ta 達

"Ta Fan Ch'in shu" 答繁欽書

T'ai-hsüeh 太學

"Ta-jen hsien-sheng chuan" 大人先生傳

Tai Liang 戴良

Tai Ming-yang 戴明揚

T'an Chia-chien 譚家健

t'an-chu 談助

T'ang Chang-ju 唐長孺

tang-ku 黨錮

T'ang Yung-t'ung 湯用彤

Tao 道

T'ao Ch'ien 陶潛

tao-li 道理

T'ao Yüan-ming chih ssu-hsiang yü ch'ing-t'an chih kuan-hsi 陶淵明之思想與清談之關係

te 德

Ting I 丁廙

Tōhō gakuhō 東方學報

Tōyō bunka no mondai 東洋文化の問題

Tōyōshi kenkyū 東洋史研究

Ts'ai Yung 蔡邕

Ts'ao Chih 曹植

Ts'ao P'i 曹丕

Ts'ao Ts'ao 曹操

Ts'ao Wei 曹魏

tseng-ta 贈答

"Tu *Jen-wu chih*" 讀人物志

"Tu *Wen-hsüan*" 讀文選

t'ung 同

Tung Chung-shu 董仲舒

tzu-ch'eng 自成

tzu-chih 自制

Tzu-chih t'ung-chien 資治通鑑

tzu-hua 自化

tzu-jan 自然

tzu-sheng 辭勝

tzu-shih 自適

tzu-te 自得

tzu-tsai 自在

tzu-tsu 自足

tzu-wei 自爲

Wang An-shih　王安石

Wang Chi-p'ei　汪繼培

Wang Ch'ung　王充

Wang Fu　王符

Wang Jung　王戎

Wang Lang　王朗

Wang Pi　王弼

Wang Seng-ch'ien　王僧虔

Wang Su　王肅

Wang Wen-kung wen-chi　王文公文集

Wang Yeh　王業

Wei Chen　衞臻

wei-ch'i　圍棋

Wei shu　魏書

Wei-Chin ch'ing-t'an ssu-hsiang ch'u-lun　魏晉清談思想初論

"Wei-Chin hsüan-hsüeh chih hsing-ch'eng chi ch'i fa-chan"　魏晉玄學之形成及其發展

Wei-Chin hsüan-hsüeh lun kao　魏晉玄學論稿

Wei-Chin Liu-ch'ao shih yen-chiu lun-wen chi　魏晉六朝詩研究論文集

Wei-Chin Nan-pei ch'ao shih lun-ts'ung　魏晉南北朝史論叢

Wen-hsüan　文選

Wen-hsüeh i-ch'an tseng-k'an　文學遺產增刊

"Wen-hua p'ien-chih lun"　文化偏至論

wu　無

wu-chih　無治

Wu [ti]　武帝

wu-wei　無爲

Yang Po-chün　楊伯峻

Yao　堯

Yen Hui　顏回

Yen K'o-chün　嚴可均

yu　有

Yü　禹

Yü Chien-hua　俞劍華

"Yu-fen"　幽憤

Yü Kuan-ying　余冠英

Yü Ying-shih 余英時

Yüan Hung 袁宏

Yüan Shu 袁淑

Yüan Tsan 袁粲

Yün-ku tsa-chi 雲谷雜記

"Yung-huai shih" 詠懷詩

The Hidden Hero: Creation and Disintegration of the Ideal of Eremitism

Wolfgang Bauer

Eremitism and individualism are two conceptions or principles that are related in a most complicated, indirect manner. It does not seem so very difficult to show that the hermit and the individualist have several important characteristics in common: the psychological distance from and critical attitude towards the masses, the reluctance to accept commitments to society, and the quest for external freedom. However, not only their motivations but also their attitudes are different from, if not contradictory to, each other in many respects. The individualist, for example, may aim at leadership in society in spite of his unwillingness to serve it, which certainly cannot be said of the hermit. And the hermit's life is essentially determined by religious or ideological considerations, sometimes to such a degree that he forgets his own person, which does not necessarily hold for the true individualist. We may say, therefore, that eremitism and individualism include and exclude each other at the same time, much like intersecting circles.

While individualism is a specific idea based on the Greek and Judeo-Christian system of thought, eremitism has been an equally important concept both in China and in the West which, for whatever reasons, reached its height in both cultures at about the same historical period, namely, the third and early fourth centuries A.D. For this reason alone, an analysis of eremitism might be helpful for an understanding of the particular nature of Chinese "individualism" or, more precisely, the nature of the counterpart or counterparts of Western individualism in China. Among numerous issues relevant for both eremetism and individualism, the philosophical ones may be most elucidating in this respect, though social and political causes must, of course, not be neglected. At the same time, it seems to be more promising to examine not only the phenomenon of eremitism as such, but also (and particularly) its fringes: the motives from which it grew and the repercussions it had on other ideas. For it is in this sphere of the "not-yet-hermit" and the "no-longer-hermit" that the quest for "individualism" really can be envisaged, more so than in the environment of the genuine hermit who has made his peace with the world.

These considerations are reflected in the subtitle of the present study: "Creation and Disintegration of the Ideal of Eremitism." The first section tries to answer the question "What makes a hermit?" on the basis of linguistic evidence and theoretical observations. The second section deals with the philosophical foundations of eremitism in China. The third section considers the various reasons for the increased influence of eremitism on political life during its "golden age," the Wei-Chin period. The fourth section traces the influence of eremitism on independent intellectual movements of later periods, such as monasticism, loyalism, and introspection of the self. The fifth section tries to clarify in retrospect which aspects of eremitism and individualism may have overlapped in China and to what extent the Chinese hermit might be called an "individualist."

What Makes a Hermit?

Terminology: Escape and Solitude

It is difficult to describe a cultural phenomenon from descriptions in a foreign language because basic concepts differ among societies. This is particularly true with regard to the "hermit" because of his long tradition in China and the West. Although we cannot embark here on a full-scale analysis of this idea as understood in the two societies, we cannot completely avoid it because, by and large, eremitism represents a negative (and therefore especially complicated) concept, similar to that of "freedom" in this regard. The difficulty of finding a common denominator for the "hermit" is often noted in the introductions to biographies of hermits in the dynastic histories.[1] While the definitions we find in these sources are sometimes revealing of the particular outlook of the writer and his time, they do not offer a general conception which is easy to apply. Thus, our approach will be to try to set forth some of the main characteristics of a hermit, taking into consideration, first of all, the terminology applied to both the hermit and the variously perceived "inner" and "outer" spheres of living.

Eremitism is determined by two complex sets of ideas which usually, though not necessarily, coincide; they are related to each other but not identical. The first set embraces the idea of escape and hiding (including any sort of retirement). Its verbal aspect implies that the hermit has to fight for his freedom against a society that does everything to keep or find him. The most central term for "escape" in Chinese, used in countless combinations,[2] is i^a, for which the corresponding character has "hare" and "to run." Less frequent but important because it functions as the relevant hexagram for "escapism" in the *Book of Changes* (I ching) is *tun*. The concept of "hiding" is represented chiefly by the word *yin* in several combinations[3] and less frequently by such concepts as yu^a, "dark,"[4] and *hsi*, "to roost."[5] The idea of "retirement," which also includes passivity, is expressed by the words *chü*, "to sit" or "to dwell [at home],"[6] and *ch'u*, "to dwell" or "to be at rest."[7] The notion of escape and hiding, essential in China for eremitism in general, is secondary to the way in which the term functions in Western languages. Only the word "anchorite" (from the Greek *anachorein*, "to retire," but not "to escape") reflects a similar sentiment.

The reverse seems to be true with regard to the second set of ideas, the central concept of which is solitude. Practically all of the relevant Western expressions stem from this concept: "hermit" or "eremite" (from the Greek *erēmos*, "lonely"), "solitary" (from the Latin *solus*, "alone"), and "monk" (from the Greek *monos*, "alone"). Interestingly enough, the concept of solitude in China is connected with the self-deprecatory designation of the ruler (*kua-jen, ku-chia*) rather than with the hermit. An exception, at least to a certain extent, is the word *tu*, "alone," which denotes an attitude close to eremitism. But it is more characteristic of the wish for independence than of a desire for isolation. This is apparent in the expression *tu-hsing*[a] (also *tu-chiai* or *chiai-shih*), which is applied to stubborn personalities. The *Hou-Han shu* [History of the Latter Han] dedicates a whole chapter to the *tu-hsing*[a]: "lone wolves" in a positive sense or even martyrs who clung to their moral ideals in spite of the opposition of the whole world. Biographies of men of a similar nature are superscribed *i-hsing*, "[men of] singular conduct," in the *Hsin Wu-tai shih* [New history of the Five Dynasties], *cho-hsing*, "[men of] extraordinary conduct," in the *Hsin T'ang shu* [New history of the T'ang], or *tu-hsing*[b], "[men of] sincere conduct," in the *Hsin Yüan shih* [New historical records of the Yüan].[8]

Thus, at least in the Chinese context, escape and hiding represent the defensive and solitude the aggressive aspect of eremitism, the latter often to such a degree that it transcends the limits of eremitism to become a justified or nonjustified opposition to state and society. At the same time, these aspects are reflected in two opposite kinds of eccentric behavior identified in the *Analects*: nervousness and timidity (*chüan*) on the one hand and madness and foolhardiness (*k'uang*) on the other.[9] They also reveal an inner contradiction of Chinese, if not of any eremitism: that between the concealment of one's own vestiges in the world and the emphasis on one's personal "will" (*chih*).[10]

Outer and Inner Forms of Eremitism: Retreat and Asceticism

Aside from these two basic aspects of eremitism (escape/hiding and solitude), another distinction is necessary which applies mainly to the particular manner of escape: that between outer and inner forms of retreat. The former is relevant to the hermit's social activities (or rather, nonactivities) and to his dwelling, the latter to his way of life, particularly to the various modes of asceticism he practices. Asceticism, playing a decisive role in anchoretical movements all over the world, is indeed nothing but a special sort of retreat, referring almost exclusively to communication with the world in one way or another—eating, drinking, sexual intercourse, speaking, and so forth. Both the outer retreat from society and the inner one, namely, asceticism, are of course closely interrelated, but what is more important is that they are certainly also stratified into degrees. As far as outer retreat is concerned, a first step towards it may be the hermit's resignation from leading posts, combined with a preference for living in smaller towns or villages rather than in the busy capital. As a next step, the hermit might leave the town or village and choose to dwell in the countryside, thereby foregoing any social activities. He may then go even further, abandoning his family and fleeing into wholly uncultivated areas, dwelling alone in the mountains and marshes or with fellow hermits (monastic eremitism) in shacks and caves, or making his way to the seashore or (especially in the West) to the desert. Only at this stage is he actually recognized as a "hermit" by the rest of society: he has left the *oikumene*, the living place of men, and entered the *anoikumene*, the part of the world deserted by actual human beings. The subsequent steps are imaginative rather than real: the hermit bids farewell to mankind altogether, vanishing into distant, fabulous countries or islands which lie behind almost unsurmountable physical obstacles such as huge mountains or vast deserts and seas. Many of the Chinese immortals (*hsien*^{a}) may be counted among such "hermits" ("earthly hermits" *ti-hsien*). The final stage of outer retreat is reached when the hermit leaves the world entirely, when he ascends to heaven "in bright daylight" as the Taoist "heavenly immortals" (*t'ien-hsien*) did, or when he becomes a heavenly saint (in Western religion) or a Buddha (in Buddhism). This stage is necessarily associated with the idea of death, although this is rarely expressed; or it may even be interpreted, by means of inversion, as an overcoming of death.

One may perhaps wonder whether the first and the last stages of retreat from the world really fall within the bounds of true eremitism. But doubtless they are all connected so that the "true" hermit as a phenomenon is understandable only in this wider context. The same holds for the various forms of inner retreat, which center around the idea of asceticism. Again, the first steps to this form of retreat may pass unnoticed: the psychological distance from the bustle of life, a certain disinterestedness in the daily routines of one's work, strange behavior, or abuse of wine and narcotics. This is often followed by a denial first of wealth and honor,[11] then of all amenities of civilized life. Subsequent stages may include the reluctance to speak, fasting, frugality in housing, and finally, of course, celibacy. Ascetic exercises characteristic of an even more rigorous stage, such as sleep deprivation, self-mutilation, or hard work, are of a different quality in that they aim, not only at "retreat," but at the "mortification" of the body and, therefore, at the separation of the hermit not only from society and his fellow men but also from all vital powers. Continuous praying or reading of sacred texts is common during this stage, although these activities may also have the general concentration of mind in view; this is certainly the objective of meditation, which is sometimes connected with asceticism. Not unlike the outer retreat described above, the logical end of this inner retreat is death: the ascetic "mortification," in its last consequence leading to an intellectual or even physical suicide, is seen as the loss of a lower mode of life in favor of a simultaneously gained higher mode. This conviction is expressed in innumerable religious scriptures, and the price of this achievement for many ascetic hermits was their lives.

There are many differences between Chinese and Western concepts of eremitism and among dissimilar concepts within China. However, it might still be possible to settle on a general definition: the hermit is a person who renounces by degrees (sometimes up to physical or intellectual suicide) contact with the human environment and the pleasures of earthly existence in order to concentrate and intensify his remaining sentiments toward higher goals. He thereby demonstrates as well his disdain of society or the whole world, for which he may be praised or condemned.

The Ideological Roots of Eremitism

Views in the Book of Changes and the Analects

The basic ideas about eremitism in China are obviously older than any philosophy of religion as such. There are numerous relevant comments found scattered throughout the *Book of Changes* which were frequently quoted by Chinese writers as a legitimation, e.g., in the relevant chapters of the dynastic histories. Still, the reasons for a hidden or solitary existence mentioned in the *Book of Changes* are anything but consistent. Autonomy and independence are given a most prominent place, in fact, at the very beginning of the book, in the first line of the first hexagram, *ch'ien* (The Creative Principle):

> The concealed dragon refrains from action. What does this signify? *Wen-yen Commentary*: According to the Master, this [symbolizes] someone dragon-like in his virtues who conceals [his light], does not change with the world, makes no name for himself, withdraws from the world without regret, cares not that no one seeks him, does what pleases him and avoids whatever might grieve him. Firm as a rock, he can by no means be uprooted. This is the concealed dragon.[12]

A similar idea is expressed in the hexagram *ku* (Decay): "He does not serve the King or the nobles. He regards his own matters as loftier [*kao*]. *Hsiang Commentary*: He does not serve the King or nobles. [His] will can be [his] law."[13]

Whereas the retreat in the two passages quoted above is obviously conceived as a fundamental, persistent attitude, it is described as depending on certain temporal circumstances only in the following quotations. The hexagram *k'un* (The Passive Principle), has the passage: "Taciturn [lit., 'tied up in a bag'] no blame, no praise. *Wen-yen Commentary*: When Heaven and Earth [cause] transformations plants and trees are exuberant, but when they are inactive [lit., 'closed'] the Superior Man [*hsien-jen*] is in hiding. The passage means to be cautious."[14] The same idea is expressed in the commentary *Hsi-tz'u*, where the important parallel between retreat and silence is also emphasized: "The way of the Princely Man is such: one time he appears [in public], another time he rests at home; one time he is silent, another time he speaks up."[15]

In both of the latter two quotations, these periods of retreat are seen as parts of an almost rhythmical process modeled after the active and passive periods of the year. The opinion that the time for retreat is during periods of menace and danger is also apparent in two hexagrams which are devoted entirely to the concept of withdrawal and hiding: *tun* (Yielding) and *ming-i* (Darkening of the Light).[16] While both portray various situations of lucky or unlucky retreat, the hexagram *tun* is altogether more favorably conceived than *ming-i* in that it implies the idea of distant dignity rather than of self-denial. On the other hand, the hexagram *ming-i* clearly plays on the hope associated with the setting sun, which invariably rises again when morning comes.

The commentaries on the *Book of Changes* quoted here originated, of course, under strong Confucian influence. In Confucian texts, the conviction that eremitism is justified only under certain conditions and for limited periods is even more strongly emphasized than it is in the *Book of Changes*. Nevertheless, this concept is not undisputed in the *Analects*, where the question of eremitism is discussed at several points (notably, at the end of chapter 14 and in chapter 19) in connection with earlier recluses.[17] The following passage (perhaps partly corrupt), while not as easily understood, is nonetheless informative because it provides a sort of classification of eremitism:

> Men who retired to privacy [*i-min*] were: Po-i, Shu-ch'i; Yü-chung, I-i, Chu-chang; Hui of Liu-hsia, and Shao-lien. The Master said: "Refusing to surrender their wills or to submit to any taint in their persons—such, I think, were Po-i and Shu-ch'i. It may be said of Hui of Liu-hsia and Shao-lien that they surrendered their wills and submitted to taint in their persons, but their words corresponded with reason and their actions were such as men are anxious to see. This is all that is to be remarked in them. It may be said of Yü-chung and I-i that, while they hid themselves in their seclusion, they gave license to their words; but in their persons they succeeded in preserving their purity and in their retirement they acted according to the exigency of the times. I [myself] am different from all these. I have no course for which I am predetermined, and no course against which I am predetermined."[18]

The classification of Po-i and Shu-ch'i, who starved themselves to death out of loyalty for the perished Shang dynasty, poses, of course, no difficulties: in a way, they are China's arch-hermits who pushed eremitism to its extreme, suicide. More difficult to interpret are their counterparts, Hui of Liu-hsia and Shao-lien, of whom at least the former is known as a sort of "antihermit." After Hui had been thrice dismissed from his office, somebody asked him whether he had not better leave his country, and he replied: "Serving men in an upright way, where shall I go to and not experience such a thrice-repeated dismissal? And if I chose to serve men in a crooked way, what necessity is there for me to leave the country of my parents?"[19] If he were to be taken as a "hermit" at all, it could only be *because* he "surrendered his will in favor of the social necessities of his time" and submitted to "taint in his person," which means that he had to isolate himself in his mind from all outside attacks. While Po-i and Shu-ch'i were oversensitive to any defilement, Hui of Liu-hsia was completely indifferent to it: "He said: 'You are you, and I am I, although you stand by my side with breast and arms bare, or with your body naked, how can you defile me?' Therefore, self-possessed [*yu-yu jan*] as he was, he kept company with men indifferently, while not losing himself."[20]

The third group of men mentioned by the Master lies somewhere between these two extremes and consists of the common hermits who try to save their lives and self-respect in periods of political danger. However, the special notice taken of their freedom of speech, in addition to the "purity" they gained in seclusion, is remarkable in its contrast to the situation of the less fortunate Hui of Liu-hsia, who had to control both his words and his actions.

The *Analects* contains yet another classification of hermits which is particularly interesting because it combines the inner and outer aspects of eremitism: asceticism and retreat. "The Master said: 'The highest virtue [*hsien*[b]] is possessed by those who retire from the whole world [or 'from their whole generation' *shih*]. Next come those who retire from a position [*ti*]. Next are those who refrain from sexual activities [*se*], and finally those who refrain from speaking [*yen*].'"[21] As we can see from this passage, the hermit, who is here called *hsien*, was held in much higher esteem by earlier than by later Confucians who, since the Han dynasty, had become the representatives of the state. It is particularly startling that the idea of timeliness is not mentioned at all in this text: the hermit is taken as a positive figure regardless of the circumstances under which he lives.

Views of the Chuang Tzu

The conception of the hermit described above is practically identical to that of the Taoists, who took a stand against life in society on principle. On closer examination, however, we may discern that the Taoists, too, were at least indirectly aware of the component of temporality in justifying their inclination to a solitary life. This is made apparent in the chapter of *Chuang Tzu* that deals with the gradual decay of an originally ideal world—"when men still attained simplicity and silence"—a decay which was caused by the progress of knowledge and culture. Only now, *after* this loss of paradise, did it become clear that

> the world has lost the Way, and the Way has lost the world; the world and the Way have lost each other.... The Way cannot go forward in the world and the world cannot go forward in the Way. So, although the sage does not retire to dwell in the midst of the mountain forest, his Virtue is already hidden. It is already hidden, and therefore he does not need to hide himself. The so-called scholars-in-hiding [*yin-shih*] of ancient times did not conceal their bodies and refuse to let them be seen; they did not shut in their words and refuse to let them out; they did not stow away their knowledge and refuse to share it. But the fate of the time was too awry. If the fate of the times had been with them and they could have done great deeds in the world, then they would have returned to Unity and left no trace behind. But the fate of the times was against them and brought them only great hardship in the world, and therefore they deepened their roots, rested in perfection, and waited. This was the way in which they kept themselves alive.[22]

At first glance these lines would appear to have been written by a Confucian.[23] But the underlying idea that it was not a bad political regime but civilization and political order as such which drove the hermit into social and mental seclusion (or, rather, left him behind) is utterly non-Confucian. The Taoist's "waiting" for the return of spontaneous life is of such grandiose dimensions that it became practically irrelevant for the individual recluse—very much in contrast to the Confucian scholar-in-hiding who was simply waiting for an enlightened king. Therefore, too, the affinity to and love of nature which was to play a significant role later on is always implied. In this sense, Taoist philosophy in general—and that contained in *Chuang Tzu*[24] in particular—may be called a philosophy of eremitism; almost every paragraph of the book is interpretable along these lines. Of more specific interest are several of the later chapters in *Chuang Tzu*, especially those on "Robber Chih" ("Tao Chih," chap. 29) and the "Old Fisherman" ("Yü Fu," chap. 31), in which Confucius is taught about the natural aims of life by these two "hiders and solitaries by profession," as we may call them. Even more important is chapter 28 on "Giving Away a Throne,"[25] which has a whole collection of stories about people (including Confucians) who prefer to decline responsibilities, honors, and riches—although for quite different reasons.

One recurring motive appearing in this context is the preservation of one's physical existence, i.e., of "life," while another is the maintenance of one's moral integrity, i.e., of "purity." These are by no means identical aims but rather conflicting ones. This is exemplified in four stories appearing at the beginning and four at the end of this chapter, all of which (except for the very last one) deal with a refusal of the throne by eminent personages. The first four stories talk about legendary hermits—Hsü Yu, Tzu-chou Chih-fu, Tzu-chou Chih-po, Shan Ch'üan, and the "Farmer of the Stone Door" (*shih-hu chih nung*)[26]—to whom Yao and Shun tried in vain to cede the empire; under the pretext of illness and weakness they declined and absconded, the "Farmer of the Stone Door" fleeing "with bag and baggage and followed by his wife and children to the shores of the sea." Of a different kind are those men who appear in the last four stories. They are, in fact, officials—Wu-tse, Pien Sui, Wu Kuang, and (last but not least) the brothers Po-i and Shu-ch'i—who decline the throne or (in the latter case) high office because they doubt the moral standard of the sovereign who wants to cede the empire to them. The former group of hermits had no reason to do this with a Yao or Shun; they shunned the position offered to them on principle. Moreover, the group of officials did not abscond in the end but committed suicide by drowning themselves. The "Robber Chih" chapter discusses officials who likewise committed suicide by "wrapping their arms around a tree or pillar," and then either starving or burning themselves to death,[27] although in this case they took their own lives on account of an insult to their honor.

Asceticism and Mourning, Suicide and Longevity

The classical prototypes for this strange gallery of personages who, though certainly not Confucians, correspond to Confucian ideals (just as the hermits fleeing Yao and Shun tally with Taoist conceptions) are Po-i and Shu-ch'i on the one hand and Ch'ü Yüan on the other. The former, whose story is given, not by chance, in the last paragraph of the chapter "Giving Away a Throne," voluntarily went into exile and death, while Ch'ü Yüan was driven to it against his will by jealous fellow officials and an incompetent prince. But what all of them had in common was the quest for purity, combined with an almost monomaniacal sense of loyalty which inevitably led to their tragic ends. The dispute recorded in the *Shih chi* [Historical records][28] and the *Ch'u-tz'u* [Songs of the South][29] between Ch'ü Yüan and the old fisherman who questioned this fatal passion for purity was carried on in literary pieces of "contre-Li-sao" and "contre-contre-Li-sao" type for almost two millennia,[30] but the basic question of whether honor or life is more important was never definitively resolved. To be sure, neither Ch'ü Yüan nor the notorious old fisherman were "hermits" in the proper sense, nor was the suicide of Ch'ü Yüan and the brothers Po-i and Shu-ch'i an accepted form of eremitism. Nevertheless, they had a tremendous influence on the development of all anchoretical ideas in China.

One reason for this was certainly the ambient gloom of these figures and their successors. The association between anchoretism and sadness was already suggested by the mourning rites which, indeed, rendered the mourner a sort of eremite for a limited period. To give an example, the pertaining regulations found in the *Li chi* prescribe for the mourner a demeanor which in every respect can be called ascetical: the mourner has to dwell on his own in a simple hut, resign from office, refrain from speaking and sexual intercourse, and adopt various other ascetical practices, e.g., fasting, sleeping in discomfort, wearing simple clothes, neglecting his hairdo, and so on.[31] In *Chuang Tzu* we have an interesting passage which even connects mourning with suicide: "There was a man of Yen Gate who, on the death of his parents, won praise by starving and disfiguring himself, and was [posthumously] rewarded with the post of Official Teacher. The other people of the village likewise starved and disfigured themselves, and more than half of them died."[32]

In fact, one is tempted to say that "mourning" might be the most common denominator for all aspects of eremitism in China. This is clearly the case with the Confucian scholar-in-waiting who "mourns" either a deceased sovereign or a fallen dynasty or, more generally, the decay of morals in his time. But it can even be seen to some extent in the attitude of the Taoist recluse (who, as a rule, strictly opposes any form of sincere or ritual mourning)[33] as he "mourns" the loss of paradisiacal life in nature. The decisive difference between them, however, is that the hermit of Taoist bent could still flee to the remaining parts of his lost paradise, to the "mountains and marshes" or the "shores of the sea," while the Confucian mourner could not and was therefore more strongly inclined toward suicide as the ultimate form of retreat.

Hints of asceticism can also be found in Taoism, but, again, they are connected with life rather than with death, for they are all connected with the search for longevity or immortality. This goal is a very old one in Taoism, already in evidence in the Taoist classics. From the very beginning the adepts obviously tried to attain it, not only on the metaphysical but also on the physical plane.[34] This is also attested by historical sources from at least the third century B.C. on. It is true that the various methods of physical exercise—breathing, fasting, sexual practices, yoga—cannot be called "ascetical" in the sense of "mortification" that we are accustomed to finding in the Western context, where such techniques really did aim at weakening the body in order to strengthen the soul. But if we take the word "asceticism" in its original meaning (from the Greek *askesis*, "exercise") it applies precisely to these Taoist practices which were designed to strengthen the body by concentrating its vital forces. Innumerable stories about Taoist hermits support the contention that this particular form of asceticism was quite the heart of the matter for those recluses and that it was an integral part of, if not the actual reason for, their solitary life.

In short, we may conclude that Chinese eremitism grew from three roots which originally had been separate and which are still discernible in later times, when eremitism had become an end in and of itself. The first root is the desire of certain individuals for autonomy as seen in various passages of the *Book of Changes*—the wish to maintain one's "will" and to rather remain a "concealed dragon" than to sacrifice oneself for ruler or society. The second root is the aspiration to save and fulfill one's life (sometimes by means of physical practices) in a natural environment where it is not endangered by politics or questionable achievements of human civilization. The third root, finally, is the retreat out of protest, search for purity,[35] or, last but not least, mourning. Whereas the second root is linked with freedom and life, the third one is closely related to their opposites: commitment and death, symbolized convincingly by those loyal men who committed suicide by "wrapping their arms around a tree." This insoluble conflict between the two primary motives of eremitism caused many difficulties for those who tried to justify their desire to retire from the world. But it also provided eremitism with an unusually intense inner life, as paradoxical concepts are wont to do.

Eremitism in Power: Justifications in the Wei-Chin Period

The Political Aspect: Protest and the Need for Security

All hermits whom we have thus far encountered in classical texts were legendary or semilegendary figures. They represent concepts rather than historical truth. Although the anchoretical ideal was frequently discussed and widely accepted in the pre-Han period, it had no real influence on political or social life. Adherents of Taoism who were unwilling to serve the state apparently preferred to refrain from entering office altogether than to withdraw after having served for a limited period, with the result that they indeed remained unknown to the world. This changed radically in the Latter Han period, probably in reaction to the harsh regime of Wang Mang, which many scholars passively opposed by retreating to private life. Their example revived the interest in earlier instances of political noncooperation and turned the rather scattered views on eremitism outlined above into a full-fledged ideological system. In the Wei-Chin period, eremitism finally evolved into a veritable mass movement within the intellectual elite, one which challenged the state in every respect.[36]

There were several reasons for this broad and almost enthusiastic acceptance of anchoretism. First of all, the atmosphere of growing political instability in general supported solitary tendencies. Moreover, two dynasties—the Ch'in and the Hsin of Wang Mang—had failed to win official legitimation, which justified in retrospect the noncooperation of numerous scholars-in-hiding. According to political theories still traceable in various early texts, down to the end of the Chou dynasty, decapitation or banishment of evil elements and unruly subjects had still been part of the ritual in the establishment of a new dynasty.[37] Legend has it, for instance, that Lü Shang had put to death all hermits who were unwilling to serve the state.[38] But in the Latter Han, the opposite gradually became standard: hermits could legitimize or delegitimize at will the reign of individual rulers or even of whole dynasties. As early as the Han, a determined recluse might be considered superior to the emperor himself. A well-known and quite early example of this situation is the story of the "Four Hoaries" (*ssu hao*), a group of four hermits who had resigned from office under Ch'in Shih Huang-ti and were reluctant to come out of hiding after the founding of the new dynasty.[39] The empress Lü finally enticed them from where they lay low and, with their help, was able to force the emperor Han Kao-tsu to withdraw the nomination of a new crown prince. On the other hand, we learn from the biographies of recluses in the *Hou-Han shu* that a hermit might have been equally prepared to follow the example of Po-i and Shu-ch'i and die for his conviction. This was the case with Kung Sheng, for example, who had been a high official under Han Ch'eng-ti and declined to serve under Wang Mang.[40] When pressed, he took to his bed, refused any food, and died fourteen days later.

Not long after the reestablishment of the Han following Wang Mang's fall, the political and moral situation began to disintegrate once more, and this, of course, did little to inspire confidence in the moral integrity of the state and in the end, it indirectly corrupted the ideal of the recluse itself. There were essentially two significant types of hermits at this time, and they were motivated by quite different, if not contradictory, reasons: the one group consisted of men who were simply scared away by the dangers connected with social obligations of any kind. They were glad to dispense with all salaries and honors in view of the fact that countless officials were being executed by the authorities in the context of never-ending political power struggles which could not be avoided by anyone wanting to pursue such a career. The other group tried to take advantage of the diminished prestige of the state, which needed the demonstrated cooperation of hermits for its own legitimation. Thus, quite a few would-be statesmen chose a solitary life in the hope that the emperor or his ministers would feel compelled to bribe them with riches to return to the court and take up leading positions. While the members of the former group may still be counted among real hermits, as their motivation still falls under the concept "preservation of life" which we have identified as one of the three roots of eremitism, the members of the latter group actually do not belong to the sphere of eremitism in the proper sense. They were already called "fake hermits"[41] at their time, and innumerable stories made reference to them in the period between the second and fifth centuries A.D. Nevertheless, the majority of hermits mentioned in the dynastic histories and other historical works apparently were true hermits. Their biographies read like descriptions of negative or hypothetical careers: sometimes entire lists of employments which were *not* taken up are provided so as to give the reader some idea of the potential rank of the hermit in question.

The Philosophical Aspect: Liberty and Nothingness

Running parallel to the developments on the political plane described above are analogous developments on the philosophical plane. They can be summarized by the catchword "nihilism," which is apt enough in that a new interpretation of the concept of "nonbeing" (*wu*) had become essential for the legitimation of individualistic trends of the time, which also affected the idea of eremitism. In Taoism, nonbeing had always been viewed as the origin of "being" (*yu*[b]) and is discussed in these terms in the *Tao-te ching*: "All creatures under Heaven are the products of being. Being itself, however, is the product of non-being."[42] This idea was still being endorsed by the Neo-Taoist philosopher Wang Pi (226-249) in his commentary to the *Tao-te ching*,[43] but this was no longer the case by the time of Kuo Hsiang's (d. 312) commentary to the *Chuang Tzu*. Kuo Hsiang sees a fundamental distinction, if not opposition, between being and nonbeing. For him, nonbeing was not an indifferent creative force but really true "nothingness" which, by not serving as a purposive creative force, allowed individual things the possibility of spontaneous development. A passage in Kuo's commentary helps to elucidate this critical distinction:

> All forms are formed by themselves [*tzu wu*]. If we go through the entire realm of existence, we shall see that there are no things...that are not transformed by themselves alone [*tu hua*] behind the phenomenal world. Hence everything created itself [*tzu tsao*] without the direction of any Creator. And since things create themselves, they are unconditioned [*wu so tai*].[44]

In reading these lines, one is reminded of the ideas of classical Western atomism as put forth in the writings of Leucippus and Democritus. This concept was later described in detail by Lucretius, who stated: "The whole of Nature is of two things built: atoms and void." Indeed, the free movement of the "atoms" is dependent on the existence of this "void" which is absolutely empty.[45] In a similar way, we observe the liberation of the individual entity—thing or person—in Kuo Hsiang's thought, which is tied in with an "atomization" of the whole universe. The key term in this context is *tzu-jan*, "being by oneself," usually translated as "spontaneous" or "natural." In Kuo's interpretation it means that all beings not only are "created by themselves" but are also "unconditioned" and "transformed by themselves only."

This philosophy, typical not only of Kuo Hsiang but in many respects of the period as a whole, had a considerable impact on the concept of eremitism. Most importantly, it diminished the difference between the hermit and the man within society, for both were now defined as entirely and exclusively dependent on their own spontaneous impulses. And it seems quite logical that in this period the concept of the "hermit in town" (*shih-yin*) or "hermit at court" (*ch'ao-yin*) came to the fore.[46] The idea of an "inner emigration" is certainly much older. There are allusions to it in the *Book of Changes*, and the biography of Tung-fang So (154-93 B.C.) in the *Shih-chi* quotes him as saying: "I have immersed myself in the vulgar and profane and found refuge from the world inside the Bronze Horse Gate. At court we can find refuge from the world and preserve ourselves whole. Why remote mountains and thatched cottages?"[47]

New, however, though essentially paradoxical, was the propinquity for open demonstration of one's inner emigration. What made the "hermit in town" a hermit at all was precisely his eccentric behavior, his constant breaking of taboos, which, indirectly, showed his attachment to the ideal of *tzu-jan*. While in earlier times "pretended madness" had been one of the most convenient excuses for resigning from office and fleeing to the wilderness as a true hermit, madness had now become, in certain cases, a welcome qualification for high appointments. There are numerous stories, e.g., in the *Shih-shuo hsin-yü* [A new account of tales of the world], particularly in the chapter entitled "Free and Unrestrained" ("Jen-tan"),[48] which discuss the shocking demeanor often associated with the abuse of wine. More interesting, because they highlight the relationship between spontaneity and sincerity, are the anecdotes about breaking the rules of mourning. Juan Chi, for instance, is reported to have attended parties while mourning his mother and, on the other hand, to have wept excessively at the funeral of a girl to whom he was not related nor had even known while she was alive.[49] No story could demonstrate better the degree to which men like Juan Chi understood themselves as eremites within society, because mourning for the parents, which usually called for a period of solitary life, no longer affected their mental attitudes.

The Aesthetic Aspect: Nature

Apart from these "hermits in town," the Wei-Chin period saw numerous other recluses flee to the wilderness—not, or at least not entirely, for such negative reasons as distaste for political life but for the positive aim of living a free and unrestricted life in nature. Here again we encounter "fake hermits," though not of the sort described above: the "fake hermits" in this instance were usually members of rich families who had built for themselves large mansions and beautiful parks not too far from the capital where they would arrange banquets for their friends.[50] They styled themselves "hermits" in elegant fashion, much like the European nobility of the mid-eighteenth century for whom (possibly under Chinese influence) the "hermitage" (*eremitage*) was an indispensible part of park and garden. Even these "fake hermits," however, exhibited a genuine appreciation for the beauties of nature, which, after all, is a major part of the real experience of the recluse. In the beginning, i.e., in the last centuries B.C., nature had not yet been seen as a pleasant place for men but rather as a place of danger. This can be inferred from, among other sources, the poem "Summons for a Recluse" ("Chao yin-shih") in the *Ch'u-tz'u*, attributed to a follower of Liu An (Huai-nan Tzu; d. 122 B.C.).[51] It portrays the menaces of wild, untamed nature in great detail and concludes with the exclamation: "O prince, return! In the mountains you cannot stay long." But in spite of the warning, this poem is one of the first (if not *the* first) which reveals an appreciation for the wonders of nature, threatening as they might be.

A sort of genre developed from the "Chao yin-shih" during the Latter Han and Wei-Chin periods which was frequently imitated later on. Gradually, the emphasis changed from cautioning against the horrors and atrocities of nature to describing its manifold beauties and, at the same time, from trying to bring the hermit back to civilization to simply visiting him in his secluded dwelling and enjoying his companionship and the pure life in the midst of crudity and chaos.[52] Thus, the "Chao yin-shih" became one of the most important roots of nature poetry. For developments in nature poetry were analogous to the hermit in town who has retreated to his own inner self rather than to the mountains and marshes. That is, within the category of nature poems there developed poems which contained descriptions of the poet's soul rather than of a real landscape.[53]

The development of the "Chao yin-shih"[54] motif reflected a new dichotomy between culture and nature which had actually begun to appear at about the same time that eremitism began to increase in importance, that is, from the end of the Han dynasty on. It was different from the traditional dichotomy between culture and wilderness that we find in late Chou and Former Han texts, for "nature" was no longer entirely untouched by civilization or quite beyond the reach of the authorities; for the first time, nature had become part of the *oikumene* to the extent that it had been "discovered" by members of society. Nobody felt it necessary to reconcile these two aspects, which in essence represent two antagonistic ways of life, more strongly than Ko Hung (284-363), who also tried to synthesize Confucianism and Taoism, the two philosophies which actually lay at the root of the conflict. The first two chapters of the *Pao-p'u Tzu, wai-p'ien* [The master who embraces simplicity, outer chapters], entitled "Chia tun," [In praise of eremitism][55] and "I-min" [The hermit],[56] deal with this problem. Both are written in the form of fictitious dialogues between a hermit and an official who have the kind of meaningful names we are used to from the *Chuang Tzu*: in the first chapter the hermit is called "Embracing Ice" (Huai-ping),[57] while the official is known as "Running to Power" (Fu-shih). These long and very elaborate dialogues draw on a wealth of historical examples, demonstrating the degree to which eremitism had evolved into a well-founded philosophy in its own right. The dialogues are remarkable in yet another respect: although Pao-p'u Tzu (Ko Hung), who acts only as an "auditor," obviously sympathizes with the hermit, the report is quite fair in that both sides are represented by their best arguments. The main point is whether or not eremitism must be regarded as high treason, since the hermit declines to serve the emperor. In both instances, the debate is won by the hermit: he convinces the official that the recluses, too, are doing their duty for the maintenance of the state. In the second chapter, the hermit says towards the end of his argument:

> One can discern that within the boundaries of the earth nobody is not the ruler's subject. Those who are at court take all efforts to regulate the common affairs, those who live in the mountain-woods cultivate their virtue in order to educate greedy and stupid people. Their methods are different but their aims are alike. All men are subjects, there is nothing beyond [the power] of the ruler, the whole world is like a house: every place where sun and moon shine, every place where rain and dew come down belongs to this realm. How could we be suspended in free space and float in the void sucking the curling vapors, and manage to live no longer on the ground and eat grain? Alas, gold and jade in the mountain, pearls and cowries in the water—even if they are not hoarded in the storehouse and magazines and not at hand for daily use, they still remain the capital of the ruler without exception. The retired scholars who do not live together with meat-eating people are not different from those [rare] objects in mountain and water. How should they not be regarded [as part] of the wealth of the country? [The hermit] Hsü Yu did not isolate himself somewhere outside the Four Oceans, the Four Hoaries did not flee to somewhere beyond the Eight Deserts.... The recluses of today, who purify their conduct in the midst of weeds and shrubs in order to exalt the Way of the former kings and to cause the people to become aware of modesty and restraint, these recluses might even have been honored by Confucians and Mohists and their demeanor might even have met with the approval of Yao and Shun. Obstinate people, however, such as [Po] and [Shu] Ch'i who did not want to eat the corn of the Chou, or as Pao Chiao who died on a bridge,[58] should never become models![59]

This seems to be a strange argument for a hermit: he wins his case by waiving his most important claim, namely, his autonomy, his independence from the demands of society. But it was, in fact, his only defense against the charge that eremitism was equivalent to disloyalty to the state and, at the same time, the only means for him to prevent the world from falling into two halves. The hermit as an "official in the wilderness" indeed acts as a herald of culture in distant, uncivilized places. It is for this reason that Ko Hung (and many writers of the Six Dynasties period) not only viewed nature as essential to the eremite but, conversely, saw the eremite as essential to nature as well: the eremite is considered the only person capable of opening the door for a mutual relationship between man and nature. There is a marvelous essay by K'ung Chih-kuei (447-501),[60] who lived during the (Liu) Sung and Nan-Ch'i dynasties, which deals with his contemporary Chou Yung, a famous official and scholar.[61] Chou had at one time been a recluse, and, in K'ung's opinion, his leaving his hiding place constituted betrayal of the mountains, trees, and other natural beings which had been his companions in solitary life:

Chou Yung is certainly an exceptional person among common men, he knows how to write, is well read and moreover engages in philosophy and history.... When he first arrived here on the Northern Mountain he wanted to excel Ch'ao Fu and Hsü Yu and to humiliate the Hundred Philosophers and the high nobility. His pride reached the sun and his austerity was reminiscent of the autumn. Sometimes he deplored that recluses had vanished forever, sometimes he was frustrated, because men such as Ch'ü Yüan appeared no more in the mountains. He would speak about the most profound problems in Buddhist sutras and examine the deepest secrets of Taoism. Wu Kuang could not be compared to him, Chüan-tzu[62] would not be his equal. But when the carriage of the imperial envoy carrying Chou Yung's nomination arrived in his valley and the imperial message reached his mountain cell he began to walk up and down restlessly and his mind was excited. His convictions changed, his love of life was roused. He looked cheerful in his cell, began to dance on his mat raising his arms, tore his garments of lotus leaves into pieces and burned them, showing his true face and behaving like an ordinary man. The curling clouds became sad and indignant, the mountain springs wept and felt sorry, woods and mountains looked forlorn, all vegetation seemed to lack something. As soon as Chou Yung finally had put on the black sash with the copper seal and had been made the head of a small district his name became quickly known in Chekiang. Once and for all he had thrown away his Taoist books and buried his Buddhist mat long ago. The flogging noise in his yamen irritated his mind and the incessant drudgery of trial cases oppressed his heart. He had ceased to sing and play the lute and given up wine and poetry. [By leaving the Northern Mountain] he had made the red cloud glisten in solitude high in the sky, the bright moon rise lonely, the green pine throw its shadow for no purpose, and the white cloud wander without companion.... The hermit's bed surrounded by orchids is empty, and so the crane cries melancholically at night. The hermit disappeared, and in the morning the apes realize this to their dismay.[63]

The Heritage of Eremitism

Buddhism and Monasticism

Chou Yung, as we learn from K'ung Chih-kuei's essay, was not only a hermit but a Buddhist as well during his sojourn in the wilderness. This is not at all surprising since in his time Buddhism had already superceded Taoism to a large extent, at least as far as the educated class was concerned. It is far more difficult to determine how much of the enormous popularity of eremitism in the Wei-Chin period can be traced to Buddhist influence. Any direct impact can most probably be excluded for the period preceding the middle of the third century A.D., but on the other hand, it appears most unlikely that Chinese thought should not have been at least indirectly influenced by Buddhism much earlier. In my opinion, hints of Buddhist imagination are discernable also in Juan Chi's well-known essay "The Biography of Master Great Man" ("Ta-jen hsien-sheng chuan") in which "Master Great Man" has successive discussions with three men: a Confucian official, a retired scholar drawn along Confucian lines who complains about the unfortunate state of the times, and a wood-gatherer of Taoist inclination who does not, like the retired scholar, care about purity but prefers to live leisurely for his own delight. "Master Great Man" regards himself as different from all three of these men but closest to the wood-gatherer, from whom he differs only in that he is of such supernatural greatness that he is able to transcend the human standards to which even the wood-gatherer remains bound. The argument of "greatness" was often used by Buddhists in discussions against Confucians and Taoists in later times, for example, in the debate on the immortality of the soul during the first half of the fifth century.[64] As we have seen, Ko Hung, who contributed significant ideas to the notion of the hermit, also seems to have been stimulated indirectly by Buddhist conceptions and modes of argumentation. This certainly does not mean that the basic ideas of Chinese eremitism were of foreign descent. It simply means that they might have been strengthened and intensified by the influx of Buddhism in this particular period. In fact, it would be quite surprising if Buddhism, as a pessimistic philosophy, had not at least gently stimulated escapist tendencies in China long before it had won over the majority of the populace. There is good reason to believe that, along with political instability and neo-Taoist philosophy, Buddhism served as a catalyst for the emergence of Chinese eremitism as a sort of independent world view in the Wei-Chin period. On the other hand, eremitism as such lost much of its appeal after the complete victory of Buddhism since it had increasingly to compete with Buddhist monasticism which, in the long run, proved stronger due to its strict organization.

As stated above, monasticism is, of course, only another and just as highly respected form of eremitism. In Christianity there was a long dispute about who was to be preferred: the hermit who lived by himself or the "cenobite" (from the Greek *koinos bios*, "common life" or "life in community"), the monastic monk. The arguments finally ran in favor of the cenobite rather than the hermit.[65] Chinese monasticism, by contrast, was definitely a foreign phenomenon and therefore must be distinguished from indigenous Chinese eremitism. Yet, even though eremitism in all its varieties has, almost down to the present, remained an important and generally accepted way of life in China, it lost its legitimacy as an end in itself due to the Buddhist victory and the subsequent era of Buddhism. Thus, the high tide of eremitism was also the beginning of its disintegration; and Buddhism, which for a short period may have indirectly helped the hermit to acquire a power he never and nowhere was to enjoy again, was also the ultimate cause of its slow but constant decline. While in the Latter Han and Wei-Chin periods the different roots of ancient eremitism gradually grew closer and in fact almost merged in the end, the reverse happened later on: anchoretical concepts and attitudes became elements of independent ideologies. It may therefore be justified to give some consideration to this "heritage of eremitism" rather than to follow up eremitism proper which, though continuing to exist, no longer continued to develop in the post-Wei-Chin period. We shall have to limit the discussion here to a few remarks on the relationship between eremitism and the following three domains: monasticism, loyalism, and the Confucian concept of "being watchful when alone" (*shen tu*).

The contrast between eremitism and monasticism is a quantitative one when viewed against the background of a pessimistic world-view like Christianity or, for that matter, Buddhism. With few exceptions, under the influence of these two religions, both monasticism and eremitism include celibacy as a conspicuous characteristic. This is, in fact, decisive but primarily because abstention from reproduction is the most radical expression of existential pessimism. As a consequence, it also entails complete isolation from the whole of common society. In Buddhism as well as in Christianity, a recluse or a monk raising a family is a contradiction in terms. It is no coincidence that the temptation of the Christian hermit is always of a sexual nature. In contrast, for the indigenous Chinese hermit, regardless of which philosophy he starts from, life-long continence is never at issue. Even Chuang Tzu, the great protagonist of eremitism in China, allegedly was married.[66] The same holds true for Lieh Tzu, whose wife, by the way, was anything but happy about his refusing attractive appointments, or so the legend goes.[67] In addition, it seems that hermits originally used to live in small groups rather than completely alone, as examplified by the Four Hoaries mentioned above who doubtless rank among the first historical hermits.

Under the impact of Buddhism, where true eremitism was of secondary importance in comparison to monasticism, these conditions altered considerably, especially with regard to Taoist eremitism. For practical rather than theoretical reasons, Taoism began to imitate Buddhism not only by establishing monasteries, where Taoists may at first have lived with their families, but also by later demanding celibacy, at least of the higher stratum of its clergy. Taoists such as K'ou Ch'ien-chih (first half of the fifth century) and Sung Wen-ming (first half of the sixth century) were particularly active in introducing these reforms.[68] They apparently saw no other way to compete with the Buddhist monks, whose austerity certainly did not leave the authorities unimpressed when it came to official disputes between Taoists and Buddhists which were frequently arranged from those times on.[69] Thus, "leaving home life" (ch'u chia) became significant in Taoism as well. In spite of such tendencies, celibacy and other ascetical practices aimed at the "mortification" of the body[70] never became as integral a part of Taoism as they had been of Buddhism from the very beginning. In fact, several Taoist schools remained unaffected by them. But they were strong enough to weaken indirectly and devalue the earlier, less stringent forms of eremitism.

On the other hand, a few key topics of indigenous Chinese eremitism were taken up and further developed by Buddhist (and later also Taoist) monasticism. For one thing, it was discussed whether a Buddhist monk should return to the world and assume an official position if the state asked him to do so. Some of these discussions are handed down to us, as, for instance, that between the second ruler of the short-lived Latter Ch'in dynasty in the north, Yao Hsing (r. 394-416), and two monks by the names of Tao-heng and Tao-piao,[71] or the even more interesting one between the usurper Huan Hsüan (369-404) and Hui-yüan.[72] Several of the arguments on both sides of this issue, particularly Yao Hsing's, resemble those with which we are familiar between hermits and officials of the same period or earlier. New, but still connected with this issue, was the controversy over whether or not a monk had to pay homage to the ruler.[73] This debate had already begun by 340 A.D. and continued for a very long time, producing a variety of solutions, one of which was that only fully ordained monks be exempted from bowing to the emperor. Concurrently, some Buddhists, such as Sun Ch'o (fourth century), argued that monks were loyal to the ruler in a different but by no means lesser way,[74] a line of argument paralleling that used by Ko Hung in defense of the recluse.

Loyalism

Despite these affirmations, it can hardly be disclaimed that both Buddhism and Taoist monasticism, much like earlier eremitism, were practically tantamount to a denial of cooperation with the state. The amazingly innovative religious activity in northern China in the middle of the twelfth century, which resulted, above all, in the emergence of Ch'üan-chen Taoism, was apparently called forth to some extent by the disinclination of many intellectuals to serve under a foreign dynasty.[75] Loyalism, of course (if it was not taken for rebellion), did not need this sort of camouflage; it had been an important peripheral feature of one of the roots of eremitism ever since Po-i and Shu-ch'i had died on Mount Shou-yang. In the Sung dynasty, however, loyalism became stressed to the point where it outshone all other anchoretical motives, and eremitism became only one of several expressions of a loyal sentiment. I need not examine once again the relation between eremitism and loyalism in the Sung and Yüan dynasties, as this was done brilliantly more than two decades ago.[76] But when looking at loyalism from the viewpoint of eremitism and not the other way around, it might be necessary to underline that, to a certain extent, loyalism was the successor of monasticism just as monasticism had been the successor of eremitism. Of course, this is *not* to say that these three were directly related, or even less that eremitism or monasticism died out entirely, but only that the crystallization point whence truly new ideas sprang, ideas relevant to a more passive and remote view of life, was shifting from one of these phenomena to the next. And so, too, was the focus of interest of the educated public shifting, a process which at the same time reflected a similar change of emphasis from Taoism to Buddhism and, finally, to Confucianism.

We may also trace the idea of loyalism back to the experience of the Wu-tai period, which perhaps yielded the lesson that no dynasty could long survive that was served by ministers like the notorious "illoyal" Feng Tao (882-954) who was condemned by Ou-yang Hsiu (1007-72) and Ssu-ma Kuang (1019-86). Or we can connect it with the story of Po-i and Shu-ch'i; or with mourning rites; or with the legendary investiture customs of banishing and killing exponents of a vanquished regime. One of its most integral components was the quest for concentration, which again asked for the elimination of desires in order to achieve an understanding of heaven, earth, and man.[77] On a superficial level, the life in retirement that was stimulated by this ideal may not appear too different from that of earlier "retired scholars" or "men-in-hiding,"

but it did differ fundamentally from all three of the original roots of
eremitism—autonomy, the preservation of natural life, and the search for
fidelity and purity—even though some connection with these roots is
plausible. And because this "eremitism" was only a matter between two
parties—the loyal subject and the object of his loyalty—it was open to
becoming "compulsory eremitism," meaning that the subject was subdued by
the object. To be sure, this had already been true, in a way, for eremitism based
on faithfulness or mourning but never in such an uncompromising, exclusive,
and exalted manner.

The scholar-in-hiding Liu Yin (1249-93)[78] cannot be called a loyalist
proper, since he was born in northern China, which was already under
Mongol rule by his time. But as one can infer from his poems in honor of Po-i
and Shu-ch'i, he was nevertheless inclined toward loyalism to the Han state. In
a self-explanatory essay, he offers us an interesting combination of the
concepts of "oneness," "absence of desire," and "aspiring to become a sage"
(which is also the title of the essay, "Hsi sheng chieh"). Precisely because of the
naiveté of this piece, which was written when the author was only eighteen, it
elucidates all the better how life in seclusion, initially inspired by external
circumstances (in this case a political regime that was despised by the author)
leads to self-cultivation and a sort of intellectual asceticism. In the
introductory description of the scenery, we encounter some epithets of the
earlier hermit, though now quite "secularized": beautiful nature, the goblet of
wine, a lute, and books. But "the wine tasting flat" indicates that Liu Yin's
mind is breaking away from this train of thought:

> It was a full-moon night of the year *ting-mao* [1267]. The autumn
> scenery appeared as if freshly bathed. The Milky Way was bright and
> sparkling white. Heaven was high and the air clear. All life was at rest. It
> was then that I sat in my central court. I had a goblet of wine, but drinking
> it, I found it flat. I had a lute, but when I struck it, no music came forth. I
> had a book from the hand of Master Chou Tun-i [1017-73], called the *I-
> t'ung*, which is subtle in meaning and difficult to grasp.... I picked it up
> and read it by the stars and the moon, until I came to the sentence: "The
> scholar aspires to becoming Heaven." This I could not comprehend.... I
> sat dozing, and only after a long time, arose again, when suddenly my
> courtyard was bathed in auspicious air; I seemed to hear the sound of feet
> on the steps, and when I looked about, I saw three men.... One of them
> said: "Lad, do you doubt my word?" I replied, asking: "Can Sagehood
> then be aspired to?" He answered: "It can.... The important thing is
> oneness [*i*]." "What is oneness?" He said: "It is the absence of
> desire.... All people in the world can be without desire." I asked if not all
> the people in the world could become Sages, and he replied: "They
> can.... Sit down, I shall discuss it with you. You have heard that in all
> Heaven and Earth, there is but one Principle [*li*] and nothing else, and
> through interactions it dispersed to become all things. In the end, it
> reassembles, once again becoming one principle. Heaven and Earth are
> man, man is Heaven and Earth. Sages and Worthies are I, I am Sages and
> Worthies.... Then what can it not achieve?"[79]

Before leaving, the master concludes his explanation by admonishing Liu
Yin "to train at achieving tranquility, satisfy the design of his bodily

organization," until he can "proceed to the level of divine wisdom and possess sincerity." We need not elaborate on the idea of "aspiring to become a sage" which is central to Neo-Confucianism and has been explained in relevant Chinese texts in a much more competent manner. What we are concerned with in the context of eremitism is the identification of "oneness" with "absence of desire" and "oneness" brought forward by a scholar who never entered office in an essay which obviously summarizes the essence of his life. To be sure, Liu Yin was no "hermit" in the traditional style. But the ideas of "absence of desire" and "oneness" seem to echo in a peculiar way the inward and outward aspects of eremitism: asceticism and escapism, both designed to unlock and to concentrate the self. While the external retreat of the official gradually became a formalized or even compulsory act based on a loyalist ideology which left the individual little freedom of choice, the internal retreat to one's own self became increasingly emphasized, and this form of retreat lacked all the spectacular attributes of eremitism in the Wei-Chin period.

Meditation and Introspection

This significant change is also apparent in the differing interpretations of the famous Confucian term *shen-tu* which, though quite old, rose to particular prominence in conjunction with the development of Neo-Confucianism. It was characteristically translated in several ways: "being watchful over oneself when alone,"[80] "vigilance in solitude,"[81] "vigilance over one's mind,"[82] "taking care of one's own will,"[83] or "self-inspection."[84] Again, this concept is only very loosely, if at all, connected with anchoretical traditions as such, but its history is still interesting for some aspects of the heritage of eremitism. As is well known, there are two frequently quoted passages in the classics in which this term occurs: the first chapter of the *Chung-yung* [The doctrine of the mean] and the sixth paragraph of the commentary to the *Ta-hsüeh* [The great learning] attributed to Tseng-tzu. The *Chung-yung* reads:

> What Heaven has conferred is called the Nature [*hsing*]. Accordance with Nature is called the Way. Cultivating the Way is called instruction. The Way cannot even for an instant be left, if it could be left it would not be the Way. Therefore the Princely Man is cautious [*chiai-shen*] of a situation where he is not seen and fearful [*k'ung-chü*] of a situation where he is not heard. Nothing is more visible than what is hidden, nothing is more manifest than what is minute. Therefore the Princely Man is *watchful when he is alone*.[85]

The *Ta-hsüeh* commentary says the following on the expression "making the thoughts sincere" (*ch'eng ch'i i*):

> What is meant by "making the thoughts sincere" is: beware of self-deception. [Your moral sentiment must be as immediate] as hating a bad smell and liking a beautiful appearance. This is called self-enjoyment. Therefore the Princely Man must be *watchful when he is alone*. There is no evil [*pu-shan*] to which the mean man, dwelling in retirement [*hsien chü*], will not proceed. However, when he sees a Princely Man, he instantly [tries to] disguise himself, concealing his evilness and displaying

his goodness. [But] when others observe his self [*chi*] as if they saw his heart and veins—of what use then is [his disguise]?...Therefore the Princely Man must be *watchful when he is alone*.[86]

The meaning of these two quotations is quite clear: there is the specific temptation for one who "is alone" or "dwells in retirement" to do evil because one's deeds are not seen or heard by others. So one might be tempted to cheat either oneself or others (both cases are mentioned in the *Ta-hsüeh* commentary along with the warning). But even though one's faults might be well hidden or very minor, they will still come to light when they have been fostered in an intimate atmosphere, i.e., when the person is by himself. This interpretation is confirmed by later treatises on the same subject. Thus, the *New Discourses* (Hsin-lun), a work of uncertain authorship but probably of the sixth century which reflects a degree of Buddhist influence,[87] has a whole paragraph on "being watchful when alone" that both paraphrases and expands upon the *Chung-yung*:

Goodness [*shan*] is the totality of conduct. It cannot be left for an instant; if it could be left it would not be goodness. Man must be good in the same way as his head needs a hat and his feet call for shoes. Now, if somebody is cultivating goodness when in public, but practicing evil when in hiding, he is like one who wears hat and shoes in the clear daylight but walks about naked and barefoot in the darkness of the night. Why then should a man being in the dark [*tsai an-mi*] break away from restraint because he is hidden? Therefore he is cautious [*chiai-shen*] of a place which eyes do not see, and fearful [*k'ung-chü*] of a place which ears do not reach: he rests in his room as if he were receiving guests and penetrates empty [areas] as if there were other men. For that reason Ch'ü Yüan did not change his correct demeanor when walking in the dark, Yen Hui did not alter his countenance when bathing at night;[88] Kou Chien[89] when arresting himself in a rock-cavern did not discontinue the ritual between ruler and subject, nor did Chi Ch'üeh[90] fail to keep to the politeness between husband and wife when tilling the field in the wilderness. All those men were watchful in their hidden and minute [position] and lived in retirement [*chü*] taking goodness for their pillow. They did not change their minds just because they were invisible to listeners. Therefore, if a person persistently remains in goodness then he will no longer have [any] woes and worries inside, no more fears and anxieties from outside. Standing erect alone, he will not be ashamed of his shadow; lying down alone, he will not be ashamed of his quilt. He can receive enlightenment from gods above while he can assure himself by human relationships below. Virtue surrounding him in public and in private, he will be blessed with happiness.[91]

This text proves that at least in the "golden age" of eremitism, "being watchful when alone" was regarded as an attitude particularly advisable for a gentleman in hiding; some of the historical examples given, like Kou Chien and Chi Ch'üeh, clearly point to those who lived temporarily in retirement for one reason or another. It was not a warning against eremitism but a warning against the moral dangers of solitary life. At the same time it applies, of course, to all other people, for, after all, there is nobody who would not be "alone" in certain periods of his existence even if only when "walking in the dark" or "bathing at night." It was doubtless in this latter sense that Chu Hsi also understood the epigram, as his commentaries on the *Chung-yung* and *Ta-hsüeh* clearly reveal.

A fundamentally different interpretation, however, came to the fore when the words "seen" and "heard" were explained in an *active* instead of in a passive sense. This perhaps occurred under the influence of the "idealistic" wing of Neo-Confucianism.[92] The whole passage suddenly acquired a touch of mysticism: "Therefore the Princely Man is cautious over what he does not see and fearful over what he does not hear. There is nothing more visible than what is hidden, nothing more manifest than what is subtle. Therefore the Princely Man is watchful [over himself] *when he is alone.*"[93] To be sure, the interpolation "over himself" is also possible in the earlier understanding of the text, but it is not requisite; and it may to a certain extent accord with yet another (though less important and less disputed) passage of the *Li chi* where we again find the term "being watchful when alone."[94] In the new interpretation of the passage, however (reflected in the translation just quoted), this interpolation is really indispensible: "invisible" and "inaudible" are no longer merely the solitary conditions that call for increased watchfulness but have become the *object* of such watchfulness and, in fact, are metaphors for the inner self. As a consequence, the word "watchful" takes on a different meaning as well: "observant" rather than "vigilant." It is therefore no exaggeration to say that in the light of this new interpretation, the statements in the *Chung-yung* about "being watchful over oneself when alone" "all seem to focus on what may be called the subjectivity of the profound person."[95]

This whole concept played an enormous role in Confucianism during the Ming, when the excessive and at times brutal power of the state caused innumerable scholars and officials to resign. It is also worth noting that during the same period new biographical anthologies of hermits were compiled, an indication that interest in escapism was once again on the rise.[96] The nature of solitary life, however, had changed. In a by now overcrowded country it was no longer as easy as it had been in the Wei-Chin period to escape into the untouched nature of "mountains and marshes," and the authorities certainly were no longer willing to tolerate a "hermit at court." So the new interpretation of the hiding place of the individual, moving from an actual locale where one is neither seen nor heard by anyone else to the innermost self, simply reflected the internalization of anchoretical ideals which could no longer be realized otherwise.

There is another essay from this period on "being watchful when alone," an essay which in every respect stands in sharp contrast to the *Hsin-lun* quoted above. It might be viewed as a comment on the *Ta-hsüeh*, for its concluding sentence makes the statement: "The gist of *The Great Learning* is shen-tu." This essay was written by the famous scholar Liu Tsung-chou (1578-1645)[97] who, though resisting the Ch'an Buddhist influence on Neo-Confucianism, advocated the practice of spending half of each day studying and the other half in meditation. His reflections about *shen-tu* show that for him the "alone" (*tu*) is no longer merely the qualification of a certain condition of human life but nothing less than the authentic designation of men's moral conscience and, at the same time, of his innermost self.

> The learning of the Princely Man, ultimately aiming at the salvation of the world, begins with [putting in order] his own situation. Aiming at [settling] his own situation, he starts [setting straight] his family and his own person, which both are connected with his self. Furthermore, in order [to cultivate] his person he has to start from his mind, his thoughts and knowledge. When he has come this far he cannot push it further, he cannot examine it further by dealing with his self. It is so hidden and subtle! This hidden and subtle place is called: "alone." What is this "alone"? Actually, it does not contain one single thing in itself, but all things are present in it. It is the focal point of highest goodness, . . . it is the basis of [all] things, and "being watchful over the alone" is the initial action for an investigation of things. To pursue the learning of the Princely Man does not mean [however] that one could refrain from acting by hiding his person [*tsang shen*], or abstain from speaking by sealing his mouth, or desist himself from all social intercourse by isolating himself from the ears and eyes of the world. He talks all day, but the reason for his talking is inaudible to others; it is only he himself who hears it. And he acts all day, but the reason for his acting is invisible to others; it is only he himself who sees it. To hear and see himself means to know himself. Wanting to get to the bottom [of this self-knowledge] we have to cause this mind of ours to settle, finding constant rest: being tranquil yet [retaining] the ability to think [*ching-an lü-te*]—this is the utmost state of "being watchful."[98]

Not much of the original eremitism remains in this line of thought. Still, Liu Tsung-chou resigned from high positions several times in his life. And when the Ming dynasty finally fell, he followed the example of Po-i and Shu-ch'i: he refused food and drink until he died.

The Hermit: An Individualist

The External Aspects of Eremitism and the Components of Individualism

Tradition is an integral part of Chinese eremitism, with special reference to the times before and after it flourished in the Wei-Chin period. In that case, however, we would have to distinguish between the hermit in a wider and in a narrower sense, the "actual" hermit on the one hand and the "not-yet-hermit" or "no-longer-hermit" (as we have termed them above) on the other. This study has tried to deal with both of them, by no means exhaustively, in an effort merely to demonstrate their interrelations. For it is here that one may hope to find the most accessible path to understanding Chinese "individualism."

Eremitism proper was, of course, most closely connected with Taoism: if Buddhism can be called a religion of monasticism, then Taoism could well be called a religion of eremitism. By comparison with Taoism, eremitism did not play as central a role in Confucianism. For Confucians, it was always taken as the exception, not the rule, and was restricted to mourning and to transitional periods of political decay (likewise associated with sorrow and affliction). On the other hand, all forms of Chinese eremitism—Taoist escape from society, Confucian "mourning" and loyalism, or for that matter, Buddhist pessimism and monasticism—obviously went along with an exaltation of the individual. Whatever the reasons for separating oneself from society, they called for a strong personality ready to set himself apart from the rest of the world, at least temporarily, and to live alone and unprotected. Thus, while it is beyond any doubt that many, if not most, hermits in China were strong individuals, we are posing quite a different question when we ask whether they were also "individualists."[99] Individualism, an intricate, multifaceted term which in itself actually represents an ideology of predominantly Western origin, certainly consists of many components, some of an active and some of a passive quality. The hermit in China, as elsewhere, felt akin to the latter but not to the former. He was possibly a "defensive" but certainly not an "aggressive" individualist, even if eremitism, as we have seen, did incorporate some aggressive aspects, at least from the viewpoint of the state. In a Western context, the defensive components of individualism may be summarized by the concept of "privacy." There are, indeed, some aspects of Chinese eremitism which suggest the idea of "privacy": the hermit "bars his door" or lives in mountain caves out of reach of ordinary human beings. Still, it is doubtful whether eremitism can be identified with the search for privacy in any respect. Isolating oneself from the civilized world by trying to flee it, or simply putting some distance between the world and oneself, does not necessarily mean that one wants in principle to isolate oneself. Quite to the contrary, this particular isolation may simultaneously mean liberation from all of the obstacles that separate an individual from the rest of nature—and, in fact, this is precisely the meaning it held for the true Taoist hermit. Thus, the "privacy" of the hermit in his seclusion quite often aimed not at the preservation of the ego but rather at its final dissolution in the cosmos and nature.

This goal is also in accord with the teaching of all major traditions of philosophical Taoism in the "golden age" of eremitism in the third and fourth centuries A.D. (although the quest for an individual immortality or longevity prevailed in religious Taoism at the same time). The longing for a final dissolution in the cosmos was paralleled and supported by the conviction of a pervading equality not only of men but of all beings, which excluded the idea of a distinctive "human dignity." In contrast, Confucianism, while making a clear distinction between human and nonhuman beings, definitely fostered the notion of "human dignity" and the concept of "equality of men" as well. But this "equality" was always seen in the context of society, where it necessarily was limited by the social position of the individual. As Hsün Tzu put it: "Men are all equal in that they are unequal."[100] Thus, everyone possessed an ego of his own, but it was impossible to separate it from the social environment and its hierarchy. There was certainly every opportunity for individual self-development, but only little autonomy in the full meaning of the word. Consequently, any retreat from society was conceived as a sort of interval in life which for this very reason could not be other than temporal—or, in the worst case, doomed the fugitive to death. In sum, while the Taoist hermit generally strove to lose immediate contact with his self, the Confucian hermit temporarily or permanently lost contact with his life which, ideally, was inseparable from society.

The Internalization of Eremitism and the Discovery of the Self

Buddhism added yet another aspect to this complicated relationship between eremitism and individualism. Confucianism had always objected to egoism, and Taoism had long since responded to the more refined desires of a civilized world, which it regarded as the source of all mischief for both the individual and society. But neither had ever negated the very existence of the ego itself: in Buddhism the desires themselves were seen as expressions of a fundamental illusion about the unreal nature of the ego. Meditation had no doubt been practiced in China long before the arrival of Buddhism. The actual end of Buddhist meditation, however, was not only the appeasement of the self, as had been the case in Taoism, but the perception of its nonexistence. It is obvious that against this background any individualism becomes entirely meaningless. But strangely enough, the growing efforts to reveal the illusionary character of the self could also lead to its opposite: namely, a rising interest in the structure of the inner self and its various components. Buddhist meditation, whether practiced in monasteries or not, was apparently based on a much more active attitude than one might expect. It tried systematically to discover the features of the self, like landmarks of an unknown continent, even while simultaneously denying the very existence of this continent. This turn from the outside to an inside world entailed significant consequences for the evolution of individualism in China. For, in spite of all the early traces of a quest for autonomy and self-development to be found, for example, in the *Book of Changes* (where it talks of men who behave like "concealed dragons" and take "their will for their law"), a more intensive self-inspection was still necessary for a system of thought which really reflected individualist tendencies to evolve.

It is perhaps only this internalization of anchoretical ideals that makes it worthwhile to study eremitism in the context of individualism—not only because it resulted in a change of emphasis from resignation to self-inspection but also because it allowed the individual to preserve fully his active powers in practical life. There were two periods in Chinese intellectual history during which this internalization was achieved in a quite different way. In the first period, it was practiced by the "hermits in town" or "hermits in court." These "hermits" had discovered that not only "nature" but every being in itself, regardless of whether or not it was physically separated from all other beings, was autonomous. Kuo Hsiang's *Chuang Tzu* commentary furnished the theoretical basis for this view of life. But the "spontaneous" conduct which the "hermits in town" considered appropriate to this new-found autonomy—drunkenness, negligence in office, the breaking of ritual taboos and the like—retained a great deal of the original hermit's passive attitude. And surprisingly enough, although they had become aware of an independent ego, this ego remained almost unconscious and anonymous, corresponding entirely to the Taoist concept of the self in general. The autonomy they were proud of was rarely accompanied by a search for self-development. It is small wonder, therefore, that the liberty of the "hermit in town" gradually degenerated into a libertinism that seemed to confirm the widespread suspicion (particularly among Confucians) that their whole philosophy was based exclusively on nihilism and egoism.

When eremitism was internalized for the second time, it was under the auspices of Neo-Confucianism. The new interpretation of the term "being watchful when alone" (demonstrated most strikingly by Liu Tsung-chou's essay quoted above) was, of course, not the starting point but merely a typical—though significant and momentous—outcome of this development. This inner emigration must certainly be viewed as a reaction to the "brutalization" of public life that began in the Yüan dynasty, just as the rise of eremitism in the Wei-Chin period is at least partly attributable to the widespread disintegration of political order. But aside from that, it was also a logical continuation of Neo-Confucian thought in Ming times. Quite in contrast to "eremitism in town," however, which evolved in a Taoist environment, the Confucian discovery of the inner self aimed at moral self-development rather than self-liberation from ethical or conventional norms. The techniques employed towards this end—meditation, "quiet-sitting," walking slowly, and regular self-examination, among others—doubtless owe much to Buddhism. But again, these physical and intellectual exercises were geared to achieving the opposite of what Buddhism had in mind, that is, not the disappearance, but the exploration and strengthening of the self so that, as the *Ta-hsüeh* promised, it might become the nucleus for a chain of reactions which would ultimately result in the salvation of the whole world.

Possibly nowhere—but certainly not in China—can the hermit be called an individualist without great reservation. Nor is eremitism simply identical with individualism, for the former lacks the active, if not aggressive, aspects which are at least as characteristic of individualism as its passive and defensive ones. Indirectly, however, eremitism contributed a great deal to the evolution of a typically Chinese variety of individualism. This indirect influence, interestingly, was at its strongest when eremitism as an ideal had already passed its height: namely, when in Neo-Confucianism the "being alone," the solitude once experienced by the hermit in his outer world, had become a metaphor for the inner self. Thus, in spite of the basic differences between eremitism and individualism, the creation—and, perhaps to an even greater extent, the disintegration—of the anchoretical ideal in China was clearly connected with individualism.

NOTES

1. See, for instance, the introductions to the *Hou-Han shu*, 12 vols. (Peking: Chung-hua Shu-chü, 1965), vol. 9, *chüan* 81, 2665-66, and the *Sung shu* [History of the Sung], 8 vols. (Peking: Chung-hua Shu-chü, 1974), vol. 8, *chüan* 93, 2275-76. Aside from studies

mentioned in notes below, namely, those by Mote (n. 76), Kung-chuan Hsiao (n. 38), Li Chi (n. 41), Wakatsuki Toshihide (n. 46), Kaguraoka Masatoshi (n. 56), and Nemoto Makoto (n. 76), the following are important for Chinese eremitism: Chiang Hsing-yü, *Chung-kuo yin-shih yü Chung-kuo wen-hua* [The Chinese hermit and Chinese culture] (Shanghai: Chung-hua Shu-chü, 1947); Kasahara Chūji, "Genjitsu no henkaku to inton-shiso" [The change of reality and the thought of eremitism], in *Ritsumeikan sōritsu gojushūnen kinen rombunshō* [A collection of essays in commemoration of the fiftieth anniversary of the founding of Ritsumeikan] (Kyoto: Ritsumeikan Daigaku, 1950), 133-75; Shiba Rokurō, *Chūgoku bungaku ni okeru kodoku-kan* [The appearance of the feeling of loneliness in Chinese literature] (Tokyo: Iwanami, 1959); Ōda Teijō, *Tōyō shisō ni okeru kodoku to mujō* [The appearance of loneliness and unfeelingness in Eastern thought] (Tokyo: Hōsei Daigaku, 1970); Fuji Masaharu, *Chūgoku no inja* [The Chinese hermit] (Tokyo: Iwanami, 1973).

2. Among others, *i-min, yin-i, kao-i, i-shih, hsi-i, i-i.*

3. For example, *yin-i, yin-shih.*

4. *Yu-jen.*

5. For example, *hsi-i, shan-hsi.*

6. Most common expression: *chü-shih.*

7. *Ch'u-shih.* Aside from these terms, there were others which pointed to eremitism only indirectly, e.g., *kao-shih,* "lofty gentleman," or *ta-shih.*

8. The terms *tu-hsing*[b] (sincere conduct) and *tu-hsing*[a] (independent conduct) go back to the same chapter, "Ju-hsing" [The conduct of the Ju], in the *Li chi* [Book of rites] which describes the demeanor of the educated official, although *tu-hsing* applied to the sage can be traced to the even earlier *Chuang Tzu.* See *Li chi chi-shuo* [Collected explanations of the *Book of Rites*] (Chung-kuo hsüeh-shu ming-chu ed.) *chüan* 10 (no. 41), 321, translated in James Legge, the *Li-Ki,* 2 vols., The Sacred Books of the East, ed. Max Müller, vols. 27 and 28 (reprint ed., Delhi: Motilal Barnasidas, 1966), 2:406 and 408; and *Chuang Tzu chi-chieh* [Collected explanations of the *Chuang Tzu*] (Chu-tzu chi-ch'eng ed.), *chüan* 23, 150, translated in Burton Watson, *The Complete Works of Chuang Tzu* (New York: Columbia University, 1968), 255: "He who does what is not good in clear and open view will be seized and punished by men. He who does what is not good in the shadow of darkness will be seized and punished by ghosts. Only he who clearly understands both men and ghosts will be able to walk alone" (or: "to conduct himself alone" [*tu-hsing*[a]]).

9. *Lun-yü cheng-i* [Corrected meanings of the *Analects*] (Chu-tzu chi-ch'eng ed.), *chüan* 13 (no. 21), 294-95, translated in James Legge, *The Chinese Classics,* 5 vols. (Hong Kong: Hong Kong University Press, 1960), 1:272.

10. Along these lines we can also trace the relation of the hermit to other groups which figure as his intellectual cousins in Chinese texts: namely, those who were "hermits" involuntarily or by profession. The companions of the "hiders" and "escapists," "noncollaborationists" and fugitives, are the exiles banished by the ruler, the most conspicuous example of whom is Ch'ü Yüan. Hiders by profession were, for example, the robbers who sometimes developed a pertinent philosophy, as we can see from Robber Chih in *Chuang Tzu.* A counterpart of the solitary is also to be found in the prisoner who does not "bar his door and refrain from going out" (*tu men pu ch'u*), as some recluses did, but is locked up by the authorities. Finally, there are solitaries by profession, such as fishermen (on lakes or rivers, not at sea) and wood-gatherers, who appear again and again as opponents in discussions with worldly-wise officials and hermits of every variety.

11. This aspect is particularly important for Chinese eremitism, in which the acceptance of poverty and the quest for solitary life are often almost identical.

12. John Blofeld, trans., *The Book of Change* (London: Allen and Unwin, 1965), 86-87.

13. Ibid., 124. The term *kao-shih,* "lofty gentleman," which is also used for hermits, is obviously based on this quotation. Slightly different in that a more passive conduct is depicted is a sentence in the hexagram *lü,* "He treads his path peacefully. Righteous persistence will bring good fortune. *Hsiang Commentary:* Righteous persistence of the recluse [*yu-jen*] will bring good fortune. He [cleaves to the] middle [path] and does not allow himself to be confused" (ibid., 21).

14. My translation. See also ibid., 92.

15. My translation. See also the German translation by Richard Wilhelm, trans., *I Ging, Das Buch der Wandlungen*, 2 vols. (reprint ed., Düsseldorf: Eugen Diederichs, n.d.), 1:232.

16. Blofeld, *Book of Change*, 152 and 157.

17. See Legge, *Chinese Classics*, 1:290-91, 331-39.

18. *Lun-yü cheng-i, chüan* 18 (no. 8), 395-97, translated in Legge, *Chinese Classics*, 1:336-37 (translation slightly modified). See also Arthur Waley, *The Analects of Confucius* (reprint ed., New York: Random House, n.d.), 221-22. I-i and Chu-chang are unknown. Waley suspects that they are not proper names at all but parts of a corrupt sentence.

19. *Lun-yü cheng-i, chüan* 18 (no. 2), 388, translated in Legge, *Chinese Classics*, 1:331-32.

20. *Meng Tzu cheng-i* [Corrected meanings of Meng Tzu] (Chu-tzu chi-ch'eng ed.), *chüan* 2A (no. 9), 144-48 (my translation). See also the translation in Legge, *Chinese Classics*, 2:206-8.

21. *Lun-yü cheng-i, chüan* 14 (no. 39), 324, translated in Legge, *Chinese Classics*, 1:290 and Waley, *Analects*, 190. Legge and Waley, however, render this passage in completely different ways.

22. *Chuang Tzu chi-chieh, chüan* 6, 98-99, translated in Watson, *Chuang Tzu*, 172-74.

23. Burton Watson mentions in a note to this passage (*Chuang Tzu*, 173) that Fukunaga Mitsuji held precisely this view.

24. In this context, several passages dealing with the concept "alone" (*tu*) are of interest, e.g., *Chuang Tzu chi-chieh, chüan* 5, 36, translated in Watson, *Chuang Tzu*, 75: "Puny and small [the sage] sticks with the rest of men. Massive and great, he perfects his Heaven alone [*tu ch'eng ch'i t'ien*]." And: "[The possessor of a state] is a thing, and yet he is not a mere thing; therefore he can treat other things as mere things. He who clearly understands that . . . is no longer a mere thing—how could he be content only to govern the hundred clans of the world and do nothing more? He will move in and out of the Six Realms, wander over the Nine Continents, going alone, coming alone [*tu wang tu lai*]. He may be called a Sole Possessor [*tu-yu chih jen*], and a man who is a Sole Possessor may be said to have reached the peak of eminence" (ibid., 68, translated in Watson, 123-24).

25. This chapter constitutes a whole, together with chapters 29 and 31, which is interrupted by chapter 30. Several stories of chapter 28 are also to be found in *Lü-shih ch'un-ch'iu* [Mr. Lü's Spring and Autumn Annals] (Chu-tzu chi-ch'eng ed.), *chüan* 2 (no. 2), 16-18, translated in Richard Wilhelm, *Frühling und Herbst des Lü Bu We* (Jena: Eugen Diederichs, 1928), 16-19.

26. This "Farmer of the Stone Door" (*shih-hu chih nung*) is possibly identical with the "Keeper of the Stone Gate" (*shih-men ch'en men*) who appears in *Lun-yü cheng-i, chüan* 14 (no. 41), 325, translated in Legge, *Chinese Classics*, 1:290.

27. *Chuang Tzu chi-chieh, chüan* 29, 198, translated in Watson, *Chuang Tzu*, 329-30: "When the world talks of worthy gentlemen, we hear 'Po I and Shu Ch'i.' Yet Po I and Shu Ch'i declined the rulership of the State of Ku-chu and instead went and starved to death on Shou-yang Mountain, with no one to bury their bones and flesh. Pao Chiao made a great show of his conduct and condemned the world; he wrapped his arms around a tree and stood there till he died. Shen-t'u Ti offered a remonstrance that was unheeded; he loaded a stone onto his back and threw himself into a river, where the fish and turtles feasted on him. Chieh Tzu-t'ui was a model of fealty, going so far as to cut a piece of flesh from his thigh to feed his lord, Duke Wen [of Chin]. But later, when Duke Wen overlooked him he went off in a rage, wrapped his arms around a tree, and burned to death. Wei Sheng made an engagement to meet a girl under the bridge. The girl failed to appear and the water began to rise, but, instead of leaving, he wrapped his arms around the pillar of the bridge and died. These six men were no different from a layed dog, a pig sacrificed to the floor, a beggar with his alms-gourd in his hand. All were ensnared by thoughts of reputation and looked lightly on death, failing to remember the Source or to cherish the years that fate had given to them." Particularly interesting is the mention of Wei Sheng, who also committed suicide by "wrapping himself" but because of his fidelity to a girl rather than to his sovereign. His story indirectly demonstrates the almost erotic relation of the official to his ruler and also the extent to which these suicides were the result of frustrated love.

28. *Shih chi*, 10 vols. (Peking: Chung-hua Shu-chü, 1959), vol. 8, *chüan* 84, 2486, translated in Burton Watson, *Records of the Grand Historian of China*, 2 vols. (New York: Columbia University Press, 1961), 1:504-7.

29. *Ch'u-tz'u* (SPPY ed.), 7.1a-3a, translated in David Hawkes, *Ch'u Tz'u, The Songs of the South* (Oxford: Clarendon Press, 1959), 90-91.

30. For the history of this literary genre, see Laurence A. Schneider, *A Madman of Ch'u: The Chinese Myth of Loyalty and Dissent* (Berkeley, University of California Press, 1980).

31. See *Li chi chi-shuo*, *chüan* 8 (no. 22), 248-49; *chüan* 10 (no. 37), 312, translated in J. J. M. De Groot, *The Religious System of China*, 2 vols. (reprint ed., Taipei: Literature House, 1964), 1:480-81, 609, and 651.

32. *Chuang Tzu chi-chieh*, *chüan* 26, 181, translated in Watson, *Chuang Tzu*, 301-2. Cf. another interesting passage in this context where Confucius advises Yen Hui to practice "fasting of the mind" (*hsin-chai*): "Make your will one! Don't listen with your ears, listen with your mind [*hsin*]. No, don't listen with your mind, but listen with your spirit [*ch'i*ᵃ]. Listening stops with the ears, the mind stops with recognition, but spirit is empty and waits on all things. The Way gathers in emptiness alone. Emptiness is the fasting of the mind" (ibid., *chüan* 4, 23, translated in Watson, 57-58).

33. See the critical remarks on the mourning for Lao Tzu (*Chuang Tzu chi-chieh*, *chüan* 3, 20, translated in Watson, *Chuang Tzu*, 52-53) and on Chuang Tzu's behavior after the death of his wife (ibid., *chüan* 18, 110, translated in Watson, 191-92).

34. See Henri Maspero, "Les procédés de 'nourrir le principe vital' dans la religion taoiste ancienne," *Journal Asiatique*, 1937 (229):177-252, 353-430.

35. In the context of the preservation of life, the aspect of purity also plays a certain role, but only in a qualified way and definitely not to the same degree as it does in the context of protest.

36. As a consequence, hermits also attracted more attention in historical writing. Although Ssu-ma Ch'ien's *Shih chi* does not contain a chapter which deals explicitly with hermits, there are two chapters which include stories of persons who may be regarded as "hermits" in one way or another: *chüan* 61 (*lieh-chuan*, *chüan* 1) has Po-i and Shu-ch'i; and *chüan* 84 (*lieh-chuan*, *chüan* 24) has Ch'ü Yüan and Chia I (the latter was exiled for his involvement in "intrigues" but was later appointed as tutor to a prince, after whose sudden death he grieved so bitterly that he died within the following year). The *Hou-Han shu* is the first of the dynastic histories to include an authentic chapter on "Hermits" ("I-min," *chüan* 83), which contains seventeen names, as well as one on "[Men of] Independent Conduct" ("Tu-hsing"ᵃ, *chüan* 81) with twenty-four names. The former chapter includes an introduction that attempts to define and classify these two groups. Chapters of a similar nature can be found in the following dynastic histories: *Chin shu*, *chüan* 94: "Yin-i," thirty-eight names; *Sung shu*, *chüan* 93: "Yin-i," eighteen names; *Nan-Ch'i shu*, *chüan* 54: "Kao-i," twelve names; *Liang shu*, *chüan* 51: "Ch'u-shih," thirteen names, and *chüan* 52: "Chih-tsu," three names; "Wei shu," *chüan* 90: "I-shih," four names; *Sui shu*, *chüan* 77: "Yin-i," four names; *Nan chih*, *chüan* 75 and 76: "Yin-i," forty-four names; *Pei shih*, *chüan* 88: "Yin-i," six names; *T'ang shu*, *chüan* 192; "Yin-i," twenty names; *Hsin T'ang shu*, *chüan* 196: "Yin-i," twenty-four names, and *chüan* 194: "Cho-hsing," seven names; *Sung shih*, *chüan* 457-59: "Yin-i," forty-three names; *Chin shih*, *chüan* 127B: "Yin-i," twelve names; *Yüan shih*, *chüan* 199: "Yin-i," six names; *Hsin Yüan shih*, *chüan* 241: "Yin-i," twenty names, and *chüan* 239 and 240: "Tu-hsing"ᵇ," one hundred twenty-four (!) names; *Ming shih*, *chüan* 298: "Yin-i," twelve names; and *Ch'ing shih kao*, *chüan* 505 and 506: "I-i," thirty-four names. No separate chapters on hermits are contained in the following: *Han shu*; *San-kuo chih*; *Ch'en shu*; *Pei-Ch'i shu*; *Chou shu*; *Wu-tai shih*; and *Hsin Wu-tai shih* (which does, however, have one on "Men of Singular Conduct": "I-hsing," *chüan* 34, six names). Among private collections of biographies of hermits which still exist or have been partly reconstructed is one attributed to Hsi K'ang (223-262). The most famous one, however, is the *Kao-shih chuan* [Biographies of lofty gentlemen] written by Huang-fu Mi (215-82) which in today's version includes ninety-one men. Huang-fu Mi was a scholar-in-hiding himself who refused to serve Emperor Chin Wu-ti and, interestingly enough, is said to have

had occasional fits of depression during which he threatened to commit suicide. In his introduction he mentions that his work was designed to supplement the *Shih-chi* and the *Han shu*, which gave too little attention to hermits and solitaries. His book became the favorite source of later encyclopedias from the *T'ai-p'ing yü-lan* [(Book for the) emperor's inspection of the T'ai-p'ing era] down to the *Ku chin t'u-shu chi-ch'eng* [Synthesis of books and illustrations of ancient and modern times], where recluses and related types of men (*tu-hsing*^a, *cho-hsing*, etc.) were frequently given a special separate section. An interesting continuation of Huang-fu Mi's *Kao-shih chuan* was compiled by Huang-fu Hsiao (1497-1546) under the title *Hsü Kao-shih chuan* (later changed to *I-min chuan* [Biographies of hermits]). It has one hundred biographies from the Chin to the Sung, including one of Huang-fu Mi himself. On the background of this text, see L. Carrington Goodrich and Chaoying Fang, *Dictionary of Ming Biography* (New York: Columbia University Press, 1976), 658.

37. On these "legendary rebels," see the literature mentioned in Joseph Needham, *Science and Civilisation in China*, 5 vols. to date (Cambridge: Cambridge University Press, 1956-), 2:115-21.

38. See, for example, *Pao-p'u tzu, wai-p'ien* (Chu-tzu chi-ch'eng ed.), *chüan* 2, 106-8, where Lü Shang is said to have put to death a certain K'uang-chüan, a fictitious name made up of the "madmen" and "timids" mentioned in the *Analects* (see n. 9 above). On Lü Shang and his relation to legendary eremitism in general, see Sarah Allan, "The Identities of Taigong wang in Zhou and Han Literatures," *Monumenta Serica*, 1972-73, 30:57-99. See also Kung-chuan Hsiao, *A History of Chinese Political Thought*, trans. Frederick W. Mote, 2 vols. (Princeton: Princeton University Press, 1979), 1:388.

39. Cf. *Shih chi*, vol. 6, *chüan* 55, 2044-47, translated in Watson, *Records*, 1:146-49.

40. *Han shu*, 12 vols. (Peking: Chung-hua Shu-chü, 1962), vol. 10, *chüan* 72 (no. 3), 3080-86.

41. On the discussion about fake hermits (*ch'ung-yin*) in introductions to biographies of hermits in the dynastic histories, see Li Chi, "The Changing Concept of the Recluse in Chinese Literature," *Harvard Journal of Asiatic Studies*, 1962-63, 24:239-41.

42. This appears in *chüan* 40, translated in Arthur Waley, *The Way and Its Power* (reprint ed., London: Allen and Unwin, 1949), 192.

43. See the translation by Ariane Rump and Wing-tsit Chan, *Commentary on the Lao Tzu by Wang Pi* (Hawaii: University of Hawaii Press, 1979).

44. See Kuo Hsiang's commentary, *Chuang Tzu chi-shih* [Collected expositions of the *Chuang Tzu*] (Chu-tzu chi-ch'eng ed.), *chüan* 2, 53, translated in Wing-tsit Chan, *A Source Book in Chinese Philosophy* (Princeton: Princeton University Press, 1963), 330-31.

45. Cf. Benjamin I. Schwartz, "On the Absence of Reductionism in Chinese Thought," *Journal of Chinese Philosophy*, 1973-74, 1:27-44; W. Bauer, "The Problem of Individualism and Egoism in Chinese Thought," in *Studia Sino-Mongolica, Festschrift für Herbert Franke* (Wiesbaden: Franz Steiner Verlag, 1979), 434-37.

46. See Li Chi, "Changing Concept of the Recluse," 241-43, and Wakatsuki Toshihide, "Chūgoku ni okeru inja-kan no hensen: Sanrin no inja kara shichō no inja e" [The change of the appearance of the hermit in China: from hermit in the mountain-forest to the hermit in town and court], *Bungei ronso*, March 1964, 8:13-20, and September 1964, 9:65-73.

47. *Shih chi*, vol. 10, *chüan* 126, 3205.

48. *Shih-shuo hsin-yü* (Chu-tzu chi-ch'eng ed.), *chüan* 23, 188-99, translated in Richard B. Mather, *Shih-shuo hsin-yü, A New Account of Tales of the World* (Minneapolis: University of Minnesota Press, 1976), 371-91.

49. *Shih-shuo hsin-yü*, *chüan* 23, 188 and 189, translated in Mather, *New Account of Tales of the World*, 372 and 374.

50. See J. D. Frodsham, "The Origin of Chinese Nature Poetry," *Asia Major*, n.s. (1960-61), 8:68-104; Obi Kōichi, *Chūgoku bungaku ni arawarete shizen to shizenkan* [The appearance and view of nature in Chinese literature] (Tokyo: Iwanami, 1969), esp. 259-87 and 530-71; Wolfgang Kubin, "Die Entwicklung der Naturanschauung in der chinesischen Literatur (Zhou bis Song)," Habilitation thesis, Freie Universität Berlin, 1981, 193-202.

51. *Ch'u-tz'u* 12.1a-3b, translated in Hawkes, *Songs of the South*, 119-20. See also A. E. Erkes, "The Chao-yin-shih 'Calling Back the Hidden Scholar' by Huai-nan-tze," *Asia Major*, 1924, 1:119-24.

52. See Jay Sailey, *The Master Who Embraces Simplicity, A Story of the Philosopher Ko Hung, A.D. 283-343* (San Francisco: Chinese Materials Center, 1978), 488-89; Kubin, "Die Entwicklung der Naturanschauung," 151-72.

53. See Andrew March, "Self and Landscape in Su Shih," *Journal of the American Oriental Society*, 1966, 86:377-96; Shuen-fu Lin, *The Transformation of the Chinese Lyrical Tradition, Chiang K'uei and Southern Sung Poetry* (Princeton University Press, 1978), 16-26; James J. Y. Liu, "Time, Space and Self in Chinese Poetry," *Chinese Literature: Essays, Articles, Reviews* (CLEAR), 1979, 1:157-79; Kubin, "Die Entwicklung der Naturanschauung," 226-96.

54. The counterpart of the "Chao yin-shih" was a poetic genre named "Seven" (*ch'i*[b]) which bears some resemblance to a poem in the *Ch'u-tz'u*, the "Summons of the Soul" ("Chao hun") written for a dead or fatally ill king (*Ch'u-tz'u*, 9.1a-15b, translated in Hawkes, *Songs of the South*, 101-9). It describes the beauties of a luxurious, cultured life as might have been common with the Han nobility in order to cause the vanishing soul to return to the body. See David Knechtges and Jerry Swanson, "Seven Stimuli for the Prince," *Monumenta Serica*, 1970-71, 29:99-116. For a convenient list of these essays, see Morohashi Tetsuji, ed., *Dai Kanwa jiten* [Great Chinese-Japanese dictionary], 13 vols. (Tokyo: Taishū-kan Shoten, 1955-59), 1:82a.

55. *Pao-p'u tzu, wai-p'ien, chüan* 1: 103-6, translated in Sailey, *Master Who Embraces Simplicity*, 3-25, and Renate Schubert, "Das erste Kapitel des *Pao-p'u tzu wai-p'ien*," *Zeitschrift der Deutschen Morgenländischen Gesellschaft*, 1970, 119:278-301.

56. *Pao-p'u tzu, wai-p'ien, chüan* 2, 106-10. On the concept of eremitism in the *Pao-p'u tzu*, see also Kaguraoka Masatoshi, "Hōbokushi ni okeru initsu shisō" [The idea of the anchorite in *Pao-p'u tzu*], *Tohō shūkyō* (July 1980), 55:51-69. Kaguraoka argues that two earlier concepts of the hermit were combined and reconciled in the *Pao-p'u tzu*: the Confucian one (represented by the word *i*) and the Taoist one (represented by the word *yin*).

57. On this name, see Sailey, *Master Who Embraces Simplicity*, 3, n. 2, referring to the *Chuang Tzu*'s use of the term *yin ping*, "drinking ice [to still a heart desiring wealth and status]."

58. Pao Chiao is apparently mixed up with Wei Sheng. See n. 37 above.

59. *Pao-p'u tzu, wai-p'ien, chüan* 2, 109.

60. K'ung Chih-kuei has a biography in *Nan-Ch'i shu* [History of the Southern Ch'i], 3 vols. (Peking: Chung-hua Shu-chü, 1972), vol. 3, *chüan* 48, 835-40.

61. Chou Yung has a biography in *Nan-Ch'i shu*, vol. 3, *chüan* 41, 730-34.

62. Wu Kuang and Chüan-tzu are two legendary hermits who have biographies in the *Lieh-hsien chuan* [Biographies of various immortals] (Ts'ung-shu chi-ch'eng ed.), *chüan* 1: 12-13, and 9-10. Wu Kuang also appears several times in the *Chuang Tzu*, e.g., in *chüan* 26 (*Chuang Tzu chi-chieh*, 181, translated in Watson, *Chuang Tzu*, 302), where he declines to accept the empire from King T'ang.

63. Juan Chi, "Ta-jen hsien-sheng chuan," in *Juan Pu-ping chi* [Collected works of Juan Pu-ping] (Han Wei Liu-ch'ao pai-san chia chi ed.), 230-36, translated in Donald Holzman, *Poetry and Politics, The Life and Works of Juan Chi, A.D. 210-263* (Cambridge: Cambridge University Press, 1976), 192-205.

64. See, for example, *Ming Fo lun* [An essay illuminating Buddhism], (Taishō daizōkyō, text no. 2109:90), translated in Walter Liebenthal, "Immortality of the Soul in Chinese Thought," *Monumenta Nipponica*, 1952, 8:380-81 "[Even before] there was no doubt that we live in Ch'ih-hsien, inside the Eight Poles. Now [we are told] there are three thousand suns and moons displayed [in the megacosmos], that twelve thousand worlds are distributed [in space]; that if one grinds to dust the earth of countries as numerous as the sand of the Ganga River as many kalpa there are, as there are dust particles; [in such an enormous universe] all that creation contains appears minute, unable to fill it.... People say: What existed before the Yellow Emperor, how far, how hazy it is! But, seen from the height of the Heavenly Course, it happened yesterday. The *Book of History* does not go

back beyond T'ang and Yü [Yao and Shun], and yet this time is called remote. . . . And there are the *Book of Poetry* and the *Book of Changes*, charming and profound. But now when in the measureless universe the three thousand suns and moons are lit and the line of their lights illuminates the twelve thousand worlds and proclaims the True [Order of Nature], then we know that what has been written by Chou Kung and K'ung Tzu answers merely the inarticulate cry of pygmy communities who call for a savior."

65. The skeptical attitude towards the hermit in Christianity can be traced back to St. Basil (second half of the fourth century). He wrote that "solitude is antagonistic to the law of love, because the solitary is bound to serve his own interests. It is bad for anybody not to have a master to rebuke faults. . . . There will always be the danger that a solitary will imagine that he has attained spiritual perfection. He cannot practise the virtues of humility, pity, and long suffering" (see Peter F. Anson, *The Call of the Desert: The Solitary Life in the Christian Church* [London: S.P.C.K., 1964], 40).

66. See n. 43 above.

67. *Chuang Tzu chi-chieh*, *chüan* 28, 189-90, translated in Watson, *Chuang Tzu*, 313-14. Compare also the story of the "Farmer of the Stone Door" mentioned above who "fled with bag and baggage to the shore of the sea."

68. See Henri Maspero, *Le Taoisme* (Paris: Civilisation du Sud, 1950), 171; Heinrich Hackmann, "Die Mönchsregeln des Klostertaoismus," *Ostasiatische Zeitschrift*, 1919-20, 8:142-70.

69. Cf. Lo Hsiang-lin, "T'ang-tai san-chiao chiang-lun k'ao" ("A study of the discussions of Confucianism, Taoism, and Buddhism in the T'ang dynasty"), *Tung-fang wen-hua*, 1954, 1:85-97.

70. Apart from sexual continence, abstention from sleep seems to be typical for asceticism and was aimed at a real "mortification" of the body. To my knowledge, it is never mentioned in earlier Taoist texts but appears frequently in such early Chinese Buddhist texts as the *Kao-seng chuan* [Biographies of eminent monks].

71. See Helwig Schmidt-Glintzer, *Das Hung-ming chi und die Aufnahme des Buddhismus in China* (Wiesbaden: Franz Steiner Verlag, 1976), 71-74.

72. Ibid., 60-66.

73. Ibid., 53-56, 66-70; Eric Zürcher, *The Buddhist Conquest of China* (Leiden: E. J. Brill, 1959), 106-8, 160-63.

74. See Schmidt-Glintzer, *Hung-ming chi*, 57-60.

75. See Ch'en Yüan, *Nan-Sung ch'u Ho-pei hsien tao-chiao k'ao* [A study of new Taoist sects in Hopei at the beginning of the southern Sung dynasty] (Peiping: n.p., 1941), 17-25.

76. Nemoto Makoto, *Sensei shakai ni okeru teiko seishin: Chūgoku teki initsu no kenkyū* [The spirit of resistance in authoritarian society: a study of Chinese eremitism] (Tokyo: Sōgen Sha, 1952); and Frederick W. Mote, "Confucian Eremitism in the Yüan Period," in *The Confucian Persuasion*, ed. Arthur F. Wright (Stanford: Stanford University Press, 1960), 202-40.

77. It is perhaps typical for this attitude that the *Hsin Wu-tai shih* uses the expression *i-hsing* ([men of] singular conduct) for the characterization of such eccentric men, who in earlier dynastic histories had been introduced under the heading "[Men of] Independent [or Extraordinary] Conduct."

78. On Liu Yin, who has a biography in the *Yüan shih*, *chüan* 171, see Mote, "Confucian Eremitism," 202-40.

79. Liu Yin, *Ching-hsiu hsien-sheng wen-chi* [Collected writings of Master Ching-hsiu] (Ts'ung-shu chi-ch'eng ed.), *chüan* 1, 1-3, translated in Mote, "Confucian Eremitism," 213-15 (translation slightly modified).

80. See Legge, *Chinese Classics*, 1:366-67, 384; Wm. Theodore de Bary, ed., introduction to *The Unfolding of Neo-Confucianism* (New York: Columbia University Press, 1975), 27; Tu Wei-ming, *Centrality and Commonality: An Essay on Chung-yung* (Honolulu: University of Hawaii Press, 1976), 2.

81. Carsun Chang, *The Development of Neo-Confucian Thought*, 2 vols. (New York: Bookman Associates, 1957-62), 2:174.

82. Ibid., 2:249.

83. Hsieh Yu-wei, "The Status of the Individual in Chinese Ethics," in *The Chinese Mind: Essentials of Chinese Philosophy and Culture*, ed. Charles A. Moore (Honolulu: East-West Center, 1967), 315.

84. Ibid.

85. Legge, *Chinese Classics*, 1:383-85; see also Tu, *Centrality and Commonality*, 2.

86. Legge, *Chinese Classics*, 1:366-67.

87. This *Hsin-lun*, which has to be distinguished from several other books with the same title (e.g., one written by Huan T'an), has been attributed to Liu Chou (fl. late fifth century A.D.), to Liu Hsieh (fl. early sixth century), and to its commentator, Yüan Hsiao-cheng (seventh century?). For an evaluation of the book, see Alfred Forke, *Geschichte der mittelalterlichen chinesischen Philosophie* (Hamburg: De Gruyter, 1964), 250-60.

88. I was unable to identify the sources of these descriptions of Ch'ü Yüan's and Yen Hui's behavior.

89. The biography of Kou Chien, king of Yüeh (r. beginning in 496 B.C.), in *Shih chi, chüan* 41, only mentions that he fasted severely after his total defeat at the East Gate of the capital of the state of Wu. Moreover, he daily drank out of a vessel filled with gall and slept on firewood in order not to forget his defeat until he finally annexed the state of Wu. See also Herbert A. Giles, *A Chinese Biographical Dictionary* (reprint ed., Taipei: Literature House, 1962), no. 982.

90. On Chi Ch'üeh (seventh century B.C.), see Giles, *Chinese Biographical Dictionary*, no. 289, where the same story is reported: "When he was laboring in the fields and his wife brought him his dinner, he would receive her with a bow as though she were some honored guest."

91. *Hsin-lun* (Han-Wei ts'ung-shu ed.), 2.6b-7b.

92. In this context, see two passages in *Wang Shou-jen, Ch'uan-hsi lu*, in *Yang-ming ch'üan-shu* [Collected works of Wang Yang-ming] (SPPY ed.), secs. 266 and 324, *chüan* 3, 12a-b, and *chüan* 3, 246, translated in Wing-tsit Chan, *Instructions for Practical Living and Other Neo-Confucian Writings by Wang Yang-ming* (New York: Columbia University Press, 1963), 218, 252-53.

93. Translated in Tu, *Centrality and Commonality*, 2. Legge, (*Chinese Classics*, 1:384) translates this as follows: "On this account, the superior man does not wait till he sees things to be cautious, nor till he hears things to be apprehensive. There is nothing more visible that what is secret, and nothing more manifest than what is minute. Therefore the superior man is watchful over himself, when he is alone."

94. See *Li chi chi-shuo*, ch. 5 (no. 10), 135. Legge (*Li Ki*, 1:401-2), translates the whole paragraph: "That in the [instituting of] rites the multitude of things was considered a mark of distinction, arose from the minds [of the framers] being directed outwards. The energy [of nature] shoots forth and is displayed everywhere in all things, with a great discriminating control over their vast multitude. In such a case, how could they keep from making multitude a mark of distinction in rites? Hence the superior men, [the framers], rejoiced in displaying [their discrimination]. But that in [the instituting of] rites the paucity of things was [also] considered a mark of distinction, arose from the minds [of the framers] being directed inwards. Extreme as is the energy [of nature] in production, it is exquisite and minute. When we look at all things under the sky, they do not seem to be in proportion to that energy. In such a case how could they keep from considering paucity a mark of distinction? Hence the superior men, [the framers], *watched carefully over the solitude* [of their own thoughts]" (emphasis added). The *shen-tu* concept is used in a similar way in texts recently discovered at Ma-wang-tui. See "Lao Tzu chia-pen chüan hou ku i-shu shih-wen" [Lao Tzu, text series A, followed by the annotated text of (four) ancient books (hitherto) lost], in *Ch'ang-sha Ma-wang-tui san hao Han mu po shu* [Books on silk (found in) Han grave no. 3 at Ma-wang-tui] (Shanghai: Wen-wu Ch'u-pan She, 1974).

95. Tu, *Centrality and Commonality*, 4.

96. Aside from the *I-min chuan* by Huang-fu Hsiao already mentioned above (n. 36), the following are of importance: Huang Chi-shui, *P'in-shih chuan* [Biographies of poor scholars], 2 *chüan*; and *I-min shih* [History of hermits], 22 *chüan*, attributed to Ch'en Chi-

ju (1558-1639), which was inaccessible to me. A printed edition of the latter work, dated 1604, is kept in the library of the Kyoto Daigaku.

97. On Liu Tsung-chou, see Arthur W. Hummel, *Eminent Chinese of the Ch'ing Period* (Washington: United States Government Printing Office, 1943), 532-33; and Tang Chun-i, "Liu Tsung-chou's Doctrine of Moral Mind and Practice and His Critique of Wang Yang-ming," *Unfolding of Neo-Confucianism*, ed. de Bary, 305-31.

98. "Chi-shan hsüeh-an" [Scholarly records of Chi-shan], in *Ming-ju hsüeh-an*, [Scholarly records of Confucian scholars of the Ming dynasty] (Chung-kuo hsüeh-shu ming-chu ed.), *chüan* 62, 713.

99. For the concept of "individualism," see Steven Lukes, *Individualism* (Oxford: Basil Blackwell, 1973).

100. *Hsün Tzu chi-chieh* [Collected explanations of Hsün Tzu], *chüan* 9, 96, translated in Homer H. Dubs, *The Works of Hsüntze* (London: Arthur Probsthain, 1928), 124.

Glossary

Ch'an 禪

Ch'ang-sha Ma-wang-tui san hao Han mu po shu　長沙馬王堆三號漢墓帛書

Ch'ao Fu 巢父

"Chao hun" 招魂

ch'ao-yin 朝隱

"Chao yin-shih" 招隱詩

Ch'en Chi-ju 陳繼儒

Ch'en shu 陳書

Ch'en Yüan 陳垣

ch'eng ch'i i 誠其意

chi 己

ch'i^a 氣

ch'i^b 七

Chi Ch'üeh 冀缺

"Chi-shan hsüeh-an" 戢山學案

Chia I 賈誼

"Chia tun" 嘉遯

chiai shen 戒愼

chiai-shih 介士

Chiang Hsing-yü 蔣星煜

Chieh Tzu-t'ui 介子推

ch'ien 乾

chih 志

"chih-tsu" 止足

Chin shih 晉史

Ch'in Shih Huang-ti 秦始皇帝

Chin Wu-ti 晉武帝

ching-an lü-te 靜安慮得

Ching-hsiu hsien-sheng wen-chi 靜修先生文集

Ch'ing shih kao 清史稿

Chiu shu 晉書

cho-hsing 卓行

Chou Kung 周公

Chou shu 周書

Chou Tun-i 周敦頤

Chou Yung 周顒

chü 居

ch'u 處

Chu-chang 朱張

ch'u chia 出家

Chu Hsi 朱熹

chü-shih 居士

ch'u-shih 處士

Ch'u-tz'u　楚辭

Fuji Masaharu　富士正晴

Ch'ü Yüan　屈原

Fukunaga Mitsuji　福永光司

chüan　狷

"Genjitsu no henkaku to inton-shisō"
現実の変革と隠遁思想

Ch'üan-chen　全眞

Han Ch'eng-ti　漢成帝

Ch'uan-hsi lu　傳習錄

Han Kao-tsu　漢高祖

Chüan-tzu　涓子

Han-shu　漢書

Chuang Tzu　莊子

"Hobokushi ni okeru initsu shisō"
抱朴子における隠逸思想

Chuang Tzu chi-chieh　莊子集解

Chuang Tzu chi-shih　莊子集釋

Hou-Han shu　後漢書

Chūgoku bungaku ni arawareta
shizen to shizen to shizenkan
中国文学に現われた自然と自然観

hsi　棲

hsi-i　棲逸

Chūgoku bungaku ni okeru kodoku-
kan　中国文学における孤独感

Hsi K'ang　嵇康

Hsi Sheng-chieh　希聖解

Hsi-tz'u　繫辭

"Chūgoku ni okeru inja-kan no
hensen: Sanrin no inja kara shi chō
no inja e" 中国における隠者の変遷
山林の隠者か弓市朝の隠者へ

hsien[a]　仙

hsien[b]　賢

Chūgoku no inja　中国の隠者

hsien-chü　閑居

Chung-kuo yin-shih yü Chung-kuo
wen-hua　中國隱士與中國文化

hsien-jen　賢人

hsin　心

ch'ung-yin　充隱

hsin-chai　心齋

Chung-yung　中庸

Hsin-lun　新論

Dai Kanwa jiten　大漢和辭典

Hsin T'ang shu　新唐書

Feng Tao　馮道

Hsin Wu-tai shih　新五代史

Fu-shih　赴勢

Hsin Yüan shih　新元史

hsing 性

Hsü Kao-shih chuan 續高士傳

Hsü Yu 許由

Hsün Tzu 荀子

Huai-nan Tzu 淮南子

Huai-ping 懷冰

Huan Hsüan 桓玄

Huan T'an 桓譚

Huang Chi-shui 黃姬水

Huang-fu Hsiao 皇甫孝

Huang-fu Mi 皇甫密

Hui of Liu-hsia 柳下惠

Hui-yüan 慧遠

i^a 逸

i^b 一

I Ching 易經

i-hsing 一行

i-i 遺逸

I-i 夷逸

i-min 逸民

I-min chuan 逸民傳

I-min shih 逸民史

i-shih 逸士

I-t'ung 易通

"Jen-tan" 任誕

"Ju-hsing" 儒行

Juan Chi 阮籍

Juan Pu-ping chi 阮步兵集

Kaguraoka Masatoshi 神樂岡昌俊

kao 高

kao-i 高逸

Kao-seng chuan 高僧傳

kao-shih 高士

Kao-shih chuan 高士傳

Kasahara Chūji 笠原仲二

Ko Hung 葛洪

Kou Chien 勾踐

K'ou Ch'ien-chih 寇謙之

ku 蠱

ku-chia 孤家

Ku chin t'u-shu chi-ch'eng 古今圖書集成

kua-jen 寡人

k'uang 狂

K'uang-chüan 狂狷

k'un 坤

K'ung Chih-kuei　孔稚珪

k'ung-chü　恐懼

K'ung Tzu　孔子

Kung Sheng　龔勝

Kuo Hsiang　郭象

Lao Tzu　老子

"Lao Tzu chia-pen chüan hou ku i-shu shih-wen"　老子甲本卷後古佚書釋文

li　理

Li chi　禮記

Li chi chi-shuo　禮記集說

Liang shu　梁書

Lieh-hsien chuan　列仙傳

Liu An　劉安

Liu Chou　劉晝

Liu Hsieh　劉勰

Liu Tsung-chou　劉宗周

Liu Yin　劉因

Lo Hsiang-lin　羅香林

lü　履

Lü [empress]　呂后

Lü Shang　呂尚

Lü-shih ch'un-ch'iu　呂氏春秋

Lun-yü cheng-i　論語正義

Meng Tzu cheng-i　孟子正義

Ming Fo lun　明佛論

ming-i　明夷

Ming-ju hsüeh-an　明儒學案

Ming shih　明史

Morohashi Tetsuji　諸橋轍次

Nan-Ch'i shu　南齊書

Nan shih　南史

Nan-Sung ch'u Ho-pei hsien tao-chiao k'ao　南宋初河北縣道教考

Nemoto Makoto　根本誠

Obi Kōichi　小尾郊一

Ōda Teijō　太田悌藏

Ou-yang Hsiu　歐陽修

Pao Chiao　鮑焦

Pao-p'u Tzu, wai-p'ien　抱朴子，外篇

Pei shih　北史

Pei-Ch'i shu　北齊書

Pien Sui　卞隨

P'in-shih chuan　貧士傳

Po-i　伯夷

pu-shan　不善

*Ritsumeikan sōritsu gojushūnen
kinen rombunshū*　立命館創立五十周
年記念論文集

San-kuo chih　三國志

se　色

*Sensei shakai ni okeru teikō seishin:
Chūgoku teki initsu no kenkyū*
専制社会における抵抗精神
中国的隠逸の研究

shan　善

Shan Ch'üan　善卷

shan-hsi　善棲

Shao-lien　少連

shen tu　愼獨

Shen-t'u Ti　申徒狄

Shiba Rokurō　斯波六郎

shih　世

Shih chi　史記

Shih-hu chih nung　石戶之農

Shih-men ch'en men　石門晨門

Shih-shuo hsin-yü　世說新語

shih-yin　市隱

Shu-ch'i　叔齊

Shun　舜

ssu hao　四皓

Ssu-ma Ch'ien　司馬遷

Ssu-ma Kuang　司馬光

Sui shu　隋書

Sun Ch'o　孫綽

Sung shih　宋史

Sung shu　宋書

Sung Wen-ming　宋文明

Ta-hsüeh　大學

"Ta-jen hsien-sheng chuan"　大人
先生傳

ta-shih　大士

T'ai-p'ing yü-lan　太平御覽

T'ang [king]　湯

T'ang shu　唐書

"T'ang-tai san-chiao chiang-lun
k'ao"　唐代三教講論考

"Tao Chih"　盜跖

Tao-heng　道恆

Tao-piao　道標

Tao-te ching　道德經

ti　地

ti-hsien　地仙

t'ien-hsien　天仙

Tōyō shisō ni okeru kodoku to mujō
東洋思想における孤独と無情

tsai an-mi　在暗密

tsang-shen 藏身

Tseng-tzu 曾子

tu 獨

tu ch'eng ch'i t'ien 獨成其天

tu-chiai 獨介

tu-hsing[a] 獨行

tu-hsing[b] 篤行

tu-hua 獨化

tu men pu ch'u 杜門不出

tu wang tu lai 獨往獨來

tu-yu chih jen 獨有之人

tun 遯 (遁)

Tung-fang So 東方朔

Tzu-chou Chih-fu 子州支父

Tzu-chou Chih-po 子州支伯

tzu-jan 自然

tzu tsao 自造

tzu wu 自物

Wakatsuki Toshihide 若槻俊秀

Wang Mang 王莽

Wang Pi 王弼

Wang Shou-jen 王守仁

Wei Sheng 尾生

Wei shu 魏書

Wen [duke] 文

wu 無

Wu Kuang 務光

wu so tai 無所待

Wu-tai shih 五代史

Wu-tse 无擇

Yao 堯

Yao Hsing 姚興

yen 言

Yen Hui 顏回

yin 隱

yin-i 隱逸

yin ping 飲冰

yin-shih 隱士

yu[a] 幽

yu[b] 有

Yü-chung 虞仲

"Yü fu" 漁父

yu-jen 幽人

yu-yu jan 由由然

Yüan Hsiao-cheng 遠孝政

Yüan shih 元史

Individualist Expressions of the Outsiders during the Six Dynasties

Richard B. Mather

In discussing "individualist expressions of the outsiders," I shall define as "outsiders" those members of the *shih/ta-fu* class[1] (the ruling elite) who for one reason or another were alienated from the conventional pursuits of their class—namely, office-holding and the fulfillment of the normal social rituals. Other classes, such as peasants, artisans, merchants, rank-and-file military men, and clerics from lower-class families, were also "outsiders" in the sense that they had no direct connection to the center of power, but since they were not judged by the same criteria as the *shih/ta-fu*, whatever eccentricities they had were in relation to a different center. The "individualists" cited in this paper will therefore be from the upper levels of early Chinese society. However, even while claiming they were "alienated" and on the outside, it is necessary to point out that they by no means rejected the fundamental world-view of the majority. In their view as well as in that of the mainstream, the universe was conceived to be a harmonious organism whose smooth operation depended on every part finding its proper place within the whole. The ruler had indeed to be ruler above, and the ruled were assigned prescribed roles below in a clearly articulated hierarchical order, perceived as replicating the order of heaven and earth. On this everyone was basically agreed.

The parting of the ways occurred when certain ritual and legal norms, which had evolved over the years and were sanctified by their attribution to sages of antiquity and their embodiment in the classics, were claimed by the majority to be the true mirror of the natural order. As Yüan Hung (328–76) said in a classic statement in his *Annals of the Later Han* (Hou-Han chi), "What is the origin of the Teaching of Names [*ming-chiao*, i.e., the accepted social code, the teaching which deals with the phenomenal world of human relations as opposed to the absolute, "nameless" world of the Tao]? In my view the meaning of 'names' [father/son, ruler/ruled, etc.] is determined by compliance with the nature of heaven and earth and by seeking the principles of naturalness [*tzu-jan*]."[2] Countering this claim, the "outsiders" charged that the norms into which contemporary society was being coerced were in reality a cruel and unnatural Procrustean bed. By raising their voices or silently acting out their protest, they were, for their part, only trying to recover the lost harmony with heaven and earth, and in the process their own integrity.

I find it fascinating that both the "holism" of the mainstream, which probably reached its clearest expression through the Neo-Confucian synthesis of the Sung and later periods, and the "individualism" of the disaffected, which, as Ying-shih Yü demonstrates elsewhere in this volume, found its truest voice during the general breakdown of values in the Wei-Chin period, start with essentially the same premises yet end with such different conclusions. Most of the unconventional characters described in this paper, by giving greater latitude to their "true selves" (as opposed to the "ephemeral selves" they manifested in response to social or political demands), became only the more unconventional and eccentric, while the Neo-Confucians, following the example of the sage himself as he reached the age of seventy, found they could "follow whatever their hearts desired without ever overstepping the bounds of propriety" (*Analects*, II:4).

The Confucian model implies that because the self is ultimately continuous with the whole it does not need to set itself apart. The "individualist" model of the Wei-Chin and Southern dynasties, on the other hand, implies that precisely because the self is continuous with heaven and earth and with "naturalness," it has to detach itself from the arbitrariness of mistaking "names"—mere human inventions—for cosmic reality. The mutually contradictory "ises" and "is nots" (*shih-fei*) of the Confucians and Mohists, for example, the one holding mourning rites to be cosmically ordained and the other holding them to be useless and wasteful, were a case in point. This inevitably put the "individualists" on a collision course with the authorities, whose role by definition was to enforce agreement between (arbitrary) names of duties (such as "mourning rites") and their actual performance.

Those who are provisionally labeled "individualists," then, are persons who affirmed their conformity to a greater whole than the one envisioned by the Confucian sages. By doing so they were also protesting what they felt to be the artificial, and therefore false, norms of contemporary society, which in their view were a bilious travesty of the cosmic order. The outsiders I will be discussing all lived during the age of disenchantment following the collapse of Han orthodoxy (roughly A.D. 250–500). Their stories derive from the somewhat fictionalized accounts in the fifth-century anecdotal collection *Shih-shuo hsin-yü* [A new account of tales of the world] and from the lives and works of reclusive poets of the fourth and fifth centuries.

An obvious example of political as well as social protest is Hsi K'ang (223-62), who, unlike his older and similarly alienated friend, Juan Chi (210-63), made no effort to camouflage his discontent and eventually lost his life under the executioner's axe. It is, in fact, on account of his forthright honesty and total lack of tact that he has been admired throughout Chinese history. Others may have *wanted* to blurt out their anger or insult the powerful in the way he did, but they usually found more devious and subtle ways of doing so. The whole coterie to which Hsi K'ang and Juan Chi are assigned—the so-called

"Seven Worthies of the Bamboo Grove"—are a somewhat idealized construct of a later generation, never clearly identified as a group before the appearance in mid-fourth-century Chien-k'ang (modern Nanking) of the book *Lives of Famous Gentlemen* (Ming-shih chuan) by the author of the *Hou-Han chi*, Yüan Hung.[3] It was partly the nostalgia of the northern emigrés in Eastern Chin south of the Yangtze which made them persist in spinning legends about the dimly remembered heroes of the lost homeland in the north. The "Seven Worthies" became a favorite topic of drawing-room conversations, and, interestingly, it was their presumed eccentricity, their emancipated life-style, their love of wine, and above all their defiance of convention which endeared them to the courtiers of Eastern Chin. If we are to believe Hsieh An (320-85), as recorded in the *Shih-shuo hsin-yü*, Yüan Hung compiled the *Ming-shih chuan* on the basis of Hsieh's own oral accounts, which the latter insisted he had just made up as a kind of joke (*chiao-kuai*), not as sober biography.[4] Reinforcing Hsieh An's disclaimer is the story found in Liu Chün's sixth-century commentary to the *Shih-shuo*, citing Tai K'uei's (d. 396) "Discourse on the Seven Worthies of the Bamboo Grove" ("Chu-lin ch'i-hsien lun"). It seems Yü Liang's (289-340) nephew once asked his uncle, who had emigrated from Lo-yang around the time of its fall in 311, about the story then circulating in Chien-k'ang that the aging Wang Jung (234–305), the youngest of the "Seven Worthies," once claimed to have been a drinking companion of Hsi K'ang and Juan Chi while they were still alive. Yü responded testily, "I never heard of such a thing while I was in Lo-yang. This story has suddenly shown up down here in Chien-k'ang, no doubt because some curiosity monger just made it up out of whole cloth."[5]

With the authenticity of the stories thus called into question even at the time of their first appearance around 340-50, it is hard to know how much of their content belongs to third-century fact and how much to fourth-century fiction. Whatever the proportions, it is evident that the mid-fourth century, when the *Ming-shih chuan* was first gaining popularity, was a time when the northern emigré population in Chiang-nan felt a need for stories about heroes who had resisted the political and moral pressures of their time. It was also a time when the cult of individual personality, exemplified by the vogue of concise but comprehensive characterization (*hsiang*) which became a favorite theme of so-called "Pure Conversation" (*ch'ing-tan*), made everyone acutely aware of the unique qualities of at least some individuals. The practice probably originated from routine character references and recommendations for civil office, which was the approved method of recruitment during the Six Dynasties. But it resulted in a genuine appreciation of individual differences. And the most interesting subjects were often found to be precisely those who differed most from the crowd.

How was Hsi K'ang different? He was quite candid about his own traits in his "Letter Breaking Off Friendship with Shan T'ao [205-83]" ("Yü Shan Chü-yüan T'ao chüeh-chiao shu"), preserved in the sixth-century *Anthology of Literature* (Wen-hsüan):

> My taste for independence [*fang*; lit., "letting myself go"] was aggravated
> by my reading of Chuang Tzu and Lao Tzu; as a result any desire for fame
> grew daily weaker and my commitment to freedom [*jen-shih*; lit., "giving
> rein to my true self"] increasingly firmer.... Furthermore, in society there
> are prescribed courtesies, and the court has its rules. When I consider the
> matter carefully, there are seven things I could never stand, and two things
> which would never be condoned.[6]

The writer goes on to enumerate these points of disagreement. The seven
things he "could never stand" were (1) getting up early for the dawn audience;
(2) being surrounded by stuffy subordinates who would hamper his freedom;
(3) kneeling for long periods or kowtowing when garbed in formal attire; (4)
having to write volumes of paperwork; (5) attending funerals and making
mawkish visits of condolence; (6) working with vulgar and conniving
politicians; and (7) the endless troubles and anxieties of official life. As for the
things that "would never be condoned," these were (1) his continual criticism
of Yao and Shun and Confucius and the Duke of Chou—the unassailable
paragons of every right-minded citizen; and (2) his penchant for speaking out
against wrongdoing whenever he saw it, regardless of the perpetrators.

Obviously, Hsi's protest was entirely personal. He liked his freedom and
hated public life, but in the political climate of his times he could not be a
private person. Critical opinions expressed in confidence to relatives or
friends came eventually to the attention of the powerful minister Chung Hui
(225-64), and because Hsi had been overheard disparaging the sage-kings of
antiquity he was branded a "corrupter of public morals" and executed in 262.
To be quite honest, however, there was rather more to it than that. He had also
been a heavy financial contributor to the unsuccessful coup of Wu-ch'iu
Chien, who in 255 had attempted to stop the rise of the Ssu-ma clan which
eventually overthrew the Wei ruling house and founded the Chin dynasty in
265. In addition, Hsi was reported to have treated Chung Hui with contempt
when the latter honored him with a personal visit. But of course the principal
reason for getting rid of him was his intransigent loyalty to the Wei royal
family of Ts'ao, to which he was related by marriage. The immediate excuse
for doing so was his imprudent defense of a friend who had been wronged by a
favorite of Chung Hui.

It is important for our purposes to see what view of human nature and
individual freedom lay behind Hsi K'ang's posture of defiance against the
orthodoxy of his times. For even though I have described his protest as
"entirely personal," it was wholly consistent with his views on the inviolability
of one's own nature (*hsing*). As he explained in his letter to Shan T'ao, "[The
gentleman] acts in accordance with his nature.... What is esteemed in human
relationships is the just estimate of another's inborn nature and helping him
realize it. When you see a straight piece of wood, you do not want to make it
into a wheel."[7] The last remark refers to Shan's reported effort to get Hsi
K'ang appointed to the post Shan was vacating.

In another essay, "On Release from Self-Interest" ("Shih-ssu lun"), Hsi
described how the gentleman "is able to transcend the Teaching of Names
[*ming-chiao*] and give free rein to naturalness [*jen tzu-jan*]." The thrust of this

essay is that the "names" of the teaching which went by this designation represented only the private interests (*ssu*) of those in power and actually went counter to the "natural" interests of the realm as a whole (*kung*).[8]

Belief in the inviolability of one's "inborn nature" was the cornerstone in Hsi Kang's and his friends' refusal to serve the faction of Ssu-ma Chao (211-65). As Angus Graham explains elsewhere in this volume, it was by no means a new idea but had its roots in the Yang Chu branch of classical Taoist thought. In the eyes of Ssu-ma Chao and Chung Hui, however, it only meant disloyalty and subversion. It is no accident that when Chung Hui put together his manifesto on the "Four Basic Relationships [Between Human Nature and Ability]" ("Ssu-pen lun"), in which he brought together the views of four persons on this subject, the two contributors who saw a direct relationship— i.e., that nature (*hsing*) and ability (*ts'ai*) are identical (*t'ung*[a]), or in agreement (*ho*)—were Chung himself and his partisan Fu Chai (205-55). The two who found them different (*i*), or separate (*li*), were Chung's political adversaries Li Feng (d. 254) and Wang Kuang (210-51), both of whom were killed in purges by the Ssu-ma faction even before Hsi K'ang.[9] The conformists apparently maintained that if a person possessed ability, his nature would automatically allow him to perform ably in office. If such a person were to decline to apply his ability in the service of the state on grounds of not wishing to violate his inborn nature, he would immediately be deemed disloyal or at least morally reprobate.

The curious thing is that when Hsi K'ang's friend Juan Chi made exactly the same claim, but concealed his feelings behind a guise of drunkenness and cryptic poetry, he escaped with his life. The classic example is the manner in which he carried out the prescribed mourning period following the death of his mother in 256. Contrary to specific instructions in the *Record of Rites* (Li-chi),[10] Juan accepted an invitation to a party at the home of Ssu-ma Chao, where he was seen helping himself generously to both meat and wine. When Ho Tseng (199-278), the commandant of the capital province, complained to the host about Juan's "unfilial" behavior, the latter pointed out how "emaciated and depressed" Juan looked, insisting he was more in need of sustenance than any of the other guests.[11] Nor was Ssu-ma Chao his only defender. P'ei K'ai (237-91), a very proper and aristocratic gentleman, paid a visit of condolence to Juan and found him drunk, disheveled, and dry-eyed, totally oblivious of his important visitor. Custom required that on such occasions the host should weep while the visitor merely paid his respects. But P'ei, who was also a very humane man, simply reversed roles and wept himself, leaving after a few words of condolence. When others criticized him for that, he explained that Juan was "beyond the realm [of ordinary morality]" (*fang-wai*).[12] In Juan's case this transcendence of ordinary morality went considerably beyond the mourning rites to infringe on even the usual taboos between the sexes. For example, Juan's sister-in-law was once about to make her usual annual visit to her parent's home. As she was leaving the Juan family compound, Juan stepped out to say goodbye, an act specifically forbidden in the *Li-chi*.[13] When reminded of this, Juan simply rejoined, "Were the rites made for people like me?"[14]

Such violations were noted, of course, because they were symbolic of something far more serious—filial piety and the separation of the sexes were held to be the very cornerstones of a stable society. But there was yet another symbol, representative of civilization itself—the wearing of clothes—which also came under attack in this period. You may recall Hsi K'ang's complaint about wearing stiff ceremonial robes while kneeling for interminable periods in court. His friend Liu Ling (d. after 265), who is known primarily for his enormous capacity for alcohol, could not even endure the casual attire one might wear within the privacy of one's own home. His biographer records that he considered the universe itself "too confining," so he would frequently remove all his clothes and sit naked in his room. Everyone has heard the story of how one day some eavesdroppers entered his house and chided him for such indecent exposure and how he retorted, "I consider heaven and earth to be my pillars and roof, and the rooms of my house to be my underpants and jacket. What are you gentlemen doing in my underpants?"[15]

All of these protests were aimed at social restraints which were deemed unnatural, or at least hypocritical. They were not the groundswell of a social revolution. Hsi K'ang was not challenging the validity of court protocol as such. He just wanted to be himself without having to be polite to stuffed shirts and nincompoops. Juan Chi was not questioning the basic assumptions of filial piety—namely, that one should love and respect one's parents in both life and death. All he did was challenge the pharisaism of those who insisted on literal fulfillment of unreasonable and anachronistic mourning regulations accumulated over the many years of Han rule. Liu Ling's going naked was not an attack on civilization, nor was he a nudist in the modern sense. His protest was not against prurient sexual taboos, but only against the invasion of his personal privacy. The "Seven Worthies of the Bamboo Grove" were individualists only to the extent that they insisted on defending the inviolability of themselves as individual persons, and they refused to bend to political and social pressures to conform to shallow and meaningless regulations. But they were not radically challenging the basic values or the hierarchical structure of the society to which they belonged, with its built-in network of mutual obligation.

The protests of the "Seven Worthies" were universally admired in the fourth century, even by conservatives. Yet there were other members of the *shih/ta-fu* class during the Six Dynasties, also establishment "dropouts" of their day, who never succeeded in winning the admiration accorded the "Seven Worthies," whose spiritual heirs they claimed to be. Such were the so-called "Eight Free Spirits" (*pa-ta*), a group including Wang Ch'eng and Hu-wu Fu-chih, among others. Since none of these men has left behind a sufficiently articulate legacy of writings to explain their private disagreement with the world, we have to draw what conclusions we can from the rather unsympathetic accounts of how they shocked their contemporaries recorded in the chapter entitled "The Free and Unrestrained" ("Jen-tan") in the *Shih-shuo hsin-yü*.[16]

The term *ta*, which I have translated as "free spirits," had in this period the special meaning "total freedom from inhibition," which implied also a kind of uninhibited or nonprejudicial wisdom. The eight individuals to whom this sobriquet was attached all gained their reputations during the darkest decade of Western Chin rule, A.D. 296-306, when the power vacuum created by the ascension of the imbecile Emperor Hui (r. 290-306) to the throne brought eight of the imperial princes into a suicidal internecine battle which weakened the state and paved the way for the domination of north China by a series of non-Han states until the unification of 589. Without defining the term, the *Shih-shuo* speaks of the group as follows: "Wang Ch'eng, Hu-wu Fu-chih, and their circle all considered giving rein to their impulses [*jen-fang*] to be "free" [*ta*], and there were some who even went naked. Yüeh Kuang laughed about it and said, 'In the Teaching of Names itself there is room for enjoyment. Why go to such lengths.' "[17]

The commentary to this passage, citing Wang Yin's fourth-century *History of the Chin* (Chin-shu), explains further:

> Toward the end of the Wei Kingdom [ca. 260] Juan Chi in his fondness for wine used to let himself go completely. Baring his head and loosening his hair, he would sit with his legs sprawled apart, completely naked. After him his disciples who valued "free wandering" [*yu*]—people like Juan Chan, Wang Ch'eng, Hsieh K'un, and Hu-wu Fu-chih—all carried on the tradition founded by Juan Chi, claiming they had attained the "root of the Great Way" [*ta-tao chih pen*]. So they doffed kerchief and cap, stripped off their clothes and exposed their genitals like so many birds and beasts. Those who went to extremes were called "unimpeded" [*t'ung*[b]], and those in the next category were called "free" [*ta*].[18]

There is clearly meant to be some kind of progression from *yu*, "free wandering" or "enjoyment," through *t'ung*[a], "clear or unimpeded passage" or "perspicacity," to the final level of freedom and transcendent wisdom represented by the word *ta*. The primary sense of this term as defined in the second-century dictionary *Explanation of Graphs and Analysis of Characters* (Shuo-wen chieh-tzu) is "to travel without meeting [any obstacle]" (*hsing pu hsiang yü yeh*). A derived meaning, occurring in texts as early as the *Tso Commentary* [Tso-chuan; fourth century B.C.], applies this "unimpeded travel" to the intelligent mind. Thus, a *ta-jen* is a transcendentally wise man who understands everything in cosmic perspective and is not constricted by the vulgar and myopic views of the crowd. Such an exalted view of the meaning of *ta*, however, was apparently not shared by critics of the "Eight Free Spirits" who saw their bizarre antics as nothing more than libertinism.

The claim of the "Eight" to have attained "the root of the Great Way" suggests that they may not have been mere libertines. It seems as though they were trying in some desperate way to recover their true selves within the natural harmony of the Tao; they had become lost in their dark world of gruesome palace intrigue, civil war, and impending invasion. Just as later the poet T'ao Ch'ien (365-427?) concluded that "in wine there is a taste of profundity,"[19] another poet of their own time, one Wang Hui, remarked, "Wine is just the thing which somehow draws a man up and sets him in a transcendent place."[20] A temporary and ultimately disappointing means to transcendence, to be sure, but one greatly favored in some quarters at the time.

The protests of the "Seven Worthies" and the "Eight Free Spirits" were partly moral—against the corruption and darkness of the age—and partly social—against outmoded rituals. Yet, on the personal side, they were also cries of anguish. Two hundred years later another rebel, living in the chaotic last years of the Eastern Chin, T'ao Ch'ien, whose memorable aphorism on wine was quoted above, reacted in a similar way to a similar environment. His response, however, was not to fight publicly but to become a recluse, living and working on a farm. Everyone is familiar with his refusal to "bend his back for a mere five pecks of rice" and his retirement to the family estate near Chiu-chiang (in modern Kiangsi) in the winter of 405, where he eked out the rest of his life on the ragged edge of starvation.[21]

We do not have to take at face value all that T'ao Ch'ien says in his poems about "getting up at dawn to clear the weeds/ And coming back with the moon, hoe on shoulder,"[22] but it is obvious that the many members of his family suffered genuine deprivation in this period and that their life-style was far from typical for their class. His rationalization for this unusual hardship is consistent through all of his poems: "I had trouble getting on with people. Taking stock, I decided for my own sake I would have to give up practical concerns and somehow or other retire from the world."[23] "From early days I have been at odds with the world;/ My instinctive love is hills and mountains. . . . / Simplicity intact, I have returned to farm. . . . / For long I was a prisoner in a cage/ And now I have my freedom back again."[24] "Accept your lot and wait until it's over,/ To stay free, crook an elbow for a pillow./ Accord with change, whatever its ups and downs-/ Follow your heart, no matter the heights and depths."[25] "I have renounced the world to have my leisure/ And occupy myself with lute and books."[26] "To cultivate the True in my poor hut/ Is perhaps the best thing I can do."[27] "It's my nature keeps me out of tune;/ To go against oneself is a real mistake."[28] "My instinct is all for freedom, . . . / Going against myself really sickens me."[29]

Even though these statements plucked at random from T'ao Ch'ien's essays and poems all celebrate the theme of "freedom," it is worthwhile to examine them a little more closely in order to understand exactly what he meant. For nowhere in the Chinese language of this period is there any word which quite corresponds to those vibrant catchwords which resonate in the breast of everyone reared on Western European values—*liberty* and *freedom*. These concepts, as I understand their definition in Stephen Lukes's valuable book, are quite complex. They imply respect for human dignity, which in turn implies *equality* under God or under the law. They also imply autonomy, privacy, and space for self-development. What T'ao Ch'ien and the others sought coincides almost exactly with the last three, but not so much with the first two. Let us look closely at the words he uses. He is "at odds with the world" (*wu shih su-yün*, lit., "doesn't fit the common rhyme-scheme") and has "trouble getting along with people." This is his primary motive for going into seclusion. It is the negative freedom of *escape* from something he cannot tolerate, very much on the same order as that of Hsi K'ang before him. But on the positive side, after escaping from the "cage" of official life, he "regains his freedom" (*fan tzu-jan*, lit., "reverts to naturalness"). *Tzu-jan* is a troublesome word. It is not exactly "freedom," as James Hightower translated it, but rather "doing what comes naturally"—something akin to, but not identical with, what we mean by "autonomy." In the next passage, "To stay free, crook an elbow for a pillow," the expression "stay free" has the literal meaning "not to injure the Void" (*shang-ch'ung*). "The Void" is metonymy for the Tao, the principle of the cosmos as well as the principle immanent within all creatures. "Not to injure the Tao" is another way of saying "to follow the Tao," to do what comes naturally. It involves a whole complex of ideas relating to harmony with the cosmos that is unrelated to Western ideas of freedom. That is why the immediately following phrases—"accord with change" (*ch'ien-hua*) and "follow your heart"(*ssu-chih*)—sound mildly contradictory to us. How can anyone follow his inner impulses and at the same time accord with external changes? But to someone accustomed to thinking of inner impulses as part of the same vital force which causes the grass to grow and the seasons to change, there is no contradiction at all. Agreement with the Tao *is* perfect freedom.

Escape from the "cage" of official life meant more to T'ao Ch'ien than freedom from irksome duties. The "leisure" he craved to "occupy [himself] with lute and books" held almost mystical overtones. It meant transcendence of the world, at the opposite remove from its dust and din. What T'ao Ch'ien was really seeking was self-cultivation. "To cultivate the True [*yang-chen*] in my poor hut" surely means to permit his "true self" to develop naturally—the self which he kept insisting was "at odds with the world." "It is my nature [*ping-ch'i*, lit., "the vital force with which I was endowed at birth"] keeps me out of tune; /To go against *oneself* [*wei-chi*] is a real mistake." What he is really saying is: "The human world has gotten out of tune with the Tao; to recover my true self and the lost harmony of the world I have no recourse but to withdraw from it."

Withdrawal from the world was nothing new in T'ao Ch'ien's day. The manner and motivation for reclusion in China is discussed by Wolfgang Bauer elsewhere in this volume. But the forms it took during the Southern Dynasties do have special coloration. Basically, all recluses were motivated by one or both of the following considerations: silent protest against an illegitimate or tyrannical government which the recluse refused to serve; or the desire for transcendence of the world through self-cultivation in an untrammeled natural environment. In spite of a venerable tradition to the contrary, I believe T'ao Ch'ien's withdrawal had little to do with the former but a great deal to do with the latter. Much has been made of his staunch loyalty to the Chin and his protest against the "usurpation" of Liu Yü, founder of the succeeding Sung dynasty (420-79). But this hardly explains why he went into seclusion a full fifteen years before that event took place. To read his poems is to become instantly aware that T'ao Ch'ien was not moved by political considerations so much as by philosophical ones, such as the meaning of life and death, which he finally came to terms with as "surrender to the cycle of things" (*tsung-lang ta-hua chung*) in the eloquent poem "Substance, Shadow, and Spirit" ("Hsing ying shen").[30]

Another poet-recluse, whose determination to renounce the world faltered by comparison with T'ao Ch'ien's apparently successful attempt, was Shen Yüeh (441-513), who was born a quarter of a century after T'ao's death and who, quite in contrast to his predecessor, served not one but *three* dynasties, in the last two of which he held very high office. In suggesting that T'ao Ch'ien's attempt at full reclusion was "apparently" successful, I mean only that most of our evidence has come from his own account. All literary biographers have learned to be very wary of taking at face value the elaborately constructed personae of writers who wish to be accepted in a particular guise that is often, in fact, largely a pose. But I do not think T'ao Ch'ien was posing. There is too much evidence even in his own account of very human frailty—moments of self-doubt and heroic whistlings in the dark—to dismiss what he is telling us as purposeful distortion. Shen Yüeh's failed attempt is equally illuminating, because he too was devastatingly honest in criticizing his own "lack of singleness" (*fei-i*).[31]

In order to clarify Shen Yüeh's personal ideal of reclusion as it related to the whole problem of protest and self-development, I will quote brief passages from his introduction to the "Lives of Recluses" ("Yin-i") in the *History of the Sung* (Sung-shu), which he edited and submitted to the Ch'i emperor in 487. In this preface he defines reclusion (*yin*) as "living with one's overt behavior [lit., "traces"] invisible to outsiders [*chi pu wai-hsien*], and one's principles [lit., "way"] unknowable [by others] [*tao pu-k'o-chih*]."[32] This does not mean physically concealing one's body (*yin-shen*), but rather "darkening one's principles" (*hui-tao*), because the condition of the world is such that they will not be understood in any case. It seems that typical reclusive behavior, like living in caves and expressing contempt for the world, is not necessarily true reclusion, because it may merely express misanthropy or an unwillingness to deal with the world. The "true recluse" moves freely in the world in times of bad government but hides his principles in his bosom. If a ruler should appear who would make use of them, he will gladly offer his services.

I am afraid that Shen Yüeh, at the time when he wrote this preface, would have found the somewhat antisocial sentiments expressed so cogently by Hsi K'ang, and even by T'ao Ch'ien, to be unworthy of his ideal. T'ao Ch'ien, in fact, though living well into the Sung era, is not included among Shen's biographies. In Shen Yüeh's view, men like T'ao Ch'ien and Hsi K'ang should have accepted office and just kept quiet. But Shen's own problem as a would-be recluse was complicated by the kaleidoscopic shifts from "good" government to "bad" and back again between 461 when he first took office and his death at age seventy-two in 513. In those forty-two years he served a total of nine emperors, four of whom had murdered their predecessors to gain the throne. Surely under those circumstances, when in the words of the *Book of Changes* (I ching) "heaven and earth were closed," it was the time for "worthy men to go into hiding."[33] But on the two occasions when Shen did attempt literally to do so (once in 494 and again in 498, when he took short leaves from the capital), his Confucian sense of duty called him back within a few months. He was trying to follow his own advice to "hide his principles" rather than his body when times were bad. But this basically Confucian philosophy of self-sacrificing service in the midst of danger was at war with another strong tendency in his life, namely, the cultivation of enlightenment (a Buddhist ideal) and of transcendence (a Taoist one), both of which required him to "hide his body" rather than his principles. He needed a mountain hermitage where he could pursue meditation and Taoist arts free of all distraction. All his life he argued with himself over whether to go or stay; it became a kind of unresolved obsession until finally, during the last six years of his life, he made his peace with both ideals. The perfect compromise was semi-reclusion in the suburbs—far enough from the uproar of the city to find quiet, yet near enough to the court to answer any urgent call. In 507 he moved into a renovated villa northeast of Chien-k'ang, where he built a landscape garden. His long poetic essay "On Living in the Suburbs" ("Chiao-chü fu") begins with a confession of his capitulation:

> Only the Perfect Man [*chih-jen*] denies himself [*fei-chi*];
> For him indeed both self and others are forgot.
> From middling wise on down to fools
> The rest all take attaining their true nature [*te-hsing*] as their field.[34]

As a Buddhist, when Shen Yüeh used the phrase "attaining their true natures," he may have had in mind the religious sense of attaining the Buddha-nature immanent in every living being, i.e., attaining enlightenment. But he had long since acknowledged that he would probably never achieve that in his lifetime,[35] so something more within the range of the "middling wise on down to fools" was more likely what he meant—that is, just to be himself, to find self-fulfillment. In other words, his mature view was very close to the views of Hsi K'ang and T'ao Ch'ien before him, since even for them, "being themselves" was in the ultimate sense to be one with the Tao.

Shen Yüeh was quite cognizant of what had happened to his thinking, as he elaborates in his lengthy apologia for living in the suburbs:

> For one like me, whose narrow, cramped ambition
> Has no design to save the world,
> I long to roost among the trees, my wings well furled,
> Or swim in mountain streams, my scales obscured.
> I have no taste for grandeur or display,
> Nor am I one who cares for bustling city streets.[36]

And again, contrasting his later with his earlier life:

> Forever cursing emptiness while seeking being,
> I always aimed at what was difficult, supposing it was easy.
> I never sought contentment from within myself,
> But only roused the more attachment by forsaking things.
> Even the gentlemen of old made this mistake,
> Which I today intend to circumvent.[37]

I have probably given undue importance to Shen Yüeh's peculiar blend of holism and individualism—the former represented by his long official career and his early views on "worthy reclusion" as expressed in the preface to the *Sung-shu* section on the "Lives of Recluses," and the latter by his abortive attempts at living in the mountains and his final compromise of living in the suburbs. I have done so to illustrate what I have found to be a very common syndrome among the *shih/ta-fu* of the Southern Dynasties—the strong political and social pressures to conform to the traditional ideal of serving in office and an intense inward psychological pressure to escape to "find oneself." Hsi K'ang figuratively thumbed his nose at society and was killed. Juan Chi employed veiled satire and lived one year longer. T'ao Ch'ien's escape was real, but it was marred by grinding poverty and physical toil, lightened only now and then by wine and poetry. Shen Yüeh wrestled all his life with the choice and finally settled, when he was nearly seventy, for an uneasy compromise.

In all these cases, including even the wild escapades of the "Eight Free Spirits," the principle of conformity to some larger "whole" than single individuals was never at issue. But the whole of the body politic or society or the family or the "realm of ordinary morality" was too confining for some of these men. To be "themselves" meant "giving free rein to naturalness," conforming to the Tao of the universe rather than the cramped, distorted values of a corrupt society.

NOTES

1. Because of disagreements among social historians over which English term to use for the ruling elite and the actual role played by them in this period, I will simply use the compound term favored by Chinese and Japanese scholars who study this period, namely, *shih/ta-fu* ("gentlemen/officials"?).

2. *Hou-Han chi, chüan* 1; quoted in Ch'en Yin-k'o, *T'ao Yüan-ming chih ssu-hsiang yü ch'ing-t'an chih kuan-hsi* [T'ao Ch'ien's thought in relation to pure conversation] (Chungking: Harvard-Yenching Institute, 1945), 26-27.

3. See Ho Ch'i-min, *Chu-lin ch'i-hsien yen-chiu* [Research on the Seven Worthies of the Bamboo Grove] (Taipei: Commercial Press, 1965), 11-15; and Donald Holzman, *La vie et la pensée de Hi Kang* (Leiden: E. J. Brill, 1957), 3-35.

4. Yang Yung, *Shih-shuo hsin-yü chiao-chien* [Collated notes on *Shih-shuo hsin-yü*] (Hong Kong: Tai Chung Bookstore, 1969), chap. 4, no. 94 (English text in Richard Mather, trans., *Shih-shuo hsin-yü: A New Account of Tales of the World* [Minneapolis: University of Minnesota Press, 1976], 140).

5. Ibid., chap. 17, no. 2 (Mather, *Tales of the World*, 323).

6. *Wen-hsüan* (Peking: Chung-hua Shu-chü, 1977), 43.3b-4a; English translation by James R. Hightower in *Anthology of Chinese Literature from Early Times to the Fourteenth Century*, ed., Cyril Birch (New York: Grove Press, 1965), 163-65.

7. Ibid.

8. See Chinese text and French translation of this treatise in Holzman, *Hi K'ang*, 176-80, 122-30. I would like to call the reader's attention to Robert G. Henricks, trans., *Philosophy and Argumentation in Third Century China: The Essays of Hsi Kang* (Princeton: Princeton University Press, 1983), 107-19.

9. *Shih-shuo hsin-yü*, chap. 23, no. 2 (Mather, *Tales of the World*, 372).

10. *Li-chi* (Tuan-chü shih-san ching wen ed.), sec. 36: "Wen-sang" [Questions about mourning rites]; translated in James Legge, *The Li Ki*, 2 vols. (Oxford: Clarendon Press, 1885), 2:375.

11. *Shih-shuo hsin-yü*, chap. 23, no. 2 (Mather, *Tales of the World*, 372).
12. Ibid., no. 11 (375).
13. *Li-chi*, sec. 1 (Legge, *Li Ki*, 1:77): "Sister-in-law and brother-in-law are not to exchange inquiries with one another."
14. *Shih-shuo hsin-yü*, chap. 23, no. 7 (Mather, *Tales of the World*, 371). For an insightful discussion of Juan Chi's attitude toward ritual, see Donald Holzman, *Poetry and Politics: The Life and Works of Juan Chi* (Cambridge: Cambridge University Press, 1976), 73-87.
15. *Shih-shuo hsin-yü*, chap. 23, no. 6 (Mather, *Tales of the World*, 374).
16. Ibid., chap. 23 (371-91).
17. Ibid., chap. 1, no. 23 (12-13).
18. Ibid.
19. "Yin-chiu" [Twenty poems after drinking wine], no. 14, in Yang Yung, *T'ao Yüan-ming chi chiao-chien* [Annotated poems of T'ao Ch'ien] (Hong Kong: Ou Hin Kee Bookstore, 1975), 159; English text in James R. Hightower, trans., *The Poetry of T'ao Ch'ien* (Oxford: Oxford University Press, 1970), 145.
20. *Shih-shuo hsin-yü*, chap. 23, no. 40 (Mather, *Tales of the World*, 389).
21. *Chin-shu* (Peking: Chung-hua Shu-chü, 1974), 94.261.
22. "Kuei yüan-t'ien chü" [Returning to the farm to dwell], no. 3 (Yang, *T'ao Yüan-ming*, 60; Hightower, *T'ao Ch'ien*, 52).
23. "Yü tzu Yen-teng su" [Testament to my sons, Yen and others], preface (Yang, *T'ao Yüan-ming*, 301; Hightower, *T'ao Ch'ien*, 5).
24. "Kuei yüan-t'ien chü," no. 1 (Yang, *T'ao Yüan-ming*, 56-57; Hightower, *T'ao Ch'ien*, 50).
25. "Wu-yüeh tan tso ho Tai chu-pu" [Written on the first day of the fifth month to match a poem by Secretary Tai] (Yang, *T'ao Yüan-ming*, 80; Hightower, *T'ao Ch'ien*, 69).
26. "Ho Kuo chu-pu" [A reply to Secretary Kuo] (Yang, *T'ao Yüan-ming*, 92-93; Hightower, *T'ao Ch'ien*, 79).
27. "Hsin-ch'ou sui ch'i-yüeh fu-chia huan Chiang-ling yeh-hsing T'u-k'ou" [Written at T'u-k'ou at night during the seventh moon of the year 401 while returning to Chiang-ling after leave] (Yang, *T'ao Yüan-ming*, 118; Hightower, *T'ao Ch'ien*, 103).
28. "Yin-chiu," no. 9 (Yang, *T'ao Yüan-ming*, 151; Hightower, *T'ao Ch'ien*, 137).
29. "Kuei-ch'ü-lai hsi tz'u" [The return], preface (Yang, *T'ao Yüan-ming*, 266; Hightower, *T'ao Ch'ien*, 44).
30. Yang, *T'ao Yüan-ming*, 50; Hightower, *T'ao Ch'ien*, 44.
31. *Liang-shu* [History of the Liang] (Peking: Chung-hua Shu-chü, 1973), 13.242.
32. *Sung-shu* (Peking: Chung-hua Shu-chü, 1974), 93.2275. See also Kamitsuka Yoshiko, "Shin Yaku no in'itsu shisō" [Shen Yüeh's thoughts on seclusion], *Nihon Chūgoku gakkai hō* (1979), 31:105-18.
33. *I ching* (Tuan-chü shih-san ching wen ed.), hexagram no. 2 (*k'un*), "Wen-yen" [Commentary on the words of the text], 3; English text in Richard Wilhelm and Cary F. Baynes, trans., *The I Ching, or Book of Changes*, 2 vols. (London: Routledge and Kegan Paul, Ltd., 1951), 2:28.
34. *Liang-shu* 13:236.
35. See, for example, Shen Yüeh's essay "Liu-tao hsiang-hsü tso-fo" [On those in the Six Dynasties eventually becoming Buddhas], in Tao-hsüan's (seventh-century) *Kuang hung-ming chi* [Expanded collection on propagating the light] (Taishō Tripitaka ed.), 52:252c-253a.
36. *Liang-shu* 13.236.
37. Ibid., 13.239.

Glossary

Ch'en Yin-k'o　陳寅恪

chi pu wai-hsien　迹不外見

Chiao-chü fu　郊居賦

chiao-kuai　狡獪

ch'ien-hua　遷化

chih-jen　至人

Chin-shu　晉書

ch'ing-t'an　清談

Chu-lin ch'i hsien-lun　竹林七賢論

Chu-lin ch'i-hsien yen-chiu　竹林七賢研究

Chung Hui　鍾會

fan tzu-jan　反自然

fang　放

fang-wai　方外

fei-chi　非己

fei-i　非一

Fu Chia　傅嘏

ho　合

Ho Ch'i-min　何啓民

Ho Kuo chu-pu　和郭主簿

Ho Tseng　何曾

Hou-Han chi　後漢紀

Hsi K'ang　嵇康

hsiang　相

hsing pu hsiang-yü yeh　行不相遇也

Hsieh An　謝安

Hsieh K'un　謝鯤

Hsin-ch'ou sui ch'i-yüeh fu-chia huan Chiang-ling yeh-hsing T'u-k'ou　辛丑歲七月赴假還江陵夜行塗口

hsing　性

Hsing ying shen　形影神

Hu-wu Fu-chih　胡母輔之

hui-tao　晦道

i　異

I ching　易經

jen-fang　任放

jen-shih　任實

Jen-tan　任誕

jen tzu-jan　任自然

Juan Chan　阮瞻

Juan Chi　阮籍

Kamitsuka Yoshiko　神塚淑子

Kuang hung-ming chi　廣弘明集

Kuei-ch'ü-lai hsi tz'u　歸去來兮辭

Kuei yüan-t'ien chü 歸園田居

k'un 坤

kung 公

li 離

Li-chi 禮記

Li Feng 李豐

Liang-shu 梁書

Liu Chün 劉峻

Liu Ling 劉伶

Liu-tao hsiang-hsü tso-fo 六道相續作佛

Liu Yü 劉裕

ming-chiao 名教

Ming-shih chuan 名士傳

pa-ta 八達

P'ei K'ai 裴楷

ping-ch'i 稟氣

shang-ch'ung 傷沖

Shen Yüeh 沈約

shih-fei 是非

Shih-shuo hsin-yü 世說新語

Shih-shuo hsin-yü chiao-chien 世說新語校箋

Shih-ssu lun 釋私論

shih/ta-fu 士大夫

Shin Yaku no in'itsu shisō 沈約の隠逸思想

Shuo-wen chieh-tzu 說文解字

ssu 私

ssu-chih 肆志

Ssu-ma 司馬

Ssu-ma Chao 司馬昭

Ssu-pen lun 四本論

Sung-shu 宋書

ta 達

ta-jen 達人

ta-tao chih-pen 大道之本

Tai K'uei 戴逵

T'ao Ch'ien 陶潛

Tao-hsüan 道宣

tao pu-k'o-chih 道不可知

T'ao Yüan-ming chi chiao-chien 陶淵明集校箋

T'ao Yüan-ming chih ssu-hsiang yü ch'ing-t'an chih kuan-hsi 陶淵明之思想與清談之關係

te-hsing 得行

ts'ai 才

Ts'ao 曹

Tso-chuan 左傳

tsung-lang ta-hua chung 縱浪大化中

t'ung[a] 同

t'ung[b] 通

tzu-jan 自然

Wang Ch'eng 王澄

Wang Hui 王薈

Wang Jung 王戎

Wang Kuang 王廣

Wang Yin 王隱

wei-chi 違己

Wen-hsüan 文選

Wen-sang 問喪

Wen-yen 文言

Wu-ch'iu Chien 毋丘檢

wu shih su-yün 無適俗韻

Wu-yüeh tan tso ho Tai chu-pu 五月旦作和戴主簿

yang-chen 養眞

Yang Yung 楊勇

yin 隱

Yin-chiu 飲酒

Yin-i 隱逸

yin-shen 隱身

yu 遊

Yü Liang 庾亮

Yü Shan Chü-yüan [T'ao] chüeh-chiao shu 與山巨源〔濤〕絕交書

Yü tzu Yen-teng su 與子儼等疏

Yüan Hung 袁宏

Yüeh Kuang 樂廣

Subjectivity in Liu Tsung-chou's Philosophical Anthropology

Tu Wei-ming

Before approaching the complex issue of the relationship between individualism and holism in Neo-Confucian thought, it is necessary to identify an appropriate point of entry, one which neither introduces a totally alien conceptual scheme nor confines the discussion to an internal dialogue. The point of entry I propose to use in this essay is the thought of Liu Tsung-chou (1578-1645), one of the most brilliant original thinkers of seventeenth-century China. Since Liu's thought, like that of many of his predecessors in the Neo-Confucian tradition, can very well be categorized as "self-cultivation" philosophy, its main concern is self-knowledge. This stress on self-knowledge may give the impression that the solitary individual is the primary datum for analysis. In reality, however, the matter requires a twofold approach. There is the individualist side, which deals with the self in a state of solitariness. The dignity, autonomy, and independence of the self are predicated on the ability of the self to know, to feel, and to will as a moral agent. There is also the holistic side: the necessity to transcend self-centeredness, to enter into meaningful communication with others, and to experience the common spring of humanity. Self-knowledge, so conceived, reveals not one's own private desires, feelings, and thoughts but the uniqueness of being human shared by all members of the human community.

The whole idea of learning for the sake of the self, which is prominent in Neo-Confucian literature, addresses issues not only of individualism but also of holism. Yet, the clear preference in Liu Tsung-chou's philosophical anthropology, his systematic and fundamental reflection on the ceaseless process of learning to be human, is to build his case on the idea of subjectivity. Lest we mistake Liu's emphasis on subjectivity as a preference for individualism, it is vitally important to note, from the outset, that subjectivity in the Neo-Confucian context is both individualistic and holistic. For the sake of convenience, we may first take the idea of subjectivity to be a movement from individualism to holism. In the course of our discussion, I want to show how insights gained from critical reflections on the Western concept of individualism[1] can be brought to bear upon the Neo-Confucian idea of subjectivity. Of course, in so doing, it is essential that the integrity of the

Chinese material—which, in the present case, means the shape of Liu's thought—be preserved. At the same time, I want to show that this kind of inquiry is in accord with the mode of reasoning inherent in Liu's logic. Since I have elsewhere explored the inseparability of subjectivity and ontological reality in Wang Yang-ming's (1472-1529) philosophy,[2] my focus here will be the Neo-Confucian claim that deep personal knowledge is the authentic way of making oneself whole. In other words, holism is achieved through deepened subjectivity.

T'ang Chün-i, in a thought-provoking article, analyzes Liu Tsung-chou's philosophy as a critique of Wang Yang-ming's *hsin-hsüeh* ("learning of the mind"), especially the later developments of Wang's teaching on *liang-chih* ("conscientious consciousness," "innate knowledge," "knowledge of the good," or "primordial knowing").[3] Fang Tung-mei, on the other hand, characterizes Liu as "an exponent of modified idealism based upon Wang Yang-ming."[4] Mou Tsung-san, while endorsing T'ang's general analysis, maintains that Liu's "internal criticism" can be understood as a refinement on Wang's formulation of the idea of *liang-chih*.[5] All of these writers seem to share the view that through critical interpretation Liu made explicit what was implicit in Wang's thought and thus brought the "learning of the mind" to its fruition.

I intend, in this exploratory essay, to probe the underlying structure of Liu's thinking, viewing it not merely as a response to Wang Yang-ming's challenge but also as an articulation of a philosophical anthropology in its own right. The focus will be Liu, the original thinker who has something profound to say about moral self-cultivation, rather than Liu, a major intellectual figure of the late Ming period. Methodologically, I propose to discuss Liu's philosophical claims as if they were addressed to a timeless and spaceless human community, while assuming that the Neo-Confucian world in the seventeenth century, with all of its cultural and social specificities, was the particular locale in which Liu philosophized in the spirit of universal moral concerns.

However, since the thinking person never thinks in a vacuum, the context in which he consciously responds to challenging situations provides a necessary background for understanding the meaning of the expressed thought. Needless to say, a familiarity with the general "discourse" by which a style of thinking has been shaped is immensely helpful for an appreciation of those subtle ideas that give the content its unique contour. If we want to know how a thinker creates a new way of perceiving reality, we need to acquire a knowledge of the intellectual world in which the presumed "new way" is both a continuation of and a departure from shared assumptions. But even the availability of a kind of "mental map" of the age can provide no more than an indication of where the thinker's difficulties arise. An appreciation of the actual process by which the thinker comes to terms with his *Problematik* requires an explanation significantly different from influence studies or contextual analyses.

The primary aim of this essay is to show how subjectivity emerges as a central issue in Liu's conception of selfhood, that is, the inner core of the personality which defines the quality of one's existence in a subtle and yet fully conscious way. Such an inquiry may help us to understand the problem, the background, and the method of addressing the perennial Confucian concern for making an ultimate commitment to the process of the goal of learning to become a sage. Furthermore, an appreciation of Liu's recommendation for "realizing humanity" may shed some light on the Neo-Confucian ideal of the unity of all things, which is predicated on a belief in the great human potential for sympathy rather than on the romantic notion of "embracing the universe."

The Problem

The difficulty in understanding Liu's philosophical anthropology as an integral part of the Confucian quest for self-knowledge derives from two sources: his fidelity to the classical tradition, centering around the *Great Learning* (Ta-hsüeh), and his unusual penchant for probing human frailty as a way of asserting personal dignity. T'ang Chün-i's description of Liu's *Problematik* is insightful:

> In Liu Tsung-chou's critique of Wang Yang-ming's thought, it is a contest for "priority or primacy" of conscientious consciousness as "willing only the good" over the "primacy or priority" of the same consciousness as "knowing good and evil." In Wang's thought, this consciousness starts with knowing good and evil; then, second, liking the former and disliking the latter; and, third, doing the former and avoiding the latter. This seems to be a psychological order conforming to common experience. However, according to Liu, this order must be converted into one which recognizes the primacy or priority of the good will as an original function of mind which is connected with another original function of mind—feeling. The knowing function is essentially determined by the orientation of the original will and its accompanying feeling, and is posterior to the will and feeling in an ontological order.[6]

T'ang's description, simply put, identifies Liu's major dissatisfaction with Yang-ming's doctrine of *liang-chih* and with his Four-Sentence Teaching—namely, the issue of the priority or primacy of willing (i^a) over knowing ($chih^a$) in the structure and function of the mind.

In Yang-ming's Four-Sentence Teaching, which represents his final statement on Confucian self-cultivation, the centrality of *liang-chih* is evident:

> There is neither good nor evil in the mind-in-itself. There are both good and evil in the activation of intentions. Knowing good and evil is the [faculty] of *liang-chih*. Doing good and removing evil is the rectification of things.[7]

For Yang-ming, moral effort begins when one is critically aware of the distinction between good and evil. At that moment, one's *liang-chih* takes cognizance of the situation and initiates the process of self-cultivation. Since Yang-ming advocates the unity of knowing and acting, to know is simultaneously to act. Yet, from Liu's point of view, this process of self-cultivation presupposes that knowing rather than willing is the foundation of morality. As a result, Yang-ming's "final statement" still falls short of grasping the root of Confucian self-cultivation.

The *locus classicus* for this issue is, of course, the text of the *Great Learning*: "When things are investigated, knowledge is extended; when knowledge is extended, the will becomes sincere; when the will is sincere, the mind is rectified; when the mind is rectified, the person is cultivated." In this brief passage, five basic concepts in Confucian thought are ordered in a specific way: *wu* (thing), *chih^a* (knowledge), *i^a* (will), *hsin* (mind), and *shen* (person). Yang-ming's attempt to underscore the primacy of knowing as an ontological ground for moral action suggests a way of reading the passages not as four discrete steps to self-cultivation but as four integrated perspectives in the same process. If we take the text of the *Great Learning* to mean four discrete steps to self-cultivation, we envision the process as a sequential development. We investigate things first in order to acquire knowledge; as knowledge is acquired, we learn to make our wills sincere; through the moral effort of making our wills sincere, we then try to rectify our minds. Only after we have rectified our minds can we begin to cultivate our persons. Thus, the investigation of things, the extension of knowledge, the sincerity of the will, and the rectification of the mind are perceived as four necessary steps by which we cultivate ourselves. Yang-ming, however, proposes that the so-called "steps" are actually integrated in a holistic process, symbolizing different degrees of refinement and subtlety in self-cultivation.

This interpretive stance, based on his theory of the "unity of knowing and acting" (*chih-hsing ho-i*), impels Yang-ming to depart significantly from the exegetical tradition which takes the "investigation of things" as a precondition for the "extension of knowledge." In Yang-ming's thought, *ko-wu* ("investigation of things") is understood as "rectification of affairs," and *chih-chih* ("extension of knowledge") is understood as the "full realization of primordial knowing." Thus, in taking "knowing" to mean more than cognition (because "knowing" entails "doing"), Yang-ming underscores the affective and conative aspects of the mind. Indeed, a distinctive feature of his "dynamic idealism" is its emphasis on the power of the will.[8] On the surface, what Liu objects to is not so much the original formulation of Yang-ming's position as the fallacious applications of the Four-Sentence Teaching in the writings of his disciples, notably Wang Chi (Lung-hsi; 1498-1583) and Wang Ken (Hsin-chai; 1483-1541).[9] Liu's insistence on the primacy of willing over knowing can thus be interpreted as a return to and a confirmation of Yang-ming's philosophical intention. However, we must not ignore the fact that Liu's intellectual self-definition is significantly different from Yang-ming's. For one thing, he believes that the so-called "fallacious applications" are rooted in the teaching of *liang-chih* itself.[10]

As T'ang notes, Liu's theoretical work is inseparable from his practical concern for providing a concrete plan for self-cultivation. The primacy of willing over knowing is, for him, "most crucial for the moral practice of becoming a sage."[11] While Liu shares with Yang-ming, and virtually all other Neo-Confucian thinkers, a faith in the perfectability of human nature through self-effort, he strongly doubts that the illumination of the mind is all that is needed. The process he envisions requires a much more subtle appreciation of the human propensity for evil. Liu's *Problematik*, in this connection, is as follows: according to Yang-ming's interpretation of the *Great Learning*, knowing good and evil entails not only liking good and disliking evil but also doing good and eradicating evil. If this is the case, the existence of evil is presupposed, and the knowledge of its existence therefore follows the experience of it. Thus, eradication of evil can never precede the experience of it. Efforts at moral self-cultivation "are one step behind the evils already done," and to pursue human perfection is no more than "to catch the tail of those evils."[12] As a result, sagehood as the most authentic manifestation of humanity is an unrealizable ideal, and the assumption that every human being is potentially a sage is unprovable.

Liu Tsung-chou's strategy to improve on Yang-ming's teaching of *liang-chih* involves two basic assumptions. He insists, on the ontological level, that human nature is ultimately good and, on the existential level, that it is absolutely necessary for each person to engage in a continuous and strenuous moral struggle against evil. In his view, the approach that combines these two basic assumptions can open a path to sagehood which avoids the two serious fallacies of the Yang-ming school: relativism (as seen in those who are overly enthusiastic, who confuse *liang-chih* with passions and claim that the dictates of all desires must be accepted as good); and absolutism (as evidenced by those who are excessively lofty, who identify *liang-chih* with a sort of objectless "sudden enlightenment" and disregard the actual growth of the moral self).[13] But Liu's concern with the perceived extremes is not merely diagnostic. He goes further, criticizing the later developments of the Yang-ming school in order to establish a more refined and more balanced way of self-cultivation.

Theoretically, Liu's intellectual enterprise begins with an inquiry into the "three major precepts" of the *Great Learning*, and particularly the third one, which states that the way of learning to be fully human consists in one's ability to "dwell in the ultimate good" (*chih yü chih-shan*). This statement might simply mean that in one's quest for perfection, one should try to the best of one's capacity to reach the optimal standard of performance in a given moral situation. Liu, however, interprets the "ultimate good" as the basis for self-cultivation. It is not merely an ideal for emulation, but the practical reason that moral action can be initiated in the first place. Moral action is possible because the ability to dwell in the ultimate good is inherent in our nature. It is our birthright, as moral agents, to manifest the ultimate good in our daily affairs. Since our nature is endowed by heaven, it is in its original state heavenly and thus divine in the fullest sense of the word. Indeed, we are heaven's co-creators: "Heaven cannot fulfill itself without human participation."[14] Thus, Liu advances the Mencian thesis that if one knows one's own human nature, one knows heaven.[15]

The idea that human nature is good in a transcendental sense underlies virtually all traditions of Neo-Confucian thought. Liu's assertion that "human nature is originally heaven,"[16] however, goes beyond the Ch'eng-Chu belief that "human nature is principle"[17] in bringing to the fore human creativity. To say that "human nature is originally heaven" implies that human nature, as originally decreed by heaven, is also generative because it is an integral part of heaven. Heaven has an infinite power of generativity. Although the idea that human participation in the cosmic transformation of heaven and earth is central to the philosophy of the *Book of Changes* and the *Doctrine of the Mean*, Liu's assumption that heaven also depends upon human activity for its own fulfillment seems unusually explicit. Therefore, for Liu, the ability to dwell in the ultimate good is not only humanly possible but morally imperative.

By establishing the claim that human nature, rather than a transcendent source, is the basis for morality, Liu's philosophical anthropology remains very much a part of the mainstream of Neo-Confucian thinking on the matter. The rhetorical context in which he articulates this particular notion is so common that even the distinction between the Ch'eng-Chu and the Lu-Wang schools, two diverging trends in Neo-Confucian thought, cannot be clearly made at this level of generality. In order to pinpoint Liu's unique contribution to this ongoing discourse, a brief discussion of what may be called the "principle of subjectivity" in Neo-Confucianism seems in order.

The Background

In an attempt to characterize the distinctive features of their spiritual quest, the Sung-Ming (tenth- to seventeenth-century) Confucians defined their Way as the "learning of human nature [*hsing*] and heavenly decree [*ming*]," the "learning of mind [*hsin*] and human nature," or the "learning of body [*shen*^{a}] and mind." These four key concepts—*hsing*, *ming*, *hsin*, and *shen*^{a}—constitute the basic problem in understanding the principle of subjectivity in Neo-Confucian thought.

The Neo-Confucian quest for the realization of the true self begins with the learning of the "body and mind." The juxtaposition of body and mind may give us the impression that the Neo-Confucians are aware of the distinction between body as the physical self and mind as the mental self. However, a distinctive feature of their mode of thinking is to transcend the distinction rather than to accept it as self-evidently true. As a result, the language of the body is laden with symbolic significance for understanding how the concept of mind (or, more appropriately, "mind-and-heart") is formulated; and, at the same time, the mind, as the master of the body, is never conceived as a disembodied spirit. The mutuality of body and mind defines the Neo-Confucian idea of the self and, indeed, the Neo-Confucian principle of subjectivity.

The body is a realm of existence in which ethico-religious values are created, maintained, and crystallized. The body is perceived not only as a gift from one's parents (hence the centrality of "filial piety" [*hsiao*] in Confucian symbolism), but also as the highest form among sentient beings endowed by heaven. Understandably, self-cultivation (*hsiu-shen*) means trimming, nourishing, and disciplining (*hsiu*) the body, rather than denying the bodily sensations through ascetic practices. The belief that the body has to be somehow surrendered and surpassed in order to permit the emergence of higher mental and spiritual values fundamentally conflicts with the Confucian assumption that human perfection is tantamount to the full realization of one's "bodily form."[18] The project of self-cultivation, in concrete terms, necessarily involves the training of the body. Rites, music, archery, charioteering, calligraphy, and arithmetic are as much physical exercise as intellectual discipline.[19] It is through the "ritualization of experience," in Erik Erikson's sense,[20] that the body matures in its self-understanding and in its communicativeness.

It is true that when Chou Tun-i (1017-73) describes human beings as receiving the "highest excellence" in the creative process of the cosmos, his main purpose is to place humanity in the pivotal position of metaphysics—as creator rather than creation in the "great transformation" (*ta-hua*).[21] But implicit in his metaphysical outlook is the assertion that the defining characteristic of being human is sensitivity, a subtle and pervasive sense of consanguinity with all modalities of being. This enables Chang Tsai (1020-77) to make the seemingly romantic observation:

> Heaven is my father and Earth is my mother, and even such a small being as I find an intimate place in their midst. Therefore that which fills the universe I regard as my body and that which directs the universe I consider as my nature. All people are my brothers and sisters, and all things are my companions.[22]

The metaphor of the body is extended by Ch'eng Hao (1132-85).

> The man of humanity regards Heaven and Earth and all things as one body. To him there is nothing that is not himself. Since he has recognized all things as himself, can there be any limit to his humanity? If things are not part of the self, naturally they have nothing to do with it. As in the case of the paralysis of the four limbs, the *ch'i* [material force, vital force] no longer penetrates them and therefore they are no longer parts of the self.[23]

On the basis of these accounts, the body can perhaps be conceived as the "house" where the human spirit dwells. The idea that the body through its sensitivity forms a communion with the myriad things can thus be understood as a concrete manifestation of the human spirit. The body, as a result, becomes an instrument for realizing spiritual values. This overt optimism about the intrinsic goodness of the body is predicated on an assumption that basic feelings, such as joy, anger, sorrow, and delight, are indications of our response to stimuli from the outside, signifying our human sensitivity toward the world around us. The notion which appears in common parlance, that it is human to experience pain and itch, may have been derived from Ch'eng Hao's medical characterization of paralysis of the four limbs as the "absence of humanity" (*pu-jen*) in the four limbs.[24] As the most sentient beings, humans are therefore endowed with the most sensitive bodies. And it is in this sense that "to embody all things in one's sensitivity is not only humanly possible but necessarily human."[25]

The self, as the human body, is thus a feeling, caring, and loving self, constantly interacting and communicating with the total environment. It responds, adapts, and internalizes the symbolic as well as physical resources that surround it, mobilizing the biological as well as the affective energies for survival, development, and fulfillment. Mencius's statement that only the sage can bring his human form to full realization of its potential is laden with ethico-religious implications, but in actual practice it also signifies that "completion" of the body is an ultimate concern. Aging is perceived as a natural process of self-realization which eventually and inevitably leads to the concluding chapter of one's life history. Premature death is regrettable; the ripe age of seventy calls for communal celebration.

Unlike the body, the mind is formless and spaceless. According to Hsün Tzu, it is vacuous, unitary, and tranquil.[26] The mind can be filled with external impressions, but it never loses its capacity for receiving new information from the outside. The mind can be attracted to a variety of subjects at the same time, but temporal fragmentation does not injure its internal coherence. And though the mind can be easily perturbed by stimuli from the immediate environment, there is always an underlying quiescence. Hsün Tzu's attempt to emphasize the cognitive function of the mind, however, represents only a minor current in Confucian thought. The predominant intellectual tradition, under the influence of Mencius, designates the mind as the creative center of morality. To be sure, a primary function of the mind is thinking (ssu).[27] But thinking, in the Mencian sense, is a transformative act, involving the total person. This is part of the reason that Mencius characterizes the mind as the "great body" (ta-t'i).[28] As the creative center of morality, the mind not only thinks but wills; and it is through willing that the mind authenticates the truthfulness of its thinking. As Mencius points out, the will is the directionality of the mind; when the mind directs, a "bodily energy" follows.[29] Actually, the conative and affective dimensions of the mind take precedence over its cognitive function. For the mind feels and wills more often and more immediately than it thinks, cogitates, and reflects.

Etymologically, the Chinese word hsin can also be rendered as "heart." To convey both senses, it is sometimes translated as "heart-mind."[30] Even though hsin is ineffable, it is directly accessible through bodily sensations. The feeling of commiseration, the sensation of being unable to bear the sufferings of another human being, is cited by Mencius to show that humaneness (jen) is an intrinsic quality of hsin. Analogously, hsin by nature is capable of making righteous judgments, intelligent choices, and appropriate social decisions. According to Mencius, the feelings of shame, of right and wrong, and of deference are natural manifestations of hsin. Respectively, each of them serves as the affective basis for realizing the moral will in righteousness (i^b), intelligence ($chih^b$), and propriety (li). Needless to say, the Mencian conception of the heart-mind is diametrically opposed to the claim that the external environment through socialization determines the shape of human conscience and consciousness.

It is also misleading, however, to characterize the Mencian position as a kind of immanentism, claiming that moral ideas are innate in the mind.

Although Mencius maintains that humaneness, righteousness, intelligence, and propriety are not drilled into us from outside, he never undermines the importance of the environment and the necessity of experiential learning. In fact, a distinctive feature of Mencian thought is its commitment to the "learning of the mind" as a comprehensive project of self-cultivation. Techniques of concentration and yoga-like practices do not feature prominently in this particular approach. The ethico-religious concern for establishing that which is great in each of us, commonly known as "establishing the will" (*li-chih*), serves as the starting point.[31] The primary concern of such a task, which means "to make a total commitment to self-realization," is to purify the will so that it can be exclusively focused on personal cultivation. Concretely, Mencius proposes that the best way to nourish the mind is to make desires few.[32] This seeming platitude is predicated on the belief that whenever the mind encounters a thing, it confronts the danger of being inadvertently led astray. More desires dictate contact with more things. As things interact with things, the mind becomes incapable of returning to its original state of equilibrium. As a result, it becomes "lost" in the changing landscape of the external world. Therefore, the minimum requirement for establishing the will is to search for the "lost mind."[33]

One of the major debates in Sung-Ming Confucianism is whether or not the mind can independently and automatically establish its own will. If the mind can, the act of willing is all that is needed as the initial step in moral self-cultivation. Lacking this capacity, methods of disciplining the mind with the explicit purpose of firming up the will must be devised. In either case, the underlying assumption of the perfectability of human nature through self-effort remains unchallenged. The difference, in Neo-Confucian terminology, lies in the relationship between mind and human nature. If human nature is such that the mind as a feeling, willing, and thinking faculty spontaneously creates moral values, then in the ultimate sense the mind defines what human nature truly is. There should not be an essential distinction between mind and human nature. On the other hand, if the mind is the actual faculty whereby one can learn to be moral but is not necessarily the ontological ground of morality, a significant distinction between mind and human nature must be recognized.

Confucians who hold the view that mind and human nature are identical stress the centrality of inward illumination and self-enlightenment of the mind as the direct and immediate path of perfecting one's nature. To them, the ontological ground for human beings to be moral is not a static structure but a dynamic process. As a process, human nature and mind can automatically engender the necessary strength for the realization of the moral self. To establish the will is perceived by them as the most efficacious way of initiating the whole process of self-realization. They further claim that the mind has no original substance of its own: its substance is shaped, as it were, by the moral effort of the will. In other words, will as the directionality of the mind defines the quality of the mind. We have a sort of paradox here. If the mind in itself is the defining characteristic of the goodness of human nature, why is there any need for moral self-cultivation? On the other hand, if it is essential to exert moral effort so that the goodness of human nature can be fully realized, does not the mind fall short of being totally self-enlightening?

This difficulty may have impelled Confucians who hold the view that mind and human nature are separable to maintain that the mind must be cultivated so that it can eventually be identified with human nature. The mind is not automatically self-illuminating. If it becomes so, it is because it has learned the art of self-mastery through a rigorous discipline. It is not enough to rely upon the power of the will. Moral self-cultivation involves at least ritual learning, book reading, and social practice. The possibility of perfecting oneself through the enlightenment of the mind without the mediation of carefully internalized methods of acquiring self-knowledge is limited. It is neither necessary nor desirable to engage oneself in the highly elusive project of bringing to fruition the moral propensity of human nature by working directly through the inner qualities of the mind; for the mind is often amorphous and the subtlety of the mind in its original state can hardly reveal itself in ordinary human existence.[34]

Although it is controversial whether or not the mind can independently establish its own will, all major Neo-Confucian thinkers accept the view that human nature, as the ordaining principle, is endowed by heaven. The *raison d'être* of human existence can thus be understood as the manifestation of the "heavenly principle" (*t'ien-li*) inherent in our nature. On the surface, this line of thinking seems compatible with the idea that human beings are divinely circumscribed. Indeed, the principle inherent in our nature is metaphorically a gift of the heavenly decree. However, unlike the circumscribed divinity which is only a pale reflection of the real divine, the principle (either as the Great Ultimate [*t'ai-chi*] or as human nature) remains the same. Implicit in this assertion is the belief that the human principle, like the ultimate principle, is a full manifestation of the heavenly decree. Since the separation of divine and mundane, sacred and secular, creator and creation, and so on, is not entertained even as a possibility in Confucian symbolism, the heavenly decree can never become the "wholly other." On the contrary, it is immanent in the basic structure of being human: if one can fully realize one's mind, one can understand human nature; through understanding human nature, one knows heaven.

The Method

Having reviewed the background of the issue, we can now place Huang Tsung-hsi's (1610-95) characterization of Liu Tsung-chou's unique contribution to Ming thought in a proper philosophical context. Huang's influential book *Ming-ju hsüeh-an* [Scholarly synopses of the Ming Confucians], provides us with an overview of Liu's "learning of the heart-and-mind." It is well known that Huang, the most famous, if not the most intimate, student of Master Liu, did much to shape the historical image of his teacher as the last towering figure of the Sung-Ming Confucian tradition. In Huang's judgment, Mastern Liu's teaching of "vigilant solitariness" (*shen-tu*) creatively crystallized the essential meaning of the Confucian Way as interpreted by the Sung philosophers and by Wang Yang-ming. By focusing on the idea of the "root of intention" (*i-ken*), Liu significantly improved on Yang-ming's theory of *liang-chih* by developing a new understanding of the critical Neo-Confucian concept of the "substance of nature" (*hsing-t'i*), the ultimate justification for human uniqueness. Since Huang's discussion of Liu's contribution in the *Ming-ju hsüeh-an* is relatively brief, even though his selection of Liu's writings and recorded conversations is quite extensive, we have little knowledge of the reasoning underlying his assessment. It will therefore be more fruitful to focus our attention on Mou Tsung-san's attempt to pinpoint the precise area in the "learning of the heart-and-mind" of Liu's original insight.

To begin, we should note that Liu was conscientiously trying to combine the insights of the two Confucian traditions mentioned above. To be specific, he wanted to reformulate the idea of the unity of mind and human nature in Wang Yang-ming's thought so that it might successfully defend itself against the criticism of being one-sidedly committed to the self-enlightening capacity of the mind. Following Mou Tsung-san's suggestion, we can perhaps characterize Liu's strategy as reformulating Yang-ming's "explicit teaching" (*hsien-chiao*) of the mind in the spirit of the "esoteric teaching" (*mi-chiao*) of "vigilant solitariness."[35] The centrality of the idea of solitariness in Liu's concept of the concrete process by which one learns to be human should become clear in the course of our discussion.

Needless to say, despite Liu's critique of Yang-ming's philosophy of *liang-chih*, he fully endorses Yang-Ming's emphasis on the centrality of inward illumination and self-enlightenment of the mind. He also shares with Yang-ming the belief that the mind can independently and automatically establish its own will. However, Liu is suspicious of the view that the knowing faculty of the mind, even with its implicit affective and conative dimensions, can really be trusted with the whole enterprise of self-cultivation. It is not what one knows but what one does not know at a given juncture of moral development that matters. The discriminating function of knowledge presupposes the dichotomy of good and evil. Such a presupposition conditions the moral agent in a divided world. Being alienated from his own nature, which is ultimately good, the moral agent can only pursue the good life in a fragmented and incremental style.

The belief that through "sudden enlightenment" the moral agent can, once and for all, dwell in the eternal bliss of the ultimate good does not provide a viable alternative either. For one thing, the supposed inward illumination of the mind can in actuality turn out to be no more than an empty vision. Yang-ming's first precept in his Four-Sentence Teaching—"the mind-in-itself is beyond good and evil"—thus begins in Liu's opinion with a wrong turn. If the substance of the mind is human nature, it should be taken as where the ultimate good dwells. The mind should not be perceived as *liang-chih*, or pure consciousness, as if the willing to be good were somehow external to its original structure. Yang-ming's second and third precepts, "in the movement of the will, there is good and evil" and "knowing good and evil is *liang-chih*," are also problematic, especially in the sense of priority. If the dichotomy of good and evil occurs in the movement of the will, primordial knowing can never precede the existence of evil. Furthermore, there is no guarantee that the act of knowing itself necessarily eradicates what the will engenders. As a result, "knowing becomes enslaved in the will; where does the good reside?"[36]

To rectify the wrong turn, Liu proposes a fine distinction between two forms of knowing. To know good and evil resembles knowing love and respect, but the resemblance is superficial. While the knowledge of love and respect is intrinsic to the feelings of love and respect, the knowledge of good and evil is extrinsic to the intuitive sense of good and evil. *Liang-chih*, in regard to love and respect, means that our primordial awareness is not adulterated by feelings of hatred and disrespect. *Liang-chih* is therefore always good. By contrast, since the knowledge of good and evil depends upon a value judgment issuing from *liang-chih*, it is inevitably a secondary procedure. Liu further proposes a more refined discrimination of the idea of the will. He believes that it is vitally important to differentiate two kinds of will. For the sake of expediency, we shall call the first "volition" (*nien*) and the second "intention" (*i*). Liu argues that Yang-ming is hampered by two problems: a misconception of the idea of the will as intention, which compels him to search for the good in the faculty of knowing, and an unsophisticated comprehension of the idea of knowledge, which compels him to search for the most refined manifestation of the good in the mind.[37]

Liu's strategy, in sum, significantly reformulates Yang-ming's Four-Sentence Teaching:

> In the movements of the mind, there is good and evil.
>
> In the tranquility of the will, there is liking the good and disliking the evil.
>
> Knowing good and evil is primordial knowing.
>
> Doing good and eliminating evil is the principle of things.[38]

In this reformulation, even though the sequence of *mind, will, knowing*, and *thing* remains unchanged and the third sentence is identical to Yang-ming's original, the meaning undergoes a profound transformation. Instead of positing as a transcendental principle that the "substance of the mind" is beyond good and evil, the mind is taken in its commonsense idea as consciousness. The will, on the other hand, assumes an active role in moral self-cultivation. Primordial knowing, accordingly, functions not as a posterior reflection on the good and evil engendered by the motions of the will; it knows as the will transforms. Understandably, Liu characterizes the will as "where the mind dwells rather than what the mind issues forth" and knowing as "implicated in the will rather than what the will gives rise to."[39] It is in this sense that Liu takes the will as the substance of the mind and contends that the act of willing, especially in the most subtle manifestation of such an act, defines the true function of the mind.

The centrality of the will in Liu's philosophical anthropology is evidenced in his distinction of the two kinds of will mentioned above. For him, volitional ideas, conditioned and shaped by past experiences, personal tastes, and instinctual demands, are not manifestations of the "pure will." Pure will, in its original state of intending, is the function of pure consciousness. As T'ang Chün-i notes, "consciousness is pure when it withdraws itself from outer or inner empirical objects, purifies itself from what it is mixed with, and sees itself as a pure subjectivity or a pure spiritual light."[40] On the other hand, if consciousness is oriented toward an object, impacted with external impressions, or mixed with ideas of the outside world, it is no longer pure. The assumption that consciousness, in its pure form, means not being conscious of something and that human beings, as their birthright, are all potentially capable of this kind of "intellectual intuition" is a salient feature of Neo-Confucian thought, indeed, of all Three Teachings in Chinese philosophy.[41] Liu's unique contribution, to quote from T'ang again, is to take pure consciousness "not merely as a pure knowing, like a light, but also as a pure feeling and a pure willing like the heat of light. Thus, pure consciousness has a life."[42]

In a deeper sense, however, Yang-ming and the majority of his followers also take pure consciousness as a vital force for ultimate self-transformation. To them, *liang-chih* as a form of pure knowing entails pure feeling and pure willing. *Liang-chih* is a transformative act as well as a reflective knowing. In the structure and function of *liang-chih*, to know involves not only "knowing that" and "knowing how" but also the evocative acts of enlightening, transforming, and, indeed, realizing. Since a defining characteristic of *liang-chih* is the unity of knowledge and action, pure consciousness is also a form of creativity. The knowing subject is thus a full-fledged creator. This seemingly Berkeleian assertion is further predicated on a belief that each human being is endowed with a godlike faculty to create through intellectual intuition. The known object becomes a living thing rather than an external fact, because the knowing subject, by an act of intention, has brought life to its existence. Yang-ming's idea that a thing is where the will resides points directly to the "idealistic" character of his thought, which seems compatible with Liu's insistence that the will as intention is a life-giving force.[43]

In what sense, then, are we to understand Liu's philosophical anthropology as reformulating Yang-ming's "explicit teaching" of the mind in the spirit of the "esoteric teaching" of "vigilant solitariness"? Mou Tsung-san suggests that we take Liu's idea of the will as a transcendental principle.[44] To be specific, the will as volition is empirical and thus operates *a posteriori*. The problem with volition so conceived is the implicit predisposition underlyling the choices of the moral agent. The will as volition is so much intertwined with the habits of the past and the partiality of the present that it can become an indulgence rather than a liberation. If we simply act according to our volition, we may find ourselves predisposed to a behavioral pattern contrary to our moral well-being. On the other hand, the will as intention is thought to be the manifestation of the pure will. The pure will, in Liu's terminology, never errs from the "ultimate good," for it, like the waves of the ocean, is a natural expression of the mind. Indeed, the pure will operates in its own intuitive way totally independent of knowledge of the senses and yet never commits an intellectual fallacy. There is, therefore, absolute certainty in doing the right thing in the right situation at the right time. The main issue, however, is to see to it that the transcendental principle is concretely applied to effect the most desirable result. In other words, there is a guarantee that the transcendental principle becomes an experienced reality rather than simply a theoretical postulate. The concept of "vigilant solitariness" speaks directly to this point.

The word *tu*, rendered here as "solitariness," also means uniqueness and absoluteness. The concept of "vigilant solitariness" occurs in both the *Great Learning* and the *Doctrine of the Mean*, denoting a method of self-cultivation with far-reaching ethico-religious implications. Although *shen-tu* is often translated as being "watchful over oneself when alone,"[45] the commonsense reading of *shen*[b] as "watchful" and *tu* as "alone" does not do justice to Liu's deliberate attempt to assign a pivotal position to the concept of *shen-tu* in his philosophical anthropology. To him, the self-discipline of being watchful over oneself when one is physically alone only scratches the surface of moral cultivation. The real challenge is to learn to be in tune with one's innermost being, that center of moral creativity which is solitary, unique, and absolute. As we have already noted, Liu takes human nature to be ultimately good, and man to be heaven's co-creator. This concomitance of heaven and man provides an ontological justification for according humanity a godlike power of creative self-transformation.

Solitariness, in this sense, denotes an ontological substance and an experienced reality. As an ontological substance, it is the heaven-endowed nature, the original mind, and the "root of intention"; as an experienced reality, it is both the unmanifested "centrality" (*chung*) and the manifested "harmony" (*ho*) of the mind.[46] While this aspect of Liu's thinking is compatible with the identity of mind and principle in the Lu-Wang tradition, the main thrust of his argument is deliberately more subtle and paradoxical. The "solitariness" (or, if you will, the uniquely human capacity for critical self-examination) inherent in our nature is a sufficient as well as a necessary cause for our moral self-perfection. Yet the concrete procedure by which we can actually initiate the whole process of fully realizing what we essentially are is by no means straightforward. For one thing, what we existentially are falls short of what we morally ought to be, which is tantamount to what our human nature ontologically is.

Since Liu rejects the claim that the mind by its enlightening knowledge can directly bring about an ultimate moral transformation of the person, "vigilant solitariness" is not simply a form of introspective knowing. Rather, it is an attempt to create an experiential basis for a penetrating, comprehensive, and continuous scrutiny of the deepest layer of one's motivational structure. The scrutiny, in this particular connection, functions both as a focused investigation of all the underlying reasons for one's action and as an overall confirmation of the unlimited possibility for personal moral growth. Self-criticism and self-respect are thus two integrated dimensions of the same process. To be thoroughly critical of everything one does, big or small, obvious or hidden, is to be totally committed to the singularity of oneself as a dynamic moral agent. This seemingly insurmountable task of self-scrutiny cannot be carried out merely at the behavioral and attitudinal levels. Unless a linkage, indeed, a channel, is established with the center of moral creativity which can bring forth an inexhaustible supply of energy for self-cultivation, there is no hope of any qualitative improvement. Sporadic efforts certainly will not do; even systematic and programmatic endeavor is not enough, if it remains in an ethical realm which fails to account for the ultimate source of morality.

In Liu's terminology, "vigilant solitariness" involves a twofold process: to "transform volitional ideas into the mind" (*hua-nien kuei-hsin*)[47] and to "manifest nature through the mind" (*i-hsin tso-hsing*).[48] The former is predicated on the belief that intention is not an expression of the mind but where the mind dwells.[49] In other words, the "root of intention" defines the "substance of the mind" (*hsin-t'i*). To transform "volitional ideas" into the mind, therefore, means to restructure volition to the extent that it becomes totally transformed into intention. Whether or not volition or volitional idea conveys the essential meaning of *nien*, the distinction Liu makes is subtle but unequivocal. Using the etymological tactic of splitting the character *nien* into the two scriptual components—*chin* (today, present) and *hsin* (mind-heart), Liu defines *nien* as *yü-ch'i* ("residual material force") of the mind.[50] T'ang Chün-i characterizes this aspect of Liu's thought as follows:

> Actually, what *yü-ch'i* denotes is the potentiality of an activity when it is gone. This is the origin of habits. Every habit, as it comes from man's past activity of consciousness, has some residual effect to compel the present consciousness to take the habitual form, called *hsi*. *Hsi* may be quite different from nature. When the present consciousness takes the habitual form of its past activity, which is different from nature, it withdraws itself backward to the habitual form and solidifies in that form, becoming partial and noncreative. This is the origin of error and evil.[51]

Nien can thus be seen as "a solidification of consciousness controlled by partial habitual form."[52]

Liu is critically aware that *nien* can be either good or bad and that it is desirable to develop the good and eliminate the bad. But he is, in principle, dissatisfied with the whole enterprise of initiating self-cultivation at this relativistic level. His quest for an absolute standard of moral excellence impels him to probe beyond objectifiable patterns of behavior, no matter how good they appear to be. He proposes that unwilled autonomous acts be thoroughly scrutinized so that one can gradually learn to act in perfect accord with the full intention of pure consciousness.[53] In practice it is unlikely that one can ever reach such a high level of intentional self-motivation that the problem of the weakness of the will is dissolved and every act is the consequence of the mind's self-illumination. To strive for it, however, is not only an authentic possibility for each human being but a moral imperative for those who take the "learning of the body and mind" seriously.

The second part of the twofold process of "vigilant solitariness" brings us to Liu's unique contribution to Neo-Confucian thought, namely his "esoteric teaching." The suggestion that true human nature can be revealed only through the intentional acts of the mind is a widely shared assumption in Sung-Ming Confucian learning. Liu's unusual move, as a response to Yang-ming's precept of *liang-chih*, is to probe the innermost structure and function of the mind. This requires an experiential understanding of the mind at the moment when its manifestation of human nature is still an incipient (*chi*) form. The possibility for an incipient manifestation to go astray is so great that unless one encounters it time and time again as a lived reality at the source, one cannot ensure its full development. Although the mind is potentially capable of fully realizing human nature, a frustrated manifestation rarely indicates what humanity really is. It is therefore vitally important to exert moral effort at the "root of intention."

However, unlike the enlightening functions of the mind, which can at least be noticed through introspection, the root of intention is ineffable in a most subtle way. It can easily escape our attention if we are not in tune with the basic rhythm of the creative life of pure consciousness. The cultivation of the root of intention, comparable to Mencius's recommendation for nourishing the mind, must be "unforgetful" (*wu-wang*) and "unhurried" (*wu-chu*).[54] While fully endorsing the Mencian belief that making desires few is the best method of nourishing the mind, Liu further suggests, in the spirit of the *Doctrine of the Mean*, a continuous interplay between the "unaroused" and "aroused" states of the mind. Specifically, he proposes that we constantly follow the ebb and flow of our feelings and emotions, mapping out the seasonal changes, as it were, in order to acquire a comprehensive understanding of where we are in our stages of moral growth.[55] As we gain awareness of our inner lives, the moral effort should be directed toward an appreciation of the inseparability of the substance and function of the mind. The more we act in accordance with the autonomy and spontaneity of the mind, the more we experience our nature as an authenticating activity rather than merely as an imagined possibility.

We must not be misled into believing, Liu cautions, that since our true nature is accessible to us through the spontaneous and autonomous functions of the mind, it guarantees a safe passage to dwelling on the ultimate good. The subtlety of the root of intention is such that as soon as the strenuous effort of "making the will sincere" (*ch'eng-i*) is discontinued, it disappears as an experienced reality. On the other hand, even though one never ceases to refine the art of bringing about the "sincerity of the will," there is always a dimension of abstruseness in the root of intention that we cannot penetrate.[56] It is in this sense that Liu considers "vigilant solitariness" the best approach to self-cultivation. The elaborate project of correcting mistakes in his seminal treatise, *Schematic of Man* [Jen-p'u], can thus be interpreted as his strategy for learning to be human by putting "vigilant solitariness" into practice as a daily ritual.

Realizing Humanity

Liu's *Schematic of Man* is, on the surface, a map, a diagram, a score, or a manual for teaching people to "change to the good and reform faults"[57] in order to become fully developed moral persons. The underlying structure of the treatise, however, is a holistic vision of self-cultivation through the practice of "vigilant solitariness." Human beings, as the most sentient beings in the universe, are "decreed" by heaven to embody the "centrality" of the cosmic transformation as their nature. They are "created," not as creatures, but as co-creators for the task of providing necessary assistance in the cosmic transformation of heaven and earth.[58] As a full member of this trinity, humanity is divine by definition, and it is human to be divine. However, although human nature is ultimately good, its way of self-manifestation is by no means transparent. The naive belief that one can become a sage through sudden enlightenment, without strenuous effort of self-cultivation, is based on a misunderstanding of the abstruseness of the original design: human nature can be manifested only through the willing, knowing, and feeling activities of the mind.

The identity of the "substance of the mind" and human nature notwithstanding, the mind needs to be disciplined, cultivated, and nourished so that the "centrality" inherent in it can manifest itself without being obstructed by enclosed and limiting selfish ideas. To realize humanity is therefore to bring the actual functions of the mind into harmony with the constituents, such as the "four beginnings" (*ssu-tuan*),[59] of human nature. Human nature so conceived is itself an activity, not merely a ground or an ideal of moral perfection. However, the form of activity human nature autonomously engenders is so subtle and incipient that it is hardly perceivable by the untutored mind. This gives rise to a paradox. The incipient activity of human nature, known as the root of intention, is actually the substance of the mind. The failure of the untutored mind to recognize this means that the mind has yet to learn to listen to its own voice. The art of "vigilant solitariness," practiced vigorously as a daily ritual, can purify one's sense perceptions and provide an experiential basis for the mind to be constantly responsive to the subtle signals of human nature.

The procedure, a ceaseless process of learning to be human, involves the following concrete steps: (1) dwelling in secluded retirement in order to experience the self in solitude; (2) divining the movement of thought in order to recognize incipient tendencies; (3) exercising caution in one's bearing in order to follow the decree of heaven; (4) strengthening the basic human relationships in order to crystallize the Way; (5) making complete the hundred practices in order to investigate one's conduct comprehensively; and (6) changing to the good and reforming faults in order to become a sage. These steps are further put in the context of a penetrating, comprehensive, and continuous project of self-criticism which identifies moral failings in terms of six major categories: the subtle faults, concealed faults, obvious faults, great faults, miscellaneous faults, and completed faults.[60]

Realizing humanity, in Liu's philosophical anthropology, entails a thorough analysis of one's behavior, attitude, motivation, and root of intention. The purpose is neither social adjustment nor personal integration in the ordinary psychological sense; it is rather the optimal manifestation of one's moral creativity as an ultimate concern. Human beings so defined are self-perfecting beings. Being human means to be ultimately self-transforming. To deepen one's subjectivity through "vigilant solitariness" is to open oneself up to the common spring of humanity. The deepened and deepening subjectivity is constantly in tune with the rhythmic pattern of heaven and earth; it is a liberation from the constraints of "opinionatedness" (*i*; ironically, this is the same character that Liu later used to mean "intention"), "stubbornness" (*pi*), "arbitrariness" (*ku*), and "self-centeredness" (*wo*).[61] Our dignity, autonomy, and self-sufficiency as human beings certainly lie in our possessing bodies and minds. Yet the reason that we really possess them is because we have learned to recognize the true face of our human nature.

In the perspective of Liu Tsung-chou's philosophical anthropology, the relationship between individualism and holism assumes a particular meaning. The dignity and autonomy of the self is predicated on one's ability to go beyond the limitation and inertia of self-centeredness through deep personal knowledge. As a result, there is a total absence of asserting one's independence as an individual vis-à-vis society. The central concern is the establishment and, more appropriately, the realization of one's true subjectivity. True subjectivity, as the genuine will beyond the restrictions of selfish desires, is not simply a state of being but also a transformative activity. It is a dynamic movement toward the ultimate good. The realization of one's true subjectivity, which can also be understood as a way of liberating oneself from obvious and insidious forms of egoism and subjectivism, necessarily involves the cultivation of a widening horizon of human understanding. The authentic way of making oneself whole is, therefore, not simply to search for that which is uniquely one's own but to acquire a taste for that quality which is uniquely human—ultimate self-transformation as a communal act. Only then can one really *know* heaven through one's own nature and thus form a trinity with heaven and earth. Holism, in this sense, is a natural outcome of subjectivity. As one authenticates one's "vigilant solitariness," one enlarges and refines one's sensitivity. The experience of "embodying" (*t'i*) the universe holistically in one's subjectivity, far from being the expansion of the ego, signifies the openness, the transparency, and the spontaneity of the cultivated self.

NOTES

1. For a critical analysis of the idea of individualism in the West, see Steven Lukes, *Individualism* (Oxford: Blackwell, 1973). For a sociopsychological study of the idea of the self, see David L. Miller, *Individualism: Personal Achievement and the Open Society* (Austin: University of Texas Press, 1967). See also Charles A. Moore, ed., *The Status of the Individual in East and West* (Honolulu: University of Hawaii Press, 1968).

2. "Subjectivity and Ontological Reality: An Interpretation of Wang Yang-ming's Mode of Thinking," *Philosophy East and West* (January-April 1973), 23(1-2):187-205.

3. T'ang Chün-i, "Liu Tsung-chou's Doctrine of Moral Mind and Practice and His Critique of Wang Yang-ming," in *The Unfolding of Neo-Confucianism*, ed. Wm. Theodore de Bary, et al. (New York: Columbia University Press, 1975), 305-31.

4. Thomé H. Fang (Fang Tung-mei), *Chinese Philosophy: Its Spirit and Its Development* (Taipei: Linking Publishing Co., 1981), 471-76.

5. Mou Tsung-san, *Ts'ung Lu Hsiang-shan tao Liu Chi-shan* [From Lu Hsiang-shan to Liu Chi-shan] (Taipei: Taiwan Hsüeh-sheng Shu-chu, 1979), 451-88.

6. T'ang Chün-i, "Liu Tsung-chou's Doctrine of Moral Mind," 313.

7. Wing-tsit Chan, trans., *A Source Book in Chinese Philosophy* (Princeton: Princeton University Press, 1963), 86.

8. Ibid., 654-91.

9. Mou Tsung-san, *Ts'ung Lu Hsiang-shan*, 451-52.

10. "Liang-chih shuo" [An essay on *Liang-chih*], in *Liu Tzu ch'üan-shu* [The complete works of Master Liu] (1822 ed.), 8.24a-26a. Hereafter cited as LTCS. See also *Yang-ming ch'üan-hsin lu* [A record of the truthful transmission of Yang-ming's teaching], in *Liu Tzu ch'üan-shu i-pien* [Supplementary edition of the complete works of Master Liu] (1850 ed.), 13.23b-24a. I am indebted to Wing-tsit Chan for calling my attention to this important text and for his kindness in making available to me his personal copy of this work, perhaps the only copy in North America. For an informative discussion on "Liang-chih shuo," see Okada Takehiko, *Ryū Nen-dai bunshū* [Literary works of Liu Nien-t'ai] (Tokyo: Metoku, 1980), 187-99.

11. T'ang Chün-i, "Liu Tsung-chou's Doctrine of Moral Mind," 313.

12. Ibid., 314.

13. "Cheng-hsüeh tsa-chieh" [Miscellaneous notes on verifying learning], item 25, in LTCS 6.14a.

14. "I-yen" [Expansive notes on the *Book of Changes*], chap. 7, in LTCS 2.14a.

15. *Mencius*, 7A:1.

16. "I-yen," 2.14a.

17. Ch'eng I, *I-shu* [Posthumous works], in *Erh Ch'eng ch'üan-shu* [Complete works of the two Ch'engs] (SPPY ed.), 18.17b.

18. *Mencius*, 6A:14; 7A:38.

19. For a brief discussion on this aspect of Confucian education, see Tu Wei-ming, "The Confucian Perception of Adulthood," in his *Humanity and Self-Cultivation: Essays in Confucian Thought* (Berkeley: Asian Humanities Press, 1980), 44.

20. Erik H. Erikson, *Toys and Reasons: Stages in the Ritualization of Experience* (New York: Norton Press, 1978).

21. Chou Tun-i, "T'ai-chi t'u-shuo" [Essay on the diagram of the Great Ultimate], in *Chu Tzu ch'üan-shu* [Complete works of Master Chu] (SPPY ed.), 1.2.

22. Chang Tsai, "Hsi-ming" [The Western Inscription], in *Chang Tzu ch'üan-shu* [Complete works of Master Chang] (SPPY ed.), 1.1a. Cf. Chan, *Source Book*, 497.

23. Ch'eng Hao, "Shih-jen" [On understanding humanity], in *I-shu*, 2A.3; Chan, *Source Book*, 497.

24. Ibid.
25. Tu Wei-ming, "The Neo-Confucian Concept of Man," in *Humanity and Self-Cultivation*, 74.
26. "Chieh-pi" [Dispelling delusions], in *Hsün Tzu yin-te* [Index to the *Hsün Tzu*] (Cambridge: Harvard-Yenching Institute, 1950), 80.34-41.
27. *Mencius*, 6A:15.
28. Ibid.
29. Ibid., 2A:2.
30. See Wm. Theodore de Bary, "The Neo-Confucian Learning of the Mind-and-Heart," in his *Neo-Confucian Orthodoxy and the Learning of the Mind-and-Heart* (New York: Columbia Press, 1981), 67-185.
31. *Mencius*, 2A:6; 6A:15. Lu Hsiang-shan's philosophical anthropology can be said to have centered around this Mencian thesis. See Mou Tsung-san, *Tsung Lu Hsiang-shan*, 3-25.
32. *Mencius*, 7B:35.
33. Ibid., 6A:11.
34. A paradigmatic example of this line of thinking is found in Chu Hsi's philosophy of mind; see Mou Tsung-san, *Hsin-t'i yü hsing-t'i* [The substance of mind and nature], 3 vols. (Taipei: Cheng-Chung Book Co., 1969), vol. 3.
35. Mou Tsung-san, *Ts'ung Lu Hsiang-shan*, 453-57.
36. "Liang-chih shuo," 8.25a.
37. Ibid., 8.25b.
38. "Hsüeh-yen" [Words on learning], pt. 1, in LTCS 10.26b. See also Huang Tsung-hsi, *Ming-ju hsüeh-an* (SPPY ed.), 62.7b.
39. Ibid., 8.25a.
40. T'ang Chün-i, "Liu Tsung-chou's Doctrine of Moral Mind," 315.
41. Mou Tsung-san, *Chih ti chih-chüeh yü Chung-kuo che-hsüeh* [Intellectual intuition and Chinese philosophy] (Taipei: Commercial Press, 1971).
42. T'ang Chün-i, "Liu Tsung-chou's Doctrine of Moral Mind," 316.
43. Wang Yang-ming, *Ch'uan-hsi lu* [Instruction for practical living], in *Wang Yang-ming ch'üan-shu* [Complete works of Wang Yang-ming], 5 vols. (Taipei: Cheng-Chung Book Co., 1955), 1:5.
44. Mou Tsung-san, *Ts'ung Lu Hsiang-shan*, 465-66.
45. Chan, *Source Book*, 89.
46. "*Chung-yung* shou-chang shuo" [An essay on the first chapter of the *Doctrine of the Mean*], in LTCS (1824-1835 ed.), 8.9a-12a. The first part of the essay (9a-10b) is missing from the Chung-hua wen-shih ts'ung-shu edition published in Taipei. The Chung-hua edition is supposed to be a photocopy of the 1822 Tao-kuang edition of the LTCS. The two pages are missing in one version of the Tao-kuang edition. The Chung-hua edition, intent on emending the defective text, supplies two handwritten pages for 9a-10b. Unfortunately, the two handwritten pages have taken material from 8.7b-9a and have thus added further confusion to the defective text. I have examined two versions of the LTCS (1824-1835 ed.) in the Harvard-Yenching collection. One of them is also defective in the same way.
47. The expression *hua-nien kuei-hsin* is found in "Hsüeh-yen," pt. 2, in LTCS 11.11b. For a focused investigation of this issue, see "Chih-nien shuo" [Theory on dealing with volition], in LTCS 8.24a-b.
48. The expression *i-hsin tso-hsing* is coined by Mou Tsung-san; see *Ts'ung Lu Hsiang-shan*, 458. The claim is fully substantiated by Liu's interpretation of human nature; see "Yüan-hsing" [On the origin of nature], in LTCS 7.1b-3a.
49. "Hsüeh-yen," pt. 2, in LTCS 11.6b.
50. Ibid., 11.11a.
51. T'ang Chün-i, "Liu Tsung-chou's Doctrine of Moral Mind," 318.
52. Ibid.
53. An example of this can be found in Liu's discourse on *hsi* (habit); see "Hsi-shuo" [On habits], in LTCS 8.19b-20b.

54. *Mencius*, 2A:2.

55. "Tu *I* t'u-shuo" [A diagrammatic note on reading the *Book of Changes*], in LTCS 2.8b-9a. See also "Hsüeh-yen," pt. 2, in LTCS 11.9a-10b.

56. "Kai-kuo shuo" [On correcting mistakes], pt. 1, in LTCS 1.13a-b.

57. *Jen-p'u*, in LTCS 1.6b.

58. *Doctrine of the Mean*, secs. 29-31. See Chan, *Source Book*, 111-12.

59. *Mencius*, 2A:6.

60. *Jen-p'u*, 1.3a-11b.

61. *Analects*, 9:4. It should be noted that the character *i* used in this context, meaning "arbitrariness of opinion," is often rendered as "selfish ideas" in Neo-Confucian terminology. Of course, the same character used in Liu's philosophical anthropology is comparable in meaning to the Mencian idea of "will" in *Mencius*, 2A:2.

Glossary

Chang Tsai 張載

Chang Tzu ch'üan-shu 張子全書

Ch'eng-Chu 程朱

Ch'eng Hao 程顥

"Cheng-hsüeh tsa-chieh" 正學雜解

ch'eng-i 誠意

Ch'eng I 程頤

ch'i 氣

chi 機

"Chieh-pi" 解蔽

chih[a] 知

chih[b] 智

chih-chih 致知

chih-hsing ho-i 知行合一

"Chih-nien shuo" 治念說

Chih ti chih-chüeh yü Chung-kuo che-hsüeh 智的直覺與中國哲學

chih yü chih-shan 止於至善

chin 今

Chou Tun-i 周敦頤

Chou Tzu ch'üan-shu 周子全書

Ch'uan-hsi lu 傳習錄

chung 中

"*Chung-yung* shou-chang shuo" 中庸首章說

Erh Ch'eng ch'üan-shu 二程全書

Fang Tung-mei 方東美

ho 和

hsi 習

"Hsi-ming" 西銘

"Hsi-shuo" 習說

hsiao 孝

hsien-chiao 顯教

hsin 心

Hsin-chai 心齋

hsin-hsüeh 心學

hsin-t'i 心體

Hsin-t'i yü hsing-t'i 心體與性體

hsing 性

hsing-t'i 性體

hsiu 修

hsiu-shen 修身

"Hsüeh-yen" 學言

Hsün Tzu 荀子

Hsün Tzu yin-te 荀子引得

hua-nien kuei-hsin 化念歸心

Huang Tsung-hsi 黃宗羲

i^a 意

i^b 義

i-hsin tso-hsing 以心著性

i-ken 意根

I-shu 遺書

"I-yen" 易衍

jen 仁

Jen-p'u 人譜

"Kai-kuo shuo" 改過說

ko-wu 格物

ku 固

li 禮

li-chih 立志

liang-chih 良知

"Liang-chih shuo" 良知說

Liu Tsung-chou 劉宗周

Liu Tzu ch'üan-shu 劉子全書

Liu Tzu ch'üan-shu i-pien 劉子全書遺編

Lu-Wang 陸王

Lung-hsi 龍谿

mi-chiao 密教

ming 命

Ming-ju hsüeh-an 明儒學案

Mou Tsung-san 牟宗三

nien 念

Okada Takehiko 岡田武彥

pi 必

pu-jen 不仁

Ryū Nen-dai bunshū 劉念台文集

shen^a 身

shen^b 愼

shen-tu 愼獨

"Shih-jen" 識仁

ssu 思

ssu-tuan 四端

Sung-Ming 宋明

ta-hua 大化

Ta-hsüeh 大學

ta-t'i 大體

t'ai-chi 太極

"T'ai-chi t'u-shuo" 太極圖說

T'ang Chün-i 唐君毅

t'i 體

t'ien-li 天理

Ts'ung Lu Hsiang-shan tao Liu Chi-shan 從陸象山到劉戢山

tu 獨

"Tu I t'u-shuo"　讀易圖說

Tu Wei-ming　杜維明

Wang Chi　王畿

Wang Ken　王艮

Wang Yang-ming　王陽明

Wang Yang-ming ch'üan-shu　王陽明全書

wo　我

wu　物

wu-chu　勿助

wu-wang　勿忘

Yang-ming ch'üan-hsin lu　陽明傳信錄

yü-ch'i　餘氣

"Yüan-hsing"　原性

Romantic Individualism in Modern Chinese Literature: Some General Explorations

*Leo Ou-fan Lee**

The term "individualism" (*ke-jen chu-i*) appears frequently in the writings of the May Fourth period, a decade of intellectual revolution (1917-27) in which traditional Chinese culture was subjected to a thorough ideological assault by a generation of radical intellectuals and writers who championed the values of "New Culture" and "New Literature." Individualism was one of the justifying principles for iconoclasm, the intellectual revolt against tradition. However, as Yü-sheng Lin has pointed out, "individualist values were not regarded in the Chinese context as self-evident and ultimate ends that should be held in and by themselves."[1] The May Fourth brand of individualism was part of an iconoclastic stance, not the basis of a system of thought; it did not constitute a mature, systematic political or philosophical doctrine. Thus, for the purposes of evaluation, May Fourth individualism might most fruitfully be viewed as a prevailing ethos focusing on the centrality of the self and its assertive independence from the bonds of traditional social relations. To this extent it is possible to characterize the May Fourth period as one of unprecedented *opposition* between the self and society, between the individual and the "whole," a conflict most articulately expressed in the literary works of the day.

Many May Fourth writers used the word "individual" (*ke-jen*) in conjunction with "individuality" (*ke-hsing*) to emphasize the primacy of the individual personality over the confining matrix of traditional values. A concomitant of individualism was "emancipation," or "liberation" (*chieh-fang*), referring to the act of freeing the self from the shackles of the traditional whole. This obvious tension between the modern concept of self in China and its traditional background is, in the final analysis, more historical and ideological than metaphysical or aesthetic. It was exacerbated by the realization that the traditional Chinese order was breaking down. China on the brink of modernity was no longer perceived as a holistic world in which

*I would like to express my appreciation to Barbara Congelosi for her exemplary editorial work on this paper, which helped to make my ideas much clearer.

239

each individual had his (or her) place. The nation was undergoing a cataclysmic transformation. May Fourth intellectuals saw themselves as living in a period of transition, a period punctuated by the kinds of conflicts, dynamic upheavals, and revolutionary changes that would reshape the old Chinese world order into a new nation-state with a new culture. This melodramatic vision was, furthermore, anchored in a new form of historicism, expressed in terms of China becoming part of mankind in its forward march toward a bright future.

In this new, universalistic scheme, the individual could perform a generative function in the creation and development of the "wholes" of modern culture and civilization. A more political manifestation of this new epistemology is what Thomas Metzger calls the "zealously ideological, heroic self"—a type which began to appear by the 1890s and has been fundamental, albeit in different ways, to Maoism and the ideology of the Kuomintang (KMT) as well as to modern revivals of Confucianism.[2] In this vision, the self is armed with a doctrinal system which explains the laws of history in the light of a fixed goal of life; the individual is filled with a fiery determination to struggle for this goal and strives to be one with history and with "the people." The key problem is, therefore, that of fusing one's heroic spirit with the rising tide of the historical force and then translating this optimistic inner vision into the outer world through writing or some other activity. For many of the period's ideologues, this fusion culminated in the victory of Mao's revolution; others perceived this revolution as an aberration and argued for a different vision of history and a different kind of fusion.

I have chosen not to treat this heroic vision of the self but to focus instead on the literary aspects of what Jaroslav Prušek calls "individualism and subjectivism." The literary expressions of the self, if not as heroic as other manifestations, are more pointedly individualistic and thus embody a crucial legacy of the May Fourth period. The May Fourth preoccupation with the self is, in my view, unique in the history of Chinese culture. It is most simply described as the combination of an obsessive concern with the significance of the human self (individualism) and a highly personal perception of reality (subjectivism). In this context, creative literature constitutes a particularly intense form of self-expression, reflecting, as Prušek notes, "the author's own feelings, moods, visions and even dreams; the artist's work approaches more and more closely to a confession in which the author reveals the different sides of his character and of his life—and especially the gloomier and more hidden sides."[3] In many such literary formulations, one finds a troubled and often conflicting relationship (in contrast to the heroic vision of a creative or accommodating fusion) between self and society and between the inner and outer realities perceived by the individual writer. It is this deep sense of disjunction which characterizes the best of May Fourth literature and which is noticeably lacking in the literature of subsequent periods.

What inspired May Fourth writers to such concern with the unique qualities of individualism and subjectivism? And how does their perception differ from its historical precedents in China and the West? This paper will attempt at least partial answers to these questions by isolating the intellectual issues of the self as formulated by some major May Fourth writers, and by exemplifying the ways in which the self is represented in conflict with society (the "whole") in selected samples of their creative writings. I have elsewhere defined the pervasive emotionality of May Fourth individualism as "romantic."[4] Perhaps the term adopted here, "romantic individualism," however amorphous, will prove more useful as a general indicator of this unique phenomenon.

Ideas of the Self

One of the most influential statements of May Fourth individualism is surely Hu Shih's famous article on Ibsenism, first published in *New Youth* (Hsin ch'ing-nien) in 1918. According to Hu Shih, the principal theme of Ibsen's drama is the damaging influence of society on the human individual; society, consisting of three great evils (law, religion, and morality), is authoritarian: "It forcibly cripples individual personality and suppresses the spirit of individual freedom and independence. When the individual personality is eliminated, and the spirit of freedom and independence is done with, society itself will also atrophy and cease to make progress."[5] Thus, Hu finds Ibsen's philosophy of "healthy individualism" vitally necessary for China and urges his compatriots to follow the example of Nora, the central character in Ibsen's *A Doll's House*, to "strive to forge an individual personality"—and, like Dr. Stockman in *An Enemy of the People*, "to be egocentric, to dare to speak the truth and fight the evil forces."[6]

Yet Hu Shih himself does not exactly favor egotistical individualism. While in a negative sense he considers the individual and society (that is, the present society) mutually harmful, he stops short of endorsing Ibsen's notion that the majority is always wrong and that only the lone individualist, such as Dr. Stockman, is right. While he supports Ibsen's idea of saving oneself, he hastens to add that "society is composed of individuals; and to save one more individual means to plant one more seed for the reconstruction of a new society."[7] Echoing Yen Fu's interpretation of Spencer, Hu Shih does not see any conflict between the individual and the collective in his positive vision of a new society and nation. In another article, "Immortalities" ("Pu-hsiu"), a manifesto of sorts for his own philosophy of life, he goes beyond the traditional "three immortalities" of establishing virtue, deeds, and words and posits a new one—that of establishing society, which Hu Shih considers "the larger self" (*ta wo*), without which no individual can exist.[8]

It is obvious that Hu Shih's May Fourth followers seized upon only one aspect of his Ibsenism—the example of Nora, interpreted in a context of self-emancipation that would free the individual personality from the shackles of traditional society and its value system. The recurrent focus of the early spate of autobiographical literature is always the young protagonist of new-style thinking who breaks away from the two major "feudal" institutions that symbolize tradition: the traditional family (immortalized in Pa Chin's celebrated novel, *Chia*, or *Family*) and the system of arranged marriage. "Breaking away from the family" (*li-chia ch'u-tsou*) thus became both a major ideological tenet and a style of behavior which signaled the first step toward liberation.

The second step was self-realization—the development and exaltation of one's new personality. On this theme, the representative spokesmen can be none other than Kuo Mo-jo and Hsü Chih-mo, two of the most famous poets of the May Fourth literary scene and leaders of the Creation and Crescent Moon societies, respectively.

Kuo Mo-jo is another grandiloquent spokesman for the self. In his early poems, he resorts to a cosmic imagery suffused with dynamism to express his sense of self-realization. We find, for instance, in a poem titled "The Heavenly Hound" ("T'ien-kou"), such observations as: "I have swallowed the entire universe/I am I!"; "I am the total energy of the entire universe"; "I am I/My ego is about to burst." Kuo's pantheistic eulogy of the ego comes closest, perhaps, to Schlegel's formulation: "It is just his individuality that is the primary and eternal element in man. To make a cult of the formation and development of this individuality would be a kind of divine egotism."[9] This statement, in turn, is echoed in Kuo's definition of pantheism, his own personal faith: "If all natural phenomena are manifestations of God, and if I also am a manifestation of God, then I am God, and all natural phenomena are manifestations of me."[10]

For Hsü Chih-mo, all human life is but "a manifestation of the self," and the fundamental act for a true human being is, as he advised his beloved Lu Hsiao-man, "to assert your own personality." This is the lesson Hsü derives from Nora: in Hsü's view, Nora must put the dignity of her own personality above any compromises or humiliations, regardless of the effects on her family and children.[11] Thus, in contrast to Hu Shih, Hsü seems to view the integrity of the individual as an end in itself—that is, without reference to any holistic framework. He calls himself an "incorrigible individualist"—"I only know, recognize, and believe in the individual"—and defines his political credo of democracy as "a pervasive individualism: the true democratic spirit is imbedded in the consciousness and conscious effort of each individual."[12] Rather than viewing the efforts of each individual as contributing to a larger system, Hsü argues for the development of individual potentialities as a way of fulfilling the self in its human meaning (to be distinguished from the "divine egotism" of Kuo Mo-jo): "I am not doing justice to myself if I cannot realize in my life what makes man man; I am not doing justice to life if in my life as a man I cannot realize what makes me me."[13] The primary motivation for Hsü's concept of self-realization is not ethical but emotional, rooted in his own experience of romantic love between the sexes.

While Hsü's dedication to individualism is total and his emotional credo utterly sincere, he does not extend his philosophy of self-realization to any intellectual concerns outside of his own emotional life. He is in no sense a profound thinker. There is no denying the fact that he succeeded in making the individual personality—especially its emotional manifestation—*the* central value in his own life and art and that, largely through his tireless promotion, the self gained unprecedented prominence in Chinese literature. But in my judgment his own poetry and prose are, like Kuo Mo-jo's, curiously unsubtle in exploring the theme and imagery of the self. The issue of self-expression in literature and in the definition of the nature and function of literature is more complicated and requires a more complex mind and less tempestuous personality than Hsü's to unravel and resolve. In this regard, there can be no better theoretician of literature in the May Fourth period than Chou Tso-jen, whose learned deliberations on the subject have already been carefully analyzed by David Pollard.[14]

Chou's numerous essays and Pollard's exegesis of them lead us to the conclusion that the idea of subjectivism is central to Chou's conception of literature. In his famous lectures on the origins of modern Chinese literature, published in 1932 under the title *Chung-kuo hsin wen-hsüeh ti yüan-liu*, Chou supplies a concise definition of literature: "Literature is something which has aesthetic form, which conveys the author's unique feelings and thoughts, and enables the reader to feel pleasure thereby."[15] There are two important implications to be derived from this statement. As Pollard explains: "The first is that the feelings and thoughts expressed must be the author's own (he should not be the spokesman for anyone else), and the second is that the effect is to give the reader 'pleasure', not instruction."[16] It can further be argued that the two points are closely interrelated. Chou is opposed to the didactic reading of literature because he considers this the major legacy of the Confucian notion of "literature as a vehicle of the Way" (*wen-i tsai tao*). In his 1932 lectures he juxtaposes it with another tradition, "poetry expressing the heart's wishes" (*shih yen chih*). As Pollard has shown, Chou considers these to be absolute alternatives; and because Chou believes that literature is essentially the expression of the author's subjective feelings, only the expressive theory is valid for him. This tradition, which reached a peak in the Kung-an and Ching-ling schools of the late Ming, is viewed by Chou as the real font of modern Chinese literature; in fact, Hu Shih's initial suggestions for literary reform (the famous "eight don'ts") are but modern reformulations of the Kung-an and Ching-ling mottos of writing.[17] It is also worth noting that Chou does not share Hu Shih's obsession with the modern vernacular (*pai-hua*), nor does he agree with Hu's contention that the classical language (*wen-yen*) is a dead language. Chou favors the use of *pai-hua* only because it is a better medium to convey the personal feelings and thoughts of modern men and women.[18]

Chou Tso-jen's explications of personal expression in literature are contained in two important essays published in the May Fourth period: "Human Literature" ("Jen ti wen-hsüeh") and "Requisites of the New Literature" ("Hsin wen-hsüeh ti yao-ch'iu"). In these essays Chou attempts to place his individualistic conception in a broad humanistic context. His humanism (*jen-tao chu-i*), which he tries to justify "scientifically," has two dimensions: he refers to mankind as a whole, an anthropological phenomenon of evolutionary progress, and also to the "discovery of man" since the Western Renaissance, which elevated the human being to central prominence.[19]

Chou's conception of man is thus a combination of these two dimensions: "He is all mankind, but also one among mankind; therefore he should plan for a life that would profit himself and others as well."[20] His conception of individuality also carries this dual meaning: "Individuality is the sole possession of the individual, yet has something basically in common with mankind."[21] As Pollard has shown, Chou's theory of humanism, if reduced to a commonplace, implies simply that "the individual is... representative of mankind," and Chou sees no conflict between the two.[22] This pan-humanist vision was very much a part of the May Fourth ethos—a kind of internationalism influenced by the likes of Romain Rolland and Tolstoy. The amorphousness of this vision provided the May Fourth writers with an easy way to transcend existing realities of Chinese society. It is interesting that as the sociopolitical realities began to loom larger in the literature of the 1930s, Chou was compelled to redefine his early humanism. The common ground between the individual and the group was becoming untenable, and Chou had to resist the sociological demands on literature—namely, that literature should perform the crucial function of social reform or at least reflect the problems of present social reality. We find in Chou's published views "a gradual but complete shift of sights from the 'large self' to the 'small self.'" Pollard argues that "in a minor way the shift was a gauge of the failing hopes of liberal Chinese intellectuals."[23] Whether or not one agrees with this generalization, it is clear that Chou reinforced his early convictions of individualism and downplayed literature's humanistic purpose. An author "can only utter subjectively the common sentiment of the people and consciously act as their interpreter."[24] And it is this individual defense of the subjective character and its nonutilitarian purpose which led to Chou's defamation in the eyes of left-wing writers even before he joined the Japanese-controlled puppet regime and became a "traitor."

If Chou Tso-jen's brand of individualism was not widely acclaimed inside China, his brother Lu Hsün (Chou Shu-jen) certainly met with the opposite reaction. His posthumous deification by Mao Tse-tung and Communist idolaters has all but eliminated the negative side of Lu Hsün, that anguished, self-doubting, and deeply introspective side which made no claims to finding the "revolutionary path" for the Chinese people. Since the term "individualism" has itself fallen into disgrace ever since the Yenan period, it is not surprising that Lu Hsün's brand of individualism has seldom been mentioned, much less analyzed with any degree of balance or insight. Yet it is my contention that Lu Hsün is one of the most individualistic of modern Chinese writers.

Lu Hsün's individualism can be traced to his years in Japan. It is intriguing to note that while the Chou brothers were exposed to the same European trends and collaborated closely on several translation projects, their respective responses to European literature were greatly at variance. Chou Tso-jen's pan-humanist reading of Russian and East European literature (for instance, he accepted Andreyev's statement that literature's "supreme achievement is to erase all barriers and distance between people")[25] did not find a ready echo in Lu Hsün. Instead, aside from a rather superficial endorsement of the downtrodden peoples of these countries, Lu Hsün sought the psychological depth in the national spirit of a people: Andreyev's stories of tormented psyches in a somber environment became his favorites. As I have argued elsewhere, Lu Hsün's initial conception of literature ran counter to the utilitarian notions of literature promulgated by Liang Ch'i-ch'ao. Lu Hsün's famous article "On Extremities in Cultural Development" ("Wen-hua p'ien-chih lun"), written in 1907, may be read as his "spiritual" interpretation of modern European history in opposition to Liang's pragmatic utilitarianism. Lu Hsün found in modern European history a subjectivist reaction to the nineteenth-century legacy of "material progress and majority rule," which had turned the European masses into a state of "insatiable materialism" and "mediocrity." Thus, only a few "farsighted, combative" individuals who rose above the mundane crowd were able to react against these excesses and swing the pendulum of European civilization in a new direction. In Lu Hsün's view, the civilization of the twentieth century, as heralded by such indomitable individuals as Stirner, Schopenhauer, Kierkegaard, Ibsen, and particularly Nietzsche, would be significantly different. Hence, he gave the following stunning advice to his countrymen:

> If we want to work out a policy for the present, we must examine the past and prepare for the future, discard the material and elevate the spiritual, rely on the individual and exclude the masses. When the individual is exalted to develop his full capacity, the country will be strengthened and will rise. Why should we be engrossed in such trivialities as gold, iron, congress, and constitutions?[26]

In a similar vein, he glorified the individual genius of such "Mara poets" as Byron, Shelley, Pushkin, Mickiewicz, Slowacki, and Sandor Pëtofe, whom Lu Hsün saw as "the warriors of the world of spirit, strong, uncompromising, sincere, truthful, and scornful of convention. Their powerful utterances brought about a national rebirth making their countries great in the world."[27]

These early statements could be called both nationalistic and romantic, and the farsighted, superhuman individuals they describe take on a solitary and commanding significance. Although most Chinese scholars of Lu Hsün have duly emphasized his nationalistic sentiments, they have largely neglected the tragic implications in his imagery. As his subsequent stories, essays, and prose-poetry written in the period from 1918 to 1925 illustrate, Lu Hsün's overarching vision is that of an alienating confrontation between the individual and the crowd. The tragic sense inherent in this vision lies in a paradox: the lone genius, alienated and persecuted by an ignorant and cruel crowd, cannot define the meaning of his own existence except by attempting to save his persecutors, even at the risk of sacrificing himself. Yet the crowd is incapable of comprehending his intention. If this tragic vision represents also the fictional projection of a self-image, we can only conclude that Lu Hsün's early thought was far from optimistic: he was deeply uncertain that a lone spiritual warrior such as himself could effect a national rebirth or awaken his countrymen from their slumbering state of existence in an unbreakable "iron

house." Thus, Lu Hsün's individualism, unlike Chou Tso-jen's, takes on a
tragic coloration bordering on existential despair: the positive, romantic gloss
of his 1907 essays is gradually replaced by a dark, brooding portrait of mental
agony on the part of tortured and solitary individuals.

While Lu Hsün never defined individualism with Chou Tso-jen's
fastidiousness, he did use the term specifically in a summary fashion in a
personal letter to Hsü Kuang-p'ing (dated 30 May 1925), who later became his
common-law wife:

> My ideas are not immediately understandable, because in them are
> contained many contradictions. If I am asked to sum them up, they
> represent perhaps the ebb and flow of two kinds of thinking—
> individualism and humanitarianism. Therefore, sometimes I suddenly
> love people, sometimes I suddenly hate people. When I work, sometimes I
> certainly work for others, but sometimes I work for my own
> pleasure.... When I talk to others, I always choose to say something
> bright, although due to some accidental carelessness I may say things
> which the ruler of hell would not object to but my "Little Devil" [Hsü
> Kuang-p'ing] is displeased to hear. In short, my ideas for others and for
> myself are different. Why so? Because my thinking is too dark. Therefore I
> can only experiment with myself but dare not invite others.[28]

This revealing passage alerts us to the two conflicting personae of Lu
Hsün: the private, introspective self, defined as individualistic, and the public
self-image that he wished to convey to others. This bifurcation between his
private and public selves inevitably heightens the tension in his creative work.
His celebrated preface to *Call to Arms* (Na-han), a collection of short stories
presumably dedicated to the May Fourth cause of cultural iconoclasm and
social change, is likewise torn by two conflicting impulses. On the one hand,
he envisions himself as a foot-soldier sounding the clarion-call to arms with
his fiction; on the other, he confesses to the genesis of his stories out of a
private act of remembrance of things past. Throughout the preface, Lu Hsün
repeatedly mentions his loneliness and isolation—a saddened sense of solitude
occasioned by memories of past failures.[29] This depressing tone serves to
dampen, if not actually contradict, his declared public purpose of reforming
society and drawing the attention of his countrymen to the need for a drastic
solution to society's ills. In fact, the same contradictory impulses tend to
permeate his entire fictional corpus—there is always an unresolved tension
between the writer's individualism and his humanitarianism. After the apex of
the May Fourth Movement in the early 1920s, Lu Hsün became increasingly
despondent and introspective, a mood that is pervasive in his second short-
story collection, tellingly titled *Wavering* (P'ang-huang), and the prose-poetry
Wild Grass (Yeh ts'ao). In these works, his private quandary seems to have
gained the upper hand over his public image—as if the author were
conducting, through his art, some painful experiment with aspects of his inner
self.

Why were the issues of individual privacy, solitude, isolation and
introspection so important to Lu Hsün and, to varying degrees, other May
Fourth writers as well? As the case of Lu Hsün has shown, his individualism

was wrapped up with the act of creative writing itself: the ways in which he brought his private travails and anxieties to bear on the larger issues of his society point to the complex roles of the modern Chinese writer.

Representations of the Self

Unlike the politician or ideologue, a writer can only communicate with his audience through his literary work. Before the introduction of collectivist methods in the 1940s, creative writing had always been a solitary and private act. However public-spirited the manifest purpose of the new literature was, its texts sometimes told a different story because of the artistic modes of representation adopted by the individual authors. A look at some prominent examples of fictional writing in the May Fourth period finds us in basic agreement with Prušek's assessment: "The most characteristic feature of Chinese literature after the literary revolution was the larger proportion of subjective elements. This would seem to be connected with the growing significance of the writer's personality, liberated from the fetters of tradition."[30] In other words, Prušek sees a direct connection between the individualism of the modern Chinese writer and the subjectivism of his art; in the May Fourth context, the latter may be regarded as a by-product of the former. If "individualism" denotes the exaltation of the writer's own personality, "subjectivism" indicates the evolution of an individualistic point of view—a perception of reality often *at odds with* the established ways of looking at things. For, in reacting against the tradition in Chinese literature in which a writer and his work partook of the values and conventions of the same cultural order by imitation and didacticism (there had been, of course, many exceptions which were conveniently ignored by the May Fourth iconoclasts), the leaders of the literary revolution—Hu Shih and Ch'en Tu-hsiu in particular—emphasized the need for originality and individuality: "Do not imitate the writings of the ancients; what you write should reflect your own personality," Hu Shih urged in one of his famous eight principles for literary reform.[31] And as Ch'en Tu-hsiu proclaimed in his manifesto of 1917: "Overthrow the stereotyped and over-ornamental literature of classicism and create the fresh and sincere literature of realism."[32]

Thus, "realism" (*hsieh-shih chu-i*) emerged as the prevalent principle of creative writing during the May Fourth period. The term in practice meant simply that a writer must write about what is most familiar to him—preferably his own personal experience—in a lively, authentic fashion. The result of early experiments in this new, realistic mode was a spate of autobiographical or quasi-autobiographical works which gave unabashed expression to the authors' own emotional experiences—an outpouring of romanticism which I have examined in another study.[33] In attempting to depict their personal experiences realistically, the early May Fourth writers were motivated by a sense of unmitigated honesty as well as confessional zeal. As the poet Li Kuang-t'ien described his fellow poet and essayist Chu Tzu-ch'ing: "Since self-emancipation was the current trend in culture and thought, and self-expression the principle of writing, to be honest in personal conduct and in creative writing thus resulted in a kind of literature of honesty which characterized Mr. Chu's early works."[34]

The same attitude tended to characterize the majority of works produced by members of the Association for Literary Studies, notably, Hsü Ti-shan, Hsü Ch'ing-wen, and Yeh Sheng-t'ao. In the case of the more flamboyant writers of the Creation Society, personal honesty is imbued with a romantic flair to create the fictional or poetic image of the author as hero. In Yü Ta-fu's first story, "Sinking" ("Ch'en-lun"), which created quite a stir because of its sexual explicitness, the protagonist—a sensitive, lonely, sexually frustrated young man—is a thinly veiled portrait of Yü himself; the plot is drawn entirely from Yü's personal experiences in Japan. Yü's "honesty" proved so successful an artistic device that in his subsequent stories he coined an obvious name for his fictional hero, Yü Chih-fu—his fictional alter ego. As Yü himself later proclaimed: "All literary works are autobiographies of their authors"; and "Because art is life, life is art, why should we separate the two?"[35] At the same time, however, Yü's autobiographical veneer is deceptive: there is, in fact, considerable distance between himself and his fictional depictions of himself. This very modern ploy, which may have been the result of Yü's reading of Western fiction and the Japanese "I-novel" (*watakushi shōsetsu*), enables Yü to go beyond the simple, honest reproduction of personal experience and achieve a degree of irony. It also allows him to probe and comment freely upon the protagonist's inner life and thoughts.

Although Yü glorifies a vision of himself as hero in his fiction, it is also a portrait of the self as an individual afflicted with an unspeakable sadness and wandering "alone on a journey" (to use the title of another story)—a weary, melancholic transient on the "road of life." In a way, Yü transforms his autobiographical stories into allegories of modern man on an aimless journey in search of meaning.[36] The art of "subjective coloring" sets Yü's protagonist against an alienating background he little understands. This became a typical set-up of early May Fourth fiction, in which the main characters are foregrounded and distanced from their objective environment—an interesting representation of the individual losing his grip on the reality of the external world. It is this quality of accentuated subjectivity which distinguishes the modern May Fourth stories from their traditional predecessors.

Lu Hsün's fiction exhibits the same sort of subjectivism, but with a more complicated device: the complex role of the narrator. His first major story, "Diary of a Madman" ("K'uang-jen jih-chi"; 1918), has been hailed as China's first modern short story. The significance of the work lies neither in its use of the modern vernacular nor, necessarily, in its striking message of the cannibalistic nature of traditional Chinese political culture (Lu Hsün was not the only one to harp on the theme of *li-chiao ch'ih-jen*, lit., "cultural rites eat people"). Rather, it lies in the unprecedented way in which Lu Hsün uses the diary device to heighten a subjective perspective. In the story, the psychological ravings of the protagonist (an individualist and loner—the first in a series of similar fictional characterizations in Lu Hsün's other stories) are framed within the diary, which is introduced by the implied author who, in a preface written in cliché-ish *wen-yen*, assumes the pose of a narrator adhering to conventional Chinese values. The ironic effect created by this complex device is more powerful than anything in Yü Ta-fu's fiction. By juxtaposing two totally different perceptions, couched in sharply differentiated languages, Lu Hsün succeeds in creating the most shattering configuration of the opposition between self and society. Insofar as the madman may be read as one of Lu Hsün's inner voices, the diary also serves as a fictional testimony of his own individualism. In Lu Hsün's subsequent stories, the fate of his tormented protagonists is told from the viewpoint of the narrators; their interactions, often fraught with dramatic tension, thus become a theatrical way of sorting out Lu Hsün's own "views, feelings, sympathy, or maybe hate" toward his countrymen and toward himself. It is also an artistic way to evoke the tension-ridden bifurcation between his individualism and humanitarianism.

A close examination of Lu Hsün's art and mentality would require at least a lengthy monograph. But even this cursory analysis should suffice to indicate that his art is closely intertwined with his individualism: it provides intricate settings with which Lu Hsün attempts not only to camouflage the workings of his inner self but also to set them *against* the outside world. Thus, it may be said that Lu Hsün's vision of reality is not objective but highly subjective. More than any other May Fourth writer, he brought modern Chinese fiction somewhat closer to the modernistic mode of twentieth-century European literature.[37]

It is well known that Lu Hsün eventually turned to the left politically, and the voluminous output of his *tsa-wen* (miscellaneous essays) in the last phase of his life (1928-36) offers sufficient proof that he managed to extricate himself from earlier periods of depression. After 1926, the end of his "wandering" period, he emerged from an agonizing quest for meaning in the boundless, barren terrain of his private psyche (depicted most vividly in *Wild Grass*) only to realize the ultimate meaninglessness of his self-torment. Thus he echoed the words of the Hungarian poet Pëtofe, "despair is as empty and vain as hope."[38]

As most Chinese scholars of Lu Hsün have pointed out, his shift from a private viewpoint to a more public stance was largely due to changed political circumstances, specifically, Chiang Kai-shek's massacre of Communists and their sympathizers in April 1927, a tragedy which left Lu Hsün profoundly disillusioned with the KMT as a revolutionary party and paved the way for his politicization toward the left. His course is typical of many other May Fourth writers. Politics and political commitment, however, are only part of public expression. It can be argued that the politicization of the May Fourth writer was an extension of his earlier views on social reformism. What is unique about the May Fourth literary scene is that, regardless of its public ideology, some writers were still able to evolve a sense of self that was mirrored in their literary works. I have suggested that the act of artistic creation is based on individualism and integrally related to the writer's personality. The cluster of values revolving around May Fourth writing and its romantic temper—self-emancipation, self-development, the release of one's emotional potentialities, independence from external restrictions, honesty and sincerity to oneself—were not construed by the more optimistic writers as contradictory to their public stance. Only the less politically oriented writers (e.g., Chou Tso-jen) or the more introspective ones (Lu Hsün and Yü Ta-fu) consciously or unconsciously perceived a conflict between individualism and humanitarianism. As I have suggested, this conflict takes shape in their literary works in the artistic evocation of an individualistic protagonist acting against a chaotic and inaccessible background. In other words, their art—and the subjective perspectives contained therein—shows a certain discrepancy with their message; the more mature a writer, the more complex and intriguing the discrepancy. From a Western critical point of view, this is not a startling discovery: a literary critic should take for granted the difference between the author and the literary text, between extrinsic message and intrinsic form. However, when we look at the phenomenon in the light of the Chinese literary tradition, the issues become more relevant.

Self, Society, and the Writer: Some Historical Reflections

For the purposes of this paper, the rich heritage of the Chinese literary tradition may be divided, on the most general level, into two broad legacies—Confucian and Taoist. Self-awareness, and its relevance to artistic creation, can be traced to Chuang Tzu, and first received substantial attention in the Wei-Chin period. This Taoist tradition, I would argue, tended to place more emphasis on a kind of artistic transcendence, whereby the individual elevates his "spirit" beyond the mundane level toward a cosmic reunion with the natural or supernatural forces. Especially in periods of sociopolitical disintegration such as the Wei-Chin, intellectuals of Taoist persuasion (such as Juan Chi, Hsi K'ang, and T'ao Ch'ien) sought escape from their troubled times by allowing the spirit to soar in the transcendent realm of art. This does not mean that a writer or artist could maintain total autonomy from mundane reality; rather, the Taoist ideal instructed only that one ought not be too attached to that reality. Beginning in the T'ang dynasty, this Taoist ideal of art gradually became enmeshed with the Confucian mainstream in a number of ways, notably through the notions of hermitage and of the place of the literary arts in the life of a Confucian scholar-official.

In the Confucian tradition, as Hsü Fu-kuan has argued, art and literature are grounded in life and society.[39] From Confucius onwards, the moral purpose has been imbedded in the very theory and practice of literature. Thus, it is impossible to speak in Confucian terms of a writer pursuing art for its own sake; creative writing was part of a scholar-official's life, but never an independent vocation. However, there may have occurred a reorientation of priorities in the seventeenth and eighteenth centuries, if not earlier. Under the influence of certain strands of Ming Confucianism, considerable energy on the part of many intellectuals went into philosophical and artistic explorations of the self and its relationship with the cosmos. Concurrently, a degree of frustration and disillusionment with officialdom also set in. By the eighteenth century (as the career of Yüan Mei indicates), entering civil service through the examination system was no longer the ultimate goal for some intellectuals; alternative avenues of individual fulfillment, especially in the area of literary arts, assumed increasing importance. For Wu Ching-tzu, author of the famous novel *The Scholars* (Ju-lin wai-shih), the entire spectrum of official enterprise was distasteful, and his ideal, as espoused in his novel, lay in the preservation of individual integrity and the refinement of individually cultivated tastes. The crowning achievement of this effort is exemplified by Ts'ao Hsüeh-ch'in's masterpiece, *Dream of the Red Chamber* (Hung-lou meng), whose multifaceted richness encompasses the splendor of his literary culture. As some intellectuals felt alienated from the state (and its Confucian ideology), the ideals of scholarship and artistic pursuits began to take priority over officialdom.

It is interesting that whereas Chou Tso-jen traced the origins of modern Chinese literature to the "personal essay" (*hsiao-p'in wen*) tradition of the late Ming and its credo that literature should "express the heart's desire," Hu Shih singled out *The Scholars* as a model novel of social criticism and the forerunner of late Ch'ing fiction. Chou and Hu discovered in past precedents what seemed to them to be genuine concerns of May Fourth literature. In their view, the new literature definitely ought not embody the prescribed values of the Confucian "way" but should rather be a medium of self-expression. However, literature as self-expression must also have a bearing on social criticism and social reform. The May Fourth writers seemed to have inherited from their Ming and Ch'ing predecessors a distaste for government service (especially when the Republican government consisted of a series of warlord regimes) and a high regard for the importance of literature. At the same time, however, as modern Chinese nationalists they felt frustrated by their inability to find a proper channel for sociopolitical service—a mentality which may have been derived from the Confucian scholar-official tradition. Thus, before new political exigencies—Chiang Kai-shek's repression of intellectuals and free expression, the rise of the Chinese Communist Party, the impending war with Japan—rechanneled their energies to goals of national survival and revolution in the early 1930s, the May Fourth writers "wandered" for a whole decade in search of a meaningful relationship between self and society and between artistic creativity and social commitment. That their selves assume an adverse position vis-à-vis social reality in much of their literature is due precisely to their exaltation of individual personality coupled with a high degree of uncertainty concerning the meaning of self. In other words, for all its prominence, the self could not be defined by modern Chinese writers in the vacuum as an end unto itself or as having an absurd existence (as in existentialism). Although Lu Hsün in his prose-poetry comes very close to the frontier of existential despair, he realizes that such a state is ultimately meaningless. Could it be that even a modernistic writer like Lu Hsün was not able to develop an existentialist epistemology of individualism unrelated philosophically to a holistic world-view?

While in the final analysis the self in modern Chinese literature is not entirely divorced from some matrix of the whole, it is also undeniable that the full-fledged manifestation of the self—to the point of opposition to the whole—did not occur in Chinese literature until the May Fourth era. It is this troubled and often adverse relationship between the self and society that forms the central motif in May Fourth literature. It is also in this regard that this modern literature can be said to be qualitatively different from its traditional counterparts[40] and that the May Fourth writers may be regarded as a species of intellectuals quite different from Metzger's political and ideological heroes.

In view of the above analysis, then, how do we compare the writers treated in this paper with Metzger's "zealously ideological, heroic" types? To be sure, the May Fourth writers did share some views with the more ideological intellectuals: most of them believed in revolution and in the need to rid China of the negative and "feudal" constraints of the past. The writers, too, wished to speak for the people, despite their relative isolation from them. As mentioned before, beginning in the late 1920s a leftist trend engulfed a large number of them, Lu Hsün included, initiating the process of politicization from "literary revolution" to "revolutionary literature." The prime movers of this trend were, in fact, the romantic individualists of the Creation Society who sought a heroic fusion with the historical high tide by announcing their melodramatic conversion to Marxism (but as seers and prophets rather than followers and true believers).

The crucial difference which marks the writers as distinct from the zealously ideological types—be they on the political left or right—was their distrust of the optimism derived from the heroic fusion of the self with the ultimate doctrinal goal. If the writers failed in contributing much intellectual meaning to the notion of the self, they were nevertheless unwilling to sacrifice it to the ideological totalism of ultimate goals. It can be said, therefore, that the most enduring legacy of the May Fourth tradition in modern Chinese literature remains its unique brand of individualism, which in turn impels the modern Chinese writer to lay claim to the supremacy of his own vision of social reality. The implication is that, by virtue of his being a writer, he possesses a better and more profound insight than the politician or ideologue into the problems of his society. If he is unwilling to provide solutions, he is equally unwilling to embrace optimistically any grandiose visions of history which do not stem from his own personal visions. Contrary to the optimism of the zealously ideological and heroic types, the more introspective writers, such as Lu Hsün and Yü Ta-fu, when confronted with the chaos of external reality, were capable of plunging themselves into anguish and self-doubt and projecting these subjective feelings in their literature. Yet, as noted earlier, this inward journey did not lead them finally to existential despair or artistic surrealism. Nor did they emulate the Neo-Taoists of the Wei-Chin period by seeking a philosophical or artistic transcendence. For the modern Chinese writer, the ultimate frame of reference remained grounded in the historical reality of his time.

It is precisely this unique frame of mind—subjectivist, *engagé*, yet nontranscendent and not ideologically totalistic—that finally brought the May Fourth writer into conflict with the Maoist cadre in later years. To be sure, most writers had already begun to renounce their individualism in the late 1920s. The focus of creative writing, particularly fiction and drama, gradually shifted from the narrow preoccupation with the author's own experience to encompass a broader social reality (such as the entire city of Shanghai in Mao Tun's *Midnight* [Tzu-yeh] or a countryside or region in the works of Lao She, Shen Ts'ung-wen, or Hsiao Hung). With some possible exceptions, however, the modern Chinese writers, while relinquishing their egos and egocentrism, continued to assert their own personal perspectives on Chinese reality. Individualism as an overt stance became, as it were, internalized in their artistic conception. The result was a literature anchored in a critical, individual perception of Chinese society which eventually clashed with Mao Tse-tung's ideological populism. The May Fourth tradition of realism with its ethos of exposé was formally denounced by Mao in his famous "Talks at the Yenan Forum" in favor of "socialist realism"—a model borrowed from Soviet Russia but given a Maoist twist to mean basically the positive extolling of "the people" as prescribed by the Party. "Individualism" in both art and politics has since taken on negative connotations.[41]

NOTES

1. Yü-sheng Lin, "Radical Iconoclasm in the May Fourth Period and the Future of Chinese Liberalism," in *Reflections on the May Fourth Movement: A Symposium*, ed. Benjamin Schwartz (Cambridge: Harvard East Asian Monographs, 1972), 25.
2. Metzger's ideas are taken from his comments on this paper at the conference. I am most grateful to him for providing this new historical angle for comparison.
3. Jaroslav Průšek, "Subjectivism and Individualism in Modern Chinese Literature," in *The Lyrical and the Epic: Studies of Modern Chinese Literature*, ed. Leo Ou-fan Lee (Bloomington: Indiana University Press, 1980), 1.
4. Leo Ou-fan Lee, *The Romantic Generation of Modern Chinese Writers* (Cambridge: Harvard University Press, 1973).
5. Hu Shih, "I-pu-sheng chu-i" [Ibsenism] in *Hu Shih wen-ts'un* [Preserved essays of Hu Shih], 4 vols. (Taipei: Yüan-tung Book Co., 1953), 1:644.
6. Hu Shih, "Chieh-shao wo tzu-chi ti ssu-hsiang" [Introducing my own thought], in *Hu Shih wen-hsüan* [Selected essays of Hu Shih] (Hong Kong: Hsien-tai Shu-tien, n.d.), 6.
7. *Hu Shih wen-ts'un*, 1:643.
8. Ibid., 1:698.
9. Quoted in Steven Lukes, *Individualism* (Oxford: Blackwell Paperbacks, 1979), 68.
10. Quoted and translated in David T. Roy, *Kuo Mo-jo: The Early Years* (Cambridge: Harvard University Press, 1971), 135.
11. Hsü Chih-mo, *Hsü Chih-mo ch'uan-chi* [The complete works of Hsü Chih-mo], 6 vols. (Taipei: Chuan-chi Wen-hsüeh Ch'u-pan-she, 1969), 4:350.
12. Ibid., 3:138.
13. Quoted in Lee, *The Romantic Generation*, 159.
14. David E. Pollard, *A Chinese Look at Literature: The Literary Values of Chou Tso-jen in Relation to the Tradition* (Berkeley: University of California Press, 1973).
15. Ibid., 26.
16. Ibid., 27.

17. Chou Tso-jen, *Chung-kuo hsin wen-hsüeh ti yüan-liu* [The origins of modern Chinese literature] (Peiping: Jen-wen Shu-tien, 1934), 92.

18. Ibid., 107-13.

19. Chou Tso-jen, "Jen ti wen-hsüeh" [Human literature], in his *I-shu yü sheng-huo* [Art and life] (Shanghai: Chung-hua Shu-chü, 1930), 12-14.

20. Quoted in David E. Pollard, "Chou Tso-jen and Cultivating One's Garden," *Asia Minor*, 1965, 11:pt. 2, 107.

21. Ibid., 191.

22. Ibid., 190.

23. Ibid., 197.

24. Chou Tso-jen, *Tzu-chi ti yüan-ti* [One's own garden] (Shanghai: Pei-hsin Shu-chü, 1923), 17.

25. Pollard, "Chou Tso-jen and Cultivating One's Garden," 184-85.

26. Lu Hsün, *Lu Hsün ch'üan-chi* [The complete works of Lu Hsün], 20 vols. (Peking: Jen-min Wen-hsüeh Ch'u-pan-she, 1973), 1:41. For a discussion of these two essays, see my article, "Genesis of a Writer: Notes on Lu Hsün's Educational Experience, 1881-1909," in *Modern Chinese Literature in the May Fourth Era*, ed. Merle Goldman (Cambridge: Harvard University Press, 1977), 166-88.

27. *Lu Hsün ch'üan-chi*, 1:99-100.

28. Ibid., 7:98.

29. Ibid., 1:269-76.

30. Prušek, "Subjectivism and Individualism," 83-84.

31. Hu Shih, "Chi Ch'en Tu-hsiu" [To Ch'en Tu-hsiu], in *Hu Shih wen-ts'un*, 1:3.

32. Quoted in ibid., 1:18.

33. Lee, *The Romantic Generation*, esp. pt. 4.

34. Li Kuang-t'ien, preface to *Chu Tzu-ch'ing hsüan-chi* [Selected writings of Chu Tzu-ch'ing] (Peking: K'ai-ming Shu-tien, 1951), 9.

35. Quoted in Lee, *The Romantic Generation*, 110.

36. See my article, "The Solitary Traveler: Images of the Self in Modern Chinese Literature," which gives a more literary survey of the transformation of the self in the changing images of the traveler in fictional works from the late Ch'ing to the present. It will be included in a collection of essays edited by Robert Hegel and Richard C. Hessney, *Expressions of Self in Chinese Literature* (New York: Columbia University Press, forthcoming).

37. I have discussed the issue of modernism in the Chinese context more extensively in an article titled "Modernism in Modern Chinese Literature: A Study (Somewhat Comparative) in Literary History," *Tamkang Review* (Spring-Summer 1980), 10 (3-4):281-307.

38. *Lu Hsün ch'üan-chi*, 1:483.

39. Hsü Fu-kuan, *Chung-kuo i-shu ching-shen* [The spirit of Chinese art] (Taipei: Hsüeh-cheng Shu-chü, 1966), chap. 1. For a brilliant analysis of Chuang Tzu's influence on Chinese aesthetics, see chap. 2.

40. In traditional Chinese literature there was, of course, extensive depiction of the self in both poetry and fiction (see the essays in the Hegel and Hessney volume). However, as C. T. Hsia has pointed out in his seminal essay on "Society and Self in the Chinese Short Story," the emergence of the "new, romantic self" did not receive full intellectual or moral approval even though the demand for self-fulfillment was already in evidence in such well-known Ming stories as "The Pearl-Sewn Shirt." See Hsia, *The Classic Chinese Novel: A Critical Introduction* (New York: Columbia University Press, 1968; paperback ed., Bloomington: Indiana University Press, 1980), 299-321.

41. A rediscovery and reevaluation of individualism is under way in post-Mao China and is especially apparent in the essays of young writers.

Glossary

Ch'en-lun 沉淪

Ch'en Tu-hsiu 陳獨秀

Chi Ch'en Tu-hsiu 寄陳獨秀

Chia 家

chieh-fang 解放

Chieh-shao wo tzu-chi ti ssu-hsiang 介紹我自己的思想

Ching-ling 竟陵

Chou Shu-jen 周樹人

Chou Tso-jen 周作人

Chu Tzu-ch'ing 朱自清

Chu Tzu-ch'ing hsüan-chi 朱自清選集

Chuang Tzu 莊子

Chung-kuo hsin wen-hsüeh ti yüan liu 中國新文學的源流

Chung-kuo i-shu ching-shen 中國藝術精神

Hsi K'ang 嵇康

Hsiao Hung 蕭紅

hsiao-p'in wen 小品文

hsieh-shih chu-i 寫實主義

Hsin ch'ing-nien 新青年

Hsin wen-hsüeh ti yao-ch'iu 新文學的要求

Hsü Chih-mo 徐志摩

Hsü Chih-mo ch'üan-chi 徐志摩全集

Hsü Ch'ing-wen 許欽文

Hsü Fu-kuan 徐復觀

Hsü Kuang-p'ing 許廣平

Hsü Ti-shan 許地山

Hu Shih 胡適

Hu Shih wen-hsüan 胡適文選

Hu Shih wen-ts'un 胡適文存

Hung-lou meng 紅樓夢

I-pu-sheng chu-i 易卜生主義

I-shu yü sheng-huo 藝術與生活

jen-tao chu-i 人道主義

Jen ti wen-hsüeh 人的文學

Ju-lin wai-shih 儒林外史

Juan Chi 阮籍

ke-hsing 個性

ke-jen 個人

ke-jen chu-i 個人主義

K'uang-jen jih-chi 狂人日記

Kung-an 公安

Kuo Mo-jo 郭沫若

Lao She 老舍

li-chia ch'u-tsou 離家出走

li-chiao ch'ih-jen 禮教吃人

Li Kuang-t'ien 李廣田

Liang Ch'i-ch'ao 梁啓超

Lu Hsiao-man 陸小曼

Lu Hsün 魯迅

Lu Hsün ch'üan-chi 魯迅全集

Mao Tse-tung 毛澤東

Mao Tun 茅盾

Na-han 吶喊

Pa Chin 巴金

pai-hua 白話

P'ang-huang 彷徨

Pu-hsiu 不朽

Shen Ts'ung-wen 沈從文

shih yen chih 詩言志

ta-wo 大我

T'ao Ch'ien 陶潛

T'ien-kou 天狗

tsa-wen 雜文

Ts'ao Hsüeh-ch'in 曹雪芹

Tzu-chi ti yüan-ti 自己的園地

Tzu-yeh 子夜

watakushi shōsetsu 私小說

Wen-hua p'ien-chih lun 文化偏至論

wen-i tsai tao 文以載道

wen-yen 文言

Wu Ching-tzu 吳敬梓

Yeh Sheng-t'ao 葉聖陶

Yeh ts'ao 野草

Yen Fu 嚴復

Yü Chih-fu 于質夫

Yü Ta-fu 郁達夫

Yüan Mei 袁枚

Part III:

The Whole and the Individual

The Family Network, the Stream of Water, and the Plant: Picturing Persons in Sung Confucianism

Donald J. Munro*

Leading intellectuals associated with China's May Fourth Movement, and particularly Ch'en Tu-hsiu (1879-1942), accused their Confucian predecessors of oppressing the individual with a feudalistic ethic that confined each person to rigid family and clan social roles.[1] The individual's choices of action were limited by the duties and obligations that accompany these social roles. Moreover, the individual had no inherent right to act other than in accordance with his respective role. Many Westerners, including this writer, have accepted the accusations of the May Fourth intellectuals. Such claims assume that persons were thought of relationally and not as discrete individuals. Roles are defined in terms of reciprocal and unchanging duties and rights vis-à-vis other people. By fulfilling roles, the person deemphasizes any unique properties he may possess as an individual. As Heinrich Popitz puts it, "The decisive fact is whether a position can develop whose rights and duties can be exercised not just by one individual in his uniqueness. Only with deindividualization are role norms formed."[2]

"Confucianism" covers a lot of ground, including state-sponsored orthodoxy and religious practices, family organization and ancestor worship, and a variety of philosophical schools. In this paper we will test the May Fourth charge with respect to one such school, Sung-dynasty Ch'eng-Chu Neo-Confucianism, examining how its adherents thought about man and the society and cosmos in which he lives. Sometimes they theorized about man and nature by employing abstractions, such as human nature, mind, heaven, destiny, principle, or "Great Ultimate." At other times they used the pictorial images suggested by graphic analogies. In effect they were using metaphors or analogies to explain man, society, or nature.

In dealing with the May Fourth claims, the study of certain analogies will serve as our methodology. Our research reveals that at least one analogy is

*I wish to thank Wm. Theodore de Bary, Irene Bloom, and Kenneth DeWoskin for constructive criticisms that I have attempted to incorporate into the present revised version of this article.

generally associated with every philosophical theory. Studying the analogies makes it possible to identify the different theories that, in their abstract formulation, are not separate but mixed in Ch'eng-Chu Neo-Confucianism. In short, the method helps to unpack the Confucian doctrine, revealing divergent strands not immediately evident to the reader. It also helps to clarify what the vague Confucian theories actually stated. We will evaluate the claim about individuals being confined to social roles by examining precisely which analogies were used to understand man and nature. Because the Sung Neo-Confucians tried to justify their ethical claims by appealing to the natural order of things, we will focus on the cosmological theories of Ch'eng I (1033-1107) and Chu Hsi (1130-1200) in evaluating the May Fourth criticism.

Analogies

For a long time, many writers in Europe believed that humans think exclusively in images. In attacking the concept of material substance, Bishop Berkeley asserted that it is an abstract idea and that we cannot have an idea of such a thing, divested of particular sensible images such as roundness or squareness.[3] The error in Berkeley's position is that people do not think only in terms of images. When they hear and understand a few sentences, they do not have a hundred images floating across their minds. They think also in words that do not suggest images.

However, the evidence suggests that some of the time people do use pictorial images in thinking. Some people think predominantly pictorially. This is true even in fields such as mathematics and physics, where one might not expect it. The mathematician S. M. Ulam wrote in his memoirs, "It is said that seventy-five percent of us have a dominant visual memory, twenty-five percent an auditory one. As for me, mine is quite visual. When I think about mathematical ideas, I see the abstract notions in symbolic pictures."[4] British-born physicist Freeman Dyson has revealed the gradual development of his own ability to mesh two modes of thought:

> Since the time of Newton, the usual way of doing theoretical physics had been to begin by writing down some equations and then to work hard calculating solutions of the equations. This was the way Hans [Bethe] and Oppy [J. Robert Oppenheimer] and Julian Schwinger did physics. Dick [Feynman] just wrote down the solutions out of his head without ever writing down the equations. He had a physical picture of the way things happen, and the picture gave him the solution directly, with a minimum of calculation. It was no wonder that people who had spent their lives solving equations were baffled by him. Their minds were analytical; his mind was pictorial. My own training, since the far-off days when I struggled with H. Y. H. Piaggio's differential equations, had been analytical. But as I listened to Dick and stared at the strange diagrams that he drew on the blackboard I gradually absorbed some of his pictorial imagination and began to feel at home in his version of the universe.[5]

Most of us probably shift back and forth from one mode to another, from the verbal or analytical (if we are not solving equations) to the pictorial and back.

When we are thinking pictorially, one of the devices we use is the metaphor, or analogy. We are not concerned here with the occasional metaphors all of us use to illustrate a point ("My daughter is like a tiger"). Nor are we concerned with the everyday metaphors that structure our ways of conceiving routine experiences. For example, George Lakoff and Mark Johnson have identified the metaphor of war as structuring our view of argument ("Your claims are indefensible...."; "He attacked every weak point in my argument.....").[6] Instead, we are interested in those metaphors or analogies that lurk behind abstract theories. They perform special functions for those theories. And because a different analogy is associated with most different theories, the repeated presence of several different analogies in one systematic philosophy can reveal much about the mix of various theories within it.

When we use the terms metaphor and analogy, we refer to a mental picture of something comprised of parts that are related in a discernible structure. A theory is one or more general rules or principles purporting to explain the relation between various facts. Because it covers many different sets of facts, the relationship between which is not immediately obvious from the facts themselves, the language of theories is abstract. By using metaphor when discussing a theory, the thinker may describe the structural relationships of the facts to which the theory applies. The theory itself may not do this in any detail. In turn, this new information can enrich the theory, making it more plausible by tightening its obvious connection to something mundane. In the end, some structural similarity is claimed between the commonplace object and the subject matter of the theory. Robert Oppenheimer describes analogies as "a special kind of similarity, which is the similarity of structure, the similarity of form, a similarity of constellation between two sets of structure, two sets of particulars, that are manifestly very different but have structured parallels."[7] And, in talking about analogy as a technique used in mathematical problem-solving, G. Polya wrote: "Analogy is a sort of similarity. Similar objects agree with each other in some respect, analogous objects agree in certain relations of their respective parts."[8] These descriptions of analogy leave open the question of the degree of similarity of structure between the analogous objects. At one end of the spectrum, the claim could be that the objects are structurally so similar that any explanation of one in terms of another has the form of a tautology.

Through the clarification of structural relationships, metaphors can solve problems internal to theories. They may also suggest to a person duties that do not follow obviously from abstract theories. Some structural aspect of a concrete object suggests duties more precisely than a theory can.

Analogies tend to limit the kinds of fact, hence the kinds of questions, that are encompassed by a theory. The thinker will exclude from consideration those facts that do not relate to the structure suggested by the metaphor. This provides momentary efficiency, which any theory requires. But it can inhibit the natural evolution of the theory by blinding its holder to new problems. Of course, a theory may rely on some device other than the metaphor to claim relations between facts or objects. Numerical classification schemes are common. Insofar as it is often difficult to identify any common structural attributes between objects that are classified together, it is difficult to make the case that analogical thinking is being employed. In his work *Symbolic Classification*, Rodney Needham says,

> In other cases—probably the majority—the ethnographic evidence provides no reason to think that the members of a symbolic class are connected by features that are common to all. The Javanese scheme of correspondence [involving the number five] is very explicit, to the point that of one member of a class it can be said that it 'is' one or another member; but beyond this statement the source offers no ground to infer that there is any common feature that unites, e.g., east, reserved, food, verandah, and propitious.[9]

The same could be said of many of the objects classified together in a set by the Chinese five-element scheme, including noses and metal, and mouths and water. While granting the existence of these classification schemes in Sung Neo-Confucianism, we will not address them particularly in this study.

Theories explain relations between facts. Sung Confucian theories of nature employ one or more specific terms for each of the abstract principles explaining these relations. There are three basic types of theories. One maintains that things are related hierarchically, often in hierarchical sets of two, and that there are rules prescribing proper behavior between them. The technical term around which this type of theory centers is li^a (rites, rules of propriety), in the sense of natural or cosmic law. Hsün Tzu was the first to give it this sense. A second type of theory maintains that all things are related in their being penetrated by a single, nonempirical, ordering unity, or in being penetrated by the same physical substance under the control of that principle. This theory uses the word li^b (principle) to refer to the cosmic order which unifies all things and events into a single intelligible pattern. Its origins go back from Ch'eng I (1033-1107), through Hua-yen Buddhism, all the way to the Neo-Taoist Wang Pi (226-49). Other technical terms such as "heaven" (*t'ien*), "decree" (*ming*), "Great Ultimate" (*T'ai-chi*), and "nature" (*hsing*) appear in statements of this theory, but each is defined as li^b viewed from differing perspectives. The theory uses the term $ch'i^a$ (material force) to refer to the interpenetrating physical substance.

Finally, there is the theory that things are related by being part of a cosmic growth process of ceaseless production and reproduction, caused by a single source of life. The world seems to be one organic entity. The "mind of heaven and earth" is responsible for the growth process; the principle of production and growth is *jen* (humaneness); and the four stages are *yüan* (originating growth), *heng* (prosperous development), li^c (advantageous gain), and *cheng* (correct firmness). Literally, they are the "four virtues" of nature,[10] which appear as explanations in the first two hexagrams of the *I ching* [Book of changes], *ch'ien*, and *k'un*.

All three theories are interrelated. Chu Hsi explains li^a (propriety) as li^b (principle), and li^b as *jen*. But each theory makes a distinctive claim about the way in which apparently disparate facts are interrelated. Therefore, we may separate them analytically. We will consider each in terms of the metaphor that stands behind it.

Each cosmological theory is holistic, treating the apparently disparate objects or facts as somehow integrated. However, the abstract theories themselves offer no compelling account of how the objects or facts to which they apply are integrated. The metaphors fill in these gaps, thereby enriching the theories.

Anyone who scans the histories of China written by foreigners during the past two decades will find the assertion that Confucians favored the analogy of the organism in explaining nature. This interpretation probably owes most to the influence of Joseph Needham, who wrote:

> But I am prepared to suggest, in view of the fact that the term Li^b [principle] always contained the notion of pattern, and that Chu Hsi himself consciously applied it so as to include the most living and vital patterns known to man, that something of the idea of "organism" was what was really at the back of the minds of the Neo-Confucians.[11]

To attribute to the Neo-Confucians the idea of organism is to assert that they interpreted nature on the analogy of the living organism. The expressions "philosophy of organism" and "organicism" can refer simply to the doctrines that stress the integration of parts of a whole, the explanation of parts in terms of the whole, and the autonomous nature of the whole. However, more than this is usually involved when the terms are used. That is, the biological overtones of an actual organism remain to inform the meaning of the terms. This certainly is the case with Needham, for whom the presence of "living and vital patterns" and developmental patterns like those of the biological organism are involved in the meaning of "the philosophy of organism," depending on the context in which he used the term.

We can readily understand why someone would treat the organism as the dominant analogy. It was one of the principal analogies used in Europe from classical Greece up to the Renaissance. Perhaps more important, an organicism involving analogizing from some form of living thing reappeared in a new form, evolutionary organicism, in the nineteenth and twentieth centuries, influenced by Darwin and the new biology. In short, the organism was a metaphor with which Europeans such as Needham were familiar through the centrality of its classical and modern roles.

Marking off the organism as the dominant analogy in Neo-Confucian thought is both important and, we believe, wrongly overstressed. It is important because organicistic metaphors from the plant world (trees and seeds of grain) play a prominent role in Neo-Confucian cosmology and ethics. It is overstressed because other structural analogies, such as the family network and the stream of water, also pervade the pictorial imagery and theoretical explanations. These are certainly no less important than those from the plant world.

The Family Network

One of the several analogies that support the abstract theoretical discussions of nature appeared early in the history of Confucian thought. This is the image of the family- or clan-based society.

The first type of abstract theory claims that nature is composed of objects integrally related to each other in a hierarchical order. Relationships of hierarchy and rules of proper behavior between them apply to all things, from the stars to human beings. They are manifest in the ways in which things are classified and are therefore intelligible. Thus, Ch'eng I says, "Therefore, we can see from the superiority of heaven and the humble status of earth, that li^a [propriety] is already established. From the arrangement of things according to types and their divisions into classes we can see that the li^a [rites] are already in operation."[12] "Nothing stands alone"[13] in this cosmos; everything comes in complementary, often hierarchical, pairs. The idea that proper relationships exist between all things is manifest in speaking of "rules of propriety" underlying their orderly divisions.

Theoretical statements about an orderly, hierarchical universe do not answer the obvious question: What holds the whole thing together? The theory needs information about the reason for the integration of its parts and the particular nature of the relationships between them. A metaphor can be helpful in this regard, because an image of a structured unit may reveal this information.

The picture of the family network does the job because the family is a unit with a clear explanation for the integration of its parts: reciprocal obligations based on what each member provides the others. Parents provide food to children, children provide old-age protection to parents; ancestors watch over the family's good fortune, and family members ritually give food and other sacrifices to ancestors. Each provision creates an obligation for the recipient. What holds the whole together is psychological expectations and reciprocal, specialized duties. This is simply commonplace knowledge.

The Sung Confucians did not themselves either think the matter through in this manner or initiate the use of the family analogy. It was a legacy of the past incorporated in their doctrines. The most prominent form in which it came to them was in the *Book of Changes*. The first two hexagrams (*ch'ien* and *k'un*) are respectively called "father" and "mother" (*k'un* being described in the original text as "mare"). As hexagrams, they pertain to nature as a whole, to heaven and earth more specifically. As seen from an early Chinese cultural perspective in the commentaries on them, they introduce to nature the idea of complementary familial obligation. *Ch'ien* has the obligation to beget children, to be creative, to nourish. *K'un* has the obligation to bear the child or to bring things to fruition. Having access to this familial image of mutual obligations means that any holistic cosmological theory has a plausible basis for explaining the interconnectedness of things in terms of complementary obligation.

In very early Confucianism, the analogy of the family was itself used to explain society. The phenomenon was not unknown in Europe. Aristotle used a similar analogy in *Metaphysics* (X11.10). Locke's target, Filmer, discussed it in *Patriarchy*. It is simply less common in European social thought and cosmologies than in Chinese. Sometime between 350 and 200 B.C. the *Hsiao ching* [Classic of filial piety] explained proper social organization as an extension of family relations: "The gentleman's service to his parents is filial; therefore, his filiality can be transferred to his prince. His service of his elder brothers is deferential; therefore, his docility stands him in good stead toward his superiors."[14] Of course, this only marked the systematic exposition of ideas that had appeared earlier. The *Mencius* states, "The root of the empire is in the state, and the root of the state is in the family."[15] A contemporary Chinese commentator has noted,

> Regarding social life, the Chinese people essentially expanded or extended family life into a larger area.... While the Chinese respect for the tutor was an extension of filial piety, the respect of friendship was, as an expansion of tutorship, also an extension of filial piety. The closely knit patterns of relatives, clansmen, fellow countrymen, and tutors, together with friends, were all interwoven around the filial axis in Chinese community.[16]

In other words, the early Confucian idea became a part of custom.

The *Classic of Filial Piety* explains the regular patterns in nature in terms of filial piety: "Filiality is the first principle of heaven, the ultimate standard of earth, the norm of conduct for the people." There are echoes of this in Sung Neo-Confucianism. Ch'eng I used the analogy of the relation between family ancestors and living family members to describe the relation of heaven to all things and of the emperor to principalities: "Heaven is the ancestor of all things. The king is the ancestor of all prefectures."[17] Analogizing from society to nature is as common as analogizing from the family.

Study of the analogies reveals several attributes of the family- or clan-based society that dominate the early Confucian strand in Sung cosmologies. Each of the core societal attributes exists in nature as well as in society. Attributing societal characteristics to nature began in the Chou-Han period, its ultimate root being the early Chou claims that the social distinctions themselves are derived from heaven.[18] Taken as a whole, the characteristics form the pictorial image of a net, comprised of central and subordinate cords. The family and society suggest a spatial image, with spatial positions attached in the net to the central cord.

The first such attribute is social roles, conceived spatially. Early Confucians had no monopoly on this idea. The *Han-fei Tzu* states that "things have their proper place, talents their proper use. When all are in their proper place, then superior and inferior may be free from action."[19] But the idea is central to Confucianism. The terms that Confucians use to denote social role all have spatial connotations and mean "position": *so*, *fen* (allocated position), and *wei*. Most frequently they stand for both commonplace social roles and the duties associated with those roles. Consistent with the spatial imagery, people can "stop" in these positions; or they can do evil by "transgressing their boundaries." The standard social roles are prince-

minister, father-son, older brother-younger brother, and husband-wife. Each
is a *fen*, which the Ch'eng brothers insist are never adequately fulfilled by their
current occupants.[20] This list expands from time to time to include such roles
as friend, sage, and scholar.[21] The duties are denoted by terms that stand both
for the obligation and for the virtue that is accomplished by doing the duty:
righteousness (*i*) as between prince and minister; familial affection as between
father and son; honesty as between friends.[22] In order to convey the idea that
the duties never change, they are called "heavenly allotments" (*t'ien fen*), and
their actual practice by people is called the "human allotment" (*jen fen*).

The second attribute is the existence of boundaries that distinguish one
social position from another. They suggest the impropriety of the occupant of
one position engaging in the activities of another position. In the philosophic
record, the roots of this attribute and the first one described go back to the
Chou-period principle of the rectification of names, requiring action
appropriate to the name of one's social role. Let the prince remain a prince, the
minister a minister, the father a father, and the son a son. In the Ch'eng-Chu
works, the idea of boundaried positions is conveyed in the expression that,
under sagely rule, "each person will occupy [or attain] his appropriate social
role" (*ke tang ch'i fen; ke te ch'i fen*).[23] Moreover, each will be and should be
(the two senses are fused) "tranquil in his position"(*ke an ch'i fen*), not seeking
the activities or privileges of some other role.

The third attribute is relational. The basic social roles come in sets of two,
in which there is a hierarchical relationship, one role carrying the duty of
exercising authority and the other obedience. The final attribute, also
relational, is the emotions that tie the various related roles together to form a
whole social organization. Viewing the social roles from the standpoint of
their changeless status, the principle that ties them together is humaneness
(*jen*). From the standpoint of their actual occupancy of the roles by actual
people, the emotions that link the positions together are love, respect, and
loyalty. Love ties parents to children and children to parents. It proceeds from
the superior to the inferior in all other sets, while respect proceeds from the
youngers to elders, or inferiors to superiors, and loyalty from subjects to
emperor. Still influenced by the family analogy from the Chou period, Ch'eng
I traced all love to family sentiments: "Benevolence focuses itself in love. No
love is greater than love for family. Therefore, Confucius said, 'Filial piety and
fraternal love are the root of all humaneness.' "[24]

The Ch'eng-Chu school of cosmology draws heavily on these attributes of
a clan-based society in interpreting nature. In so doing, it draws on a pictorial
image of hierarchically arranged positions whose respective spaces are
surrounded by boundaries that are interwoven to form a flexible net. The
pictorial image of a net is suggested by the fact that the major sets of social
relations (sovereign-subject, father-son, husband-wife) are called the three
kang. *Kang* is the principal rope in a net, to which other ropes are attached.
The sovereign, father, and husband are pictured as central ropes to which
others attach. Contemporary Chinese writers continue to refer to the explicit
image of the net when describing these *kang*.[25] Furthermore, Sung writers
refer to an artery through which a vital force flows from a central base,

connecting all kin, both the living and their ancestral spirits: "Each kinship group has its own central base. Descendants' bodies are here and ancestors' vital force is here. There is an artery that links them."[26]

Each societal attribute we have just identified applies to nature. First, not only persons, but all objects in nature have allotted positions within whose "space" or with whose duties they must abide: "The sage has an impartial mind. He exhausts the principles of heaven, earth, and all things so that each may gain its proper place [*fen*]."[27] And "Each of all things and affairs has its place [*so*]. When it obtains its place there is tranquility; when it loses it there is disorder."[28] Moreover, "the heavenly order [*t'ien hsü*] is natural sequence. It teaches the prince to rest in the position [*wei*] of prince."[29] Boundaries between positions exist throughout nature, not just in society. This is conveyed in the quotation, paraphrase, or echo of passages from the *ken* hexagram in the *Book of Changes*. The *ken* hexagram means "keeping still." Most frequently quoted is the commentary "Keeping his stopping still [i.e., quiet] means stopping in his place."[30] In referring to this, the *Erh-Ch'eng ch'üan-shu* [Complete works of the two Ch'eng brothers] says, "*Ken* means stopping it in its place [*so*]. When all things stop in their places, there is no indeterminate position [*fen*]."[31] "Stopping in its place" means doing what is appropriate for something occupying that position and not transgressing the established boundaries. The texts speak of things (*wu*), not simply of people: "The *ken* hexagram only makes clear that the myriad things should have their own stopping places."[32] A planet has a proper position and should not encroach on the orbit of another heavenly body. The superior man who wishes to pattern himself on nature's order looks to the *ken* hexagram for guidance: "The superior man observes the *ken* hexagram and thinks of what his stopping place is and of not going beyond his position [*wei*]."[33]

Extending the family analogy to nature introduces the attribute of hierarchical relationship, involving authority and obedience. The hexagrams *ch'ien* and *k'un* designate principles that apply throughout nature. Analogizing from family to universe, Chu Hsi says that just as a person's father and mother are his parents, so are *ch'ien* and *k'un* the parents of the world.[34] Just as *ch'ien* is the ruler of *k'un*, so are the husband the ruler of the wife and the natural principles the rulers of matter (*ch'i*[a]).[35] In human society, the rules of propriety (*li*) include the proper duties and expectations of persons related in the hierarchical sets. By analogy, the rules of propriety describe such relationships in nature at large: "From the arrangement of things according to types ... we can see that the *li* are already in operation."[36]

Social roles come in hierarchical sets. Such sets are found in nature as well. Furthermore, Chu Hsi regularly describes the source of natural pattern (*li*[b]; principle) that is at the core of his entire doctrine as the ruler (*tsai*; *chu tsai*).[37] "That which causes material force to be able to move or be still is *li*[b], which acts as ruler." And he says that when we speak of *li*[b], not as "one," but from the standpoint of the many phenomena in which it is manifest, we must remember the rank differences it instituted among things, "just like in the human family."[38]

There are passages about all things coming in sets of two that contain no reference to the analogy of family or society. For example, "Among all things in the universe, there is none that does not have its complementary opposite. Where there is yin, there is yang; where there is humaneness, there is righteousness; where there is good, there is evil; where there is speech, there is silence; and where there is action, there is tranquility."[39] The idea of authority-obedience is muted in this statement of relationships. The idea of complementarity is heightened, as evidenced by the juxtaposition of humaneness and righteousness (*i*), and action and tranquility. The principle of complementary opposites is presented as the way in which the production and reproduction of things in the world occur: "All principles necessarily have opposites; this is the origin of production and reproduction."[40] In the beginning there was only the one material force (*ch'i*[a]). It became the two material forces, yin and yang, which produced all things in the universe. Thus, all things have their opposites. Where there is birth, there is death, and so forth.[41] Though the societal analogy is absent in these passages, the existence of such a classification system reinforces the assignment of persons to social roles that come in sets of two.

The final attribute of the family or society is the emotion that links the various positions together. This is love, the emotional counterpart of the life force that parents give their children. As the cosmic principle of life, this love is humaneness.[42] Almost every social virtue is defined as some form of *jen*, the cosmic principle of growth or creativity. This is true of respect (*ching*),[43] reciprocity (*shu*),[44] loyalty (*chung*),[45] and impartiality (*kung*).[46]

Sung claims about a natural or cosmic counterpart for boundaried and hierarchical social positions, linked by duties and emotions, served as a powerful argument in favor of the naturalness of social roles and helped to enforce compliance with the rules and feelings attached to those roles. This provides some basis for the May Fourth Movement charge that Neo-Confucianism supported constraining social roles. This is confirmed by consideration of the highest virtue of which the ideal man or sage is capable, unselfish impartiality, which is rendered by a variety of expressions: *kung* (impartiality), *kung hsin* (impartial mind), *wu wo* (no self), and *wu szu yü* (without private desires), among others.

The family analogy required us to think of a person relationally, in terms of hierarchical links and authority. Thus, broadly defined, impartiality is seeing the self in terms of natural relationships. And this way of viewing the self must occur automatically, without purposive effort (the idea of avoiding purposive effort owes something to Taoism and Ch'an Buddhism). The cardinal sin, selfishness, is to perceive the self separately from those particular relations. The contrast between this view and the portrait of the individual associated with the individualisms that arose in Renaissance Europe is readily apparent.

Because a part of the cosmology explains nature by employing the family or society analogy, unselfish impartiality often means fulfilling the natural duties encompassed in natural social roles or obeying the natural rules governing other things. Selfishness means failure to abide with and fulfill those duties. The roles and duties are specified in the early rules of propriety (li^a) or in the "heavenly principles" (*t'ien li*, when those were thought of synonymously with the rules of propriety) or in the heavenly allotments (*t'ien fen*) or in human relationships (*jen lun*). The following passages typify this sense of unselfish impartiality:

> When one can conquer the self and get rid of the selfish mind, one naturally can return to the rules of propriety.[47]

> In looking, hearing, speaking, and acting, when one does nothing contrary to principle, this is acting according to the rules of propriety. The rules of propriety are principle. Whatever is not in accord with heavenly principle is selfish desire.[48]

> Being basically without selfish intention is nothing but obeying heavenly principle.[49]

Rather than show discipline by conforming to duty, the selfish person satisfies his private desires. In this manner, the Ch'eng-Chu writers equated the distinction between unselfish impartiality (*kung*) and selfishness (*szu* or *szu yü*) with the early Confucian contrast between doing what is right (*i*) and doing what brings personal gain (li^c).[50]

This sense of impartiality explains many of the Ch'eng-Chu criticisms of Buddhism. The Buddhists fail to abide by the duties of the natural social roles into which humans must fit. This failure to regard themselves in terms of such relationships constitutes selfishness: "The reason those Buddhists want to destroy heavenly principles and get rid of human relations is because they are selfish."[51] In addition, they fail to note the other natural rules to which they are subject, such as the rule of complementary pairs. Where there is joy, there is suffering; and where there is life, there is death. Buddhists are bound as well as other human beings to obey these rules. Yet they try to avoid suffering and death, which illustrates their selfishness.[52] The contrast between the Confucian sage and the Buddhist on all of these issues is apparent in these words: "The sage develops to the utmost his selfless mind and exhausts the principles of heaven, earth, and all things so that each thing can occupy its proper place. However, the Buddhists do everything for their personal selfishness."[53]

One of the main analogies used to explain the mind equates selfless impartiality with discipline. This describes the relation of master and servant. In the psyche of the selfless person, the moral mind (awareness of eternal principles) is master and the human mind (awareness of bodily needs and sensations) obeys. The good person, the selfless person, is one who obeys the rigid rules of his social roles.

Discipline. Submergence of personal desires that do not conform to role duties. The selfless impartiality required by the family or society analogy ensures order. No wonder those in positions of power continued to bless it and to link it with order. We should not overstate Chu Hsi's own attachment to discipline. However, his treatment of selfishness in this connection was sufficiently open-ended to permit partisan interpretation by future rulers who did prize role obedience as fundamental to order.

The Stream of Water

Of all of the metaphors and analogies in the *Chu Tzu yü-lei* [Classified conversations of Master Chu], the one most frequently encountered is water. In contrast to the family metaphor, it reinforces an egalitarian perspective on man by claiming that humans equally share in the same principle of value and order. But this is rushing the argument.

The common phrase that sums up the second cosmological theory is *li i fen shu*: "Principle is one, but its manifestations are many." W. T. Chan has traced this expression back to Tao Sheng (d. 434). Ch'eng I used it in his commentary on the *Book of Changes*.[54] Principle (li^b) is at once the natural ordering pattern in all things and the reason for their coming into existence and remaining as they are. Considered as one, principle is the same as the Great Ultimate (*T'ai-chi*), which is the aggregate of all principles: "The principles of all things taken as one make up the Great Ultimate." Considered as many, the li^b is present in individuals as their natures, *hsing*. The theory derives in part from the Chinese Buddhist doctrine that the Buddha nature is One (One Mind), and yet it is present in all people. Each individual has the Buddha nature. Both the T'ien-t'ai and Hua-yen schools refer to dharmas as manifestations of li^b, which cannot be divided. In addition, the Hua-yen school considers that each thing manifests individually the entire li^b, making it all the more a macrocosm-microcosm theory. There is a suggestion of the notion that dharmas (including persons) manifesting the same li^b are of equal worth.

In the works of Chu Hsi, depending on context, the phrase *li i fen shu* and similar references to a one-many relationship can be interpreted in any of the following ways. First, there is one Great Ultimate, the aggregation of all principles. It is a macrocosm of all that exists, yet each thing is a microcosm, possessing the Great Ultimate within itself. Second, we can talk about the one ordering principle or pattern of the universe, or we can refer to the principle's presence in individual things as their particular natures, partially a function of their material endowment (*ch'i chih chih hsing*). Material endowment is what divides things into classes such as animals and birds, and each class has its own li^b. Third, there is one natural obligation for humans, namely, love. But love can be manifested in a variety of forms, such as filiality, brotherly love, or loyalty. The egalitarian perspective derives its basis from the first two of these. Each individual human shares in the one unifying principle.

The idea of a unity that remains a whole in spite of being present in apparently discrete individual things is difficult for most people to grasp. Plato acknowledged this fact in criticizing his own doctrine of the Forms:

> How are we to conceive that each of them [i.e., each Form] being always one and the same and subject neither to generation nor destruction, nevertheless is, to begin with, most assuredly this single unity and yet subsequently comes to be in the infinite number of things that come into being—an identical unity being thus found simultaneously in unity and in plurality. Is it torn in pieces, or does the whole of it, and this would seem the extreme impossibility, get apart from itself?[55]

The Neo-Confucian response to this conceptual problem was to employ several graphic analogies to facilitate recognition and understanding.

Using the analogy of the moon and its reflection in its entirety in the myriad streams, Chu Hsi tried to explain the nature of the relationship between the Great Ultimate and the individual rocks, flowers, fish, and humans in which it is present.

> [Someone asked], "Then there is the reality of the single li^b [principle], and all things manifest it as their essence. Therefore among all things, each possesses the single Great Ultimate. But in this case, is the Great Ultimate cut up into parts?" Chu Hsi answered, "Originally there is only the single Great Ultimate, and all things receive it in its entirety. It is like the moon in the heavens. There is only one moon, and yet it spreads out over all the rivers and we see it [reflected] everywhere. We cannot say it is divided up into parts."[56]

Chu Hsi did not use this particular analogy often. However, the passage just cited is widely known, probably because it purports to clarify, through graphic analogy, the complex relationship of one and many. The analogy itself derives from Buddhism. The Indian sutras, translated into Chinese, employ the analogy chiefly to convey the idea of illusion or of the derivative nature of things. Reflected moons are unreal, just as the objects perceived by human consciousness or contemplated by conceptual thought are unreal.[57] The important idea here pertains to the reflection, not to the moon per se. Thus, the *Laṅkāvatāra-sūtra* makes the following point: "The *skandhas* [components of personality] . . . are similar to reflections of trees in water; they should be seen as a mock show, and a dream."[58] However, in Chinese works favored by the distinctively Chinese Buddhist schools, the moon analogy, while perhaps retaining its original Indian sense, is also used to explain the one-many, macrocosm-microcosm relationship. Thus, an eighth-century Ch'an Buddhist work states:

> The one Buddha nature perfectly penetrates all natures.
> One dharma everywhere comprises all dharmas.
> One moon everywhere is manifest in all bodies of water.
> All the moons reflected in the water are gathered together in the one
>   moon that they reflect.
> The Dharma-body of all Buddhas penetrates selfhood.
> Selfhood at the same time is one with the Tathāgata.
> One stage in the Path is equivalent to all stages.[59]

There is a reason why Chu Hsi did not make use of the moon metaphor more frequently. For this Confucian, the chief problem in the one-many theory is not explaining reality-illusion, but explaining *how* the one-many relationship can take place, precisely the problem that plagued Plato. The moon metaphor does not suggest as plausible an answer to this problem as does the water metaphor. The water metaphor can be found in the Chou texts, but it was more immediately familiar by its prominence in the Hua-yen Buddhist texts.[60] This familiar metaphor provided our second holistic theory with an explanation of how disparate things are integrated to form a whole: interpenetration.

The dynamics of water include a known process of flow, from one source into a chain of interconnecting channels or ditches. The water analogy thus describes a familiar or plausible picture of penetration by one flowing substance as the means whereby the linkage between all things takes place. At the transcendental level, all things are penetrated by the flow of sincerity or integrity (*ch'eng*), or, generally, principle (*li^b*).[61] Unlike the carpenter who remains distinct from the house he builds, this "originator" maintains an integral connection to the things through which it flows:

> Great is the *ch'ien* Beginning. Everything begins as a result of it. It is the source of Integrity. This is to refer comprehensively to one single flowing source. The *ch'ien* changes and each thing gains its proper nature. Integrity flows forth and each thing has its own settling place. When it is a person, it is this Integrity. When it is a thing, it is this Integrity. Therefore we say, "Integrity is thus established. It is like water. Its emergence involves just one source. After it flows forth and branches into a myriad outlets there is still only this [single] water."[62]

"Natural principle" is thus embodied by a single entity such as water, which, as rain, falls distinctively in various places. At the same time, if we leave the transcendental level, we find that material force (*ch'i^a*) connects all things by flowing streamlike through them, as water through the gills of a fish; the nonempirical principle (*li^b*) in its flow determines the order of the actual vitality in matter.[63] The relationship among apparently disparate concrete things, as well as the relationship among apparently disparate principles, is described in terms of interpenetration by that which flows respectively through either the nonempirical order or the physical realm.

At the empirical level, there is the general material force (*ch'i^a*) that links all things, and there is the specific material force (also *ch'i^a*) that links past and future clansmen as a unit, also conceived as similar to a water flow: "My material force is the material force of my ancestors, and this also constitutes a single material force."[64] Actually, the *ch'i^a* continually changes in accordance with the yin-yang and five-element cycles. The implication is that the material force of which humans and other things are composed scatters at death. However, Chu Hsi also accepted traditional beliefs about ancestors, namely, that they are capable of some identity after death so that they can respond as personal clan ancestors to sacrifices. This means that the *ch'i^a* of ancestors, though dispersed, can be called back and temporarily reaccumulate as a result of the sacrifice. In this temporary state, the ancestors have some personal identity. Chu Hsi needed a theory of a diffuse unity that could still somehow link the many ancestral spirits and their mortal descendants. He found it by applying to *ch'i^a* the analogy of a body of water (the diffuse unity) with its waves (the personalized spirits and mortals).

> After all, descendants are composed of the material force of their ancestors. Although the ancestors' material force disperses, the root of the [kinship group] is here. If descendants manifest fully their integrity and respectfulness, then they can successfully summon their ancestors' material force to accumulate here. It is like water making waves. Later water is not the same as former water. The later waves are not the same as

the former waves. But all together there is only this one body of water making waves. The descendants' material force and the ancestors' material force also are like this. Naturally, the ancestors' material force had dispersed at one point. But its root is still here. Since the root is still here, one can also accumulate material force here. This matter is difficult to explain.[65]

Not only are all things united as a result of being composed of the same material force, but also all living and dead members of kinship groups remain unified through participation in some particularistic material force. The material force accumulates substantially in one place, suggestive of a root from which branches eventually develop and fan out but never separate from the root. In the analogy drawn above, that source may be the ancestral temple, where the special force accumulates. The communication between descendants who sacrifice and ancestors who respond, as required by the demands of traditional Confucianism, is made possible by the existence of a material continuum linking the living who sacrifice in the temple with their ancestors. But, in a departure from traditional Confucianism that was inspired by the one-many idea of Buddhism, we learn that it is not permissible to think of the material force of ancestral spirits as entirely distinct from that of living family members. Specific material force must always be conceived as part of an undivided whole, in which descendants as well as ancestral spirits participate. This idea is consistent with the new naturalistic elements introduced in Neo-Confucianism.

The difficult philosophical question of how something like a spirit can have the separate identity required for communication with kin through sacrifice yet also be part of the same undifferentiated whole remains unresolved. The analogy of water gives an apparent pictorial solution, but it cannot be stretched far enough to justify this premise. No wonder Chu Hsi says that "this matter is difficult to explain."

At the level of the individual person, Chu Hsi speaks of the "love flowing forth" and Ch'eng I of "man's mind flowing in all directions."[66] Flowing into the individual from one source, they flow out from him to other objects, linking them together. The metaphor that describes the third type of theory, the plant sprout, is an equally common way of describing this outreach from the individual to others. In addition, it clarifies what it is that flows between things: the life force that unites all things as they develop through the four-stage growth pattern.

Another philosophical problem that the water analogy helps to resolve is how principle (li^b) can be localized so that we can look for the li^b of a particular thing, e.g., an individual person. There is nothing inherent in the conception of li^b that provides a clear idea as to where or how li^b is located in things. Water, however, is localized by means of a container ($ch'i^b$), such as a bowl. Thus, a container must be found for li^b, and this is some physical substance that can surround it. "Without physical substance, there would be no place for the nature endowed by heaven to be; like a spoonful of water, without the thing to hold it the water would have no place to settle."[67] Its container is its $ch'i^b$, which, in the individual, is the mind.

A third problem for which the analogy supplies a solution is the cause of evil or error. Water is subject to pollution from its surroundings, including its container. Hence, the purity of li^b will be subject to contamination from its container, the physical endowment. The variation of actual human nature from one individual to the next is a function of "the differing colors of the bowls" or the "cleanliness" of the bowls or channels in which the water is located.[68]

There is some disjunction between the actual existence of human evil, attributed to selfishness, and Chu Hsi's claims about the possible triumph of order (li^b). The theory offers no clear basis for such a claim, but the water analogy does. It offers a relationship between an inevitable force (water from its spring) and temporary obstacles to its flow. "Humaneness is like a water source and selfishness is like sand and stone that are obstacles to its flow. Impartiality [kung] is getting rid of the sand and stone. Without sand and stone, water can flow. Without selfishness, humaneness can be recovered."[69]

Finally, the analogy tries to explain how disparate values are related. The "principle is one, its manifestations are many" theory implies that values are related but provides no basis for this assertion. The water analogy provides an explanation: the relation between source and what emanates from the source.

> Just as in the case of a water source flowing into a thousand streams, one cannot deny that the water flowing downward into them is not the water of a single source. Man has just one mind. The filiality of serving parents, the loyalty from serving one's prince and the brotherly respect from serving elders are all this one mind.[70]

In other words, humaneness (jen) is the ultimate source, from which the moral sense, propriety, and knowledge all flow. Or, structured another way, humaneness is the source, filiality and brotherly love are the first pond into which it flows, loving all people the second, and loving all things the third.[71]

Of course, like all deep structural analogies, while the water image provides solutions to some problems by clarifying structural relationships, it blinds its user to other problems. Not all attributes of the physical objects in the metaphor can apply to phenomena to which the theory applies. For example, it is easy to say that the dirt on a bowl can interact with the clean water it contains (both are material); but how does a person's formless, transcendental nature interact with his physical self? They are entirely different kinds of things. We know how bowls get dirty, but why are the physical natures of some people corrupt and others not? Where does evil come from? Finally, can qualities from the physical world apply meaningfully to the transcendental? We can speak of larger or smaller amounts of water, but what does it mean, as Chu Hsi sometimes says, to speak of larger or smaller quantities of principle in a thing?[72]

Chu Hsi's own ethical system is the ultimate beneficiary of solving the problems raised by the water analogy. The demonstration that all things are linked together by something that interpenetrates them is the bottom-line argument for fulfilling role duties for the sake of the whole. At the same time, however, the theory and its associated image of the flow of pure water tell us that all things have equal worth. There is something pure in each. Therefore, we have an obligation to love all things, whether this purity is manifest or not.

The portrait of nature conveyed by the water analogy, which is anchored in Hua-yen Buddhism, stands in contrast to the portrait derived from the family or society analogy. Therefore, it helps us to evaluate the first of the two May Fourth claims about social roles in Ch'eng-Chu Neo-Confucianism. According to the analogies based on the water image, the cosmos is either devoid of hierarchy or hierarchy is minimized. The nature of the relation of one thing to another is egalitarian. The Great Ultimate is equally present in all things, making them of equal worth. Unlike the image of social space with its boundaries, the Great Ultimate is not divisible. It is devoid of barriers. The relationship of each thing tò another is one of indivisible parts of a whole.

The attempt to mesh these two incompatible cosmologies is symbolized in the statement of Ch'eng I that "the rules of propriety [li^a] are principle [li^b]."[73] The rules of propriety suggest hierarchy and status barriers; principle suggests unity and equal value. In conclusion, then, the differing relationships suggested by two types of analogy have revealed two patterns. One was symbolized by the hexagrams *ch'ien* and *k'un* as father and mother, by the idea of positions alloted by heaven (*t'ien fen*), and by "the rules of propriety as the order of heaven and earth."[74] The other was suggested by the water that remains one and pure, though its channels are many and dirty. The former type suggests that things are related as part of a hierarchical network; the latter indicates that things are related as undifferentiated parts of a unitary whole.

The network image seems to lock the individual into a set of social roles that restricts his attention to a limited group with whom he has reciprocal duties or rights. The picture of the stream assures him that all persons have equal worth because the li^b is present in them; by implication, they should be equally objects of his love, which should not be focused on a limited group. The two analogies seem to leave the individual with a conflict of duties.

The Plant

Another explanatory theory in Ch'eng-Chu Neo-Confucianism claims that things have a common source of life and its continued maintenance, the Great Ultimate, or the "mind of heaven and earth." One name of this source is humaneness (*jen*), the principle of life, which ensures that all things develop through a similarly staged life process.[75] Things thus related form a holistic unity. Whereas the previous theory concerned an interpenetrating principle that controls an interpenetrating material force, this theory adds to the cosmology some new ideas: source of life, principle of life, life or vitality as the quality of the material force, and stages. These ideas had not been present in the one-many Buddhist doctrine inherited by Chu Hsi. Through his formulations, they become superimposed on it.

The following excerpts are representative of Chu Hsi's discussion of the abstract theory:

Movement also is not the mind of heaven and earth. It is only that through which we see that mind. For example, in the tenth month, how can we not be said to have the Mind of Heaven and Earth? It flows through all.... Of [the four stages of nature], *yüan, heng, li*, *cheng, yüan* [originating growth] is the time when the young sprouts begin to come up, *heng* [prosperous development] is the time when leaves and branches grow.[76]

If we wish to understand the meaning of *jen*, we should know that it is present in an all-pervasive, genial material force. This material force is the yang and spring material of heaven and earth. Its principle is the mind of heaven and earth that produces things.... This idea, then, is of something devoid of selfish destruction. With it, a person regards other men and himself as one, other things and himself as one.[77]

But if you gather together the facts from all around you, you will realize a most important matter of priority [*ta t'ou-nao*].... For example, from the font of commiseration one can infer the existence of the *jen* that exists in the mind. Among the heavenly virtues, *jen* is the originating growth, and the originating growth is the active yang aspect of the Great Ultimate.... If now we clearly take note of the Great Ultimate, then we definitely will be able to note all the principles and their instances in the world as coming from it.[78]

Like the previous two holistic theories, this one draws on a deep structural metaphor to argue for the structural integration of the apparently disparate facts to which it applies. A case could be made that the deep metaphor is the human organism. After all, the Sung philosophers do occasionally use the term *t'i* (body) to refer to the organic whole composed of heaven, earth, and all things, with its mind and its pervasive life force. The use of *t'i* is as much a statement about how the humane person should empathetically regard things as about the actual structure of things. Ch'eng Hao said, "The humane man forms one body with things as a complete whole";[79] Ch'eng I said, "The humane man regards heaven, earth, and all things as one body."[80] There is classical precedent for explaining the cosmos as one body akin to that of an animal. The term *ti-mai*, "pulses of the earth," appears in the second century B.C. in the *Shih chi* [Records of the Grand Historian].[81] Religious Taoists used the metaphor of the human body in their cosmologies. Chu Hsi himself occasionally explains the structure of the universe by analogy to man: "Heaven is a great man, while man is a small heaven"; and "The circular shape of man's feet is like the earth."[82] But these references are extremely rare. Far more frequently, Chu Hsi draws on the structure of a plant to explain the theory of the cosmos and man's relation to it that is described in the passages just cited.

One problem with the idea of "one body" is that it does not provide adequate clarification of possible relationships to resolve the conflict between routine duties to family or prince and duties to strangers. Most references to "one body," though harking back to the Buddhist sources, echo most immediately Chang Tsai's (1020-77) essay "Hsi-ming" [The Western inscription]: "Heaven is my father and earth is my mother.... All people are my brothers and sisters, and all things are my companions."[83] The trouble is that this only perpetuates the tension between hierarchy and equality. It keeps the basic familial social roles (father, mother, brother) as required by the network image, yet it treats all things as equally one's companions. Superficially, many of the Neo-Confucian texts have regularly inconsistent references to "regarding things and the self as equal" and voice criticisms of Buddhists for not differentiating between people. No wonder Chu Hsi had to resort to a different metaphor: the plant.

The plant image constitutes the best vehicle for conveying simultaneously both how the disparate facts or things are interrelated (organically) and also how nature manifests dynamic activity that people can so readily understand (seasonally changing plant growth). The relation between things like a root or a seed and buds, flowers, fruit, and leaves is an organic interconnection of things linked in a single life process. This provides the abstract theory with the idea necessary to explain its holistic claims about the integration of parts. The root by itself carries the idea of the source of life, as required by the abstract theory.

Given that our third cosmological theory incorporates the principle of life, the introduction of the plant metaphor communicates the dynamic of the principle in its application of the idea of cycles of change to all things (derived from the *Book of Changes*' explanations of the first two hexagrams, *ch'ien* and *k'un*: the developmental stages of originating growth, prosperous development, advantageous gain, and correct firmness). Chu Hsi associated these with the four seasons.[84] Thus, the four-season growth process of plants characterizes all the myriad things that exist in the universe: all things must pass through the stages of sprouting, development, fruition, and death and preparation for renewal, in a never-ending cycle.[85] The metaphor has enriched the abstract theory with both a portrait of structural relationships between source (root/seed) and parts and a known process of change by stages. For these reasons, then, Ch'eng I says, "*Li*[b] is like a tree one hundred feet high, which constitutes one continuous whole from its roots to its branches and leaves."[86] And Chu Hsi, who speaks of "the thousand branches and myriad leaves of the principle of nature,"[87] describes the Great Ultimate as follows:

> The Great Ultimate is like a tree which in growing upward divides as branches, and divides again to produce flowers and leaves. Production of life without cease. When you get to the point of what is inside the fruit, there is both the principle of the production of life without cease, of life going forth, and also the limitless Great Ultimate, which is even more ceaseless.[88]

When localized in man, the metaphor of the plant explains man's mind, the repository of the life principle at the human level. Chu Hsi speaks of the mind as being like a seed of grain that contains the principle of life, *jen*.[89] This means that the mind is capable of going through a process of growth akin (though not identical) to that of a plant. Humaneness cosmically (the mind of heaven and earth) or in man's mind is associated with the four stages.[90] More specifically, it is identified with *yüan* (originating growth), or spring, the source of life and first stage in the cyclical process. In fact, in man's mind, humaneness in action is love that develops progressively from love of kin to love of other people to love of other things in the world.[91] This love grows out of the root or seed in man's mind, as do all of the other cardinal virtues of man. The metaphor of the root goes back to the first chapter of the *Analects*, where we learn that filiality is the root of humaneness. Chu Hsi had to explain this as meaning that filiality is the first behavioral step (root meaning "primary") in actually practicing humaneness to others. This is because his theory is that principle/humaneness/human nature is the immaterial structure (root meaning "nonempirical basis") from which *all* behavioral forms of love actualize.[92] Thus, humaneness is the root, filiality and brotherly love the sprouts, or principle is the root and love is the sprout, not vice versa.

To structure the mind by means of the plant analogy is to say that the mind's major active traits are vitality and affection. The European, accustomed to thinking of man as a rational animal and of the mind as a reasoning instrument, is bewildered by the metaphor of the seed of grain. It becomes intelligible to him if he understands that Ch'eng I and Chu Hsi were pointing up the dominance of nonrational traits in the mind: vitality and the expansive feeling of love. A trait from the affective side of the psyche constitutes the quintessentially human quality of mind in contrast to reason, which was assigned that role in Europe from Aristotle to Descartes.

Localized in the individual mind, the plant metaphor permits a resolution of the conflict of duties implied for man by the previous two theories and left unresolved in "The Western Inscription": isolated in his actual network with its role duties, the individual must still treat all other men as brothers.

The solution pertains to the expansive spatial capabilities (growth) of something that is basically private, subjective, and boundaried. Though locked in his network, the individual's *mind* need not be private and boundaried any more than the vital force need remain in its husk or root. The analogies provide a persuasive argument for mental expansiveness by structuring it as a known natural process: contained shell, emergence of life from within it, staged growth. The reader can thereby comprehend that through his mind he can go beyond the actual network bonds:

> Someone asked: "In the statement by one of the Ch'eng brothers, 'Man's mind should be alive, flowing everywhere without end and not located in just one spot,' how should we understand 'alive'?" Chu Hsi replied, "When the mind is unselfish, it can thrust out. Being alive is not being dead."[93]

That which is alive expands, as does the sprouting seed. If we identify love and life, we can think of love expanding. The analogy provides us the structure to think in these terms. In the end, we realize that the mind awaits only the proper nourishment or cultivation to grow. To grow outward, to thrust outward, means that the self expands, as the individual person embraces more and more people and things. He knows them (their principles) and loves them. Thus, they become part of him. The boundaries that limited him fall away as his mind "grows" or projects itself beyond his physical person to embody all those things beyond him. The boundaried self expands to be replaced by the expanded self.

The central problem in self-cultivation is not the proper exercise of free will, as is hypothesized in so much of Western ethics. Rather, it is how to remove obstacles that prevent the natural growth of the mind through principle; or how to remove obstacles that block the water (principle) from flowing forth, to use the previous metaphor, or that distort incoming impressions. This means that the problem is identifying and then removing selfish thoughts.

The four stages of growth solve the problem of preferential treatment for those in the immediate network. The initial sprouts are filial and brotherly affection within the family network, followed by growth in affection for other people and things.[94] The progressive outward extension of affection to others is as natural as the stages from seed to ripened ear of grain.

If one function of the sprout analogies is to suggest the mind's expansion capabilities, the other is to provide optimism and argument. The actual virtuous life is possible because it is a manifestation of a potentiality already there, as living seed or root: actual compassion derives from the innate principle of humaneness. And one should be compassionate, because that is fulfillment of something natural.

In addition to implying the mind's ability to expand through love to embrace gradually all things, the plant analogies suggest three other concrete ways in which the individual can "form one body," or participate in the cosmic family. He is in an endless life cycle, like a seed, and can produce offspring, just as he was produced from a prior seed. Next, if he attains an official position, he can nourish the minds of others through educational and economic policies. Finally, by unblocking the selfish thoughts that impede the flow of the vital forces through himself, he can unlock energy for the performance of all of these tasks. Thus, plant analogies are the source of concrete actions that make intelligible the theory of forming one body. By alerting us to the four paths just mentioned, they clarify the vague description in the *Doctrine of the Mean* to which the Sung writers refer in speaking of the individual who is able to effect this union: "Able to assist the transforming and nourishing powers of heaven and earth, he may with heaven and earth form a ternion."[95]

The plant metaphor places the individual in a context in which the idea is to transcend social role boundaries. Whereas in the theory illustrated by the family network the virtue of unselfish impartiality was equated with obedience to one's particular social roles, the plant metaphor requires a new definition of this virtue. In contrast to the meaning previously depicted, at the core of which is an acute sense of social place, we find impartiality described as the absence of such boundaried positions. Chang Tsai said, "Selfishness means being spatially bounded" (*wo yu fang yeh*, meaning that there are things outside the self).[96] Chu Hsi put it this way:

> The operation of the principle of the mind penetrates all. . . . If there is a single thing not yet entered, the reaching is not yet complete, and there are things not yet embraced. This shows that the mind still excludes something. For selfishness separates and obstructs, and consequently one and others stand in opposition.[97]

Selfishness is quite commonly described as the state in which the mind still has something outside itself (*hsin wei yu wai* or *yu wai chih hsin*).

This second kind of impartiality is a way of looking at the world and feeling about it. As described by our Sung writers, it blends into the picture of the indivisible water or moon. "Impartial [*kung*], then everything is one with myself. Selfish, then all things are different from each other."[98] For impartial persons, all things form one body.

Concretely, impartiality takes several different forms. One is compassion. "The way of humaneness is difficult to describe; only the word 'impartiality' comes close to it."[99] And: "The humane man regards heaven, earth, and all things as one body; there is nothing not himself."[100] Commentators treat the Mencian mind of commiseration as the mind that views all things as one body. Another form consists in knowing the principles of all things. The terms used for "to know" are revealing of the image: *t'i* (to embody) and *t'ung* (to penetrate).[101] Ch'eng I says, "When one has no selfish subjectivity, there will be no occasion when he is acted on in which he will not penetrate everything."[102] Commentators describe the mind that has embodied all things as "vastly impartial" (*ta kung*).[103] *Kung* itself is used to describe both impartial love, noted just above, and also impartial cognition: "Although one can *kung* all the affairs of the world, if one does it with selfish intentions, it is not *kung* at all."[104] Furthermore, the impartial person, empty of prejudice, is responsive to the influences of all things.

In sum, the metaphysical portrait anchored in the analogies of water and plants leads us to a conception of unselfish impartiality not as the disciplined assumption of social roles, but as the possession of an expanded mind that embraces emotionally and cognitively all things, an obvious goal for the person who realizes that all things form one body.[105] Obedience and the expression of differential emotions were the basis for participation in the network of relationships in the case of the family metaphor. Empathy and knowing are the basis in the latter two analogies.

In Chinese Buddhism, the difference between illusion and reality poses an important question. In post-Cartesian Western philosophy, the big question is the split between appearance and reality. The Cartesian problem rests on the assumption that the mind receives pictures of external objects that are subjective copies or representations of them: Do the mind pictures (how things appear to us) accurately copy reality? The Neo-Confucian cosmological view that we have just described points to neither of these as significant philosophical issues. Instead, it directs us to the difference between the partial (*p'ien*) and impartial perspective, partial and impartial knowledge, partial and impartial love. The correct course is to try continually to expand the perspective, knowledge, and love. Being impartial, one embraces all cognitively and affectively.

There is a remarkable convergence between the Neo-Confucian cosmological picture associated with the plant analogy and that which was dominant in Europe from the Greek age to the Renaissance. One form of classical Western organicism employed the analogy of the human organism to explain society and nature. A life force (*psyche* or soul) permeates nature, providing motion or life, which are identical. Mind gives order to the motions of the life force, serving as the source of the regular quantitative changes that make possible natural sciences. Plato described this world as "a living creature with soul and reason."[106] Life and mind exist in the organism and in nature. Occasionally, more complex correspondences appeared. Distinguishing in the organism and in society the head that rules and the body that obeys, John of Salisbury (twelfth century) spoke of the prince as head, the senate as heart, the soldiers and officials as hands, the financial officers as stomach, and the peasants as feet.[107]

But this is not the cosmological or sociological theory that reveals the dramatic convergence. That distinction belongs to Aristotle's theory, worked out in the *Physics*. It certainly overshadowed in influence any Platonic physics through the Middle Ages. Early in that work, Aristotle takes as his theme the "nature" (*phusis*) of things. He says, "For those things are natural which, by a continuous movement originated from an internal principle, arrive at some completion."[108] His account, he says, pertains to animals, plants, and the elements earth, air, fire, water, and their inorganic compounds. "Each of them," he says, "has within itself a principle of motion and of stationariness (in respect of place, or of growth and decrease, or by way of alteration."[109] We can refer to that principle of motion as the thing's nature as well. Motion is the fulfillment of what exists potentially, by which the thing's end, or form, is achieved. The key ideas in Aristotle's account of a thing's nature are: growth, internal principle of motion, teleology. The whole theory is inspired by the picture of something concrete that grows. In speculating about the underlying analogy, we have a choice of plants or living animals. The strongest case can be made that it was the latter, that is, living animals as things that move themselves and grow to a point of completion.[110] In the end, Christian theologians drew support for their ethical doctrines from the theory in much the same spirit as did the Neo-Confucians.

During the Renaissance, the organic analogy faded from cosmologies, to be replaced by the machine. However, many of the most influential theories of the state in nineteenth-century Germany drew on the human organism for explanation: the state possesses the attributes of human personality, or it goes through developmental ages akin to human life periods, or its beginnings and development are similar to the birth and developmental biology of the animal. Joseph von Görres and Karl Salomon Zacharia were influential in this approach.[111]

In France and England, the new nineteenth-century organicism had something of the character of a romantic reaction against the world and society as machine. Nor was it restricted to theories of the state. It differed from the classical organicisms in its rejection of two attributes of the earlier doctrines. It avoided claims about near identity between parts of the universe or society and parts of an animal organism and made no claims about an omnipresent vital force (Bergson is an exception).

In declaring these assumptions invalid, the new organicism pointed instead to three structural features of organisms that are present in society and/or nature. The first is the fact that the character of any part is determined by its relationships. The image is of integrated parts. Thus, the object of any study is the organizational relationships of parts, rather than the individual parts themselves. The organicist biologist Joseph Needham, in an article on the organicist philosopher Whitehead, wrote, "The fate of a given monad, protein molecule, atomic group, or what have you, in the original egg [under study by an embryologist] is a function of its position in the whole."[112] The second is the existence of envelopes in space. Different levels of organization occur, one within another. In the organism, the envelopes proceed from protons and electrons to atoms to molecules to cells to organs and tissues to functioning bodies; once again, the image of integration. The third is the existence of continuous, linear, ladderlike development leading to higher forms of organization. "Higher" is conceived descriptively, in the sense of increased complexity and interdependency of parts. It also indicates greater worth.[113] Steps on the ladder suggest stages of development. Organisms, societies, and nature progress up the ladder. The forms of existence are not static. The first two attributes owe much to Darwin, the third to the eighteenth-century fascination with progress, as popularized by Condorcet and others.

Ch'eng-Chu cosmology is partially organicistic, in some ways similar to the classical Western organicisms, though not to the nineteenth-century variety. Unlike Western organicism, it derives more from the plant metaphor than from the human organism. However, the analogy of a living plant is only one of three analogies that dominate the theories of nature. There is a danger in overstating the organicistic analogy and ignoring the others, among them, the family network and stream of water. Of course, sometimes we use the term organicist loosely to refer to the belief that the world consists of whole objects (including the world itself), the parts of which are so integrated that a part is only understandable in terms of its relation to other parts. If we use the term loosely, it becomes just a synonym for a holism.

We have separated out three different cosmological theories and their associated deep structural metaphors, but have left unexplored the mingling and interweaving of all three theories and their metaphors in the actual writings. In those texts, love flows forth as water from a spring into various ponds, as well as grows forth from a root. The exercise of this love enables the individual to fulfill his social roles. The mind of heaven and earth flows through all things, revealing itself in the growth of young sprout.

Conclusion

Our study of the three types of cosmological theory provides a response to the May Fourth Movement criticism from the perspective of one form of Confucianism. There is a side to Sung Neo-Confucian thought that supports confining the individual to rigid family and clan social roles. However, there is another side that emphasizes his obligations to all things, in some way equal in worth, beyond the family. The obligations may be fulfilled through expanding his concern mentally beyond the immediate social role situation. So there is a Confucian alternative to rigid social role constraint. But it is not the freedom from communal ties or cultivation of unique traits that the modern European individualist might expect. Rather, it is yet another kind of selflessness, in which the individual mentally transcends his tight little familial island and gradually yet simultaneously comes to know and empathize with an ever wider group of people and things. Selflessness as discipline is seen in the subordination of the individual's own immediately experienced desires or interests as he identifies with those of others.

Our three metaphors permit us to put the theories together and describe them pictorially, as the Sung thinkers did. One schema might depict the mind as a channel, through which flows a gaseous life force. In special forms, this force penetrates members of individual families and their ancestors. In a less specific form, it is all-pervasive. The life force flows through the channel unless obstacles block it, and that flow permits the mind to expand continually in stages. At the same time, the early growth of the mind is manifest in the warm feelings and energy needed for the proper fulfillment of routine familial and social roles. Later growth provides the feelings and energy by means of which the individual's mind embraces other people, birds, beasts, and plants.

In spite of their differences, the three theories explain things and persons relationally. A person is either the father of X, the older brother of Y, or the husband of Z, or he is an inseparable part of some whole such as the "one body" permeated by the life force. In this regard, the Sung Neo-Confucian portrait of man stands in dramatic contrast to the view of man associated with the new analogy of a social contract that began to dominate Western explanations of society in the seventeenth century. As one historian of the English Renaissance put it, "Society, in fact, was no longer conceived as an 'organism,' but as a joint stock company."[114] Unlike classical Western organicisms and Ch'eng-Chu relationalism, parties to contracts participate as equal, discrete individuals. They are not explained relationally. They have properties as individuals, not as occupants of social roles or as parts of a whole like a stream or a plant. Depending on the thinker, these properties are reason, desires, rights, capacities, or needs. Also in contrast to classical Western organicisms and Ch'eng-Chu portraits of the natural society is the premise in Western contract theory that the ruler is either an equal or a subordinate to the other contract participants, rather than their natural head. The society that emerges from their agreement is artificial, not natural.

The metaphors associated with the three holisms enrich our understanding of what a holism is. First, we have learned that a holistic theory describes in some way the relationships among multiple facts or objects: for example, one possible relationship is the natural integration or inseparability of parts, with a visual image of a commonplace physical object supposedly demonstrating the character of that integration. Second, each set of things to which a given theory applies has an autonomous existence that is different from that of its parts and from that of other wholes. We can picture each set of related parts or facts behaving in unique, predictable ways. Families and trees reproduce in predictable ways over time; their parts retain relationships of certain kinds. Streams move in ways we know and can predict and which we know are different from the movement of sheep. Objects to which the theories associated with those metaphors apply will behave together in some unique way.

The modern fate of these three holisms is a mixed bag. The "one in many" theories, resting respectively on the image of the stream and the plant root, found a modern custodian in Hsiung Shih-li (1885-1968). He both revitalized several of the traditional metaphors and added to them elements from the modern organicisms as reflected in the work of Henri Bergson. T'ang Chün-i (1909-78) inherited this legacy from Hsiung. The theory of natural boundaried positions, anchored in the metaphor of the family network, is extinct. In its place we have had new theories of human society and nature. They derive from Darwin, Condorcet, and Marx. Behind them lurks the image of the ladder. Rungs on the ladder. Stages of human development or natural evolution. Chinese Marxist writers have favored the term "heavenly ladder" (*t'ien t'i*) to describe social changes, such as the institution of communes that at one time were said to lead upward to a final utopia. But that is another story. The theories of the new age still ahead of us will employ new analogies, some of which we may be able to guess (the computer, which causes theories to use words like "feedback," "input," "programming," and "interface") and some of which we cannot even imagine.

NOTES

1. Chow Tse-tung, *The May Fourth Movement* (Cambridge: Harvard University Press, 1960), 302.
2. Heinrich Popitz, "The Concept of Social Role as an Element of Sociological Theory," in *Role*, ed. John A. Jackson, Sociological Studies no. 4 (Cambridge: Cambridge University Press, 1972), 17.
3. George Berkeley, "Three Dialogues," in *Essays, Principles, Dialogues*, ed. Mary W. Calkins (New York: Charles Scribner's Sons, 1929), 251-52.
4. S. M. Ulam, *Adventures of a Mathematician* (New York: Charles Scribner's Sons, 1976), 183.
5. Freeman Dyson, "Disturbing the Universe," *The New Yorker*, 13 August 1979, 69.
6. George Lakoff and Mark Johnson, "Conceptual Metaphor in Everyday Language," *The Journal of Philosophy* (August 1980), 77(8):455.
7. Robert Oppenheimer, "Analogy in Science," *American Psychologist* (1956), 2(3):127-35. Quoted in Donald A. Schon, *Displacement of Concepts* (London: Tavistock Publications, 1963), 39.
8. G. Polya, *How to Solve It* (Princeton: Princeton University Press, 1945), quoted in Schon, *Displacement of Concepts*, 38.
9. Rodney Needham, *Symbolic Classification* (Santa Monica: Goodyear, 1979), 63-64.
10. Translations of these four terms come from Derk Bodde. See Fung Yu-lan, *History of Chinese Philosophy*, trans. Derk Bodde, 2 vols. (Princeton: Princeton University Press, 1952), 2:636.
11. Joseph Needham, *Science and Civilisation in China*, 5 vols. to date (Cambridge: Cambridge University Press, 1956-), 2:474.

12. Ch'eng Hao and Ch'eng I, *Li hsü* [Preface on rites], in *Ho-nan Ch'eng shih i-wen* [Literary legacy of the two Ch'engs of Honan province], appended to the *Erh-Ch'eng ch'üan-shu* (SPPY ed.), 2.1b.

13. *Chu Tzu ch'üan-shu* [Complete works of Master Chu], facsimile reprint of the 1885 reissue of the 1715 ed., 2 vols. (Taipei: Kuang-hsüeh she, 1977), 46.15a-b (2:1022).

14. *Hsiao ching*, trans. Sister Mary Lelia Makra (New York: St. John's University Press, 1961), 31.

15. *Mencius*, 4A:5.

16. Hsieh Yü-wei, "Filial Piety and Chinese Society," in *Philosophy and Culture East and West*, ed. Charles A. Moore (Honolulu: University of Hawaii Press, 1962), 424.

17. Ch'eng I, *I chuan* [Commentary on the *Book of Changes*], in *Erh-Ch'eng ch'üan-shu*, 1.2b.

18. The *Shu ching* [Book of documents] contains the passage, "From Heaven are the social arrangements with their several duties" (*t'ien hsü yu tien*), and "From Heaven are the social distinctions with their several ceremonies" (*t'ien chih yu li*). See James Legge, trans., *The Chinese Classics*, 5 vols. (Hong Kong: Hong Kong University Press, 1960), vol. 3: *The Shoo King* or *The Book of Historical Documents*, "The Counsels of Kaou-Yaou," 3/3/6, 73. Chu Hsi quotes from the passage.

   The *Tso chuan* lists four ranks of rulers (king, duke, minister, and knight) and six of ruled in an apparent attempt to pair ten social positions with the ten time divisions of the day. See *Tso chuan*, Chao kung 7. Hsün Tzu analogized from the set of ritualized rules (*li*) that order a hierarchical society to the "rules" that account for orderly behavior by planets and rivers: "*Li* is that whereby Heaven and Earth unite, whereby the sun and moon are bright, whereby the four seasons are ordered, whereby the stars move in the courses, whereby rivers flow" (from Homer H. Dubs, trans., *The Works of Hsüntze* [London: Probsthain, 1928], 223.)

   By Han times we begin to find the analogy of social space with inviolable boundaries (i.e., social duties and rights exclusive for a given group) applied to the cosmos: "Each of the five elements circulates according to its sequence; each of them exercises its own capacities in the performance of its official duties. Thus wood occupies the eastern quarter where it rules over the forces of spring" (from Fung Yu-lan, *History of Chinese Philosophy*, 2:21). And: "The five fluids come forward in turn, each of them takes precedence once. When they do not keep to their proper sphere, there is disaster; when they do, everything is well ordered" (from the *Huang Ti nei ching su wen* [The Yellow Emperor's classic of internal medicine], quoted in Alfred Forke, *World Conception of the Chinese* [London: Probsthain, 1952], 252). The Taoist Hsi K'ang (223-262) differentiated his proper cosmic place from any Confucian social place, from which we know that social and cosmic place did not always overlap. See Richard B. Mather, "The Controversy over Conformity and Naturalness During the Six Dynasties," *Journal of the History of Religions*, 1969-70, 9(2-3):166, 168. Correspondences between man and nature in the Han period also derive from analogizing from the human organism, with its emotions and will, to heaven and nature.

19. Burton Watson, trans., *Han Fei-tzu* (New York: Columbia University Press, 1964), 35.

20. Ch'eng Hao and Ch'eng I, *I-shu* [Written legacy], in *Erh-Ch'eng ch'üan-shu* 1.2a.

21. Ibid., 4.4a.

22. *Chu Tzu ch'üan-shu* 60.14a-b (2:1312).

23. Ch'eng Hao and Ch'eng I, *I-shu* 14.2a.

24. Ibid., 18.1b.

25. Fung Yu-lan, "The Philosophy at the Basis of Traditional Chinese Society," in *Ideological Differences and World Order*, ed. Filmer S. C. Northrop (New Haven: Yale University Press, 1949), 26.

26. Chu Hsi, *Chu Tzu yü-lei t'a-ch'üan* [Complete edition of the classified conversations of Master Chu Hsi], ed. Li Ching-te (1270) (Kyōto Yamagataya Shoshi ed., 1668; reprint ed. in 8 vols., Kyoto: Chūbun Shoten, 1973), 3.16b (1:234) [3.13a; 1:135]. For purposes of cross reference, the page references in brackets following any citation from the *Chu Tzu yü-lei t'a-ch'üan* are to the corresponding passages in the *Chu Tzu yü-lei* (1473; reprint ed. in 8 vols., Taipei: Cheng-chung Shu-chü, 1962); the first set of numbers indicates the *chüan* and page; the second set gives the volume number and the consecutive pagination.

27. Ch'eng Hao and Ch'eng I, *Ts'ui-yen* [Pure words], in *Erh-Ch'eng ch'üan-shu*, 1.9a.
28. Ch'eng I, *I-chuan* 4.20b.
29. Chu Hsi, *Chu Tzu yü-lei t'a-ch'üan* 78.44b (5:4210) [78.35a; 5:3269].
30. *The I Ching or Book of Changes*, trans. Richard Wilhelm (English translation by Cary F. Baynes), 2 vols. (London: Routledge and Kegan Paul, Ltd., 1960), *Ken*, 2:303.
31. Ch'eng Hao and Ch'eng I, *Ts'ui-yen* 1.29a.
32. Ch'eng Hao and Ch'eng I, *I-shu* 6.3a.
33. Ch'eng I, *I chuan* 4.21a.
34. *Chu Tzu ch'üan-shu* 19.8b (1:413), 53.59a (2:1195). See also Ch'eng I, *I chuan*, pref., 1a.
35. Chu Hsi, *Chu Tzu yü-lei t'a-ch'üan* 52.31a (4:2675) [52.24b; 3:2058].
36. See n. 12 above.
37. Ch'eng Hao and Ch'eng I, *I-shu* 11.11b.
38. See the discussion and citations in Hou Wai-lu, *Chung-kuo ssu-hsiang t'ung-shih* [General history of Chinese thought], 4 vols. (Peking: Jen-min ch'u-pan she, 1963), 4B:607, 622.
39. *Chu Tzu ch'üan-shu* 46.13a (2:1021).
40. Ch'eng Hao and Ch'eng I, *Ts'ui-yen* 1.2a.
41. *Chu Tzu ch'üan-shu* 48.3b (2:1047).
42. Ch'eng Hao and Ch'eng I, *I-shu* 18.2a.
43. Ibid., 11.2a.
44. Ch'eng Hao and Ch'eng I, *Wai-shu* [Additional works], in *Erh-Ch'eng ch'üan-shu* 7.1a.
45. Ibid.
46. *Chu Tzu yü-lei t'a-ch'üan* 94.42b (6:4986) [94.33b; 6:3878].
47. Ibid., 2A.4b. See also Ch'eng Hao and Ch'eng I, *Ts'ui-yen* 1.21b.
48. Ch'eng Hao and Ch'eng I, *I-shu* 15.1b.
49. Ibid., 2A.16a.
50. Ibid., 17.2b.
51. *Chu Tzu ch'üan-shu* 7.29a-29b (1:169).
52. Ch'eng Hao and Ch'eng I, *I-shu* 2A.13a.
53. Ibid., 14.2a.
54. W. T. Chan, "The Neo-Confucian Concept of *Li* as Principle," *Tsing-hua Journal of Chinese Studies* (February 1964), 4(2):134.
55. *Philebus* 15b, in *The Collected Dialogues of Plato*, ed. Edith Hamilton and Huntington Cairns (New York: Bollingen, 1961), 1091.
56. *Chu Tzu ch'üan-shu* 52.37b (2:1154), 49.10b (2:1066).
57. Étienne LaMotte, *La Somme du Grand Véhicule d'Asanga Mahāyānasamgraha* (Louvain: Institut Orientaliste Louvain-La-Neuve, 1973), 124. I am indebted to Luis Gómez of the University of Michigan, for references to the Buddhist sources.
58. Edward Conze, ed., *Buddhist Texts Through the Ages* (New York: Philosophical Library, 1954), 214.
59. From a work attributed to a monk who was possibly a T'ien T'ai master before becoming a Ch'an master. Takakusu Junjiro and Watanabe Kaikyoku, eds., *Taishō Shinshū Daizōkyō*, 85 vols. (Tokyo: The Taishō Shinshū Daizōkyō kanko kai, 1927; reprint, 1968), work no. 207b, vol. 50, 460c, lines 13-15. Luis Gómez assisted me with this translation. For a similar T'ien T'ai reference, see also work no. 1509, vol. 25, 101b, 102b.
60. This metaphor can be found in the early classical texts, where it usually explains three theoretical claims: the course of natural changes moves ceaselessly on, like water gushing from a spring (*Analects*, 9:16); some behavior is natural or spontaneous to man, like his attraction to a virtuous model, and cannot be stopped any more than the downward flow of water (*Mencius*, 4B:18); and the mind can be kept clear, so as to determine right and wrong correctly, like water in a pan that remains undisturbed by externals (*Hsün Tzu*, "Chieh pi" [Removing becloudings]). Some of these meanings appear later.

The new function of the metaphor, to illustrate the implications of the one-many relationship, appears prominently first in Chinese Buddhist texts such as those of the Hua-yen school. Fa-tsang (643-712) has a theory to the effect that we can distinguish between li^b principle, or the "realm of principle" (*li fa chieh*), which cannot be divided, and phenomena (*shih*) which are divisible and individuated. The former, the *dharmatā*, is "what is depended on" and the latter "that which depends" or arises through causation. Water explains what "dependency" might mean, conveying a sense of something underlying something else— the *dharmatā* is the ocean and the events and things of the world are waves: "The leaping waves of the phenomenal world, boiling as in a cauldron, are the functioning of the complete and genuine substance" (Fung Yu-lan, *History of Chinese Philosophy*, 2:348). Writers in the Yogācara school use water to explain the unclear mind (which is likened to muddy water) and the uninterrupted presence of the *ālaya* consciousness in cause-effect sequences (onward flow of the torrent, though whipped by the wind into waves). See Daisetz T. Suzuki, trans., *The Laṅkāvatāra-sūtra* (London: Routledge and Kegan Paul, Ltd., 1973), 190; and Alex Wayman, "The Mirror as a Pan-Buddhist Metaphor-Simile," *History of Religions* (May 1974), 13(4):255. Chu Hsi refers to the Buddhist use of the latter of these two; see *Chu Tzu ch'üan-shu* 44.9a (2:991). Water also suggests pure consciousness or the Buddha nature, and ice, or the reflections in it, suggests illusion, or conceptual thought; Hou Wai-lu, *Chung-kuo ssu-hsiang*, 4A:558.

61. Chu Hsi, *Chu Tzu yü-lei t'a-ch'üan* 18.10b-11a (2:952-53) [18.8b; 2:700]. Chu Hsi regularly speaks of the *Tao-li* (natural principles) flowing forth everywhere.

62. *Chu Tzu ch'üan-shu* 52.25a (2:1148).

63. On the flow of the material force through man, see Chu Hsi, *Chu Tzu yü-lei ta-chüan* 4.22b (1:296) [4.17b; 1:82].

64. Ibid., 3.16a (1:233) [3.12b; 1:134]. *Chu Tzu yü-lei t'a-ch'üan* 4.22b (1:296) [4.17b; 1:182].

65. Ibid., 3.17a (1:235) [3.13a; 1:135]. Sung Neo-Confucians also use the Buddhist analogy of water and ice. In Buddhism, ice suggests illusion temporarily clouding a Buddha nature that is universal and clear, as is the ocean water in its unfrozen state. See Hou Wai-lu, *Chung-kuo ssu-hsiang* 4A:268.

66. *Chu Tzu ch'üan-shu* 44.9b (2:991).

67. Chu Hsi, *Chu Tzu yü-lei t'a-ch'üan* 4.12b (1:276) [4.10a; 1:167]. See also *Chu Tzu ch'üan-shu* 44.14a (2:994).

68. Chu Hsi, *Chu Tzu yü-lei t'a-ch'üan* 4.19a (1:289) [4.14b-15a; 1:176-77].

69. Ibid., 95.43b (6:5068) [95.34a-b; 6:3957-58].

70. Ibid., 27.20b (2:1540) [27.15a-b; 2:1161-62].

71. Ibid., 20.18b (2:1088) [20.14b; 2:806].

72. Ibid., 4.3b (1:258) [4.2a; 1:51].

73. Ch'eng Hao and Ch'eng I, *I-shu* 15.1b.

74. Ibid., 18.32b.

75. *Chu Tzu ch'üan-shu* 49.23b (2:1072).

76. Ibid., 44.7a (2:990).

77. Ibid., 47.1b (2:1026).

78. Ibid., 46.13b (2:1021).

79. Ch'eng Hao and Ch'eng I, *I-shu* 2A.3a.

80. Ch'eng Hao and Ch'eng I, *Ts'ui-yen* 1.7b.

81. Professor Yü Ying-shih brought this to my attention. As Kristofer Schipper has shown, figures associated with the Heavenly Masters movement of the late second century A.D. linked the three parts of the body (head, chest, belly) with the Three Masters who should rule a social movement and with the three Heavens with their three ethers that rule the universe. A Taoist-influenced T'ang medical text states, "The heart has the function of ruler and the lungs are the transmitting officers giving forth regulations; the liver is the general devising strategems." See Kristofer Schipper, "The Taoist Body," *History of Religions* (February-May 1948), 17(3-4):355-81.

82. Yung Sik Kim, "The World View of Chu Hsi (1130-1200): Knowledge About the Natural World in *Chu Tzu ch'üan-shu*" (Ph.D. diss., Princeton University, 1979), 281-82. The first quotation is from *Chu Tzu ch'üan-shu* 23.2a (1:508); the second is from the same work, 29.4a (1:641).

83. Wing-tsit Chan, trans., *Reflections on Things at Hand* (New York: Columbia University Press, 1967), 77, 284.

84. Chu Hsi, *Chu Tzu yü-lei t'a-ch'üan* 68.7a (5:3549) [68.6b; 5:2748].

85. *Chu Tzu ch'üan-shu* 52.19b (2:1145).

86. Ch'eng Hao and Ch'eng I, *I-shu* 15.8a.

87. Chu Hsi, *Chu Tzu yü-lei t'a-ch'üan* 20.18a (2:1087) [20.14b; 2:806].

88. Ibid., 75.20b-21a (5:4032-33) [75.18b; 5:3130].

89. *Chu Tzu ch'üan-shu* 44.7b (2:990).

90. *Chu Tzu yü-lei t'a-ch'üan* 20.20a-b (2:1091-92) [20.16a; 2:809].

91. Ibid., 20.29a (2:1109) [20.23a; 2:823].

92. Ibid., 20.17a (2:1085) [20.13b; 2:804].

93. *Chu Tzu ch'üan-shu* 44.9b (2:991).

94. *Chu Tzu yü-lei t'a-ch'üan* 20.17a-20a (2:1085-91) [20.13b-16a; 2:804-9].

95. *Doctrine of the Mean*, sec. 22.

96. Chan, *Reflections on Things at Hand*, 71.

97. Ibid., 75. The passage is from the *Chu Tzu yü-lei t'a-ch'üan* 98.12b-13a (7:5214) [98.11a; 6:4059]. The context is a passage from a work of Chang Tsai.

98. Ch'eng Hao and Ch'eng I, *I-shu* 15.1b.

99. Ch'eng Hao and Ch'eng I, *Ts'ui-yen* 1.2b.

100. Ibid., 1.7b.

101. *Chu Tzu ch'üan-shu* 44.12b (2:993).

102. Chan, *Reflections on Things at Hand*, 45.

103. Chu Hsi and Lü Tsu-ch'ien, *Chin ssu-lu*, [Reflections on things at hand], ed. Chang Po-shing (1651-1725) (Taipei: Shih-chieh Shu-chü, 1967), 2.71.

104. Ch'eng Hao and Ch'eng I, *Ts'ui-yen* 1.38a.

105. *Chu Tzu ch'üan-shu* has an excellent example of this kind of selflessness (44.11b) [2:992].

106. Francis M. Cornford, *Plato's Timaeus* (New York: Library of Liberal Arts, 1959), 30a, 20.

107. David G. Hale, *The Body Politic* (The Hague: Mouton, 1971), 39.

108. *Physics* 199b, in *The Basic Works of Aristotle*, ed. Richard McKeon (New York: Random House, 1941), 251.

109. *Physics* 192b, in ibid., 236.

110. In discussing the difference between natural and manufactured objects, Aristotle focuses on the fact that the former initiate motion from within. He is able to defend this thesis so long as he is talking about animals but not when he is talking about inanimate things. For a brief account of the influence of the analogy of living animals on Aristotle's physics, see Bertrand Russell, *A History of Western Philosophy* (New York: Simon and Schuster, 1945), chap. 23.

111. Francis William Coker, *Organismic Theories of the State* (New York: Columbia University Press, 1910).

112. Joseph Needham, "A Biologist's View of Whitehead's Philosophy," in *The Philosophy of Alfred North Whitehead*, ed. Paul A. Schilpp (La Salle, Ill.: Open Court, 1971), 261.

113. Robin G. Collingwood, *The Idea of Nature* (Oxford: Oxford University Press, 1945), 135.

114. Vivian de S. Pinto, *The English Renaissance: 1510-1688* (London: Cresset P., 1966), quoted in Hale, *The Body Politic*, 13.

Glossary

Ch'an 禪

Chang Po-hsing 張伯行

Chang Tsai 張載

Chao kung 昭公

cheng 貞

ch'eng 誠

Ch'eng Hao 程顥

Ch'eng I 程頤

ch'i[a] 氣

ch'i[b] 器

ch'i chih chih hsing 氣質之性

ch'ien 乾

Chin ssu-lu 近思錄

ching 敬

Chu Hsi 朱熹

chu tsai 主宰

Chu Tzu ch'üan-shu 朱子全書

Chu Tzu yü-lei 朱子語類

Chu Tzu yü-lei ta-ch'üan 朱子語類大全

chung 忠

Chung-Kuo ssu-hsiang t'ung-shih 中國思想通史

Erh-Ch'eng ch'üan-shu 二程全書

Fa-tsang 法藏

fen 分

Han Fei-tzu 韓非子

heng 亨

Ho-nan Ch'eng shih i-wen 河南程氏遺文

Hou Wai-lu 侯外廬

Hsi K'ang 嵇康

Hsi-ming 西銘

Hsiao ching 孝經

hsin wei yu wai 心爲有外

hsing 性

Hsiung Shih-li 熊十力

Hsün Tzu 荀子

Hua-yen 華嚴

Huang Ti nei ching su wen 黃帝內經素問

i 義

I ching 易經

I chuan 易傳

I-shu 遺書

jen 仁

jen fen   人分

jen lun   人倫

kang   綱

ke an ch'i fen   各安其分

ke tang ch'i fen; ke te ch'i fen
各當其分; 各得其分

ken   艮

k'un   坤

kung   公

kung hsin   公心

li[a]   禮

li[b]   理

li[c]   利

Li Ching-te   黎靖德

li fa chieh   理法界

Li hsü   禮序

li-i fen-shu   理一分殊

Lü Tsu-ch'ien   呂祖謙

ming   命

p'ien   偏

shih   事

Shih chi   史記

shu   恕

Shu ching   書經

so   所

szu   私

szu yü   私欲

ta kung   大公

ta t'ou-nao   大頭腦

T'ai-chi   太極

Taishō Sinshū Daizōkyō   大正新修
大藏經

Takakusu Junjirō   高楠順次郎

T'ang Chün-i   唐君毅

tao-li   道理

Tao Sheng   道生

t'i   體

ti-mai   地脈

t'ien   天

t'ien chih yu li   天秩有禮

t'ien fen   天分

t'ien hsü   天敍

t'ien hsü yu tien   天敍有典

t'ien li   天理

T'ien-t'ai   天台

t'ien t'i   天梯

tsai   宰

Tso chuan   左傳

Ts'ui-yen 粹言

t'ung 通

Wai-shu 外書

Wang Pi 王弼

Watanabe Kaikyoku 渡邊海旭

wei 位

wo yu fang yeh 我有方也

wu 物

wu szu yü 無私欲

wu wo 無我

yu wai chih hsin 有外之心

yüan 元

On the Matter of the Mind: The Metaphysical Basis of the Expanded Self

Irene Bloom

> Without the mind of heaven and earth to produce things, there would not be this body of mine. Only when there is this body of blood-and-*ch'i* is the mind of heaven and earth to produce things made complete.
>
> Chu Hsi

Introduction

It has been suggested that the Western idea of the person derives from two sources, the theater and law: both the *dramatis personae* of the stage and the possessors of legal rights and liabilities in Roman law were agents of choice. A signal contribution of Christianity, in this view, was to bring together these two concepts and to extend the attribution of personhood to every human being:

> In fusing the legal and dramatic concepts of a person, Christianity made every human being with a will, qualify as a person, in order to make them all equally qualified to receive divine judgment. With this introduction of a conception of unitary and equal persons, Christianity at one stroke changed both the rule of law and the idea of persons.[1]

In Christian thought, the will—and, crucially, a free will—was to assume importance as the unifying center of the person:

> Because persons are primarily agents of principle, their integrity requires freedom; because they are judged liable, their powers must be autonomous. But when this criterion for personhood is carried to its logical extreme, the scope of agency moves inward, away from social dramas, to the choices of the soul, or to the operations of the mind. What, after all, is it that is ultimately responsible, but only the will? It is the will that chooses motives, that accepts or rejects desires, principles. To the extent that such activities of the soul or the mind must remain autonomous, unconditioned, free, they are in principle indifferent not only to social class but to physical presence. To find the primary, uncaused cause of action—where that action is to be judged eternally liable—is to look for a simplicity and unity that is its own agency. The shadow of disembodiment that was implicit in the idea of a legal person moves forward, stands stage center: we have a person who is a pure *res cogitans* (or, in the religious versions, one that can survive death).[2]

While the dualism of soul and body, of a rational and appetitive nature, had been established in Western thought since Plato, it was in the later Christian context that the mind/body dualism became bound up with problems of individuation. Souls that are equal in the eyes of God become the theologically, morally, and psychologically significant part of persons and the capacity for choice the determinant of a unique personal identity. In the later history of the individual in the West, at the point when it becomes relevant to speak of "individualism," this capacity for autonomous choice and action—which necessarily rests with the conscious mind as distinct from (and not infrequently at odds with) the physical body—remains fundamental and, if anything, assumes even greater importance.[3]

In classical China, where persons were characteristically defined in terms of biological inheritance, identities and roles were not chosen but received along with the gift of life itself. This biological conception of the person no doubt owed much to the social and psychological pattern known as familism which, while drawing on very ancient pre-Confucian sources, became an essential part of the evolving Confucian value system. Early Confucian sources suggest that the person was conceived in the first instance as the flesh-and-blood (more literally, the blood-and-*ch'i*) product of his parents' procreation, and his body was regarded as the original source of his integrity, his essential inheritance from those who gave him life. Perhaps because a person was seen as existing in primary relation to his immediate forebears, and through them and their progenitors in turn to heaven or nature, rather than in direct relation to God as the creator of individual human lives, natural and repeatable patterns of human relatedness were emphasized rather than the unique career of an individual soul.

A person is born a son or a daughter, may be or become a brother or a sister, and in the natural course of human events will become a father or mother of children and a friend to other persons. Some men, albeit relatively few, become ministers to the sovereign. While, logically, only the first two relations are strictly involuntary, psychologically, only the last—the relation between minister and sovereign—is in the strictest sense voluntary. Even here, the choice which attracts greater notice is not that of serving but of declining to serve, precisely because it entails withdrawal from one of the primary human relationships and thus must be explained or justified, usually in terms of some moral failing on the part of the ruler.[4]

The fact that individuals are represented in the Confucian setting as part of a relationship also profoundly conditions the way moral responsibility is construed. That Confucius could respond to a question from Duke Ching of Ch'i concerning proper government by saying, "The ruler is ruler, the minister is minister, the father is father, and the son is son,"[5] obviously suggests both a degree of prior consensus about the moral and behavioral implications of these roles and a tendency for ethical thought to focus on the ways in which fundamental human relationships are understood and enacted. Considering what is known of the tenor of life during the time of Confucius, the buffeting which he apparently experienced in his own life, and the divergent standards adopted by contending schools of thought, it is remarkable how muted are any hints of moral ambiguity in the *Analects*. The clarity and resolution brought to bear by Confucius on moral problems, his secure sense of what the issues were and how they were to be determined, must certainly have owed something to the fact that he could find a high degree of stability attaching to particular human relationships and to the identities that derived from those relationships.[6]

Compare Plato and Confucius on similar cases. It would appear that in the evolution of the Chinese ethical tradition, as of the Greek, there must at some stage have been ambivalence over how to weigh competing claims in the agonizing situation that arises when filial devotion conflicts with public responsibility. That human dilemma is perhaps too fundamental ever to be decisively resolved in any society, though the way the problem is framed in philosophical and literary contexts is, of course, revealing. The dialogue of Plato's *Euthyphro* opens as Euthyphro, standing both within and without the relationship of son to father, prepares to prosecute his father for murder. Socrates, who professes surprise at the strength of Euthyphro's determination in the matter, presses him to support his contention that he has reliable knowledge of what is holy and unholy, pleasing and displeasing to the gods. Euthyphro's defense is found wanting, and Socrates remains skeptical, but the case clearly involves the broader issue of justice and its relation to holiness, which at the close of the dialogue remains significantly unresolved, open for further deliberation.[7]

No such ambiguity remains following Confucius's rejoinder to the Duke of She concerning the man praised by the duke as "Upright Kung" because he bore witness against his father for stealing a sheep: "Among us, in our part of the country, those who are upright are different from this. The father shields the son, and the son shields the father. Uprightness is to be found in this."[8] The fact that this exchange is recorded in the *Analects* implies that the moral responsibility of a son toward a father must have been an open issue in the time of Confucius and, given the strength of Legalism in succeeding centuries, it must have remained a live issue long after that. But, unlike Plato's Socrates, who reaches no firm conclusion about what constitutes appropriate behavior for a son when his father has committed a crime, Confucius for his part returns without hesitation to the primacy of the relationship between father and son. In the later Confucian context this relationship would always be primary and, in conventional morality, usually determinative, a characteristic disposition that may conceivably have precluded for many centuries the emergence of a more abstract concept of justice. Equally important, with time the relationship, more than simply governing the duties and obligations inherent in the human encounters that flowed from it, so thoroughly penetrated the identity of the person that alternative definitions came to appear false and unnatural.

If the idea of the person as an agent of choice was indeed from quite an early period a dominant concept in the West, but not in China, where biological and familial ties provided the enduring metaphors, what inferences may be drawn concerning the philosophical and religious understanding of man in China as contrasted with the West? Mindful of the considerable risks that attend any cross-cultural comparisons, which often obscure more than they illumine because they reflect insufficiently the variety and complexity that characterize any major tradition, I should like nonetheless to hazard the following generalization concerning eschatology and the metaphysics of the person in the Western Christian as contrasted with the Confucian tradition.

As has already been suggested, the liability of the person to divine judgment and the prospect of eternal bliss or damnation based on this final judgment is a central theme in Western Christian thought. When it comes to the ultimate determination of eternal reward or punishment, it is the irreducible core of the individual, his conscious self, that must be held accountable, for one is considered liable for what one has done consciously and voluntarily. It was on the basis of a long tradition of this kind that John Locke in *An Essay Concerning Human Understanding* would define the person as "a forensic term, appropriating actions and their merit,"[9] specify consciousness as the criterion for personal identity, and represent the overriding issue involved in the problem of identity and diversity as the responsibility held by persons, individually, for determining their own spiritual destiny.[10]

In classical Confucianism, the bodily and ultimately perishable aspect of the human being was, to my knowledge, never excluded as part of the definition of the person, nor was the career of a discrete individual soul ever projected as a journey into eternity. Rather than seeing the person in terms of liability and reward, considerations of urgent consequence to the individual who would ultimately depart from the world alone, having created his own destiny, Confucians typically saw the person in terms of creativity and communication, capacities which disposed him to form part of a nexus. Important to the definition of the person are the biological continuity of life, the maintenance of distinctively human modes of interaction and relatedness, and temporary but nonetheless meaningful participation in the ongoing processes of life as a whole. Viewed in a temporal framework, the career of the self is not infinitely extended, though, given the importance attached to biological and psychological relatedness, its metaphysical basis is significantly expanded. What follows represents an attempt to explain more fully what is intended by this statement.

Confucius and Mencius on the Mind

In his brief but richly provocative essay, *Confucius—the Secular as Sacred*, Herbert Fingarette has suggested that the Confucius of the *Analects*

> does not elaborate the language of choice and responsibility as these are
> intimately intertwined with the idea of the ontologically ultimate power of
> the individual to select from genuine alternatives to create his own
> spiritual destiny, and with the related ideas of spiritual guilt, and
> repentance and retribution for such guilt.[11]

In Fingarette's view, the absence of any disposition on the part of Confucius to focus on the element of choice is interpretable in terms of a remoteness from the psychological modes of understanding associated in the West with concern for "an inner core of one's being, 'the self.'"[12] Rather, the Confucian commitment is to something with deep roots in the common ground of a still fertile antiquity, to "traditionally ceremonially defined social comportment," that is, to li^a, "ritual."[13] Seeing the notion of choice as part of a complex of ideas which includes moral responsibility, guilt, retributive punishment, and repentance, Fingarette contends that the entire complex is missing from the moral reflections of Confucius.

Fingarette suggests, as have some previous writers on the subject, a distinction between a Western concept of guilt, in which the object of guilt is oneself, and a Chinese concept of shame, which, having a more external referent, is "an attack upon some specific action or outer condition."[14] He continues,

> Although the opportunity for explicitly and richly elaborating the notion of choice is latent in the central imagery of the Path [i.e., the Tao], that opportunity is with remarkable thoroughness ignored. And, although there are isolated references to a moral illness, self-accusations, and inner examination—each potentially so fertile and apt for use by one concerned with responsibility, guilt, and repentance—none of these is developed or in any way further remarked upon by Confucius.... [A]lthough there is more frequent and systematic reference to shame, this is associated with specific external possessions, conduct or status; it is a moral sentiment focused upon one's status and conduct in relation to the world rather than an inward charge against one's stained, corrupt self. The absence of the choice-responsibility-guilt complex of concepts, taken in textual context, warrants the inference in connection with such an insightful philosopher of human nature and morality, that the concepts in question and their related imagery, were not rejected by Confucius but rather were simply not present in his thinking at all.[15]

The conclusion is that, for Confucius, "Man is not an ultimately autonomous being who has an inner and decisive power, intrinsic to him, a power to select among real alternatives and thereby to shape a life for himself. Instead he is born as 'raw material' who must be civilized by education and thus become a truly human man."[16]

The argument here is intriguing, in part convincing, and yet, I believe, in at least one crucial respect problematic. The difficulty lies in the recurrent suggestion that the apparent absence in Confucian thought of a developed concern with the inward life explains the disinterest of Confucius in the matter of choice. Such a view seems to emerge from a comparison with Western thought which, when seen in historical perspective, is of doubtful validity. To compare, for example, Augustine's agony over the "disease of my soul" with Confucius's lament over the moral insensibility of Tsai Yü, whom he likens to rotton wood which cannot be carved or a wall of dried dung which cannot be trowelled,[17] is, of course, to juxtapose two very different metaphors for moral failing. As Fingarette perceives it,

> Here [with Tsai Yü] the active disease, the fulminating world of Augustine, is replaced by a state of moral deadness, of passivity and inherent insensitivity to moral values. Tsai Yü is at the utmost stage of the loss of capacity to be a moral human being. But in Augustine's imagery, the intensity and dynamism of the corrupting guilt are the measure of the vitality of his moral concern and of his imminent conversion.[18]

Leaving aside the question of whether the brevity of Confucius's remark about Tsai Yü allows the secure conclusion that he is "at the utmost stage of the loss of capacity to be a moral human being," what is omitted from consideration here is the historical perspective. Quite apart from the admittedly great cultural divide between them, Confucius and Augustine are separated by some nine centuries. Part of the originality of Augustine, who has been described as "the first Christian philosopher,"[19] and "the first philosopher of the Will,"[20] was, as Hannah Arendt has observed, that the inspiration he drew from Latin sources so profoundly and enduringly informed his Christian reflections. If we acknowledge that the starting point of Augustine's philosophical development was a highly pragmatic Roman and Stoic quest for private happiness,[21] then the depth of his concern with the interior life should be understood neither as an expression of a continuous feature of Western thought nor as a departure from earlier tendencies, but as the result of a confluence in the mind of an extraordinarily creative thinker of strands which had earlier been distinct, leading to a development fresh with him and fraught with significance for the later history of Christian thought:

> We find this pragmatic concern for private happiness throughout the Middle Ages; it underlies the hope for eternal salvation and the fear of eternal damnation and clarifies many otherwise abstruse speculations whose Roman origins are otherwise difficult to detect. That the Roman Catholic Church, despite the decisive influx of Greek philosophy, remained so profoundly Roman was due in no small measure to the strange coincidence that her first and most influential philosopher should also have been the first man of thought to draw his deepest inspiration from Latin sources and experiences. In Augustine, the striving for eternal life as the *summum bonum* and the interpretation of eternal death as the *summum malum* reached the highest level of articulation because he combined them with the new era's discovery of an *inward* life. He understood that the exclusive interest in this inner self meant that "I have become a question for myself" (*"quaestio mihi factus sum"*)—a question that philosophy as it was then taught and learned neither raised nor answered.[22]

In the case of Augustine, this discovery of the inward life and depth of interest in the inner self were bound up with an inclination to raise questions about the self and the nature of mind that is not found with comparable intensity in any previous thinker.

The point to be made here is that "the idea of the ontologically ultimate power of the individual to select from genuine alternatives to create his own spiritual destiny" is a relatively late development in the West. Though Fingarette in his discussion of the matter of choice does not explicitly delve into the Confucian concept of the will, this is clearly what is at issue here.

When he speaks of a view of man as "an ultimately autonomous being who has an inner and decisive power... to select among real alternatives," it is apparently not a Greek or a Roman but a later Christian concept of the will that he had in mind as a basis for comparison, such an idea having been unknown to Plato or Aristotle, the Stoics, or even to the early Christians.[23] Instead of viewing the Confucian commitment to ritual practice as an alternative to interest in or exploration of an interior life, which is the underlying interpretive theme of Fingarette's essay, it may be more appropriate to approach the problem historically. This would involve the recognition that the concern with an interior life developed in China, as in the West, over time and in the course of sustained reflections on the nature of man and his relation to the infinite. In the West the confluence of two traditions, Latin and Christian, appears to have been decisive. Similarly, in China the most searching questions concerning the nature of the mind emerged from the conflict and interaction between Confucianism and Buddhism which culminated during the eleventh and twelfth centuries in the Neo-Confucian tradition.

All of this is not intended to question the cogency of Fingarette's observation concerning the absence of a developed imagery of choice in the *Analects*, but rather to suggest that choice is not only and necessarily to be viewed as part of the complex of ideas which involves moral responsibility, guilt, retributive punishment, and repentance, as it is at the point when we encounter the Augustinian notion of *liberum arbitrium*, or free will. Obviously, all human beings make choices of varying degrees of moral and practical significance all the time, with some degree of self-consciousness. What is variable among individuals, living in the presence of a variety of religious and philosophical traditions and in the context of different cultures, is the way choices are perceived: which situations are viewed as morally problematic, which options present themselves for serious consideration, what immediate or ultimate criteria are adduced—or simply felt—as applicable to any given instance, what degree of emotional intensity or anguish is invested in the choice. With the example of Augustine in mind, one is prompted to speculate that the greater the degree of conflict perceived within the individual—for example, as between mind and body, reason and desires, a purer or baser self—or the greater the distance between the individual and infinite, the greater the drama that is likely to attend the problem of choice.[24] It may not be overbold to suggest that in the Confucian setting these conflicts are minimal and the distances less than formidable.

Perhaps the most striking contrast between concepts of the person in classical China and the West is found in the fact that, unlike either their Greek contemporaries or later Christian thinkers, early Confucians showed little inclination to counterpose mind and body (still less, soul and body) as competing contenders for mastery of the person whose identity they comprise. The very conception of *hsin*[a] as mind-and-heart, the seat of the affections (*ch'ing*) as well as of thought or reflective consciousness (*ssu*), had

associations which were visceral rather than cerebral. Such a conceptualization was in itself conducive to (or reflective of) a holistic rather than a dualistic
understanding of the person. Nor was there in the thought of Confucius or
Mencius a sharp conflict between a rational faculty and the desires or
passions. Whereas Aristotle in the *Eudemian Ethics* introduced the notion of
προαίρεόις, or purposive choice, to reconcile the antagonistic elements of
reason and desire,[25] Mencius appears to have been conscious of no such
conflict. At only one point in the *Mencius* is there reference to a need to
restrain the desires, and here Mencius says simply:

> To nourish the mind there is nothing better than to make the desires few.
> Here is a man whose desires are few: in some things he may not be able to
> keep his heart [or mind], but they will be few. Here is a man whose desires
> are many: in some things he may be able to keep his heart [or mind], but
> they will be few.[26]

Unlike Aristotle, who, perceiving a tension between a rational faculty and the
desires, thinks in terms of a faculty of choice which can make judgments as to
the appropriate means toward the end of happiness, Mencius perceives a need
for concentration or purification of the mind so as to preserve it (*ts'un*). The
desires are inimical to reason, or to balance, not by their nature, but only by
their number: the primary problem is to avoid distraction of the mind and an
attendant loss of direction and purpose.

   This may afford some explanation for the fact that, characteristically, in
the *Mencius*, as in the *Analects*, the term *chih*[a], or will, has the sense of
resolve, purpose, or determination. Confucius refers to setting the will on
learning,[27] on humaneness,[28] on the Tao,[29] and to "learning extensively and
having a sincere will" (*po-hsüeh erh tu-chih*).[30] Mencius speaks of setting the
will on humaneness[31] and on the Tao[32] and of "establishing the will" (*li-
chih*).[33] It is possible to "focus the mind and apply the will" (*chuan-hsin chih-
chih*) to the mastery of an art such as playing chess.[34] Frequently, one realizes
(or does *not* realize) his will, or, perhaps more aptly, his intention or ambition
(*te-chih*).[35] That the will has little to do with choice and much to do with
resolve, commitment, or determination is evident from what may happen to it
in the course of interaction between the self and others. As Confucius
observes, the will of even a common man cannot be taken away from him,[36]
yet the will of a worthy man may under certain circumstances be
surrendered.[37] King Hsüan of Ch'i asks Mencius to "assist" his will,[38] and the
concern of a man of culture is, according to Mencius, to "exalt his will."[39]

   Choices must, of course, be made, but they tend on the whole not to be
dramatized. When Mencius is challenged with the suggestion of an apparent
conflict between ritual practice and practical necessity—i.e., between the
ritual that requires that males and females not allow their hands to touch in
giving or receiving anything and a man's need to use his hand to save his
drowning sister-in-law—there is no need to agonize over the decision.[40]
Naturally, a sister-in-law in danger of drowning must be rescued, just as a
child teetering on the edge of a well must be pulled to safety, and for the same
psychomoral reasons. Here Mencius characterizes the situation as one in
which *ch'üan*, or in Legge's translation, "peculiar exigency" is involved. There

is no way that a ritual, properly understood, can outweigh the natural and appropriate dictates of the human mind/ heart. Like *ching*[a] (enduring or pervading principles), *li*[a] can at most provide a general model or form which will require adaptation according to given circumstances. But when his adversary taxes Mencius with the analogy of an entire world that is drowning ("The whole kingdom is drowning. How strange that you will not rescue it!"), Mencius insists on the need to rescue the world not by morally unconventional means but on the basis of the Tao.[41]

Neither *li*[a] nor *ching*[a], both of which are bound up with human forms and creations,[42] have anything like the weight or authority of the omniscient, omnipotent, and transcendent Judeo-Christian God whose will may represent a powerful counterforce to the human will. The issue of divine versus human authority does not arise. It is almost inconceivable that in the Confucian setting an individual could be confronted with so terrible a dilemma as that of Abraham when he is called upon by God to sacrifice Isaac, his only son, on the altar of faith and obedience.[43] The idea that an earnest follower of the Tao might be required by heaven to repress the most natural and spontaneous promptings of his mind/ heart would have neither a metaphysical basis nor a teleological point.

Perhaps most significant for the metaphysics of the person is the fact that the mind is understood as both the unifying center of the person and the unifying element among persons. It is the agency of communication through which the person recognizes his fundamental relatedness to others and to the totality of being. Human minds are understood to have common dispositions, to function analogously, and to develop in similar ways. In Mencius's view, the shared dispositions, known as the "four beginnings" (*ssu-tuan*) of virtue, are essential to being human. That moral action is not a matter of conscious deliberation or choice, and hence the subject of alternative interpretations or judgments, is the obvious point of Mencius's discussion of the "four beginnings"—the sense (literally, the mind/ heart) of pity and commiseration, the mind/ heart of shame and dislike, the mind/ heart of modesty and yielding, and the mind/ heart of right and wrong.[44]

Interestingly, Mencius offers an argument for only the first of these—that most famous and powerful argument that the mind that prompts any human being who sees a child about to fall into a well to move to save the child is one that has functioned spontaneously and naturally in the way *every* human mind can reliably be expected to do:

> When I say that all men have a mind/ heart which cannot bear to see the sufferings of others, my meaning may be illustrated thus: even now-a-days, if men suddenly see a child about to fall into a well, they will without exception experience a feeling of alarm and distress. They will feel so, not as a ground on which they may gain the favour of the child's parents, nor as a ground on which they may seek the praise of their neighbours and friends, nor from a dislike to the reputation of having been unmoved by such a thing.[45]

In this example, which becomes prototypical in Confucian ethics, there is no question either of conflicting impulses or of ulterior motives. Perception and action are so closely joined that there is no interlude for conscious deliberation.[46] The conviction that human beings in general can be counted on to feel impelled to save children from falling into wells enables Mencius to sustain a more expansive confidence concerning the other mental promptings, which he also takes to be natural and spontaneous. "To lack the mind of pity and commiseration is not to be human; to lack the mind of shame and dislike is not to be human; to lack the mind of modesty and yielding is not to be human; to lack the mind of right and wrong is not to be human."[47] This is not injunction, but description, or even definition. The existence of these "four beginnings" which, under normal circumstances, develop into the four cardinal virtues of humaneness, righteousness, propriety, and wisdom, figures into the psychological and motivational structure of the person in precisely the same way that the four limbs constitute his external physical form, a point about which Mencius is explicit.[48]

If there is any choice involved in the development of the "four beginnings" into the four virtues of humaneness, righteousness, propriety, and wisdom, it is again primarily a negative and even a destructive one.[49] To possess the "four beginnings" while asserting that one cannot develop them is considered self-injury, literally, "self-destruction" (tzu-tsei). It follows that asserting that one's ruler is unable to develop these beginnings is injuring or destroying one's ruler.[50] Here the image of "self-injury" or "self-destruction" is strong enough to suggest that the negation really amounts to foreclosing on one's own humanity. The choice, if it can be considered as such, is so drained of tension as to be unengaging as an ethical issue. More likely, the notion of choice is not the relevant one here at all, for to talk about not developing the "four beginnings" is to say nothing significant about the human mind in respect to its freedom, but only to acknowledge its susceptibility to injury and abuse. I. A. Richards was most discerning in his perception that the failure of the human mind to develop and function as it should is seen by Mencius as "accidentally frustrated potentiality."[51]

Rather than the particular pattern established through the exercise of choice by a deliberative faculty possessed by the individual, what is critical in the Mencian context is the common pattern established through the common or analogous development of a mind understood to be shared with others. Mencius's affirmation that ordinary human beings are not only capable of becoming sages but are fundamentally like sages represents a profound conviction about the essential nature of the human mind: "Thus all things which are the same in kind are like to one another. Why should we doubt in regard to man, as if he were a solitary exception to this? The sage and we are the same in kind."[52] The evidence for likemindedness is found, tellingly, through resort to the analogy of a similarity of sense experience:

> Men's mouths agree in having the same relishes; their ears agree in enjoying the same sounds; their eyes agree in recognizing the same beauty: shall their minds alone be without that which they similarly approve? It is, I say, principles and righteousness. The sages only apprehended before me that of which my mind approves along with other men. Therefore principles and righteousness are agreeable to my mind, just as the flesh of grass-fed and grain-fed animals is to my mouth.[53]

Just as there are no disputes in matters of taste, so there are no significant differences in matters of morals, which are, for Mencius, analogous to matters of taste.[54]

It is characteristic of Mencius's perception of a unity of mind and body that he saw a necessary connection between maintaining a sense of moral balance and nourishing the psychophysical energy or *ch'i*—that is, between "holding firm one's will" (*chih ch'i chih*) and "doing no violence to one's *ch'i*" (*wu pao ch'i ch'i*). But Mencius's sense of the relation between moral balance and psychophysical energy goes beyond the dualistic wisdom of *mens sana in corpore sano* in that it reflects not so much a recognition that mind and body interact (a point that was apparently uncontested) as a conviction that there is a fundamental connection between the health of the individual and his capacity to relate to others. The well-being of the individual is both the condition for and the consequence of a harmonious interaction with a larger whole that ultimately includes "all between heaven and earth."

Questioned about his contention that his superiority to his philosophical adversary Kao Tzu lay in his understanding of words and skill in nourishing his "vast, flowing *ch'i*" (*hao-jan chih ch'i*), Mencius (stipulating that this "vast, flowing *ch'i*" is "difficult to describe") goes on to characterize it as follows:

> This is *ch'i*. It is consummately great and consummately strong. Being nourished by righteousness, and sustaining no injury, it fills up all between heaven and earth. This is *ch'i*. It is the counterpart of righteousness and the Way. Without it, man is in a state of starvation. It is not produced by the accumulation of righteous deeds; it is not to be obtained by incidental acts of righteousness. If one's actions cause the mind to feel discontented, it becomes starved. I therefore said Kao Tzu never understood righteousness because he makes it something external.[55]

It is of the utmost consequence for the metaphysics of the person in the Confucian tradition that for Mencius, as for the later Neo-Confucian thinkers who drew on his authority, *ch'i* is both part of the individual endowment and also a transpersonal reality. It is when the individual endowment of *ch'i* is properly nourished that the continuity of the individual with a larger and more encompassing reality becomes evident; honoring this sense of continuity with all living things in turn contributes to the well-being of the person. Through his complement of *ch'i* the individual is both vital and one with other living beings; when this *ch'i* is constantly guided by the mind, it is itself nourished and strengthened. Mencius stresses that while the *ch'i* is to be guided by the will, which is its leader or instructor (*shuai*), the individual complement of *ch'i* must not be injured.[56] The famous Mencian formula, "Always be doing something, but without fixation" (*pi yu shih yen erh wu cheng*), conveys the sense that the conscious mind must lead and direct without forcing or distorting the normal and natural development of the complete individual.[57] The moral mind and the vital *ch'i* connect the individual with other living beings but are also possessed by him as his own endowment as a discrete person. Neither the transpersonal reality nor the personal endowment should be neglected or compromised.

The injunction that one must "neither forget" the need for appropriate moral cultivation "nor help things grow" in such a way as to damage one's psychophysical resources is indicative not only of the psychophysical basis of Mencian ethics, but also of an underlying metaphysics of the person in which mutuality and reciprocity are essential concepts.[58] This metaphysical position, coupled with the Confucian perception of human beings as essentially similar by nature, forms the basis for an enduring element in Confucian thinking about the relation between the individual and the whole. With relatedness and complementarity being understood as a fundamental metaphysical reality as well as an evident psychological necessity, it is natural that *jen*, or humaneness (expressive of the idea of responsiveness, mutual regard, and shared responsibility), should have become primary among the Confucian virtues.[59] *Jen*, for Mencius, defines the human ("Humaneness is what it means to be human"), epitomizes the human mind ("Humaneness is man's mind"),[60] and determines the moral capacity of the individual to exert positive influence over others. The idea of *jen*, already central for Mencius, was to take on even greater importance for the Sung Neo-Confucians, for whom it would acquire metaphysical status as well.

Reflections on the Mind in the Ch'eng-Chu School of the Sung

Keith Campbell has observed that a presupposition of the mind/body problem found in the mainstream of Western philosophy is a particular idea of individuality:

> Whatever we think minds are, the Mind-Body problem presupposes that each normal adult has a mind, has the whole of a mind, has only one mind, and has a mind nobody else has. Maybe this is not the truth. Parmenides and Spinoza both affirmed that all things are one, and our minds, which seem to be distinct, are in reality but aspects of the single divine universe. In Hindu thought the mind's destiny is seen as reunion with the divine mind of which it is a temporarily dislocated part. Jung's notion of a collective unconscious belongs to the same family of ideas which deny that different people, with different bodies, have different and separate minds.
>
> It is clear that without the assumption of individuality our Mind-Body problem quite evaporates. We would have to grapple instead with questions about how the one mind is shared out, and how it is that we know our own thoughts by introspection, but not those of others. There would be many problems. But the question: What is the relation between my body and my mind, and between your body and your mind, which does not hold between my body and your mind? would no longer be a question about any real aspect of our situation. It would just lapse.[61]

Conceivably, this formulation of alternative views of mind—mind possessed either individually or collectively—does not exhaust all of the possibilities. An examination of Neo-Confucian concepts of mind, which drew on classical Confucian views, especially that of Mencius, but developed them more fully, suggests that the mind is seen as operating between these two poles, as being the agent which establishes—or, perhaps more precisely, recovers—a relation between the one and the many, the part and the whole.

Here, the assumptions about the mind and the philosophical problems associated with it differ from those inherent in the dominant Western or Indian formulations. The starting point in thinking about mind in the Ch'eng-Chu tradition is neither that minds are discrete (that the individual "has a mind, has the whole of a mind, has only one mind, and has a mind nobody else has"), nor that mind is ultimately one (in the Hindu sense of mind as a part or aspect of a collective whole). In the philosophy of mind of Chu Hsi (1130-1200), mind as such is relational. The human mind, while individually endowed along with *ch'i*, is like all other human minds, structured so as to make possible both personal integration and active communication with others, and capable in its fullest development of being united with the mind of heaven and earth. The assumption is not that mind (as distinct from body) represents the essential as opposed to the contingent self, but that through the agency of the mind the self has access to the more complete reality of which it is an integral part.

The proper function of the mind in the Ch'eng-Chu perspective is to recognize and internalize the metaphysical and moral relation between the individual and the totality of being. That the individual actually exists does not present itself as a problem, hence the need to establish certainty about personal reality has no particular urgency. Neither the Cartesian *cogito ergo sum* nor the kind of epistemological and metaphysical problem that prompted that solution[62] would have appeared particularly relevant to Neo-Confucians at almost any stage in the evolution of Neo-Confucian thought. The same may be said about the mirror image of this problem in the Vedānta of Śaṁkara—the converse notion that the doubting self cannot be doubted inasmuch as "the interior Self is well known to exist on account of its immediate (intuitive) presentation."[63] The Sung Neo-Confucians are prompted neither to doubt the real existence of the person nor to dismiss the validity of such doubts. The problems involved in the Sung Neo-Confucian concept of mind are, by contrast, not those typically associated with either the position that makes mind the basis of individuality or the position that makes mind the ground of unity. Rather, the problems have to do with assessments of the mind's innate intuitive and communicative capacities and the requirements for their full development. Given the essential similarities perceived to exist among persons on the basis of a common human nature, there is the question of how minds endowed from the same source, sharing a common substance and similar dispositions and developing analogously, may nonetheless be different—that is, more or less capable of internalizing the relation between the individual and the larger whole. Given the fact that the mind is essentially relational, what metaphysical explanation is there for the fact that it does not always ideally fulfill its functions?

Here it is relevant to observe that Sung Neo-Confucian concepts of mind were defined and redefined through the responses of eleventh- and twelfth-century thinkers to the powerful and long-standing assault of Buddhism on the Confucian concept of the person. Clearly, it was on the ground of the metaphysical status of the person that the clash of Buddhism with traditional

Chinese values and beliefs had been most intense. Indian Buddhism had begun with a direct challenge both to earlier philosophical and religious conceptions and to conventional notions of personhood,[64] and, however, marked the differences between the Buddhist perspective on the person and earlier Brahmanic views, the disparity between Buddhist and classical Confucian ideas was greater still.

One of the striking features of classical Confucian thinking about the person is a reliable sense of a naturally integrated person and an integral lifetime. That is, the Confucian metaphysics of the person, with its notable avoidance of any mind/body or cognitive/affective dualism, joined with Chinese historical-mindedness, with its tendency to accept the ordinary cycle of a natural human lifetime as significant both in itself and as a connecting link between preceding and succeeding generations. However, Confucian security proved insufficient to withstand altogether the shock of Buddhist skepticism concerning the conditions for personal unity. The physical body, which had been accepted naturalistically, took on the taint of impurity, its ultimate perishability viewed as a warning of the tenuousness and fragility of the relation among its parts. The mind, which Confucians had respected as the master of the person, was seen as prey to all manner of deceptions and delusions, even while it was recognized as the agency whereby enlightenment to the truth of emptiness might finally be achieved. The historical time frame was found to be illusory, and, with the doctrine of karma, doubt was cast even on the possibility of "passing this way but once."

The career of Buddhism in China offers a fascinating example of the operation of dialectic in the life of the mind. That is, an object which is being negated (in this case the notion of a naturally integrated person) must not only at one stage be affirmed as negated (as asserted in Mādhyamika dialectic), it must also be scrutinized (the more so, perhaps, in that so much of Buddhist teaching about the person tended to undermine the validity of sense data and the lessons of ordinary human experience). Buddhism, while controverting earlier concepts of the self and the nature of the mind, also introduced certain questions which, once raised, could never quite be expunged as philosophically significant. Buddhist solutions might be rejected, but the questions that had been raised in the course of several centuries of Buddhist-Confucian interchange could not simply be dismissed. They had to be resolved in new ways, and this, presumably, is what the Neo-Confucians of the eleventh and twelfth centuries were engaged in when they confronted two problems: the relation between ideal and concrete or physical reality and the relation between human moral potential and the present promptings of the human mind/heart. As these problems are framed here, there are suggestions of dualism—not, in the first case, a mind/body dualism or, in the second, a cognitive/affective dualism, but in both cases a dualism of actual and potential moral capacity.

In thinking about the individuation of the person and his development as a knowing subject and intentional agent, Chang Tsai (1020-1077), Ch'eng I (1033-1107), and Chu Hsi adopted certain terms and categories which were without provenance in the Confucian classics. Several of these pertained to human nature, the innovation being the idea that persons possess two natures, an original nature (*pen-hsing*) associated with principle (*li^b*), which is pure and perfectly good, and a physical nature (*ch'i-chih chih hsing*) associated with material force (*ch'i*), which harbors the "selfish human desires" (*ssu-yü*). Chang Tsai initiated the idea of the distinct physical nature:

> With the existence of physical form, there exists physical nature. If one skillfully returns to the original nature endowed by heaven and earth, then it will be preserved. Therefore in physical nature there is that which the superior man denies to be his nature.[65]

Chang contraposed the original nature and the discrete physical endowment, identifying the physical endowment as the source of one-sidedness and partiality. Ch'eng I extended this idea by proposing a dichotomy between a common human nature, which is uniformly good by virtue of its association with *li^b*, and capacity (*ts'ai*), which is variable in its quality owing to its association with clear or turbid *ch'i*.[66] Chu Hsi, endorsing this idea and recognizing that it was without classical precedent, commented that

> The doctrine of physical nature originated with Chang [Tsai] and Ch'eng [I]. It made a tremendous contribution to the Confucian school and is a great help to us students. None before them enunciated such a doctrine. Hence with the establishment of the doctrine of Chang and Ch'eng, the theories [of human nature] of all previous philosophers collapse.[67]

The introduction by Chang Tsai and Ch'eng I of a dualism between an original or "ideal" nature and the physical nature, and their acceptance of its epistemological corollary, which was to discount the importance of sense experience,[68] may, in fact, suggest Buddhist influence. But it is nonetheless clear that these two philosophers were impelled by the most Confucian of concerns, which was, essentially, to reestablish a psychophysical basis for an integrated person and to recover the metaphysical basis for an expanded self. This they achieved, as had Mencius, through their concept of mind.

The role of the mind in Chang Tsai's system was to connect the nature and the feelings.[69] The statement *hsin t'ung hsing ch'ing che yeh* ("the mind connects [or commands] the nature and feelings") and the underlying conception of a mind capable of uniting substance and function represent one of Chang's most significant contributions to the Neo-Confucian metaphysics of the person. Another formulation of this idea by Chang in the *Cheng-meng* [Correcting youthful illusions], which had it that "in the uniting of nature and consciousness, there is the mind" (*ho hsing yü chih-chüeh yu hsin chih ming*),[70] was less acceptable to Chu Hsi because the distinction between the nature and consciousness seemed to have been overdrawn almost to the point of reifying the nature, so that the suggestion of disembodiment was barely suppressed.[71] But the idea of the mind connecting (or, as Chu Hsi interpreted it, "commanding") the nature and feelings gave clarity to an integrated conception of the person. The ideal pattern presented by the original nature and the individual psychophysical manifestations deriving from the physical nature came together in the mind.

Chang Tsai also had some seminal reflections on the integrative capacity of the mind, and his statement in the *Cheng-meng* about "enlarging one's mind" so as to "enter into all things in the world" highlights the second major function of the mind in the Sung Neo-Confucian context, that of providing the metaphysical basis for the expanded self:

> By enlarging one's mind one can enter into all things in the world. As long as anything is not yet entered into, there is still something outside the mind. The mind of ordinary people is limited to the narrowness of what is seen and what is heard. The sage, however, fully develops his nature and does not allow what is seen or heard to fetter his mind. He regards everything in the world to be his own self. This is why Mencius said that if one exerts his mind to the utmost, he can know nature and heaven. Heaven is so vast that there is nothing outside of it. Therefore the mind that leaves something outside is not capable of uniting itself with the mind of heaven. Knowledge coming from seeing and hearing is knowledge obtained from contact with things. It is not knowledge obtained through one's moral nature. Knowledge obtained through one's moral nature does not originate from seeing and hearing.[72]

Here Chang asserts that the human mind, possessed by all alike but employed most effectively by the sage, is capable of being enlarged through an expansion of ethical consciousness. When one expands one's mind (*ta ch'i hsin*) one is able to enter into all things in the world (*t'i t'ien-hsia chih wu*). The kind of mental operation implied by the term *t'i* in this context may elude precise definition. The suggestion, however, is that of incorporating an object of consciousness into oneself, or, in a profound way, projecting oneself into the position of the other so that the fact of relatedness is fully internalized.

This bears some similarity to what Herbert Fingarette describes as "imaginative analogizing of self with other" as a focus of ethical concern in the *Analects*,[73] though among Neo-Confucians of the Ch'eng-Chu tradition the idea takes on a more inclusive character and, with Chu Hsi himself, a decidedly intellectualist cast. In Chu's reading of the *Cheng-meng*, the word *t'i* is understood as "entering into"—literally, introducing one's mind into things or situating one's mind within things (*chih hsin tsai wu chung*) so as to acquire insight into their principle. He states that the process described by Chang Tsai is like the investigation of things and the extension of knowledge in the program of the *Great Learning*.[74] It is clear that the essential Confucian link between epistemology and ethics, cast into some doubt in the Mahayana Buddhist context in which ethical conduct had something of the character of supererogation, is reasserted as at once necessary and natural because it derives from the structure of human personality. Knowing in the Confucian perspective always includes awareness of the emotions, dispositions, and needs of others, and here the range of concern is broadened to include all things.

The achievement Chang had in mind, the expansion of the self, was evidently an empathetic identification between the self and things such that subject/object dualism might be relinquished along with the sense that there is anything alien to one's own mind. Like the Buddhists, Chang found that sensory knowledge could be a distraction or a fetter insofar as "contact with things" fostered arbitrary distinctions between the self and things of the "external" world. Unlike the Buddhists, he visualized no inevitable dissolution of the natural boundaries of the self once the metaphysical reality had been clarified through "knowledge obtained through one's moral nature." In that the mind was the agency whereby the self was both integrated and expanded, "regarding everything in the world as one's self" implied neither self-negation nor self-abnegation but self-fulfillment. Chang reaffirmed the Mencian confidence that by exerting one's mind to the utmost one would know one's nature and that by knowing one's nature one would know heaven. He may even have gone beyond Mencius in his assertion that the human mind could not only know heaven but ultimately unite with the mind of heaven.

Ch'eng I's epistemological perspective was similar to Chang Tsai's. In postulating the identity of human nature and principle, Ch'eng, too, felt that he was reaffirming the most fundamental contribution of Mencius to the Confucian philosophy of man.[75] There was also some similarity in their views of mind. As Chu Hsi would observe, " 'Mind is one. At times one speaks of it in terms of substance and at times one speaks of it in terms of function.' This statement of I-ch'uan's [Ch'eng I's] is similar to Heng-ch'ü's [Chang Tsai's] idea that 'the mind commands the nature and feelings.' "[76]

In the metaphysics of the person developed by Chang Tsai and Ch'eng I, the rudiments of Chu Hsi's metaphysics of the person are prefigured. The basic ideas were elaborated and refined by Chu Hsi in his mature philosophy of mind.[77] But these essential elements—the idea of a nature which has ideal and physical aspects and a mind which both commands and unifies these aspects and potentially connects the individual with a larger social and cosmic whole—are retained. Mind, for Chu Hsi, or that aspect of the mind which was understood as the master of the person, is always understood to be associated with *ch'i*. "Mind," Chu says, "is the spirit of *ch'i*" (*hsin che ch'i chih ching-shuang*).[78] Mind is also seen as the residence or repository of *li^b*, or principle; without mind, *li^b* would be metaphysically stranded.[79] "The nature," he observes, "is principle. The mind is what contains and holds [these principles], distributes them, and causes them to function."[80] "The nature is the principle which the mind possesses. The mind is the ground where principles congregate."[81] "That whereby consciousness exists is the principle of the mind; that which is capable of consciousness is the intelligence of *ch'i*."[82] Chu Hsi often returns to Chang Tsai's pregnant formulation, "the mind connects [or commands] the nature and feelings," which he found to be the most incisive of any made by the Northern Sung masters on the metaphysics of the person.[83] As he puts it in one of his many discussions and elaborations of this statement:

> The nature is principle. The nature is substance and the feelings are function. The nature and feelings both issue from the mind. Therefore the mind is able to command them. The word "command" [*t'ung*] is like the "command" in "commanding troops" and refers to the means whereby one controls them. Thus humaneness [*jen*], righteousness [*i^a*], propriety [*li^a*], and wisdom [*chih^b*] are the nature, and Mencius said that humaneness, righteousness, propriety, and wisdom are rooted in the

mind. Pity and commiseration, shame and dislike, modesty and yielding, and right and wrong are essentially feelings, and Mencius spoke of the mind of pity and commiseration, the mind of shame and dislike, the mind of modesty and yielding, and the mind of right and wrong. From the fact that he spoke of them in this way one can see that the mind can command the nature and feelings. Within the one mind there are naturally movement and tranquillity. Tranquillity is the nature. Movement is the feelings.[84]

With the Sung Neo-Confucians, mind, as the unifying center of the person and the agency which integrates the individual and the whole, is conceived in terms similar to those of Mencius, yet the differences are also noteworthy. Part of the *problematik* of Neo-Confucianism lies in the fact that the integration of the person is no longer natural, as it was with Mencius. It can no longer be taken for granted but has to be accomplished, both theoretically and practically, through an enormous effort of mind, if the moral possibilities of human nature are to be called forth. Mind becomes a central concern in the Sung, and it is not difficult to discern both similarities with Buddhist thinking on the mind and signs of an intense reaction against Buddhism. In their habit of discounting sense knowledge and deprecating the "selfish human desires," the Neo-Confucians reveal at least an affinity with the Buddhists. Yet in their gravitation toward a concept of *moral* mind/heart as the commander of an integrated person capable of significant moral expression and development, their rejection of Buddhist metaphysical assumptions is clear.[85]

Of overriding importance for the Neo-Confucian concept of mind is the fact that a mind/body dualism is all but excluded by the representation of the mind in Ch'eng-Chu thought, no less than in the Lu Hsiang-shan tradition, as the unifying center of the person. The dualism of an ideal and a physical reality, of the universality of principle and the particularity of the psycho-physical endowment, is no doubt real and important. Yet much of what Chu Hsi has to say about the mind, the nature, and the feelings serves to confirm that the mind is effective as the agency of integration. "The nature is the principle of the mind; the feelings are the movement of the nature; the mind is the master of the nature and feelings."[86] Individually endowed, mind is nonetheless capable of attaining a transpersonal reality; functioning as consciousness, it is nonetheless a vehicle for principle, which is at once its substance or content and its metaphysical source or ground.[87] Mind is individual in its association with *ch'i* and transpersonal in its association with *li*[b], functional in its association with *ch'i* and the feelings and substantial in its association with *li*[b] and nature.[88] It is clearly relevant to our discussion of individualism and holism in the Confucian philosophical perspective to note that the primary object of cultivation in Chu Hsi's *hsin-hsüeh*, or "learning of the mind/heart," is to ensure that the "human mind" (*jen-hsin*) which is endowed in the psychophysically discrete individual becomes more and more closely attuned to the "mind of Tao" (*Tao-hsin*) which is an expression of the unity or wholeness of principle.

One of the metaphysical grounds for optimism concerning the concinnity of the part to the whole was discovered in the concept of the oneness of principle and the diversity of its particularizations (*li-i fen-shu*). Whatever Chu Hsi may ultimately have owed to Hua-yen Buddhism for the metaphysical doctrine of the one and the many and the coimplication of all phenomenal reality,[89] he came to the doctrine through the mediation of Ch'eng I and Li T'ung (1093-1163), whose purposes had been primarily ethical and resolutely anti-Buddhist. Ch'eng I, with whom its Neo-Confucian formulation seems to have originated, perceived the idea of *li-i fen-shu* to be implicit in the ethical perspective found in Chang Tsai's "Hsi-ming" [Western inscription]. Here the naturalness, intimacy, and intensity of Confucian familism (interpreted by Ch'eng I in terms of diverse particularizations) were preserved as the basis for an all-embracing ethical universalism (understood by Ch'eng in terms of the oneness of principle.)[90] Li T'ung, too, had attended to the ethical imperative which he found inherent in *li-i fen-shu*,[91] and for Chu Hsi the concept worked both metaphysically and morally.

In Chu Hsi's terms, *li-i fen-shu* expressed the relation between li^b and *ch'i*. When questioned about this relation, he replied, "I-ch'uan expressed it very well when he said that 'principle is one; its particularizations are diverse.' When heaven, earth, and the myriad things are spoken of together, there is only one principle. As applied to human beings, however, there is one principle in each individual."[92] Here the relation is established between a metaphysical unity based on the oneness of principle and a phenomenal diversity based on the particularizations or differentiations of principle in a variety of physical forms. The particularity of principle is not an illusion ultimately to be dispelled, but, in line with Chu Hsi's belief that *ch'i* is the abiding place of li^b ("without which li^b would have no place to dwell"),[93] *ch'i* is recognized as the vital element, the stuff of life without which life itself would be inconceivable.

For Chu Hsi, as for Ch'eng I, the path of ethical cultivation is plotted to direct individuals in working through particularity toward the unifying source in a single universal principle. Chu Hsi differs from the Buddhists in that he does not perceive the process of cultivation through which the individual is accommodated to the whole as involving dissolution of the consciousness of individual self or the abandonment of the vital intuitions of discreteness, diversity, or personality. For him, cultivation entails expansion of the sense of self through an enhanced awareness of the moral nature (identified in the Ch'eng-Chu framework with principle) and an enlarged sense of the relatedness of all life. In other words, the moral development of the person involves overcoming the unclarity of mind that derives from indulgence of the "selfish human desires," the product of the individual psychophysical endowment. The process is thought to entail not inhibition of personality, but release from the obscurity and selfishness which demean and diminish the self. The human mind, containing principle and connecting or commanding the nature and feelings, is ideally equipped to work through particularity toward unity; it loses nothing in the process but the confines of selfishness and isolation.

If a comparison of this view with Western perspectives on the mind is pressed, it would appear that the characteristic agency of the human mind as conceived by the Sung Neo-Confucians is not to exercise choice and to confirm the possibility of human autonomy but to recognize connections and recover the metaphysical grounds for relatedness and communication. Chu Hsi's discussions of the will suggest that his view, while again going beyond Mencius, involves no radical divergence from the primary view of will as resolve, purpose, or determination. It is commitment to a goal, or, perhaps, the strength and resolution with which one applies his mind to a goal. Questioned about the passage in *Analects* 2:4 in which Confucius describes the maturation of his mind beginning with "setting his will on learning," Chu Hsi approves the suggestion that the will is the directedness of the mind (*hsin yu suo chih wei chih chih*). He adds, however, that there is another implication:

> There are in the world a thousand forks and ten thousand roads, but the sage was not inclined toward any other road, but only this one road. The will lies in the deep recesses of the mind, and therefore the doctors say that the will belongs to the kidneys.[94] Among students of today there are none who do not pursue learning, yet one cannot say of all of them that they have "set their will on learning." If one can set his will on learning, then he naturally cannot stop. If one "learns and constantly practices what he learns,"[95] to the point that he achieves pleasure from it, then each step follows in turn. It is like a person who in cold months is spontaneously inclined toward a place where there is fire and in hot months is spontaneously inclined toward a place where there is a breeze. In serving his sovereign he is motivated by reverence; in serving his parents he is motivated by filiality. Although in the course of it there are difficulties, he does not shrink from difficulty but carries out these actions with thoroughness.[96]

The image of the fork in the road does appear here, yet the issue is not the choice between alternatives. Confucius exercises his will in committing himself entirely to the one road of learning. Learning at this juncture evolves its own internal momentum: when he has gone beyond the casual pursuit of learning, which can be interrupted in response to other demands, and "set the will on learning," he is inspired by total dedication to the goal—"he naturally cannot stop." As was the case with Mencius, who perceived in human beings a natural or spontaneous orientation toward a moral action—"virtually a moral tropism," as Arthur Danto puts it—Chu Hsi here likens the impulse to moral action to a thermotropism.[97] Mencius had suggested a cognitive requirement for the full development of the "four beginnings" of virtue, saying, "Since all men have these four principles in themselves, let them know how to give them all their development and completion and the issue will be like that of fire, which has begun to burn, or that of a spring which has begun to find vent."[98] With Chu Hsi, who put even greater stress on cognitive development, the will must be engaged and the direction and course set before the impulse begins to operate reliably, at which point there is no longer a question of choice between conflicting demands or competing claims.

Despite the complexity of Chu Hsi's views on *li*[b] and *ch'i* and the relation between the original nature and the physical nature, the will properly stands in much the same relation to the physical powers that it had for Mencius, who said that "the will comes first and the *ch'i* follows it." In a remark which, according to Ch'ien Mu, was made toward the close of his life, Chu Hsi expressed the following view:

> Although there are certainly times when people's physical powers are strong or weak, the willpower never fails. If one constantly maintains this will, then even if one's physical powers fail utterly, the will is not implicated. As in my case with this old ailment of mine now causing me to fail utterly, it is not that I do not know that each day I ought to give myself leave to arise late in order to care for the illness. But in my mind I am naturally not at ease, and by the fifth watch I can no longer sleep. Although I would like to force myself to sleep, this mind of mine is that of a person who has already gotten up and is unwilling to remain in bed. From this one may know that if people can maintain this willpower, it will definitely not be taken away[99] by their physical powers. Those who are moved by their physical powers are just people who "do violence to themselves" and "throw themselves away."[100]

The terms quite inadequately translated here as "physical powers" and "willpower" are, literally, "blood-*ch'i*" (*hsüeh-ch'i*) and "will-*ch'i*" (*chih-ch'i*). In the previous passage quoted, the will was ascribed to the "deepest recesses of the mind" (*hsin chih shen ch'u*); here, it is seen to operate at what in modern parlance might be called the level of the subconscious. Chu Hsi is evidently reporting his own personal experience: his account suggests a psychic momentum so powerful that neither failing physical stamina nor the ordinary dictates of prudence could interfere or intervene in its functioning.

In his later years Chu Hsi endorsed Hu Hung's view that equal weight should be given to establishing the will (*li-chih*) through learning and maintaining the will (*chih-chih*) through reverence or seriousness (*ching*[b]). This exertion of the will, which might be understood to entail constant and rigorous effort but *not* the need to overcome a conflict of Augustinian dimensions, is sustained by the groundedness of the person in a broader metaphysical reality and supported by an intense conviction of the significance of his moral endeavor:

> Wu-feng [Hu Hung, 1100-1155] said, "To carry out learning lies in establishing the will. Abiding in reverence is in order to maintain one's will." These words are most excellent. Yin and yang stand in opposition to one another, but once the will is established, the self is established in yang. Although at times one may lose his footing and enter yin, once he realizes it, he will again return to yang. Scholars of today all say that another is a Yao or a Shun while I am an ordinary man. How can I be a Yao or a Shun? Those who say this are not as good as the Buddhist Sudhana,[101] who said, "I have already issued forth with the bodhi-mind. Regardless of what I do, I shall become a Buddha." He can still manage to become a Buddha, yet I cannot manage to become a Yao or a Shun!
>
> I therefore asked: "Establishing one's will is certainly right. But how does one establish one's will?" Answer: One establishes it through starting from the beginning and establishing the fundamental. In one's body one participates in heaven and earth, and as an ordinary man one brings peace to the world. There is truly this principle.[102]

What validated such an exertion of the will and sustained Chu Hsi's confidence in the ability of even an ordinary man to aspire to the accomplishments of the sages was that he saw *jen*, or humaneness, as the original substance of the human mind as well as its character or communicative capacity. As has already been noted, Chu accepted Chang Tsai's moral epistemology as expressed in Chang's assertion that "by enlarging one's mind, one can enter into all things in the world." Though Chang had not used the term *jen* in the "Ta-hsin" [Enlarging the mind] section of the *Cheng-meng*, Chu understood the communicative capacity of the mind that Chang was talking about in this passage to be the very essence of *jen*. As he put it,

> In the passage, "By enlarging one's mind, one can enter into all things in the world," the expression "enter into" is like "*jen* entering into all affairs and being present universally."[103] It means that the principle of the mind flows like the blood system which circulates throughout the body. If there is one thing which is not yet entered into, then there is somewhere it has not extended, its inclusiveness is incomplete, and there is something outside the mind. Then egoism (*ssu-i*) causes separation and things and the self are contraposed, so that we cannot be sure that even those closest to us will not be left outside. Therefore the mind that leaves anything outside is not capable of uniting itself with the mind of Heaven.[104]

It is precisely this capacity of the mind to unite with the mind of heaven—that is, to overcome any sense of opposition between self and other and to enter into a productive moral relation with all things—that Chu Hsi understood as the essential character of *jen*, the complete substance of the mind. In contrast to the Buddhist ideal of homelessness, Chang Tsai had in the "Western Inscription" discovered his home everywhere and in everything. The sense of being fully at home in the world at large was cultivated also by Chu, who, evoking the spirit of Chang Tsai and recalling the language of Mencius, said, "When this mind is broad and without the slightest trace of selfishness, having precisely the same compass as heaven and earth, this is 'dwelling in the wide house of the world,' this is dwelling in *jen*."[105]

Wing-tsit Chan and Ch'ien Mu have observed that the concept of *jen* becomes with Chu Hsi a metaphysical as well as a moral concept.[106] There is even one sense in which it is the primary metaphysical concept. In Ch'ien Mu's view, it is only in understanding Chu Hsi's idea of *jen* that one fully appreciates his theory of *li*[b] and *ch'i*, the relation between them, and the dynamic quality of both in his system.[107] Following the lead of the Ch'eng brothers, who saw *jen* as a generative principle, resembling a seed and conveying the impulse to life and growth in the natural world,[108] Chu identified the original substance of the human mind with the mind of heaven and earth and with the creative spirit or life force in the universe. Like the Ch'engs, he saw *jen* as encompassing all four primary virtues;[109] he also made the correspondence with the natural world by observing that the spirit of spring and of creation extended through and unified the entire cycle of life:

> Humaneness [*jen*], righteousness, propriety, and wisdom are origination, flourishing, advantage, and correctness.[110] If in spring there were not the potential to bring forth, then when it came to summer there would be no cause for growth, in autumn and winter there would be no capacity to gather in and to store.
>
> The life force [*ch'i*] of the growth of spring permeates the whole, and in humaneness is contained the impulse to movement and goodness.[111]

In the process that begins with the appearance of the barest touch of green in the tree and continues gradually through the innumerable transformations involved in the production of branches, leaves, flowers, and fruit is displayed the impulse to production and reproduction (*sheng-sheng*). Of this impulse to bring forth life, Chu Hsi remarks, "If it were not for humaneness and love [*ai*], why should it be thus?"[112] Underlying Chu's confidence in the human capacity for moral development and effective moral action is his belief that the mind of heaven and earth to produce things (*t'ien-ti sheng-wu chih hsin*) and to effect the myriad transformations of the natural process is the same mind which is shared by human beings and other living things. "Humaneness," he says, "is the mind of heaven and earth to produce things and is what human beings and things receive for their mind."[113] Ch'ien Mu crystallizes the metaphysical significance of this statement as follows:

> What can be perceived as uniting heaven and earth and the myriad things is simply a unitary *ch'i*. The mind is this *ch'i* in its most spiritual aspect [*ch'i ch'i chih tsui ching-shuang che*]. Heaven and earth have a mind, and the myriad things also have a mind. *Jen* is the vital principle and the vital impulse within this *ch'i*.[114]

Donald Munro suggests that this Neo-Confucian doctrine of *jen* bears some resemblance to animism in that it focuses on the impulse to life and procreativity in all things.[115] It is, of course, true that the Latin word *anima*, or "breath," from which the term derives, suggests a possible parallel with the notion of *ch'i*. However, it is the contrast between the two terms as they evolved that is the more striking, the term *anima* being associated with soul or spirit as *distinct* from matter, the term *ch'i* implying no such separation. The doctrine of "animism," introduced by Georg Ernst Stahl in the early eighteenth century, turns on the idea that a discrete immaterial soul, distinct from matter, resides within animate objects and determines their organic development. For Chu Hsi, not only does *ch'i* encompass both the material and spiritual realms (the very distinction between them would probably have been unintelligible to him), but the terms *kuei* and *shen* (often translated as "spirits" or "positive and negative spiritual forces") are the dynamics of the process of coming and going, expansion and contraction, gathering and scattering of the unitary *ch'i* discussed by Ch'ien Mu in the preceding quotation.[116]

It is also noteworthy that, while Chu Hsi placed human creativity and procreativity within the larger context of nature as a whole, consistently emphasizing the continuity of life, he also seems to have believed that, in moral terms, there is a considerable gap between human beings and other living things. Human beings are distinguished from other living things by the quality of their *ch'i* and the nature of their consciousness—more specifically, by their capacity for mutual involvement and concern. In addition to the impulse to live and love of life, which are shared universally, human beings have the potential to participate more broadly in heaven and earth and, through the habits and rituals of caring and nurturing and the ordering of life through government, to assist in the processes of production and transformation.[117] Such a view does not vitiate his perception that between one human being and another the discrepancies are comparatively small. Sages are distinguished from ordinary human beings by virtue of their capacity to fulfill their distinctively human potential by relieving the mind of the distortion, selfishness, and narrowness normally attendant upon its specific endowment and by allowing the mind to reflect its affinity with the endowment of heaven in its correctness, universality, and breadth—that is, by fulfilling the humaneness of the mind.[118]

This impetus toward an expanded self, so clear in Chu Hsi's metaphysics and in the metaphysics of the Ming thinkers who followed him, is integrally bound up with his understanding of the mind as relational by its nature. As he put it when questioned about Mencius's idea of "enlarging" and "completing" the "four beginnings":

> To "enlarge" is to expand [*chang-k'ai*]. To "complete" is to fulfill [*fang-man*]. The mind of pity and commiseration is not just something that occurs at the time one sees a child [falling into a well], for it is thus in every activity. If today you extend it in one activity and tomorrow you extend it in another, gradually it will be fully released. From one's household it will extend to the state, and from the state to the world, and it will be sufficient to preserve all within the four seas. This is "completing" so as to attain full development.
>   Question: Are "enlarging" and "completing" the same as fully developing the self and extending the self?
>   Answer: It is simply to enlarge and complete it where once there were boundaries. It is like when the hand picks up a brush, puts it to paper, and forms characters. One cannot say that the hand is of one sort while the characters are another. The child falling into the well over there and the mind of pity and commiseration in me are just one thing. One cannot say that the child falling into the well belongs to that "other," while the mind of pity and commiseration belongs to me.[119]

To "enlarge and complete [the self] where once there were boundaries" is not to obliterate the distinction between self and other but to recognize the implications of human interrelatedness and interaction and to perceive that the self is actually realized in responsiveness rather than in isolation. This idea is more than moral, however; it is also metaphysical. Chu Hsi is making a statement about the nature of consciousness which, seen from the perspective of twentieth-century Western philosophy, has a decidedly modern cast.

Coda

In *The Possibility of Altruism*, Thomas Nagel draws attention to the importance in assessing ethical motivation of establishing what are the central elements in an agent's metaphysical conception of himself. He contrasts Kant's view, in which the central element is freedom, with his own, in which it is "the conception of oneself as merely a person among others equally real."[120] One could conceivably argue that both elements have some place in the metaphysics of the Sung Neo-Confucians and of their successors in the Yüan and Ming. However, the conception of freedom is somewhat different. It is a spiritual freedom of the kind described by Professor de Bary in his discussion of Li T'ung and his sense of *sa-lo* in this volume and also, as the final quotation from Chu Hsi suggests, the freedom of communication and interaction unimpeded by boundaries which are indefensible metaphysically as well as morally. Autonomy and choice in the Kantian sense are here not primary concepts; the sense of being involved in mankind and in a larger continuity of being is associated, rather, with openness, receptivity, personal integration, and interpersonal communication. Chu Hsi, like Mencius, would hardly have demurred at seeing himself as "merely a person among others equally real"— that was implicit in the concept of *jen*—though perhaps the adverb "merely" might better be omitted. In the modern West, entering a "post-individualist" age,[121] there may be reason to view oneself as "*merely* a person among others equally real." In the "Western Inscription" Chang Tsai might describe himself as "such a small creature" (*tzu-miao*), but in Neo-Confucian terms one is never "merely" a person because he is part of an interaction in which the part and the whole are interdependent.

In terms of our discussion of individualism and holism, the appropriate conclusion may be that, in classical Confucianism and Neo-Confucianism alike, the metaphysics of the person was such that the individual and the whole were seen in dynamic terms as part of an interaction. Confucian thinkers were keenly aware that human beings are not born, nor do they grow, mature, or reach fulfillment independent of familial and societal context. At the same time they focused on the fact that society depends on the actions of individuals. It is the textures of ordinary human lives that make a society what it is, and ordinary human lives may be tellingly affected by the actions of extraordinary individuals. In a Confucian perspective, the ordinary human relationships, particularly those between parents and children, mattered enormously. So did the exemplary capacity of the noble or profound person and the sage. For Chu Hsi, the central element in the metaphysical conception of the person is the mind's capacity to connect the individual and the whole, each of which requires the other. This sense of interdependence is perhaps nowhere more clearly expressed than in this simple statement: "Without the mind of heaven and earth to produce things, there would not be this body of mine. Only when there is this body of blood-and-*ch'i* is the mind of heaven and earth to produce things made complete."[122]

NOTES

Author's note: I have been both helped and heartened in the preparation of this paper by exchanges with Peter Bol, Wing-tsit Chan, Arthur C. Danto, Wm. Theodore de Bary, Terry Kelleher, Lydia Lenaghan, Michael J. Mooney, W. Scott Morton, Donald J. Munro, Wang Yuquan, and Pei-yi Wu. My thanks are due to each of them, but all are, of course, free from any taint deriving from my own errors of fact or interpretation.

1. Amelie Oksenberg Rorty, "A Literary Postscript: Characters, Persons, Selves, Individuals," in *The Identities of Persons*, ed. Amelie Oksenberg Rorty (Berkeley and Los Angeles: University of California Press, 1976), 310. I have reservations about the statement that the change brought about by the fusion of Latin and Christian concepts of the person was accomplished "at one stroke," but, allowing for some literary license, Professor Rorty's characterization of the significance of that development is apt.
2. Ibid., 311-12.
3. Steven Lukes, *Individualism* (Oxford: Basil Blackwell, 1973), 131-32.
4. This was, obviously, over the course of many centuries, an issue of urgent importance to potential officials who had to decide in different contexts whether or not to serve. It is discussed in many sources. I do not wish to oversimplify the problem but only to suggest that it is most commonly the refusal to serve which, for Confucians, required justification. Of the sources in which this issue is raised, perhaps none are more indicative of the general orientation of Confucius himself in this matter than the famous passages in the *Analects* 18:6 and 18:7. The latter concludes with the statement of the disciple Tzu-lu, who criticizes the example of the vanished recluse: "Not to take office is not righteous. If the relations between old and young may not be neglected, how is it that he sets aside the duties that should be observed between sovereign and minister? Wishing to maintain his personal purity, he allows that great relation to come to confusion. A superior man takes office, and performs the righteous duties belonging to it. As to the failure of right principles to make progress, he is aware of that" (translation by James Legge in *The Chinese Classics*, 7 vols. [Oxford: Oxford University Press, 1892], 1:335-36).
5. *Analects*, 12:11.
6. I do not know whether studies have been made that would shed light on the perceived stability of the kinship system and of familial relationships in the Spring and Autumn period, but it seems reasonable to assume that, relative to Greece during the same period, a greater degree of perceived stability must have attached to familial relationships in China. In *The Hellenic World*, Alvin W. Gouldner speculates that among the psychic costs of slavery in ancient Greece was "its possibly adverse effects on the capacity of the male to make a deep psychic investment in his wife," because defeat in war might result in the enslavement of anyone—man, woman, or child. The radical insecurities faced by everyone, regardless of class, and the constant possibility that women and children could be lost to one through being enslaved, militated, he argues, against deep emotional involvement. In support of this idea he notes that, in Homer and throughout classical Greek literature, there were no ordinary words that specifically meant "husband" and "wife." Among the further psychic consequences of slavery, according to Gouldner, "One is its unpredictable character that would only heighten the anxiety concerning it and, in particular, would tend to disrupt the connection between what a man did and what happened to him. The reassuring feeling that social reality is intrinsically orderly would surely be undermined by the apparent unpredictability of what could occur." See Alvin W. Gouldner, *The Hellenic World: A Sociological Analysis* (New York: Harper Torchbooks, 1969), 26-27. The *Tso chuan* affords evidence that during the turbulent Spring and Autumn period in China rulers and ministers of states defeated in war frequently experienced social degradation. Hsü Cho-yün observes that, "The familial solidarity of nobles within a state, and the class

solidarity of nobility among the states, gradually broke down in the Ch'un-Ch'iu [Spring and Autumn] period.... Wars were harder fought and more frequent, and their consequences were more serious. The leading citizens of a conquered state and the officers of a defeated army lost all social status; and since at least 110 states were conquered during the Ch'un-Ch'iu period, it is clear that large numbers of people were forced to undergo this humiliation" (Hsü Cho-yün, *Ancient China in Transition* [Stanford: Stanford University Press, 1969], 77). Whether or not it was at all common for rulers of defeated states to be reduced to slave status, as Hsü seems to suggest (ibid., 60-62), is open to some question. Professor Wang Yuquan's view is that most likely this fate was suffered only by rulers of "barbarian" states such as Ch'u or by nobility of the Sung state; rulers who were related to the Chou house were probably not so threatened (personal communication). Clearly, a study which explored the question of the psychic consequences of the upheavals of the Spring and Autumn period and their bearing on Confucian perceptions of the stability of personal and familial relationships would be extremely illuminating.

7. *Euthyphro*, especially 9c-d and 12d-e, in *The Collected Dialogues of Plato*, ed. Edith Hamilton and Huntington Cairns (Princeton: Princeton University Press, Bollingen series, 1961), 177, 181.

8. *Analects*, 13:18 (translation adapted from Legge, *The Chinese Classics*, 1:270). Legge's very revealing comment on this passage is that "Anybody but a Chinese will say that both the duke's view of the subject and the sage's were incomplete."

9. John Locke, *An Essay Concerning Human Understanding*, 2 vols. (New York: Dover Publications, 1959), 1:467.

10. As Locke puts it in his chapter "Of Identity and Diversity" concerning the nature of the person, "It is a forensic term, appropriating actions and their merit; and so belongs only to intelligent agents, capable of a law, and happiness, and misery. This personality extends itself beyond present existence to what is past, only by consciousness,—whereby it becomes concerned and accountable; owns and imputes to itself past actions, just upon the same ground and for the same reason as it does the present. All which is founded in a concern for happiness, the unavoidable concomitant of consciousness; that which is conscious of pleasure and pain, desiring that that self that is conscious should be happy. And therefore whatever past actions it cannot reconcile or *appropriate* to that present self by consciousness, it can be no more concerned in than if they had never been done: and to receive pleasure or pain, i.e., reward or punishment, on the account of any such action, is all one as to be made happy or miserable in its first being, without any demerit at all. For, supposing a *man* punished now for what he had done in another life, whereof he could be made to have no consciousness at all, what difference is there between that punishment and being *created* miserable? And therefore ... the apostle tells us, that, at the great day, when every one shall 'receive according to his doings, the secrets of all hearts shall be laid open.' The sentence shall be justified by the consciousness all persons shall have, that *they themselves*, in what bodies soever they appear, or what substances soever that consciousness adheres to, are the *same* that committed those actions, and deserve punishment for them" (ibid., 467-68; italics in the original).

11. Herbert Fingarette, *Confucius-The Secular as Sacred* (New York: Harper Torchbooks, 1972), 18.

12. Ibid., 30.

13. Ibid.

14. Ibid.

15. Ibid., 34.

16. Ibid., 34-35.

17. *Analects*, 5:9.

18. Fingarette, *Confucius*, 31.

19. Hannah Arendt, *The Life of the Mind*, 2 vols. (New York: Harcourt Brace Jovanovich, 1978), vol. 2, *Willing*, 84.

20. Ibid.

21. Ibid., 85.

22. Ibid.

23. Donald Munro looks to Lucretius, among the Romans, as offering a discussion of free will
and refers to the passage in *De Rerum Natura* 2.251-93 where Lucretius introduces the
theory of the swerve of the atom (παρέγκλσις *clinamen, declinatio, inclinatio*) as a way of
acounting for the fact that the mind in living things exerts control over the motions of the
body (Munro, personal communication; see also his introduction to this volume). Were it
not for the swerve, asks Lucretius, "whence comes this free will in living creatures all over
the earth, whence I say is this will wrested from the fates [*libera per terras unde haec
animantibus exstat, unde est haec, inquam, fatis avolsa voluntas*] by which we proceed
whither pleasure leads each, swerving also our motions not at fixed times and places, but
just where our mind has taken us? For undoubtedly it is his own will in each that begins
these things, and from the will movements go rippling through the limbs" (Lucretius, *De
Rerum Natura*, with an English translation by W. H. D. Rouse [Cambridge, Mass.:
Harvard University Press, and London: William Heinemann, Loeb Classical Library,
1975], 114-15). Cyril Bailey, author of one of the standard English commentaries on
Lucretius, contends that the poet's target in this passage is Democritus, and the object of
the maneuver is to find an escape from the crushing determinism of Democritus' atomism.
David J. Furley in his illuminating study *Aristotle and Epicurus on Voluntary Action* (in
Two Studies in the Greek Atomists [Princeton: Princeton University Press, 1967], 161-237)
argues persuasively that what concerns Lucretius is *not* Democritus but Aristotle and the
Aristotelian distinction between voluntary and involuntary action in the *Nicomachean
Ethics* and *De Motu Animalium*. He notes (214-15) that in the other passage in *De Rerum
Natura* in which Lucretius discusses voluntary action (4.877-906), the idea of the swerve
does not occur at all, which supports his view that the swerve, while playing an important
role in Epicurean cosmology, "plays a purely negative role in Epicurean psychology" (232).
As he puts it, the swerve "saves *voluntas* from necessity . . . but it does not feature in every
act of *voluntas*" (ibid.). Whether, following Bailey, one adopts the more traditional
interpretation, or, following Furley, a carefully documented revisionist view, it is difficult
to see that the "free will" of Lucretius is really comparable to the concept which was later to
be found in Augustine. It is noteworthy that there is nothing in *De Rerum Natura* 2.251-93
which explicitly states that this "will wrested from the fates" is, in fact, a moral will, nor is
this "free will in living creatures all over the earth" even defined as a distinctively human
faculty. On Furley's argument, Lucretius was following Aristotle in attempting to open a
space in which moral action could occur, but he is at pains to state that, for Aristotle, "the
criterion of the voluntary act is not that it is 'spontaneous,' or 'freely chosen,' or that 'he
could have done otherwise,' but that the source of the action cannot be traced back to
something outside the agent" (220). On the matter of choice among the Epicureans, Furley
writes, "The wise Epicurean is not to be pictured as asserting himself by repeated 'acts of
volition' against the temptations of the world, but as having learned not to be tempted. His
'freedom' does not consist in being presented with possible alternatives, and in choosing
one when he might have chosen the other. It consists rather in the fact that his *psyche* is the
product of his own actions and is not unalterably swayed by some 'destiny' from the time
before his birth" (235). Simply stated, choice, for Lucretius, does not occupy a larger role
than did προαίρεόις for Aristotle. I am grateful to Professor Lydia Lenaghan of the
Department of Classics, Barnard College, for having drawn my attention both to Cyril
Bailey's study, *The Greek Atomists and Epicurus* (Oxford: Clarendon Press, 1928) and to
Furley's more recent work. On the relative lateness of the idea of a will which freely chooses
among alternative courses of action (i.e., the Augustinian idea), see also Arendt, *Life of the
Mind*, 2:15-17 ff. This is also the major thesis of a brilliant study by Albrecht Dihle, *The
Theory of Will in Classical Antiquity* (Berkeley and Los Angeles: University of California
Press, 1982).

24. Augustine's *Confessions* contains many illustrations of the intense sense of conflict within
the self. See, for example, Book VIII, sec. 8, which begins, "My inner self was a house
divided against itself." See also Book VIII, sec. 10: "When I was trying to reach a decision
about serving the Lord my God, as I had long intended to do, it was I who willed to take this

course and again it was I who willed not to take it. It was I and I alone. But I neither willed to do it nor refused to do it with my full will. So I was at odds with myself. I was throwing myself into confusion. All this happened to me although I did not want it, but it did not prove that there was some second mind in me besides my own. It only meant that my mind was being punished. *My action did not come from me, but from the sinful principle that dwells in me.* It was part of the punishment of a sin freely committed by Adam, my first father" (translation by R. S. Pine-Coffin, *Confessions* [Harmondsworth, Middlesex: Penguin Books, 1961], 170, 173; italicized quotation is from Paul's *Epistle to the Romans* 7:17).

25. *Eudemian Ethics*, II, 10.1226b in *Aristotle*, 23 vols. (London: William Heinemann, and Cambridge, Mass.: Harvard University Press, Loeb Classical Library, 1971), 20:292. The concept of προαίρεόις is also discussed by Aristotle in other writings, including the *Nicomachean Ethics* III, 1.1111b, though its function is less clearly defined there. On the function of προαίρεόις in the *Eudemian Ethics*, see Arendt, *Life of the Mind*, 2:60-62.

26. *Mencius*, 7B:35 (translation by Legge, *The Chinese Classics*, 2:497).

27. *Analects*, 2:4.

28. *Analects*, 4:4.

29. *Analects*, 4:9, 7:6.

30. *Analects*, 19:6.

31. *Mencius*, 4A:9, 6B:8, 6B:9.

32. *Mencius*, 7A:24.

33. *Mencius*, 5B:1, 7B:15.

34. *Mencius*, 6A:9.

35. *Mencius*, 3B:2, 4B:1.

36. *Analects*, 9:25.

37. *Analects*, 18:8.

38. *Mencius*, 1A:7.

39. *Mencius*, 7A:33.

40. *Mencius*, 4A:17.

41. *Mencius*, 4A:17. A. S. Cua points to the indeterminacy of the concept of *tao*, along with the characteristic Confucian emphasis on harmony, as elements bearing on perceptions of conflict in a Confucian moral perspective. As he puts it, "To adopt *tao* or *jen* as a governing ideal of one's life does not imply a determinate conception of the ideal to be realized. It is to adopt an attitude and to resolve, with one's mind and heart (*hsin*), to look at things and events in a way in which they can become constituents in a harmonious unity that is not specified in advance of man's confrontation with changes in the natural world. To adopt this ideal attitude is to see human life in its morally excellent form, as possessing a coherence in which apparently conflicting elements are viewed as eligible elements of an achievable harmonious order. The presence of conflicting elements in experience is a fact to be acknowledged. This acknowledgement brings with it the necessity of reconciliation. . . . Since the desired coherence of the moral order is not spelled out a priori, the harmonization of conflicting elements in experience is essentially a *creative* endeavor on the part of both the Confucian moral thinker and agent" (*The Unity of Knowledge and Action: A Study in Wang Yang-ming's Moral Psychology* [Honolulu: The University Press of Hawaii, 1982], 53).

42. Peter Boodberg's observation on *li*[a] was that "As is well known, the character *li* is composed of two elements: the so-called radical (semantic determinative) for 'rite,' 'worship of the numina,' appearing in most graphs relating to religious beliefs and ritual practices, and a 'phonetic' part representing a vase or ritual vessel. The only other common Chinese character with the same 'phonetic' is *t'i*, 'body,' 'human body,' 'to embody,' 'embodiment,' 'form,' (its radical is 'bone,' 'skeletal structure'). This would seem to indicate that for the ancient Chinese this particular word for 'vessel' connoted something like 'morphon' and, in a way curiously parallel to the use of *skeuos* in Greek and of 'vessel' in our own scriptural language, served as a metonym for 'human body.' 'Form,' that is, 'organic' rather than geometrical form, then, appears to be the link between the two words,

as evidenced by the ancient Chinese scholiasts who repeatedly used *t'i* to define *li* in their glosses. Another favorite paronym for *li* is *ti*, 'order,''series,''sequence.' From the above we must deduce that, for the ancient Chinese, *li* was a concept situated somewhere near the point of intersection of notions that we could express by such words as 'corporate form,' 'worshipful acconformation,' 'formal accorporation,' 'eumorphosis,' 'social coordination,' or 'corpor-ordination.' It would seem that 'Form,' with a capital, to be understood as ritual form, social form, or good form, and so qualified whenever occasion would require, serves best as the simplest equivalent of the Chinese term." See "The Semasiology of Some Primary Confucian Concepts," in *Philosophy East and West* 2:4 (January 1953), 326-27. The word *ching*[a] is, of course, made up of the radical for "silk" and a phonetic representing underground streams. Its primary meaning is, in Karlgren's summary, the "warp in a loom, meridians of longitude; ("warp" in the body:) larger blood vessels, nerves; (the moral "warp":) rules of conduct, rule, law, classical book, canon... regulate; follow a rule, pass along; pass, past, already." See Bernard Karlgren, *Analytic Dictionary of Chinese and Sino-Japanese* (New York: Dover, 1974), 136. Both *li*[a] and *ching*[a] have some significant reference to things made by human beings and also to the human body. This is not to suggest that either is distinct from natural forms but only that both are evocative of the most characteristically human creations.

43. *Genesis*, 22.
44. *Mencius*, 2A:6 (translation by Legge in *The Chinese Classics*, 2:202-4).
45. Ibid.
46. In the words of Arthur Danto regarding this famous example of the person observing the child by the well: "I think that what Mencius is saying is that you cannot simply observe the child falling into the well as a matter of fact; you don't just register that as a feature of the world. To register it is *ipso facto* to act. The mind and body are united in the sense that perception and action are virtually a seamless package, at which point we can say that the question of 'what to do' can never arise for a person who sees the world morally in that way. He has no choice; there is virtually a moral tropism... almost as if there were some enzyme operating there" (from the transcript of the conference prepared by Robert Eno).
47. *Mencius*, 2A:6. Legge, *The Chinese Classics*, 2:202.
48. *Mencius*, 2A:6. Legge, *The Chinese Classics*, 2:203.
49. For a somewhat different approach to this passage, see David Shepherd Nivision, "Mencius and Motivation," in *Studies in Classical Chinese Thought*, ed. Henry Rosemont, Jr. and Benjamin I. Schwartz, *Journal of the American Academy of Religion Thematic Issue* (September 1979), 47 (3 S):417-32, esp. 423.
50. *Mencius*, 2A:6. Legge, *The Chinese Classics*, 2:203.
51. I. A. Richards, *Mencius on the Mind* (1932; reprint ed., London: Routledge and Kegan Paul, 1964), 79.
52. *Mencius*, 6A:7. Legge, *The Chinese Classics*, 2:404-5.
53. *Mencius*, 6A:7. Legge, *The Chinese Classics*, 2:406-7.
54. One might argue that Hsün Tzu places more emphasis on volition than Mencius and adduce as evidence for this the famous passage in the "Chieh-pi" [Dispelling obsession] chapter in which he represents the mind as "the ruler of the body and the master of its godlike intelligence" (*hsin che hsing chih chün yeh, erh shen-ming chih chu yeh*). Here Hsün Tzu says of the mind that, "It gives commands but is not subject to them. Of its own volition it prohibits or permits, snatches or accepts, goes or stops. Thus the mouth can be forced to speak or to be silent; the body can be forced to crouch or to extend itself; but the mind cannot be made to change its opinion. What it considers right it will accept; what it considers wrong it will reject. Hence we may say that it is the nature of the mind that no prohibition may be placed on its selections." See Burton Watson, trans., *Hsün Tzu: Basic Writings* (New York: Columbia University Press, 1963), 129. But the ensuing passage makes clear that the emphasis here is not on moral autonomy or choice but on self-control, concentration, and the capacity to hold on to unity so that competing claims will not cause the mind to be distracted, unbalanced, or divided.
55. *Mencius*, 2A:2. Legge, *The Chinese Classics*, 2:190.

56. *Mencius*, 2A:2. Legge, *The Chinese Classics*, 2:188, 190-91.

57. *Mencius*, 2A:2.

58. See the very useful discussion by Herbert Fingarette of the concept of *jen* and the *Analects* in his article "Following the 'One Thread' of the *Analects*," in *Studies in Classical Chinese Thought, Journal of the American Academy of Religion Thematic Issue* (September 1979) 47 (3 S):373-99, esp. 395-99. Professor Fingarette sees the Confucian concepts of *chung*, *hsin*[b], and *shu* as being oriented toward the integrity of individual persons. He comments: "A natural outcome of the focus on persons, rather than the group as such, could be some form of individualism—familiar enough to us in the West, but also familiar in post-Confucian texts as early as the *Great Learning* where we find the idea that 'the cultivation of the self is the root.' Such a purely individualistic notion, however, is *not* to be found in the *Analects*. One never finds there the proposal that the ultimate value is either individual happiness, or in some more Chinese sense, the moral flowering of the *individual* self. In the *Analects*, the individual self is never spoken of as either root *or* flower. Human relations are always conceived as relations of person-to-person, though always and essentially within a *communal framework*. . . . In sum, the one thread—*chung-hsin* and *shu*—leads us to an ideal of the person-with-person engagement that is a basic reality in Confucius' vision of man. We might call this ideal relation, using 'man' in its honorific sense, the man-to-man relation, or perhaps preferably, man-with-man. In the Chinese of the *Analects*, it is *jen*. The character *jen* presents to us, both in its written form and in its meaning, the quintessential vision of a world in which the basic human reality is man as two, person-with-person" (397). Professor Fingarette goes on to observe that the reason that *jen* cannot be defined is that "no determinate act can be equivalent to *jen* for the act must be inspired by *shu*, and *shu* is precisely that direct, imaginative analogizing of self with other that is independent of rules, formulas, or generalized descriptions or argument. . . . *Jen* is not a specific act as such, but a dynamic stance, a way of being engaged with another person. It is the stance-in-action of being truly humanly engaged" (389). The important point made here, I believe, is that the concern of Confucius with the integrity of individual persons and the "deeply communal coloration" of his thought are not divergent but mutually supportive tendencies.

59. *Mencius*, 7B:16.

60. *Mencius*, 6A:11.

61. Keith Campbell, *Body and Mind* (Notre Dame: University of Notre Dame Press, 1980), 6-7. I am indebted to Donald Munro for calling my attention to this discussion.

62. I have in mind here, of course, Descartes' famous exercise in doubting in the First Meditation and its resolution in the Second Meditation. See René Descartes, *Meditations on the First Philosophy in Which the Existence of God and the Real Distinction Between the Soul and the Body of Man Are Demonstrated*, in F. E. Sutcliffe, trans., *Discourse on Method and the Meditations* (Harmondsworth, Middlesex: Penguin Books, 1968), 95-112.

63. Translated in Sarvepalli Radhakrishnan and Charles A. Moore, eds., *A Source Book in Indian Philosophy* (Princeton: Princeton University Press, 1957), 510. Śaṁkara also says, "The existence of *Brahman* is known on the ground of its being the Self of every one. For every one is conscious of the existence of (his) Self, and never thinks 'I am not.' If the existence of the Self were not known, every one would think 'I am not.' And this Self (of whose existence all are conscious) is *Brahman*" (ibid., 511).

64. See, for example, this cautionary advice from the *Majjhima-nikāya* I, 8: "An uninstructed ordinary person is not wisely reflecting if he thinks 'In the past was I, was I not, what was I, what was I like, having been what what was I?' Or if he thinks, 'In the future will I be, will I not be, what will I be, what will I be like, having been what what will I be?' Or if he is subjectively doubtful now in the present and thinks, 'Am I, am I not, what am I, what like, whence has this being come, wheregoing will it come to be?' To one who is thus not wisely reflecting, one of six speculative views may arise as though it were real and true: 'There is self for me; there is not self for me; simply by self am I aware of self; simply by self am I aware of not-self; simply by not-self am I aware of self.' Or he may have a speculative view such as this: 'That self of mind that speaks and knows, which experiences now here, now

there the results of karma that was lovely or evil, that self of mine is permanent, stable, eternal, it will stand fast like unto the eternal'—this is called speculative view, holding a speculative view, the wilds, wriggling, scuffling, and fettering of speculative views" (translated in Edward Conze, ed., *Buddhist Texts Through the Ages* [New York: Harper Torchbooks, 1964], 74).

65. Chang Tsai, *Cheng-meng* [Correcting youthful illusions], "Ch'eng-ming" [Sincerity and enlightenment], in *Chang Tzu ch'üan-shu* [Complete writings of Master Chang Tsai] (SPPY ed.), 2.18b-19a (translated in Wing-tsit Chan, *A Source Book in Chinese Philosophy* [Princeton: Princeton University Press, 1963], 511).

66. See, for example, *Ho-nan Ch'eng-shih i-shu* [Written legacy of the Masters Ch'eng of Honan], hereafter, *I-shu*, 19.4b, in *Erh-Ch'eng ch'üan-shu* [Complete writings of the two Ch'engs] (SPPY ed.).

67. Chu Hsi's commentary on Chang Tsai's *Cheng-meng*, "Ch'eng-ming," in *Chang Tzu ch'üan-shu* 2.19a-b (translated in Chan, *Source Book*, 511).

68. See, for example, Chang Tsai's statement in the opening passage of the "Ch'eng-ming" section of the *Cheng-meng* (in *Chang Tzu ch'üan-shu* 2.17a): "Knowledge gained through enlightenment which is the result of sincerity is the innate knowledge of one's natural character (*t'ien-te liang-chih*). It is not the small knowledge of what is heard or seen" (translated in Chan, *Source Book*, 507). Ch'eng I's view, as seen, for example, in *I-shu* 25.2a, was similar: "The knowledge obtained through hearing and seeing is not the knowledge obtained through moral nature. When a thing (the body) comes into contact with things, the knowledge so obtained is not from within. This is what is meant by extensive learning and much ability today. The knowledge obtained from moral nature does not depend on seeing and hearing" (translated in Chan, *Source Book*, 570).

69. *Chang Tzu ch'üan-shu*, 14.2a.

70. Chang Tsai, *Cheng-meng*, "T'ai-ho" [Great harmony], in *Chang Tzu ch'üan-shu* 2.3b (translated in Chan, *Source Book*, 504).

71. *Chu Tzu ch'üan-shu* [Complete writings of Master Chu Hsi] (1714 ed.), 44.5a.

72. Chang Tsai, *Cheng-meng*, "Ta-hsin" [Enlarging the mind], *Chang Tzu ch'üan-shu* 2.21a.

73. See n. 58 above.

74. Professor Wing-tsit Chan has pointed out to me that Chu Hsi was here following the use of the term *t'i* in the *Doctrine of the Mean*, 16.2. Thus, the *t'i* was not like the *t'i* of substance as contrasted with *yung* of function. See *Chu Tzu yü-lei* [Classified conversations of Master Chu] (1473; reprint ed., Taipei: Cheng-chung shu-chu, 1970), 98.11a.

75. See, for example, *I-shu*, 22A.11a.

76. *Chu Tzu yü-lei* 95.1b, quoting *I-ch'üan wen-chi* [Collection of literary works of Ch'eng I] 5.12a (in *Erh-Ch'eng ch'üan-shu*) and *Chang Tzu ch'üan-shu* 14.2a. As Professor Wing-tsit Chan has pointed out, this view of mind as one in substance and function represented a self-correction on the part of Ch'eng I whose earlier view had involved a sharper dichotomy of mind and principle. It is especially interesting that Chu Hsi saw this particular formulation of Ch'eng I's as according most fully with Chang Tsai's view. See Wing-tsit Chan, "Patterns for Neo-Confucianism: Why Chu Hsi Differed from Ch'eng I," *Journal of Chinese Philosophy* (June 1978), 5(2):117.

77. The ways in which Chu Hsi built on and modified Ch'eng I's ideas concerning the mind, the nature, and the feelings are explored in Wing-tsit Chan's important essay, "Patterns for Neo-Confucianism," esp. 116-20.

78. *Chu Tzu yü-lei* 5.3b.

79. *Chu Tzu yü-lei* 5.3a.

80. *Chu Tzu yü-lei* 5.6a.

81. Ibid.

82. *Chu Tzu yü-lei* 5.3b.

83. *Chu Tzu yü-lei* 98.6b.

84. *Chu Tzu yü-lei* 98.7a.

85. Donald Munro suggests that, while Chu Hsi does avoid a mind/body dualism and total denigration of the human desires, there is nonetheless "a hierarchical distinction between

the nature and feelings." An apparent concomitant of this distinction, in Professor Munro's view, is "a tendency to trivialize a whole range of human experience—that which is characterized by imbalance or disequilibrium"(personal communication). This tendency may well exist among some Neo-Confucians and it may again reflect both their rejection of Buddhism and their preoccupation with some of its central insights. On the one hand, the style of some of the earlier Ch'an masters—their studied *ir*reverence and almost calculated irrationality—was evidently repudiated by Neo-Confucians who set so much store by reverence or seriousness. Most of the major figures in the Ch'eng-Chu tradition not only disapproved of Buddhism but condemned with considerable fervor what they saw as Buddhist "selfishness" and its ruinous effects on social cohesiveness and order. On the other hand, quite a number of Sung Neo-Confucians apparently shared Buddhist wariness of the human desires and many adopted the practice of quiet-sitting (*ching-tso*) as a means of achieving self-control and clarity of mind. As Wm. Theodore de Bary has observed with respect to the Ming reaction to some aspects of Ch'eng-Chu thought, "Controversy arose . . . over Chu Hsi's philosophy of human nature, which was seen as attributing evil to man's physical nature. There is little basis for this in Chu's theoretical position, as Fung Yu-lan pointed out in discussing Chu's later critics. What may well have fueled the issue, however, was the practical implication of quiet-sitting as a discipline of the mind over the bodily desires, opposing a pure and quiescent principle to disturbing psychophysical influences on the mind. Together with the religious intensity of its practitioners, this produced a strong puritanical strain in the Ch'eng-Chu school." See Wm. Theodore de Bary, ed., "Introduction," *The Unfolding of Neo-Confucianism* (New York: Columbia University Press, 1975), 14-15. However, as Professor de Bary also points out, it is noteworthy that on the subject of the human emotions Chu Hsi's views did differ, often quite considerably, from those of Chou Tun-i, Chang Tsai, and even Ch'eng I. A careful study of this facet of Chu Hsi's thought would represent an important contribution to our understanding of his philosophy and provide a basis for examining more thoroughly the relation between this aspect of Neo-Confucian thought and wider trends in the Sung period.

86. *Chu Tzu yü-lei* 5:6b.
87. For a fuller discussion of this, see Chan, "Patterns for Neo-Confucianism."
88. In Wing-tsit Chan's view, it is in the mature and developed concept of balance between substance and function that Chu Hsi went most significantly beyond Ch'eng I, whose primary emphasis was on substance. As he puts it ("Patterns for Neo-Confucianism," 118): "The reason why the mind is the master of nature and feelings is because 'The mind is the abode of intelligence and the master of the whole body.' Again, 'The mind is the intelligence of man and can therefore possess all principles and respond to all things.' Needless to say, intelligence is substance and response is function. Because of this substance and function relationship, nature and feelings are not only combined in the mind but also under its control. Nature as substance cannot be separated from feelings as function. It is wrong therefore for the Buddhists merely to try to see the mind or for Lu Hsiang-shan and company merely to concentrate on the mind. Just as substance can only be seen in function, so nature must be manifested in feelings. Feelings can be either good or evil. It all depends on their master, the mind, whether it can regulate them to the proper degree. This is old philosophy taught in the *Doctrine of the Mean*, but the logic is new. This new dimension was created not by Ch'eng I, but by Chu Hsi."
89. See Chan, *Source Book*, 639; Fung Yu-lan, *History of Chinese Philosophy*, trans. Derk Bodde, 2 vols. (Princeton: Princeton University Press, 1967), 2:541-42. See also the discussions of this concept in the articles by Donald J. Munro and Wm. Theodore de Bary in this volume.
90. *I-ch'üan wen-chi* 5.12b.
91. See especially *Yen-p'ing ta-wen* [Dialogues with Yen-p'ing], in Okada Takehiko, ed., *Kinsei kanseki sōkan, shisō hen*, 22 vols. (Kyoto: Chūbun shuppansha, 1972), 8:99-101. See also the discussion by Wm. Theodore de Bary in this volume.
92. *Chu Tzu yü-lei* 1.1b (translation adapted from Chan, *Source Book*, 635).

93. *Chu Tzu yü-lei* 1.2b.

94. See, for example, *Huang-ti nei-ching su-wen* [The Yellow Emperor's classic of internal medicine], ch. 7, sec. 23 (Kuo-hsüeh chi-pen ts'ung-shu ed.), pt. I, 88. Ilza Veith, trans., *The Yellow Emperor's Classic of Internal Medicine* (1949; reprint ed., Berkeley and Los Angeles: University of California Press, 1970), 208: "The five viscera hide and store the following: the heart stores and harbors the divine spirit [*shen*]; the lungs harbor the animal spirits [*p'o*]; the liver harbors the soul and the spiritual faculties [*hun*]; the spleen harbors ideas and opinions [*i*[b]]; and the kidneys harbor willpower and ambition [*chih*[a]]. This explains what is stored away and harbored by the five viscera."

95. *Analects*, 1.1.

96. *Chu Tzu yü-lei* 23.15a. Quoted in Ch'ien Mu, *Chu Tzu hsin hsüeh-an*, 5 vols. (Taipei: San-min shu-chü, 1971), 2:368.

97. See n. 46 above.

98. *Mencius*, 2A:6. Legge, *The Chinese Classics*, 2:203.

99. Chu Hsi uses the same verb *to* used by Confucius in *Analects*, 9:25, where he says, "The commander of the forces of a large state may be carried off, but the will of even a common man cannot be taken [*to*] from him." Legge, *The Chinese Classics* 1:224.

100. *Chu Tzu yü-lei* 104.11a, quoting *Mencius*, 4A:10. The entire passage is quoted in Ch'ien Mu, *Chu Tzu hsin hsüeh-an*, 2:370-71.

101. His quest is recounted in the *Hua-yen ching* [Flower garland sutra], "Ju fa-chieh p'in" [Entering the dharma realm], in *Taishō Shinshū dai-zōkyō*, nos. 278 and 279.

102. *Chu Tzu yü-lei* 118.3a-b. Quoted in Ch'ien Mu, *Chu Tzu hsin hsüeh-an*, 2:366.

103. Quoting from *Cheng-meng*, "T'ien-tao," in *Chang Tzu ch'üan-shu* 2.11b.

104. *Chu Tzu yü-lei* 98.11a.

105. *Chu Tzu yü-lei* 55.8a. Chu Hsi here alludes to *Mencius*, 3B:2.

106. Wing-tsit Chan, "Chu Hsi's Completion of Neo-Confucianism," in *Études Song—Sung Studies in Memoriam Étienne Balazs*, ed., Francoise Aubin, ser. II, no. 1 (1973), 72-73. Ch'ien Mu, *Chu Tzu hsin hsüeh-an*, 1:345-65.

107. Ch'ien Mu, *Chu Tzu hsin hsüeh-an*, 1:345-49.

108. *I-shu* 18.2a.

109. See, for example, *Chu Tzu yü-lei* 6.7b, 20.16b, 17a-b, 24a-b; 95.1b-2a. See also "Yü-shan chiang-i" [Lecture at Yü-shan] in *Chu Tzu wen-chi* (SPPY ed., published as *Chu Tzu ta-ch'üan*) 74:19a.

110. Alluding to the opening phrase of the *Book of Changes*, *ch'ien* hexagram.

111. *Chu Tzu yü-lei* 20.24b.

112. *Chu Tzu yü-lei* 17.12a.

113. *Chu Tzu yü-lei* 95.22a.

114. Ch'ien Mu, *Chu Tzu hsin hsüeh-an*, 1:359.

115. With reference to the idea of *jen* as a generative principle and Chu Hsi's identification of the original substance of the human mind with the mind of heaven and earth and with the creative spirit or life force of the universe, Professor Munro asks, "What are the boundaries between [this] position . . . and the position we pejoratively call 'animism'? . . . Specifically, can we be concrete about what it is to 'participate in the transforming processes of heaven and earth'? Does it mean simply that humans sire or bear children just as other things reproduce? Does it mean that they feel love for family members and try to create conditions of love in larger groups in which they participate? What is dynamic creativity?" (from the transcript of the conference proceedings prepared by Robert Eno).

116. See, for example, *Chu Tzu yü-lei* 3.7a. Interestingly, Joseph Needham in his discussion of Sung Neo-Confucianism in *Science and Civilisation in China*, 5 vols. to date (Cambridge: Cambridge University Press, 1956-), vol. 2, turns at the end of his discussion of the Sung to seventeenth-century European developments. Referring to the need for the Cambridge Platonists to extricate themselves "from the animism of the Neo-Platonists," he suggests that the Sung Neo-Confucian conception of *li* and *ch'i* offered a conceptual vehicle by which this process might have occurred. As Needham puts it, "With all their biological insight, sadly lacking otherwise in the early Newtonian period, the Cambridge divines and

naturalists remained fundamentally vitalist, and the substitution of *archaei* for souls did not really help. Spiritualism had been ingrained for centuries in Europe, as we saw [Needham, *Science and Civilisation*, 2:294ff.] from the fortunes of the macrocosm-microcosm analogy there. Confronted with a mathematised universe, it had either to retire into the fastnesses of ecclesiastical authority, or (more nobly) to send the rational theologians into a counter-attack in which vitalism was opposed to mathematics. Yet in the seventeenth century the only path truly leading beyond Descartes (and his apparently irretrievable bifurcation of Nature) did not turn away from mathematics, it passed directly through its midst; this was the path which Leibniz took. It could only have been taken in the light of an organicism from which every animistic residue, every component other than the pure organising relations themselves, had disappeared. Perhaps Neo-Confucian Li showed the way for the purification of Neo-Platonic plastic nature" (504).

117. Ch'ien Mu, *Chu Tzu hsin hsüeh-an*, 1:357.
118. *Chu Tzu yü-lei* 36.24a.
119. *Chu Tzu yü-lei* 53.15a-b.
120. Thomas Nagel, *The Possibility of Altruism* (Princeton: Princeton University Press, 1978), 14.
121. See Fred R. Dallmayr, *Twilight of Subjectivity: Contributions to a Post-Individualist Theory of Politics* (Amherst: University of Massachusetts Press, 1981).
122. *Chu Tzu yü-lei* 53.3a.

Glossary

ai 愛

chang-k'ai 張開

Chang Tsai 張載

Chang Tzu ch'üan-shu 張子全書

Cheng-meng 正蒙

Ch'eng I 程頤

Ch'eng-Chu 程朱

"Ch'eng-ming" 誠明

ch'i 氣

ch'i ch'i chih tsui ching-shuang che 其氣之最精爽者

ch'i-chih chih hsing 氣質之性

"chieh-pi" 解蔽

ch'ien 乾

Ch'ien Mu 錢穆

chih[a] 志

chih[b] 智

chih-ch'i 志氣

chih ch'i chih 持其志

chih-chih 持志

chih hsin tsai wu chung 置心在物中

ching[a] 經

ching[b] 敬

Ching [duke of Ch'i] 景

ch'ing 情

ching-tso 靜坐

Chou Tun-i 周敦頤

Chu Hsi 朱熹

Chu Tzu ch'üan-shu 朱子全書

Chu Tzu hsin hsüeh-an 朱子新學案

Chu Tzu ta-ch'üan 朱子大全

Chu Tzu wen-chi 朱子文集

Chu Tzu yü-lei 朱子語類

ch'üan 權

chuan-hsin chih-chih 專心致志

chung 忠

Erh-Ch'eng ch'üan-shu 二程全書

fang-man 放滿

hao-jan chih ch'i 浩然之氣

Heng-ch'ü 橫渠

ho hsing yü chih chüeh yu hsin chih ming 合性與知覺有心之名

Ho-nan Ch'eng-shih i-shu 河南程氏遺書

"Hsi-ming" 西銘

hsin[a] 心

hsin[b] 信

hsin che ch'i chih ching-shuang
心者氣之精爽

hsin che hsing chih chün yeh, erh
shen-ming chih chu yeh 心者形之
君也，而神明之主也

hsin chih shen ch'u 心之深處

hsin-hsüeh 心學

hsin t'ung hsing ch'ing che yeh
心統性情者也

hsin yu suo chih wei chih chih
心有所之謂之志

Hsüan [king of Ch'i] 宣

hsüeh-ch'i 血氣

Hsün Tzu 荀子

Hu Hung 胡宏

Hua-yen 華嚴

Hua-yen ching 華嚴經

Huang-ti nei-ching su-wen 黃帝
內經素問

hun 魂

i[a] 義

i[b] 意

I-ch'uan 伊川

I-ch'uan wen-chi 伊川文集

jen 仁

jen-hsin 人心

"Ju fa-chieh p'in" 入法界品

Kao Tzu 告子

Kinsei kanseki sōkan, shisōhen
近世漢籍叢刊，思想編

kuei 鬼

li[a] 禮

li[b] 理

li-chih 立志

li-i fen-shu 理一分殊

Li T'ung 李侗

Lu Hsiang-shan 陸象山

Okada Takehiko 岡田武彥

pen-hsing 本性

pi yu shih yen erh wu cheng 必有
事焉而勿正

po-hsüeh erh tu-chih 博學而篤志

p'o 魄

sa-lo 洒落

shen 神

sheng-sheng 生生

shu 恕

shuai 帥

Shun 舜

ssu 思

ssu-i 私意

ssu-tuan 四端

ssu-yü 私欲

ta ch'i hsin 大其心

"Ta-hsin" 大心

"T'ai-ho" 太和

Taishō Shinshū dai-zōkyō 大正新脩大藏經

Tao-hsin 道心

te-chih 得志

ti 第

t'i 體

t'i t'ien-hsia chih wu 體天下之物

"T'ien-tao" 天道

t'ien-te liang-chih 天德良知

t'ien-ti sheng-wu chih hsin 天地生物之心

to 奪

ts'ai 才

Tsai Yü 宰予

Tso chuan 左傳

ts'un 存

t'ung 統

Tzu-lu 子路

tzu-miao 茲藐

tzu-tsei 自賊

Wang Yuquan 王毓銓

Wu-feng 五峯

wu pao ch'i ch'i 無暴其氣

Yao 堯

Yen-p'ing ta-wen 延平答問

"Yü-shan chiang-i" 玉山講義

yung 用

Neo-Confucian Individualism and Holism

Wm. Theodore de Bary

By this point in the volume, the reader will already have encountered a variety of "individualisms" and "holisms" and may not appreciate being told that the forms these concepts take in Neo-Confucianism are no less diverse. As "Neo-Confucianism" itself is a Western term for the new phase of Confucian thought arising in the Sung period (966-1279) and extending down into the twentieth century, its use in the West has had the advantage that it could collectively represent all of the new trends emerging from the Confucian revival in the Sung.[1] Often this new thought has been identified with one particular movement, the Ch'eng-Chu school, which, though only a segment of the whole, later came to be viewed as orthodox. In the early phase of the movement this claim to orthodoxy was expressed in the term "Learning [or School] of the Way" (tao-hsüeh). But there were other names for this teaching too: "Way of the Sages" or "Way to Sagehood" (sheng-jen chih tao); "Learning of the Sages" (sheng-hsüeh); "Learning of the Mind-and-Heart" (hsin-hsüeh); "Learning of Human Nature and Principle" (hsing-li hsüeh), or, in abbreviated form, the "School [or Learning] of Principle" (li-hsüeh).

For simplicity's sake, I shall focus here on the Ch'eng-Chu teaching as the most representative form of Neo-Confucian learning and the most formative influence on later thought with respect to the issue of individualism and holism.

Chu Hsi's (1130-1200) thought begins and ends with the aim of "learning for the sake of one's self" (wei-chi chih hsüeh), a phrase which recalls Confucius's dictum in the Analects (14:25) that learning should be for the sake of one's self and not for the sake of pleasing others. This aim, which set such a high value on the individual self, was put before Chu early in life by his father; it was what later motivated his studies under his teacher Li T'ung (1093-1163), what guided him in his official educational duties and what inspired his thinking to the end of his scholarly career.[2] For many of his later followers, it was also what distinguished true Confucian teaching from any other.[3]

What this had to do with "individualism," a Western concept introduced to the East Asian scene only in the nineteenth century, remains a question. The simplest answer is that it has little directly to do with the later Western forms of individualism in China but much to do with native Chinese forms that appear in the Sung and Ming periods, most notably in the school of Wang Yang-ming. These Neo-Confucian forms of individualism must be understood in the light of both the Confucian tradition Chu invoked and the circumstances of his own age, for it was in explaining his view of the self in the Sung context that he resorted to the earlier language of Confucius.

Seen in the larger perspective of Confucian thought, the phrase "for the sake of one's self" should be taken as expressive, not of a radical individualism which asserts the complete autonomy of the self or sees the individual as in opposition to society, but of a Confucian personalism which affirms the importance of the self or person (*shen* or *tzu*) as the dynamic center of a larger social whole, biological continuum, and moral/spiritual community. In the Sung this Confucian view of the person or self becomes noticeably enlarged, in ways that reflect the expansive economic, social, and cultural trends of the times. If one thinks of Confucian tradition as the larger continuum of which Neo-Confucianism is its later, mature phase, one may say that Neo-Confucian individualism represents a subspecies of Confucian personalism. On the one hand, it partook of individualistic tendencies broadly manifested in Sung thought—in Ch'an Buddhism, for instance, and in Confucians outside the Ch'eng-Chu school like Su Tung-p'o and Lu Hsiang-shan. On the other hand, Confucian tradition imposed upon these tendencies certain restraints which, along with limiting factors in the physical and social environment, shaped and contained this individualism so that, as compared to modern Western varieties which have stressed freedom from any form of constraint, i.e., in terms of "liberty," "liberation," etc., it might be viewed as remaining for the most part within the more modest limits of Confucian personalism, which saw the individual as fulfilling himself through the social process and a moral and spiritual communion with others.

Often this process was described as "getting or finding [the Way] oneself" (*tzu-te*), a concept I have discussed in *The Liberal Tradition in China*. Here it may suffice to explain that "getting" or "finding" the Way in oneself suggests the Way as embracing the self and others and implies the essential harmony of the self, the Way, and others as something to be realized through one's efforts at self-cultivation. There is no fundamental opposition here between the one and the many; nor is there, in the end, a loss of personhood or individuality through the total absorption of the self into the one. Instead, what Chu Hsi seeks is a self-realization in which man fulfills all that is distinctively human while participating in the creative work of heaven and earth. The individualism under discussion here is in keeping with that conception.

In his writings Chu Hsi addressed an educated elite which thought of itself as occupying positions of leadership in the family, the school, the community, and the state. Traditionally, Confucians had viewed these as primary roles of the individual, corresponding to the moral duties which Confucius said must have first claim on one's attention, after which, if one had time and energy to spare, one could devote oneself to "letters" (*wen*). The Neo-Confucians reconfirmed this priority in the Sung, but as a class in more comfortable circumstances they also enjoyed more leisure for cultural activities than most of their forebears; along with it there were increased material and technical means at their disposal. Generally speaking, the centers of Neo-Confucian scholarship were also areas which led in agricultural production, trade, and population growth in the late T'ang and Sung period, i.e., modern Kiangsu, Chekiang, Kiangsi, Fukien, Szechuan, and—for political and cultural reasons rather than economic—the capital region in north central China.[4] Whatever it may have lacked in military prowess, the Sung certainly did not want for brilliant cultural achievements, and it is no surprise that the outburst of individual creativity in arts and letters, especially the greater freedom of individual expression in painting, calligraphy, and other arts taken up by scholar-officials, should have expressed itself also in Neo-Confucian thought.[5]

The term *wen* represented something more than letters and polite culture, however. A follower of Hu Yüan (993-1059) spoke of *wen* as the literary expression or cultural transmission of the Confucian Way.[6] In this sense *wen* stood for the highest values of the culture, human civilization as carrying out the Way and the will of heaven. Confucius had talked of his own mission in the world as bound up with "this culture" (*ssu-wen*), and many Neo-Confucians likewise took it as their personal responsibility in life to make the Way manifest in the world through "this culture."[7]

In so doing, the Neo-Confucians, as an educated elite in relatively prosperous times, dedicated their new affluence and leisure to serious purposes, attempting to convert them into a higher form of culture. They did this with a sense of vocation as leaders in the society who felt keenly their responsibility to meet the social and cultural crises of their time. It was this humane concern which led them to reinterpret and revitalize tradition so that, instead of merely perpetuating antiquarian studies, it would express the highest aspirations of the Confucian elite as bearers of that culture in the Sung.[8]

In this broader and deeper conception of *wen*, the cultural activities of the Neo-Confucian scholar ranged from the substantive business of moral self-cultivation to the study of classical texts, literary activities, and historical or practical learning of some social benefit. In the Ch'eng-Chu school these were viewed as complementary activities, sometimes summed up in terms of "dwelling in reverence and fathoming principle" (*chü-ching ch'iung-li*, i.e., spiritual/moral and intellectual pursuits); or "quiet-sitting and book learning"(*ching-tso, tu-shu*), i.e., contemplative practice and scholarly study); or "preserving one's moral nature and pursuing scholarly inquiry" (*tsun te-hsing, tao wen-hsüeh*). These activities went hand-in-hand. Book learning was meant to enhance and enrich one's moral cultivation, while the latter served to deepen one's scholarly understanding. Thus, even "learning for the sake of one's self" was intimately bound up with how one read the classics; and classical studies, always a major occupation of the Confucian, involved not only textual research but also the application of textual learning to practical activities through which the Neo-Confucian pursued his self-cultivation. In this sense, "learning for the sake of one's self " was to be understood, not as opposed to activities in behalf of others, but rather as a constant attention to one's self-development and self-integration in the midst of such activities.

From this point of view, then, we may say that "learning for the sake of one's self" as the substantive pursuit of the Neo-Confucian was revealed not only through his functional roles in society (*yung*) but in how he related to his tradition, to his culture (*wen*), in all of the senses described above. It may well be that in all major ethico-religious traditions some relation to the scriptures is important to the process of self-discovery and self-definition and that St. Augustine's *tolle lege* ("take up and read")—or, by contrast, the Zen master's tearing up of the scriptures—are paradigmatic acts of almost universal significance. Nevertheless, there has probably been no other tradition so clearly committed to scholarship as the Confucian, and in the absence of sacerdotal, pastoral, or monastic activities, book learning and literary activity have been even more central tasks for the Confucian than they were for the Christian, the Jew, or the Muslim.

Accordingly, it is through these activities that we find the Neo-Confucian celebrating certain individualistic qualities associated with the autonomous mind—self-consciousness, critical awareness, creative thought, independent initiative and judgment—which find their way into the basic texts and commentaries of the Ch'eng-Chu school. In other words, Sung individualism asserted itself as a natural outgrowth of the high degree of cultural activity sustained in the Sung by the members of the scholar-official class and by the classes supporting them. Likewise, in Sung politics, Neo-Confucians advocated a more independent role for scholars at court. Meanwhile, in the social sphere, there was no doubt less allowance made for the individual; rather, a greater accommodation to others was stressed.

To sum up, then, the types of individualism asserted here reflect the following features of Sung society and culture: (1) the special status and functions of the scholar-official class; (2) the rising affluence and rich culture of the period; (3) a religious atmosphere pervaded by a Ch'an Buddhist spirituality which had already put the problem of the self high on the human agenda; and (4) the interaction of these factors with a Confucian humanistic tradition already disposed to value highly the cultural and political contributions of the individual scholar.

In Chu Hsi's terms, the essential nature of the self was the same in all these contexts. It is not he, but we who, from the hindsight of history, find the fullest expression of this individualism in certain areas most significant for his class and his time. In principle Chu Hsi would probably still insist that, whatever the limiting factors in particular situations, the highest priority should always attach to the fulfillment of the person, i.e., to the fullest development and exercise of individual human capabilities within the given circumstances.

Individualism and Holism

If self-fulfillment for the Neo-Confucian meant a personal realization of the Way, the Way itself partook of both unity and diversity. Functionally speaking, it could take the several forms of the "Way of the Teacher," "Way of the Ruler," "Way of the Emperors and Kings," "Way of the Minister," "Way of the Parent," etc., which have been cited as the principal roles of the Neo-Confucian.[9] These are familiar categories in Neo-Confucian ethical teaching. And in his discussion of the Way of the Great Learning, one of Chu Hsi's most significant attempts to formulate the basis of a public morality, he asserts that, depending on the circumstances of the individual, self-fulfillment—how one "rests in the highest good" or "fulfills the ultimate of heavenly principle"—will be defined in terms of what is proper to one's own function or station, i.e., in relation to one or more of these "ways."[10]

Still, these functional roles, and their appropriate "ways," do not completely define the selfhood or personhood of the individual, which is more than the sum of its functional parts. It is sagehood, the working model of self-cultivation, and the Way of the Sage which represent the integrating ideal of selfhood in the Ch'eng-Chu system; that is, the process by which the individual realizes in his own life the values of the Way and, by achieving a unique personalization of that Way, fulfills at once, as Chu Hsi puts it, both "the whole substance" of his nature and its "great functioning" in the world.

To some extent, this Way could be conceptualized and described, as the Sung masters attempted to do out of the conviction that the reality of sagehood was comprehensible in rational terms—up to a point. Neo-Confucians stopped short of a complete definition, recognizing that the perfection of virtue was not a fixed quantity but, in the form of human love and creativity, opened out indefinitely onto a larger vista of reality which had to be conceived holistically. As Chu Hsi said of *jen* (humanity, humaneness): "This principle cannot easily be conveyed in words. If a fixed definition is given to it, then violence might be done to its all-encompassing nature."[11]

Man's place in this larger and also deeper universe was presented by Chu Hsi in the first chapter of *Reflections on Things at Hand* (Chin-ssu lu), entitled "The Substance of the Way" ("Tao t'i"), as well as in his comments on earlier Confucian teachings related to the metaphysical or spiritual aspects of the Way. As his title *Chin-ssu lu* implied, the Way was something near at hand, simple and ordinary. Hence Chu had mixed feelings about putting the metaphysical aspect up front in chapter one. He did so, however, in order to provide a philosophical framework for the pursuit of sagehood—one which set forth his own philosophical assumptions in contrast to those of Buddhism and Taoism.

Neo-Confucians often quoted Confucius's saying, "Hearing the Way in the morning, one can die content in the evening" (*Analects*, 4:8). This suggested a religious or mystical conception of the Way and of self-identification with it as the ultimate in human fulfillment. Other passages in the *Analects*, cryptic in themselves and often uncertain of interpretation, were cited as expressing the essential quality of the Way under its numinous aspect. One example, frequently mentioned, is the characterization of the Way as the inexhaustible and unceasing stream of life. Ch'eng I quotes Confucius (*Analects*, 9:16):

"Confucius, standing by a stream, said: It passes on like this. He meant
that the nature of the Way is like this. Here we must find out for
ourselves." Chang I [a student of Ch'eng I] said, "This means infinity."
The teacher said, "Of course it means infinity, but how can this single idea
of infinity tell everything about the passing stream?"[12]

The reality Ch'eng I speaks of here is something to be experienced for
oneself; it cannot be defined even in an expression like "infinity," though
"infinity" is the word insofar as words will go. A similar conception underlay
Chu Hsi's choice of the opening lines of Chou Tun-i's *Diagram of the Supreme
Ultimate Explained* (T'ai-chi-t'u chieh) as the first principle to be asserted in
Reflections on Things at Hand: "Indeterminate and yet the Supreme
Ultimate" (*wu-chi erh t'ai-chi*).[13] Thus, he characterized the ultimate reality
principle as nonfinite and open-ended while at the same time fixed and
definite as a normative principle.

The significance of this characterization derives from the Neo-Confucian
encounter with Taoism and Buddhism, in which the former sought to reaffirm
the fundamental reality of enduring values against the Taoist teaching of
nothingness (*wu*) and Buddhist doctrine of emptiness (*k'ung*). Yet, in
reasserting the Supreme Ultimate from the *Book of Changes* as the first
principle of being, Chu Hsi felt the need to take into account the Taoist view of
change and the Buddhism law of impermanence. Simply to assert immutable
principles would not do, unless one could also establish their simultaneous
immanence in and transcendence of the world of change.[14] To say that the
ultimate reality principle was "nonfinite," "limitless," and "indeterminate"
meant that it was not itself a thing subject to change. Thus, Chu Hsi said that
wu-chi meant absence of "shape and form," of "sound or smell," "direction,"
or "position."[15] To speak of principle as the Supreme Ultimate gave it a
definite moral significance, while speaking of it as nonfinite or indeterminate
would preclude its being taken for a thing.[16]

Modern writers have tended, for a variety of reasons, to focus on Ch'eng-
Chu thought as a philosophy of principle and on the Supreme Ultimate as the
quintessence of principle. But little has been said about *wu-chi*, an equally
fundamental aspect of reality for Chu Hsi. One form taken by the former line
of interpretation has been to see man and the human order as completely
defined by a hierarchical structure of immanent natural laws, so that man's
nature is bounded by rigid moral norms, rationalistically conceived to support
the claims of the established order on the individual. Thus, Neo-Confucianism
has been described as having a "closed character."[17] Self-cultivation is viewed
essentially as a process of bringing oneself into conformity with established
norms, and Neo-Confucian teaching is seen as lending itself to, if not enlisting
in, the ideological service of authoritarian regimes.

Important as rational and moral principle were to the Ch'eng-Chu school,
it is wrong to disregard the nonfinite, formless, and indefinable aspect of *wu-
chi* as if this were only a minor concession to Taoism or an eclectic element of
no intrinsic significance for Chu's philosophy. There was nothing adventitious
about this conception, arrived at in the mature development of Chu's thought.

It was discussed by him at length and strongly defended against pointed opposition.[18] In Chu's debate with Lu Hsiang-shan it was a central issue. Lu saw *wu-chi* as a throwback to Taoism and therefore incompatible with true Confucian teaching. Chu responded that *wu-chi* should not be taken as Taoist nothingness, a first principle out of which existent things emerged.[19] *Wu-chi* and *t'ai-chi* were inseparable aspects, not successive stages, of being.[20] They were simultaneous aspects of a Way that was in one sense indeterminate and yet in another sense the supreme value and ultimate end of all things.[21]

Although Chu asserted this dichotomy as a cosmological principle governing all creation, for him as for Chou Tun-i its primary significance lay in its application to man and the cultivation of sagehood. In man the Supreme Ultimate was the principle of perfection in the mind-and-heart, sometimes projected as the ideal of sagehood toward which self-cultivation was directed by the practice of "abiding in reverence and fathoming principle."[22] Yet, the closer one came to attaining the fullness of virtue—exemplified in the sage as sincerity or integrity (*ch'eng*) and asserted for all men as the "highest good" (*chih-shan*) for each—the more open-ended the process was seen to be and the less bounded the self. This is the meaning of Ch'eng I's assertion about the expansiveness of the self that comes with self-mastery: "If one can subdue oneself, his mind will become broad and generous and his body will become big and be at ease," and it is why Chu Hsi refused to define "humanity" (*jen*) in words lest it seem to set a limit on man's identifying with the infinite mind of heaven-and-earth.[23]

This also helps us to understand what Chu Hsi has in mind when he discusses the "highest good" in the *Great Learning* (Ta-hsüeh) as the goal of universal self-cultivation. Chu explains this in *Questions and Answers Concerning the Great Learning* (Ta-hsüeh huo-wen). He speaks of the reality of *wu-chi* manifesting itself in the utmost refinement and spirituality of the creative process, by which yin-yang and the five agents combine in man, and he receives as his endowment from heaven all of the inherent principles (i.e., the inner structures, or patterns, which make things what they are and should be) which will be applicable to daily human affairs.[24] The ultimate quintessence of these principles as the Supreme Ultimate or Norm is also infinite and inexpressible, but since one cannot help giving it a name, it is called "the highest good."[25] Attainment of this "highest good" comes through experiencing the Supreme Ultimate as "one undifferentiated Unity."[26] In the "square inch" of man's mind there is this empty spirituality which contains all principles. It is the wondrous, endlessly creative center of the human mind-and-heart; it is what distinguishes man from beast in the higher reach and refinement of his spirituality and what enables man, through the attainment of the highest good or Supreme Ultimate, to join heaven-and-earth in the work of creation.[27]

Much of Chu Hsi's discussion of human nature and the mind must be understood in the light of these two fundamental characteristics of all reality. Thus, the nature of man (*hsing*), which unifies all of the principles that make man what he should be, is, metaphysically speaking, the Supreme Ultimate (*t'ai-chi*) in each individual. Its particularity is defined in terms of a person's lot, or share in life (*fen*), which determines the specific conditions under which this perfection is to be achieved and the functions through which the utmost degree of sincerity or integrity (*ch'eng*) is to be made manifest. Its universality involves participation in a process that is as limitless and indefinable (*wu-chi*) as the creative love which unites heaven, earth, and all things. In a letter responding to a question concerning his important lecture at the Jade Mountain, Chu said: "The nature is the substance of the undifferentiated Supreme Ultimate. In a fundamental sense it cannot be expressed in words, but it contains all principles including the four great constitutive virtues, which, if they are to be given names, are humaneness, righteousness, decorum, and wisdom."[28]

In this passage Chu Hsi, while offering a definite method for the cultivation of this nature, describes the culmination of the process in terms suggestive of the inexpressible. For example—and it became a celebrated example in the Ch'eng-Chu school—Chu attached a special note to his commentary on the "investigation of things and extension of knowledge" in *Sentences and Phrases of the Great Learning* (Ta-hsüeh chang-chu), and he elaborated further on this theme in his *Questions and Answers on the Great Learning*. First, the commentary based on Ch'eng I:

> The foregoing fifth chapter of the commentary explained the meaning of "investigation of things and the extension of knowledge," but it is now lost. I have ventured to draw upon the ideas of Master Ch'eng [I] to supply it. That the "extension of knowledge consists in the investigation of things" means that, wishing to extend one's knowledge, one must fathom the principles in each thing or affair as it presents itself to us. The spiritual intelligence of man always seeks to know, and the things and affairs of this world all have their principles. But if there are principles yet unfathomed, man's knowledge is incomplete. Therefore the *Great Learning*, at the outset of its instruction, insists that the student, in regard to the things and affairs of the world, proceed from what he already knows of their principles and fathom them to their utmost limit. After exerting himself for a long time, one day he will experience a breakthrough to integral comprehension. Then there will be nothing in the multiplicity of things external or internal, fine or coarse, that is beyond one's reach, and nothing in the whole substance and great functioning of the mind that will not be fully clarified. This is what is meant by the investigation of things, the extension of knowledge.[29]

Now, for the *Questions and Answers on the Great Learning*:

> In the spirit of learning what one studies is nothing but the mind and principles. Though the mind is the master of this one person, its empty, spiritual substance can command all the principles under heaven, and though the principles are dispersed in things, their operation [or function], in all its subtlety and refinement, does not lie beyond this one man's mind. Initially there is no distinction to be made between the internal or external, fine or coarse, but if one is unaware of the spirituality of the mind-and-heart and thus unable to preserve it, obscurations and vexations will prevent one from fathoming the fine subtlety of the principles. Unable to understand their fine subtlety and having no way to

fathom them, one would be prevented by partiality, narrow-mindedness, and obstinacy from exhaustively exercising the whole substance of the mind-and-heart.

Thus the sage provided instruction so that man would become aware of this spiritual intelligence in the silence of his own mind and preserve it in dignity [of demeanor] and single-minded composure [quiescent unity] as the basis of his fathoming of principle; and [it was also] so that man would understand the subtlety of principles, fathom them through scholarly study and discussion, and accomplish the work of exhaustively exercising the mind, so that the broad and narrow interpenetrate one another and action and quiescence sustain one another. From the start there is no distinction to be made between what is internal or external, fine or coarse, but with the persistent and genuine accumulation of effort, there will be a breakthrough to integral comprehension, and having come to understand all things in their undifferentiated unity, in the end there will be no distinctions of internal or external, fine or coarse to speak of.

Nowadays people want to oversimplify the matter and wrap it up in mystery so as to make it seem like a profound and impenetrable doctrine of some very special sort. They would have scholars misdirect their minds to something outside words and letters, saying that only in this manner can the way be apprehended. This is all attributable to the seductive and misleading doctrines of Buddhism in recent times, and it would be a great error to let this be put forward to the detriment of the ancients' real learning of "clarifying virtue" and "renewing the people."[30]

The direct meaning and significance of these passages may be summed up as: (1) the need to study things and affairs in order to understand their principles; (2) a belief in the intelligibility of principle; (3) the characterization of the mind as "empty and spiritual" (in the sense of unlimited receptivity and permeability) while at the same time replete with principle (in the sense of the mind and things being similarly structured so that there is a natural affinity between them); (4) the view of the cumulative nature of learning and the increasing coherence of principles as pursued both extensively in things and intensively within the self; (5) the culmination of this learning in a comprehensive understanding of things in their undifferentiated unity or wholeness (*kuan-t'ung*), which eventually dawns on one (i.e., an understanding which is not necessarily an exhaustive knowledge of things in their particularity but which brings a fusion of cognitive awareness and affective response, overcoming the dichotomy of self and other, inner and outer, etc.); (6) the view that this holistic understanding, though it goes beyond words, is not to be confused with a Buddhist enlightenment which transcends morality and reason; and (7) the conviction that growth in learning leads to the fullest possible manifestation of the "whole substance and great functioning" of man's nature and of individual selfhood or personhood.

Admittedly, the text is not without its ambiguities, and these led to controversy among later Neo-Confucians. How extensive did the search for an exhaustive knowledge of the principles in things need to be? For some later critics, this seemed to require a lifetime of prolonged study, as if scholarly achievement had become a prerequisite to achieving sagehood. Chu undoubtedly believed that study and investigation were lifetime pursuits, yet here he is talking about a certain stage in the pursuit of learning when one's understanding finally brings a sense of being at home with oneself and the world. Chu does not actually stipulate that this sense of wholeness and fulfillment requires a mastery of all the principles in things; it is more likely that what he had in mind was a process of learning, both cognitive and affective, which brought one's capacity for empathetic understanding to the point where nothing in the world seemed alien to one.

Presumably, this deep sense of being at home with oneself and things, of overcoming the dichotomy between self and other, inner and outer, also meant understanding one's own role and destiny in a manner similar to Confucius's "learning the imperative of heaven" (t'ien-ming) at the age of fifty. This is now seen in Chu Hsi's terms under the two basic aspects of knowing the principle or the ground of one's being (so-i-jan chih ku) and the principle of what a thing should be (so-tang-jan chih tse). Since each individual has his own principle and Supreme Ultimate, his integrated comprehension of the wholeness of things would include an insight into heaven's imperative under both these aspects as the basis of his individuality in relation to the Way as a whole.[31] Moreover, being established through the conjunction of man's heavenly nature (principle) with his physical nature, like the principle inherent in each seed of grain, this particularity of the individual would be recognized as a compound of the physical and emotional nature with the moral and rational. It was not just an abstract norm.[32]

As a succinct statement of Chu Hsi's mature views on the method and goal of self-cultivation, and one which appeared prominently in a basic text of the Neo-Confucian school—the first among the Four Books in the new curriculum—the passage in Chu's commentary on the Great Learning had extraordinary importance and influence. The further attention which Chu gave to it in Questions and Answers on the Great Learning not only amplified the rather terse language of the Sentences and Phrases and expanded its significance but also demonstrated that this idea was no mere afterthought or casual comment of Chu's but rather the culmination of a long development in his thinking about the central concepts in Sung philosophy.

This philosophical dialogue goes back almost to the start of his intellectual and spiritual quest in colloquy with his teacher Li T'ung (1093-1163). It transpired in fulfillment of his father's injunction to Chu that he should pursue "learning for one's own sake," something which Chu said he only seriously began under the tutelage of Li T'ung.[33] Chu Hsi's Responses of Yen-p'ing (Yen-p'ing ta-wen) records his conversations and correspondence with Li in the years from 1157 to 1162. In the immediate background of this exchange is Chu's youthful fascination with Ch'an Buddhism, and in the direct foreground of the discussions are issues arising from the Buddhist-Confucian encounter. They are issues which significantly affect our understanding of Chu Hsi's holism as well as the alternatives he considered before arriving at his final position. Though we cannot review here the whole sorting-out process he went through, neither can we bypass it completely if we are to grasp the significance of Chu's holistic conception of self-fulfillment as compared to others proposed at that time.

The key terms in which this holism is discussed came down to Li T'ung and Chu Hsi from the Ch'eng brothers (Ch'eng I taught the teacher of the teacher of Li T'ung) and their uncle Chang Tsai (1020-1077). One of these expressions was Ch'eng's "unity of principle and diversity of its particularizations" (*li-i fen-shu*). Another was Ch'eng Hao's doctrine of the "humaneness which forms one body with heaven-and-earth and all things" (*t'ien-ti wan-wu i-t'i chih jen*),[34] also spoken of by him holistically as "totally forming the same body [substance] with things" (*hun-jan yü wu t'ung-t'i*).[35] Still another formulation was Chang Tsai's description of man, set forth in his "Western Inscription" ("Hsi-ming"), as sharing in the same substance and having a fundamental affinity with heaven-and-earth and all things. Chu drew upon these conceptions while also qualifying them in important respects. Together they provide the context for Chu's enigmatic expression, "a breakthrough to integral comprehension" (*huo-jan kuan-t'ung*), which is the culmination of the learning process and the fulfillment of self-cultivation as described in Chu's commentaries above.

As Li T'ung explained to Chu the significance of the "unity of principle and diversity of its particularizations," he took issue with the idea of principle or substance as separable from practice or function. Some persons held that there was no essential difference in principle between Confucianism and Buddhism, since Confucian "humaneness" (*jen*) could be equated with Buddhist "compassion" (*tz'u*). According to this view, the only significant difference between the two teachings lay in the functional aspect—i.e., Buddhism's lack of a practical program such as Confucianism offered for dealing with the needs of human society. Li, however, and Chu following him, contended that the difference in practice also pointed to a difference in principle. One could not expect Confucian practice to follow from Buddhist principle, nor could one accept as true principle what did not lead to Confucian ethical practice. Hence, there could be no dichotomizing, as in Buddhism, of principle and practice to represent two different orders of reality, principle real and undifferentiated, practice less real because it pertained to the world of differentiation and discrimination.[36] To substantiate principle, one must realize one's humanity in the midst of practice, i.e., by coming to terms with one's individual lot (*fen*) or station in life and its differentiated duties, thus fulfilling one's own particular nature as well as joining oneself to the creative principle underlying all things. This is what was meant by realizing the unity of principle and the diversity of its particularizations.[37] It was also what distinguished Confucianism as "real or practical learning" from the "empty learning" of Buddhism, which viewed the world of action as a secondary or qualified order of reality in comparison to the essential truth of Buddhist emptiness. In this way the reality of the individual was affirmed along with the unity of principle, so that self-realization involved no loss of individuality through absorption into the whole. In the end true individuality merged with, rather than was submerged in, holistic unity.

Li T'ung was willing to concede neither the Buddhist bifurcation of reality on two levels of truth nor the need for transcendental enlightenment as the precondition for coping with the world. For him, on the contrary, true self-realization and spiritual freedom were to be attained in the performance of the moral task.[38] To describe the characteristic spirit of the sage, Li borrowed an expression from Huang T'ien-chien's (1045-1105)[39] portrayal of Chou Tun-i as having achieved a state of mind that was "free, pure, and unobstructed [sa-lo] like a breeze on a sunny day or the clear moon."[40] This characterization later was included by Chu Hsi in his presentation of the "Dispositions [or Characteristics] of the Sages and Worthies" in *Reflections on Things at Hand*.[41] Chu also expressed his admiration for like qualities in Li T'ung, who had overcome his own wayward disposition to achieve a lofty state of mind, serenity of soul, and unfathomable profundity. It was a freedom of spirit attained by liberating oneself from all selfishness, obstinacy, and rigidity. In this state one's mind was completely impartial and open to reality. Principle inherent in one's nature could then express itself freely and clearly, with no selfish obstructions.[42]

As Li is quoted in the *Responses of Yen-p'ing*:

> If in encountering things and affairs one can have not one iota of selfish obstinacy or rigidity, then that is to be "free, pure, and unobstructed." In other words, this is to be large-minded, open, and fair. It is to be completely one with principle and the Way. If in encountering things one is not able to enter into them completely [it means that] in one's mind-and-heart, one has not freed oneself from all trace of partiality, or in other words that one is still obstinate and rigid. None of this will do.[43]

Elsewhere Li likened this state of mind to the "evening spirit" spoken of by Mencius, a spirit nourished by the restorative influence of the night (*Mencius*, 6A:8).[44] He also explained that it was a state of mind in which one naturally followed principle and the latter imposed no restraint. Indeed, if one felt any constraint, said Li, he would know he was not proceeding on the right course.[45]

Achieving this state in which the mind and principle had become one was not something to be accomplished in one stroke or by a headlong effort. It required constant attentiveness to one matter or affair after another, in the manner of Ch'eng I's "holding to reverence" (*chih-ching*) or "abiding in reverence" (*chü-ching*).[46] The mind should be allowed to dwell on each matter until principle in the mind and the principle in things became completely fused.[47] "If you go from one thing to another without really comprehending each in turn, it is of no use."[48] After a long while this cumulative exercise would produce a natural sense of ease and freedom in the mind-and-heart.[49]

Chu Hsi saw this method of Li's in the light of Ch'eng I's practice of the investigation of things and the fathoming of principle (*ko-wu ch'iung-li*). In the *Reflections on Things at Hand*, he quoted Ch'eng I as saying "when the mind is at ease, it naturally perceives principle."[50] And again, "one must investigate one item today and another tomorrow. When one has accumulated much knowledge, he will naturally achieve a thorough understanding like a sudden release."[51] This is similar to Chu Hsi's own account of the investigation of things culminating in a breakthrough to integral comprehension and a sense of total clarity, as set forth in his commentary on the *Great Learning* and elaborated in the *Questions and Answers on the Great Learning*. His final view, as expressed in the latter text, summed up a lifetime of study and reflection on the Neo-Confucian kōan Li T'ung had passed on to him and Cheng I's teachings had helped him solve.[52]

As a form of praxis in self-cultivation Li T'ung strongly recommended quiet-sitting (*ching-tso*), which he also described as "sitting in silence and clearing the mind" (*mo-tso ch'eng-hsin*).[53] Influenced though it was by Ch'an Buddhism's "sitting in meditation" (*tso-ch'an*), this practice had been adapted to Neo-Confucian purposes and conformed to its own life-style.[54] Li believed that quiet-sitting would settle the mind and leave it with the transparency of still water, in which heaven's principle and one's own moral stance in relation to a given matter would emerge clearly.[55]

> The way of learning does not lie in too many words. It is just sitting silently, clearing the mind, and experiencing heavenly principle. Then even the slightest sign of selfish desire will not go undetected or unchecked. . . .
>
> Generally speaking, if one has doubts as to how to proceed, one should sit silently and look within oneself. Then one's moral obligations are sure to be revealed clearly, heavenly principle is sure to be observed, and one can detect the point at which one's effort should be applied in daily affairs.[56]

For Li T'ung, this introspective practice was intended as a spiritual discipline to nourish the mind and keep it in a constant state of attentiveness, mindfulness, or readiness for action in daily life. While it focused on the unmanifest state of the mind-and-heart, before the activation and articulation of the feelings, it was not understood as opposed to rational discourse or scholarly learning. Li T'ung rejected the notion of "sudden enlightenment" in Ch'an Buddhism, with its transcendence of discursive knowledge. When Chu came to Li after his experiments with Ch'an, Li directed him to study the Confucian classics, which would engage him in rational discourse concerning the moral life. The kind of insight or enlightenment sought by Confucius should not be limited to words, but neither could it dispense with them. "Holding to reverence" through quiet-sitting went hand-in-hand with book learning, i.e., study of the classics.[57] Thus, the deep personal experience of truth, as taught by Li, should be of the wondrousness or mystery which is at the very heart of discursive knowledge itself. In other words, it should help one to understand the wonder of creation in the most ordinary things and to recognize in the numinous aspect of things something of enduring value, rather than the momentary reflection of an emptiness of which nothing can finally be predicated. Here the magic of the word expresses the wondrous functioning (*miao-yung*) of substantial Confucian principle, as contrasted to the "mysterious being" (*miao-yu*), which arises from Emptiness but which, in Ch'an Buddhism, one should not try to put in words (*pu-li wen-tzu*).

Combining as it did objective observation and personal intuition, this method could produce a kind of enlightenment (*chüeh-wu*), but Li T'ung preferred to express it as "finding the Way in oneself through personal experience" (*t'i-jen tzu-te*).[58] Chu Hsi also spoke of "finding the Way in oneself" and of "personal realization," but in the passages cited above from his commentaries, he preferred to express it in terms of achieving the "whole substance and great functioning" of the mind. The reasons for this are better understood if we look at the alternative formulations which Chu considered before arriving at his final position.

Chu had some reservations about the method of quiet-sitting precisely because it smacked too much of quietism, and because as a means of "nourishing principle in the mind" it seemed to concentrate on substance (i.e., the mind in its quiescent state) at the possible expense of function—a concern he felt even over Ch'eng's emphasis on the unity of principle.[59] Chu sought a formulation that would better express Li's own insistence on the need to combine the "unity of principle" with the "diversity of its [functional] particularizations."

Among the theories which Chu evaluated in this connection was Ch'eng Hao's "humaneness which forms one body with heaven-and-earth and all things."[60] Properly understood, this was a doctrine to which Chu could give his blessing, and with that it remained one of the most influential Neo-Confucian concepts down into modern times.[61] But without some qualification, it could easily be misinterpreted as putting primary stress on the sense of man's unity with the universe at the expense of the differentiated functions through which man's humaneness must in fact be realized. That is, a subjective experience or mystical feeling of oneness with the universe could become the counterfeit of a true holistic self-realization through moral effort and practical action. For Chu Hsi, a genuine holism could only mean the simultaneous realization of the "whole substance and great functioning" of human nature because the humaneness which forms "one body with heaven, earth and all things" cannot be simply a subjective experience of undifferentiated unity—it must also express itself in loving actions of a particular sort.

Similar problems were involved in the extensive discussions of the Ch'eng brothers, Li T'ung, and Chu Hsi over the meaning and significance of the "Western Inscription" of Chang Tsai. The brevity of this text is out of all proportion to the wide attention it has commanded and the enormous influence it has exerted. As the succinct expression of a quintessentially Chinese mysticism of the human order, it appealed almost immediately to the humanistic religiosity of the Confucians and quickly became established as a classic statement of Neo-Confucian holism, being included in innumerable anthologies from Chu Hsi's *Reflections on Things at Hand* and the official Ming *Compendium on Human Nature and Principle* (Hsing-li ta-ch'üan) of 1415 to the Ch'ing dynasty's *Essential Ideas Concerning Human Nature and Principle* (Hsing-li ching-i) of 1715, to name only a few.

The essential spirit of the work may be conveyed in a few lines:

> Heaven is my father and Earth is my mother, and even such a small creature as I find an intimate place in their midst.

Therefore that which fills the universe I regard as my body and that which directs the universe I consider as my nature.

All people are my brothers and sisters, and all things are my companions.

The great ruler [the emperor] is the eldest son of my parents [Heaven and Earth], and the great ministers are his stewards. Respect the aged—this is the way to treat them as elders should be treated. Show deep love toward the orphaned and the weak—this is the way to treat them as the young should be treated. The sage identifies his character with that of Heaven and Earth, and the worthy is the most outstanding man. Even those who are tired, infirm, crippled, or sick; those who have no brothers or children, wives or husbands, are all my brothers who are in distress and have no one to turn to.

When the time comes, to keep himself from harm—this is the care of a son. To rejoice in Heaven and to have no anxiety—this is filial piety at its purest.

He who disobeys [the Principle of Nature] violates virtue. He who destroys humanity is a robber. He who promotes evil lacks [moral] capacity. But he who puts his moral nature into practice and brings his physical existence into complete fulfillment can match [Heaven and Earth].

One who knows the principles of transformation will skillfully carry forward the undertakings [of Heaven and Earth], and one who penetrates spirit to the highest degree will skillfully carry out their will.

Wealth, honor, blessing, and benefits are meant for the enrichment of my life, while poverty, humble station, and sorrow are meant to help me to fulfillment.

In life I follow and serve [Heaven and Earth]. In death I will be at peace.[62]

Critical discussion of the meaning of the text has tended to concede its importance as a basic affirmation of man's creative role in the universe, while seeking to amend it in one direction or another. Recent exceptions to this have been critics who see it as expressing a paternalistic philosophy readily exploitable by the traditional ruling elite, though Shimada Kenji has shown that in fact it was most often invoked by idealistic reformers and revolutionaries, not by defenders of the status quo.[63] This question need not concern us here, but insofar as Neo-Confucian holism had a vital connection with Sung-Ming individualism, certain points in the "Western Inscription" are worth noting: (1) the strong affirmation of human life as grounded in the creative power of heaven-and-earth, and human love as an expression of that creative energy; (2) the sense of unity with the cosmos and continuity with all life; (3) the positive view of individual life in the context of the family and community, offering the prospect of a self-fulfillment that includes, but goes beyond, the meeting of one's social obligations; (4) the value of worldly goods and meaningfulness of human experience as contributing to self-fulfillment over a lifetime; and (5) the priority given to filial piety over loyalty to the emperor and the stress on self-respect and self-preservation as a filial duty.

From this it is plain what a high value Chang Tsai sets on the individual self and its potential for creative communion with heaven-and-earth. Questions arose almost immediately, however, over his emphasis on man's

oneness with the universe and all things—to the neglect, some thought, of the
performance of those specific duties which alone could give practical
realization to man's humanity. It was objected that Chang preached a doctrine
of universal love hardly different from Mo Tzu's or from Buddhist
compassion, both of which were undifferentiated with respect to the priorities
and form of ethical action appropriate to specific human relationships.
Against this, the Ch'engs, Li T'ung, and Chu Hsi pointed to some of the
specific duties referred to by Chang and asserted that, on the contrary, the
"Western Inscription" served uniquely to express the proper relation between
substance and function, unity in principle and diversity in particular
applications.[64] Nevertheless, Chu Hsi saw a need in this discussion for greater
clarity as to the relation between humanity (humaneness) and love, substance
and function, the unity of principle and the diversity of its particularizations.

Ch'eng I had already raised this issue in his discussions of humanity with
his students, and Chu quoted him in *Reflections on Things at Hand* in a way
which expressed the irreducibly individual, and at the same time holistic,
character of its realization:

> It is up to you gentlemen to think for yourselves and personally realize
> what humanity is. Because Mencius said: "The feeling of commiseration is
> what we call humanity" [6A:6] later scholars have therefore considered
> love to be humanity. But love is feeling, whereas humanity is the nature.
> How can love be taken exclusively as humanity? Mencius said that the
> feeling of commiseration is the beginning of humanity. Since it is called
> the beginning of humanity, it should not be called humanity itself.[65]

In his "Treatise on Humanity" ("Jen shuo") and his "Lecture at the Jade
Mountain" ("Yü-shan chiang-i"), Chu developed the distinction between
humanity as the principle (substance) of love and love as the functioning of
humanity. Confusion of the two led, at one extreme, to the identification of
human nature or humanity with raw emotion or a diffuse humanitarian
sentimentality, and, at the other, to a kind of undifferentiated consciousness
which denied the value distinctions so vital to the practice of genuine
humaneness. To avoid these pitfalls, Chu would ground human love in a
larger cosmic principle, the life-giving energy and creature-loving mind-and-
heart of heaven-and-earth, while also subordinating it to the higher end of
perfecting human nature to attain the Supreme Ultimate. At the same time he
would confirm as function the concrete reality of the love expressed in the
mind-and-heart of man and given specific, practical application in human
society.

In Chu Hsi's words:

> In the teachings [of Confucius, it is said], "Subdue oneself and return to
> decorum." This means that if we can overcome and eliminate selfishness
> and return to the Principle of Nature [*t'ien-li*, Principle of Heaven], then
> the substance of this mind [that is, *jen*], will be present everywhere and its
> function will always be operative. It is also said, "Be respectful in private
> life, be serious in handling affairs, and be loyal in dealing with others."
> These are also ways to preserve this mind. Again, it is said, "Be filial in

serving parents," "Be respectful in serving elder brothers," and "Be loving in dealing with all things." These are ways to put this mind into practice.

Furthermore, to talk about *jen* in general terms of the self and things as "one body" may lead one to be vague, confused, neglectful, and make no effort to be vigilant. The bad effect—and there has been—may be to consider other things as oneself. [On the other hand] to talk about love exclusively in terms of consciousness will lead people to be nervous, impatient, and devoid of any quality of depth. The bad effect—and there has been—may be to take desire in itself as principle. In one case, the mind is forgetful [and careless]. In the other case there is an artificial effort to get results. Both are wrong.[66]

Here Chu argues against a concept of the self and things as forming one body if it means an identification so vague and a compassion so diffuse that one fails realistically to meet the concrete needs of the self and things in their own particularity, as in the case of the Bodhisattva's sacrificing himself to feed the starving tiger, a gesture so extravagant and unrealistic as to be meaningless.[67] This is to put undue emphasis on substance to the neglect of function. On the other hand, if one pursues consciousness—"using the mind to pursue the mind"—without regard to the larger ends that should guide the emotion of love, it can lead to an impatience for getting immediate results that is detrimental to one's true emotional and moral development. This is to put undue emphasis on function (immediate utility) at the expense of substance (the perfecting of one's humaneness).

In his commentary on the "extension of knowledge" in the *Great Learning*, Chu had described cognitive learning as the initial stage in a process of self-cultivation that should lead to the realization of the "whole substance and great functioning" of man's nature. By "whole substance" he meant "humanity," seen in the larger dimensions of man's oneness with heaven, earth, and all things and also as the directive principle which gave ultimate meaning and significance to human life. By "great functioning" he meant the exercise of the full range of human faculties—intellectual, moral, emotional, and spiritual—which could participate in the creative work of heaven-and-earth, especially in meeting the needs of human society.

When in the *Questions and Answers on the Great Learning* Chu speaks of the mind as "empty and spiritual yet replete with principle," he alludes to the infinite and limitless (*wu-chi*) aspect of the unity of the Supreme Ultimate, which is also the "highest good" to be realized in man on the basis of the "unity of principle and diversity of its particularizations." "The highest good," in the language of the *Great Learning*, represents the Supreme Ultimate in each individual as defined by his own share in heaven's endowment, his station and duties in life, and the circumstances which condition his actions. It is what is most appropriate for him in the context of these givens.[68] As for the "Supreme Ultimate," which is the rough equivalent of the "highest good" in the language of the *Changes* and Chou Tun-i, Professor Chan has summed up Chu Hsi's view as follows:

> According to him, the Great Ultimate is at once the one principle and the sum total of all principles. At the same time, since everything has principle, everything has the Great Ultimate in it. Consequently, the

Great Ultimate involves all things as a whole and at the same time every individual thing involves the Great Ultimate. In other words, the universe is a macrocosm while everything is a microcosm. In a sense the pattern was hinted [at] by Chou Tun-i in his T'ung-shu [Comprehending the Changes] where he said, "The many are [ultimately] one and the one is actually differentiated in the many. The one and the many each has its own correct state of being. The great and the small each has its definite function."[69]

When Chu describes the culmination of the learning process as a "breakthrough to comprehensive understanding," he expresses the idea of an enlightenment that comprehends both the unity and diversity, the infinity and ultimacy, of principle in the mind and things. This implies an understanding of the total functioning of the substance of the mind in all its dimensions and faculties, an "enlightenment" that includes the cognitive and affective aspects of the mind-and-heart, yet goes beyond them in the same sense that Chu intended when he spoke of humanity as the guiding principle of love.

This, then, was the ideal of self-cultivation for Chu Hsi, which would define the kind of individual fulfillment he envisaged for man. It is also "finding the Way in oneself" in the deeper sense of tzu-te spoken of in his summing up of the significance of the Doctrine of the Mean, which, he says, "speaks of the meritorious achievements and transforming influence of the sages and spiritual men in the highest degree. It was Tzu Ssu's desire that the learner should search within himself and find it [the Way] within himself."[70] For Chu, too, it represented the final fruit, even if it could not be a "definitive" result, of his lifelong search to achieve "learning for the sake of one's self."

The doctrine of the "whole substance and great functioning" of man's nature, in the terms it is expressed here, remains true to Chu's conception of the Supreme Ultimate as a nature that is both formed and yet-to-be formed, possessing in man an essential goodness that is still to be perfected. Among the various tendencies in Sung Neo-Confucian thought it was the Ch'eng-Chu school that particularly insisted on the goodness of human nature. This was a goodness which implied man's freedom to choose the path of self-improvement and self-perfection, to transform his actual nature so as to achieve, or at least approximate, sagehood. Understood as yet-unformed and, indeed, limitless (wu-chi), that nature contained within it the possibility of achieving self-transcendence as well as self-fulfillment. Accepting the limits imposed by what was given (one's lot, station, condition, and disposition as "decreed" by heaven), and while still living within the form of things, one could by the exercise of that freedom pass beyond the limits of the given. In this sense Chu was affirming both the inherent dignity of the person and his inalienable freedom to opt for a self-fulfillment yet to be discovered within himself.

If this sounds rather too free-wheeling for "orthodoxy," it must immediately be said that Chu tried to hedge it around with safeguards, conscious of the dangers which atttended such a sense of freedom—the danger of self-delusion which may arise from failure to fully exercise one's cognitive faculties in relation to knowable facts and principles; the danger of being carried away by vague mystical feelings not substantiated in actual conduct or experience; and the danger, on the other hand, of pursuing immediate utility without due regard for the nature of oneself and things, and so on. The balance Chu sought to achieve through self-cultivation was a precarious one, as he himself implied in his discussion of the mind of man as unstable and the mind of the Way as barely perceptible. Holism could easily become its own worst enemy if its component parts were not kept in line with the Way. So embracing was Chu's synthesis that later scholars—including Wang Yang-ming himself—could find some warrant there for views much in contrast to other emphases in Chu's thought.

Chu Hsi's system has long been recognized as the great synthesis of the philosophical speculation and dialogue carried on in the Sung. Here we can see that it also serves as the practical synthesis of the methods for attaining sagehood or enlightenment discussed in that time. In the words "integral comprehension" (*kuan-t'ung*), Chu Hsi's description of individual fulfillment expresses one of the highest ideals of Sung thought and scholarship. To penetrate, comprehend, and coordinate the full range of knowledge, and to bring it into a unity, was the aim of several major works of the period: Chou Tun-i's *Comprehending the Changes* (T'ung shu); the *Comprehensive Mirror for Aid in Government* (Tzu-chih t'ung-chien) of Ssu-ma Kuang, the *Comprehensive Treatises* (T'ung-chih) of Cheng Ch'iao (1104-1162); and in the late Sung, the *Comprehensive Inquiry into Literary Remains* (Wen-hsien t'ung-k'ao) of Ma Tuan-lin (1254-1325). The "comprehensiveness" (*t'ung*) spoken of in these titles reflects the prevailing ideal of broad and comprehensive scholarship (*po-hsüeh*) that Chu Hsi tried to harmonize with its polar opposite, the Confucian ideal of integrated learning, the "one thread running through it all" (*i-kuan*) spoken of in the *Analects*.

Whether succeeding ages could sustain this magisterial view of learning would be a real question, but that it challenged them to achieve such an ideal of individual fulfillment is attested by the successive generations of scholars and thinkers who set themselves to this task in Yüan, Ming, and Ch'ing China, Yi-dynasty Korea, and Tokugawa Japan.

As it came from the hands of Chu Hsi, the Neo-Confucian "learning for one's own sake" rearticulated a perennial Confucian personalism, marked now by individualistic tendencies typical of the Sung period. That is, it expressed a more expansive view of the self responding to new opportunities and challenges. In the more complex society of the Sung, the literatus had to articulate a new sense of himself vis-à-vis the demands these times made upon him—the demand for loyalty to a state grown increasingly autocratic and bureaucratic; the conflicting claims of partisan politics; the need for functional specialization in many areas of life; the relative priority of book learning and moral cultivation in the face of a daunting proliferation of scholarly literature; and—to cite just one more challenge to his social conscience—the moral vacuum left by Ch'an Buddhism in the wake of its drive for a transmoral liberation.

To call this simply "Neo-Confucian individualism" would be to risk misunderstanding: it would seem to exaggerate the special features of the

Sung "self" and to remove it from the social matrix and historical continuum in which the Confucian concept of personhood is embedded. To view it, on the other hand, simply as an exhumed "personalism" of the classical variety, reaffirmed in a traditionalistic manner, might be to ignore the specific qualities of Sung life and culture, qualities which encouraged a new sense of human creativity and individual autonomy. The Sung environment produced imaginative reinterpretations of the classics and histories and new views of the nature, substance, and functioning of the self, which, though coined in the continuing dialogue with Buddhism and Taoism, produced a heightened sense of the human potential—moral, intellectual, aesthetic, and spiritual—to be realized through the effort of self-cultivation.

If what is "new," or "partly new," in these Neo-Confucian theories reflects the changed circumstances in which the Sung literatus performed the political, scholarly, and literary functions of his class, it is also true that the continuing quest for self-fulfillment, the aspiration for a learning which went beyond all worldly gain or social function, generated a dynamic spirituality and forms of self-expression quite unprecedented in past tradition. Indeed, this radical testing of the limits of the self eventually evoked the censure of more traditional scholars, faithful above all to the original core of Confucian teaching, and led them to repudiate the grandiose conceptions of the self envisioned by Sung thinkers. The intensity of this reaction in seventeenth- and eighteenth-century China and Japan is, however, a measure of the challenge which Neo-Confucian individualism was seen to offer to established values and institutions. There was here a potential for radical activism which remained one aspect, though until now largely a neglected one,[71] of the Neo-Confucian legacy to modern times.

If we review this development in terms of "individualism" and "holism" and consider these two terms as represented in Confucian thinking by the "self" and the "Way," it is evident that for Chu Hsi, as for his tradition, these were properly seen as complementary conceptions, not opposed values. One's moral nature, according to the *Doctrine of the Mean*, comes from heaven and is ordained toward a perfection specifically defined by the lot or share (*fen*) in life also granted by heaven—that is, by the working out of one's own destiny in the circumstances decreed by heaven. Thus, a distinctive fulfillment for each individual is ordained for him as his own Supreme Ultimate, the highest good uniquely defined within the limits of his own lot in life. Whether this should be likened to what is sometimes called the "unique value" or "dignity" of the individual in the West may be a semantic question, but there can be no doubt that Chu Hsi saw the individual as partaking of the supreme value of the Way in his own concrete particularity, or that Chu Hsi assigned man a high dignity by virtue of his role in the creative process of heaven-and-earth.

In these terms, the more profound one's participation in the Way of heaven-and-earth, the more deeply rooted one's own individuality becomes. This allows for nonconformity to prevailing social or political trends, but not unconformity to the Way. On this basis, then, holism may be seen as implicit in the Confucian sense of individuality.

On the social level the same is true. In terms of the "Three Structural Principles" (*san kang ling*) of the *Great Learning* as explained by Chu Hsi, the ordering of human society starts with self-cultivation, but true cultivation of one's nature, one's humanity, implies the extension of this process to all mankind by assisting everyone to achieve self-perfection. For the ruler and those who participate in rulership it becomes their duty—part of their own self-cultivation—to provide the means for others' achievement of self-perfection. To the extent, then, that fulfillment of the highest good/Supreme Ultimate in each person corresponds to what one might call the development of his own individuality or personhood, the extension of this principle to all men as the precondition for "ordering the state and pacifying the world" amounts to recognizing the need for a more generalized individual*ism* and not just the valuing of individual*ity* in certain persons or the members of a certain class.[72]

This is not an insignificant distinction. In the Chinese cultural tradition—most evidently in painting, calligraphy, and poetry—individuality had long been prized. Taoism, Neo-Taoism, and Ch'an Buddhism had each focused attention on the radically "individual" character of self-realization. Far more rare is it to find such emphasis on self-fulfillment in the context of a public philosophy which asserts as a social value the inseparability of one person's fulfillment from all others. (Mahayana salvation, while implicating all beings, was not predicated upon any assertion of social or political claims.)

In this sense, Chu Hsi's teaching may be seen as approaching a doctrine of individualism. In another sense, the hierarchical social arrangements which Chu saw as necessary to the maintenance of order among men—and without which no individual entitlements could be incorporated into an institutional structure—would no doubt appear to modern egalitarians as imposing severe limits on the realization of many individuals' full potentialities. Many Neo-Confucians no doubt accepted the inevitability of such limitations, while others saw in heaven's principles (*t'ien-li*) the basis for a pushing-back of these limits and in heaven's unfailing creativity (*sheng-sheng*) the prospect of richer opportunities for individual fulfillment.[73]

NOTES

1. Fung Yu-lan, *History of Chinese Philosophy*, trans. Derk Bodde, 2 vols. (Princeton: Princeton University Press, 1953), vol. 2; Carsun Chang, *The Development of Neo-Confucian Thought*, 2 vols. (New York: Bookman Associates, 1957 and 1962); Alfred Forke, *Geschichte der neueren Chinesischen Philosophie* (Hamburg: Cram, De Gruyter, 1964), bk. 1, chap. 1.

2. Chu Hsi, *Chu Tzu wen-chi* [Collected writings of Master Chu], in *Chu Tzu ta-ch'üan* [Great compendium of Master Chu] (SPPY ed.), 74.1b, 19b; see also "Chu Hsi and Liberal Education," in my *The Liberal Tradition in China* (Hong Kong and New York: Chinese University of Hong Kong Press, 1983).

3. See Abe Takeo, *Gendaishi no kenkyū* [Researches in Yüan history] (Tokyo: Sōbunsha, 1972), 45-57; Chang Chiu-shao, "Wu Tang yüan-hsü" [Preface of Wu Tang], in *Li-hsüeh lei-pien* [Classified collection of the learning of principle] (Ssu-k'u ch'üan-shu chen-pen ed., 6th ser.), 2b; Chang Po-hsing, *Hsing-li ching-i* [Imperial compilation of essential ideas on nature

and principle] (1850 ed.), 7.12a. Martina Deuchler, "Self-Cultivation for the Governance of Men," *Asiatische Studien*, 1980, 34(2):16.

4. See Robert Hartwell, "Patterns of Settlement, the Structure of Government, and the Social Transformation of the Chinese Political Elite, ca. 750-1550" (Paper presented to the Columbia University Seminar on Traditional China, 9 September 1980), esp. 18-19; and Shiba Yoshinobu, *Commerce and Society in Sung China*, trans. Mark Elvin, Michigan Abstracts of Chinese and Japanese Works on Chinese History, no. 2 (Ann Arbor: Center for Chinese Studies, 1970), esp. 45-50, 202-13; Saeki Tomi, *Sō no shin bunka* [The new culture of the Sung] (Tokyo: Jimbutsu Ōraisha, 1967), 141-68, 370-85.

5. See Saeki Tomi, *Sō no shin bunka*, 381-85.

6. Huang Tsung-hsi and Ch'üan Tsu-wang, *Sung Yüan hsüeh-an* [Scholarly materials from the Sung and the Yüan] (Taipei: Ho-lu T'u-shu Ch'u-pan-she, 1975), 1.26.

7. See Chu Hsi, "Ta Lü Tzu-yüeh" [Letter to Lü Tsu-ch'ien], in *Chu Tzu wen-chi* 47.17b; and my *Neo-Confucian Orthodoxy and the Learning of the Mind-and-Heart* (New York: Columbia University Press, 1981), 8, 22-24.

8. See Saeki Tomi, *Sō no shin bunka*, 370ff. On the crisis in education from the lack of a sense of higher purpose, see Thomas H. C. Lee, "Life in the Schools of Sung China," *Journal of Asian Studies* (November 1977), 37(1):58-59.

9. T'ang Chün-i, *Chung-kuo che-hsüeh yüan-lun, Yüan chiao pien* [Original discourses on Chinese philosophy, basic teachings] (Hong Kong: New Asia Research Institute, 1975), 2, points out that the early leaders of the Confucian revival in the Sung particularly emphasized the "Way of the Teacher" (*shih-tao*).

10. *Ta-hsüeh chang-chü*, in *Ssu-shu chi-chu* [Collected commentaries on the four books] (Chung-kuo tzu-hsüeh ming-chu chi-ch'eng ed.), 1a-b, 6a-b (7-8, 17-18); *Ta-hsüeh huo-wen* (Kinsei kanseki sōkan, shosō samplen ed.), 4b (8). (Page numbers in parentheses refer to consecutive pagination in reprint edition cited.)

11. *Chu Tzu yü-lei* [Classified conversations of Master Chu] (Taipei: Cheng-chung Shu-chü, 1970), 20.21a (759). (Note: page references appearing in parentheses after citations of the *Chu Tzu yü-lei* provide the reader with a cross-reference to the Chūbun Shuppansha ed. [1979].)

12. Ch'eng I, *I-shu* [Written legacy], in *Erh-Ch'eng ch'üan-shu* [Complete works of the two Ch'engs] (SPPY ed.), 19.3b; Mao Hsing-lai, *Chin-ssu lu chi-chu* [Collected notes on the *Chin-ssu lu*] (Ssu-k'u shan-pen ts'ung-shu ch'u-pien ed.), 3.13b; Wing-tsit Chan, *Reflections on Things at Hand* (New York: Columbia University Press, 1967), 99-100.

13. Chu Hsi, *T'ai-chi-t'u chieh*, in *Chou-Chang ch'üan-shu* [Complete works of Chou and Chang] (Kinsei kanseki sōkan, shisōhen ed.), 39; Mao Hsing-lai, *Chin-ssu lu chi-chu*, 1a-2a; Chan, *Things at Hand*, 5.

14. *Chu Tzu yü-lei* 94.2b (3758).

15. Chu Hsi, *T'ai-chi-t'u chieh*, 43; Mao Hsing-lai, *Chin-ssu lu chi-chu* 1.1b; *Chu Tzu wen-chi* 36.9b. *Chu Tzu yü-lei* 94.1a, 5b (3755, 3764).

16. *Chu Tzu yü-lei* 94.1a-b, 4a-b, 6a (3755-56, 3762-63, 3765); *Chu Tzu wen-chi* 36.14a.

17. Masao Masuyama, *Studies in the Intellectual History of Modern Japan* (Princeton: Princeton University Press, 1975), 20-31; see also de Bary, *Principle and Practicality* (New York: Columbia University Press, 1979), 136-38; Ishida Ichirō, "Tokugawa hōken shakai to Shushigakuha no shisō" [Tokugawa feudal society and Neo-Confucian thought], partial English translation in *Philosophical Studies of Japan* (1964), 5:17-24.

18. This development and discussion is analyzed in detail by Tomoeda Ryūtarō in his *Shushi no shisō keisei*, rev. ed. (Tokyo: Shunju-sha, 1979), 142, 154-57, 183-84, 214-18, 227-38.

19. *Chu Tzu wen-chi* 36.10a-b, 11b-12a.

20. *Chu Tzu yü-lei* 94.1b, 2a (3756-57).

21. See also Tomoeda Ryūtarō, *Shushi no shisō keisei*, 227-38.

22. Ibid., 238ff.

23. Ch'eng I, *Wai-shu* [Outer works], in *Erh-Ch'eng ch'üan-shu* 3.1b, quoted in Mao Hsing-lai, *Chin-ssu lu chi-chu* 5.14a; Chan, *Things at Hand*, 165; *Chu Tzu yü-lei* 20.21a (759).

24. See Chu Hsi, *Ta-hsüeh huo-wen*, 2b-3a (4-5).

25. Ibid., 4b (3).
26. See Tomoeda Ryūtarō, *Shushi no shisō keisei*, 15.
27. Chu Hsi, *Ta-hsüeh huo-wen*, 3a-b (5-6).
28. "Ta Ch'en Ch'i-shih" [Reply to Ch'en Ch'i-shih], in *Chu Tzu wen-chi* 58.21a-b.
29. *Ta-hsüeh chang-chü*, 6a-b (17-18).
30. *Ta-hsüeh huo-wen*, 20b-21a (39-41).
31. Chu Hsi, "Wei-cheng" [Governing], in *Lun-yü chi-chu* [Collected commentaries on the *Analects*], in *Ssu-shu chi-chu* 2.9a; *Ta-hsüeh huo-wen*, 4b-7a (8-13); *Chu Tzu yü-lei* 1.1a-b, 23.16b, 117.9a (1, 892, 4491).
32. *Chu Tzu yü-lei* 94.8a-b (3769-70).
33. *Chu Tzu wen-chi* 38.34a-b (first letter in response to Chiang Yüan-shih). For the sequence of Chu's learning experiences, see Wing-tsit Chan, "Patterns for Neo-Confucianism: Why Chu Hsi Differed from Ch'eng I," *Journal of Chinese Philosophy* (June 1978), 5(2):101-26; and Tomoeda Ryūtarō, *Shushi no shisō keisei*.
34. Ch'eng I, *I-shu* 2A.2a.
35. Ibid., 2A.3a; Tomoeda Ryūtarō, *Shushi no shisō keisei*, 110.
36. Okada Takehiko, "Shushi no chichi to shi," *Seinan gakuin daigaku bunri ronshū* (March 1974), 14:pt. 2, 70.
37. Chu Hsi, *Yen-p'ing ta-wen* (Kinsei kanseki sōkan, shisōhen ed.), 70, 89–92, 99–103. Iki Hiroyuki, "*Empei tomon* wo yomu" [On reading *Responses of Yen-p'ing*], in *Tōyō no risō to eichi* [The ideals and wisdom of the East], ed. Okada Takehiko (Fukuoka: Tōyō Shisō Kenkyukai, 1963), 51–64.
38. Chu Hsi, *Yen-p'ing ta-wen*, 111.
39. Huang T'ing-chien, *Sung-shih* [Sung history], 444.1; *Sung-Yüan hsüeh-an* 19.28.
40. Chu Hsi, *Yen-p'ing ta-wen*, 65, quoting Huang T'ing-chien's preface to the poetry (*shih*) of Chou Tun-i found in *Yü-chang Huang hsien-sheng wen-chi* [Collected writings of Mr. Huang of Yü-chang] (SPTK ed.), 1.14b.
41. Mao Hsing-lai, *Chin-ssu lu chi-chu* 14.6a; Chan, *Things at Hand*, 298.
42. *Yen-p'ing ta-wen*, 83-84.
43. Ibid., 67-68.
44. Ibid., 60, 63-64.
45. Ibid., 62.
46. Ibid., 61-62.
47. Ibid., 62.
48. *Yen-p'ing ta-wen fu-lu* [Supplement to the *Responses of Yen-p'ing*] (Kinsei kanseki sōkan, shisōhen ed.), 135.
49. Ibid.
50. Mao Hsing-lai, *Chin-ssu lu chi-chu* 3.11a, no. 25; Chan, *Things at Hand*, 7.
51. Ch'eng I, *I-shu* 18. 5b; Mao Hsing-lai, *Chin-ssu lu chi-chu* 3.5b, no. 9; Chan, *Things at Hand*, 92.
52. *Yen-p'ing ta-wen*, 72, 109; Mou Tsung-san, *Hsin-t'i yü hsing-ti* [Substance of mind and substance of its nature], 3 vols. (Taipei: Cheng-chung Book Company, 1969), vol. 3, chaps. 2-4; Tomoeda Ryūtarō, Introduction to *Yen-p'ing ta-wen* (Kinsei kanseki sōkan, shisōhen ed.), 1-11; Okada Takehiko, "Shushi no chichi to shi," 85, 93.
53. Chu Hsi, *Yen-p'ing ta-wen*, 93, 111, 114; Okada Takehiko, "Shushi no chichi to shi," 86.
54. Cf. my "Neo-Confucian Cultivation and Enlightenment," in *The Unfolding of Neo-Confucianism*, ed. Wm. Theodore de Bary (New York: Columbia University Press, 1975), 170-72.
55. Chu Hsi, *Yen-p'ing ta-wen*, 42, 63, 114; Okada Takehiko, "Shushi no chichi to shi," 86.
56. Chu Hsi, *Yen-p'ing ta-wen*, 114.
57. Tomoeda Ryūtarō, Introduction to *Yen-p'ing ta-wen*, 9-10.
58. Chu Hsi, *Yen-p'ing ta-wen*, 92, 102, 107, 109; Tomoeda Ryūtarō, *Shushi no shisō keisei*, 248; Okada Takehiko, "Shushi no chichi to shi," 81-82.
59. Tomoeda Ryūtarō, *Shushi no shisō keisei*, 60; Chan, "Patterns for Neo-Confucianism," 112-13.

60. Ch'eng I, *I-shu* 24.2a.

61. The classic study of the evolution of this doctrine and its relation to modern reformism and radicalism is Shimada Kenji's "Subjective Idealism in Sung and Post-Sung China: The All Things are One Theory of *Jen*," *Tōhōgaku-hō* (March 1958), 28:1-80.

62. Adapted from Wing-tsit Chan, *A Source Book in Chinese Philosophy* (Princeton: Princeton University Press, 1963), 497-98.

63. Shimada Kenji, *Shushigaku to Yōmeigaku* [The learning of Chu Hsi and Wang Yang-ming] (Tokyo: Iwanami, 1967), 67-70.

64. Ch'eng I, *I-ch'uan wen-chi* [Collected writings of Ch'eng I], in *Erh-Ch'eng ch'üan-shu* 5.11b; Mao Hsing-lai, *Chin-ssu lu chi-chu* 2.42b-46b; *Chu Tzu yü-lei* 98.12a-20b (pp. 4003-16); *Yen-p'ing ta-wen*, 26-29; Chan, *Source Book*, 498-99, and *Things at Hand*, 79-81.

65. Ch'eng I, *I-shu* 18.1a; Mao Hsing-lai, *Chin-ssu lu chi-chu* 1.31b-32a (translated in Chan, *Things at Hand*, 27).

66. "Jen shuo," in *Chu Tzu wen-chi* 67.21b; translation adapted from Chan, *Source Book*, 596.

67. *Chu Tzu yü-lei* 126.20b (4858).

68. *Ta-hsüeh chang-chü*, 4a-5a (13-15); *Ta-hsüeh huo-wen*, 4a, 5b, 7b, 8b, 11a, 13a-14a, 18b, 31b (7, 10, 14, 16, 21, 25-27, 36, 62).

69. Chan, "Patterns for Neo-Confucianism," 110.

70. Chu Hsi, *Chung-yung chang-chü* [Commentary on the *Mean*], in *Ssu-shu chi-chu*, 49.

71. The notable exception, of course, is the work of Shimada Kenji. See n. 61 above.

72. Chu Hsi, *Ta-hsüeh chang-chü*, 1a-6a (7-17). See also my "Individualism and Humanitarianism in Late Ming Thought," in *Self and Society in Ming Thought*, ed. Wm. Theodore de Bary (New York: Columbia University Press, 1970), 146-48.

73. Cf. Matsumoto Sannosuke, "The Idea of Heaven: A Tokugawa Foundation for Natural Rights Theory," in *Japanese Thought in the Tokugawa Period*, ed. T. Najita and I. Scheiner (Chicago: University of Chicago Press, 1978), 181-97.

Glossary

Abe Takeo 安部健夫

Ch'an 禪

Chang Chiu-shao 張九韶

Chang I 張繹

Chang Po-hsing 張伯行

Chang Tsai 張載

ch'eng 誠

Cheng Ch'iao 鄭樵

Ch'eng-Chu hsüeh 程朱學

Ch'eng Hao 程顥

Ch'eng I 程頤

Chiang Yüan-shih 江元適

chih-ching 持敬

chih-shan 至善

Chin-ssu lu 近思錄

Chin-ssu lu chi-chu 近思錄集註

ching-tso 靜坐

Chou-Chang ch'üan-shu 周張全書

Chou Tun-i 周敦頤

chü-ching 居敬

chü-ching ch'iung-li 居敬窮理

Chu Hsi 朱熹

Chu Tzu ta-ch'üan 朱子大全

Chu Tzu wen-chi 朱子文集

Chu Tzu yü-lei 朱子語類

Ch'üan Tsu-wang 全祖望

chüeh-wu 覺悟

Chung-kuo che-hsüeh yüan-lun, Yüan chiao pien 中國哲學原論原教編

Chung-yung chang-chü 中庸章句

Empei to mon wo yomu 延平答問を讀む

Erh-Ch'eng ch'üan-shu 二程全書

fen 分

Gendaishi no kenkyū 元代史の研究

Hsi-ming 西銘

hsin-hsüeh 心學

Hsin-t'i yü hsing-ti 心體與性體

hsing 性

Hsing-li ching-i 性理精義

hsing-li hsüeh 性理學

Hsing-li ta-ch'üan 性理大全

Hu Yüan 胡瑗

Huang T'ing-chien 黃庭堅

Huang Tsung-hsi 黃宗羲

hun-jan yü wu t'ung-t'i 渾然與物同體

huo-jan kuan-t'ung 豁然貫通

I-ch'uan wen-chi 伊川文集

i-kuan 一貫

I-shu 遺書

Iki Hiroyuki 猪城博之

Ishida Ichirō 石田一郎

jen 仁

Jen shuo 仁說

ko-wu ch'iung-li 格物窮理

kuan-t'ung 貫通

k'ung 空

li-hsüeh 理學

Li-hsüeh lei-pien 理學類編

li-i fen-shu 理一分殊

Li T'ung 李侗

Lu Hsiang-shan 陸象山

Lun-yü chi-chu 論語集註

Ma Tuan-lin 馬端臨

Mao Hsing-lai 茅星來

miao-yu 妙有

miao-yung 妙用

mo-tso ch'eng hsin 默坐澄心

Mo Tzu 墨子

Mou Tsung-san 牟宗三

Okada Takehiko 岡田武彥

po-hsüeh 博學

pu-li wen-tzu 不立文字

sa-lo 洒落

Saeki Tomi 佐伯富

san kang ling 三綱領

shen 身

sheng-hsüeh 聖學

sheng-jen chih tao 聖人之道

sheng-sheng 生生

shih 詩

shih-tao 師道

Shimada Kenji 島田虔次

Shushi no chichi to shi 朱子の父と師

Shushi no shisō keisei 朱子の思想形成

Shushigaku to Yōmeigaku 朱子学と陽明学

so-i-jan chih ku 所以然之故

Sō no shin bunka 宋の新文化

so-tang-jan chih tse 所當然之則

Ssu-ma Kuang 司馬光

Ssu-shu chi-chu 四書集註

ssu-wen 斯文

Su Tung-p'o 蘇東坡

Sung-shih 宋史

Sung Yüan hsüeh-an 宋元學案

Ta Ch'en Ch'i-chih 答陳器之

Ta-hsüeh 大學

Ta-hsüeh chang-chü 大學章句

Ta-hsüeh huo-wen 大學或問

Ta Lü Tzu-yüeh 答呂子約

T'ai-chi-t'u chieh 太極圖解

T'ang Chün-i 唐君毅

tao-hsüeh 道學

tao t'i 道體

t'i-jen tzu-te 體認自得

t'ien-li 天理

t'ien-ming 天命

t'ien-ti wan-wu i-t'i chih jen
天地萬物一體之仁

Tokugawa hōken shakai to Shushi-gakuha no shisō 德川封建社会と
朱子学派の思想

Tomoeda Ryūtarō 友枝龍太郎

tso-ch'an 坐禪

tsun te-hsing, tao wen-hsüeh 尊德
性道問學

T'ung-chih 通志

T'ung-shu 通書

tzu 自

tz'u 慈

Tzu-chih t'ung-chien 資治通鑑

Tzu Ssu 子思

tzu-te 自得

Wai-shu 外書

Wang Yang-ming 王陽明

wei-cheng 爲政

wei-chih chih hsüeh 爲己之學

wen 文

Wen-hsien t'ung-k'ao 文獻通考

wu 無

wu-chi erh t'ai-chi 無極而太極

Wu Tang yüan-hsü 吳當原序

Yen-p'ing ta-wen 延平答問

Yen-p'ing ta-wen fu-lu 延平答問附
錄

Yü-chang Huang hsien-sheng wen-chi 豫章黃先生文集

Yü-shan chiang-i 玉山講義

yung 用

Punishment and Dignity in China

Chad Hansen

Chinese thought is nonindividualistic. That claim would be less difficult to evaluate if we could distinguish clearly between an individualistic and a nonindividualistic moral theory. But it seems as if the very idea of a morality involves reference to the free actions of autonomous, rational, individual persons. Our notion of society is that of an emergent and artificial structure made up of individuals and fueled by the psychological drives of those individuals.

This essay outlines a plausible and coherent nonindividualistic ethical-political theory and argues that attributing this theory to classical Chinese thinkers explains their philosophical writings better than the alternative assumption, viz., that Chinese thinkers were individualists. The argument that Chinese thought is not individualistic is not an argument by inductive enumeration. It is rather an argument about which interpretive theory best explains classical Chinese ethical and political writings. An interpretive theory that attributes nonindividualist assumptions, for example, explains some of the well-known contrasts between Chinese and Western ethical views, such as group responsibility and the aversion to the rule of law. If we assumed that the basic classical Chinese ethical outlook were as individualistic as our own, we would find it relatively more difficult to understand how a Chinese thinker would come to such views.

The nonindividualist background beliefs that I attribute to classical Chinese philosophers form a shared base from which different philosophers of China depart in various directions—some, e.g., Mencius, in the *direction* of individualism. The assumptions primarily underlie realistic Confucianism (e.g., Hsün Tzu), Mohism, Taoism, and Legalism. I contend that these background beliefs form a coherent and interesting nonindividualist point of view—one which can be plausibly explained as consistent with the background assumptions of Chinese moral philosophers.

This project inherently involves some simplifying generalizations. In addition to trying to outline a single framework to characterize a complex Chinese tradition, I must also presuppose some contrastive framework to characterize Western individualistic ethical thought. Fortunately, Anglo-American philosophers are converging on a near consensus about the "essence" of Western morality. Recent moral philosophy has been dominated by the view that Western ethics is fundamentally Kantian as opposed to utilitarian. This consensus has it that consequentialism, even an altruistic version like utilitarianism, represents a revolutionary revision in Western morality. Rawls, for example, argues that utilitarianism does not take individuals as seriously as does Western ethical "intuition."[1] That is, utilitarianism maximizes some "good"—no matter who enjoys it. Even if the good were human perfection rather than units of pleasure or happiness, utilitarianism per se would not prefer *individual* perfection to family, village, or state perfection.[2] Donagan argues that the "common morality" of the West is more adequately captured by Kantian categorical principles of respect for rational individuals than by utilitarian maximization,[3] and Dworkin represents Western "concurrent morality" as a justifying theory of our legal practices which, in contrast to utilitarianism, "takes rights seriously."[4]

The difference between Chinese and Western ethical theories centers around the dignity of the individual, the issue which distinguishes Kantian from consequentialist theories. As noted above, utilitaranism is a consequentialist theory which prescribes maximizing some good no matter who enjoys it or how it is distributed. Classical Chinese theories, I contend, are all rather more like consequentialist than Kantian systems. The consequentialist features are reflected in political doctrines—especially in the view of law and punishment. In defending this interpretation, I will focus on philosophical doctrines which have parallels in Western political theory to show how the Chinese counterparts presuppose a less individualistic view of human moral psychology, of society, and of our role in nature.

This interpretive theory is initially motivated by a set of interesting features of Chinese ethical writings. First, Chinese philosophers do not have an undefined or primitive concept that plays the role in their political theories that "justice" does in Western thought. Their political theories are, in general, teleological, and the central concepts, such as benevolence (*jen*) and order (*chih*), reflect welfare concerns. Classical Western examples of justice, like keeping promises and telling the truth, seldom emerge as examples in pre-Han Chinese ethical writing. Second, theoretical justifications of (or opposition to) law and punishment seldom turn on standard retributive considerations, i.e., justifiable vengeance, payment of debts, or the like. Third, there is no discussion of "rights"—in fact, no such term enters the Chinese vocabulary until comparatively modern times. Finally, the concept of the rule of law, although formulated in Chinese political theories, is typically rejected or tolerated uncomfortably, especially by Confucianism, the dominant school of political theory.

These contrasts arise in an otherwise familiar moral point of view. Chinese political theories are forms of universal altruism and share with Western "justice" a clear concern with distributive equality.[5] It is not that the Chinese view is one which, while coherent, is based on bizarre background beliefs—like the Hindu doctrine which rationalizes away apparent injustice to individuals by appeal to a belief in reincarnation and Karma.[6] It is rather that

Chinese theories are based on a different conception of moral personhood—and whether or not the Western conception of a person is a more plausible one is philosophically controversial (though it is not a controversy I shall discuss much here). Historically, the Western conception of personhood grew out of a supernatural analysis of human action—one which links it to "divine reason." In fact, the Chinese view is coherent with a relatively "naturalistic" analysis of human action. The Chinese moral tradition can be understood as acknowledging that human actions are continuous with natural events and that human intelligent behavior is conditioned by social practices, natural feelings, intuitions, and the like, rather than by any nonnatural or abstract "reason."

Given these basic differences in background beliefs about moral personality, we should be suspicious of interpretations that impute to Chinese philosophers anything resembling a Kantian concern for individuals. The arguments for individual rights and for the proposition that dignity and respect are owed to rational individuals as such do not compel agreement in a Chinese context where these background conceptions differ.

Background Conceptions of Justice

Assumptions about moral agents (persons) and their relation to society and the world are presupposed in the justification of normative principles. The differences in these background assumptions explain why philosophers from the Chinese philosophical tradition would see less justification for the cluster of values we call "individualism." The moral conceptions we are using to contrast the two traditions are those cited by Rawls in his elaboration of a hypothetical choice justification of the principles of justice.[7] Rawls suggests that such a justification presupposes a conception of a moral agent—a person—and a conception of a well-ordered society in a world of a certain description. If we thought of people as essentially egoistic, competitive, and impulsive, we would choose principles allowing freer use of coercion than if we thought of people as essentially social, inclined to common pursuits, and capable of governing their impulses by a conception of shared principles. Similarly, if we assumed that there were no scarcity, or, conversely, that there were overwhelming scarcity, we would find certain principles worthless. Let us analyze the Chinese counterparts of these central evaluative conceptions.

The Concept of a Person

Moral Autonomy

That the traditional morality of China does have a close analogue to the Western conception of individual dignity seems to be the view of Herbert Fingarette: "By analogy, Confucius may be taken to imply that the individual human being, too, has ultimate dignity, sacred dignity by virtue of his role in rite, in ceremony, in *li*."[8] While it is, of course, plausible that Confucius has a high regard for humans in his scale of values and, further, that he presupposes that all humans "participate in" the *li*, it does not follow that Confucian ethical theory implies an analogue of Kantian dignity. Confucius suggests neither that people choose the *li* nor that they may legitimately require justifications of it. Thus, Fingarette links Confucian "individual dignity" to participation in merely conventional behavior patterns.

One absolutely central aspect of the concept of moral autonomy in Western philosophy involves distinguishing morality proper from conventional mores. In Kant's system, this aspect is expressed by the conception of persons as autonomous—as law-givers to themselves. This autonomous, self-regulating rule system might be the product of intuition or reason. If reason is the faculty of moral agents which generates the autonomous regulation, then I can legitimately expect a rational justification of prescriptions to which I am asked to conform. If the faculty is intuition, then my intuitions might come to be in conflict with conventional moral beliefs. In these cases, it is not enough merely to say "this is the way it is done!" To think of moral principles as exhausted by an elaborate, traditional code is to deny an aspect of dignity that is fundamental to the Kantian point of view.

This basic element of autonomy in Western ethical theory generates the distinction between codes of etiquette, fashion, or customs, on the one hand, and morality on the other. Etiquette, fashion, and customs are products of history. They are, from the moral point of view, accidental. One can always ask whether one ought to follow accepted and established prescriptions. It does not follow from the mere existence of any such system that its prescriptions are morally correct.

It may fairly be asked if Confucius's traditionalist political philosophy has this distinct concept of morality at all. Ethical theorizing begins when we distinguish morality from tradition. Not having such a distinction is plausibly the definitional equivalent of lacking a concept of morality as such. If we see Confucian traditionalism in this light, we could follow Philippa Foot and describe the differences between Western ethics and Confucianism not as "differences in moral outlook, but rather as a difference between a moral and a nonmoral point of view."[9] This does not mean that the human good is not valued in Confucian ethics, but the concept of Kantian dignity, or respect for the individual, involves more than merely basing moral calculation on what is good for humans. It is a claim that individual persons deserve respect because they have a special kind of epistemic, justificational, and motivational relation to moral principles. What is significant about morality (as opposed to traditional mores) is that it is independent of any particular cultural system of rules and provides a framework from which we can evaluate such cultural systems.

Fingarette's Confucius is especially vulnerable to the charge of "mere" traditionalism because Fingarette chooses to emphasize *li* as the central concept in his treatment of Confucius. Despite the manifest importance of *li* (ritual) in Confucius's thought, there are other terms which arguably might reflect a distinct notion of morality, e.g., *jen* (typically translated "benevolence" or "goodness") and *i* (typically "righteousness," "duty," or "sense of duty"). *Jen* is conspicuously undefined in Confucius's *Analects*. Interpretations vary widely but seem to converge on the claim that whatever *jen* is, it does not prescribe any actions conflicting with *li*. It is more like an appropriate "attitude" one should take in following the traditional code.[10] *I*, on the other hand, can be regarded as a potentially distinct concept—one which is best translated as "morality" in both the *Mo Tzu* and the *Mencius*. But the *Analects* neither contrasts *i* with *li* nor suggests that *i* is a standard for evaluating traditional codes like *li*—nor even that *i* is a part of *li*.

The first clear use of *i* as a conception of morality, distinct from traditional rules, appears to have emerged in opposition to Confucianism and tends to confirm the hypothesis that Confucius himself never distinguished the two. Mo Tzu criticized Confucian *li* theory for confusing traditional rules with *i* (morality). Thus, it is Mo Tzu who first makes theoretically explicit the distinction between morality and traditionally accepted mores.

> Mo Tzu said: This is because they confuse what is habitual with what is proper, and what is customary with what is right [*i*]. In ancient times east of the state of Yüeh lived the people of the land of K'ai-shu. When their first son was born, they cut him up and ate him, saying that this would be beneficial to the next son. When their fathers died, they loaded their mothers on their backs, carried them off and abandoned them, saying, "One can't live in the same house with the wife of a ghost!" These were regarded by the superiors as rule of government and by the people as accepted procedure. They continued to practice these customs and did not give them up, carried them out and did not abandon them. And yet can we actually say that they represent the way of benevolence and righteousness [*jen-i*]? This is what it means to accept what is habitual as proper and what is customary as right.[11]

Mo Tzu thus makes a clear distinction between custom and morality (*i*) and, following Mo Tzu, this distinction becomes common property among classical philosophers of all schools. Mencius, writing in response to Mo Tzu's critique, emphasizes the pair *jen-i* and, in comparison to Confucius, enormously downplays the conventional *li*. He defends the Confucian burial tradition against Mo Tzu's attack in ways which are implicitly universalistic.

> In great antiquity there were some who did not bury their parents. When their parents died, they took them up and threw them in a ditch. Later when they passed by them and saw foxes and wild cats eating them and flies and gnats eating them, their perspiration started out upon their foreheads, they looked askance and could not bear to look straight. Now the perspiration was not for the sake of other people. It was something at the bottom of their hearts that showed in their expressions. They immediately went home and returned with baskets and spades and covered the bodies. If it was indeed right to cover them, then there must be certain moral patterns which made filial sons and men of humanity inter their parents.[12]

Sensitized to Mo Tzu's distinction, Mencius defends the Confucian *li* by arguing that they are rules which are generated by the innate tendencies of human nature (which means they are commanded by heaven). This makes the justification of the practice of *li* relatively independent of tradition and custom.

The Taoists, too, make the distinction between what is right and what is social convention, although they use it to deny, as Nietzsche and as emotivists do, that there are any standards of judgment of the type required for morality—namely, standards that are independent of conventional or natural predispositions of judgment. They use the distinction to deny that there is any point of view from which all proposed conventional mores might be judged: "Then we have the rights and wrongs of the Confucians and Mohists. What one calls right, the other calls wrong; what one calls wrong the other calls right."[13] Whatever we say of Confucius himself, Mo Tzu and the philosophers who follow him do make a clear distinction between morality and convention. But there is no hint of a theoretical assumption that our epistemic access to morality comes from a faculty of reason. That morality is separate from custom or tradition and that morality is based on reason are distinct claims.

Reason and Rationality

Western theories of moral psychology from Plato to Rawls (minus the Romantics and an occasional moral-sense theorist) have assumed that the faculty of reason gives the individual access to moral truth. Traditional Chinese moral psychology does not include the doctrine that human individuals have a faculty of reason or that any such faculty is the source of moral judgment.[14] Mo Tzu suggested that his *yen* (words) were "irresistible" to people who heard them, but he did not attribute the compulsion to any distinct mental faculty.[15] Mencius, too, held that all humans must in some sense recognize the rights and wrongs (*shih-fei*) of morality, but not in the sense of grasping rational moral principles and beliefs. He teaches, rather, that people just have innate inclinations to act and react morally.

> Therefore I say there is a common taste for flavor in our mouths, a common sense for sound in our ears, and a common sense for beauty in our eyes. Can it be that in our hearts/minds alone we are not alike? What is it that we have in common in our minds? It is moral patterns. The sage is the first to possess what is common in our minds. Therefore moral patterns please our heart/minds as beef and mutton and pork please our mouths.[16]

While we can approximately describe Mencius's position as intuitionist, it is important to note that the "outputs" of Mencius's heart/mind are patterns of behavior, not knowledge of the truth of prescriptive utterances. Further, unlike Aristotle's moral intuitions, Mencius's are never characterized as "rational." The use of "heart/mind" as a translation of *hsin* reflects the response-oriented, noncongnitive nature of the patterns that Mencius says are innate.

For a similar reason, it is a mistake to regard Taoism as "consciously anti-rational."[17] There was no distinct concept of a rational faculty or a reasoning process for Taoists to oppose. The Taoists do, as noted above, reject the suggestion that there are absolute or neutral grounds of judgments of right and wrong, but their introduction of skepticism into the tradition would have had a much different flavor if that tradition had claimed that reason gives us access to objective moral principles.

In the Western tradition, especially as synthesized by Kant, the content of ultimate normative principles is respect for the faculty that gives us access to the moral law. We owe respect to rational beings. Individual persons have a fundamental dignity as rational beings—as capable of prescribing to themselves, ascertaining and conforming to the moral law. Not only is morality something distinct from particular historical conventions, it is a body of prescriptive principles accessible to and dictated by a particular faculty—the faculty of reason. In contrast, in neither metaethics nor moral psychology do we find an unambiguous classical Chinese counterpart of the concept of rationality. Rational functions, such as the ability to make inferences and practical judgments, are attributed to the heart/mind as an undifferentiated part of the process by which the action guiding moral "feelings" are "aroused" by external events. Normative theory in China, therefore, absent the theory of persons as rational agents, is unlikely to reflect Kantian principles of respect for individuals.

Beliefs and Desires

"Reason" has been part of the Western conception of a person for so long that it is difficult for us to imagine what a different view of persons would be like. Yet, the classical Chinese concept grows out of obvious features of human social life which we all acknowledge. Fingarette persuasively describes some of the underlying assumptions of Confucius's view of humankind.

> However, men are by no means conceived as being mere standardized units mechanically carrying out prescribed routines in the service of some cosmic or social law. Nor are they self-sufficient, individual souls who happen to consent to a social contract. Men become truly human as their raw impulse is shaped by *li*. And *li* is the fulfillment of human impulse, the civilized expression of it—not a formalistic dehumanization. *Li* is the specifically humanizing form of the dynamic relation of man-to-man.[18]

Humans are naturally inclined to pick up ritual embellishments of impulses to action. Reason, of course, is one aspect of this characteristic of human nature where the conventions or rituals are used in calculation or deduction and argument. But the Confucian focus is on the conventions which regulate the social aspects of our lives. These conventions forge modes of being social, of interacting and coordinating behavior. Confucius does promote education in the practice of *li* (ritual), and he sees human nature as realized rather than constrained or distorted by training and participation in the *li*. Confucius conceives of the human as a "ceremonial being." An inclination to ritual togetherness is, for him, a natural property of humans.[19]

The stress on the social, malleable nature of humans as absorbers of convention rather than on their autonomy, independence, and uniqueness as reasoners is reflected in other very interesting differences both in the philosophy of mind and in epistemology. Western "reason" developed in juxtaposition to two companion concepts—belief and desire. The faculty of reason operates on beliefs. It includes operations such as drawing inferences, proposing explanations, and assessing and ranking outcomes in deliberation about practical matters. In the first two activities, reason operates on private, propositional attitudes—"beliefs." The third underlines the Western view of voluntary, free action. In the standard explanation of human action, practical reason operates on beliefs in the context of desires. The faculty of reason combines, for example, a desire for a lichee together with a belief that a bundle of lichees is in the bottom drawer of the refrigerator. This produces a new desire to open the bottom drawer of the refrigerator. That derived desire causes the action.

Chinese action theory and philosophy of mind divide the functions differently—in ways which help explain why absorption of social convention rather than independent rational discovery remains the focal point of the theory of human nature. Classical Chinese philosophers focus on names (distinction making) and desires rather than beliefs and desires. To be able to acquire a shared naming convention a human must have or acquire the ability to make a distinction—a *shih* (this), *fei* (not this). Along with this ability comes a socially appropriate attitude toward the things distinguished in this way and a set of dispositions (desires) involving them. Chinese philosophers fasten on these acquired discrimination abilities and the attitudes (desires) which accompany them rather than on the creation and modification of beliefs. Our "raw impulses" are tuned when we internalize ways of classifying and categorizing things. Thus, language shapes behavior.

Confucians worried that the associated distinctions, along with the names, might not be used in uniform ways and that the actions generated by the accompanying attitudes consequently might not be "in accord." Hence the importance of "rectification of names" (*cheng-ming*), which guarantees that the attitudes and actions are directed at appropriate targets.

> If names are not rectified, then language will not be in accord. If language is not in accord then undertakings cannot be completed. If undertakings are not completed then ritual and music will not flourish. If ritual and music do not flourish then punishments will not be on target, if punishments are not on target the people will not know how to move hand or foot.[20]

The Western concept of belief cannot be analyzed as merely a disposition to speech or other behavior. Beliefs have contents, and these contents are expressed in sentences or propositions, as opposed to names. Chinese philosophers of language, for the most part, do not deal with sentences or sentence counterparts like judgment, belief, opinions, and so forth.[21] Their theories converge on names (words). This orientation reinforces the view of humans as shaped by acquired social forms. Our focus on the social rather than the autonomous nature of language users is related in obvious ways to whether we attend to words or to sentences. Contrast the ways in which the sentences and words[22] we use reflect social influence. All the words in my repertoire have been learned. My use of words either does or does not conform to the linguistic practices of my community, and I tend, unconsciously, to shape my desires and actions to the distinctions marked by my set of socially given descriptive terms. By contrast, it would not even make sense to speak of my repertoire of sentences. While I have been exposed to sentences in all of my learning, the sentences I utter or write are not thought of as learned in the same sense that my vocabulary is. Thus, my beliefs, as expressed by sentences, are not as obviously social products as are my conceptual distinctions. The notion of reason has an obvious role to play in explaining my beliefs, but social practice explains my distinction-making ability—my use of words.

The Chinese focus on names and feelings (or desires) as opposed to beliefs and their concern with the traditional attitude toward the social shaping of feeling, together with the relative absence of a conception of reason, are, I am suggesting, all related phenomena. From the earliest ethical theory, it has been understood (most clearly by the Taoists) that the important elements in human motivation come from acquired social forms. Some argued that there were innate inclinations to moral feelings in the human heart. No Chinese philosopher ever proposed that morality came from the operation of an asocial faculty of reason.

Mencius stands almost alone among classical Chinese ethical theorists in arguing for the innateness of moral feelings. He almost totally denies human dependence on social convention for the attitudes which guide action. Still, Mencius does not claim that the feelings are products of a faculty which resembles reason in any substantial sense. Mencius's favorite analogy is to the growth of a plant where the structure of the adult plant is implicit in the seed and, except for deprivation, is not changed by environment. Like the maturing plant, the heart/mind's inclinations to action are present in the heart/mind as tendencies, which become stronger and more discriminating as one's moral heart matures. The heart/mind directs actions in accordance with its "fonts"; it does not yield prescriptive formulae which can be rationally analyzed and discussed. It instead produces, in concrete situations of choice, assents and dissents (*shih* [this : right] judgments and *fei* [not this : wrong] judgments) which are pro and con attitudes toward actions, not evaluative propositions for belief. Mencius's view is that raw impulse naturally (that is, asocially) grows into sagelike behavior, consistently and perfectly moral, when allowed free development.

In its claim of autonomy from social inculcation, Mencius's theory is the classical Chinese ethical theory closest to Kantianism. Access to the particular prescriptions is, in principle, available to each human. The distinction of right and wrong is not a matter of social conventions appropriately manipulated by social institutions but is part of the innate feeling structure of human nature. Individual expressions of similar sentiments might be found in Confucius or *Hsün Tzu*. Hsün Tzu, for example, talks of a mind which "gives commands but is not subject to them," a mind "which cannot be forced to change its opinion... whose selections cannot be prohibited."[23] But, both of them focus on learning from external sources—the *li*. Confucius follows his heart's desire only after seventy years of study and practice have shaped his heart to respond spontaneously in accord with traditional norms.[24] Despite certain similarities to Kant, however, Mencius's ethical perspective is not Kantian. Kant would reject Mencius's account of morality for the same reason he rejects Hume's. Mencius does not treat the prescriptions of morality as "given" by rational beings to themselves. Being based on a set of psychological propensities, instincts and tendencies, the behaviors generated by Mencius's heart/mind would not be categorical dictates of reason, but rather of sentiment. While Mencius's humans are autonomous relative to social practices and conventions, they are not autonomous relative to natural human inclinations—the "heavenly feelings." Heaven built those reactions in. Humans do not choose to be endowed with an evaluating mind—though they may choose whether or not to cultivate it.

The Well-Ordered Society

The concept of a well-ordered society is the second idealized moral conception that Rawls regards as underpinning any justification of fundamental moral principles. Rawls presents his principles as those which would be chosen as principles for criticizing social institutions in the abstract, hypothetical situation of choice. This device, in which we imagine (or project into past history) a presocial deliberation on whether or not to have a social structure, is a familiar theme in Western political theory.

There is a parallel hypothetical choice argument in classical Chinese ethics that illuminates the differences between the Chinese and Western conceptions of a well-ordered society. Mo Tzu's arguments for universal love and for "Agreeing with the Superior" ("Shang t'ung") are both elaborated via a hypothetical choice:

> Mo Tzu said: In ancient times, when mankind was first born and before there were any laws or government, it may be said that every man's view of things was different. One man had one view, two men had two views, ten men had ten views—the more men, the more views. Moreover, each man believed his own views were correct and disapproved of those of others, so that people spent their time condemning one another. Within the family fathers and sons, older and younger brothers grew to hate each other and the family split up, unable to live in harmony, while throughout the world, people all resorted to water, fire, and poison in an effort to do each other injury. Those with strength to spare refused to help out others, those with surplus wealth would let it rot before they would share it, and those with beneficial doctrines to teach would keep them secret and refuse to impart them. The world was as chaotic as though it were inhabited by birds and beasts alone.
>
> To anyone who examined the cause, it was obvious that this chaos came about because of the absence of rulers and leaders. Therefore the most worthy and able man in the world was selected and set up as the Son of Heaven....
>
> When all these officials had been installed, the Son of Heaven proclaimed the principle of his rule to the people of the world, saying, "Upon hearing of good or evil, one shall report it to his superior. What the superior considers right, all shall consider right; what the superior considers wrong all shall consider wrong."[25]

The above passage argues for an authority structure but not for a specific normative principle. Mo Tzu, however, is committed to a specific principle—the principle of universal altruism or utility—and he justifies it most of the time by appeal to divine command. In one interesting passage, however, he employs another hypothetical choice argument, one which proves only that a person would prefer that society be governed by the principle—not that the person himself ought to adopt the principle on prudential grounds. It is also interesting to note that the "universal love" justification is nonegoistic, i.e., it presupposes that we are interested in the welfare of others—especially those in our family.

> Suppose that here is a broad plain, a vast wilderness, and a man is buckling on his armor and donning his helmet to set out for the field of battle, where the fortunes of life and death are unknown; or he is setting out in his lord's name upon a distant mission to Pa or Yüeh, Ch'i or Ching, and his return is uncertain. Now let us ask, to whom would he entrust the support of his parents and the care of his wife and children? Would it be to the universal-minded man, or to the partial man? It seems to me that, on occasions like these, there are no fools in the world. Though one may disapprove of universality himself, he would surely think it best to entrust his family to the universal-minded man. Thus people condemn universality in words but adopt it in practice, and word and deed belie each other. I cannot understand how the men of the world can hear about this doctrine of universality and still criticize it![26]

The underlying contrasts found in the context of the surface similarity between this argument and typical Western counterparts should clarify the fundamental differences between the two traditions. Mo Tzu, like Hobbes, presents a quasi-historical account of the development/justification of the institution of government authority. Both also rely on a vivid description of a "state of nature" which would ensue if these or similar institutions were not set up.

The differences between Mo Tzu and Hobbes are more intriguing than the similarities. Some bear on the concept of a person. The historical people in Mo Tzu's "original position" are not represented as egoistic. They are not portrayed as maximizers of satisfaction. On the contrary, they are explicitly assumed to be motivated by *i* (morality).[27] The problem envisioned by Mo Tzu is not the amoral nature of human motivation, but the need for social agreement about moral distinctions. Mo Tzu takes the efficiency cost of moral diversity—the confusion and inefficiency resulting from the absence of a common *shih* and *fei*—to be the justification for having a system of authority dictating our attitudes.

Accordingly, Mo Tzu's description of the state of nature does not concentrate as much as Hobbes's on the human potential for destructive violence and does not justify characterizing this state of affairs as a state of war with every man against every other man. Mo Tzu describes inefficiency, not war: the failure to utilize talents, to distribute wealth, to spread valuable teachings. Mo Tzu characterizes it as a state similar to that of animals (who are not constantly at war) in that there are no shared moral standards.

The actors in Mo Tzu's state of nature do not have a natural "right" to punish those who threaten their lives or property. "Entitlement" notions do not play an important role in Mo Tzu's hypothetical choice. Accordingly, he does not represent the decision to set up an emperor as a contract, covenant, or promise. He does not mention any renunciation or transfer of rights. The legitimacy of the result is not held to rest on a hypothetical act of consent. The assumptions behind Mo Tzu's choice theory are, in fact, much more purely consequentialist than are Hobbes's justifications. They involve almost no assumptions of justice, retribution, deserts, obligations, or commitments.

Punishment is mentioned in some versions of Mo Tzu's argument for agreement with the superior. However, no hint that punishment has other than a consequentalist basis ever emerges. People are punished to induce their cooperation with this beneficial system, not for violations of particular rules (laws).

This observation points to a salient contrast between the Chinese and traditional Western views of society. The state and the ruler which are justified by the argument do not carry out their function by passing laws for protecting lives and property and by punishing violations of those laws by force. Instead the society works via a harmony of moral judgments. No one is empowered with the authority to formulate new rules. The hierarchy resembles a judiciary more than a legislature. The officials hear cases; they judge them to be *shih* or *fei* (right or wrong); the others in the hierarchy make their words and judgments conform to those above them. The process most resembles that of a judicial system in that judges in lower courts follow the precedents set by higher courts. A host of officials is required because there are simply too many cases for one "worthy" to hear them all. In Mo Tzu's idealized society, the outcome is that the society agrees to adopt and enforce a uniform, positive morality rather than enpowering a body or person to pass and enforce positive laws.

The theory is not necessarily relativistic, however. Mo Tzu does not advocate the uniform acceptance of just any positive morality (though that would satisfy the need for harmonious efficiency). The emperor models his judgments after heaven's will, which Mo Tzu assumes to be utilitarian. Mo Tzu advocates the inculcation of utilitarianism as a shared positive morality, whereas Confucius favored the inculcation of traditional *li*.

Put in the least flattering way, Mo Tzu advocates what liberalism would characterize as mind control. The description suggests that government's primary concern should be with the people's moral distinctions and secondarily with their actions. Mo Tzu assumes that people are naturally motivated by *i* and that government should fix *i* in order to achieve cooperative and efficient social interaction.

Mo Tzu's system of agreement with the superior is authoritarian and in basic structure is quite similar to Confucius's theory of the role of government. Confucius also advocated inculcating moral behavior through model emulation and through "rectification of names." A Confucian official ought, in the same way as Mo Tzu's superiors, to rectify the names so that the society has uniform evaluative attitudes. The Confucian superior or sage acts as the model of these attitudes. The traditional rules (*li*) are used in the place of the rule of maximizing utility, and the Confucian scholar or sage rectifies names to get agreement on the behavior the *li* requires. The society thus comes to share an interpretation of the *li* in action.

Mohists and Confucians disagree about the appropriate standard, but not about the appropriateness of shaping the people's moral motivations. Both assume that people are naturally moved to action by shared standards of naming, discriminating, and evaluating, and both share the goal of social order achieved by universal acceptance of a body of prescriptive discourse (a *tao*). Confucius's ideal of a well-ordered society, like Mo Tzu's, resembles a judicial system rooted in a positive morality more than it does a legal system.

Confucius explicitly opposes laws and punishments on several grounds. A legal system, he argues, is an arrangement which stimulates prudential or selfish calculation more than it does moral calculation.[28] Laws are inefficient in the long run. By inculcating selfishness, a rule of law requires spiraling elaboration to restrain the clever pursuit of "self" by those who are glib. One's goal, according to Confucius, should be to eliminate litigation.[29] Laws inevitably proliferate and finally undermine the social-moral potential of humanity.

So the concept of a well-ordered society for both Confucius and Mo Tzu excludes the rule of law. Both envision a society governed by a shared conception of value with seemingly authoritative mechanisms for "fixing" the fuzzy edges of the conception. The hierarchy—a meritocracy in both cases—fixes the conception by making judgments (assigning names to things or pronouncing them *shih* or *fei*) which become examples to the people.

Classical China does have a "Legalist" school which advocates "administration of *fa* (laws)," in contrast to the Confucian "administration of *li* (ritual)." The traditional enmity between Legalists and Confucians has blurred the degree to which the Legalists agree with the basic premises of the Confucian and Mohist conceptions of the well-ordered society. Legalism agrees with Confucianism and Mohism that government is supposed to inculcate social values. The disagreement centers on the source and content of the values and the degree to which punishment may be used in achieving conformity. Confucius's is a society in which positive morality is interpreted as if it were law; Mo Tzu's standards follow from utilitarian considerations; and the Legalists enforce the emperor's edicts.

All three schools tolerate or advocate some use of "punishment." None, however, justifies the institution of punishment retributively. Neither Confucius nor Mo Tzu is enthusiastic about punishment, but both acknowledge that it can be a part of the well-ordered society. Mo Tzu allows the use of punishment to coerce people into the system of agreement with the superior. Chinese legal theorists do say that the severity of individual acts of punishment should reflect the severity of the crime, and the Legalists argue for uniform and impartial application of punishment. Again, however, justification of these punishment strategies usually rests on consequentialist grounds—what beneficial social results the punishment will effect. Confucians traditionally rejected this equalizing aspect of Legalist use of laws—also on consequentialist grounds. In fact, despite disagreement about how much reliance should be placed on punishment, all three schools regard it as a tool for achieving the goal of social control: punishment and reward are motivational techniques.

The concept of persons as rational agents is intimately connected with theories of retribution. In cases where we suppose a person's rational faculties to be deficient (e.g., the mentally impaired, children, nonhumans), if we can be said to use punishment at all, its purpose can only be that of channeling their behavior to some consequentialist end—their own or our good. When dealing with those we consider fully rational agents, by contrast, we suppose that punishment may be justified when a wrong is done even though that punishment may have no demonstrable salubrious consequence. This acceptance of purely retributive justification presumably signals a connection between the concepts of reason and free or voluntary action—but this is not an issue I propose to explore further here.

Traditional Chinese attitudes toward the rule of law throw light on current legal developments in China. The People's Republic is openly acknowledging its desire to promote something more like the Western rule of law. The government now allows coverage of certain trials, and travelers are frequently allowed to see courts in operation. The functioning of the modern Chinese court reflects the traditional ambivalence toward a strictly retributive rule of law. In a murder trial presented for Western press coverage, the court's charge did not mention any specific statute which prevented or provided the penalty for murder. The judge charged the defendant not merely with violating a law but also with failing to study well and to conform to shared communist ideals. The latter was an especially grievous fault since the accused came from a working-class family and thus had no "congenital excuse" for his defects in character! The defendant's plea, similarly, stressed his low political consciousness, and he apologized for not having internalized the ideals of the socialist system (freedom of choice for women, less emphasis on "saving face," etc.). The judge delivered the sentence, not in the spirit of retribution or as a deserved sanction, but as a way of moving the culprit aside so social progress could go on.[30]

This promotion of the rule of law reflects the repudiation of aspects of Maoism in China today. It could be argued that Mao's policies in this regard were aiming even closer to the Mohist and Confucian version of the well-ordered society but with conformity of political consciousness taking the place of conformity to *li* (ritual) or to *i* (morality). It is interesting to reflect on the contrast between a Western "rule of law" and this traditional model to see how the different conceptions of personhood and society inform the contrasting social institutions.

Teleology and the Justification of Law and Punishment

The ambivalent attitude toward punishment in China shows how the concept of individual dignity is involved in justifying the institution of legal punishment. Confucian theoretical opposition to punishment is a coherent extension of the moral point of view I am attributing to the classical Chinese tradition. The classical Chinese aversion to legal process, the minimal tolerance of punishment, and the analysis of persons as "shaped and polished" by authoritative inculcation of evaluative conventions are best explained together. An adequate justification, if one can be made at all, of adopting the rule of law along with a system of retributive punishment requires appeal to the rights of individuals based on the Kantian principle of respecting the dignity of individuals as rational beings. Consequentalist justifications, as I argue below, are dubious. Thus, individualism and advocacy of the rule of law and punishment go hand in hand.

In discussing the justification of punishment, I am, of course, concerned about the institution of punishment, not specific acts of punishment. The justification of a particular act of punishing is undeniably "retributive" and would appeal to the rules of the uniform practice of the institution.

Some argue that the justification of the institution of punishment *must* be consequentalist, since a retributivist argument for retributive institutions seems circular.[31] The usual consequentalist justification of the institution of punishment goes as follows. The total good is maximized by a system which controls behavior in the common interest through threat of punishment. The threat is made credible by actually inflicting punishment with enough frequency to convince rational actors that the punishment-cost multiplied by the probability of incurring that cost is higher than the expected benefits of doing the illegal act. This form of the argument emerges commonly in Legalist writings.

> What is stopped by heavy penalties would not in all cases be stopped by light penalties; whereas what is stopped by light penalties would in all cases also be prevented by severe penalties. Therefore, where the ruler establishes severe penalties all wrong-doing ceases. If all wrong-doing ceases, how can the people suffer any harm?[32]

This extreme Legalist view did not dominate Chinese philosophy to the same extent as it did Chinese politics. The classic Confucian criticism of this Legalist argument for impartial punishment was also consequentalist. It did not presuppose a concept of humanity that was radically different from that of the Legalists. In particular, it does not necessarily presuppose that humans are innately good: "Confucius said, 'Lead them with government and order them with punishment and the people will avoid wrongdoing but they will have no shame. Lead them with virtue and order them with rites and they will have shame and reform themselves.'"[33] Confucius's analysis assumes only that the people can make choices according to either a selfish, prudential point of view or a shared, conventional one. He need only insist that both are possible. Thus, his argument holds that a social order based on passing laws and attaching punishments stimulates the habit of making prudential or selfish calculations and, correspondingly, depresses the equally possible development of a regulative social orientation. People are thus literally *made* selfish (individualists?) by legal institutions.

The Legalists, in their justification of punishment, also need not claim that humans lack social attitudes or the potential to deliberate from a shared point of view. Their chief defense appeals to the urgency of achieving order. It is not that people could not, in principle, be developed as Confucius hoped, but that given the objective situation, it would take too long. There is a difference in the relative optimism about human nature between Han-fei Tzu and Confucius, but it is a difference in degree, not in kind.

> When you don't have rags to wear, don't wait for fancy embroidery. For in governing a state, when urgent matters have not been accomplished, efforts should not be directed toward things that can wait. If in governmental measures one neglects ordinary affairs of the people and what even simple folks can understand, but admires the doctrines of the highest wisdom, that would be contrary to the way of orderly government.[34]

Now, a consequentialist justification of punishment fails if it merely contains the observation that a system which incorporates punishment creates a higher net utility than no system at all. Consequentalist justifications of institutionalized punishment must be comparative advantage justifications between alternative strategies. They must demonstrate not merely that punishment works to reduce pain (or some other harm) more than it directly causes it via the punishments themselves, but, further, that the net advantage of a system of direct imposition of retributive punishment is higher than for *any alternative method* of social control.

One alternative method for utility calculation was presented by Herbert Morris in his classic article "Persons and Punishment."[35] Morris considers a system which would make massive use of psychotherapy, drugs, hypnosis, preemptive commitment to mental institutions, and the like. The utilitarian must prefer the therapy model to the punishment model since it is both more effective in reducing crime and less dependent on the direct imposition of pain. The intent of Morris's argument, however, is to justify punishment. He attempts to show that the therapy model is a morally unacceptable alternative institution, and his argument is that it violates our rights—our dignity. To apply a therapy system on us violates our rights; and since the alternative is a system of punishment, we have a right to punishment as the preferred system of social control.

Morris's argument links the rule of law and punishment. There are possible systems of social control which are superior to punishment on consequentialist grounds and are still not as odious as his therapy model. Let us consider an alternative quasi-legal institution inspired by Confucian and Mohist ideals, which, in some ways, resembles recent practice in Maoist China.

One thing American visitors had noted in Maoist China was the absence of obvious official coercive power—which belied the view of China as a regimented society. There were probably fewer uniformed policemen on the streets than in America and far fewer guns or night-sticks in evidence. The visitor was likely to be regaled with claims about the near absence of crime despite obvious urbanization, overcrowding, poverty, and a rather robust historical tradition of organized banditry, piracy, and the like.

Drugs, hypnosis, and mental hospitals were not the route China was following, however. The most plausible institutional explanation of the remarkable domestic order in Maoist China revolves around the institution of the "study session." Practically everyone (at least in urban environments) participated in regular meetings to discuss practical business, to encourage appropriate attitudes, and to criticize deviant behavior.

Empirical analysis of the institution of the study session in China is beyond the scope of this paper. Whether or not China's study sessions actually work as defenders and apologists say, the model provides us with a useful basis for constructing hypothetical alternatives to punishment. I will henceforth speak of a hypothetical "Chinina" with social control exercised through something like study sessions. The analogy to China serves only to suggest that such a social arrangement is within the realm of possibility for some societies. If anything, it is closer to practical possibility than is the massive use of psychotherapy and drugs in crime prevention.

In Chinina we will allow that the system might still employ promulgated laws. These might be evolved principles of "common law" growing out of Mo Tzu's utilitarian principle, or they might be made up of currently authorized slogans together with some sort of recognized procedure for interpreting them in action, or there might even be a body of legislative enactments. The important thing is only that there be an accepted body of rules for which enforcement by predominantly persuasive techniques is institutionalized.

Anyone who holds that the concept of law entails punishment may not consider the envisioned system of Chinina a legal system. The appropriateness of the term is not central to the argument here. What is important to the present argument is only that the citizens of Chinina can identify certain rules as prescriptions to which government institutions promote conformity.

Now, the techniques used in promoting the desired behavior in the institutionalized study sessions would all fall under the broad heading of "persuasion." The paradigm would be winning someone over by presenting an argument—getting someone to see the point of conformity. No doubt peer pressure, desire for acceptance, exhaustion of excuses, opportunity for advancement, good jobs, tenure, etc., would function as they do in our society to further conformity. The system might be backed, as was Mo Tzu's, by a coercive force. That force, however, would be employed only to obtain participation in the persuasive system—i.e., attendance and sincere participation in the periodic discussions. Even that could normally be a matter of persuasion. We know enough about human nature and motivation to predict that such a system could work. It is not obvious that further coercion or the threat of coercion would be necessary to obtain a suitably high level of conformity under this system (though it surely could be argued that Mao's China used coercion more extensively than this and that more might be necessary on first implementation in a society like our own).

Many of the objections that might have been raised to the therapy model do not apply to Chinina. One could hardly say that such an institutional structure violated our rational nature. By depending mainly on argument and persuasion, it seems rather to presuppose it. There would be no obvious violations of due process since no one would have therapy forced on them. They would only be confronted verbally and asked to answer for their behavior in terms of shared conceptions. Such a "moral reeducation" might be regarded as equivalent to punishment in the sense that it would be employed only in response to the commission of some act held judicially to violate the shared rules of behavior. But it would not involve the idea that the society was "harming" the criminal to restore a moral balance.

The point is not that such a system would totally eliminate crime. In principle, a consequentialist justification of this system would be successful even if there were more crime than we presently experience, since there would also be lower negative utility from the actual infliction of punishment, from the fear of punishment, from the costs of punishment to the families involved, and so forth. The appeal to the actual practices in China only serves to suggest to us that the claim that such a system could work is more plausible than the Western doctrines of psychological egoism and original sin would suggest. The possibility of a nonpunishment system requires far less sanguine assumptions about human nature than do various forms of anarchism—or, for that matter, Marxism. Roughly, in fact, the assumptions about human nature and society which would justify such a system are those we find in Confucianism and Mohism.

A powerful consequentialist argument for this system—especially from the perspective of underdeveloped societies—is that it is temptingly cost-effective. From the social point of view, one must include in the cost of a legal system the salaries of all lawyers, judges, policemen, prison guards, as well as the cost of prison construction, prisoner support, etc. An underdeveloped country motivated by purely consequentialist considerations would find a system of persuasion economically irresistible.

There are costs, however. The total man-hours spent in meetings must be calculated as a negative utility (unless the sessions could be made far more pleasant than the average Sunday-school encounter). There would be difficulties among friends growing out of resentment of criticisms or pressure applied at the meetings. Surely the boredom implicit in such regularized conformity must be reckoned a cost. Millean concerns about the narrow range of choices available need not be dismissed. Nonconformity often yields social exploration of private life-styles which turn out to be quite satisfying, but a system such as our Chinina model does not necessarily rule these out, since the institutions are to focus only on particular public prescriptions. Further, one can expect not to be persuaded by groups of utilitarians to abandon nonconforming behavior which increases utility.

At the same time there would be a separate set of advantages. The nation could mobilize to concerted efforts at tasks which could hardly be handled in a traditional legal framework, e.g., the elimination of flies, sparrows, and spitting. Energy conservation, elimination of sexism, and so forth, which a system of coercion could achieve only at great cost, could be efficiently promoted through an institution of persuasion.

The techniques used in Chinina's system are simply a rather more intense application of the socialization process of growing up—adjusting, harmonizing, and adapting to our social environment. It is here, of course, that the strongest objection to this conception of a "well-ordered society" emerges. It does treat us as children. While we recognize the need for paternalistic inculcation of a system of values, we also feel that adults have an inherent dignity which forbids indiscriminate application of these techniques beyond a certain maturity. We object to the direct institutional "giving" of our conception of an appropriate life-style, of a conception of justice and right, even though we recognize that such inculcation is going on haphazardly all the time. But what kind of objection is it? Are the conceptions wrong? To insist they are, in this allegedly ideal utilitarian context at least, begs the question.

The consequentalist social arrangement of our hypothetical Chinina suggests that the development of moral values is an accident of culture and requires a social inculcation process—whether in the form of study sessions or television advertising and dramatization. Objection to the system seems to come from rather strong assumptions of individualism. These assumptions would be based on the Kantian view that we should regulate our lives by principles which are dictates of pure reason and that the conceptions by which we govern our lives are not, in the sense required for our notion of moral autonomy, merely social nor merely dependent on particular institutional practices. Those conceptions should, instead, be extracultural dictates of reason, accessible to each person in the absence of any special teaching.

Chinina's persuasion institutions are, of course, only one possible institutional arrangement that could achieve what is envisioned by Mo Tzu's agreement with the superior or Confucius's rectification of names. The point of both the modern and ancient systems appears to be that widespread agreement in moral judgment justifies adopting some institutional framework for shaping evaluative attitudes. The Chinina model presupposes something else about moral agency which we also associate with China—group sanctions. If my coworker in our study session is not persuaded of the norms contributing to utility, I may appropriately incur a sanction. Such attitudes are well entrenched in China's Legalist ideology. Shang Yang's original reforms (556 B.C.) "ordered the people to be organized in groups of fives and tens, mutually to control one another and to share in one another's punishments."[36]

Moral Responsibility and the Cosmos

The idea of group responsibility is least appealing when one considers sharing punishments. However, even when punishment is not at issue, the concept conflicts with Western intuitions. It suggests that we are responsible for the effect we have on the behavior of others. Consequentialism, which gives no special place to individuals, would appear to be consonant with such a view. We do the act which will have the best consequences as far as we can tell, and our calculation of those consequences must include prediction of how others will react to what we do or say. Manipulating others into doing the right act is clearly compatible with—and plausibly required by— consequentialism. It appears, however, to conflict with a principle of Western law and common morality cited by Donagan: "However, neither in law nor in common morality is it held that the causal 'reach' of an action can extend to any and every subsequent event that would not have occurred had it not occurred."[37] Confucian, Mohist, and Legalist moral theory appear at odds with traditional Western morality in this respect. The sage or fully moral actor would be able to influence all the outcomes by his action. This idea is expressed most forcefully in one of the "Four Books" of Confucianism.

> Only those who are absolutely sincere can fully develop their nature. If they can fully develop their nature, they can fully develop the nature of others. If they can fully develop the nature of others, they can then fully develop the nature of things. If they can fully develop the nature of things, they can assist in the transforming and nourishing process of Heaven and Earth, they can thus form a trinity with Heaven and Earth.[38]

As Wing-tsit Chan observes in his comment on this passage, this is an expression of the "unity of humanity and Heaven or Nature." It is an ideal expressed in Mencius's "floodlike *ch'i*"[39] which will fill up all between heaven and earth, in Hsün Tzu's rhapsodizing about the man of enlightenment who "surveys all heaven and earth, governs all beings, and masters the great principle of all that is in the universe,"[40] or by Confucius's man of *jen* (benevolence) who must "establish" others to establish himself.[41] All these images are expressions of a Confucian view of the continuity of humanity and the natural course of events. As such, they conflict with the conception of human action implicit in Western morality. As Donagan puts it, "The Hebrew-Christian tradition, as I understand it, conceives human actions as interventions by human agents in the ordinary course of nature, thereby presupposing a distinction between event causation and agent causation."[42]

The point of all this can be appreciated by focusing on telling the truth. An approach which held that causal responsibility did not extend to the actions of other rational agents would support a relatively categorical prescription to tell the truth. One would not be responsible for the way another person used the truthful information conveyed to him. Of course, no Confucian urges lying, but the emphasis in Confucian as well as Mohist discussions of language use is on its tendency to promote good behavior rather than on its semantic truth.[43] Confucius talks of language's being carried out in behavior; Mo Tzu advocates "making constant" language which promotes certain beneficial behavior.[44] Fingarette is correct about a Chinese awareness of the "performative" element of language. Speaking is acting. One's moral reach extends through the effects one's words have on others.

One consequence of this "cosmic responsibility" view of our place in nature is the Neo-Confucian sense of predicament outlined by Metzger. Neo-Confucians believed in Mencius's doctrine that they could cultivate a way which linked them with the whole cosmos. Feeling responsible, ultimately, for the working of the system, they were frustrated and disillusioned when their practice of the way did not produce utopia.

> Admittedly, in saying that Neo-Confucians had a sense of predicament, we are saying something about them that they would not have said. The wholeness of the cosmos was for them something ever there which had been perfectly understood by the sages and which they were now in the process of once again properly understanding. Continually trying to brush aside the problems impeding this understanding, they were intent on making increasingly evident this glorious oneness existing beyond any predicament whatsoever. We skeptics of the twentieth century, however, know little about any such oneness.[45]

The Confucian moral point of view, then, includes a view of the entire cosmos as a sphere of human action—an outlook compatible with consequentialism. Nature is continuous and one's actions have consequences. The fact that certain consequence sequences include the deliberate actions of other persons does not alter the moral significance to a Confucian sage. Ideally, he should be able to select the correct words or action for the situation and the people involved so as to maximize the good.

Conclusion: Suitably Restricted

Traditional Chinese views of the world, society, and human nature differ in important ways from their counterparts assumed by our theoretical analysis of Western "common morality." The Chinese conceptions are: (1) a naturalistic, holistic conception of the place of humans in nature; (2) a conception of the well-ordered society as a peaceful cooperative structure produced by a shared moral cultivation; and (3) a conception of human action which presents that motivation as socially given—in particular, through learning how to use words. Human action is not explained by a belief-desire contrast, and it does not invoke the notion of reason. These ideas contrast with the conceptions behind a Kantian value system based on "individual dignity." Furthermore, the conceptions themselves are neither philosophically indefensible nor palpably superstitious. They are background conceptions which would seem to gird a utilitarian morality—one which would, as Rawls suggests, take less seriously than does our own tradition the differences among individuals.

This essay has been concerned mainly with the classical Chinese schools—the Confucius-Hsün Tzu wing of Confucianism along with Mohism and

Legalism—in suggesting these contrasts. It should be noted that Mencius's intuitionism is a system of moral thought in China which moves in an individualistic direction from this theoretical base. Moreover, traditional Neo-Confucian thought is more akin to Mencius's version of Confucianism than it is to Hsün Tzu's, and Neo-Confucianism also includes aspects borrowed from Buddhism which, *prima facie* at least, are more "internal"(less social) than was classical Confucianism. I commend the analysis of the rich and detailed traditions of Buddhism and the various branches of Neo-Confucianism along these lines as worthy topics for further research and discussion. But I also would argue that both the Mencius (Neo-Confucian) and Buddhist views of human nature are *prima facie* less plausible than the naturalistic Confucian-Mohist views. In addition, Maoism rejects the Mencius-like assumptions of an innate human nature and, arguably, goes back to the Mo Tzu-Hsün Tzu view of an educable, changeable human nature.

At the same time, many of the doctrines of Neo-Confucians, e.g., the relative dislike of punishment and the view of humans as cosmic citizens ultimately participating with heaven in "transforming heaven and earth," reflect the impact of the classical tradition as I have described it. The downplaying of punishment as a form of social control does seem to be a sign of a less individualistic conception of human action. If punishment can be justified, it must be by an appeal to individual dignity—not to general utility. And any categorical imperative to tell the truth or keep promises appears to rest on a metaphysical distinction between human action and the course of nature. The fact that the concept of law, retributive justice, categorical honesty, etc., play a less central role in Chinese moral reasoning tends to confirm that, in general, it is based on less individualistic background assumptions.

I do not insist, however, that a naturalistic conception of human nature, together with an awareness of the way in which human nature is shaped by culture, is incompatible with individualism or with a strong sense of the dignity of the individual. But it remains to be shown how we could justify Western moral attitudes given such difference in background conceptions. Reasonable people sitting down together in a disciplined dialogue *should* be able (in principle and in the long run and so forth) to reach agreement on fundamental moral principles. But the case for some of our favorite moral principles may not be found particularly compelling by genuinely moral and reasonable discussants from the Chinese philosophical tradition.

NOTES

1. John Rawls, *A Theory of Justice* (Cambridge: Harvard University Press, 1971).
2. It is important to note that in classical Chinese, terms like *jen* (human) do not have their own principles of individuation. So merely talking of the perfection of *jen* does not entail that the goal is individualistic. For a Confucian the goal is more plausibly the perfection of the familial system or the social whole.
3. Alan Donagan, *The Theory of Morality* (Chicago: University of Chicago Press, 1977), 26.
4. Ronald Dworkin, *Taking Rights Seriously* (Cambridge: Harvard University Press, 1977), 57.

5. One could argue that the concern is merely what would be required by utilitarian principles, together with an intuitive feeling for diminishing marginal utility.

6. Donagan, *Morality*, 33-35. I acknowledge some effect of Buddhism on the cultural tradition, but I do not think that Buddhism changed the conceptions of the world as a context of moral action, of society, or of persons into a Hindu conception. Rather, Buddhism strengthened the altruistic and monistic naturalism already inherent in the classical tradition and mainly focused attention on the achievement of sagehood. But the traditional Confucian moral content of that ideal has remained intact.

7. John Rawls, "Kantian Constructivism in Moral Theory: The Dewey Lectures 1980," *The Journal of Philosophy* (September 1980), 77(9):520.

8. Herbert Fingarette, *Confucius-The Secular as Sacred* (New York: Harper and Row, 1972), 75. It should be noted that although in this passage Fingarette uses the word "individual," he, too, dissents from the view that Confucianism saw moral issues in terms of the individual. He actually argues that there is a Confucian concept of the dignity of *jen* (humanity). So Fingarette may not in fact disagree with my main conclusions in this paper.

9. Philippa Foot, "Moral Arguments," *Mind* (1958), 67(268):502-13.

10. Fingarette, *Confucius*, 42. Mencius makes *jen* the centerpiece of his philosophy in ways which seem to be more clearly related to an absolute morality.

11. Mo Tzu, *A Concordance to Mo Tzu*, Harvard-Yenching Institute Sinological Index Series, supp. no. 21 (Taipei: Chinese Materials and Research Aids Service Center, Inc., 1974), 39/25/75-77 (translation in Burton Watson, *Mo Tzu: Basic Writings* [New York: Columbia University Press, 1963], 75).

12. Mencius, *A Concordance to Meng Tzu*, Harvard-Yenching Institute Sinological Index Series, vol. 17 (Taipei: Chinese Materials and Research Aids Service Center, Inc., 1973), 21/3A/5 (translation in Wing-tsit Chan, *A Source Book in Chinese Philosophy* [Princeton: Princeton University Press, 1963], 71).

13. Burton Watson, trans., *Chuang Tzu: Basic Writings* (New York: Columbia University Press, 1964), 34.

14. "Reason" has been offered as a translation for some very central concepts in Chinese thought, e.g., *tao*, by Paul Carus, trans., *The Canon of Reason and Virtue* (Chicago: Open Court Publishing Co., 1970), and *li*, by Percy Bruce, *Chu Hsi and His Masters* (London: Probsthain, 1932). The only support for such translations is that these concepts do play one of the roles of "reason" in some Western systems—the role of a metaphysical principle of order. But in the West that role is parasitic on the notion of reason as a mental processing faculty or a logical property. No psychological or logical counterparts underlie the proposed equivalents in Chinese thought. The proposed equivalents of "reason" function primarily as metaphysical structures and only derivatively as psychological faculties.

15. *Mo Tzu*, 84/47/54.

16. *Mencius*, 44/6A/7. Although the translation follows Chan, *Source Book*, 56, I have succumbed to the temptation to change the translation of *li* (principle) to *li* (pattern) in accordance with my own view that the *li* are not formulae, but patterns or tendencies of human behavior.

17. This view is nearly universal among intellectual historians. Graham uses the characterization in talking about Chuang Tzu (A. C. Graham, *Later Mohist Logic, Ethics and Sciences* [Hong Kong and London: The Chinese University of Hong Kong Press and The School of Oriental and African Studies, University of London, 1978], 21). Paradoxically, Graham has done more than any other scholar in recent times to uncover a coherent interpretation of Chuang Tzu's philosophical position.

18. Fingarette, *Confucius*, 7.

19. Ibid., 15.

20. *A Concordance to the Analects of Confucius*, Harvard-Yenching Institute Sinological Index Series, vol. 16 (Taipei: Chinese Materials and Research Aids Service Center, Inc., 1972), 25/13/3.

21. Graham (*Mohist Logic*, 25) claims that the sentence *was* eventually discovered by the Later Mohists but that the discovery was difficult. I would add that it was incomplete.

22. Pre-Han talk of names should be read as talk about words. The Neo-Mohists follow most other writers of the time in using *ming* (name) to refer to terms without regard for the most typical part of speech they play. Even sentential operators are called *ming* (names).

23. Burton Watson, trans., *Hsün Tzu: Basic Writings* (New York: Columbia University Press, 1963), 129.

24. *Analects*, 2:4.

25. Watson, *Mo Tzu*, 34-35.

26. Ibid., 42.

27. Watson translated *i* (morality) as "view of things."

28. *Analects*, 2:3.

29. Ibid., 12:13.

30. *New York Times Magazine*, 14 January 1979.

31. Stanley Benn, "Punishment," in *The Encyclopedia of Philosophy*, ed. Paul Edwards, 8 vols. (Taipei: Red Bridge, 1970), 7:29-36.

32. Lord Shang, quoted in Kuan-chuan Hsiao, *A History of Chinese Political Thought*, Princeton Library of Asian Translations, vol. 1 (Princeton: Princeton University Press, 1979), 400.

33. *Analects*, 2:3.

34. Han-fei Tzu, quoted in Chan, *Source Book*, 259.

35. Herbert Morris, "Persons and Punishment," *The Monist* (October 1968), 52(4):475-501.

36. Lord Shang, quoted in Hsiao, *Political Thought*, 372.

37. Donagan, *Morality*, 42.

38. *The Doctrine of the Mean*, sec. 22 (translated in Chan, *Source Book*, 107-8).

39. *Mencius*, 11/2A/2.

40. Watson, *Hsün Tzu*, 129.

41. *Analects*, 6:30.

42. Donagan, *Morality*, 46.

43. *Analects*, 13:3.

44. *Mo Tzu*, 80/46/37.

45. Thomas Metzger, *Escape from Predicament: Neo-Confucianism and China's Evolving Political Culture* (New York: Columbia University Press, 1977), 160.

Glossary

cheng-ming 正名

ch'i 氣

chih 治

Chuang Tzu 莊子

fa 法

fei 非

Han-fei Tzu 韓非子

hsin 心

Hsün Tzu 荀子

i 義

jen 仁

jen-i 仁義

li 禮

ming 名

Mo Tzu 墨子

"Shang t'ung" 尙同

Shang Yang 商鞅

shih 是

shih-fei 是非

tao 道

yen 言

Postscript

Philosophical Individualism in Chinese and Western Thought

Arthur C. Danto

While it may reasonably be asked where, if not in the writings of its philosophers, the philosophy of a culture is to be found—or how, if not by comparing their philosophers, one is to compare the philosophies of distinct cultures—there is often enough disparity between a culture's philosophy and its philosophers to justify a degree of circumspection in drawing inferences from one to the other. And this is so even when philosophers have played a historical role in forming the "philosophy" of their culture, as Confucius certainly did in China and Aristotle no less clearly did in our own. So before drawing some summary contrasts, I would like to lay down a few caveats.

Dieter Henrich wrote, in the preface to a study of Kant, that "we really still don't know how to interpret philosophical texts." I think he is right, in part because philosophical expression belongs to a distinct literary genre not even its best practitioners fully comprehend. This was brought home to me when a sensitive interpreter of Chuang Tzu complained that it is very difficult to distill any propositions out of Chuang Tzu. Rather than posing a problem, it seemed to me, this might be the beginning of a solution to how that text is to be read: it may just be the most important fact about that amazing and tantalizing thinker's work that it is not primarily, if at all, a repository of buried propositions—utterances whose destiny is caricatured in the wisdom of the fortune cookie. It was Wittgenstein (another fortune-cookie writer) who observed that philosophy is not a set of philosophical propositions but a certain kind of activity. One of my favorite passages in the *Analects* is where Confucius says that if he gives someone three corners who cannot find the fourth corner for himself, he cannot teach that person. The "fourth corner" for reading the *Analects* might consist in supposing them to be a body of existential enthymemes, in which the reader has not only to find the missing corner for himself, but the whole force of the philosophy only emerges through the experience of *seeking* that corner. So the passages are, in effect, spiritual exercises for developing one's moral muscles, and the power of the work consists in a human product defined by a certain competence. The competence bears distinct analogies with what we have been taught to identify as linguistic competence, that is, the power to produce and understand novel sentences without having to teach or learn the meanings of those sentences. The minister must have that sort of competence in order to administer successfully, and so it is to those who would acquire what I call "ministerial competence" that the *Analects* is addressed, and its enthymemic structure is a means to that end. So we do not engage, or ought not engage, with the *Analects* across the distance that normally separates reader from text, when it is the purpose of the texts to instruct or entertain. The purpose of *this* text is rather the transformation of its readers and the changing of their lives and so to overcome itself as a text in discharging that function. It completely disarms the text, then, to immortalize it, as it gets to be enshrined and canonized in the subsequent history of China.

At least four of the great philosophical texts of ancient China—the *Analects*, the *Chuang Tzu*, the *Tao-te ching*, and the books of Mencius—are so far from being merely propositional that we have to think carefully before we decide whether the texts which seem to be so—the *Hsün Tzu*, the *Han-fei Tzu*—really are so. Each of these books defines a mode of life, so we accept them by living in ways the books help us to live, rather than by simply reading them. They are like garments which have to be worn: if you do not put them on, they are deeply empty and existentially shapeless. And each of them demands a kind of exclusivity, as the lives they shape us into cannot all be lived at once.

What I have said regarding Chinese texts is to a large degree true of philosophical texts the world over, for when we recognize the amazing variety of textual forms in which philosophy is presented, the thought is irresistible that unless a philosopher has invented a wholly novel form, he has not really achieved true originality in his thought either. In comparison with the variety of philosophical writing, there is a steady predictability to poetry, drama, or fiction, which to me at least suggests that these are more limited and, if you wish, less dangerous enterprises. A thinker like Nietzsche, for example, invented perhaps ten distinct philosophical genres, to the point where, I am told, a practiced reader of his work can tell to which text a particular fragment must belong, so suffused is each part with the style of the whole. Since stylistic affiliation to a parent text is presupposed, there is a serious question of the degree to which we are justified in pulling propositions out of Nietzsche—as much so as with Chuang Tzu—and whether they could be detached and asserted on their own. Kierkegaard's thought is similarly not to be torn out of the disjunctive texts, the jokebooks, the para-sermons, proto-diaries, mock elocutions, and postscripts through which the philosophy is conveyed. And the history of philosophical literature is the history of dialogues, fragments, lecture notes, examinations, essays, meditations, critiques, discourses, letters, summae, encyclopedias, testaments, investigations, *Vorlesungen, Aufbauen,* poems, pensées, tractatuses, confessions, and a whirl of other subtler, unnamed forms, which, if they do not altogether defy generalization, demand a singular discernment on the part of the generalizer and *some* explanation of this profusion.

For the past seventy-five years, in my own philosophical world, the favored form of expression has clearly been modeled on the scientific report, a communication of limited results for the information of coworkers engaged in an activity somewhat equivalent to what Thomas Kuhn has taught us to construe as Normal Science. The professional philosophical paper, addressed to the professional philosophical readership, draws a sharp circumference around its audience, the lives of whom have nevertheless been transformed by their belief in a nontransformative relationship between them and these texts: the power of this kind of communication is concealed by a rhetoric of implied impersonality, objectivity, truth, argument, stylelessness, and the use of displayed technical formulae (which are almost always paraphrased in the vernacular, as though the writer were, after all, not confident of his reader's equipment). There will be no duller book, should some contemporary seek to be the Diogenes Laertius of our time, than the "Lives of the Contemporary American Philosophers." Strictly speaking, we do not have lives so much as careers, and the categories of the curriculum vitae—education, publications, honors—as much defines the shape of conduct as the rules of monastic order did for the Benedictines. In brief, philosophical writings today as much define a form of life and a relationship between reader and writer as any ever have.

I am not denying that there are philosophical truths. Philosophy is no more merely a form of literature than it is only a way of life. It lies at the intersection of science and art and religion, and its own nature remains its deepest problem and, in the end, possibly its only problem. I shall not, of course, try to define philosophy here. I seek only to stress that there are ways of reading philosophical texts which may say more about the philosophy of a culture than any propositions one may elicit from the texts taken as merely advancing propositions. In any case there is a problem of reading which hardly has been broached.

My second caveat is that there may be a great many categories and distinctions which have the utmost cultural importance, but which nevertheless go utterly unremarked in the philosophical texts of the culture. So the *absence* of something from those texts does not necessarily say anything very much about the philosophy of culture in which the text belongs. How much of first importance to us as human beings really finds voice in our most important philosophical texts? I was made shockingly aware of this when I was asked, a year ago, to comment on a talk by Judith Shklar delivered as a Thrilling Lecture at Columbia. Her talk was about cruelty, and her commendable undertaking was to "put cruelty first" as the worst of human vices. Very few philosophers in our tradition have put it first, in that sense, and neither do many of our religions. What I found in preparing my remarks was the almost complete *absence* from the great moral texts of Western thought of even a mention of cruelty. Montaigne and Machiavelli excepted, until Schopenhauer and Nietzsche no one seems to have singled out cruelty as something to think about philosophically. Compared with discussions of why we ought to keep our promises or tell the truth, the scant literature here is as obvious as it is exiguous. Hastings' *Encyclopedia of Religion and Ethics*, for example, does not even have an article on it. (Or, more accurately, under "Cruelty" it says, "See Humanitarianism," and that item concerns cruelty to animals—as though cruelty to man by man had not even enough historical significance to merit discussion.) One could hardly deduce from the literature on ethics the gory moral history of our civilization—the treatment of Protestants by Catholics in Montaigne's France, or of Catholics by Protestants in Donne's England, or of everyone by everyone at one time or another. A recent and profoundly influential paper in moral theory by a British writer (Philippa Foot) is constructed on the example of rudeness— coming to a garden party in offensively run-down clothes—and another writer, considered of some consequence in contemporary moral psychology, illustrates moral weakness with the example of taking an extra piece of dessert at high table. These efforts were published late in the twentieth century, by writers cognizant of the Nazis and aware of the Gulag, and at a time when torture was practiced as routinely and bureaucratically as the collection of taxes by (according to Amnesty International estimates) seventy-odd countries around the globe. I don't blame the philosophers for using the examples they do, and it may be the case that they could not have made the points they needed for their analyses by using routine examples of banal evil. But were everything except philosophy erased from the documents of our time, future readers would infer that *we lived in a golden age!*

I have no explanation for this silence on such a seemingly central issue. I might never have noticed it had I not been charged with responding to Ms. Shklar's paper. But it cannot be the only such silence, and I would require a lot of evidence from a culture before I would be ready to infer the absence of some concept in that culture's philosophy from the mere fact that it is absent in the writings of the culture's philosophers. The fact that a certain notion is identified with individualism in one set of philosophical writings and is found quite lacking in another says little in the final analysis as to whether or not individualism was important in the latter.

These caveats registered, I want now to make a few comparative observations. To begin with, neither the Western nor the Chinese tradition impresses me as especially favorable to individualistic theory, though one or another species of "individualism" appears early in each. A more radical individualism than that of Protagoras could hardly be imagined. His *homo mensura* theory is that each man lives in his own world, effectively incommensurable with each other world, and that whatever man believes about his world is true, exactly because his beliefs define that world. So everyone is always right and no one wrong; contradiction is impossible. Protagoras presented himself as a teacher, indeed, a teacher of virtue. There has to be an inconsistency between his profession and his doctrine because something has to count as wrong if there is to be ethics and something has to count as false if there is inconsistency. The great heroic struggle in ancient philosophy was between Protagoras and Socrates over the possibility of falsehood, and hence the possibility of a truth that meant something. And, of course, Socrates needed this to uphold his teaching that evil is a matter of ignorance if ignorance is a matter of false belief. So false beliefs must be possible, the question being how, if Protagoras is right. The question of objective truth, and hence the possibility of knowledge of objective truth which must be public and invariant to individuals, was set up on Socratic beginnings and has given shape to the *Problematik* of Western philosophical thought ever since. The desire, and then the power, to find the truth, enshrined in the fateful definition of man as a rational animal by Aristotle, specified an anthropology for Western philosophy in which cognitive individualism could have no place—nor could it have one until the anthropology became modified in the direction of Protagorean individualism, a position which has continued to haunt, and sometimes to tempt, philosophy in our hemisphere. Even moral theory has been phrased in cognitive terms, and for Kant the test of a moral principle is precisely the degree to which it could coherently be willed as an objective truth of nature—a *universal law*. It is with regard to this model that the examples used in moral theory must be understood—rather than in terms of their immediate moral urgency, as in the case of the concept of cruelty.

In Confucianism, human essence is defined in terms of the Five Relations, implying that one is human just to the degree that one satisfies or fulfills these vital relationships. Indirectly, therefore, one is taught to repudiate any concept of man as an individual apart from these relations, as in the celebrated eccentricities of Chuang Tzu. The eremetic, rootless wanderer, tracing a faint path of spiritual fulfillment through the fogs and clouds of a knobby universe which has no more need of him than he of fellow humans, must have impressed the Chinese thinker as poetic but improbable, and in any case inconsistent with the human essence construed as irreducibly relational—when one strips the relationships off, nothing recognizably human remains to tread the paths of nothingness. The temptation to shed these relationships may very well have been, in the abstract, as tempting to the Chinese thinker as the stunning of reason through intoxication and frenzy has been to the West. But these are furloughs from our essence, transitory abandonments of the heart of our being, to which we are inevitably returned.

Let me revert for a moment to our own moral theory, of which, it seems to me, Kant must be the most representative of our theorists, as moral principles in his theory are imperatives holding over rational beings as a class. The rational being is perceived as a legislator, but each legislator enacts only those principles any other legislator would enact upon suitable ratiocination—in the end, everyone must think alike. Rationality has an implicit antagonism to authority; opposition to authority implies an individualism, but it is, in fact, only a false one, as may be seen from this sketch of Kant's theory. The Kingdom of Ends, each member of which is autonomous and defined by the moral will, sounds like the epitome of an individualistic theory, but it does not work out that way—the form of moral precepts is universal, and their content is what any rational being would endorse.

It has been held against Kant that he evolved his moral theory for what must be construed as almost pure rational beings, beings without those interests which arise from the animal side of our nature, and that he did so almost as though ethics had nothing to do with that. Even so, Kant is consistent with a tradition which holds that reason is, as Aristotle puts it, "the best thing in us," and the life of reason the best life, indeed, a divine life. Aristotle, who also points out that we are social animals, seems as little impressed with that fact as Descartes evidently was with the fact that we all were once children. The ideal since Plato has been that we should live as the gods live, that "we should, so far as we can, make ourselves immortal and strain every nerve to live in accordance with the best thing in us." Animality, then, is something to be striven against, an obstacle to the best life, a thought which recommended itself vehemently to Christianity as though ethics were not, as the Chinese realized, required precisely because we are not like gods. Human beings have needs and vulnerabilities, and a structure is needed to accommodate them existentially, even if aspects of this structure are not reflected in our ("our") concept of the best life, which is rational self-sufficiency.

Self-sufficiency becomes an impossible ideal in China as well, but what is expunged from our moral self-image in the West is the basis of our moral self-image there: the unit of moral discourse is not the principles of a moral act but a total moral life, and the questions have to do with what we should do and how we should act as we move from stage to stage. Thus, the moral exemplar is less the being who has managed to slough off existential impediments to the life of pure reason than the being who is wise through having lived a suitable life and can give us guidance as we seek our own way.

Moral education in the West, or at least in Western theory, has concerned the education of the will. The bulk of the *Republic* concerns the education of guardians. These were the social counterparts to the psychological faculty of the will and were charged with the duty of executing the mandates of reason, which naturally ruled but required enactment; hence, the complicity of the will. The *weak* will would be personally destructive and socially disastrous, but the centrality of will in moral theory in the West cannot be overestimated. In Kant we read that only the good will is unconditionally good, and the ideal will is the *holy* will, which spontaneously enacts only what is rational: as though will and reason were one. The will plays no such exalted role in moral psychology in China. The moral organ would, I suppose, be judgment, concerned to apply principles to circumstances in which it requires all the guidance it can get and for which life must be the ultimate teacher. But this is precisely reflected in the Chinese texts, construed as gymnasia for the education of a judgment which must operate in the absence of rules and whose agent must deal with situations as they arise within the structures we, of course, all share, of total lives. So the Chinese mind moves by case to case through cases, and universalization would be something his wisdom would make him diffident to try.

The major differences in the two traditions arise, I think, from the two modes of antiindividualism, cognitive and vital, which are implied by their basic anthropologies. But having offered this one corner, I leave it to others to pick up the other three.

Index

altruism, 360, 369. *See also* empathy; humaneness; impartiality; *jen*; *kung*; sympathy

Analects, 87, 162-63, 200, 278, 295, 296, 308, 331, 335, 349, 363, 385-86

analogy: family network, 264-69, 277, 279, 282, 284; fork in the road, 312; jade stone, 104; ladder, 284; moon, 271; organicism, 262-63, 276, 281; plant, 263, 275-82, 284, 340, 367; theories, in Sung school, 262-63; water, 80, 263, 270-75, 282, 284, 286-87 n. 60. *See also* metaphor

anarchism, in Chinese political thinking, 26, 122-23, 376

ancestors, and *ch'i* (vital force), 272-73

arbitrariness (*ku*), 232

Aristotle (384-322 B.C.), 14, 264-65, 278, 281, 299, 300, 364, 385, 389

art, 114, 250-53

asceticism, 159, 166, 176-77. *See also* eremetism

Association for Literary Studies, 247-48

Augustine (354-430), 23, 297, 298, 299, 313, 334

autobiography, and realism, 247

autonomy: in classical philosophy, 11-14, 299; in Confucianism, 96, 181, 297, 312, 332, 361-65; defined, 11; and dignity, 14, 16, 206; and individualism, 1, 2, 11-14, 206-7, 293-94; and morality, 361-64; and personhood, 293; and privacy, 86, 88, 92, 94-95; self-conception, 166, 171, 317; and social convention, 367; in Taoism, 13-14

being (*yu*), 134

belief, as part of reason, 364-65

bonds, three and six rules (*san-kang liu-chi*), 121-25, 235, 266-67, 351

Boodberg, Peter, 321-22 n. 42

Book of Changes. See I-ching

Buddhism: appearance and reality, 280; Ch'an, 179, 343; compassion (*tzu*), 341, 346; development, 26-29; Hua-yen school, 50,

262, 270, 271, 275, 286 n. 10 and n. 60, 311; influences, 178, 305-7, 381 n. 6; on one-many, 273, 275, 286-87 n. 60, 311; on personhood, 306; on self, 20, 308; T'ien-t'ai school, 270. *See also* eremitism; mind; morality

cardinal relations. *See lun* (relations)

Chan, W. T., 270, 347, 378

Chang Tsai (1020-1077), 221, 276, 279, 311; on mind, 307-8, 311, 324 n. 68; on nature/feeling dualism, 325 n. 85; on personhood, 306-7, 317; on self-fulfillment, 341, 345; "Western Inscription," 341, 344-45

change, 110, 111, 116, 277

characterology, 126, 130, 132

charity, principle of, 40

Ch'en Tu-hsiu (1879-1942), 247, 259

ch'eng (correct firmness), 262, 276

ch'eng (integrity, sincerity), 272, 337, 338

Ch'eng-Chu school (origins in eleventh and twelfth centuries), 18, 23; on the body, 221; on cosmology, 266-67, 282; criticism of Buddhism, 269; on cultivation of nature, 338; holism in, 18, 78; on mind, 305, 309, 310, 314; and Neo-Confucianism, 331-51; on personhood, 306-7; on relationalism, 283

Ch'eng Hao (1132-1185). *See* Ch'eng-Chu school

Ch'eng I (1033-1107), 262, 264, 265, 270, 273, 275, 276, 278, 280, 324 n. 68, 324-25 n. 85. *See also* Ch'eng-Chu school

cheng-ming (rectification of names), 60, 266, 366-67, 370-71, 377

ch'i (matter, vital force), 262, 267, 272-76, 278-9, 282-3, 293-4, 303, 305, 307, 309-10, 311-17 *passim*, 326-27 n. 116, 378

chien ai (universal love), 77

chih (intelligence or wisdom), 222, 302, 309, 315, 338

chih. See will

Michigan Monographs in Chinese Studies

Michigan Abstracts of Chinese and Japanese Works on Chinese History

The Michigan Monographs and Michigan Abstracts series are available from:

Center for Chinese Studies Publications
The University of Michigan
104 Lane Hall
Ann Arbor, Michigan 48109